Lecture Notes in Computer Science 15238

The series Lecture Notes in Computer Science (LNCS), including its subseries Lecture Notes in Artificial Intelligence (LNAI) and Lecture Notes in Bioinformatics (LNBI), has established itself as a medium for the publication of new developments in computer science and information technology research, teaching, and education.

LNCS enjoys close cooperation with the computer science R & D community, the series counts many renowned academics among its volume editors and paper authors, and collaborates with prestigious societies. Its mission is to serve this international community by providing an invaluable service, mainly focused on the publication of conference and workshop proceedings and postproceedings. LNCS commenced publication in 1973.

Wolfgang Maass · Hyoil Han · Hasan Yasar ·
Nick Multari
Editors

Conceptual Modeling

43rd International Conference, ER 2024
Pittsburgh, PA, USA, October 28–31, 2024
Proceedings

Springer

Editors
Wolfgang Maass
Saarland University and German Research Center for Artificial Intelligence (DFKI)
Saarbrücken, Germany

Hasan Yasar
Software Engineering Institute – Carnegie Mellon University
Pittsburgh, PA, USA

Hyoil Han
Illinois State University
Normal, IL, USA

Nick Multari
Pacific Northwest National Laboratory
Richland, WA, USA

ISSN 0302-9743 ISSN 1611-3349 (electronic)
Lecture Notes in Computer Science
ISBN 978-3-031-75871-3 ISBN 978-3-031-75872-0 (eBook)
https://doi.org/10.1007/978-3-031-75872-0

This Springer imprint is published by the registered company Springer Nature Switzerland AG
The registered company address is: Gewerbestrasse 11, 6330 Cham, Switzerland

Preface

This volume of the Lecture Notes in Computer Science series contains the proceedings of the 43nd International Conference on Conceptual Modeling – ER 2024, held in Pittsburgh, PA, USA, during October 28–31. Pittsburgh, PA, known as the "Steel City," has a rich history rooted in the steel industry, which fueled the city's growth during the nineteenth and early twentieth centuries, making it a powerhouse of American manufacturing. Today, Pittsburgh has reinvented itself as a hub for technology, healthcare, and education, showcasing its resilience and strength through economic transformation and innovation. Carnegie Mellon University (CMU) is a global leader in computer science and artificial intelligence, renowned for pioneering research and breakthroughs that have significantly shaped the field, including advancements in machine learning, robotics, natural language processing, engineering, and cybersecurity.

The ER Conference, with a 43-year tradition of showcasing high-end results in the field of conceptual modeling, is evolving to embrace the rapidly expanding landscape of artificial intelligence and beyond. This year, the conference broadened its scope, inviting discussions on how conceptual modeling can redefine its role within the AI domain, including areas like data preparation and model development. Furthermore, the conference addressed the integration of conceptual modeling in critical AI-related topics such as explainable AI, AI software engineering, and the ethical, societal, and legal implications of AI technologies. This expansion reflects the growing need to explore how conceptual modeling can contribute to the responsible and effective development of AI systems.

ER 2024 continued to honor its roots by providing a platform for a broad spectrum of traditional topics in conceptual modeling, including the latest research and practices in areas such as theories of concepts and ontologies, process modeling, goal modeling, and more. The call for papers invited submissions of original research that explore new foundations, establish connections, and extend applications beyond the current boundaries of the discipline. It also welcomed industry reports and vision papers, reflecting the conference's commitment to both theoretical advancements and practical applications. This approach ensured that ER 2024 remained a vital forum for advancing both the traditional and emerging aspects of conceptual modeling.

ER 2024 received a total of 213 paper submissions, including 113 for the main conference and 100 for the ER forum and workshops. The double-blind review process began with 14 submissions being desk-rejected by the program co-chairs for being incomplete or outside the conference's scope. The remaining submissions underwent independent evaluations by at least three Program Committee (PC) members, followed by a detailed discussion phase moderated by senior PC members who provided meta-reviews summarizing and explaining recommendations to the authors. Co-chairs reviewed all recommendations, sought revisions of reviews and meta-reviews, and made the final decisions. A thorough plagiarism check using Springer's iThenticate tool led to additional discussions among the co-chairs and Steering Committee, resulting in four rejections.

Ultimately, 22 submissions were accepted based on their novelty and contributions to advancing the state of the art, with 14 directly accepted and eight conditionally accepted pending minor revisions verified by the PC chairs. This rigorous process culminated in an acceptance rate of 19.46%, with the final volume featuring 22 high-quality papers. Additionally, five submissions were transferred to the ER Forum, and nine were redirected for consideration at ER workshops.

The main conference included sessions on Research papers, Keynotes, Tutorials, Panels, the Forum for short visionary papers, Posters, and Demos. The three invited keynote presentations were "Explanation, semantics, and ontology" by Nicola Guarino, retired research associate at the Institute of Cognitive Sciences and Technologies of the Italian National Research Council (ISTC-CNR), and former director of the ISTC-CNR Laboratory for Applied Ontology (LOA); "New Technology, Same Basics" by Paul D. Nielsen, Director and Chief Executive Officer of the Carnegie Mellon University Software Engineering Institute (CMU SEI); and "Wood Wide Models" by Pradeep Ravikumar, Professor in the Machine Learning Department, School of Computer Science at Carnegie Mellon University.

On behalf of our community, we extend our gratitude to the keynote speakers for sharing their invaluable insights into the evolution of conceptual modeling research over the past 43 years and its future. The three tutorials, selected through an open call, tackled timely and relevant topics that lie at the heart of our community's interests. As the editors of this volume, we sincerely thank all the authors who submitted their novel research contributions to the conference, as well as the members of the Program Committee and Senior Program Committee for their dedication and expertise in the rigorous review and discussion of submissions. We are deeply grateful to the Organizing Committee for meticulously managing all aspects of the conference, including promotion, submission management, portal design, and effective communication throughout the event. Special thanks also go to the Software Engineering Institute (SEI) at Carnegie Mellon University for graciously hosting ER 2024. While this volume showcases the scientific achievements that brought our community together in Pittsburgh it also reflects the vibrant global network of researchers in the field of conceptual modeling. This year, we were joined by nine authors from Africa, 96 from Asia, 283 from Europe, 74 from North America, 18 from Oceania, and 58 from South America, highlighting our truly international community that continues to grow and thrive.

September 2024

Wolfgang Maass
Hyoil Han
Hasan Yasar
Nick Multari

Organization

Honorary Chair

Paul Nielsen	Carnegie Mellon University, USA

General Chair

Hasan Yasar	Carnegie Mellon University, USA

Chief Coordinator

Peter Chen	Carnegie Mellon University, USA

Distinguished Advisors

Kenneth M. Ford	Florida Institute for Human and Machine Cognition, USA
Jeffrey J. P. Tsai	Asia University, Taiwan

Program Co-chairs

Hyoil Han	Illinois State University, USA
Wolfgang Maass	German Research Center for Artificial Intelligence (DFKI) and Saarland University, Germany
Nick Multari	Pacific Northwest National Lab, USA

Forum Chairs

Sotirios Liaskos	York University, Canada
Patrick Marcel	University of Orléans, France

ER Steering Committee Liaisons

Stephen W. Liddle	Brigham Young University, USA
Il-Yeol Song	Drexel University, USA

Panels Chairs

Oscar Pastor	Universidad Politécnica de Valencia, Spain
Veda Storey	Georgia State University, USA

Posters and Demos Chairs

Sergio de Cesare	University of Westminster, UK
Frederik Gailly	Ghent University, Belgium

Workshops Chairs

Motoshi Saeki	Nanzan University, Japan
Leah Wong (Retired)	NIWC Pacific, USA

Tutorials Chairs

Carlos Ordonez	University of Houston, USA
Juan Carlos Trujillo Mondéjar	University of Alicante, Spain

CEUR Proceedings Chair

Enrico Gallinucci	University of Bologna, Italy

Publicity Chairs

Anna Bernasconi	Politecnico di Milano, Italy
Claudenir M. Fonseca	University of Twente, The Netherlands

Sponsorship Chairs

Michele Falce	CMU SEI, USA
Hasan Yasar	Carnegie Mellon University, USA

Industrial Track Chairs

Sharma Chakravarthy	University of Texas at Arlington, USA
Paul B. Losiewicz	Quanterion Solutions Inc., USA

Senior Program Committee

Jacky Akoka	CEDRIC-CNAM, IMT-TEM, France
João Paulo A. Almeida	Federal University of Espírito Santo, Brazil
Paolo Atzeni	Università Roma Tre, Italy
Stefano Ceri	Politecnico di Milano, Italy
Ho-Jin Choi	KAIST, South Korea
Isabelle Comyn-Wattiau	ESSEC Business School, France
Gill Dobbie	University of Auckland, New Zealand
Aldo Gangemi	Università di Bologna, Italy
Nicola Guarino	ISTC-CNR, Italy
Giancarlo Guizzardi	University of Twente, The Netherlands
Manfred Jeusfeld	University of Skövde, Sweden
Paul Johannesson	Stockholm University, Sweden
Alberto Laender	Federal University of Minas Gerais, Brazil
Carson Leung	University of Manitoba, Canada
Stephen W. Liddle	Brigham Young University, USA
Sebastian Link	University of Auckland, New Zealand
Heinrich C. Mayr	Alpen-Adria-Universität Klagenfurt, Austria
John Mylopoulos	University of Ottawa, Canada
Shamkant Navathe	Georgia Institute of Technology, USA
Carlos Ordonez	University of Houston, USA
José Palazzo Moreira de Oliveira	Federal University of Rio Grande do Sul, Brazil
Jeffrey Parsons	Memorial University of Newfoundland, Canada
Oscar Pastor	Universidad Politécnica de Valencia, Spain
Henderik A. Proper	TU Wien, Austria
Jolita Ralyté	University of Geneva, Switzerland
Colette Rolland	Université Paris 1 Panthéon-Sorbonne, France
Motoshi Saeki	Tokyo Institute of Technology, Japan
Peretz Shoval	Ben-Gurion University of the Negev, Israel

Pnina Soffer	University of Haifa, Israel
Veda Storey	GSU, USA
Bernhard Thalheim	Christian-Albrechts-Universität zu Kiel, Germany
Juan Trujillo	Universidad de Alicante, Spain
Gerd Wagner	Brandenburg University of Technology at Cottbus, Germany
Chao Wang	Chongqing Normal University, China
Chaokun Wang	Tsinghua University, China
Isabelle Comyn-Wattiau	Essec Business School, France
Carson Woo	University of British Columbia, Canada
Eric Yu	University of Toronto, Canada
Jelena Zdravkovic	Stockholm University, Sweden

Program Committee

Jun Miyazaki	Institute of Science Tokyo, Japan
Mara Abel	Federal University of Rio Grande do Sul, Brazil
Anurag Acharya	Florida International University, USA
João Araújo	Universidade NOVA de Lisboa, Portugal
Alessandro Artale	Free University of Bozen-Bolzano, Italy
Sören Auer	TIB Leibniz Information Center Science & Technology and University of Hannover, Germany
David Aveiro	Madeira University, Portugal
Claudia Ayala	Universitat Politècnica de Catalunya, Spain
Wolf-Tilo Balke	TU Braunschweig, Germany
Monalessa Barcellos	Federal University of Espírito Santo, Brazil
Robin Bergenthum	FernUniversität in Hagen, Germany
Anna Bernasconi	Politecnico di Milano, Italy
Sourav Bhowmick	Nanyang Technological University, Singapore
Devis Bianchini	University of Brescia, Italy
Sandro Bimonte	INRAE, France
Luiz Olavo Bonino Da Silva Santos	University of Twente, Netherlands
José Borbinha	INESC-ID, Universidade de Lisboa, Portugal
Dominik Bork	TU Wien, Austria
Shawn Bowers	Gonzaga University, USA
Stephane Bressan	National University of Singapore, Singapore
Robert Andrei Buchmann	Babeş-Bolyai University of Cluj Napoca, Romania
Jordi Cabot	ICREA – UOC, Spain

Diego Calvanese	Free University of Bozen-Bolzano, Italy
Cinzia Cappiello	Politecnico di Milano, Italy
Stefano Ceri	Politecnico di Milano, Italy
Luca Cernuzzi	Universidad Católica "Nuestra Señora de la Asunción", Paraguay
Sharma Chakravarthy	University of Texas at Arlington, USA
Jianhua Chen	Louisiana State University, USA
Suphamit Chittayasothorn	King Mongkut's Institute of Technology Ladkrabang, Thailand
Yong Suk Choi	Hanyang University, South Korea
Soon Chun	City University of New York, USA
Tony Clark	Aston University, UK
Loek Cleophas	TU Eindhoven and Stellenbosch University, Netherlands
Rogério Costa	Polytechnic of Leiria, Portugal
Dolors Costal	Universitat Politècnica de Catalunya, Spain
Jérôme Darmont	Université de Lyon, France
Sergio de Cesare	University of Westminster, UK
Johann Eder	Alpen-Adria-Universität Klagenfurt, Austria
Vadim Ermolayev	Ukrainian Catholic University, Ukraine
Rik Eshuis	Eindhoven University of Technology, The Netherlands
Luís Ferreira Pires	University of Twente, The Netherlands
Peter Fettke	German Research Center for Artificial Intelligence (DFKI) and Saarland University, Germany
Hans-Georg Fill	University of Fribourg, Switzerland
Claudenir M. Fonseca	University of Twente, The Netherlands
Enrico Franconi	Free University of Bozen-Bolzano, Italy
Mattia Fumagalli	Free University of Bozen-Bolzano, Italy
Frederik Gailly	Ghent University, Belgium
Enrico Gallinucci	University of Bologna, Italy
Yunjun Gao	Zhejiang University, China
Faiez Gargouri	University of Sfax, Tunisia
Chang Ge	University of Minnesota, USA
Sepideh Ghanavati	University of Maine, USA
Asif Qumer Gill	University of Technology, Sydney, Australia
Cesar Gonzalez-Perez	Incipit CSIC, Spain
Jaap Gordijn	Vrije Universiteit Amsterdam, Netherlands
Guido Governatori	Independent Researcher, Australia
Georg Grossmann	University of South Australia, Australia
Sergio Guerreiro	INESC-ID/University of Lisbon, Portugal

Renata Guizzardi	University of Twente, The Netherlands
Simon Hacks	Stockholm University, Sweden
Siegfried Handschuh	University of St. Gallen, Switzerland
Sven Hartmann	Clausthal University of Technology, Germany
Martin Henkel	Stockholm University, Sweden
Sabine Janzen	German Research Center for Artificial Intelligence (DFKI), Germany
Jinhang Jiang	McKesson, USA
Paul Johannesson	Stockholm University, Sweden
Dimitris Karagiannis	University of Vienna, Austria
Kamalakar Karlapalem	IIIT Hyderabad, India
Julius Köpke	Universität Klagenfurt, Austria
Agnes Koschmider	Kiel University, Germany
Thomas Kühne	Victoria University of Wellington, New Zealand
Vinay Kulkarni	Tata Consultancy Services Research, India
John Lalor	University of Notre Dame, USA
Ralf Laue	University of Applied Sciences Zwickau, Germany
Jeee-Hyong Lee	Sungkyunkwan University, South Korea
Moonkun Lee	Chonbuk National University, South Korea
WooKey Lee	Inha University, South Korea
Maurizio Lenzerini	Sapienza University of Rome, Italy
Jingjing Li	University of Virginia, USA
Tong Li	Beijing University of Technology, China
Sotirios Liaskos	York University, Canada
Sergio Lifschitz	PUC-Rio, Brazil
Chun-Han Lin	National Taiwan Normal University, Taiwan
Tok Wang Ling	National University of Singapore, Singapore
Mengchi Liu	Carleton University, Canada
Jim Logan	Dassault Systèmes, USA
Peter Loos	IWi at DFKI, Saarland University, Germany
Hui Ma	Victoria University of Wellington, New Zealand
Zoltan Mann	University of Amsterdam, Netherlands
Beatriz Marín	Universitat Politècnica de València, Spain
Wolfgang Mayer	University of South Australia, Australia
Jose-Norberto Mazón	University of Alicante, Spain
Massimo Mecella	Sapienza University of Rome, Italy
Miguel Mira da Silva	INOV, University of Lisbon, Portugal
Daniel Moldt	University of Hamburg, Germany
Jose Morales	CMU SEI, USA
João Moreira	University of Twente, Netherlands
Haralambos Mouratidis	University of Essex, UK

Júlio César Nardi	Federal Institute of Espírito Santo, Brazil
Bernd Neumayr	Johannes Kepler University Linz, Austria
Wilfred Ng	Hong Kong University of Science and Technology, China
Selmin Nurcan	Université Paris 1 Panthéon – Sorbonne, France
Anne Ngu	Texas State University, USA
Andreas Oberweis	Karlsruhe Institute of Technology, Germany
Leo Obrst	MITRE, USA
Alessandro Oltramari	Bosch Research and Technology Center, USA
Andreas L. Opdahl	University of Bergen, Norway
Elda Paja	IT University of Copenhagen, Denmark
José Palazzo	Federal University of Rio Grande do Sul, Brazil
José M. Parente de Oliveira	Aeronautics Institute of Technology, Brazil
Robert Pergl	Czech Technical University in Prague, Czechia
Barbara Pernici	Politecnico di Milano, Italy
Geert Poels	Ghent University, Belgium
Fabio Porto	National Laboratory of Scientific Computation, Brazil
Christoph Quix	Hochschule Niederrhein University of Applied Sciences, Germany
Maxx Richard Rahman	Saarland University, Germany
Mostafizur Rahman	Rakuten Institute of Technology, Japan
Jan Recker	University of Hamburg, Germany
Jana-Rebecca Rehse	University of Mannheim, Germany
Manfred Reichert	University of Ulm, Germany
Hajo A. Reijers	Utrecht University, Netherlands
Iris Reinhartz-Berger	University of Haifa, Israel
Wolfgang Reisig	Humboldt-Universitaet zu Berlin, Germany
Stefanie Rinderle-Ma	Technical University of Munich, Germany
Syed Rizvi	Amity University Lucknow, India
Tarmo Robal	Tallinn University of Technology, Estonia
Ben Roelens	Open Universiteit, Ghent University, Netherlands
Michael Rosemann	Queensland University of Technology, Australia
Kristina Rosenthal	Hochschule Niederrhein University of Applied Sciences, Germany
Matti Rossi	Aalto University, Finland
Marcela Ruiz	Zurich University of Applied Sciences, Switzerland
Bernhard Rumpe	RWTH Aachen University, Germany
Tiago Sales	University of Twente, Netherlands
Maribel Yasmina Santos	University of Minho, Portugal
Estefania Serral	KU Leuven, Belgium

Jiaxing Shang	Chongqing University, China
Shivam Sharma	Pacific Northwest National Laboratory, USA
Cogan Shimizu	Wright State University, USA
Samira Si-Said Cherfi	CEDRIC – Conservatoire National des Arts et Métiers, France
Joy Smith	University of Twente, Netherlands
Monique Snoeck	KU Leuven, Belgium
Vítor E. Silva Souza	Federal University of Espírito Santo, Brazil
Stefan Strecker	University of Hagen, Germany
Markus Stumptner	University of South Australia, Australia
Arnon Sturm	Ben-Gurion University of the Negev, Israel
David Sundaram	University of Auckland, New Zealand
Angelo Susi	Fondazione Bruno Kessler, Italy
Valentina Tamma	University of Liverpool, UK
Victoria Torres	Universitat Politècnica de València, Spain
Marina Tropmann-Frick	Hamburg University of Applied Sciences, Germany
Panos Vassiliadis	University of Ioannina, Greece
Srikar Velichety	University of Memphis, USA
Andreas Vogelsang	University of Cologne, Germany
Hongzhi Wang	Harbin Institute of Technology, Canada
Yves Wautelet	Katholieke Universiteit Leuven, Belgium
Barbara Weber	University of St. Gallen, Switzerland
Hans Weigand	Tilburg University, Netherlands
Manuel Wimmer	Johannes Kepler University Linz, Austria
Robert Wrembel	Poznań University of Technology, Poland
Zhen Yang	Beijing University of Technology, China
Robin Yeman	CMU SEI, USA
Eric Yu	University of Toronto, Canada
Apostolos Zarras	University of Ioannina, Greece
Heinz Züllighoven	Ingenieurbüro Dr. Züllighoven, Germany

Additional Reviewers

Syed Juned Ali
Keshav Bansal
Souvik Barat
Kelly Rosa Braghetto
Sven Christ
Matthias Ehrendorfer
Martin Eisenberg
Joan Giner Miguelez
Jenny Guber
Seung-Ho Han
Maximilian Harms
Jonghwan Hyeon
Eojin Joo
Youngjun Lee
Daniel Lehner
Ben Liu
Alexander Lüpges
Adrian Costin Marin
Sergio Morales
Fabian Muff
Katerina Papantoniou
José Fabián Reyes Román
Suman Roychoudhury
Gengyuan Shi
Oliver Tautz
Wilfrid Utz
Isadora Valle Sousa
Beate Wais
Philip Winkler
Yorck Zisgen

Steering Committee

Chair

Jeffrey Parsons — Memorial University of Newfoundland, Canada

Vice-chair

Giancarlo Guizzardi — University of Twente, The Netherlands

Treasurer

Stephen W. Liddle — Brigham Young University, USA

Steering Committee Members

Peter P. Chen
Isabelle Comyn-Wattiau
Ulrich Frank
Giancarlo Guizzardi
Jennifer Horkoff
Paul Johannesson
Gerti Kappel
Kamal Karlapalem
Alberto Laender
Stephen W. Liddle
Tok Wang Ling
Sebastian Link
Hui Ma
João Paulo A. Almeida

Jeffrey Parsons
Oscar Pastor
Jolita Ralyte
Sudha Ram
Motoshi Saeki
Vítor Estêvão Silva Souza
Il-Yeol Song
Veda Storey
Juan Carlos Trujillo
Carson Woo
Eric Yu
Heinrich Mayr

Keynote Speeches

Towards Explanatory Conceptual Models: A Systematic Approach Based on Ontological Analysis

Nicola Guarino

Institute of Cognitive Sciences and Technologies of the Italian National Research Council (ISTC-CNR), Italy
nicola.guarino@cnr.it

A widespread requirement for conceptual models is that they need to have some kind of formal semantics in order to be used, and especially in order to be shared. In this talk I will defend that just having a formal semantics is not enough: in order to be shared and integrated, conceptual models need to be explained in terms of their ontological commitments to the world. I will distinguish therefore between ordinary conceptual models, which typically describe a domain in terms of its relevant entities and relationships, and have therefore a merely descriptive role, and explanatory conceptual models, which aim at explaining why those relationships hold. I will propose then a systematic approach to expand an ordinary model at two different levels of explanatory detail, based on the ontological notion of truth-making.

New Technology, Same Basics

Paul Nielsen

Carnegie Mellon University Software Engineering Institute (CMU SEI), USA
nielsen@sei.cmu.edu

Who hasn't dabbled with popular Artificial Intelligence (AI) Large Language Models such as Gemini or ChatGPT, either as part of a project or just to see what it might produce? AI's popularity and the idea that AI can transform human effort is everywhere in our scientific and industrial communities. AI clearly is a growing business driver.

And AI has value for conceptional modeling. For instance, natural language processing can help in identifying the relational data of entities and generative AI and inverse relationship approaches can help create deeply insightful entity relationship (ER) diagrams and models for systems. To get the usable, reliable AI systems people want, designers and developers need to learn how to repeatably build sound AI systems. With those systems, we will see improvements in areas such as modeling (e.g., digital twins for smart cyber-physical systems), security engineering to defend large-scale systems, and the use of modern software practices (e.g., in developing threat models for DevSecOps).

To build sound AI systems repeatably, we need to pursue these system qualities: robust, secure, scalable, and human centered. Those quality attributes form the basis for AI Engineering discipline. There is much work to do to create and implement the AI Engineering discipline in areas such as making a commitment to moving R&D in practice to get ahead of the galloping use of AI tools, recognition that we cannot abandon good practices such as practicing cyber hygiene and the use of modern software engineering practices, and the creation of a new concept of the digital-engineering-aware workforce able to interact effectively with AI models.

New Technology, Same Basics

Wood Wide Models

Pradeep Ravikumar

Machine Learning Department, School of Computer Science
at Carnegie Mellon University
pradeepr@cs.cmu.edu

Foundation models are monolithic models that are trained on a broad set of data, and which are then in principle fine-tuned to various specific tasks. But they are ill-suited to many heterogeneous settings, for instance numeric tabular data, or numeric time-series data, where training a single monolithic model over a large collection of such datasets is not meaningful. For instance, why should numeric time series of stock prices have anything to do with time series comprising the vital signs of an ICU patient? For such settings, we propose the class of wood wide models.

The wood wide web is often used to describe an underground network of fungal threads that connect many trees and plants together, which stands in contrast to a large concrete foundation on top of which we might build specialized buildings. Analogously, in contrast to a single foundation model upon which one might build specialized models, we have many smaller wood wide models that all borrow subtler ingredients from each other. But to be able to share nutrients from the wood wide web, trees need a special root-based architecture that can connect to these fungal threads. Accordingly, to operationalize wood wide models, we develop a novel neuro-symbolic architecture that we term "neuro-causal" that uses a synthesis of deep neural models and causal graphical models to automatically infer higher-level symbolic information from lower-level "raw features", while also allowing for rich relationships among the symbolic variables. Neuro-causal models retain the flexibility of modern deep neural network architectures while simultaneously capturing statistical semantics such as identifiability and causality, which are important to discuss ideal, target representations and their tradeoffs. But most interestingly, these can further form a web of wood wide models when they borrow in part from a shared conceptual ontology, as well as causal mechanisms. We provide conditions under which this entire architecture can be recovered uniquely. We also discuss efficient algorithms and provide experiments illustrating the algorithms in practice.

Tutorials

Data Fabric: Technologies, Modeling and Applications

Kamalakar Karlapalem[1], Radha Krishna Pisipati[2], and Satyanarayana R. Valluri[3]

[1] Data Science and Analytics Centre, IIIT-Hyderabad, India
kamal@iiit.ac.in
[2] Department of Computer Science and Engineering, National Institute of Technology Warangal, India
[3] Databricks Inc., California, USA

Data Fabric is an amalgamation of various database system technologies, offering extensive research opportunities for deploying end-to-end data management platform-based solutions. These platforms have seen advancements in middleware, advanced and powerful ETL pipelines, and generative AI-supported data pipelines with unified storage and compute to establish compliance and governance and reduce latency. Deployed systems using technologies such as data mesh, data lakes, data warehouses, and cloud databases serve as data sources, and the data fabric solution manages data, query, and analytics pipelines by leveraging distributed computing capabilities and dynamically routing queries for optimal performance without centralizing data storage. Understanding the interconnections (technology and applications) among source systems, data fabric, domain, and application is crucial for establishing correct and complete data fabric solutions for user applications. This paper presents a holistic view of data fabric technologies and addresses the importance of understanding the interconnections among source data systems, data fabric, domain, and application, focusing on metadata and application development. For metadata, we envisage an ER model solution to provide an overall conceptual data landscape for the underlying data systems for a data fabric.

Data Fabric: Technologies, Modeling and Applications

Spatial Conceptual Modeling: Introduction to the MM-AR Metamodeling Platform and the Augmented Reality Workflow Modeling Language

Fabian Muff, Hans-Georg Fill, and Daniel Borcard

University of Fribourg, Research Group Digitalization and Information Systems
{fabian.muff,daniel.borcard,hans-georg.fill}@unifr.ch

This tutorial introduces the concept of Spatial Conceptual Modeling and MM-AR, a new web-based, 2D/3D metamodeling platform. It covers the prototypical implementation of MM-AR and the Augmented Reality Workflow Modeling Language (ARWFML) together with use cases and a hands-on session.

A Deep Dive into Benchmarking Ontology Reasoners: Techniques, Tools, and Insights

Gunjan Singh and Raghava Mutharaju

IIIT-Delhi, India
{gunjans,raghava.mutharaju}@iiitd.ac.in

Ontology-based reasoners are crucial for knowledge representation and reasoning across various domains, including healthcare and finance, as they facilitate informed decision-making. This tutorial will guide participants through key performance metrics, experimental design strategies, and data considerations required for effective benchmarking, equipping them with the knowledge to evaluate and enhance the capabilities of the reasoners.

Contents

Process Modeling

Enhancing BERT Performance: Multi-teacher Adversarial Distillation with Clean and Robust Guidance ... 3
Xunjin Wu, Jingfei Chang, Wen Cheng, Yunxiang Wu, Yong Li, and Lingfang Zeng

On the Task-Specific Effects of Fragmentation in Modular Process Models ... 18
Amine Abbad-Andaloussi, Clemens Schreiber, and Barbara Weber

A Universal Prompting Strategy for Extracting Process Model Information from Natural Language Text Using Large Language Models ... 38
Julian Neuberger, Lars Ackermann, Han van der Aa, and Stefan Jablonski

Agent System Event Data: Concepts, Dimensions, Applications ... 56
Qingtan Shen, Artem Polyvyanyy, Nir Lipovetzky, and Timotheus Kampik

Advanced Modeling Languages

Multi-faceted Evaluation of Modeling Languages for Augmented Reality Applications The Case of ARWFML ... 75
Fabian Muff and Hans-Georg Fill

Application of the Tree-of-Thoughts Framework to LLM-Enabled Domain Modeling ... 94
Jonathan Silva, Qin Ma, Jordi Cabot, Pierre Kelsen, and Henderik A. Proper

ECQL: Towards Succinct and Extensible Modeling of Multi-model Query Results ... 112
Gengyuan Shi, Chaokun Wang, and Yabin Liu

Ontological Modeling

An Analysis of the Semantic Foundation of KerML and SysML v2 ... 133
João Paulo A. Almeida, Luís Ferreira Pires, Giancarlo Guizzardi, and Gerd Wagner

Portions of Matter and Their Existential Events: An Ontology-Based Conceptual Model ... 152
Lucas Valadares Vieira, Fabricio Henrique Rodrigues, and Mara Abel

Model-Driven Design and Generation of Training Simulators for Reinforcement Learning ... 170
Sotirios Liaskos, Shakil M. Khan, John Mylopoulos, and Reza Golipour

Domain and Goal Modeling

Generating Secure Workflow Designs from Requirements Goal Models Using Patterns ... 195
Sotirios Liaskos, Ibrahim Jaouhar, Syed Muhammad Danish, and Shakil M. Khan

Modeling and Reasoning About Explanation Requirements Using Goal Models ... 215
Sotirios Liaskos, John Mylopoulos, Alex Borgida, and Shakil M. Khan

Enhancing Domain Modeling with Pre-trained Large Language Models: An Automated Assistant for Domain Modelers ... 235
Dominik Prokop, Štěpán Stenchlák, Petr Škoda, Jakub Klímek, and Martin Nečaský

Language Models and Conceptual Modeling

How are LLMs Used for Conceptual Modeling? An Exploratory Study on Interaction Behavior and User Perception ... 257
Syed Juned Ali, Iris Reinhartz-Berger, and Dominik Bork

Small, Medium, and Large Language Models for Text-to-SQL ... 276
Aiko Oliveira, Eduardo Nascimento, João Pinheiro, Caio Viktor S. Avila, Gustavo Coelho, Lucas Feijó, Yenier Izquierdo, Grettel García, Luiz André P. Paes Leme, Melissa Lemos, and Marco A. Casanova

Establishing Traceability Between Natural Language Requirements and Software Artifacts by Combining RAG and LLMs ... 295
Syed Juned Ali, Varun Naganathan, and Dominik Bork

Applications of Conceptual Modeling

GenACT: An Ontology-Based Temporal Web Data Generator 317
Gunjan Singh, Udit Arora, Shashikant Kumar, Riccardo Tommasini, Pieter Bonte, Sumit Bhatia, and Raghava Mutharaju

SAQI: An Ontology Based Knowledge Graph Platform for Social Air Quality Index 337
Saad Ahmad, Sudhir Attri, Ruchi Dwivedi, Muzamil Yaqoob, Aasim Khan, Praveen Priyadarshi, and Raghava Mutharaju

Conceptual Framework for Designing Hippocratic APIs 355
Sarmad Rezayat, Gerrit Burmester, Hui Ma, and Sven Hartmann

The Role-Artifact-Function Framework for Understanding Digital Identity Models 377
Frederico Schardong and Ricardo Custódio

Ontological Foundations of Resilience 396
Pedro Paulo F. Barcelos, Rodrigo F. Calhau, Ítalo Oliveira, Tiago Prince Sales, Frederik Gailly, Geert Poels, and Giancarlo Guizzardi

Conceptual Modelling Method for Digital Twins 417
Emilio Carrión, Óscar Pastor, and Pedro Valderas

Author Index 437

Process Modeling

Enhancing BERT Performance: Multi-teacher Adversarial Distillation with Clean and Robust Guidance

Xunjin Wu, Jingfei Chang, Wen Cheng(✉), Yunxiang Wu, Yong Li, and Lingfang Zeng(✉)

Zhejiang Lab, Hangzhou, China
{wuxunjin,chengwen,zenglf}@zhejianglab.cn

Abstract. The BERT model has slow inference speed due to the massive parameters, and it is susceptible to adversarial attacks due to lack of robustness. Knowledge distillation tackles the first issue by compressing the model, while adversarial training resolves the second issue by incorporating disturbances into training. However, existing knowledge distillation methods often struggle to balance between model accuracy and robustness. To address this, we propose a multi-teacher adversarial distillation approach for the BERT model. Our approach employs a clean teacher, providing soft labels to guide the student model in learning the clean samples, and a robust teacher, which employs adversarial training and semi-supervised learning to guide the student model in learning adversarial samples. Additionally, we introduce adaptive loss weights, which enable the student model to focus on the more challenging knowledge during training process. We validate the effectiveness of our proposed approach through experiments with various adversarial attack methods. On the typical text classification dataset IMDB, we improve the robust accuracy of the student DistilBERT model from 19.78 to 35.17, while maintaining a high clean accuracy of 93.17.

Keywords: BERT · Knowledge Distillation · Adversarial Training

1 Introduction

In the field of natural language processing research, pre-trained large language models based on the Transformer architecture, such as BERT [1], have achieved significant performance in various downstream tasks. However, the BERT models have a huge number of parameters, which makes their inference speed slow. To mitigate this issue, knowledge distillation methods [2] train smaller, less accurate student network to imitate larger and more accurate teacher network, which transfers the knowledge and compresses the model parameters. When distilling a large BERT model into a lightweight BERT model using knowledge distillation, it prevents the student model from overly relying on the true labels of training samples. Instead, the student learns the generalization capabilities of the teacher

W. Maass et al. (Eds.): ER 2024, LNCS 15238, pp. 3–17, 2025.
https://doi.org/10.1007/978-3-031-75872-0_1

model through the output logits, intermediate layers, or the Transformer's self-attention layers.

Currently, training a BERT model requires large-scale corpus datasets, but a significant portion of the corpus datasets have low quality. Some of them are artificially synthesized, while some are generated by large language models like ChatGPT [3], and some are adversarial examples from adversarial attack. As shown in Fig. 1, adversarial attack is a method to confuse model predictions by adding small but destructive perturbations to input samples, transforming clean texts like "This movie was pretty poor" into adversarial texts like "That movie was petty por". Adversarial attack changes characters, words, or sentences, leading to a significant drop in model prediction accuracy and posing a challenge to the application of the language model.

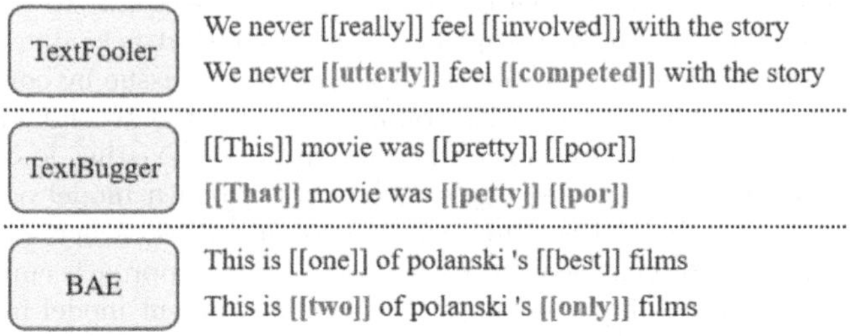

Fig. 1. Examples of adversarial attack strategies that convert the clean texts into the adversarial texts.

To mitigate the impact of adversarial samples, adversarial training methods is usually adopted. Adversarial training methods search for appropriate perturbations, and enable the model to learn features which are invariant to perturbations, thereby improving the robustness of the model. However, existing adversarial training methods often lead to a decrease in the accuracy of model recognition for clean samples.

In general, smaller models tend to have lower robustness, while larger models with good robustness face issues related to slower model inference speed and deployment difficulties. Adversarial distillation methods combine knowledge distillation and adversarial training, achieving model compression and enhancing model robustness. However, they share similar issues with adversarial training methods. In adversarial distillation, the student model mimics the probability distribution of the teacher model's predictions on adversarial samples. In contrast, in conventional distillation methods, the student model mimics the probability distribution of the teacher model's predictions on clean samples. Consequently, the accuracy of predicting clean samples may relatively decrease in adversarial distillation methods.

To address the above issues, this paper proposes a multi-teacher adversarial distillation method for the BERT model. The main contributions of this paper can be summarized as follows:

- We employ two teacher models: a clean teacher model that utilizes knowledge distillation to produce soft labels, guiding the student to recognize the clean samples, and a robust teacher model that utilizes adversarial training, guiding the student to recognize the adversarial samples. This overcomes the shortcoming of previous knowledge distillation work that couldn't balance the accuracy and robustness of student model effectively.
- During the training process, we dynamically adjust the loss weights for multi-teacher adversarial distillation, therefore, we can force the student model to focus on the knowledge which it cannot handle well. For example, when the distillation loss is large, we increase the weight of the student model learning from the clean teacher model. When the consistency loss is large, we can increase the weight of the student model learning from the robust teacher model. The adaptive loss weight updating strategy controls the student model's scale to learn from clean samples and adversarial samples.
- Through massive experiments, we validate the effectiveness of the proposed multi-teacher adversarial distillation method, as well as the impact of each component of the method.

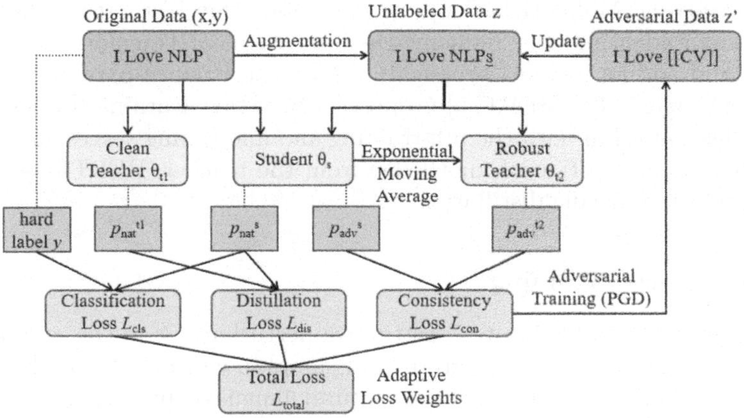

Fig. 2. Framework for multi-teacher adversarial distillation, where the original clean data (x, y) is augmented to obtain unlabeled data z, and then updated to adversarial sample z' based on consistency loss and PGD adversarial training algorithm.

2 Related Work

2.1 Knowledge Distillation

Hinton [2] first introduces the knowledge distillation method, where a smaller student model learns from a more complex teacher model to achieve knowledge transfer and model parameter compression. In traditional supervised learning, models aim to fit the probability distribution of their predictions to the true label distribution, while ignoring the hidden information contained in the probability distribution over non-correct classes. Knowledge distillation, as illustrated in Eq. (1), utilizes soft labels, denoted as q_i, produced by the teacher model to guide the student model. These soft labels are adjusted by a temperature parameter T, enabling the student model to learn smoother probability distributions and thus enhance its generalization ability.

$$q_i = \frac{exp(z_i/T)}{\Sigma_j exp(z_j/T)} \tag{1}$$

BERT [1] is a pre-trained language model based on the Transformer architecture, which uses a masking mechanism to give each word representation contextual information. It has demonstrated outstanding performance in the field of natural language processing. However, BERT models have a large number of parameters, and to make them more deployable, there have been many efforts to distill knowledge from BERT models to create lightweight variants. DistilBERT [4] aligns the student's outputs with soft labels from the teacher and uses cosine loss to align the directions of teacher and student hidden vectors, mitigating the risk of overfitting. MobileBERT [5] introduces bottleneck structures in both the teacher and student models, reducing the dimensions of Transformer inputs and outputs, and adding forward propagation layers to balance parameter ratios in the student model. TinyBERT [6] proposes a two-stage learning framework that involves distillation in both the pre-training and fine-tuning stages, ensuring the comprehensive acquisition of knowledge from the teacher, BERT-base, in both general and task-specific distillation.

2.2 Adversarial Training

Adversarial attacks add tiny yet destructive perturbations to the original input samples, converting them into adversarial samples, causing the model to make incorrect predictions. In the field of natural language processing, adversarial attack methods usually find the most important words or characters, and then modify them, such as TextFooler [7], TextBugger [8], BAE [9]. To defend against the adversarial attacks, Madry [10] proposes the Projected Gradient Descent Attack (PGD) algorithm, which formulates adversarial training as a min-max two-stage optimization problem.

$$\underset{\theta}{min}\mathbb{E}_{(x,y)\sim D}[\underset{r\in S}{max}L(\theta, x+r, y)] \tag{2}$$

As shown in Eq. (2), in the first stage, the algorithm seeks to find the optimal adversarial sample by maximizing the model's loss function L with respect to the data (x, y) from distribution D and model parameters θ. In the second stage, given the adversarial sample $(x+r, y)$, the algorithm optimizes the model parameters to minimize the loss function L, thereby enhancing the model's robustness.

2.3 Adversarial Distillation

Adversarial distillation methods combine adversarial training with knowledge distillation, allowing for defense against adversarial attacks while achieving model compression. Li [11] evaluates the robustness of multiple knowledge distillation methods under adversarial attacks, they adopt better training and data augmentation strategies, proposing a distillation method called ComKD, that balances robustness and generalization capabilities within and outside the domain. In the RSLAD [12] method, the teacher model guides the student model with robust soft labels, enabling the student model to better handle adversarial attacks while maintaining the generalization ability learned from the teacher model's normal training. Similar to our work, MTARD [13] introduces multi-teacher adversarial distillation for convolutional neural networks, but it is mainly applied in the field of computer vision rather than natural language processing.

Compared to existing knowledge distillation methods, our approach adopts adversarial training to update adversarial samples, which helps the model to be invariant to small perturbations. And an adaptive loss function weights updating strategy is employed, which allows student to focus more on the knowledge that is currently challenging. At the same time, we adopt the semi-supervised learning method Mean Teacher [14] to update the parameters of the robust teacher model, which provides smooth targets for the student, reducing its sensitivity to adversarial samples and improving overall robustness.

3 Methodology

As shown in Fig. 2, our multi-teacher adversarial distillation method takes original labeled text data and generates unlabeled adversarial data through data augmentation. A clean teacher model guides the student network to learn the correct classification ability for the original labeled text data, and a robust teacher model guides the student model to learn robustness for the unlabeled adversarial data.

3.1 Multi-teacher Adversarial Distillation

The original labeled training data (x, y) is input into the student model θ_s and clean teacher model θ_{t1} and obtain the prediction results. The student model learns the soft label p_{t1} output by the teacher model through knowledge distillation with temperature parameter T. As depicted in Eq. (3), we calculate the classification loss L_{cls} between the student model prediction result $p^s_{nat} = \theta_s(x)$ and the true hard label y, and the distillation loss L_{dis} between the soft label and the student model prediction result $p^{t1}_{nat} = \theta_{t1}(x)$. Where CE represents the cross-entropy loss function:

$$\begin{aligned} L_{cls} &= CE(y, p^s_{nat}) \\ L_{dis} &= CE(softmax(p^{t1}_{nat}/T), p^s_{nat}). \end{aligned} \tag{3}$$

To enhance data diversity, we utilize the nlpaug 1[1] library for text data augmentation of the original labeled data. Three text data augmentation methods are adopted: synonym replacement, which means randomly replacing words with synonyms; contextual word embedding method, which means augmenting words in sentences without altering the context; back-translation method, which means translating sentences into another language and then back into the original language. Since the augmented data may alter the semantics of the original data, we remove the labels. The original labeled data (x, y) is divided into three equal parts, where each part is augmented using one of the three methods, and then merged together into unlabeled data z.

The unlabeled data z is input to the student model θ_s and robust teacher model θ_{t2}, obtaining the prediction results $p^s_{adv} = \theta_s(z)$ and $p^{t2}_{adv} = \theta_{t2}(z)$, then the consistency loss L_{con} between the student and teacher predictions is calculated, which adopts the mean squared error loss function (MSE):

$$L_{con} = MSE(p^s_{adv}, p^{t2}_{adv}). \tag{4}$$

We carefully consider the choice of loss functions to effectively train the student model under the guidance of both clean and robust teacher models. The use of cross-entropy loss in Eq. (3) is motivated by its prevalence in classification tasks, where it provides a robust measure of the difference between predicted probabilities and true labels. This facilitates the student model's learning from clean samples as well as the soft labels from the clean teacher.

In contrast, the mean squared error loss, utilized in the consistency loss Eq. (4), serves to quantify the difference between the student model's predictions on adversarial samples and those of the robust teacher. This choice is deliberate, as it emphasizes the model's ability to maintain consistency under perturbations, which is crucial for robustness against adversarial attacks.

We aim for the robust teacher to guide the student in resisting adversarial attacks, so we adopt the PGD [10] adversarial training strategy, based on the min-max optimization problem of adversarial training. First, we maximize the consistency loss L_{con}, and iteratively approach the optimal perturbation r in the direction of gradient ascent through multiple small steps. If it exceeds a certain constraint space S, it is mapped back to the boundary of the space to ensure that the perturbation magnitude is not too large, and the adversarial sample is updated to $z' = z + r$:

$$\begin{aligned} r = z' - z = & \underset{\|z'-z\|_p \leq \varepsilon}{argmax}\, MSE\left(\theta_{t2}\left(z'\right), \theta_s\left(z'\right)\right) \\ r^{t+1} = & Clip_{\|r\|_p \leq \varepsilon}\left(r^t + \eta g\left(r^t\right) / \left\|g\left(r^t\right)\right\|_2\right) \\ g\left(r^t\right) = & \nabla_r MSE\left(\theta_{t2}\left(z + r^t\right), \theta_s\left(z + r^t\right)\right). \end{aligned} \tag{5}$$

where $t = 1, ..., K$, and K, ϵ, η are the number of disturbance, disturbance amplitude, and disturbance step size, respectively, $\|r\|_p \leq \varepsilon$ is the constrained

[1] https://github.com/makcedward/nlpaug.

space, $Clip_{\|r\|_p \leq \varepsilon}$ is the operation of mapping back to the constrained space boundary.

3.2 Adaptive Loss Weights and Mean Teacher Strategy

We employ the stochastic gradient descent (SGD) to optimize the parameters of the student model θ_s with the objective of minimizing the overall loss function L_{total}:

$$\begin{aligned} \underset{\theta_s}{argmin} L_{total} &= CE\left(y, \theta_s(x)\right) \\ &+ w_1 CE\left(softmax\left(\theta_{t1}(x)/T\right), \theta_s(x)\right) \\ &+ w_2 MSE\left(\theta_{t2}\left(z'\right), \theta_s\left(z'\right)\right). \end{aligned} \tag{6}$$

where w_1 and w_2 are the weights of distillation loss and consistency loss, reflecting the proportion of knowledge learned by the student model from the clean teacher and robust teacher, respectively.

$$\begin{aligned} w_1 &= exp\left(L_{dis}/L_{cls} - 1\right) \\ w_2 &= exp\left(L_{con}/L_{cls} - 1\right) \end{aligned} \tag{7}$$

As illustrated in Eq. (7), we adjust the weights of each loss function, so that the proportion of student model learning from true labels, distilled soft labels, adversarial robust knowledge dynamically changes with the training process:

Initially, the weights w_1 and w_2 are all set to 1.

During the training process, when the proportion of distillation loss compared to classification loss L_{dis}/L_{cls} is relatively large, it indicates that there is a large gap between the prediction of student and the soft label of clean teacher, so that more knowledge can be acquired from the clean teacher, therefore, the weight of the distillation loss w_1 is increased.

On the other hand, when the proportion of consistency loss compared to classification loss L_{con}/L_{cls} is relatively large, it indicates that there is a large gap between the predictions of student and robust teacher, so that more knowledge can be acquired from the robust teacher, therefore, the weight of the consistency loss w_2 is increased.

In the later stage of training, the student model has acquired strong ability to recognize both clean and adversarial samples, with w_1 and w_2 being quite small, and student learns more from the true labels rather than clean or robust teacher.

The advantage of adaptive loss is that the student model pays more attention to the knowledge that it is currently difficult to learn.

In general, a well-performing model should produce similar outputs for similar inputs. Therefore, we employ the Mean Teacher [14] semi-supervised learning mothod, where the parameters of the robust teacher model θ_{t2} are updated as the exponential moving average (EMA) of the student model's parameters θ_s. This consistency regularization allows the student model to learn smooth output targets from the robust teacher model, reducing the sensitivity of the student model

Algorithm 1: Multi-Teacher Distillation

input : Training data (x, y), augmented unlabeled data z.

for $Epoch \leftarrow 0$ **to** $MaxEpoch$ **do**
- Get the model predictions;
- Get L_{cls},L_{dis},L_{con} by Eqs. (3) and (4);
- Update adversarial data by Eq. (5);
- **for** $i \leftarrow 0$ **to** $MaxStep$ **do**
  - Update student by Eqs. (6) and (7);
  - Update robust teacher by Eq. (8);

output: Trained student BERT model θ_s.

to adversarial samples. The smoothing coefficient α signifies the extent to which historical teacher model information is preserved during the training iteration at round i. The first term encompasses historical data from the robust teacher model's parameters, while the second term incorporates information from the current iteration step of the student model:

$$\theta_{t2}^{i} = \alpha\theta_{t2}^{i-1} + (1 - \alpha)\theta_{s}^{i}. \tag{8}$$

The overall training algorithm for our proposed multi-teacher adversarial distillation is summarized in Algorithm 1.

4 Experiment

4.1 Datasets and Evaluation Metric

Our proposed algorithm is evaluated on four text classification datasets: AG News [15], IMDB [16], MR [17], and SST-2 [18]. For the evaluation of the models after training, we utilize the test set for all datasets except SST-2, for which we utilize the develop set since the test set labels are unavailable. After training, our evaluation process follows a two-step approach, we first evaluate the accuracy of the trained student model on the original test samples. Subsequently, we utilize the TextAttack [19] library to perturb the original test samples using adversarial attack strategies, such as TextFooler [7], TextBugger [8] and BAE [9]. As an indicator for evaluating the robustness of the distilled student model, we compare the original accuracy and robust accuracy, the smaller the difference between the two, the more difficult it is to perform adversarial attacks on the model, and the better the model's robustness.

4.2 Baseline Models

We utilize the pre-trained 12-layer BERT-base model from HuggingFace[2] library as our clean teacher model, and we initialize both the robust teacher model and

[2] https://huggingface.co/.

the student model with the pre-trained 6-layer DistilBERT [4], the latter is the distilled version of BERT-base, with less parameters. The student model trained using our multi-teacher adversarial distillation algorithm is denoted as MT-DistilBERT. We compare the clean and robust accuracy of MT-DistilBERT with the pre-trained BERT-base and DistilBERT models, along with the existing advanced BERT distillation methods, namely MobileBERT [5] and TinyBERT [6], TinyBERT adopts the same 6-layer architecture as DistilBERT, while MobileBERT is distilled by compressing the dimensions of the 24-layer BERT-large model.

4.3 Implementation Details

To determine the hyper-parameters, we conduct a grid search based on empirical parameters from previous knowledge distillation researches, including the learning rate, batch size, and the temperature parameter for the distillation process. We identify the optimal combination that yields the best performance on a validation set.

During the training process, we fine-tune the student DistilBERT model using the Adam optimizer with a learning rate of $2 * 10^{-5}$ for 3 epochs with a batch size of 4. The temperature parameter for the distillation process, denoted as T, is set to 3, as it provides a good balance between learning from the teacher model's soft label and the real sample's hard label.

Additionally, we incorporate a dropout layer with a rate of 0.2 before the final two fully-connected layers in the BERT model, in order to prevent overfitting, especially given that the student model is smaller than the teacher. Dropout layer works by randomly deactivating a subset of neurons during training, which promotes model generalization. A dropout rate of 0.2 is chosen after empirical testing to balance regularization and model capacity.

For updating the parameters of the robust teacher model, the EMA (Exponential Moving Average) smoothing coefficient α is 0.999. For PGD (Projected Gradient Descent) training, we define the following hyperparameters: the number of perturbation iterations K is set to 3, the perturbation magnitude ϵ is set at 1.0, and the perturbation step size η is 0.3.

4.4 Experimental Results

Main Results: The performance of different models is presented in Table 1, which contains clean accuracy and robust accuracy under various adversarial attack strategies, namely Textfooler, TextBugger and BAE. TextFooler is the strongest among the three adversarial attack methods, because the robust accuracy of each model decreases the most relative to the clean accuracy. Notably, although for the clean accuracy, our proposed MT-DistilBERT slightly lags behind its clean teacher model (BERT-base) and other BERT distillation methods (MobileBERT and TinyBERT) on most datasets, MT-DistilBERT achieves the highest robust accuracy, indicating superior robustness against adversarial attacks. It indicates that our method can effectively improve the robustness of the model, and meanwhile the clean accuracy of the model is not significantly decreased.

Table 1. Performance of the models on AG News, IMDB, MR and SST-2 datasets, clean means clean accuracy without attack on the original data, while the others are robust accuracy under different adversarial attacks.

		Dataset			
Attack	Model	AG	IMDB	MR	SST-2
Clean	BERT-base	94.31%	91.68%	83.30%	92.24%
	DistilBERT	92.68%	90.50%	82.93%	91.85%
	MobileBERT	94.92%	92.37%	85.22%	92.55%
	TinyBERT	**95.75%**	**94.12%**	**86.18%**	**93.50%**
	MT-DistilBERT(ours)	94.24%	93.17%	84.41%	92.14%
TextFooler	BERT-base	37.40%	36.30%	3.25%	2.44%
	DistilBERT	35.77%	18.70%	0.00%	6.37%
	MobileBERT	33.33%	29.27%	1.63%	3.25%
	TinyBERT	32.52%	**30.92%**	0.81%	4.96%
	MT-DistilBERT(ours)	**41.71%**	30.89%	**8.09%**	**7.26%**
TextBugger	BERT-base	48.78%	31.71%	26.83%	30.08%
	DistilBERT	46.34%	18.70%	13.82%	5.69%
	MobileBERT	33.33%	32.52%	25.73%	27.64%
	TinyBERT	47.97%	28.46%	30.08%	38.21%
	MT-DistilBERT(ours)	**50.28%**	**35.13%**	**36.99%**	**42.17%**
BAE	BERT-base	67.24%	29.27%	25.20%	35.77%
	DistilBERT	69.67%	21.95%	27.64%	25.45%
	MobileBERT	63.98%	35.77%	23.58%	34.96%
	TinyBERT	**76.67%**	24.39%	30.08%	35.86%
	MT-DistilBERT(ours)	72.11%	**39.45%**	**33.32%**	**38.42%**

Ablation Studies on Loss Functions: We conduct ablation experiments to prove the significance of individual components of the proposed multi-teacher adversarial distillation approach. To figure out how different model loss functions affect accuracy and robustness, four combinations are examined:

1) the classification loss only, where student model is trained solely using the clean labeled data, $L_{total} = L_{cls}$;

2) inclusion of classification loss and distillation loss, where student model learns from labeled data and soft labels provided by the clean teacher model, $L_{total} = L_{cls} + w_1 L_{dis}$;

3) combination of classification loss and consistency loss, where student model learns from labeled data and robust information from the robust teacher model, $L_{total} = L_{cls} + w_2 L_{con}$;

4) the full combination of classification loss, distillation loss and consistency loss, where student model learns from labeled data, soft labels from the clean teacher model, and robust information from the robust teacher model, $L_{total} = L_{cls} + w_1 L_{dis} + w_2 L_{con}$. The MT-DistilBERT's performance on the IMDB dataset, shown in Fig. 3, demonstrates that the full combination of loss functions yields the most robust student model. This underscores that multi-teacher adversarial distillation, as compared to guidance from either a single clean teacher or a single robust teacher, significantly enhances the student model's capacity to defend against adversarial samples, and meanwhile maintaining a high accuracy in clean sample predictions. In addition, we can see that adding distillation loss, which represents the knowledge of clean teacher, leads to certain improvements in both clean accuracy and robust accuracy. While introducing consistency loss, which represents the knowledge of a robust teacher, may reduce clean accuracy but significantly enhance robust accuracy.

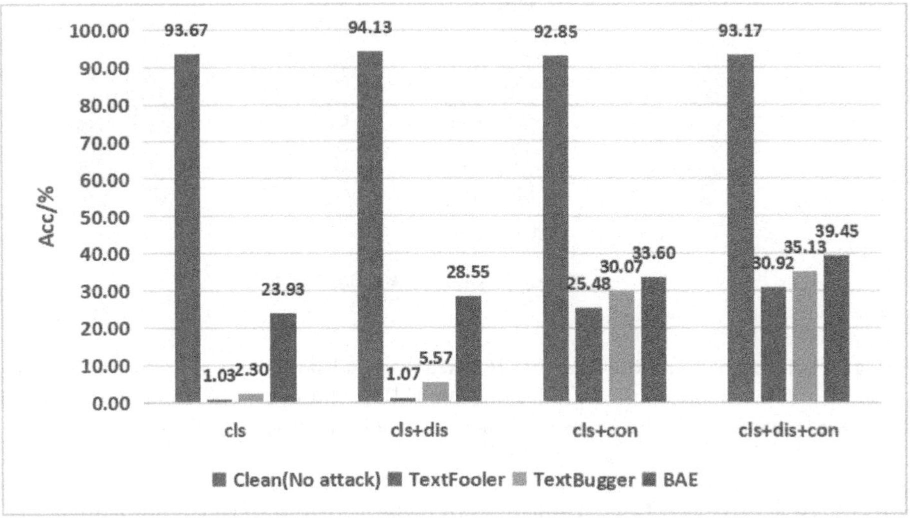

Fig. 3. Performance of DistilBERT student trained with diverse loss functions on IMDB dataset. Clean presents the original accuracy with no attack, and the others are robust accuracy under the three attack metrics using TextAttack.

Impact of Adversarial Training: For the adversarial data, we first augment the labeled data to produce unlabeled data, then update it by employing PGD adversarial training during the model training process. So we conduct ablation study to show the impact of PGD adversarial training on model performance. We consider two combinations of loss functions that will utilize PGD adversarial training, as mentioned earlier: $L_{total} = L_{cls} + w_2 L_{con}$, as well as $L_{total} = L_{cls} + w_1 L_{dis} + w_2 L_{con}$, which corresponds to scenarios where the student model is guided by a single robust teacher and multi-teacher distillation, respectively.

We compare the data z obtained from text data augmentation only and the data $z' = z + r$ obtained from PGD adversarial training, by Eq. (5), as the unlabeled adversarial data. The clean accuracy and robust accuracy for the four experimental settings are shown in Fig. 4, where robust accuracy is the average under the three adversarial attacks, TextFooler, TextBugger and BAE. It is evident that updating the adversarial samples through PGD adversarial training yields a substantial robustness improvement of the student model, whether we apply robust teacher guidance or multi teacher distillation.

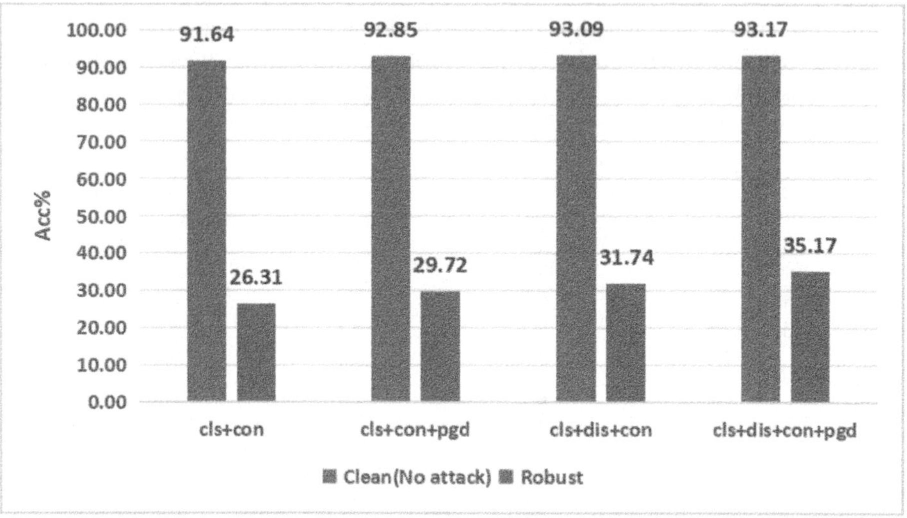

Fig. 4. Performance of MT-DistilBERT with or without pgd adversarial training method, and with diverse loss functions on IMDB dataset. The robust accuracy is the average accuracy under three adversarial attack metrics.

Impact of Adaptive Loss Weights: In order to validate the significance of the proposed adaptive loss weights updating strategy, we compare the training with adaptive loss weights to the training with fixed loss weights. The latter applies fixed and equal loss function weights, i.e., $w_1=w_2=1$. As shown in Fig. 5, whether using clean teachers, robust teachers, or multi-teacher distillation, employing adaptive loss function weights results in higher clean and robust accuracy for the student model compared to fixed weights. This demonstrates the effectiveness of the method, as it enables the student to focus more on the knowledge with larger loss and poorer performance.

5 Relevance to Conceptual Modeling

Conceptual modeling is about representing and structuring knowledge in a manner that is accessible for decision-making. Our method, through the use of a clean

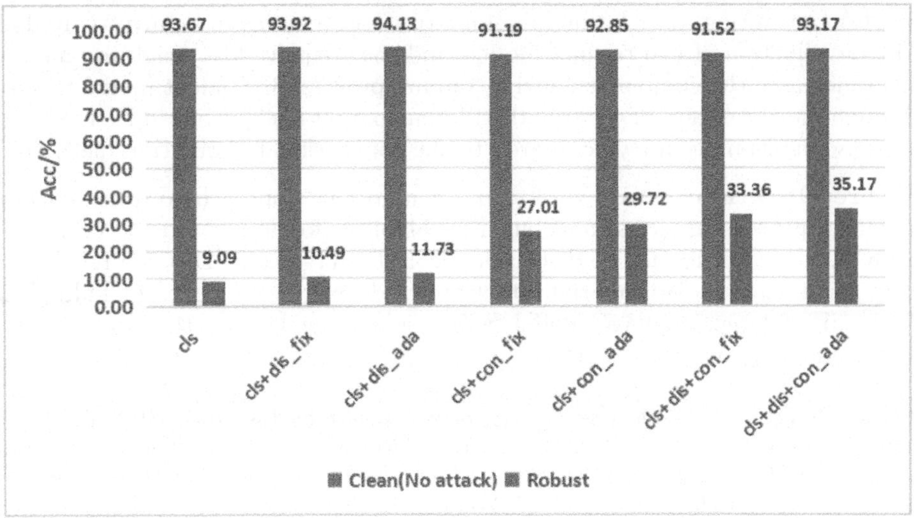

Fig. 5. Performance of MT-DistilBERT with adaptive or fixed loss weights. The robust accuracy is the average accuracy under three adversarial attack metrics.

teacher and a robust teacher, effectively transfers the knowledge embedded in a larger BERT model to a smaller student model. This transfer of knowledge is aligned to the way conceptual models convey the essence of complex systems, making them more manageable.

Besides, conceptual models are designed to be robust against various forms of uncertainty. Similarly, our method seeks to enhance the robustness of the BERT model against adversarial attacks, which can be seen as a form of uncertainty in the input data. By training the student model to recognize both clean and adversarial samples, our method reflects the elasticity required to construct good conceptual models that can adapt to changes in the environment.

6 Conclusion and Discussion

Main Findings: Our proposed multi-teacher adversarial distillation approach has significantly improved the student BERT model's robust accuracy for adversarial samples, while maintaining the high accuracy for clean samples, with the guidance of two teacher BERT models. Moreover, adaptive loss weights enable the student to focus on knowledge with poor performance, which may vary with the training phase.

Extensive experiments have demonstrated the effectiveness of multi-teacher adversarial distillation on typical text classification datasets compared to existing BERT distillation methods.

Limitations: Despite the promising results, our study has several limitations: 1. Our method is evaluated primarily on text classification tasks. The generalizability of our approach to other natural language processing tasks, such as question answering, translation or summarization, remains to be investigated. 2. The introduction of two teacher models and the adaptive loss weighting mechanism increases the complexity of the training process. 3. Student model trained through multi-teacher adversarial distillation exhibit a slight but indeed existing decrease in clean accuracy compared to the conventional distillation methods.

Future Direction: Future work could extend this approach to other natural language processing tasks, and ensure scalability for larger models or larger-scale datasets, not limited to distillation from BERT-base to DistilBERT. There are tons of emerging adversarial attacks towards language models, including the Jailbreak of large language model, which is a crucial trend that we will pay attention to in our future work.

Acknowledgments. This work is supported in part by the National Natural Science Foundation of China (U22A6001), the National Key R&D Program of China (2022YFB4500405, 2023YFB4503005), the Zhejiang provincial "Ten Thousand Talents Program" (2021R52007), and the Young Scientists Fund of the National Natural Science Foundation of China (62306286).

Disclosure of Interests. The authors have no competing interests to declare that are relevant to the content of this article.

References

1. Kenton, J.D.M.-W.C., Toutanova, L.K.: Bert: pre-training of deep bidirectional transformers for language understanding. In: Proceedings of NAACL-HLT, pp. 4171–4186 (2019)
2. Hinton, G., Vinyals, O., Dean, J.: Distilling the knowledge in a neural network. arXiv preprint arXiv:1503.02531 (2015)
3. OpenAI. Chatgpt: optimizing language models for dialogue (2022)
4. Sanh, V., Debut, L., Chaumond, J., Wolf, T.: Distilbert, a distilled version of bert: smaller, faster, cheaper and lighter. arXiv preprint arXiv:1910.01108 (2019)
5. Sun, Z., Yu, H., Song, X., Liu, R., Yang, Y., Zhou, D.: Mobilebert: a compact task-agnostic bert for resource-limited devices. In: Proceedings of the 58th Annual Meeting of the Association for Computational Linguistics, pp. 2158–2170 (2020)
6. Jiao, X., et al.: Tinybert: distilling bert for natural language understanding. In: Findings of the Association for Computational Linguistics: EMNLP 2020, pp. 4163–4174 (2020)
7. Jin, D., Jin, Z., Zhou, J.T., Szolovits, P.: Is bert really robust? a strong baseline for natural language attack on text classification and entailment. Proc. AAAI Conf. Artif. Intell. **34**(05), 8018–8025 (2020)
8. Li, J., Ji, S., Du, T., Li, B., Wang, T.: Textbugger: generating adversarial text against real-world applications. In: Proceedings 2019 Network and Distributed System Security Symposium. Internet Society (2019)
9. Garg, S., Ramakrishnan, G.: Bae: bert-based adversarial examples for text classification. In: Proceedings of the 2020 Conference on Empirical Methods in Natural Language Processing (EMNLP), pp. 6174–6181 (2020)

10. Madry, A., Makelov, A., Schmidt, L., Tsipras, D., Vladu, A.: Towards deep learning models resistant to adversarial attacks. In: International Conference on Learning Representations (2018)
11. Li, T., Rashid, A., Jafari, A., Sharma, P., Ghodsi, A., Rezagholizadeh, M.: How to select one among all? an empirical study towards the robustness of knowledge distillation in natural language understanding. In: Findings of the Association for Computational Linguistics: EMNLP 2021, pp. 750–762 (2021)
12. Zi, B., Zhao, S., Ma, X., Jiang, Y.-G.: Revisiting adversarial robustness distillation: robust soft labels make student better. In: Proceedings of the IEEE/CVF International Conference on Computer Vision, pp. 16443–16452 (2021)
13. Zhao, S., Wang, X., Wei, X.: Mitigating the accuracy-robustness trade-off via multi-teacher adversarial distillation. arXiv preprint arXiv:2306.16170 (2023)
14. Tarvainen, A., Valpola, H.: Mean teachers are better role models: weight-averaged consistency targets improve semi-supervised deep learning results. Adv. Neural Inf. Process. Syst. **30** (2017)
15. Zhang, X., Zhao, J., LeCun, Y.: Character-level convolutional networks for text classification. Adv. Neural Inf. Process. Syst. **28** (2015)
16. Maas, A., Daly, R.E., Pham, P.T., Huang, D., Ng, A.Y., Potts, C.: Learning word vectors for sentiment analysis. In: Proceedings of the 49th Annual Meeting of the Association for Computational Linguistics: Human Language Technologies, pp. 142–150 (2011)
17. Pang, B., Lee, L.: Seeing stars: exploiting class relationships for sentiment categorization with respect to rating scales. In: Proceedings of the 43rd Annual Meeting on Association for Computational Linguistics, pp. 115–124 (2005)
18. Socher, R., et al.: Recursive deep models for semantic compositionality over a sentiment treebank. In: Proceedings of the 2013 Conference on Empirical Methods in Natural Language Processing, pp. 1631–1642 (2013)
19. Morris, J., Lifland, E., Yoo, J.Y., Grigsby, J., Jin, D., Qi, Y.: Textattack: a framework for adversarial attacks, data augmentation, and adversarial training in NLP. In: Proceedings of the 2020 Conference on Empirical Methods in Natural Language Processing: System Demonstrations, pp. 119–126 (2020)

On the Task-Specific Effects of Fragmentation in Modular Process Models

Amine Abbad-Andaloussi[1(✉)], Clemens Schreiber[2], and Barbara Weber[1]

[1] University of St. Gallen, St. Gallen, Switzerland
{amine.abbad-andaloussi,barbara.weber}@unisg.ch
[2] Karlsruhe Institute of Technology, Karlsruhe, Germany
clemens.schreiber@kit.edu

Abstract. Modularization has been extensively investigated for its role in enhancing the comprehension of process models by dividing them into smaller, self-contained and manageable modules. However, existing studies have reported inconclusive results, prompting further exploration into when modularization supports or impedes process comprehension. Among the key factors suggested to influence the effect of modularization is the type of the task at hand. Indeed, the fragmentation of information across several modules caused by modularization can challenge readers' comprehension of process models, especially if the task is not confined to a single module. While the effect of fragmentation has been explored for flow-based tasks, requiring understanding procedural aspects of process models, our work extends to circumstantial tasks, which instead demand comprehending model rules and constraints that rely on the broader context associated with specific process parts. Using eye-tracking, we investigate how the fragmentation of information caused by modularization impacts cognitive integration (i.e., the collection and synthesis of dispersed information) and its subsequent effect on cognitive load and model comprehension. Our findings demonstrate that fragmentation significantly affects cognitive integration in flow-based tasks only. Moreover, our results show that cognitive integration is linked to both cognitive load and readers' comprehension of process models. The outcome of this work provides a detailed model, explaining the task-specific effects of fragmentation. Practically, our findings highlight the need for modeling tools that dynamically adjust their user interface to reduce cognitive integration demands, thereby enhancing model comprehension.

Keywords: Process model Comprehension · Eye-tracking · Cognitive Integration · Cognitive Load

1 Introduction

Understanding complex processes using process models is key to performing management and technical tasks, ranging from strategic decision making to effective process redesign and enhancement [18,28]. Modularization has been widely

W. Maass et al. (Eds.): ER 2024, LNCS 15238, pp. 18–37, 2025.
https://doi.org/10.1007/978-3-031-75872-0_2

investigated, in this vein, for its role in supporting the comprehension of complex processes through the division of these processes into smaller, self-contained, and manageable modules (cf. overview in [62]). Yet, there is no consensus on whether modularization supports or hinders model comprehension. which prompts further exploration into the conditions under which modularization is beneficial [62].

One critical factor that influences the effectiveness of modularization is the type of task at hand [51, 62]. Modularized models inherently cause information to be fragmented across several modules, affecting readers' mental effort (i.e., cognitive load) and task performance (in terms of model comprehension) in a manner that varies with the task type [51]. Indeed, previous research [51] has shown that local tasks, which require information located within a single module, are generally unaffected by such fragmentation. In contrast, global tasks, which require information from multiple modules, suffer due to the increased effort imposed by the split attention effect and the need to cognitively integrate information from different locations [51, 62]. However, these findings have been predominantly based on flow-based tasks [51, 62]. These tasks (also called sequential tasks) require understanding the procedural aspects of the process [19, 23, 45, 57]. A typical example of a flow-based comprehension task involves determining whether, in a given model, an activity can be executed before or after another one.

This paper broadens the scope of existing research [51, 62] by incorporating circumstantial tasks in the investigation of fragmentation caused by modularization. Unlike flow-based tasks, circumstantial tasks require an understanding of the broader context associated with specific parts of the process. These tasks often involve rules or constraints that are not strictly sequential but are dependent on certain state changes within the process [19, 23, 45, 57]. A typical example of a circumstantial comprehension task involves determining whether, in a given model, certain activities can only be executed when an object in the process gets into a specific state. Both flow-based and circumstantial tasks are needed in practice. Flow-based tasks are common to understand routine and procedural process operations, whereas circumstantial tasks are critical in comprehending the circumstances under which a particular process outcome can occur [19, 23, 45, 57]. Moreover, our paper delves further into the investigation of the interplay between fragmentation and cognitive load as well as task performance by introducing cognitive integration (i.e., the collection and synthesis of information distributed over several locations [13]) as a mediating variable. Cognitive integration is thereby considered as a driver for readers' cognitive load and task performance. Furthermore, our work expands the research on flow-based and circumstantial tasks by integrating cognitive integration into the investigation of these tasks, which previous studies have not thoroughly explored [19, 23, 45, 57]. Additionally, it contributes to the growing research stream that examines how distinct task characteristics affect process model comprehension [34, 44, 48, 51].

Our research questions can be summarized as follows: **RQ1. How does fragmentation in modular process models impact readers' cognitive integration in flow-based and circumstantial comprehension tasks?** and **RQ2. How does cognitive integration affect readers' cognitive load and**

task performance? To answer these questions, we designed and conducted an eye-tracking experiment, aiming to obtain detailed insights into readers' cognitive integration through their visual behavior during different comprehension tasks. Also, this technology allows to objectively assess readers' cognitive load. In our experiment, we used horizontal modularization, a technique that involves breaking down a system into interconnected modules without imposing hierarchical constraints [33,59]. This approach facilitates the modeling of knowledge-intensive and flexible processes [1,26], and is frequently used to model case-based processes [1,26]. It has also been shown to enhance process model comprehension [59]. Specifically, we adopt the fragment-based approach [26] within the horizontal modularization paradigm. Our findings indicate that the fragmentation of information caused by modularization affects readers' cognitive integration differently in flow-based local and global tasks, whereas cognitive integration remains equally high in both circumstantial local and global tasks. The implications of this work extend to both research and practice. Especially, in research, our work provides a more detailed model that explains the effect of fragmentation on cognitive integration and its subsequent effect on cognitive load and task performance while considering both flow-based and circumstantial tasks. Practically, our findings raise the need for advanced tool support that can dynamically adjust their user interface to reduce readers' cognitive integration demands and thus lower their cognitive load and increase their performance.

The remainder of this paper is structured as follows. Section 2 presents the background and related work. Section 3 describes our empirical research method. Section 4 presents our findings. Then, Sect. 5 discusses these findings, relates them to the existing literature, and highlights the implications of our research and its threats. Finally, Sect. 6 concludes the paper and sets directions for future work.

2 Background and Related Work

This section presents the background and related work, Sect. 2.1 provides an overview of process model comprehension, Sect. 2.2 introduces the different facets of modularization and the associated effects. Section 2.3 introduces cognitive integration, cognitive load and process comprehension measures.

2.1 Process Model Comprehension

Existing research on process model comprehension can be organized into three key streams: (1) research focused on the *presentation* of process models, which can be further divided into those focused on presentation mediums and tools (e.g., [3,54]) and those investigating the syntax, semantics and pragmatics of process models (e.g., [21,22,36,49,52,58–60]). (2) Research focused on the *users* of process models, notably looking into domain knowledge, expertise and educational aspects (e.g., [8,32,37,47]). (3) Research exploring the characteristics of the *tasks* for which process models are used and their impact on process model comprehension (e.g., [16,34,48,50,51,62]). Therein, authors have, for instance, investigated the difference between schema-based tasks (i.e., requiring information shown explicitly in the model) versus non-schema-based tasks (i.e., requiring knowledge beyond the explicit information provided by the model) [48], local tasks (i.e., addressing a single module of a modular process model) versus global tasks (i.e., addressing many modules of a modular process model) [50,51,62], and flow-based tasks (i.e., examining the procedural aspects of processes) versus circumstantial tasks (i.e., examining the rules and constraints within the process that are not strictly sequential but are dependent on certain state changes) [19,23,45,57]. Our work contributes to the stream of research focused on the task characteristics by examining the interplay between local and global tasks, both in flow-based and circumstantial contexts. To the best of our knowledge, such a combination has not yet been explored in the literature.

2.2 Modularization

Modularization in Process Models. Modularization refers to the technique of dividing a system into interconnected, self-contained modules [43]. The literature on process modeling identifies three distinct forms of modularization: vertical, horizontal, and orthogonal [33,59]. Vertical modularization organizes the process into hierarchical modules [33,59]. In contrast, horizontal modularization splits the process into various linked modules without imposing a hierarchical structure [33,59]. Orthogonal modularization organizes the process based on cross-cutting concerns such as privacy and security, spanning over several parts of the process [33,59]. Given that horizontal modularization facilitates the division of process modules without any restrictions on hierarchical relationships or cross-cutting concerns, it emerges as a more universally applicable method.

The Fragment-based Modeling Approach. This approach [26] is a representative for horizontal modularization. It is based on the Business Process Modeling and Notation (BPMN) [41]. At the design stage, complex processes are segmented into smaller, independently modeled modules (i.e., called *fragments*) that are interconnected through the use of data objects. These objects are linked to specific process activities and serve to define the pre- and post-conditions constraining their execution. Each data object is further associated with a specific data class and is assigned a state. The different states and their progression are organized into a structure known as a lifecycle, which is a labeled transition system. Transitions between states occur as a result of executing a process activity. At run time, the fragments can be executed in different orders. Therein, the interaction protocol between the different fragments, defining how they could possibly be combined, is handled through the data objects and their lifecycles. Since the connections among the fragments do not have to follow a hierarchical structure, the fragment-based approach reflects very well the core principle of horizontal modularization.

Figure 1 depicts an example of a logistics process modeled using the fragment-based approach. This figure shows 2 out of 6 fragments and one out of 3 life-

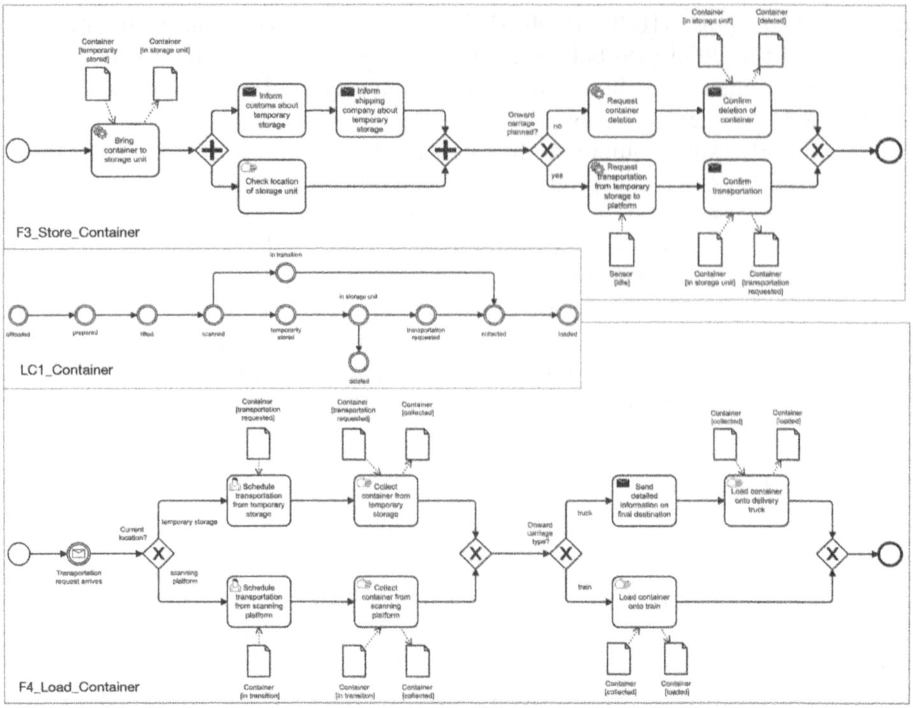

Fig. 1. Example of a process modeled using the fragment-based approach. A better resolution is available in our online Appendix (See Footnote 1).

cycles that we have actually used in our experiment (cf. Sect. 3.2). The fragments *F3_Store_Container* and *F4_Load_Container* use the data-object *Container* to interact with each other. The lifecycle of this data object is shown in *LC1_Container*. To demonstrate the interaction between the two fragments, in *F3_Store_Container*, when the activity *Confirm transportation* is executed, the state of the data object *Container* moves from *[in storage unit]* to *[transportation requested]*. Consequently, the execution of the activity *Schedule transportation from temporary storage* becomes enabled in *F4_Load_Container*.

Besides the fragment-based approach, various techniques have been suggested in the literature to decompose processes horizontally. For example, events have been used to connect process fragments (cf. overview in [31]). Our study, however, uses the fragment-based approach [26] because it is rooted in BPMN [41]—the process modeling language standard in the industry. Moreover, this approach has clear execution semantics driven by pre- and post-conditions, assigned as data objects to the process activities. These semantics enhance the expressiveness of the approach and enable capturing complex process behavior efficiently.

The Task-specific Effect of Fragmentation in Modular Process Models. Depending on the characteristics of the task at hand, modularization could have varying effects [50,51,62]. Indeed, modularization could lead to fragmentation when the task-relevant information span multiple modules [7,51,62]. This hypothesis was specifically tested in [50,51], where the authors have found that global tasks, addressing several process modules, are more impeded by the effect fragmentation than local tasks, addressing a single module. This effect translated into higher cognitive load and lower task performance (in terms of model comprehension) in global tasks compared to the local ones. While the authors in [50,51], focused on flow-based tasks, our study broadens the scope to circumstantial tasks. Moreover, it uses cognitive integration [13] as a factor that mediates the relationship between fragmentation, and cognitive load as well as task performance.

2.3 Cognitive Integration, Cognitive Load and Comprehension

Cognitive Integration. This process involves merging information from various sources [13]. In process modeling research, eye-tracking data have indicated that visual associations act as a good indicator of cognitive integration [13]. The run count measure is a key metric for capturing readers' visual associations as documented in [13]. It quantifies the number of times a reader enters and exits areas of interest (i.e., process model elements) that are relevant to solving a specific task. While the authors in [13] have linked this measure to task performance, its relationship with cognitive load still requires statistical evidence. Such evidence would establish the relationship between cognitive integration and cognitive load. Motivated by the goal to substantiate this relationship, our work first confirms the impact of cognitive integration on task performance, as reported in [13], and extends the investigation to also assess the effect of cognitive integration on cognitive load in the context of process comprehension tasks.

Cognitive Load. Cognitive load defines the strain imposed on the human working memory when executing a mental task [14,42]. The cognitive load theory (CLT) posits that human performance is constrained by their cognitive load [14,42]. When reaching high levels of cognitive load (also called cognitive overload), their performance is likely to drop [14,42], leading them to misinterpret the process behavior in the context of comprehension tasks. Cognitive load can be quantified using subjective and objective measures. The subjective measures rely on self-reporting where users are asked to subjectively assess the difficulty they perceived when solving a given task. In the literature [5,50,51,62], this is typically administrated using a 5-point Likert scale ([0: "very easy", 4: "very difficult"]). The objective measures, in turn, are usually based on users' behavioral and physiological reactions to cognitive load. In this regard, eye-tracking technology can provide interesting insights [14,27,56]. Unlike the subjective assessment of perceived difficulty that is collected in a retrospective manner, eye-tracking continuously captures users' visual behavioral and physiological reactions to cognitive load throughout the entire task, offering detailed temporal insights [27]. Central to eye-tracking is the notion of a fixation, which refers to the time period the human eyes remain still at a specific location in a stimulus [27]. According to the eye-mind hypothesis, our eyes fixate on what our minds are actively processing [30]. Based on that, the work by Glöckner and Herbold [24] suggests that fixations longer than 250 ms are indicative of mental processing, which accentuates as the duration of the fixation increases, signifying progressively deeper levels of mental processing. Fixation-based measures have been applied in several studies to capture users' cognitive load [5,50,51,55,59]. The *low/high index of pupil activity* (LHIPA) [17] is another approach to objectively assess cognitive load. This index differentiates lower and higher oscillations in pupil frequencies, with lower values indicating higher levels of cognitive load. The LHIPA measure has been used in a set of studies as a robust indicator of cognitive load [6,50,51].

Task Performance in Terms of Process Comprehension. Users' performance has been assessed through various metrics (cf. overview in [20]). These metrics often evaluate both the correctness of the operations required by a task and the time needed to complete these operations. A particularly insightful metric that encapsulates both aspects is the comprehension efficiency measure. This measure, is calculated as the ratio of task correctness to the task duration [38]. Higher values indicate higher comprehension efficiency.

Overall, as outlined in Sect. 1, our study investigates the effect of fragmentation on cognitive integration and its subsequent influence on cognitive load and task performance, considering both flow-based and circumstantial tasks. Drawing on existing literature, we are capturing cognitive integration using the run count measure, cognitive load using a 5-point Likert scale of perceived difficulty, mental processing fixations, and LHIPA; and finally, task performance using the comprehension efficiency measure.

3 Research Method

3.1 Research Model

The Task-Dependent Effect of Fragmentation on Cognitive Integration. As specified in Sect. 2.2, modularization can lead to fragmentation [43,51,62]. Hence, when solving tasks that require information covering several modules, readers would engage in a complex process of collecting and synthesizing this information, known as cognitive integration [13]. We advance that this effect can be observed by contrasting local tasks confined to a single module with global tasks spanning several modules. This effect is, however, expected to occur only when the tasks address procedural aspects of the process (i.e., flow-based tasks). This is because, for flow-based local tasks, the procedural information needed to complete the task is readily available within a single, self-contained module, reducing the need for extensive cognitive integration. Whereas for flow-based global tasks, the procedural information is spread across multiple modules, necessitating a significant amount of cognitive integration as readers must trace the dependencies between process activities that are not immediately visible within a single module. When it comes to circumstantial tasks, we expect that the differentiation between local and global tasks in terms of cognitive integration would not be as pronounced as for flow-based tasks. Indeed for both circumstantial local and global tasks, a substantial level of cognitive integration is required as readers need to understand the rules and constraints closely tied to the different process activities and how these integrate and affect the process behavior.

Based on these assumptions, we expect the relationship between fragmentation and cognitive integration to be moderated by the task perspective (i.e., flow-based or circumstantial). This is because the task perspective factor can affect the strength of the aforementioned relationship depending on its levels [25,40]. Hence, our first hypothesis can be formulated as follows: **H1: The effect of fragmentation on cognitive integration in process model comprehension is moderated by the task perspective.**

The Effects of Cognitive Integration on Cognitive Load and Task Performance. Cognitive integration involves the collection and synthesis of information from various sources [13]. Throughout this process, readers must identify each piece of information relevant to their task and temporarily store it in working memory until all the other corresponding pieces of information are located and assembled together. Considering the limited capacity of the working memory, the increased need for information intake occurring during cognitive integration is expected to yield high levels of cognitive load [14,39,53]. Higher demands for cognitive integration are also expected to yield lower task performance. Indeed, when task-relevant information is consolidated in one place and only low cognitive integration is needed, mapping this information to the reader's existing mental scheme (i.e., mental structure capturing well-integrated chunks of knowledge) is simpler, than in cases where the information is dispersed over several places and high cognitive integration is needed [11,29]. In such scenarios, readers should combine and reorganize information before finding a fit with their mental scheme [11,29]. This process is expected to take longer and plausibly be more prone to errors, which would translate to reduced comprehension efficiency and thus low task performance.

Based on these assumptions, we formulate our second hypothesis as follows: **H2: Readers' cognitive integration during process comprehension can explain their cognitive load and task performance.**

Research Model Overview. Overall our study aims to investigate the complex relationship between *fragmentation* in modular process models, denoting our independent variable, and readers' *cognitive load* as well as *task performance*, both denoting our dependent variables. We use *task perspective* as a moderator and *cognitive integration* as a mediator [25,40]. An overview of our research model is depicted in Fig. 2. Fragmentation is operationalized with local and global tasks. Cognitive load is operationalized with both objective measures derived from fixation and pupil measurements (i.e., mental processing fixations above 250ms [24] and LHIPA [17]) and a subjective 5-point Likert scale of perceived difficulty. Task performance is operationalized with comprehension efficiency [38]. The task perspective, in turn, is operationalized with flow-based and circumstantial tasks [23]. Cognitive integration is operationalized through visual associations captured with the run count measure [13].

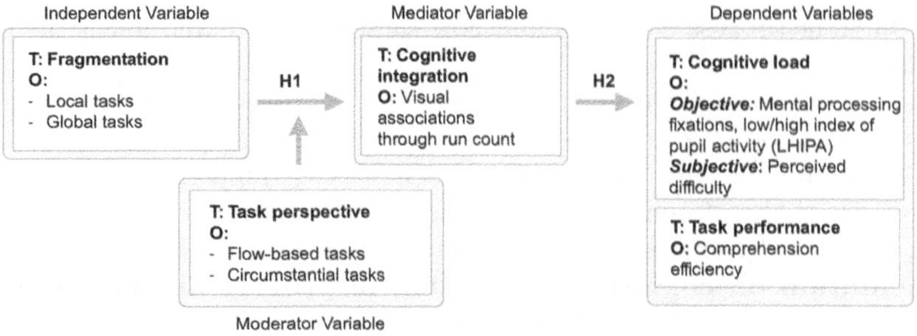

Fig. 2. Research model **T**: theoretical construct. **O**: Operationalization of construct.

3.2 Material and Participants

Material. The material designed for this experiment covers a large process model, capturing a logistics process, and a collection of tasks with different characteristics. Using the fragment-based approach [26], the logistics process is divided into six distinct fragments modeling (1) the offloading of a container upon its arrival at a port, (2) the scanning of the container, (3) the procedure for storing the container, (4) the loading of the container for delivery, (5) the management of information pertaining to the container, and (6) the analysis and reporting of any shakes that occur during the container's handling at the port. The communication between these fragments is carried out through 3 data objects: i.e., container, sensor, and an enterprise resource planning (ERP) file. Throughout the process execution, each object can take a set of possible states which are represented in three respective object life cycles. A portion of this logistics process is depicted in Fig. 1, while the full process is available as part of the experiment material uploaded to our online Appendix[1]. To avoid confounding factors, the process fragments were designed with similar essential and accidental complexity [2,9]. For the former, each fragment has 6 to 8 activities and 2 to 4 exclusive or parallel gateways. As for the latter, the layout of the models was carefully designed and all the activities were labeled using the verb-object naming convention [15,36]. Details specific to real logistic processes were removed from the models to avoid the impact of domain knowledge and the use of common sense.

The experiment includes a set of 8 *flow-based* and 6 *circumstantial* tasks, half of which (4 flow-based, 3 circumstantial) address *local* aspects that can be found within a single process fragment and the other half address *global* aspects

[1] See https://github.com/aminobest/ER2024Fragmentation.

that require information spread over two process fragments. The flow-based tasks address popular workflow patterns including sequencing, choice, concurrency, and iteration (e.g., for sequencing: "The activity X needs to be executed before the activity Y"); whereas the circumstantial tasks focus on the overall pre- and post-conditions governing the execution of the process activities [19,23,45,57] (e.g., pre-conditions: "The activities X and Y can only be executed if the object O is in the state [state1]"). All these tasks comprise a statement that readers need to validate, by selecting one of the following options: *true, false, I don't know*, after checking the given set of process model fragments. To avoid task-related confounding factors, each pair of tasks compared according to our research model (i.e., flow-based local vs. flow-based global; circumstantial local vs. circumstantial global) comprises statements that are formulated exactly in the same way, addresses two process activities only and has the same answers (both true or both false). The material of this experiment including all the used tasks and process fragments is available in our online Appendix (See Footnote 1).

Participants. We recruited 46 participants for this experiment which took place at the University of St Gallen in Switzerland (22 participants), Karlsruhe Institute of Technology in Germany (17 participants), the research center Forschungszentrum für Informatik FZI in Karlsruhe (4 participants) and Promatis an IT-consulting company in Karlsruhe (3 participants). The participants ranged in age from 20 to 50 years, with the majority (63%) aged between 20 and 30 years. Their professional backgrounds fell into three primary categories: researchers with PhDs or higher (22 individuals), students (17 individuals), and those from an industry or IT-admin background (7 individuals). The participants had varying expertise in BPMN. To facilitate their involvement in the experiment, we conducted a standardized familiarization session and assessed their understanding through a quiz. Moreover, to minimize confounding effects due to differences in expertise, a within-subject design was used. Each participant repeatedly encountered flow-based local, flow-based global, circumstantial local and circumstantial global tasks. Although their background might influence the tasks' outcome, the within-subject design ensures that all treatments are equally affected, allowing for reliable conclusions about their distinct effects. Detailed demographics are available in our online Appendix (See Footnote 1).

3.3 Experiment Procedure

Every participant attended a separate experiment session that lasted approximately one hour. The sessions were conducted in a controlled laboratory setting. The session's procedure began by acquainting the participant with BPMN and the fragment-based modeling approach [26], followed by a brief quiz comprising two comprehension tasks to ensure good understanding of the modeling approach. During the quiz, participants were permitted to ask questions and receive feedback on their answers. All the participants passed the quiz and therefore could participate in the experiment. Prior to the main experiment's part, participants had to fill out a demographic survey asking about their background and experience in process modeling and checking their physical ability to participate in an eye-tracking experiment. The experiment then proceeded with two test tasks designed to help participants become familiar with the experimental setup. These initial tasks were not included in the final data analysis to prevent any biases stemming from the participants' unfamiliarity with the experimental setup. To counter any potential learning effect, the tasks were randomized and presented in varying sequences to different participants. For each task, participants were given the 6 process model fragments of the logistic process (cf. Sect. 3.2) and were asked to validate a statement about this process. Following that, a 5-point Likert scale was administered to assess their perceived difficulty of that task.

3.4 Data Collection and Analysis Approaches

Data Collection. The first phase of data collection involved the gathering of demographic data as outlined in Sect. 3.3. The second phase involved eye-tracking. Therein, we used a Tobii X3-120 eye-tracker attached to a 24" monitor. To ensure consistent recording quality, lab lighting was adjusted according to established guidelines [27]. The open-source eye-tracking software EyeMind [6] was used to run the experiment protocol and to automatically link eye-tracking data with the underlying elements of the process model fragments.

Data Analysis. From the 46 participants, we collected a total of 644 data points per measure, distributed as follows: 184 data points for flow-based local and global tasks *each*, and 138 for circumstantial local and global tasks *each*. For one participant (SP11), the data for a flow-based local task and a flow-based global task were removed due to an issue during data collection, as the participant accidentally skipped these tasks.

We investigated the effect of fragmentation on readers' cognitive integration, considering the task perspective as a moderator variable (i.e., Hypothesis **H1**, cf. Sect. 3.1 and Fig. 2). As explained in Sect. 3.1 fragmentation was operationalized with local and global tasks, while cognitive integration was operationalized using the run count measure, which we calculated by counting the number of entries and exits to the process model elements relevant for each specific task (similar to [13]). The visits to these elements were automatically derived thanks to the automated mapping between eye-tracking data and the underlying process model elements granted by EyeMind [6]. The task perspective, in turn, was operationalized using flow-based and circumstantial tasks. At first, we computed the mean run count for flow-based local, flow-based global, circumstantial local and circumstantial global tasks. This allowed us to compare local vs global flow-based tasks as well as local vs global circumstantial tasks. These comparisons are shown on the left side of Table 1. For the inferential tests, to eliminate interdependencies between data points, we averaged the measurements to derive a single data point per participant, measure and condition (flow-based local, flow-based global, circumstantial local, and circumstantial global). Then, we used the MEMORE approach [40] to test for the moderating effect of the task perspective. MEMORE is adequate for repeated measures collected following a within-subject design. For this specific test, to meet the normal distribution assumption of MEMORE moderation analysis, we applied a log transformation to the run count measures and conducted the Shapiro-Wilk test to ensure that the data is normally distributed. As a second approach, we applied the non-parametric Wilcoxon Signed-Rank test (single-tailed) to compare the run count of flow-based local versus flow-based global tasks and the run count of circumstantial local versus circumstantial global tasks separately. Wilcoxon Signed-Rank test is adequate for repeated measures collected following a within-subject design and does not impose assumptions on the normality of the data. Using MEMORE to test for the moderating effect along with splitting the data and running separate Wilcoxon tests enhances the certainty regarding the moderating effect of the task perspective. The inferential tests are shown on the right side of Table 1.

Following that, we investigated the effect of cognitive integration on cognitive load and task performance (i.e., Hypothesis **H2**, cf. Sect. 3.1 and Fig. 2). Herein, we conducted a regression analysis of cognitive integration, operationalized with the run count measure, against cognitive load and task performance, operationalized with the measures shown in Fig. 2. The mental processing fixations and the LHIPA measures were derived respectively considering the gaze data and pupil data collected throughout each task. The fixations were derived using the Identification by Velocity Threshold-Algorithm (IVT) [27] and a threshold was set to keep only fixations associated with mental processing operations (i.e., with a duration >250 ms) [24]. The LHIPA, in turn, was calculated after cleaning the pupil data using the Cheetah Pipeline [63] and applying the LHIPA algorithm documented in [17]. The perceived difficulty measure was obtained from the 5-point Likert scale survey that the participants had to fill in after each task. The comprehension efficiency measure was calculated by dividing the task correctness by the time taken to complete that task in milliseconds. To run the regression analysis, we used the Robust linear Model Regression (RLM) approach, which is less sensitive to the assumption of normally distributed data. To avoid inter-dependencies between the data points when using RLM, we averaged each used measure to derive one data point per participant and measure. Then, to check whether the relationship between the run count measure and the dependent variables holds under the different conditions, we repeated the regression analysis for each level of each condition. The results are reported in Table 2. Detailed documentation of our analysis approach can be found in the Python notebook provided as part of the online Appendix (See Footnote 1).

4 Findings

The Task-specific Effect of Fragmentation on Cognitive Integration. The results summarized in Table 1 address **RQ1** (cf. Sect. 1). The left side of the table shows the descriptive statistics corresponding to the mean run count measured when solving flow-based local, flow-based global, circumstantial local, and circumstantial global tasks. Note that to investigate Hypothesis H1, the comparisons are done horizontally between local and global tasks (cf. Fig. 2). These statistics suggest that flow-based global tasks yield a higher run count than flow-based local tasks. However, for circumstantial global and local tasks, no clear difference in the means of run count is apparent. The inferential statistics shown on the right side of Table 1 confirm these observations as the mean difference of the former comparison is significant (both p-values of MEMORE and Wilcoxon tests $<.001$), while the mean difference of the latter comparison is not significant (p-value MEMORE=0.690, p-value Wilcoxon=0.667). Overall, these results support **H1** (*The effect of fragmentation on cognitive integration in process model comprehension is moderated by the task perspective*) as the task perspective (flow-based versus circumstantial) affects the relationship between fragmentation and cognitive integration. This finding is discussed in Sect. 5.

Table 1. Analysis of readers' cognitive integration when solving different types of tasks, via the run count measure. M: mean. *p*-value Wilcoxon is the result of the Wilcoxon Signed-Rank test. *p*-value MEMORE is the result of the MEMORE moderation analysis. Additional statistics provided by MEMORE (i.e., effect, standard error, t, confidence intervals) are provided in our online appendix as part of the analysis notebook (See Footnote 1).

Task perspective	Measure	Descriptive		Inferential	
		Local M	Global M	*p*-value *MEMORE*	*p*-value *Wilcoxon*
Flow-based	Run count	16.159	31.578	**<.001**	**<.001**
Circumstantial	Run count	20.962	20.379	0.690	0.667

Effect of Cognitive Integration on Cognitive Load and Task Performance. The findings summarized in Table 2 address **RQ2** (cf. Sect. 1). The influence of cognitive integration on cognitive load and performance across different task types—whether flow-based, circumstantial, local, or global—is evident. The regression analysis results indicate a significant impact of run count on both the objective cognitive load measures (i.e., mental processing fixations and low/high index of pupil activity LHIPA) and the comprehension efficiency measure, as indicated by the respective p-values in Table 2. However, the effect of run count on subjective perceived difficulty across three task types (flow-based local, flow-based global, and circumstantial global) is not significant. Moreover, the signs of the coefficient measures in Table 2 show that for all the tests with a significant effect, increases in run count lead to higher mental processing fixations as well as lower LHIPA and comprehension efficiency. These trends suggest that increased run count yields higher cognitive load and lower task performance (cf. Sect. 2.3). These results support **H2** (*Readers' cognitive integration during process comprehension can explain their cognitive load and task performance*) considering objective measures only. This finding is discussed in Sect. 5.

Table 2. Regression Analysis. Full statistics including the coef., standard error, z-score, and confidence intervals for the different regressions including the intercepts are provided in our online appendix as part of the analysis notebook (See Footnote 1). Abbreviations: Gr.: Group, Dep.: Dependent, Indep.: Independent, Var.: Variable, Coef.: Coefficient, Flow.: Flow-based, Circms.:Circumstantial.

Gr.	Indep. var.	Dep. var.	Coef.	p-value
Flow. local	Run count	Mental processing fixations	1.185	**<.001**
		Low/High Index of Pupil Activity	−0.009	**0.038**
		Perceived difficulty	0.006	0.561
		Comprehension efficiency	−4.89e-04	**<.001**
Flow. global	Run count	Mental processing fixations	1.966	**<.001**
		Low/High Index of Pupil Activity	−0.006	**0.012**
		Perceived difficulty	0.020	**0.005**
		Comprehension efficiency	−1.75e-04	**<.001**
Circms. local	Run count	Mental processing fixations	1.569	**<.001**
		Low/High Index of Pupil Activity	−0.011	**0.009**
		Perceived difficulty	0.008	0.518
		Comprehension efficiency	−2.79e-04	**0.001**
Circms. global	Run count	Mental processing fixations	1.456	**0.025**
		Low/High Index of Pupil Activity	−0.011	**0.040**
		Perceived difficulty	−0.016	0.414
		Comprehension efficiency	−2.54e-04	**0.006**

5 Discussion

This section synthesizes the findings presented in Sect. 4, discusses them in relation to existing literature and outlines their implications. Regarding our first hypothesis (i.e., **H1**, cf. Sect. 3.1), our results show a significant relationship between fragmentation in modular process models and readers' cognitive integration when solving flow-based tasks. Indeed, for flow-based global tasks, fragmentation caused an increase in readers' run count, which reflects higher visual associations and thus more cognitive integration [13], compared to flow-based local tasks. However, for circumstantial tasks, no significant differences were observed. The lack of a significant effect thereby aligns with our initial assumption in Sect. 3.1, suggesting that cognitive integration demands are inherent to circumstantial tasks, regardless of the degree of fragmentation. This proposition is supported by the descriptive statistics in Table 1, where the run count was equally high in both local and global circumstantial tasks. Our findings align with those reported in [44], suggesting that difficulty increases proportionately with the size of the task-relevant region in the model. This can be interpreted within our context to mean that tasks involving larger portions of the model likely demand more cognitive integration. Circumstantial tasks inherently require synthesizing context beyond the explicit control-flow depicted in the model, which typically involves more extensive regions of the model compared to flow-based local tasks. This broader scope likely explains the consistently high demands for cognitive integration in circumstantial tasks. Similarly, when comparing flow-based local and global tasks, the latter span multiple process fragments, corresponding to a broader area of the overall process and thus yielding higher demands for cognitive integration. With respect to the second hypothesis (i.e., **H2**, cf. Sect. 3.1), our results demonstrate that changes in readers' cognitive load and task performance can be explained by their cognitive integration efforts as captured by the run count measure. Indeed, the impact of this measure on the number of mental processing fixations, LHIPA, and readers' comprehension efficiency was consistent across all task types (flow-based local, flow-based global, circumstantial local, and circumstantial global). In contrast, the subjective perceived difficulty measure, which relies on participants' self-assessment using a Likert scale, was not significantly impacted by changes in run count in three out of the four task types. This discrepancy might be attributed to the nature of subjective measures, which are typically collected post-hoc (i.e., by the end of the task), thus failing to capture the continuous variations in cognitive load experienced throughout a task [14]. Moreover, subjective assessments are threatened by meta-cognitive biases where participants underestimate the difficulty of the task at hand or feel reluctance to report it [14]. Moreover, questionnaires used to capture users' cognitive load subjectively may be prone to interpretation ambiguities in some circumstances [14].

Our research has implications for both research and practice. For the former, our findings contribute to the body of existing research investigating the comprehension of modular process models [12,46,50,51,54,59,62], specifically those focused on the cognitive effects of fragmentation [50,51,62]. Additionally, our results highlight the importance of potential moderating factors, such as the task perspective (flow-based or circumstantial), which could influence the degree to which different levels of fragmentation affect cognitive integration. This underscores the need to carefully interpret existing theories. Furthermore, as the previous studies [19,23,45,57] investigating flow-based and circumstantial tasks did not incorporate cognitive integration into their theoretical frameworks, our work enriches this stream of research by considering a key factor that turned out to be significantly impacting users' cognitive load and task performance in our study. By considering the task perspective, our research further complements the insights on the impacts of cognitive integration in [13], which was rather focused on the model representation perspective. Also, our research expands the theoretical framework in [13] by delivering statistical evidence linking cognitive integration not only to users' performance but also to cognitive load.

At a practical level, our findings raise the need for enhanced tool support to mitigate the negative impacts of cognitive integration on cognitive load and task performance. For example, guided simulations can assist readers in mentally offloading [62] the complex relationships and interplay between different parts of process models [10] - whether these parts are contained within the same file (e.g., the same process model fragment or sub-process) or distributed across multiple files. Several studies in the literature have recognized guided simulations for their effectiveness in enhancing process model comprehension (e.g., [8,10,35]). However, it remains to be seen whether the benefits of guided simulations extend beyond flow-based tasks to support circumstantial tasks as well, which may require more than a single or a few trace simulations to develop an overarching understanding of the model. Another proposal is to use natural language processing (NLP) techniques to automatically identify the task-relevant parts of the process model from the task prompt, then augmented with the capabilities of large language models (LLMs), generate coherent explanations of how the task-relevant parts of the process model are interlinked. Such technology could significantly reduce the cognitive integration burden on users during comprehension tasks.

Threats to Validity. Our study is subject to internal, construct, and external validity threats [61]. To mitigate the internal validity threats, we addressed potential learning effects by randomizing the experiment's tasks, ensuring that these effects are spread uniformly across all tasks. Moreover, each task was designed to reference different combinations of activities within the process models, and tasks compared in a pairwise manner during the analysis were consistently formulated and have identical answers (either both true or both false). To mitigate the threats to construct validity, we selected measures that capture cognitive integration, cognitive load, and comprehension from studies that have successfully used them in their empirical studies (cf. Sect. 2.3). To mitigate the threats to external validity, despite the difficulty of organizing eye-tracking experiments, we recruited a large number of participants (46), making our study among the extensive ones in the process comprehension research involving eye-tracking. This relatively large sample enhances the generalizability of our findings. Moreover, the fragment-based approach [26] we used is based on BPMN [41], the de-facto process modeling language, and reflects the horizontal modularization approach which is commonly found in software engineering, particularly in architectures like microservices and service-oriented architectures. This relevance to current professional practices further supports the external validity of our research, suggesting that our findings can be applied outside lab environments and potentially beyond process modeling research.

6 Conclusion and Future Work

In this study, we examined the effects of fragmentation on readers' cognitive integration across both flow-based and circumstantial comprehension tasks that address local and global aspects. Additionally, we investigated whether cognitive integration could explain variations in cognitive load and task performance. Our findings highlight a significant relationship between fragmentation and increased cognitive integration in flow-based global tasks, as opposed to local ones. However, in circumstantial tasks, fragmentation did not significantly impact cognitive integration, which remained high for both local and global tasks, indicating that such tasks inherently demand high levels of cognitive integration, regardless of fragmentation. Moreover, our results confirm that cognitive integration affects both readers' cognitive load and their task performance.

An important direction for future work is to delve further into how to support circumstantial tasks on modular process models to reduce readers' cognitive integration effort. Adapting these models to describe processes following a constraint-based declarative approach rather than an imperative one could be beneficial for circumstantial tasks, but may have the opposite effect on flow-based tasks [19]. Therefore, other alternatives that focus on augmenting existing process representations with additional artifacts would be more adequate [4]. Notably, one can investigate whether guided simulations could bring enhanced support to both local and global circumstantial tasks. Finally, the NLP and LLM-based approaches discussed in Sect. 6 are also worth evaluating.

References

1. Van der Aalst, W.M., Weske, M., Grünbauer, D.: Case handling: a new paradigm for business process support. Data Knowl. Eng. **53**(2), 129–162 (2005)
2. Abbad-Andaloussi, A.: On the relationship between source-code metrics and cognitive load: a systematic tertiary review. J. Syst. Softw. **198**, 111619 (2023). https://doi.org/10.1016/j.jss.2023.111619
3. Abbad Andaloussi, A., Buch-Lorentsen, J., López, H.A., Slaats, T., Weber, B.: Exploring the modeling of declarative processes using a hybrid approach. In: Laender, A.H.F., Pernici, B., Lim, E.-P., de Oliveira, J.P.M. (eds.) ER 2019. LNCS, vol. 11788, pp. 162–170. Springer, Cham (2019). https://doi.org/10.1007/978-3-030-33223-5_14
4. Abbad-Andaloussi, A., Burattin, A., Slaats, T., Kindler, E., Weber, B.: On the declarative paradigm in hybrid business process representations: a conceptual framework and a systematic literature study. Inf. Syst. **91**, 101505 (2020)
5. Abbad-Andaloussi, A., Burattin, A., Slaats, T., Kindler, E., Weber, B.: Complexity in declarative process models: metrics and multi-modal assessment of cognitive load. Exp. Syst. Appl. **233**, 12092 (2023). https://doi.org/10.1016/j.eswa.2023.120924
6. Abbad-Andaloussi, A., Lübke, D., Weber, B.: Conducting eye-tracking studies on large and interactive process models using eyemind. SoftwareX **24**, 101564 (2023). https://doi.org/10.1016/j.softx.2023.101564
7. Abbad Andaloussi, A., Soffer, P., Slaats, T., Burattin, A., Weber, B.: The impact of modularization on the understandability of declarative process models: a research model. In: Davis, F.D., Riedl, R., vom Brocke, J., Léger, P.-M., Randolph, A.B., Fischer, T. (eds.) NeuroIS 2020. LNISO, vol. 43, pp. 133–144. Springer, Cham (2020). https://doi.org/10.1007/978-3-030-60073-0_15
8. Abbad-Andaloussi, A., Zerbato, F., Burattin, A., Slaats, T., Hildebrandt, T.T., Weber, B.: Exploring how users engage with hybrid process artifacts based on declarative process models: a behavioral analysis based on eye-tracking and think-aloud. Softw. Syst. Model. **20**, 1437–1464 (2021)
9. Antinyan, V.: Evaluating essential and accidental code complexity triggers by practitioners' perception. IEEE Software **37**(6), 86–93 (2020). https://doi.org/10.1109/ms.2020.2976072
10. Aysolmaz, B., Reijers, H.A.: Animation as a dynamic visualization technique for improving process model comprehension. Inf. Manag. **58**(5), 103478 (2021)
11. Baddeley, A.: Working memory. Science **255**(5044), 556–559 (1992)

12. Baß, J., Winter, M., Pryss, R., Reichert, M.: Exploring comprehension strategies of modular process models: a combined eye-tracking and concurrent think-aloud study. Brain Sci. **14**(4), 303 (2024)
13. Bera, P., Soffer, P., Parsons, J.: Using eye tracking to expose cognitive processes in understanding conceptual models. MIS Q. **43**(4), 1105–1126 (2019)
14. Chen, F., et al.: Robust Multimodal Cognitive Load Measurement. HIS, Springer, Cham (2016). https://doi.org/10.1007/978-3-319-31700-7
15. Corradini, F., et al.: A guidelines framework for understandable BPMN models. Data Know. Eng. **113**, 129–154 (2018)
16. Dobesova, Z., Malcik, M.: Workflow diagrams and pupil dilatation in eye-tracking testing. In: ICETA 2015, pp. 1–6. IEEE (2015)
17. Duchowski, A.T., Krejtz, K., Gehrer, N.A., Bafna, T., Bækgaard, P.: The low/high index of pupillary activity. In: CHI Conference on Human Factors in Computing Systems, pp. 1–12 (2020)
18. Dumas, M., La Rosa, M., Mendling, J., Reijers, H.A.: Fundamentals of Business Process Management. Springer, Heidelberg (2013). https://doi.org/10.1007/978-3-642-33143-5
19. Fahland, D., et al.: Declarative versus imperative process modeling languages: the issue of understandability. In: Halpin, T., et al. (eds.) BPMDS/EMMSAD -2009. LNBIP, vol. 29, pp. 353–366. Springer, Heidelberg (2009). https://doi.org/10.1007/978-3-642-01862-6_29
20. Figl, K.: Comprehension of procedural visual business process models: a literature review. Bus. Inf. Syst. Eng. **59**, 41–67 (2017)
21. Figl, K., Di Ciccio, C., Reijers, H.A.: Do declarative process models help to reduce cognitive biases related to business rules? In: Dobbie, G., Frank, U., Kappel, G., Liddle, S.W., Mayr, H.C. (eds.) ER 2020. LNCS, vol. 12400, pp. 119–133. Springer, Cham (2020). https://doi.org/10.1007/978-3-030-62522-1_9
22. Franceschetti, M., Abbad-Andaloussi, A., Schreiber, C., A. López, H., Weber, B.: Exploring the cognitive effects of ambiguity in process models. In: International Conference on Business Process Management. Springer (2024)
23. Gilmore, D.J., Green, T.R.G.: Comprehension and recall of miniature programs. Int. J. Man Mach. Stud. **21**(1), 31–48 (1984)
24. Glöckner, A., Herbold, A.K.: Information processing in decisions under risk: Evidence for compensatory strategies based on automatic processes. In: MPI Collective Goods Preprint (2008/42) (2008)
25. Hair, J.F., Hult, G.T.M., Ringle, C.M., Sarstedt, M., Danks, N.P., Ray, S.: Moderation analysis. In: Partial Least Squares Structural Equation Modeling (PLS-SEM) Using R. CCB, pp. 155–172. Springer, Cham (2021). https://doi.org/10.1007/978-3-030-80519-7_8
26. Hewelt, M., Weske, M.: A hybrid approach for flexible case modeling and execution. In: La Rosa, M., Loos, P., Pastor, O. (eds.) BPM 2016. LNBIP, vol. 260, pp. 38–54. Springer, Cham (2016). https://doi.org/10.1007/978-3-319-45468-9_3
27. Holmqvist, K., Nyström, M., Andersson, R., Dewhurst, R., Jarodzka, H., van de Weijer, J.: Eye Tracking: A Comprehensive Guide to Methods and Measures. OUP, Oxford (2011)
28. Indulska, M., Green, P., Recker, J., Rosemann, M.: Business process modeling: perceived benefits. In: Laender, A.H.F., Castano, S., Dayal, U., Casati, F., de Oliveira, J.P.M. (eds.) ER 2009. LNCS, vol. 5829, pp. 458–471. Springer, Heidelberg (2009). https://doi.org/10.1007/978-3-642-04840-1_34

29. Jeffries, R., Turner, A.A., Poison, P.G., Atwood, M.E.: The processes involved in designing software. In: Cognitive Skills and Their Acquisition, pp. 255–283. Psychology Press (2013)
30. Just, M.A., Carpenter, P.A.: A theory of reading: from eye fixations to comprehension. Psychol. Rev. **87**(4), 329 (1980)
31. Krumeich, J., Weis, B., Werth, D., Loos, P.: Event-driven business process management: where are we now?: a comprehensive synthesis and analysis of literature. Bus. Process. Manag. J. **20**(4), 615–633 (2014)
32. Kummer, T.F., Recker, J., Mendling, J.: Enhancing understandability of process models through cultural-dependent color adjustments. Decis. Support Syst. **87**, 1–12 (2016)
33. La Rosa, M., Wohed, P., Mendling, J., Ter Hofstede, A.H., Reijers, H.A., van der Aalst, W.M.: Managing process model complexity via abstract syntax modifications. IEEE Trans. Industr. Inf. **7**(4), 614–629 (2011)
34. Mandelburger, M.M., Mendling, J.: Cognitive diagram understanding and task performance in systems analysis and design. MIS Q. **45**(4), 2101–2157 (2021)
35. Maslov, I., Poelmans, S.: Facilitating the comprehension of business process models for unexperienced modelers using token-based animations. Inf. Manag. **61**(5), 103967 (2024). https://doi.org/10.1016/j.im.2024.103967
36. Mendling, J., Reijers, H.A., van der Aalst, W.M.: Seven process modeling guidelines (7pmg). Inf. Softw. Technol. **52**(2), 127–136 (2010)
37. Mendling, J., Strembeck, M.: Influence factors of understanding business process models. In: Abramowicz, W., Fensel, D. (eds.) BIS 2008. LNBIP, vol. 7, pp. 142–153. Springer, Heidelberg (2008). https://doi.org/10.1007/978-3-540-79396-0_13
38. Mendling, J., Strembeck, M., Recker, J.: Factors of process model comprehension-findings from a series of experiments. Decis. Support Syst. **53**(1), 195–206 (2012)
39. Miller, G.A.: The magical number seven, plus or minus two: some limits on our capacity for processing information. Psychol. Rev. **63**(2), 81 (1956)
40. Montoya, A.K.: Moderation analysis in two-instance repeated measures designs: probing methods and multiple moderator models. Behav. Res. Methods **51**, 61–82 (2019)
41. OMG.: Business process modeling notation v 2.0 (2006). https://www.omg.org/spec/BPMN/2.0/
42. Paas, F., Tuovinen, J.E., Tabbers, H., Van Gerven, P.W.M.: Cognitive load measurement as a means to advance cognitive load theory. Educ. Psychol. **38**(1), 63–71 (2003). https://doi.org/10.1207/S15326985EP3801_8
43. Parnas, D.L.: On the criteria to be used in decomposing systems into modules. Commun. ACM **15**(12), 1053–1058 (1972)
44. Petrusel, R., Mendling, J., Reijers, H.A.: How visual cognition influences process model comprehension. Decis. Support Syst. **96**, 1–16 (2017)
45. Pichler, P., Weber, B., Zugal, S., Pinggera, J., Mendling, J., Reijers, H.A.: Imperative versus declarative process modeling languages: an empirical investigation. In: Daniel, F., Barkaoui, K., Dustdar, S. (eds.) BPM 2011. LNBIP, vol. 99, pp. 383–394. Springer, Heidelberg (2012). https://doi.org/10.1007/978-3-642-28108-2_37
46. Reijers, H., Mendling, J.: Modularity in process models: review and effects. In: Dumas, M., Reichert, M., Shan, M.-C. (eds.) BPM 2008. LNCS, vol. 5240, pp. 20–35. Springer, Heidelberg (2008). https://doi.org/10.1007/978-3-540-85758-7_5
47. Reijers, H.A., Mendling, J.: A study into the factors that influence the understandability of business process models. IEEE Trans. Syst. Man Cybern. **41**(3), 449–462 (2010)

48. Ritchi, H., Jans, M., Mendling, J., Reijers, H.A.: The influence of business process representation on performance of different task types. J. Inf. Syst. **34**(1), 167–194 (2019). https://doi.org/10.2308/isys-52385
49. Sánchez-González, L., García, F., Mendling, J., Ruiz, F.: Quality assessment of business process models based on thresholds. In: Meersman, R., Dillon, T., Herrero, P. (eds.) OTM 2010. LNCS, vol. 6426, pp. 78–95. Springer, Heidelberg (2010). https://doi.org/10.1007/978-3-642-16934-2_9
50. Schreiber, C., Abbad-Andaloussi, A., Weber, B.: On the cognitive effects of abstraction and fragmentation in modularized process models. In: Di Francescomarino, C., Burattin, A., Janiesch, C., Sadiq, S. (eds.) BPM 2023, pp. 359–376. Springer, Cham (2023). https://doi.org/10.1007/978-3-031-41620-0_21
51. Schreiber, C., Abbad-Andaloussi, A., Weber, B.: On the cognitive and behavioral effects of abstraction and fragmentation in modularized process models. Inf. Syst. **125**, 102424 (2024)
52. Trinh, D.M.T., Abbad-Andaloussi, A., López, H.A.: On the semantic transparency of declarative process models: the case of constraints. In: Sellami, M., Vidal, M.-E., van Dongen, B., Gaaloul, W., Panetto, H. (eds.) CoopIS 2023, pp. 217–236. Springer, Cham (2024). https://doi.org/10.1007/978-3-031-46846-9_12
53. Tulving, E., Craik, F.I.: The Oxford Handbook of Memory. Oxford University Press (2000)
54. Turetken, O., Rompen, T., Vanderfeesten, I., Dikici, A., van Moll, J.: The effect of modularity representation and presentation medium on the understandability of business process models in BPMN. In: La Rosa, M., Loos, P., Pastor, O. (eds.) BPM 2016. LNCS, vol. 9850, pp. 289–307. Springer, Cham (2016). https://doi.org/10.1007/978-3-319-45348-4_17
55. Wang, W., Chen, T., Indulska, M., Sadiq, S., Weber, B.: Business process and rule integration approaches-an empirical analysis of model understanding. Inf. Syst. **104**, 101901 (2022)
56. Weber, B., Fischer, T., Riedl, R.: Brain and autonomic nervous system activity measurement in software engineering: a systematic literature review. J. Syst. Softw. **178** (2021)
57. Weidlich, M., et al.: The impact of sequential and circumstantial changes on process models. In: ER-POIS@ CAiSE, pp. 43–54. Citeseer (2010)
58. Winter, M., Neumann, H., Pryss, R., Probst, T., Reichert, M.: Defining gaze patterns for process model literacy-exploring visual routines in process models with diverse mappings. Expert Syst. Appl. **213**, 119217 (2023)
59. Winter, M., Pryss, R., Probst, T., Baß, J., Reichert, M.: Measuring the cognitive complexity in the comprehension of modular process models. IEEE Trans. Cognit. Develop. Syst. **14**(1), 164–180 (2022)
60. Winter, M., et al.: Are non-experts able to comprehend business process models–study insights involving novices and experts. arXiv preprint arXiv:2107.02030 (2021)
61. Wohlin, C., et al.: Experimentation in Software Engineering. Springer, Heidelberg (2012). https://doi.org/10.1007/978-3-642-29044-2
62. Zugal, S.: Applying cognitive psychology for improving the creation, understanding and maintenance of business process models. Ph.D. thesis, University of Innsbruck (2013)
63. Zugal, S., Pinggera, J., Neurauter, M., Maran, T., Weber, B.: Cheetah experimental platform web 1.0: cleaning pupillary data. arXiv preprint arXiv:1703.09468 (2017)

A Universal Prompting Strategy for Extracting Process Model Information from Natural Language Text Using Large Language Models

Julian Neuberger[1(✉)], Lars Ackermann[1], Han van der Aa[2], and Stefan Jablonski[1]

[1] University of Bayreuth, Bayreuth, Germany
{Julian.Neuberger,Lars.Ackermann,Stefan.Jablonski}@uni-bayreuth.de
[2] University of Vienna, Vienna, Austria
han.van.der.aa@univie.ac.at

Abstract. Over the past decade, extensive research efforts have been dedicated to the extraction of information from textual process descriptions. Despite the remarkable progress witnessed in natural language processing (NLP), information extraction within the Business Process Management domain remains predominantly reliant on rule-based systems and machine learning methodologies. Data scarcity has so far prevented the successful application of deep learning techniques. However, the rapid progress in generative large language models (LLMs) makes it possible to solve many NLP tasks with very high quality without the need for extensive data. Therefore, we systematically investigate the potential of LLMs for extracting information from textual process descriptions, targeting the detection of process elements such as activities and actors, and relations between them. Based on a novel prompting strategy, we show that LLMs are able to outperform state-of-the-art machine learning approaches with absolute performance improvements of up to 8% F_1 score across three different datasets. We evaluate our prompting strategy on eight different LLMs, showing it is universally applicable, while also analyzing the impact of certain prompt parts on extraction quality. The number of example texts, the specificity of definitions, and the rigour of format instructions are identified as key for improving the accuracy of extracted information. Our code, prompts, and data are publicly available at https://github.com/JulianNeuberger/llm-process-generation/tree/er2024.

Keywords: Process Information Extraction · Large Language Models · AI-assisted Conceptual Modeling · Business Process Modeling

1 Introduction

In the field of Business Process Management (BPM), process models are established tools for designing, implementing, enacting, and analyzing enterprise pro-

W. Maass et al. (Eds.): ER 2024, LNCS 15238, pp. 38–55, 2025.
https://doi.org/10.1007/978-3-031-75872-0_3

cesses [12]. However, the manual creation of these models is very time-consuming and accounts for around 60% of the total time spent on process management [16]. In order to reduce this effort, the automatic creation of these models based on a variety of information sources is a research focus in the field of BPM [5,16]. In this respect, the paper at hand contributes to the extraction of process-relevant information from natural language information sources.

Information on organizational processes is frequently contained in a range of textual documents, such as process descriptions, rules and regulations, and work instructions [1,4]. Recognizing this, a variety of techniques has been developed that aim to automatically extract process information from texts in order to subsequently turn it into process models [2,8,16]. This two-step procedure, in which information is extracted first and turned into a process model second, comes with several advantages in comparison to a direct text-to-model transformation approach: (1) The result quality can be evaluated with established means from the information-extraction domain, (2) extracted information can be transformed in more than one target process modeling language[1], and (3) it is possible to use extracted process information for other purposes such as, for instance, compliance checking, formal reasoning [3,26], and process querying [19].

The goal, scope, and challenges of information extraction depend on the input document type and content, as well as the desired output, i.e., the information to be extracted. Still, the extraction of process information from text generally involves: (1) the identification of textual mentions of process entities, such as activities, process participants, and business objects, and (2) relations between these entities, such as sequential dependencies, exclusivity, and assignments (e.g., who performs which step). As an illustration, Fig. 1 shows a fragment of a textual description and two instantiations of the extraction task, focused on the information necessary for a model in Business Process Model and Notation (BPMN)[2] model [9] (upper part) and for declarative process modeling [2] (lower part). As shown, they involve different entities and relations, which each need to be inferred from the unstructured textual input.

A key problem is that the extraction of process information is still largely rule-based [23]. However, crafting useful rules is complicated, requires an extensive understanding of the process itself, and the rules are hard to transfer across organizations or text sources. To overcome this, recent work proposed the use of machine learning techniques [23], though these are hampered by data scarcity. Work that strives towards using pre-trained generative LLMs, e.g., GPT-3 [8] aims to circumvent this concern. However, the work in [8] only presents a preliminary study, with limitations in terms of analyzed datasets, extracted information, and result discussion. Therefore, this paper aims to provide deeper insights into the usability of LLMs for process information extraction and specifically includes the following core contributions: **(I)** It presents challenges that make the

[1] This is inspired by the paradigm of *interlingua-based machine translation* [27], which reduces the number of translation systems for n languages from n^2 to $2n$.

[2] https://www.omg.org/bpmn/, accessed June 2, 2024.

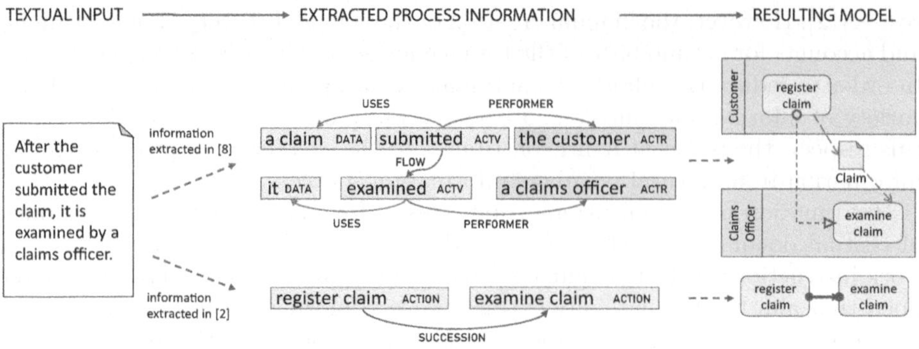

Fig. 1. Fragment of a larger text describing a business process of an insurance company. Different methodologies may extract different process relevant information, depending on the target modelling notation or use case.

extraction of process-relevant information in particular a difficult task (Sect. 2). **(II)** As our main contribution, it proposes a novel, task-specific, and rigorously empirically validated prompting strategy for solving the aforementioned information extraction tasks (Sect. 4). **(III)** It provides the currently most comprehensive study of using LLMs for extracting business process relevant information from natural language text (Sects. 5 and 6). To this end we rigorously compare our prompting strategy on multiple datasets with state-of-the-art approaches and achieve up to 7% higher absolute F_1 scores compared to machine learning methods and up to 8% compared to rule-based methods. **(IV)** By testing our prompting strategy with eight state-of-the-art LLMs, we empirically demonstrate the generality of both our results and the applicability of our prompting strategy. **(V)** An ablation study (Sect. 6.2) shows that common best practices in prompt engineering are only of limited use for process information extraction. Thus, we also define guidelines for using LLMs for process information extraction (Sect. 6.4).

The rest of this paper is structured as follows. Section 2 describes the information extraction tasks and its challenges in detail. Section 3 summarizes the current state of the art in dealing with these tasks. After that we, describe our prompting strategy, the experiments, and corresponding results (Sects. 4, 5, 6). Section 7 describes limitations and future work.

2 Task Descriptions and Challenges

In this section, we describe the three main (sub)tasks of process information extraction (Sect. 2.1), before highlighting a range of challenges associated with such extraction and with the use of LLMs for it (Sects. 2.2, 2.3).

2.1 Task Descriptions

Our work focuses on three established subtasks of (process) information extraction from text: Mention Detection (MD), Entity Resolution (ER), and Relation Extraction (RE) [2,7,23,26].

Mention Detection (MD) is concerned with finding and extracting text fragments that contain process relevant information, such as activities (or actions), process-relevant objects or data (i.e., business objects), or involved persons and departments (i.e., actors). For instance, in Fig. 1, the upper example shows mentions of *data*, *actions*, and *actor*, whereas the lower one focuses on *activities*. This definition is similar to Named Entity Recognition (NER), though we also extract spans not covered by the traditional definition of NER, e.g., activities.

Entity Resolution (ER) aims to recognize when different mentions refer to the same process entity. For example, in Fig. 1, successful ER would identify that the word *it* in "it is examined" corresponds to the *claim* mentioned in the previous phrase. Another common example is using ER to recognize that the same actor (across mentions) performs different steps. ER is a super-set of co-reference resolution and anaphora resolution [29] and is a crucial step when dealing with process-related texts, which frequently involve repeated mentions across sentences or even paragraphs [23].

Relation Extraction (RE) is the task of detecting and classifying relations between mentions. Relations are usually directed and have one (unary relation), or two (binary relations) arguments. For instance, the upper example in Fig. 1 shows three kinds of relations: *uses* signals which data objects are used by an activity, *performer* captures which actor performed an activity, and *flow* captures a sequential relation between two activities. RE is crucial when it comes to information extraction in our context, given that processes inherently involve process steps (i.e., activities) that are connected to each other through relations. Note that we regard constraint extraction [2,26] (CE), which relates to declarative process modeling, as an RE problem: constraints have one or two arguments, are directed, and carry type information (e.g., *Succession*, *Init*).

2.2 Challenges of Process Information Extraction from Text

Information extraction, a common task in natural language processing (NLP), faces general challenges, which are also well-known in BPM literature [1,15], and often central elements of interest in the design of rule-based and learning-based systems alike [2,23]. Simply using LLMs for process information extraction solves some of these challenges and justifies the investigation of their applicability.

In the context of process-related texts ***Linguistic Variance*** means that the same behavior or process characteristics can be described in a variety of ways such as, for instance, active and passive voice. ***Context Cues*** are a challenge in that single words can fundamentally alter the meaning of a process description (e.g., *"first, a claim is created" and inverted semantics in "finally, a claim is created"*. Processes are typically described in sequential form, although they usually contain branches (e.g. XOR decision branches). This results in ***Long-distance Relations*** that existing approaches struggle with [23] or cannot handle [2]. ***Implicit and Ambiguous Information*** such as the "examination target" in *"after registering the file in the database, it needs to be examined"* needs to be interpreted [3,15]. Research indicates a negative correlation between correctness of extracted process information and ***Text Length*** [7]. Finally, the application of deep learning is hindered by the fact that the largest available data set contains only 45 human-annotated process descriptions [9] (***Small Datasets***).

LLMs are able to overcome the above challenges [32], which is why this paper analyzes their suitability for process information extraction, as proposed in previous work [6,8]. However, LLMs require great care in the formulation of the input (prompts) [8,22,31–33]. In [22] authors argue: "a good prompt can be worth hundreds of labeled data points". For this reason, the core of the present work lies in the development (Sect. 4) and evaluation (Sects. 5 and 6.2) of suitable prompts for process information extraction.

2.3 Challenges of Process Information Extraction Using LLMs

Using LLMs for process information extraction from texts helps with linguistic challenges, but adds itself several additional challenges. We discuss these here and reference them later in Sect. 6.4 to show how we can deal with them.

(C1) Limited Output Control. Input and output consist of plain text. Given that the input for inference is raw text, it inherently suits LLMs for our tasks (cf. Section 2.1). However, as the expected output should adhere to a specific schema, it becomes necessary to instruct the LLM to conform to this schema. Moreover, this principle necessitates a robust output parser, as LLMs tend to exhibit variability in their output, which presently cannot be entirely eradicated. Having only limited control over generated output is especially problematic for the BPM domain, where definitions for relevant information often overlap, e.g., *actions* (just predicate) versus *activities* (predicate and object).

(C2) Input Presentation Dependencies. Although LLMs provide an interface for natural language input, the quantity, form and level of detail must be carefully matched to the task at hand. The LLM faces the challenge of determining the importance of the input components. Furthermore, while LLMs emulate human reasoning, the interpretation of inputs may diverge significantly from that of human beings, thereby rendering prompt optimization a trial-and-error process. This challenge is further aggravated by some elements of process models, that are complex to explain concisely, e.g., parallel and exclusive workflows.

(C3) Black-box. Deep learning methods generally suffer from challenges concerning explainability of predictions [34], which is also true for LLMs. Contrary to classical learning methods, such as decision trees, LLMs offer no fail safe mechanism to validate extraction rules. This is problematic for business process information extraction in particular, since recent work focuses on "human-in-the-loop" systems [30], where the human must be able to follow system decisions.

(C4) Data Unawareness. In contrast to generative AI models trained on task-specific data, an LLM is usually not aware of the particular dataset it is tasked to process. Thus, using LLMs to process a particular dataset requires to form instructions that precisely describe all relevant details of a dataset. The generalizing capabilities of LLMs can be an additional hurdle in this context, especially, when declarative process models are concerned, where a multitude of constraint types exist. The LLM is likely to know of these through the pre-training process, and therefore may extract irrelevant ones for a given dataset.

(C5) Costly Experiments. Applying LLMs usually requires usage of commercial APIs (e.g., OpenAI), which come with downsides: (i) a token limit restricting the maximum input and output size and (ii) fees based on the number of tokens processed. In view of the many possible variations in the influencing parameters, conducting experiments can be cost-intensive. This is especially true for the BPM domain, where the density of information in process descriptions is very high, needing many output tokens to extract and encode it.

3 Related Work

Related approaches are divided into rule-based, machine learning (ML)-based, deep learning-based, and LLM-based process information extraction. An approach is considered related if it solves at least one of the tasks in Sect. 2.1.

Rule-Based Approaches. Rule-based approaches leverage linguistic features to extract information from natural language process descriptions through explicitly coded mapping rules. For instance, Friedrich et al.'s seminal work [16] employs syntax features and word information from a lexical database to identify patterns at both sentence and document levels for BPMN model creation. Other approaches like those in [26,28] adopt similar techniques for automatic text annotation, employing regular expressions for syntactic dependency trees, and part-of-speech tags, showcasing superior performance on novel datasets. Additionally, [2] presents a rule-based technique, currently leading in extracting declarative process models from raw text using syntax parsing and word-level features. Similar advancements are seen in [9,14], the latter integrating ML-based entity MD with subsequent rule-based RE. Furthermore, [21] focuses on extracting Dynamic Condition Response (DCR) graphs. Recent studies suggest that while rule-based approaches can be tailored to specific tasks and data sets, they can hardly deal with ambiguity and linguistic variance. [8,23].

ML-Based Approaches. [23] presents a ML extraction pipeline based on [9] and is used as a baseline for our comparative evaluation (Sect. 6). The deep-learning approach presented in [25] classifies text fragments analyzing the input text on several levels of granularity. However, extracting these fragments is not part of the approach, which simplifies the task of MD to mention classification, i.e., locating the information to extract is omitted. Though the work presented in [6] overcomes this limitation and outperforms the approach, it does not support RE. In general, techniques of this paradigm either struggle to deal with linguistic variability and ambiguity, or they require vast amounts of training data, making them particularly unfeasible for small datasets (see Sect. 2.2).

LLM-Based Approaches. Bellan et al. [8] utilize pre-trained LLMs to cope with data scarcity, yet their approach exhibits three primary weaknesses: *(i)* It is restricted to a subset of entity types, namely *activities*, *participants*, a *performs* relation, and a *direct-consequences* relation, *(ii)* it lacks strict output formatting, hindering automated result processing, unlike our prompting strategy, and *(iii)* its evaluation is limited to 7 of the 45 process descriptions from the PET dataset, whereas we evaluate our modular prompt on the entire dataset, plus two validation datasets. Thus, direct comparison between [8] and our work is not feasible. Nonetheless, as in [8], our modular prompt also descriptive instructions with input examples accompanied by their expected outputs. Although process models are generated using LLMs in [18], the work is not comparable to ours, as [18] requires human involvement and only supports the extraction of activities and their arrangement in a directed graph (e.g., actors and data are missing).

4 LLM-Based Process Model Extraction from Text

Extracting process information with LLMs requires a *prompt design* that addresses the challenges mentioned in Sect. 2.3. Thus, a prompt structure consisting of the three modules *Context*, *Task Description* and *Restrictions* is described below at the example of the Mention Detection task. However, the prompting strategies for the remaining tasks (Sect. 2.1) are analogous.

High-Level Prompt Structure. LLMs take freely formulated text as input, which is called the prompt. To this end we base our prompts on an ablation study (Sect. 6.2), which is used to identify beneficial and detrimental prompt components. To do this, we first need a modular prompt design so that we can specifically remove individual components in the study to examine their benefits and ultimately to only keep the advantageous components. Adhering to the best practices outlined in [31], our initial prompt design is structured into three modules (see Fig. 2): *(A)* a context description framing the process information extraction task on a high level, *(B)* a detailed task description, and *(C)* constraints that further restrict the context and the output format, and contains disambiguation hints. To design potentially relevant components for all three modules we rely on general design patterns [11,22,31,33]. Therefore, in the next subsection, the three modules are specified and discussed in terms of how they address the LLM-specific challenges outlined in Sect. 2.3.

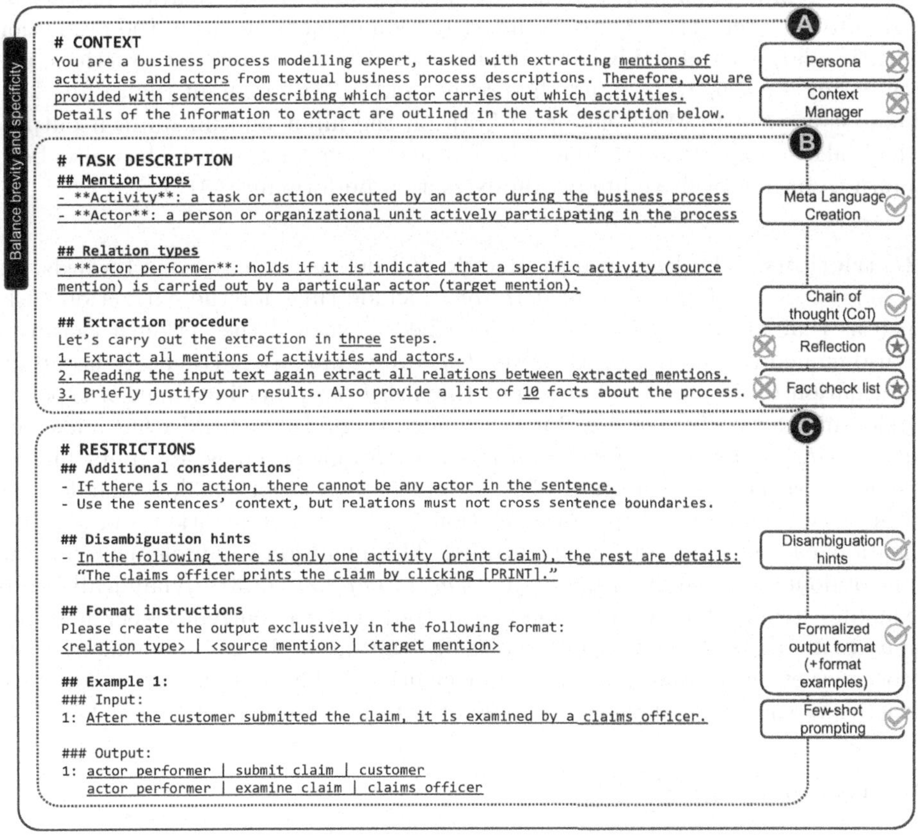

Fig. 2. Modular prompt structure (underlined = task-specific content, boxes = design pattern, ✓ = useful, ☒ = non-useful, ★ = use in prompt engineering).

Context and Task Description. In module *(A)* we use the *persona* design pattern [33] to control the language style of generation results. We assign it the role of a process modeling expert. This is followed by the *context manager* design pattern [33], which includes a general description of the information extraction task (i.e., objectives and a description of the input specifics). This limits the information basis the LLM may use, mitigating the risk of hallucination.

Module *(B)* is mainly concerned with defining the specifics of the process information extraction task. Its backbone is the *creation of a meta language*

[33], which defines the types of elements to extract from the input text. Figure 2 provides an example that defines activities and actors as mention types and a relation called *actor performer* that associates actions with their performers, following our running example from Fig. 1. Another widespread best practice is known as *chain of thought (CoT)* [31,32], whereby the actual task is broken down into individual steps. Thus, our prompt divides the relation extraction task into two steps that separate the extraction of mentions from the prediction of their relations and a third step, which combines two more best practices, i.e., generating a *list of facts* about the process and *reflection* about the results [33]. These cause the LLM to elaborate both on the input and on its own output, which allows experts to validate the extracted information and has also been shown to have a positive impact on extraction performance [31,32].

Restrictions. The last prompt module *(C)* defines expectations towards the LLM's output. *Additional considerations* include rules for the extraction task, such as that an actor can only be described as such if the action it performs is also named (compare Fig. 2). *Disambiguation hints* are particularly useful for information types that are hard to distinguish from other information types or irrelevant information. In Fig. 2 it is intended to guide the LLM what makes up an *Activity*, if the input gives additional, irrelevant specifics. Prompts further include a schematic definition of a *formal output format* [33], which for the exemplary prompt is a tuple of a relation type, a source mention and a target mention, each separated by a pipe symbol. The definition is complemented by an (out-of-domain) example. Finally, *few-shot prompting* [22,31] dynamically adds examples for input and corresponding output. For the current paper few-shot samples are pairs of raw textual process descriptions and a task-dependent set of process-relevant information (e.g., actor mentions). This design pattern and best practice is known to alleviate the issue of *data unawareness* of LLMs [17,20].

5 Experiment Setup

In this section we define the experiments we run to evaluate the usefulness of LLMs for process information extraction[3]. It covers an overview of the datasets we use, including the respective baselines, and a definition of metrics we apply.

We use three well-known datasets for evaluating our prompts. One of these (PET) represents the current state of the art, both in terms of size, as well as the process information techniques developed for it. The other datasets feature different characteristics, making them relevant for validation experiments. This lets us gain insights into the robustness of an LLM as a process information extractor, as well as how it behaves when applied to other process modeling languages. We call the best approaches for extracting the information from these datasets *baselines*, and use them in Sect. 6 as comparisons with various LLMs.

[3] Code at https://github.com/JulianNeuberger/llm-process-generation/tree/er2024 .

PET [9]: This is the largest dataset currently available. It contains 45 documents with annotations for information especially useful for creating process models in BPMN. These include 7 types of mentions such as activities, actors, data objects, but also 6 relation types. These cover the behavioural process perspective (*Flow*), data perspective (*uses*, and organizational perspective (*actor, performer*). Additionally, this dataset features relations that span multiple sentences. It therefore tests the ability of approaches to reason across wider spans of text. We use an extended version of this dataset, which includes data for the ER task, as presented in [23]. The currently best approach for extracting information is using conditional random fields for MD, a pre-trained neural co-reference resolver for ER, and a decision tree ensemble for RE [23]. We use scores as reported in [23], which have corresponding publicly available code and can be reproduced with it.

DECON [2]: This collection of 17 textual process descriptions is annotated with a set of 5 Declare [24] Constraint types between business process relevant activities. Additionally, constraints may be negated, as well as unary, i.e., constraining a single action. Annotations are given on a sentence level, and only sentences that describe at least one constraint are contained in the dataset. The expected (ground-truth) activities are already transformed into Declare-conform phrases, i.e., the activity description "*The claim is registered*" should be extracted as "*register claim*". It does not contain an approach for MD in isolation, and only contains mentions of type action. The authors of [2] propose a rule-based approach combining multiple NLP techniques, e.g., *typed dependency relations.*

ATDP [26]: This dataset uses 18 textual descriptions, that largely overlap with the ones from [2], but also contains sentences, that describe no constraint. As such, this dataset tests approaches for their ability to judge whether or not sentences contain relevant information, before extracting constraints. Furthermore, the set of constraints was expanded to eight types. Additionally, this dataset also provides annotations of actions, conditions, entities, and events, which we used in an MD setting. Quishpi et al. proposed a rule-based ensemble of patterns for MD and CE on typed dependency structures [26].

We use the well established metrics *Precision* P and *Recall* R for our experiments. P is a measure of how well an extraction approach is able to avoid false positives, i.e., assigning the wrong type to mentions and relations, or extracting them, where they are not expected. R on the other hand measures how much of the expected information (true positives) is found. The two metrics are typically aggregated via their harmonic mean $F_1 = 2\frac{P \cdot R}{P+R}$. Following [26], we use $P = \frac{\#correct}{\#pred}$ and $R = \frac{\#correct}{\#gold}$, with $\#correct$ as the number of correct predictions, $\#pred$ the number of total predictions, and $\#gold$ as the number of expected mentions or relations. For a fair assessment, we count predictions as correct in exactly the way described by the work we compare the LLM to.

6 Results

Table 1 shows the results we observed when running the experiments as described in Sect. 5 with an optimized prompt, that follows the recommendations we found in our study of best practices (Sect. 6.2). All results use GPT-4o, the latest version of OpenAI's GPT with *temperature* = 0. *top_p* is unchanged, as per OpenAI's recommendation, when using temperature based sampling.[4]

For the reference dataset PET, our experiments show that GPT-4o is capable of an absolute F_1 score improvement of 5% for MD, 22% for ER, and 17% for RE. Remarkably, for RE, GPT-4o is able to match and outperform the machine learnt baseline, which was trained on 36 manually annotated documents [23], without any labeled data (zero-shot). For MD it reaches similar scores, even when not given any examples, compared to the machine learnt baseline, which was trained using 36 manually annotated documents [9]. For real-world application this means that LLMs can be used in business process information extraction scenarios, even if the organization has not a single manually annotated training example. This is an exciting find, as it promises significant speed-up of model creating tasks of practitioners across business domains.

Table 1. Results for each dataset and the different extraction stages, compared to baseline results using GPT-4o.

	Dataset	DECON			ATDP			PET		
	Metric	P	R	F_1	P	R	F_1	P	R	F_1
MentionDetection	Baseline	*no baseline*			0.62	**0.82**	0.71	**0.73**	0.64	0.69
	Zero-shot	0.72	0.75	0.73	0.58	0.77	0.66	0.65	0.71	0.68
	1-shot	0.87	**0.80**	0.83	0.63	0.77	0.69	0.72	0.75	0.73
	3-shot	**0.88**	0.79	**0.83**	**0.68**	0.79	**0.73**	0.72	**0.77**	**0.74**
EntityResolution	Baseline	*no data*			*no data*			0.55	**0.51**	0.52
	Zero-shot							0.67	0.55	0.60
	1-shot							0.76	**0.70**	0.73
	3-shot							**0.79**	**0.70**	**0.74**
RelationExtraction	Baseline	0.77	0.72	0.74	**0.58**	0.64	0.61	0.79	0.66	0.72
	Zero-shot	0.66	0.75	0.70	0.49	0.66	0.57	0.88	0.85	0.86
	1-shot	0.76	0.82	0.79	**0.58**	**0.73**	**0.64**	0.90	0.89	0.89
	3-shot	**0.79**	**0.85**	**0.82**	**0.58**	0.72	**0.64**	**0.90**	**0.89**	**0.89**

When evaluating on the validation datasets (cf. Section 5), we found that GPT-4o is able to match and out-perform the rule-based systems in all cases, most notably improving F_1 scores for RE on dataset DECON by an absolute 8%. Our result for MD on dataset DECON has no corresponding baseline, as the

[4] see OpenAI's source code, accessed June 3, 2024.

authors of [2] did not report values for MD in isolation. Errors and ambiguities are common in dataset ATDP hindering machine learning methods in learning valid extraction rules. This also adversely affects the extraction accuracy of GPT-4, when extracting the same types of constraints in the ATDP dataset compared to the DECON dataset. We discuss this further in Sect. 6.4. Since the importance of ER only recently gained attention [23, 26], the reference dataset PET is currently the only dataset providing data for evaluation of this task.

6.1 Model Comparison

We originally developed our prompts for GPT-4 version *GPT-4-0125-preview*, to assess how well our prompting strategy generalizes to other models we prompted a total of eight models for the MD and RE tasks on PET. We selected models following AlpacaEval[5], which is designed for testing the instruction following capabilities of LMMs [13]. At the time of writing model *YI Large Preview* was not publicly accessible and could not be considered in our comparison, even though it ranked third on AlpacaEval.

Results for the comparison can be found in Table 2. We set the temperature for all models to 0. All GPT models perform on similar levels, with the exception of GPT3.5, which is significantly smaller compared to GPT-4 models. For the zero-shot RE task GPT3.5 even failed to produce responses for most documents, leading to very low recall. Claude3 Opus seems to be as capable as GPT-4, its smaller variant Sonnet performs significantly worse on zero-shot tasks, but is able to produce comparable results given three examples. Llama 3 70B Instruct is an open-weight model and could be run locally, i.e., it is useful for using our prompting strategy in scenarios where sending data to an API is not possible. Llama 3 70B Instruct seems to be nearly as capable as the closed-weights Claude 3 Sonnet and is therefore viable in a few-shot setting.

Table 2. Comparison of our prompts across different models. Best results per task and metric are set **bold**.

Task	PET MD (Zero-shot)			PET MD (3-shot)			PET RE (Zero-shot)			PET RE (3-shot)		
Model	P	R	F_1	P	R	F_1	P	R	F_1	P	R	F_1
GPT-4o	0.58	0.69	0.63	0.68	0.77	0.72	**0.88**	**0.85**	**0.86**	0.90	0.89	0.89
GPT-4-2024-04-09	0.63	0.67	0.65	**0.73**	0.76	**0.74**	0.87	0.79	0.83	0.89	0.88	0.88
GPT-4-0125-preview	**0.65**	0.71	**0.68**	0.72	0.77	**0.74**	0.87	**0.85**	**0.86**	0.89	0.87	0.88
GPT-3.5-0125	0.35	0.50	0.42	0.51	0.70	0.59	0.51	0.06	0.11	0.74	0.64	0.69
Claude 3 Opus	0.55	**0.72**	0.63	0.66	**0.80**	0.73	0.86	**0.85**	**0.86**	**0.92**	**0.91**	**0.91**
Claude 3 Sonnet	0.46	0.65	0.54	0.63	0.78	0.70	0.78	0.67	0.72	0.91	0.87	0.89
Llama 3 70B Instruct	0.56	0.64	0.59	0.62	0.71	0.67	0.76	0.66	0.70	0.88	0.81	0.84
Qwen1.5 72B Chat	0.32	0.33	0.33	0.53	0.65	0.59	0.61	0.65	0.63	0.74	0.77	0.75

[5] See https://tatsu-lab.github.io/alpaca_eval/, last accessed May 30, 2024.

6.2 Ablation Study

We conduct an ablation study to assess the usefulness of the best practices presented in Sect. 4 and to measure the impact of the prompt's main components. This study is run on the reference dataset (PET), as it is the largest one and used by recent publications [8,9,23]. To obtain a baseline for the tasks of MD and RE, we use a prompt that implements the best practices as shown in Fig. 2 and run it on the *GPT-4-0125-preview* model. We then purposefully remove specific components from this prompt, namely the *format examples*, the *context manager*, the *persona*, the definition of mention and relation types (*meta language*), the instruction to think in several steps (*chain of thought*), any *disambiguation* hints, and the instruction to generate explanations (*reflection*) and a *fact check list* about the process. Additionally, we also use a prompt with very short descriptions of relations and types (*balancing brevity and specificity*). We run each prompt in the zero-shot setting and record the observed F_1 score, as well as the parsing errors that occurred.

Table 3 provides detailed results. Removing examples has a significant negative effect (−0.22 for MD and −0.07 for RE), mainly rooted in the number of parsing errors that are made (919 for MD), as well as directionality of relations for the RE task (confusing source and target mentions). Removing the context manager and persona only has minor effects (±0.01 per task), suggesting lower relevance for process information extraction compared to other NLP settings.

Table 3. Changes in F_1 score of GPT-4, without specific prompt components given in Fig. 2. Column *relative* F_1 shows difference to the baseline prompt, *Useful* shows a ✓, if we recommend this component in prompts for process information extraction and ★ for prompt engineering and data curating only.

	Mention Detection (MD)			Relation Extraction (RE)			
Experiment	Relative F_1	Absolute F_1	Parsing Errors	Relative F_1	Absolute F_1	Parsing Errors	Useful
Baseline	–	0.59	0	–	0.77	0	
No Format Examples	−0.22	0.37	919	−0.07	0.70	1	✓
No Context Manager	+0.01	0.60	0	−0.01	0.76	0	
No Persona	+0.01	0.59	1	+0.01	0.78	0	
No Meta Language	−0.09	0.49	2	−0.05	0.72	0	✓
No Chain of Thought	−0.01	0.57	1	−0.02	0.75	0	✓
No Disambiguation	−0.03	0.55	0	−0.01	0.76	1	✓
No Reflection	+0.04	0.63	0	+0.02	0.79	0	★
No Fact Check List	+0.03	0.62	1	−0.02	0.75	0	★
Very Short Prompt	−0.04	0.54	1	−0.03	0.74	0	✓

In addition to removing prompt components, we also tested using GPT in an older, less capable, but much cheaper version, GPT-3.5. Running the baseline prompt, results in a significant drop in extraction quality, with $F_1 = 0.27$ for MD and $F_1 = 0.56$ for RE. Splitting the baseline prompt into multiple prompts, each focusing on only one mention type, lets us prompt GPT-4 repeatedly for the same document. These highly specialized prompts are called "agents", which pass information between each other. For example, we instruct the first agent to extract *Actions*, which are passed to other agents extracting *Actors* and *Business Objects* respectively. This lets us exploit the inherent dependency between these elements. If no Action is detected in a sentence, then there is likely no relevant Actor or Business Object, even if there are nouns that would qualify from a linguistic standpoint. This way of prompting leads to an absolute improvement of +0.08 in F_1 score for both the MD and RE tasks.

6.3 Stability of Results

LLMs are notorious for their non-deterministic output [10], which often puts the validity and stability of results into question. To assess the severity of these problems with our prompting strategy, we repeated the extraction of mentions (MD) and relations (RE) on all documents of PET five times. In each iteration we used gpt-4o-2024-05-13 as a model in a 1-shot setting and recorded the micro F_1 score. We then calculated mean (0.70 for MD, 0.89 for RE), standard deviation (0.003 for MD, 0.002 for RE), minimum (0.69 for MD, 0.89 for RE), and maximum (0.70 for MD, 0.89 for RE). While there are fluctuations in results, they are so minor that they do not call the validity of our results into question.

6.4 Lessons Learned

Using LLMs for extracting process relevant information brings with it a category of challenges, which we already discussed in Sect. 2.3. Solving these is paramount for successful application of LLMs. In this section we discuss how we approached these challenges and what lessons we learned.

(C1) Limited Output Control. The expected output format, as well as the form of extracted information, can mainly be influenced by the prompt components *Meta Language* and *Format Examples*. Adding these results in significantly improved F_1 scores, (+0.22 and +0.05 respectively for MD on PET). These improvements are explained by less parsing errors (919 less for MD on PET), and better recall and precision in detecting mentions. LLMs also run the risk of being "stochastic parrots", simply synthesizing linguistically correct phrases, based on their training data [10]. In our experiments we observed changes in F_1 of maximally −0.02 for rephrased prompts. This indicates robustness of our prompts and suitability of LLMs as an tool for business process information extraction.

(C2) Black-Box. A valuable advantage of utilizing LLMs is their ability to reflect, thereby providing justification for their generated results. Figure 3 shows three examples of justifications for extraction results in the ATDP dataset (see Sect. 2.1). Case I shows the ideal outcome where prediction and expected constraint are identical. Note, that the justification even refers to the meta-language provided in the prompt (compare Sect. 4). In case II, the prediction and the gold standard constraint do not match, because of an error in the gold standard data, following [2], which defines completing a process as a *meta action* that can not be part of any constraint. The dataset creators are alerted of this issue by the LLM, since it plausibly justifies why *send out report* marks the end of a process instance. Finally, in case III the extraction result is controversial, since the sentence is ambiguous. If we consider the term *immediately* to encompass both actions, they are constrained by an *existence* constraint. Alternatively, viewing *check quantity* as a subtask of *process part list* suggests only one action needs modeling. Using such reflective explanations make LLMs useful for "human-in-the-loop" systems, which are already applied in fields like process mining [30].

(C3) Input Presentation ependencies. Adding more text to prompts sometimes has an adverse effect, reducing extraction quality (Sect. 2.3). This makes optimizing prompts difficult, since it is not clear, if adding additional disambiguation hints or longer definitions would improve the result. Using partial extraction prompts helps with this issue, as the sections regarding *Meta Language Creation* can be focused on a few types. Depending on the task, there may even be inter-dependency between information, that can be efficiently exploited in this way.

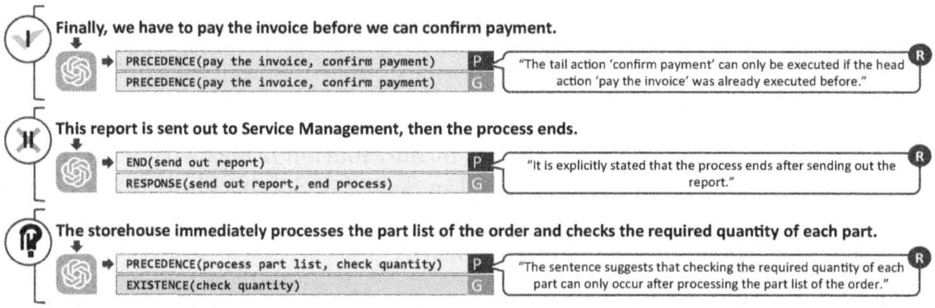

Fig. 3. Reflection example with Predicted and Gold standard constraints: (I) perfect match, (II) gold standard error, (III) ambiguous case

(C4) Data Unawareness. This issue arises, when LLMs are used in a zero-shot setting. There, the components *Meta Language*, and *Format Examples* are the only ways to "teach" the model how to perform the task. Applying the pattern of *few-shot prompting*, i.e., using labeled data in a few-shot setting was beneficial. This makes the use of an LLM more akin to training a machine learning model, but with significantly lower data requirements. In our experiments, three examples were sufficient to achieve better extraction results than those of machine learning models trained with more than ten times of the data.

(C5) Costly Experiments. This is a major drawback of LLM based process information extraction. The most capable LLMs are hosted as cloud-based solutions and are priced per token. We found that limiting the number of examples to 1 resulted in the best cost-value ratio. Additionally, our experiments showed that leaving out the prompt components *Context Manager*, *Persona*, and *Disambiguation* is a valid way to limit the number of tokens sent per request, albeit with potential minor decreases in extraction accuracy. Prompting LLMs without the request for a *Fact List*, nor *Explanations* for extracted information greatly reduces the amount of tokens as well, especially useful after prompt engineering or data curating (during "*inference*"). Alternatively one can switch to cheaper models, i.e., *LLama 3 72B*, if the drop in performance is acceptable.

7 Conclusion

Summary. This paper presents an extensive study on the usefulness of LLMs for the extraction of process information from natural language text. We collected linguistic challenges and discuss how LLMs are uniquely fit for solving them. We also discussed challenges that arise through the use of LLMs and show how other communities propose to deal with these (or similar) concerns through prompt engineering. We present experimental results on three process information extraction datasets, which at least match the current state of the art on these datasets and in most cases improve it by as much as 8% in the F_1 metric. This shows the suitability of LLMs as a method for extracting business process relevant information from natural language process descriptions. To flesh out this notion, we analyze how well our prompting strategy can be applied to different LLMs without changing them, showing their universal nature. We expect LLMs to be a benchmark in the process information extraction domain for the foreseeable future, as limitations in dataset quality and quantity, combined with the need for complex reasoning make it very hard to train large extraction approaches from scratch. We make all our code, prompts, and LLM answers available, to support further research.

Limitations. A limitation of our work is that the list of prompt components we present may not be exhaustive, and they may have interactions that our ablation study does not capture. Additionally, some models suffer from hallucinations, especially Qwen1.5 and Llama 3, which hallucinate non-existent entity and relation types – 20 and 37 instances in the worst cases respectively. However, the severity of this problem diminishes in the few-shot setting (0 and 4 instances respectively in the worst case). We plan on analyzing how our prompts could be enhanced to improve instruction following for these models. Lastly, the current pricing models prohibit large-scale application of the most capable model to process information extraction. Alternatives (e.g., Llama) avoid this issue, but require more labeled examples to reach comparable levels of performance. This limitation may change in the near future, as more cost-efficient models and specialized hardware reduce costs to acceptable levels. Alternatively, very capable—and therefore expensive—LLMs could be used to create and curate training data for smaller local models, leveraging the reasoning capabilities of LLMs indirectly.

Future Work. In future work we aim to use LLMs as tools to support labeling of new data. Current datasets are limited in origin, i.e., they usually describe processes from municipalities or small service providers. We plan to analyze the ability of LLMs to generalize beyond the domains with available labeled data and highlight the promising flexibility observed in our current experiments. Additionally, using GPT-4o's image processing and generation capabilities could be a promising line of research for direct text to model transformation. Finally, our results show very limited improvement in extraction quality, when the prompt includes a role the LLM is restricted to (persona). A slight variation of this idea is to describe the target audience of extraction results in the prompt, to further improve the quality of extracted process information.

References

1. Van der Aa, H., Carmona Vargas, J., Leopold, H., Mendling, J., Padró, L.: Challenges and opportunities of applying natural language processing in business process management. In: COLING (2018)
2. van der Aa, H., Di Ciccio, C., Leopold, H., Reijers, H.A.: Extracting declarative process models from natural language. In: CAiSE (2019)
3. Van der Aa, H., Leopold, H., Reijers, H.A.: Checking process compliance against natural language specifications using behavioral spaces. IS (2018)
4. van der Aa, H., Leopold, H., van de Weerd, I., Reijers, H.A.: Causes and consequences of fragmented process information: Insights from a case study. In: AMCIS (2017)
5. van der Aalst, W.: Process Mining. Springer Berlin Heidelberg, Berlin, Heidelberg (2016). https://doi.org/10.1007/978-3-662-49851-4
6. Ackermann, L., Neuberger, J., Jablonski, S.: Data-driven annotation of textual process descriptions based on formal meaning representations. In: La Rosa, M., Sadiq, S., Teniente, E. (eds.) Advanced Information Systems Engineering: 33rd International Conference, CAiSE 2021, Melbourne, VIC, Australia, June 28 – July 2, 2021, Proceedings, pp. 75–90. Springer International Publishing, Cham (2021). https://doi.org/10.1007/978-3-030-79382-1_5
7. Ackermann, L., Neuberger, J., Käppel, M., Jablonski, S.: Bridging research fields: An empirical study on joint, neural relation extraction techniques. In: CAiSE (2023)
8. Bellan, P., Dragoni, M., Ghidini, C.: Extracting business process entities and relations from text using pre-trained language models and in-context learning. In: EDOC (2022)
9. Bellan, P., Ghidini, C., Dragoni, M., Ponzetto, S.P., van der Aa, H.: Process extraction from natural language text: the PET dataset and annotation guidelines. In: NL4AI (2022)
10. Bender, E.M., Gebru, T., McMillan-Major, A., Shmitchell, S.: On the dangers of stochastic parrots: Can language models be too big? In: ACM FAccT (2021)
11. Cui, L., Wu, Y., Liu, J., Yang, S., Zhang, Y.: Template-based named entity recognition using bart. arXiv preprint arXiv:2106.01760 (2021)
12. Davies, I., Green, P., Rosemann, M., Indulska, M., Gallo, S.: How do practitioners use conceptual modeling in practice? Data Knowl. Eng. **58**(3), 358–380 (2006)
13. Dubois, Y., et al.: Alpacafarm: A simulation framework for methods that learn from human feedback. Adv. Neural Inform. Process. Syst. **36** (2024)
14. Ferreira., R.C.B., Thom., L.H., Fantinato., M.: A semi-automatic approach to identify business process elements in natural language texts. In: ICEIS (2017)

15. Franceschetti, M., Seiger, R., López, H.A., Burattin, A., García-Bañuelos, L., Weber, B.: A characterisation of ambiguity in BPM. In: Almeida, J.P.A., Borbinha, J., Guizzardi, G., Link, S., Zdravkovic, J. (eds.) Conceptual Modeling: 42nd International Conference, ER 2023, Lisbon, Portugal, November 6–9, 2023, Proceedings, pp. 277–295. Springer Nature Switzerland, Cham (2023). https://doi.org/10.1007/978-3-031-47262-6_15
16. Friedrich, F., Mendling, J., Puhlmann, F.: Process model generation from natural language text. In: CAiSE (2011)
17. Kaddour, J., Harris, J., Mozes, M., Bradley, H., Raileanu, R., McHardy, R.: Challenges and applications of large language models. arXiv preprint (2023)
18. Kourani, H., Berti, A., Schuster, D., van der Aalst, W.M.: Process modeling with large language models. arXiv preprint arXiv:2403.07541 (2024)
19. Leopold, H., van der Aa, H., Pittke, F., Raffel, M., Mendling, J., Reijers, H.A.: Searching textual and model-based process descriptions based on a unified data format. SoSym **18**, 1179–1194 (2019)
20. Lewis, P., et al.: Retrieval-augmented generation for knowledge-intensive nlp tasks: Adv. Neural. Inf. Process. Syst. **33**, 9459–9474 (2020)
21. López-Acosta, H.A., Hildebrandt, T., Debois, S., Marquard, M.: The process highlighter: From texts to declarative processes and back. In: CEUR Workshop Proceedings, pp. 66–70. CEUR Workshop Proceedings (2018)
22. Min, B., et al.: Recent advances in natural language processing via large pre-trained language models: a survey. ACM Comput. Surv. **56**(2), 1–40 (2023)
23. Neuberger, J., Ackermann, L., Jablonski, S.: Beyond rule-based named entity recognition and relation extraction for process model generation from natural language text. In: CoopIS (2023)
24. Pesic, M., Schonenberg, H., Van der Aalst, W.M.: Declare: full support for loosely-structured processes. In: 11th IEEE International Enterprise Distributed Object Computing Conference (EDOC 2007), pp. 287–287. IEEE (2007)
25. Qian, C., et al.: An approach for process model extraction by multi-grained text classification. In: CAiSE (2020)
26. Quishpi, L., Carmona, J., Padró, L.: Extracting annotations from textual descriptions of processes. In: BPM 2020 (2020)
27. Richens, R.H.: Interlingual machine translation. Comput. J. **1**(3), 144–147 (1958)
28. Sànchez-Ferreres, J., Burattin, A., Carmona, J., Montali, M., Padró, L., Quishpi, L.: Unleashing textual descriptions of business processes. In: SoSyM (2021)
29. Sukthanker, R., Poria, S., Cambria, E., Thirunavukarasu, R.: Anaphora and coreference resolution: A review. Information Fusion (2020)
30. Ter Hofstede, A.H., et al.: Process-data quality: The true frontier of process mining. In: ACM JDIQ (2023)
31. Törnberg, P.: Best practices for text annotation with large language models. arXiv preprint arXiv:2402.05129 (2024)
32. Wei, J., et al.: Chain-of-thought prompting elicits reasoning in large language models. In: NIPS (2022)
33. White, J., et al.: A prompt pattern catalog to enhance prompt engineering with chatgpt. arXiv preprint arXiv:2302.11382 (2023)
34. Xu, F., Uszkoreit, H., Du, Y., Fan, W., Zhao, D., Zhu, J.: Explainable ai: brief survey on history, research areas, approaches and challenges. In: NLPCC (2019)

Agent System Event Data: Concepts, Dimensions, Applications

Qingtan Shen[1(✉)], Artem Polyvyanyy[1], Nir Lipovetzky[1], and Timotheus Kampik[2]

[1] The University of Melbourne, Parkville, VIC 3010, Australia
{qingtan.shen1,artem.polyvyanyy,nir.lipovetzky}@unimelb.edu.au
[2] SAP, Walldorf, Germany
timotheus.kampik@sap.com

Abstract. Event data is a collection of recorded events that capture performed actions and observed states of business processes supported by information systems. It describes the times of event occurrences, event types, event attributes, and process cases of events identified by one or more objects the events relate to. Process mining uses event data to analyze and improve the processes in organizations. These processes are often performed by actors or agents, such as employees, resources, and systems, in different roles within organizations. In this paper, we present Agent System Event Data (ASED), a new type of event data that describes business processes as interactions of agents. ASED provides a new scope for analyzing individual agents involved in multiple processes, interactions of agents, and systems of agents that enact the processes. We formalize ASED as a conceptual data model, discuss its dimensional data modeling aspects, and argue that event data, in general, benefits from dimensional representation. We review existing event data types and discuss the complementary nature of existing models and ASED. Finally, we validate ASED by demonstrating its ability to express existing business process compliance rules, significantly expanding the scope of compliance analysis addressed by existing data models.

Keywords: Process mining · event logs · event data · agent system mining

1 Introduction

Process mining is a research discipline at the intersection of data science and business process management [3]. It studies methods and tools to extract insights from event logs recorded during the execution of business processes. An event log is a starting point of every process mining study, consisting of events recorded by information systems during executions of business processes. Each event record can contain information about the triggering activity and process instance, as well as related business objects, activities, resources, and agents. By leveraging event logs, organizations can achieve operational transparency, uncover inefficiencies, and make data-driven decisions [2].

The success of a process mining study hinges on the adept extraction of relevant event data from the information systems that execute a given process. Over the last

W. Maass et al. (Eds.): ER 2024, LNCS 15238, pp. 56–72, 2025.
https://doi.org/10.1007/978-3-031-75872-0_4

two decades, the process mining community has meticulously crafted a data model for event data, encapsulating crucial entities and their interrelationships. This conventional event data model, as described by the XES standard [1], serves as a cornerstone for developing new process mining algorithms and analytics, as well as for preparing event data for use by these techniques. Recently, new process mining paradigms, like Object-Centric Process Mining (OCPM) [4], Robotic Process Mining (RPM) [20], and Agent System Mining (ASM) [28] have emerged. These approaches challenge conventional assumptions about event data, striving to establish effective models that are streamlined in their conceptualization and operationalization while robust in their expressiveness and capacity to facilitate analysis of intricate scenarios.

This paper reviews existing event data models and leverages insights gained to propose a new data model for ASM. ASM, a type of process mining, aims to understand and improve organizations by interpreting them as agent-based systems. In these systems, autonomous agents, including people, machines, and AI, independently perceive their environment, make decisions, and take actions to achieve their goals. These agents interact dynamically and unpredictably with each other and their environment, posing challenges in analyzing their behavior. ASM addresses this by utilizing event data generated by such agent-based systems. Specifically, this paper makes these contributions:

- Introduces the Agent System Event Data (ASED) model, providing a new conceptual framework for event data in Agent System Mining.
- Identifies that ASED has features of a dimensional data model widely used in data warehouses and advocates for the general use of dimensional modeling for event data in process mining.
- Studies the relationship between the ASED model and other event data models in process mining, highlighting the complementary nature of existing data models.
- Validates, by means of a publicly available implementation applied over real-world event data, the ASED model by showing its ability to express a wide range of process compliance rules related to roles, resources, and agents in processes.[1]

The paper proceeds as follows. The next section reviews related work on data models for representing event data in process mining. Then, Sect. 3 presents event data models that are commonly used in process mining. Next, Sect. 4 introduces the ASED model and discusses its dimensional nature and its relationship with the other event data models. Section 5 validates ASED by studying its ability to express business process compliance rules. Finally, Sect. 6 states concluding remarks.

2 Related Work

In this section, we explore various types of process mining, primarily focusing on the process discovery problem studied within the domain. Process discovery involves constructing process models from event data [2].

Event data used as input for conventional process discovery techniques typically includes events with three essential attributes: *activity*, *case identifier*, and *timestamp*.

[1] The ASED model for the BPIC 2013 event log (10.4121/uuid:500573e6-accc-4b0c-9576-aa5468b10cee) and an implementation of the compliance rules over ASED is available at https://doi.org/10.26188/26868592.v1 and https://doi.org/10.26188/26868442.v2, respectively.

Thus, an event represents an activity triggered at a specific timestamp within a given process case. Events sharing the same case identifier, ordered by their timestamps, collectively describe the execution of a process instance, also known as a *trace*. This trace delineates the sequence of activities executed and the events they triggered.

Traditional process mining techniques typically focus on modeling and analyzing processes based on cases captured as a reference to a single object. To overcome this limitation, object-centric process mining (OCPM) methods have been developed to mine and analyze processes involving multiple object types. OCPM can be applied to event logs containing information about events, activities, and the objects and object types associated with each activity [6]. Events processed by OCPM methods can relate to any number of objects; for example, a delivery event may involve both a package and the items inside it simultaneously. The fundamental concept of OCPM is to create a flattened event log for each object type and apply process discovery methods to construct models for each of them [6]. Subsequently, a merging step is applied to combine these object-type models into a comprehensive process model based on the relationships between different objects. Van der Aalst [5] outlined three benefits of OCPM methods. Firstly, data extraction becomes more efficient by focusing on the relationship between events and objects without considering case information. Secondly, relationships between objects can be mined and analyzed from event logs without requiring additional information. Thirdly, object-centric process models can provide visualization of the relationships between objects. OCPM techniques have been applied in various domains. For instance, Li and de Carvalho [21] applied OCPM to social media data to analyze dependencies and relationships between activities and objects. Also, Hobeck and Weber [15] used OCPM on blockchain data to generate an object-centric, directly-follows graph depicting relationships between contracts, markets, and transactions as objects.

Robotic Process Mining (RPM) [20] is defined as a class of techniques to identify candidate routines and use these routines to discover specifications that can be executed by Robotic Process Automation (RPA) bots. The input data, also called the User Interaction (UI) log, is collected from user-driven tasks, which refer to the data generated from interactions between a user and software applications. A UI log is a sequence of events completed by a single user in a single workstation. Each event has a timestamp and is characterized by an event type (e.g., *open email*); no case information is stored in the UI log. An event may have some attributes to store more information. For example, if an event has the type *open file*, then the file name can be stored as an event attribute. The RPM pipeline first preprocesses the input UI log, filters out noise, then identifies suitable event sequences for automation, and finally extracts executable specifications for these sequences. RPM is applied to select sequences of repetitive work that are suitable for automation, to apply RPA, and then to execute scripts for encoding the fine-grained interactions that automate the selected work sequences.

A Multi-Agent System (MAS) is a collection of agents that achieve common or conflicting goals through interactions. Business processes whose participants act independently towards their goals while interacting with other entities, e.g., social interactions over business activities [16], can naturally be modeled as MAS. Agent-Based Modeling (ABM) is a technique that can be applied to describe an organization as a system composed of autonomous agents [28]. Unlike classical process discovery techniques employed to discover a Petri net or BPMN model, agent system mining combines ABM and process mining techniques, aiming to infer the design of a MAS by automatically constructing it from event data. A MAS model often contains two types of components: agent models and models of their interactions. Agent models capture the behaviors of autonomous agents that participate in the system, while interaction models describe patterns of agent interactions. ASM studies ways to construct MAS models from event data, and it comes with at least two benefits compared to classical process discovery methods. Firstly, ASM analyses the behavior of process participants and their interactions [28], which can avoid constructing unreadable models with activities from the same agent scattered across distant parts of the model. Secondly, MAS models constructed by ASM discovery do not necessarily grow in complexity with event data volume growth [28]. Tour et al. [29] introduced the first divide-and-conquer algorithm, called Agent Miner, for automatically discovering a MAS model from event data. The algorithm discovers an interaction model of agents and then each agent's behavior to fit the interaction model.

3 Event Data Models

This section discusses data-driven, event-centric conceptual data models. In the process mining community, Message Sequence Charts (MSCs) that utilize two syntactical constructs, agents and messages, are applied to model message sending and receiving between agents [19], while in the MAS community, several meta-models for agent systems are well-established. Prominently, the AALAADIN meta-model [14] is designed to show the coordination and negotiation schemas of MAS, and the JaCaMo meta-model [9] shows the dependencies, connections, and conceptual mappings between three agent-oriented programming dimensions: environment, agent, and organization. However, these meta-models are not event-centric. In Sects. 3.1 to 3.3, we present conventional, object-centric, and user interaction event-centric conceptual data models.

3.1 Conventional Event Data

Conventional event data is a collection of observed and recorded events. Many technologies, including process mining [3] and process querying [24], are applied to event data. Figure 1 shows the conceptual model of conventional event data [6].

An *event* is a record that documents an activity or change within a system or application. It is defined as a mapping from attribute names to attribute values. According to the design in Fig. 1, an event is triggered by exactly one activity, while each activity can trigger multiple events, and it is meaningless to keep records of activities that trigger no events. In addition, each event refers to a process *case* and has a *timestamp*.

An event attribute refers to further specific information associated with an event, beyond the standard event attributes of activity, case, and timestamp, providing various perspectives on the data. Typically, each event encompasses multiple attributes designed to capture different aspects of the event. It is worth noting that some activities may lack event attributes entirely, and presenting irrelevant attributes for such activities serves no purpose. An event can possess any number of event attributes, with each attribute value precisely corresponding to one event and one event attribute. Events may utilize

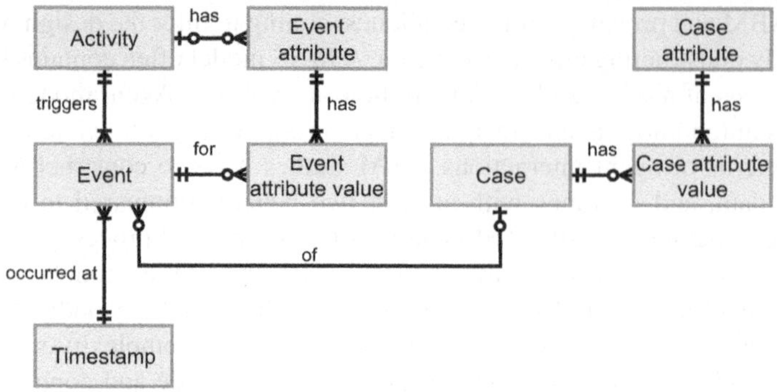

Fig. 1. Conventional event data model [6]

the same attribute to capture information from similar perspectives. However, some events may lack attributes or attribute values. Thus, the relationship between event and event attribute value is mandatory-to-optional. Nevertheless, if an activity with multiple attributes triggers an event, every attribute must have a value corresponding to the event.

A case represents a chronological sequence of events that traverse a particular process. A case can comprise any number of events, and some events may not be associated with any specific case. In conventional event data, it is typically assumed that an event cannot be linked to more than one case. Thus, the relationship between events and cases in the design in Fig. 1 captures this relation as many events can relate to one case. Similarly to events and activities, a case may possess any number of case attributes. Case attributes encapsulate aggregated knowledge derived from all events within the case, enabling the application of querying and other analytical techniques at a higher level of abstraction.

3.2 Object-Centric Event Data

Van der Aalst [6] introduced an Object-Centric Event Data (OCED) model. Similar to the conventional event data model, the OCED model in Fig. 2 has entities and relationships for storing information about events and activities. In addition, OCED supports collecting information about objects; hence, the corresponding entities and relationships are added to the OCED meta-model. Every object has one object type, e.g., object O_1 can be of type package, while object O_2 can be of type item. An event can relate to any number of objects, and an object can relate to any number of events. For example, objects O_1 and O_2 can be involved in the same delivery event. Similarly, object O_1 can be involved in multiple events, e.g., a delivery event and a payment event. An object type can have any number of object attributes, and these attributes should have values. An attribute value of an object can differ across different timestamps, which supports updating a single object attribute instead of updating the complete object. For example, the location attribute of object O_1 can be updated at different timestamps. Different objects may have relationships, e.g., item O_2 is in package O_1. The OCED model resolves the convergence and divergence problems common in convention event

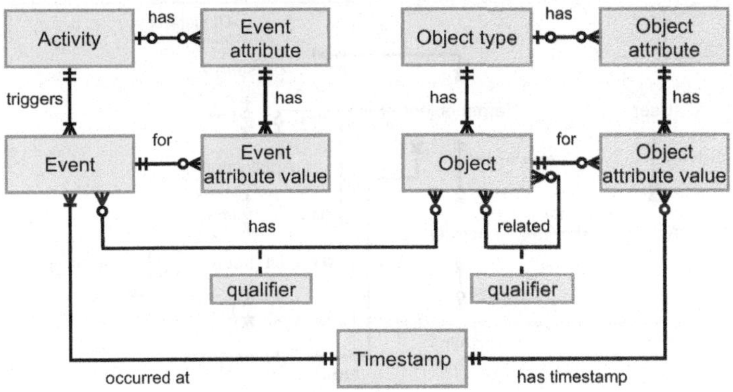

Fig. 2. Object-centric event data model [6]

data [4]. The convergence problem happens when events that involve more than one object are replicated. For instance, when O_1 and O_2 are delivered together, two events are often used to describe this delivery activity in the conventional event data. The divergence problem happens when events that relate to the same object are scattered across different cases. OCED can solve this issue by constructing a case of events for each object. OCED can be used, for instance, in graph embeddings to capture information about the structure of object relationships for subsequent process mining analysis [8].

3.3 User Interaction Event Data

Abb and Rehse [7] presented a User Interaction Event Data (UIED) model for storing low-level activities performed by users during the execution of tasks using software systems. Figure 3 shows the UIED model. Each event in the UIED describes a single interaction between a user and an interface. The activity entity combines the action and the target part of the UIED. It corresponds to the event entity in the conventional event data model. An activity combines a single user and a single target object. The action entity combines the user entity and the activity entity and stores the behavior the user performs using the input devices, such as *click on mouse*. A user can execute any number of actions, while an action can only be performed by exactly one user. The target object entity records the information about the interface object over which the action is executed. The tree-shaped UI component hierarchy is introduced to capture different levels of knowledge about the target object. Each target object refers to such UI hierarchy components. The lowest-level elements of the interface are stored in the UI element entity, such as buttons, text boxes, and their current states. Lowest-level elements can be combined into UI groups based on their functionality, such as the login task. The relationship between UI groups is also modeled in UIED, which is useful for mining the interactions between high level functions. The UI application and the UI system entities can store higher-level interface information, e.g., the process instance and the system-level action, respectively. Although one can apply OCED to user interaction data and store the information about users and UI objects as objects, UIED has two benefits.

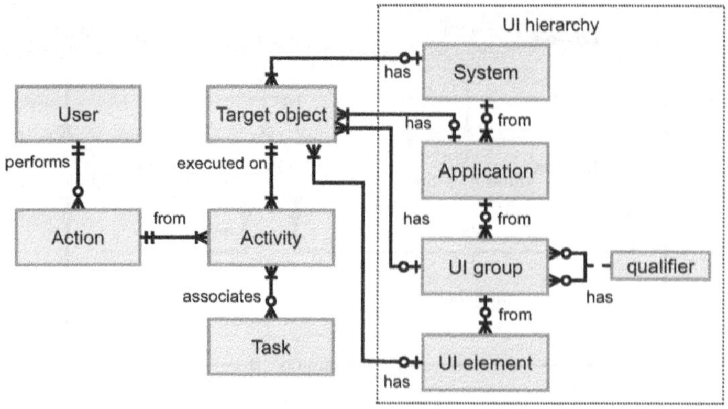

Fig. 3. User interaction event data model [7]

Firstly, for different events, UIED can store dynamic object attributes attached to these events in the entities from the UI hierarchy component. Secondly, object attributes can be shared in different object types based on their UI hierarchy components. However, storing the same target object with different attributes can lead to redundancy.

4 Agent System Event Data

This section presents our Agent System Event Data (ASED) model (Sect. 4.1), discusses the aspects that characterize ASED as a dimensional model (Sect. 4.2), explains the relation of ASED to other event data models (Sect. 4.3), and shows that publicly available event data can already be represented using ASED (Sect. 4.4).

4.1 Entities and Relationships

Figure 4a shows the ASED model captured using the ER notation. The entities of the model can be split into three categories: conventional process mining entities (highlighted with blue background in the figure), process entity (green), and MAS entities (red). Next, we discuss entities from each of these categories in detail, emphasizing the relevant relationships within and across the categories.

Conventional Entities. Four entities in the ASED model are borrowed from the conventional model. These are the *Event*, *Case*, *Timestamp*, and *Activity* entities. Similar to the conventional process mining, we assume that each event has exactly one process *Case* it refers to and is triggered by exactly one *Activity* at exactly one *Timestamp*. In turn, an *Activity*, *Case*, and *Timestamp* can refer to multiple events. The meaning of these entities is the same as in the conventional process mining; cf. Sect. 3.1.

Similar to the *Event* and *Case* entities in the conventional data model, every entity of the ASED model can have multiple and arbitrary attribute values, implemented as the *AttributeValue* entity shown in Fig. 4b. This associative entity implements a many-to-many relationship between *Entity* and *Attribute*, with a particular value stored as

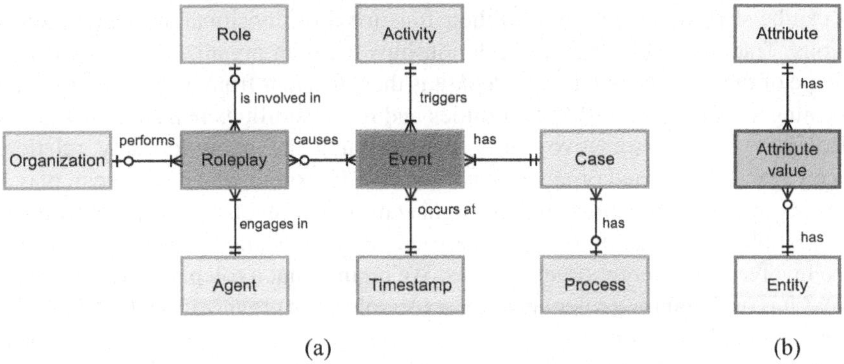

Fig. 4. (a) The Agent System Event Data model and (b) tracking of entity attributes

an attribute of this association. In a concrete implementation of the ASED model, this pattern of attribute values can be replicated for any group of entities in the model. Specifically, every such replica should create copies of *Attribute* and *AttributeValue* entities, specific to the selected group of ASED entities, and link all the entities in the group to the *AttributeValue* entity replica via the one-to-many relationship.

Process Entity. A *Process* is a collection of activities that, when performed, leads to an objective of an organization, for instance, an insurance claim handling process, an implementation of a clinical guideline, or a process of issuing a birth certificate. A *Case* refers to an instance of a process. For example, an insurer usually handles multiple instances of a health insurance process, one per claim, with concrete activities executed to settle the claim. In conventional process mining, it is assumed that the same process triggers all events in an event log. An agent in an organization is often simultaneously involved in multiple instances of different processes. For instance, a financial officer can be simultaneously involved in multiple instances of risk management and financial reporting processes. To understand the essence of the agent's performance, including context switches and task prioritization and transition planning, one needs to expand the scope of event data to the overall landscape of processes in an organization. Thus, in the ASED model, a *Process* must have at least one *Case*, whereas, to ensure compatibility with conventional event data, it is optional for a *Case* to refer to one *Process*.

MAS Entities. An *Agent* is a person or machine that can perform activities to produce specified effects. In an organization, examples of agents include employees, manufacturing equipment, and AI agents performing automated decision-making. A *Role* defines duties and expectations associated with a particular job in an organization, such as specific activities that an agent in this role is responsible for. An agent can relate to multiple roles. For example, an academic can simultaneously relate to the roles of a lecturer to teach classes and a researcher to produce new knowledge. An *Organization* is a group of agents with a particular purpose, for example, a government department, a business, or a healthcare institution. One can also interpret a group of agents as an organizational unit, a distinct team or a division within an organization. Organization units can be structured according to their functional or divisional aspects within organizations. Tracking such structural relationships between organization units is beyond the scope of the ASED model. A *Roleplay* is then an agent from a specific organization performing an activity to fulfill their duties and responsibilities in a specific role.

Roleplay is an associative entity that captures the many-to-many relationship between agents, roles, and organizations. As already explained, an agent can play multiple roles in an organization, and an organization can involve multiple agents. Similarly, multiple agents can play the same role. Also, the same agent and the same role can be involved in different organizations. We require that a roleplay refers to an agent, whereas it is optional for a roleplay to refer to a role or an organization. In the latter case, we assume that the agent plays some default role in a default organization. The cardinality of the relationship between *Roleplay* and *Event* is many-to-many. Indeed, an agent from an organizatoin playing a role can do that multiple times to cause many events. For instance, an academic from a research group writing a research paper wearing their "scientist hat" can trigger many events, including paper submission, paper review, and camera-ready version submission. At the same time, an event, in general, can be caused by several roleplays. For example, a supervisory meeting event for a research fellow may refer to the fellow, their principal and co-supervisors, collaborators, and research partners, each being in a corresponding roleplay for their organization with respect to this event. To ensure compatibility with the conventional event data, it is optional for an event to refer to a roleplay. In contrast, the existence of a roleplay instance must be justified by relating it to an event.

4.2 Dimensions

Dimensional modeling is a data modeling technique used in data warehousing to organize and structure data for efficient querying and analysis [22,23]. At the core of dimensional modeling is the concept of a star schema, which consists of a central fact table surrounded by dimension tables. The fact table contains quantitative measures or metrics (facts) related to a business process or event, while dimension tables provide descriptive attributes for analyzing the facts. Dimension tables typically represent entities such as time, location, and objects that characterize the facts in the fact table, and they serve as entry points for querying and filtering data in the fact table. The simple and intuitive structure of a star schema facilitates fast and easy query performance, as well as simplified data retrieval and analysis.

In a star schema, the fact table serves as the focal point for analyzing information and trends, while dimensional tables provide context for interpreting the facts. This model facilitates multidimensional analysis of the data, supporting complex reporting requirements. Additionally, the denormalized structure of a star schema minimizes join operations in queries, leading to improved query performance and reduced database complexity. Overall, dimensional modeling and star schemas provide a flexible and scalable framework for organizing and analyzing data, making it a popular choice for decision support and business intelligence applications.

The ASED model adheres to the structure of a star schema, or a dimensional model, commonly encountered in data warehouses. Within this schema, the *Event* entity and the *Roleplay* entity can be seen as two fact tables, while *Activity*, *Case*, *Timestamp*,

Agent, *Role*, and *Organization* are dimensional tables that characterize the facts. In addition, the *Process* entity refines the *Case* entity to define a normalized dimensional hierarchy [23]. It is worth noting that the *Roleplay* entity and the *Event* entity are in a many-to-many relationship, deviating from the typical structure of a star schema in which a fact table is related to dimensional tables via one-to-many relationships. Such a many-to-many relationship can be implemented using an auxiliary table *RoleplayTo-Event* in which the related identifier of roleplays and events are matched. Also, note that this deviation from a conventional dimensional design can be addressed through various means. For example, the relationship between *Event* and *Roleplay* can be constrained to a many-to-one relationship by tracking only dominant roleplays for each event [23]. Alternatively, a many-to-many relationship can be interpreted as multiple one-to-one relationships, assuming each event is associated with several roleplays, each corresponding to a distinct role.

We recommend dimensional modeling as a preferred approach for capturing event data in process mining due to its ability to efficiently organize and analyze complex relationships between entities that identify events. By organizing event data into fact tables and dimension tables providing descriptive attributes, dimensional modeling facilitates the exploration and analysis of events from multiple perspectives. This approach allows process mining practitioners to quickly identify patterns, trends, and correlations within event data, enabling insights into process behavior, performance, and compliance. The denormalized structure of star schemas supports faster query performance and streamlined data retrieval [24]. Furthermore, the multidimensional nature of dimensional modeling supports advanced analytical techniques, such as OLAP (Online Analytical Processing), enabling interactive and dynamic exploration of event data across various dimensions. Overall, dimensional modeling offers a robust framework for capturing, organizing, and analyzing event data in process mining, empowering organizations to extract valuable insights and optimize their business processes effectively.

4.3 Compatibility

ASED can be applied in different process mining paradigms, such as Agent System Mining, Robotic Process Mining (or Task Mining), and Object-Centric Process Mining, see Sect. 2 for the discussion of these process mining types. In this section, we discuss the relation between ASED and event data models used in these process mining types.

Agent System Mining. Agent System Mining (ASM) requires a collection of event data, each characterized by a case identifier, a timestamp, an activity, and an agent. In classical event data, the case identifier and activity that triggered an event are stored within the *Case* entity and the *Event* entity, respectively, and the agent information is stored within the event attributes. In ASED, all agent attributes are stored in the *Agent* entity, whereas the other three types of information are stored in the same entities as in classical event data. Existing algorithms for discovering agent-based models from event data in ASM require that every event is triggered by exactly one agent [29]. These algorithms can be extended to benefit from the ability of ASED to express the fact that an event can be triggered by several agents playing different roles in different organizations. In addition, ASED, for the first time, argues that event data may encompass data stemming from multiple processes, a phenomenon that ASM can benefit from when analyzing agents' performance across different functions [28]. Future work in ASM will explore the benefits of ASED and the boundaries of what models can be inferred based on the available concepts, and which analysis these concepts can support.

Task Mining. ASED can be applied to support user interaction mining techniques. One can interpret the *Agent* and *Role* entities in ASED as the *User* and *Action* entities in UIED, respectively, while the *Event* entity can be interpreted as the *Activity* entity in UIED. In ASED, multiple agents (users) can be involved in the same event, e.g., an online meeting. The information related to these user actions is stored in the Roleplay entity. This many-to-many relationship is useful when doing task mining on collaboration platforms that track interactions between users. In terms of dimensional modeling, the *Event* entity in ASED is a fact table characterized by the dimensions referred to by the keys of the *Roleplay*, *Activity*, and *Timestamp* entities. Hierarchical dimensional tables can also be used to characterize the *Target object* entity to store attributes from the UI hierarchy component. Such dimensional tables can support efficient querying and are suitable for mining the relationships between different UI levels. Furthermore, the *Task* entity in UEID can be interpreted as the *Process* entity in ASED, while the *Target object* entity in UIED can be accepted as the *Activity* entity in ASED. Consequently, one can combine the features of ASED and UIED by linking the UI hierarchy concepts in UIED to the *Activity* entity in ASED, obtaining the benefits of both designs.

Object-Centric Process Mining. Object-Centric Event Data (OCED) can be integrated with ASED by relating the *Event* entity in ASED with the *Object* entity in OCED. The relationship between the ASED *Event* entity and the OCED *Object* entity should also be borrowed from the OCED model; that is, it is a many-to-many relationship. The other entities and relationships from both ASED and OCED should then be included in the integrated event data model without further modifications. In such an integrated data model, one can capture relationships between agents, events, and objects, benefiting from both original designs. Consequently, according to the integrated model, an event can be triggered by any number of agents playing different roles in their organizations. At the same time, an event in such an integrated world can be related to any number of objects, providing scopes for identifying process cases as various combinations of objects. This ability to identify process cases as combinations of objects involved in the occurrence of events constitutes the main benefit of OCED over the conventional event data model [5]. Such an integrated data mode supports the querying of the information between agents and objects. In addition, it can be used to study resource allocation across various processes and cases. Finally, such an integrated model supports tracking of the relationships between objects and processes and between objects and organizations. This is particularly useful for relating business objects to relevant departments and processes within organizations.

4.4 Feasibility

As ASED is a new data model, there are no publicly available event datasets captured in ASED. In this section, we study the feasibility of obtaining an event dataset that adheres to the ASED requirements by converting a publicly available conventional event log to ASED. Specifically, we convert the BPIC 2013 event log[2] into the ASED format. The BPIC 2013 event log is an extract of the Volvo IT Incident and Problem Management event log, which stores information about agents, resources, organizations, and processes as event attributes. We implemented the ASED model as a relational database.[3] The attributes of the various ASED entities were obtained based on the available attributes of the *Event* entity from the BPIC 2013 event log. The implementation of the conversion is publicly available.[4] We also make publicly available the result of the conversion of the BPIC 2013 event log into the ASED dataset. To facilitate accessibility of the results, we store the tables of the derived schema in the CSV format[5], and keep the timestamp values in the event fact table. In the converted ASED event log, each event is performed by a single roleplay. However, in general, it is possible to map conventional events to ASED events performed by several roleplays. For example, such a situation may arise when the attributes of some specific events contain information about more than one agent, their roles, and organizations. Alternatively, one can decide to cluster conventional events into high-level ASED events and model them as such caused by all the roleplays involved in the corresponding low-level events. However, such a clustering step may require additional information besides the conventional event log, e.g., configuration of the clustering technique or manual definitions of high-level events.

5 Process Compliance

Next, we validate the ability to express process compliance rules that relate to the management of agents, roles, and organizations in processes over the ASED data model. To identify relevant compliance rules, we performed a literature search. We executed the query "*(process compliance) AND (role OR resource OR agent OR object)*" on Web of Science to search for relevant papers. On May 17, 2024, this query returned 58 papers. After screening the titles, abstracts, and the full content of the papers, we identified 8 papers that discuss process compliance rules of interest. We examined these papers and extracted *all* relevant compliance rules from them, resulting in a total of 40 identified rules. Each of these compliance rules was evaluated to determine if it can be implemented over all event data models discussed in Sect. 3 and ASED. The conventional event data and OCED cannot express any of these 40 compliance rules, while UIED can express some of the rules that address the relationship between agents and activities. The summary of the rules supported by ASED and UIED is given in Table 1.

The identified compliance rules address relationships between multiple attributes, such as role, case, agent, and time. Most of these rules can be implemented over the ASED model, as is documented in the last column of Table 1. We implemented all compliance rules supported by ASED.[6] In addition, we converted BPIC 2013, a publicly available industrial event log, to ASED (see Footnote 5). We evaluated the implemented rules over the obtained ASED model to validate the claims of ASED support in Table 1.

[2] https://doi.org/10.4121/uuid:500573e6-accc-4b0c-9576-aa5468b10cee.

[3] https://doi.org/10.26188/26868532.v1.

[4] https://doi.org/10.26188/26868586.v1.

[5] https://doi.org/10.26188/26868592.v1.

[6] https://doi.org/10.26188/26868442.v2.

Table 1. Process compliance rules, where T_1, T_2, and T_3 refer to tasks/activities, A_1 and A_2 refer to agents, R_1 and R_2 refer to roles, O_1 and O_2 refer to organizations (organization units), P_1 and P_2 refer to processes, and M refers to a time period; "✓" – rule supported; "×" – rule not supported; "AS" – Agent System Event Data; "UI" – User Interaction Event Data

No.	Compliance rules	Ref.	UI	AS
1	T_1 must be done by A_1	[11]	✓	✓
2	A_1 is responsible for T_1	[11]	×	×
3	T_1 must be done by R_1	[11,13,26]	×	✓
4	T_1 must be done by O_1	[11]	×	✓
5	T_1 must be done by an agent in list $[A_1, A_2, \ldots]$	[11]	✓	✓
6	An agent in list $[A_1, A_2, \ldots]$ is responsible for T_1	[11]	×	×
7	T_1 must be done by a role in list $[R_1, R_2, \ldots]$	[11,18]	×	✓
8	T_1 must be done by an organization in list $[O_1, O_2, \ldots]$	[11]	×	✓
9	T_1, T_2 should not be done by the same agent in one case	[13]	×	✓
10	T_1, T_2 should not be done by the same role in one case	[13]	×	✓
11	T_1, T_2 must be done by the same agent in one case	[13]	×	✓
12	T_1, T_2 must be done by the same role but different agents in one case	[13]	×	✓
13	R_1, R_2 must be involved together in T_1	[13]	×	✓
14	A_1, A_2 must be involved together in T_1	[13]	×	✓
15	A_1 should not play only role R_1 in the whole process	[12]	×	✓
16	The number of roles A_1 plays in the whole process is limited	[12]	×	✓
17	The number of cases A_1 participates in is limited	[12]	×	✓
18	A_1 should not play different roles in the same case	[12]	×	✓
19	If A_1 does T_1 in R_1, then A_1 should not do T_2 in R_2 in the same case	[12]	×	✓
20	If A_1 does T_1, then A_1 must perform T_2 in same case	[17]	×	✓
21	If O_1 does T_1, then this T_1 must be done by A_1 in O_1	[17]	×	✓
22	If A_1 in O_1 does T_1, then O_2 must perform T_2 earlier in same case	[17]	×	✓
23	If O_1 does T_1, then O_2 must perform T_2 later in same case	[17]	×	✓
24	If T_1, T_2 are directly followed, then they cannot done by a same agent	[17]	×	✓
25	R_1 is always responsible for R_2	[27]	×	×
26	Number of activities done by A_1 in the whole process is limited	[18]	×	✓
27	Number of activities done by R_1 in the whole process is limited	[18]	×	✓
28	Two tasks from two cases of different processes should not be done by the same role	[18]	×	✓
29	At least one activity in a case must be done by roles in the middle level	[18]	×	×
30	R_1 can perform a maximum of N activities in any case of P_1	[18]	×	✓
31	T_1, T_2 should be done by different organizations	[25]	×	✓
32	If A_1 does T_1 and not T_2 in period M, then A_1 must do T_3 later	[25]	✓	✓
33	If A_1 does T_1 and not T_2 in period M, then R_1 must do T_3 later	[25]	×	✓
34	T_1 must be done by an agent with R_1 in O_1	[26]	×	✓
35	If T_1 occurs before T_2 in a case, they must be done by the same agent	[26]	✓	✓
36	If T_1 occurs before T_2 in a case, they must be done by agents from O_1	[26]	×	✓
37	If T_1 is done by A_1 in R_1, T_2 should be done by a lower-level role before	[26]	×	×
38	If T_1 and T_2 are done by the same organization and T_3 occurs, T_3 should be done by R_1	[26]	×	✓
39	If A_1 does T_1, T_2 sequentially, then A_1 must in O_1	[26]	×	✓
40	If T_1, T_2 occurs before T_3, then T_1, T_2 must be done by agents in O_1	[26]	×	✓

Table 2. (a) Instances of the *Event* entity, (b) instances of the *Roleplay* entity, and (c) relationships between the *Event* and *Role* entities

(a)

ID	Case	Activity	Timestamp
E_1	C_1	T_1	*2010-03-31 14:59*
E_2	C_1	T_1	*2010-03-31 15:00*
E_3	C_1	T_2	*2010-03-31 15:45*
E_4	C_1	T_1	*2010-04-06 14:44*
E_5	C_1	T_2	*2010-04-06 14:45*

(b)

ID	Agent	Role	Organization
RP_1	A_1	R_1	O_1
RP_2	A_1	R_2	O_1
RP_3	A_2	R_2	O_1
RP_4	A_2	R_1	O_1
RP_5	A_3	R_1	O_1

(c)

Event	Roleplay
E_1	RP_1
E_2	RP_1
E_3	RP_2
E_4	RP_3
E_5	RP_4

For example, one can implement the rule "A_1 *(an agent) should not play different roles in the same case*" (Rule 18 in Table 1) by checking, for each case, if A_1 is involved only in one role associated with all events that relate to that case. This logic over the ASED model is captured in Algorithm 1. Table 2a and 2b lists instances of the *Event* and *Role* entities, respectively, while Table 2c implements the *EventToRoleplay* relationship by relating events to roleplays that were involved in triggering them. Consider that Table 2a stores all events from case C_1. Table 2c suggests that four roleplays were involved in this case. These roleplays can be used to extract roles and agents that define them; see Table 2b. Assume that Algorithm 1 is invoked for the input of agent identifier A_1 and entity instances and relationships in Tables 2a to 2c. As there is only one case (C_1), the `for` loop at Algorithm 2 of the algorithm will execute once. In this only iteration, the *eids* variable will be assigned set $\{E_1, E_2, E_3, E_4, E_5\}$; this is the set of all events in the currently analyzed case (cf. Algorithm 3). Then, at Algorithm 4, all roleplays relevant to the events in *eids* are extracted. Hence, it holds that *rids* is equal to $\{RP_1, RP_2, RP_3, RP_4\}$. At Algorithm 5, the algorithm computes all roles the requested agent (A_1) played in roleplays from *rids* and stores them in *roles*. If the number of played roles exceeds one ($|roles| > 1$), the case is added to the *res* set, which was initialized as the empty set at Algorithm 1. If the returned set *res* is empty, there are no cases in which the agent plays more than one role, and thus, the rule is satisfied; otherwise, the rule is violated. As *res* contains C_1, compliance rule 18 is violated on this example input.

The ASED model does not support five of the surveyed compliance rules (cf. Table 1). Rules 2 and 6 refer to the responsibilities of agents when performing activities. For example, Rule 2 "A_1 *is responsible for* T_1" requests to check that agent A_1 always acts in the highest role when performing activity T_1. This check can be performed in two steps. Firstly, one needs to confirm that A_1 is involved in the execution of T_1. Secondly, when a group of agents is involved in the execution of T_1, one needs to confirm that A_1 has the highest-level role in this agent group [11]. ASED supports checking the first step, while the second step cannot be checked because ASED does not explicitly model the hierarchy of roles. Therefore, Rules 2 and 6 cannot be checked over ASED. Rule 25 requests that "R_1 *is always responsible for* R_2," meaning that if R_2 is involved in a case, then R_1 must also be involved in the same case, and the role level of R_1 must be higher than R_2 [18]. Again, we cannot check this rule without knowing the

Algorithm 1: Compliance rule 18 from 1 over ASED

Input: An agent identifier aid, instances of the *Event* and *Roleplay* entities, and an *EventToRoleplay* relationship between the *Event* and *Roleplay* entities.
Output: The set of all case identifiers in which agent aid plays more than one role.

$res \leftarrow \emptyset$;
for $c \in$ *Case* **do**
  $eids \leftarrow \{e.ID \mid e \in \textit{Event} \wedge e.Case = c.ID\}$;
  $rids \leftarrow \{e2r.Roleplay \mid e2r \in \textit{EventToRoleplay} \wedge e2r.Event \in eids\}$;
  $roles \leftarrow \{r.Role \mid r \in \textit{Roleplay} \wedge r.ID \in rids \wedge r.Agent = aid\}$;
  if $|roles| > 1$ **then** $res \leftarrow res \cup \{c.ID\}$
return res

role levels. The knowledge of role hierarchy is also necessary when checking Rules 29 and 37. Therefore, to support checking these five rules, one should model role levels explicitly or infer them from available data.

It is significantly more challenging to check the compliance rules from Table 1 over other event data models. In the conventional model, it is impossible to check the rules by relying only on event attributes, as the semantics of such attributes are unspecified. For instance, it is not possible to match agents and roles if an event has two attributes storing information about agents and two attributes storing information about roles unless some additional knowledge about the mapping is available. Specifically, the event "*hold a meeting*" may involve many participants in different roles, and it may be necessary to relate participants to corresponding roles. OCED does not model agents, roles, roleplays, or organizations explicitly. However, the generic nature of OCED, implemented via objects and their qualified relationships, allows for the encompassing of any data schema, including ASED. This approach, however, requires external schema knowledge that is not initially available in OCED. The original OCED model, hence, cannot support any compliance rules listed in Table 1. UIED can describe hierarchies of roles and store agent information in the target object entity. However, it is not possible to express that a specific agent can play different roles. These aspects of UIED make it suitable for implementing only four compliance rules out of those listed in Table 1.

As all compliance rules currently not supported by ASED relate to responsibilities of agents [10], the extension of ASED toward modeling of responsibilities of agents or inference of responsibilities based on ASED is future work.

6 Conclusion

This paper presents Agent System Event Data (ASED), a model aimed at conceptualizing the event data used in Agent System Mining. We provide a detailed exposition of ASED and conduct a comprehensive review of various event data models in process mining, elucidating the relationship between ASED and the existing models. Furthermore, we subject ASED to a rigorous validation by demonstrating how ASED can be used to verify a diverse array of process compliance rules pertaining to roles, agents, and resources. Through this validation, we confirm that ASED significantly expands the coverage of compliance rules supported by existing event data models.

Several limitations of this work should be acknowledged. First, one can conduct a systematic literature review to expand the list of identified relevant compliance rules used to validate the ASED model. Second, ASED currently lacks the capability to model responsibilities of agents and superior-subordinate relationships between agents. Lastly, the discussion of ASED's feasibility does not account for the practicality of directly recording the data generated by existing information systems. Future work will aim to address these limitations. Lastly, we plan to explore the ability of ASED to facilitate the discovery of agent-based models from event data.

Acknowledgment. This work was in part supported by the Australian Research Council project DP220101516.

References

1. IEEE Standard for eXtensible Event Stream (XES) for achieving interoperability in event logs and event streams. IEEE Std 1849-2023 (Revision of IEEE Std 1849-2016) (2023)
2. van der Aalst, W.M.P.: Process mining: overview and opportunities. ACM Trans. Manag. Inf. Syst. **3**(2), 7:1–7:17 (2012)
3. van der Aalst, W.M.P.: Process Mining—Data Science in Action. 2nd edn. (2016)
4. Aalst, W.M.P.: Object-centric process mining: dealing with divergence and convergence in event data. In: Ölveczky, P.C., Salaün, G. (eds.) SEFM 2019. LNCS, vol. 11724, pp. 3–25. Springer, Cham (2019). https://doi.org/10.1007/978-3-030-30446-1_1
5. van der Aalst, W.M.P.: Object-Centric Process Mining: An Introduction. In: ICTAC Summmer School, LNCS, vol. 13490, pp. 73–105, Springer (2021). https://doi.org/10.1007/978-3-031-43678-9_3
6. van der Aalst, W.M.P.: Object-centric process mining: unraveling the fabric of real processes. Mathematics **11**(12), 2691 (2023)
7. Abb, L., Rehse, J.: A reference data model for process-related user interaction logs. Di Ciccio, C., Dijkman, R., del Río Ortega, A., Rinderle-Ma, S. (eds.) BPM, LNCS, vol. 13420, pp. 57–74, Springer, Cham (2022). https://doi.org/10.1007/978-3-031-16103-2_7
8. Adams, J.N., Park, G., van der Aalst, W.M.P.: Preserving complex object-centric graph structures to improve machine learning tasks in process mining. Eng. Appl. Artif. Intell. **125**, 106764 (2023)
9. Boissier, O., Bordini, R.H., Hübner, J.F., Ricci, A., Santi, A.: Multi-agent oriented programming with JaCaMo. Sci. Comput. Program. **78**(6), 747–761 (2013)
10. Cabanillas, C., Resinas, M., Ruiz-Cortés, A.: Automated resource assignment in BPMN models using RACI matrices. In: Meersman, R., et al. (eds.) OTM 2012. LNCS, vol. 7565, pp. 56–73. Springer, Heidelberg (2012). https://doi.org/10.1007/978-3-642-33606-5_5
11. Cabanillas, C., Resinas, M., Ruiz-Cortés, A.: Introducing a mashup-based approach for design-time compliance checking in business processes. In: Bajec, M., Eder, J. (eds.) CAiSE 2012. LNBIP, vol. 112, pp. 337–350. Springer, Heidelberg (2012). https://doi.org/10.1007/978-3-642-31069-0_28
12. Dalpiaz, F., Cardoso, E., Canobbio, G., Giorgini, P., Mylopoulos, J.: Social specifications of business processes with Azzurra. In: RCIS, pp. 7–18, IEEE (2015)
13. Elgammal, A., Türetken, O., van den Heuvel, W., Papazoglou, M.P.: Formalizing and applying compliance patterns for business process compliance. Softw. Syst. Model. **15**(1), 119–146 (2016). https://doi.org/10.1007/s10270-014-0395-3

14. Ferber, J., Gutknecht, O.: A meta-model for the analysis and design of organizations in multi-agent systems. In: ICMAS, pp. 128–135, IEEE Computer Society (1998)
15. Hobeck, R., Weber, I.: Towards object-centric process mining for blockchain applications. In: Köpke, J., et al. (eds.) BPM Blockchain and RPA Forum, LNBIP, vol. 491, pp. 51–65, Springer, Cham (2023). https://doi.org/10.1007/978-3-031-43433-4_4
16. Ito, S., Vymetal, D., Sperka, R., Halaska, M.: Process mining of a multi-agent business simulator. Comput. Math. Organ. Theory **24**(4), 500–531 (2018)
17. Knuplesch, D., Reichert, M.: A visual language for modeling multiple perspectives of business process compliance rules. Softw. Syst. Model. **16**(3), 715–736 (2017)
18. Kumar, A., Liu, R.: A rule-based framework using role patterns for business process compliance. In: Bassiliades, N., Governatori, G., Paschke, A. (eds.) RuleML 2008. LNCS, vol. 5321, pp. 58–72. Springer, Heidelberg (2008). https://doi.org/10.1007/978-3-540-88808-6_9
19. Lassen, K.B., van Dongen, B.F.: Translating message sequence charts to other process languages using process mining. Trans. Petri Nets Other Model. Concurr. **1**, 71–85 (2008)
20. Leno, V., Polyvyanyy, A., Dumas, M., Rosa, M.L., Maggi, F.M.: Robotic process mining: vision and challenges. Bus. Inf. Syst. Eng. **63**(3), 301–314 (2021)
21. Li, G., de Carvalho, R.M.: Process mining in social media: applying object-centric behavioral constraint models. IEEE Access **7**, 84360–84373 (2019)
22. Moody, D.L., Kortink, M.A.: From ER models to dimensional models: bridging the gap between OLTP and OLAP design, Part 1. J. Bus. Intell. **8**, 7–24 (2003)
23. Moody, D.L., Kortink, M.A.: From ER models to dimensional models Part II: advanced design issues. J. Bus. Intell. **8**, 20–29 (2003)
24. Polyvyanyy, A.: Process Querying Methods. Springer, Cham (2022). https://doi.org/10.1007/978-3-030-92875-9
25. Sadiq, S.W., Governatori, G., Namiri, K.: Modeling control objectives for business process compliance. In: Alonso, G., Dadam, P., Rosemann, M. (eds.) BPM, LNCS, vol. 4714, pp. 149–164, Springer, Heidelberg (2007)
26. Semmelrodt, F., Knuplesch, D., Reichert, M.: Modeling the resource perspective of business process compliance rules with the extended compliance rule graph. In: Bider, I., et al (eds.) BMMDS/EMMSAD, LNBIP, vol. 175, pp. 48–63, Springer, Heidelberg (2014)
27. Soto, M., Münch, J.: Focused identification of process model changes. In: Wang, Q., Pfahl, D., Raffo, D.M. (eds.) ICSP, LNCS, vol. 4470, pp. 182–194, Springer, Heidelberg (2007)
28. Tour, A., Polyvyanyy, A., Kalenkova, A.A.: Agent system mining: vision, benefits, and challenges. IEEE Access **9**, 99480–99494 (2021)
29. Tour, A., Polyvyanyy, A., Kalenkova, A.A., Senderovich, A.: Agent miner: an algorithm for discovering agent systems from event data. In: Di Francescomarino, C., Burattin, A., Janiesch, C., Sadiq, S. (eds.) BPM, LNCS, vol. 14159, pp. 284–302, Springer, Cham (2023). https://doi.org/10.1007/978-3-031-41620-0_17

Advanced Modeling Languages

Multi-faceted Evaluation of Modeling Languages for Augmented Reality Applications The Case of ARWFML

Fabian Muff(✉) and Hans-Georg Fill

University of Fribourg, Research Group Digitalization and Information Systems, Fribourg, Switzerland
{fabian.muff,hans-georg.fill}@unifr.ch

Abstract. The evaluation of modeling languages for augmented reality applications poses particular challenges due to the three-dimensional environment they target. The previously introduced Augmented Reality Workflow Modeling Language (ARWFML) enables the model-based creation of augmented reality scenarios without programming knowledge. Building upon the first design cycle of the language's specification, this paper presents two further design iterations for refining the language based on multi-faceted evaluations. These include a comparative evaluation of implementation options and workflow capabilities, the introduction of a 3D notation, and the development of a new 3D modeling environment. On this basis, a comprehensibility study of the language was conducted. Thereby, we show how modeling languages for augmented reality can be evolved towards a maturity level suitable for empirical evaluations.

Keywords: Augmented Reality · Domain-specific Modeling Language · Metamodeling

1 Introduction

Augmented Reality (AR) software applications are widely used today to superimpose any type of virtual information on the real world to enhance human perception, e.g., for purposes such as machine maintenance, training, or medical applications [23]. In the past, several model-based approaches have been proposed to facilitate the creation of such applications, e.g., [5,8,11,12,19–21]. At their core, they aim to simplify the creation of AR scenarios by freeing users from the need for specialized programming skills. Thereby, these modeling languages have to satisfy a number of specific requirements to cover basic and advanced augmented reality concepts. In addition, the inherent focus on three-dimensional

Financial support is gratefully acknowledged by the Smart Living Lab funded by the University of Fribourg, EPFL, and HEIA-FR.

W. Maass et al. (Eds.): ER 2024, LNCS 15238, pp. 75–93, 2025.
https://doi.org/10.1007/978-3-031-75872-0_5

environments poses additional challenges for the design and usage of such languages. In a previous design cycle, the Augmented Reality Workflow Modeling Language (ARWFML) was proposed as a novel approach to modeling AR scenarios. As a result of the first design cycle, the approach was demonstrated to encompass a more extensive range of AR concepts than any preceding approach, thereby leading to a greater degree of expressiveness [16]. In the course of a second design cycle, the language was implemented on the two-dimensional (2D) *ADOxx* metamodeling platform. The goal of this implementation was to assess the technical feasibility of the language specification by translating it into the *ADOxx* metamodeling concepts and to provide the basis for subsequent practical evaluations. Although this implementation was successfully achieved, some shortcomings were identified due to the limitation of *ADOxx* to 2D modeling environments [7].

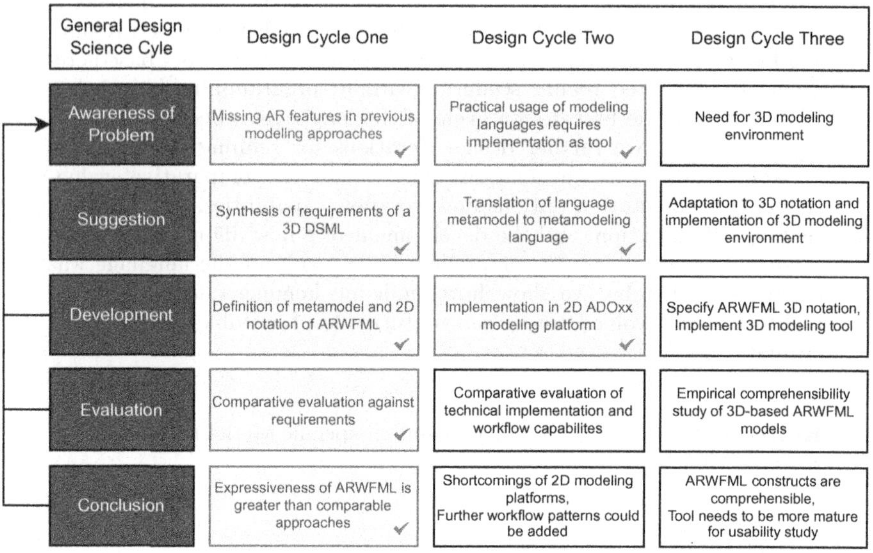

Fig. 1. Design cycles for advancing the *ARWFML* language [16], following *Design Science Research Methods* [15]. The light gray areas have already been addressed.

Therefore, in this paper, we continue to evaluate this previous implementation in comparison to similar approaches following design science research (DSR) methodologies [15] – see Fig. 1. Based on expert feedback received in this second design cycle, we conducted a comparison of the language's workflow capabilities with those of other languages. Subsequently, we will report on how we addressed the identified shortcomings in a third design cycle and finally arrived at a new implementation that is ready for assessing the comprehensibility of the language concepts in an empirical study. The main contributions of this paper are (i) detailed insights into the evaluation process of modeling languages for the domain of augmented reality by using *ARWFML* as a concrete example, (ii) a comparison of technical features of AR modeling language implementations including their workflow capabilities, and (iii) the results from an empirical study for testing the comprehensibility of *ARWFML* constructs. Thereby, we aim to inform how such evaluations can be accomplished for similar approaches.

The paper is structured as follows. Section 2 provides a brief revisit of *ARWFML* and a comparative evaluation of its technical implementation to related approaches in Sect. 2.1. Section 2.2 focuses on those approaches capable of creating AR workflow scenarios and compares them against the most relevant workflow patterns. This is followed by a description of the third design cycle in Sect. 3, which includes the design of a new three-dimensional notation for *ARWFML* in Sect. 3.1, a newly developed, 3D-enhanced modeling environment presented in Sect. 3.2, and the results of an empirical comprehensibility study of the extended *ARWFML* language in Sect. 3.3. The paper ends with a conclusion and an outlook in Sect. 4.

2 Outline of ARWFML and Comparative Evaluation of Related Approaches in the Second Design Cycle

The *Augmented Reality Workflow Modeling Language* (ARWFML) is a domain-specific visual modeling language that allows the modeling of complex augmented reality workflows for different application scenarios [16]. It includes three different types of visual models: *ObjectSpace* models for defining the general AR environment, *FlowScene* models for defining the AR workflow, and *Statechange* models for specifying the different changes of virtual objects within this workflow. *ARWFML*'s high level of abstraction frees users from the need to have technical expertise in AR application development, allowing them to focus on the content and functionality of AR scenarios. The created *ARWFML* models are to be interpreted by an AR execution engine running AR experiences based on the loaded models. In a first design cycle, the *ARWFML* metamodel has been specified and compared against requirements for model-based AR approaches. *ARWFML* was shown to cover more requirements than any previous approach. Figure 2 shows the visual elements of *ARWFML*. In a second design cycle, the *ARWFML* metamodel has been translated to the *ADOxx* metamodeling language, and the language has been implemented on the 2D *ADOxx* metamodeling platform by considering agile modeling method engineering principles [4,7].

2.1 Comparative Evaluation of Technical Implementation

In the following, we continue with the evaluation of *ARWFML* in the second design cycle. When evaluating modeling approaches for AR scenarios, it is not sufficient to consider only the language requirements for AR concepts as previously for *ARWFML* [16]. It is also necessary to consider how such modeling languages can be technically implemented, including the elicitation and execution of models to create AR scenarios and the necessary technical requirements.

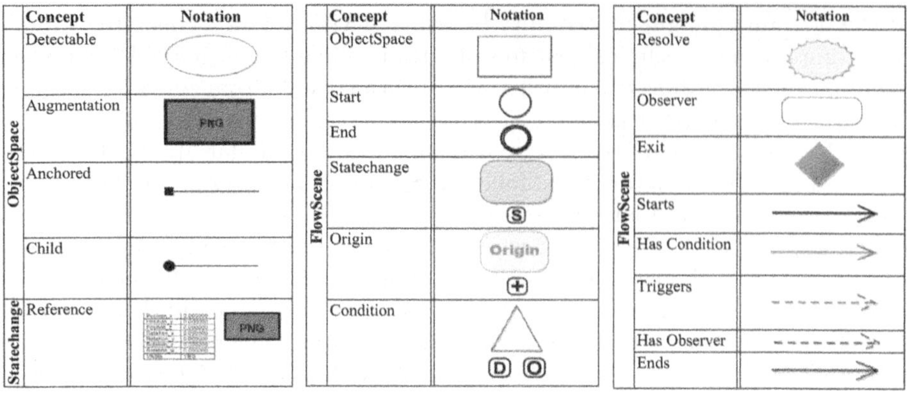

Fig. 2. 2D notation of of the *ARWFML* language concepts, separated by the three different language types *ObjectSpace*, *Statechange*, and *FlowScene*.

The reason for this is that the elicitation of models for 3D space, which is a prerequisite for AR scenarios, cannot be accomplished in 2D-based modeling environments. In addition, for languages that define workflows, it is important to verify the ability of a language to cover different workflow patterns [2]. Ultimately, the question arises as to what methods can be used to evaluate the modeling approaches in more detail. Thus, for the evaluation part of the second design cycle, in the following, we conduct a comparative evaluation of the technical implementation, including the workflow capabilities, and evaluation types of the major related approaches compared to *ARWFML*—see Table 1. The comparison considers the dimensions *Language Type*, *Model Elicitation Environment*, *Model Execution*, and *Resulting Environment*. Furthermore, the approaches are compared in their capabilities to define workflows *(Workflow)* and applied type of evaluation *(Type of Evaluation)*—see Table 1.

The *SSIML* and *X3D* approach by Lenk et al. [12] investigated model-driven development and round-trip engineering for 3D web applications by converting text-based models to code for 3D experiences. Ruminski and Walczak [20] and Lechner [11] introduced the textual declarative languages *CARL* and *ARML 2.0* for modeling augmented reality experiences that can be interpreted by an execution engine or as browser standard and offer 3D environments for their specification. Grambow et al. [8] presented the *BPMN-CARX* approach, a visual extension of the BPMN language. Models can be interpreted in a run-time environment as AR experiences. Ruiz-Rube et al. [19] introduced *ARE4DSL*, a text-based model-driven development approach for the generation of code that produces AR model editors. The resulting applications are geared towards modeling itself rather than developing AR applications in general. Campos-Lopez et al. [5] proposed *ALTER*, an automated textual approach to build augmented reality interfaces. Models are interpreted to run as a domain-specific language in an AR interface. Lastly, Wild et al. [21,22] proposed an approach called *ARLEM*, for the definition of AR learning activities. A reference implementation allows for immersive model creation in three-dimensional space and the runtime interpretation in an AR application.

Table 1. Comparison table for related AR modeling approaches. (D): Domain-specific languages. (P): Language profiles. (Y): Dimension covered by approach. (N): Dimension not covered by approach.

	SSIML/ X3D [12]	CARL [20]	BPMN-CARX [8]	ARML [11]	ARE4DSL [19]	ALTER [5]	ARLEM [21]	ARWFML [16]
Language Type								
DSML/Profile	D	D	P	D	D	D	D	D
Model Elicitation Environment								
Textual	Y	Y	Y	Y	Y	Y	Y	Y
Visual 2D	N	N	Y	N	N	N	N	Y
Visual 3D	N	N	N	N	N	N	N	N
Immersive	N	N	N	N	N	N	Y	N
Model Execution								
Code Generation	Y	N	N	N	Y	N	N	N
Model Interpretation	N	Y	Y	Y	N	Y	Y	Y
Resulting Environment								
3D Experience	Y	Y	Y	Y	N	N	Y	Y
Modeling Environment	N	N	N	N	Y	Y	Y	N
Workflow								
Workflow Execution	N	N	Y	N	N	N	Y	Y
Type of Evaluation								
Use Case Demonstration	Y	Y	Y	Y	Y	Y	Y	Y
Implementation	Y	Y	Y	N	Y	Y	Y	Y
Empirical Comprehen- sibility Study	N	N	N	N	N	N	N	N
Empirical Tool Usability Study	N	N	N	N	Y	Y	N	N
Empirical Simulation	N	N	Y	N	N	N	N	N

Only the three approaches *BPMN-CARX* [8], *ARLEM* [21] and *ARWFML* [16] offer workflow capabilities for specifying complex branching in AR experiences. Regarding the type of evaluation considered by the different approaches, all of them demonstrated use cases. All approaches, except *ARML 2.0* [11], have been evaluated with a first implementation as a proof of concept. No approach evaluated the comprehensibility of the proposed language, and only *ARE4DSL* [19] and *ALTER* [5] have been evaluated regarding the usability of the proposed prototype. In addition, *BPMN-CARX* [8] has been evaluated by conducting an empirical simulation. *ARWFML* has also been implemented and use cases have been shown on the basis of the two-dimensional *ADOxx* metamodeling platform [7]. However, the second design cycle showed that a further evaluation of the workflow requirements is necessary on the level of the *ARWFML* metamodel. Furthermore, the language should be empirically evaluated by users to assess its practical feasibility. Therefore, in the next section, we advance to an evaluation of *ARWFML* against common workflow patterns, which will be followed by the description of the third design cycle to establish the foundations for a first empirical evaluation in Sect. 3.

2.2 Evaluation of Workflow Capabilities

Modeling languages for depicting and executing workflows have a long tradition. They permit to structure sequences of activities to complete tasks and may support different types of patterns, which characterize the expressiveness of a language. The most significant patterns were summarized by van der Aalst et al. [1,2]. Typical examples for workflow modeling languages include Petri nets [18] or BPMN[1].

In the following, we compare *ARWFML* against two other AR modeling languages that enable the specification of workflows based on 20 core workflow patterns [2]. Various additional patterns exist. However, van der Aalst et al. mention that these 20 are the most significant patterns [1]. Furthermore, we present a use case for an *ARWFML FlowScene* model that illustrates all the workflow patterns supported by *ARWFML*. Based on this analysis, we derive further language requirements that will be considered in subsequent design iterations. Table 2 shows a summary of the modeling languages *BPMN-CARX*, *ARLEM*, and *ARWFML* regarding 20 selected workflow patterns.

The analysis reveals significant differences in the workflow capabilities of each modeling language. *BPMN-CARX* shows the most comprehensive support, successfully implementing 15 of the 20 analyzed patterns. This includes comprehensive support for all basic control flow patterns and the majority of advanced branching, synchronization, and multiple instances patterns, indicating a flexible approach to complex workflow scenarios. Since *BPMN-CARX* is an extension of the BPMN modeling language, it comes with the extensive capabilities of the base language and allows for very complex workflows. Conversely, the language is constrained by its focus on process flows in general, with only basic annotations of tasks with AR functionalities. It is not tailored for the definition of spatial models, whereas the other two approaches are explicitly developed for defining workflows for AR.

In contrast, *ARLEM* supports only four patterns. Three basic control flow patterns, and arbitrary cycles. This suggests a focus on simpler, more linear workflows without the need for complex synchronization. *ARLEM*, as well as *ARWFML* do not support patterns involving multiple instances and state-based decisions. Multiple instance patterns describe situations where there are multiple threads of execution active in a process model, each relating to the same activity [2]. Given that there can be only one instance of an AR experience at a given time, these patterns are not considered in *ARLEM*, nor *ARWFML*. The limited support of workflow patterns can restrict the use of *ARLEM* in more complex or variable workflow scenarios. It is important to note that *ARLEM* is designed to define learning experiences and does not claim to allow the definition of highly complex scenarios.

ARWFML supports eight workflow patterns, including the most basic control flow patterns, which are essential for straightforward sequential and parallel processes. This includes the *Sequence*, *Parallel Split*, and *Simple Merge* patterns. However, it shows limitations in handling more complex synchronization

[1] https://www.omg.org/spec/BPMN/2.0/ last visited on: 25.04.2024.

Table 2. Comparison of support of workflow patterns according to [2] by three AR modeling languages. (Y): Full support. (N): No support. (∼): Partial support.

Workflow Pattern	BPMN-CARX [8]	ARLEM [21]	ARWFML [16]
Basic Control Flow Patterns			
Pattern 1 (Sequence)	Y	Y	Y
Pattern 2 (Parallel Split)	Y	N	Y
Pattern 3 (Synchronization)	Y	N	N
Pattern 4 (Exclusive Choice)	Y	Y	N
Pattern 5 (Simple Merge)	Y	Y	Y
Advanced Branching and Synchronization Patterns			
Pattern 6 (Multi - choice)	Y	N	Y
Pattern 7 (Synchronizing Merge)	∼	N	N
Pattern 8 (Multi - merge)	Y	N	Y
Pattern 9 (Discriminator)	∼	N	N
Structural Patterns			
Pattern 10 (Arbitrary Cycles)	Y	Y	Y
Pattern 11 (Implicit Termination)	Y	N	Y
Patterns involving Multiple Instances			
Pattern 12 (Multiple Instances Without Synchronization)	Y	N	N
Pattern 13 (Multiple Instances With a Priori Design Time Knowledge)	Y	N	N
Pattern 14 (Multiple Instances With a Priori Runtime Knowledge)	Y	N	N
Pattern 15 (Multiple Instances Without a Priori Runtime Knowledge)	N	N	N
State-based Patterns			
Pattern 16 (Deferred Choice)	Y	N	N
Pattern 17 (Interleaved Parallel Routing)	∼	N	N
Pattern 18 (Milestone)	N	N	N
Cancellation Patterns			
Pattern 19 (Cancel Activity)	Y	N	N
Pattern 20 (Cancel Case)	Y	N	Y
$\sum$ **(fully supported)**	**15**	**4**	**8**

and exclusive choice patterns, which are critical for dynamic decision-making scenarios in workflows. In advanced branching and synchronization, *ARWFML* supports patterns like *Multi-choice* and *Multi-merge*. It lacks support for the *Synchronizing Merge* and *Discriminator* patterns, indicating some limitations in splitting and merging multiple concurrent paths within a workflow. The language's support extends to structural patterns, particularly handling arbitrary cycles and implicit terminations effectively. As stated previously, it is not feasible to execute multiple instances of an AR workflow on a single device concurrently, given that there is only one AR session running at a time. Thus, patterns involving multiple instances are not considered. Furthermore, state-based patterns such as *Deferred Choice*, *Interleaved Parallel Routing*, or *Milestone* are not yet supported by *ARWFML*. Cancellation is possible through the *Cancel Case* pattern. Given that *ARWFML* does not have the concept of activities, the *Cancel Activity* pattern is not applicable.

To demonstrate the workflow patterns supported by *ARWFML*, Fig. 3 shows an example of a *FlowScene* model. All supported workflow patterns are indicated

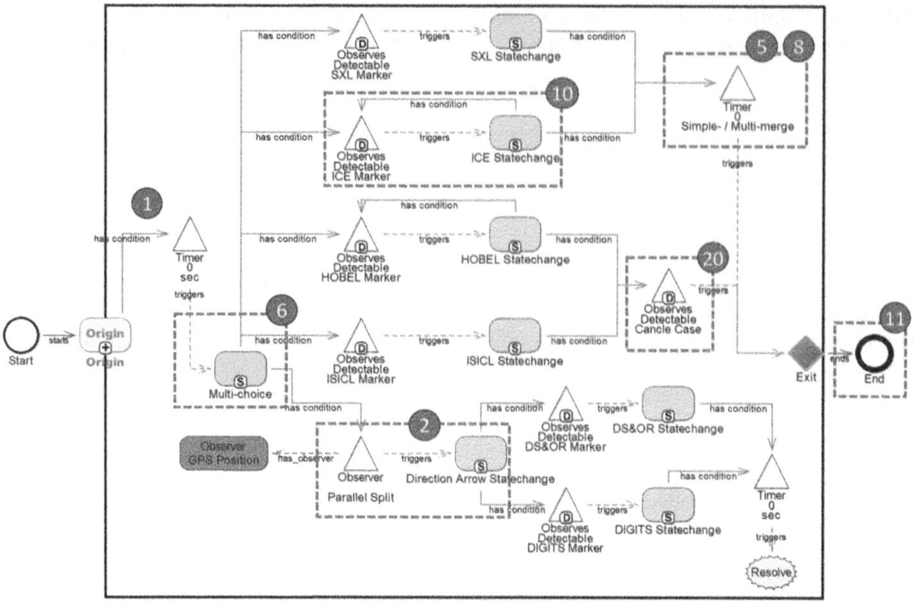

Fig. 3. *ARWFML FlowScene* model illustrating the eight supported workflow patterns by *ARWFML*. Each pattern in the model is marked with a red circle indicating the number of the workflow pattern according to Table 2. (1) *Sequence*; (2) *Parallel Split*; (5) *Simple Merge*; (6) *Multi-choice*; (8) *Multi-merge*; (10) *Arbitrary Cycles*; (11) *Implicit Termination*; (20) *Cancel Case*.

with the corresponding pattern number in the model. The use case presented in this example depicts a scenario in which an AR user has the potential to visit various research groups on a university campus. At the physical location of each research group on the campus, a marker is placed. As soon as the user comes within proximity to the marker, visual information about the research group is displayed in AR. There are various conditions and paths that can be activated, such as the initiation of a flow, only if the user is within the specified range of *GPS* coordinates. Some areas may be revisited multiple times (*Arbitrary Cycle*), while others may only be visited once.

In summary, *BPMN-CARX* stands out as the most versatile and capable language, especially for environments where complex, multi-faceted workflows are common, but it lacks simplicity since it is based on the BPMN modeling language. *ARLEM* might be more suited for simpler and less dynamic environments. *ARWFML* provides a robust foundation for fundamental and some advanced workflow scenarios. However, further development may be necessary to fully support the more complex and dynamic patterns required in highly variable and decision-intensive workflows. For example, by modifying the *ARWFML* metamodel to allow exclusive choices in the condition concept and introducing the possibility of defining synchronization conditions, patterns 3, 4, 7, and 9 could be supported. Furthermore, by extending the observer concept with incoming messages, pattern 16 could be supported. This would result in the number of supported patterns increasing to 13, thereby approaching the number of patterns that can be supported by the BPMN modeling language. Thus, we will tackle these changes in a fourth design cycle. Before doing so, in the next section, we will advance with a first empirical evaluation of the comprehensibility of the language in its current form by users and show the corresponding challenges.

3 Third Design Cycle: Towards Empirical Evaluations

As discussed in Sect. 2, different paths can be taken to evaluate AR modeling languages. The most common approaches include use case demonstrations, e.g., [5,8,11,12,19–21] and proof of concept implementations, e.g., [5,8,12,19–21]. When considering the involvement of users, recent approaches conducted usability [5,19], or simulation studies [8]. Simulation studies and usability studies are strongly dependent on software tools. As a result, they do not evaluate the modeling language itself, but rather a combination of the modeling language and the implementation in the tool. Thus, the evaluation of the comprehensibility of the modeling language should be first conducted independently of the software tool, e.g., as proposed by Bork et al. [3].

However, since *ARWFML* is a domain-specific modeling language that allows for the modeling of 3D *ObjectSpaces* and *Augmentations* therein, the previously developed 2D notation was found to be inadequate [16]. As a consequence, it was necessary to design a new three-dimensional notation of the *ARWFML* language constructs. With the help of this 3D notation, models that are more adequate for an empirical evaluation of the comprehensibility can be provided. The question of how these models are created arises. In principle, mock-up tools (e.g., Figma[2]), image editing software (e.g., Adobe Photoshop[3]), or 3D scene editing tools (e.g., Blender[4]) could be used. However, the definition of valid conceptual models with these purely graphical tools poses a challenge, as the creation may easily lead to formal inaccuracies and inconsistencies, and thus invalid models. Consequently, for the purpose of conducting a user-based comprehensibility study, it was necessary to develop a novel 3D-enabled modeling environment that facilitates the generation of formally accurate models in 3D notation.

3.1 Preliminaries: Adaptation of ARWFML to 3D

In the third iteration of the DSR research project, the 2D notation of *ARWFML* (see Fig. 2) has been adapted to a 3D notation (see Fig. 4). It is important to note that *ARWFML* contains three-dimensional dynamic visualizations for the classes Detectable, *Augmentation*, and Reference. Figure 4 shows examples of dynamic visualizations of these classes in column "Dynamic Example". For

[2] https://www.figma.com/community.
[3] https://www.adobe.com/products/photoshop.html.
[4] https://www.blender.org/.

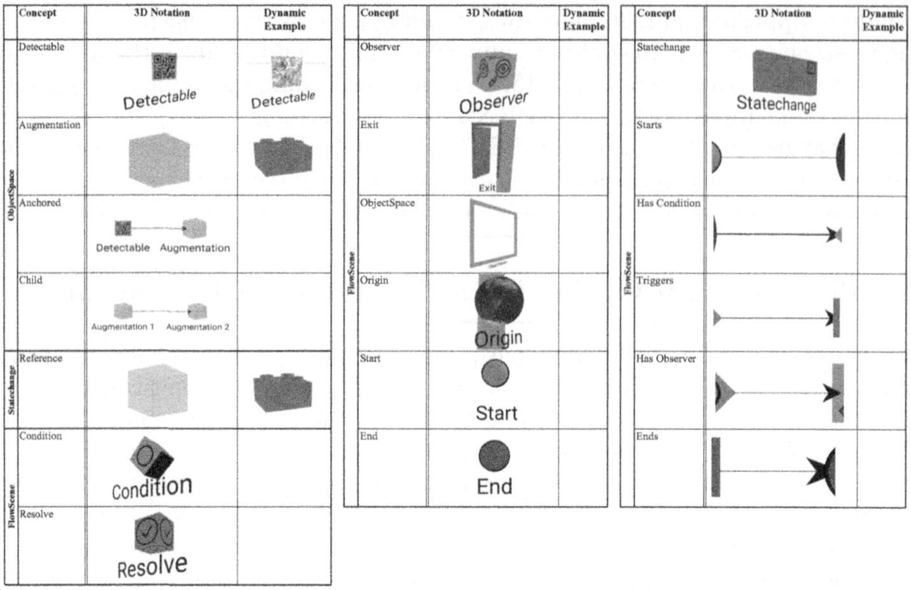

Fig. 4. 3D notation of of the *ARWFML* language concepts grouped by the *SceneTypes ObjectSpace*, *Statechange*, and *FlowScene*. For each *SceneType*, the visual notation is shown in the *3D Notation* column. If there is a dynamic visualization depending on attribute values, an example visualization appears in the *Dynamic Example* column.

the *Detectables*, an illustrative example of a special color marker that can be identified by computer vision algorithms is provided. As an illustration of an *Augmentation*, a 3D object in the form of a green color brick that can be 3D visualized in an AR application is presented. As the Reference class is linked to *Augmentations*, the dynamic visualization of References displays the same 3D model as the referenced *Augmentation*, in this example also the green color brick.

3.2 The 3D Modeling Environment M2AR

In order to facilitate the creation of 3D-enhanced *ARWFML* models, a new modeling environment, designated as *M2AR*, has been developed. *M2AR* is a web-based modeling environment that enables the creation of traditional 2D models as well as models in three-dimensional space [17]. The platform is based on the 3D JavaScript library *THREE.js*[5] and the mixed reality immersive web standard WebXR [9].

On this new platform, the novel 3D notation for *ARWFML* was implemented in a way that facilitates spatial alignment of disparate three-dimensional objects. This is particularly advantageous when modeling *Statechanges*, as they define the

[5] https://github.com/mrdoob/three.js/.

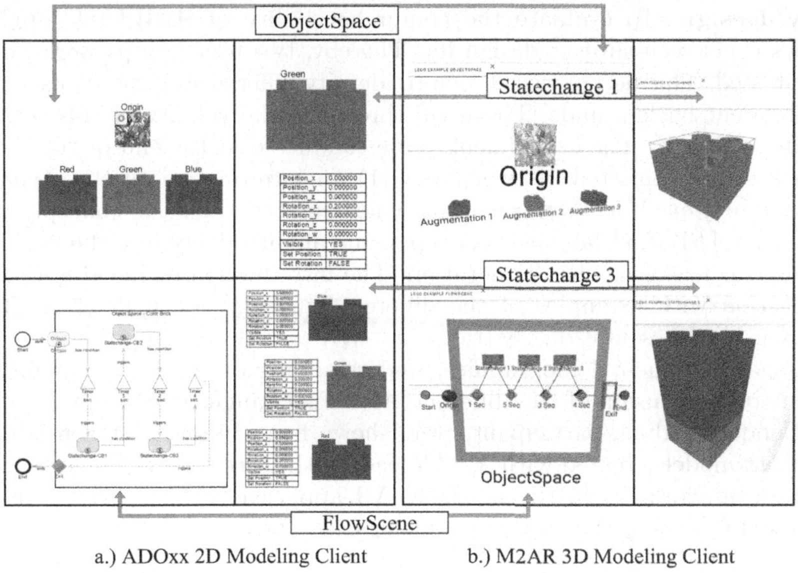

Fig. 5. Visual comparison of *ObjectSpace*, *Statechange*, and *FlowScene* models in (a.) 2D notation of *ARWFML* in the *ADOxx* modeling tool from the first design cycle and (b.) the new 3D notation in the new *M2AR* modeling client.

manner in which the various *Augmentations* are represented in the real world. This addresses the necessity for an environment that permits three-dimensional spatial modeling, derived at the conclusion of the initial design cycle described in [16]. Figure 5 illustrates a comparison of *ARWFML* model excerpts of the 2D notation modeled in the *ADOxx* implementation from the second design cycle (cf. [16]) and the 3D notation in the new *M2AR* modeling environment.

M2AR is a prototypical modeling environment that has not yet reached a level of maturity sufficient to empirically evaluate its usability due to the high expectations users have for such tools today. However, it allows expert modelers to create valid *ARWFML* models that can then be interpreted by an *AR Engine* that takes models from the 3D modeling client as input to execute modeled AR applications. Consequently, models created with *M2AR* are well-suited for an empirical evaluation of the comprehensibility of the modeling language.

3.3 Empirical User Study for ARWFML Model Comprehensibility

This section presents the design and findings of an empirical user study conducted to assess the comprehensibility of *ARWFML* in 3D notation. We describe the study design, followed by data on the experimental subjects, the evaluation metrics used, the study results, and a discussion of potential threats to the study's internal and external validity.

Study Design: To evaluate the comprehensibility of *ARWFML*, our study employs a between-subject design [6]. Thereby, two user groups were independently tested. This design was chosen to identify differences between user groups with different backgrounds. The main threats to the validity of this setup will be addressed later. The experiments were conducted at the end of 2023.

Each study consisted of two parts: (1) an introduction to the *Augmented Reality Workflow Modeling Language*, which covered the basic concepts of AR, the specific *ARWFML* language concepts, and an introduction to the new *M2AR* environment featuring the 3D notation. The introduction included a 45-minute presentation with examples of the different language concepts of *ARWFML*. Following the presentation, participants were asked to complete a questionnaire regarding their demographics, understanding of *ARWFML* models, and general comprehension of the different *ARWFML* language concepts. To assess model understanding, participants were shown five sections of screenshots from *ARWFML* models created with *M2AR*, each with three different possibilities for the resulting workflow in the resulting AR application. The participants were then asked to choose the correct result for each question.

Table 3. Categories of survey question (Q1–Q5) for evaluating *ARWFML* model understanding.

Q	Use Case	Purpose
Q1	Color Brick	Prediction of outcome showing different Statechanges.
Q2	Color Brick	Prediction of outcome when differing Conditions.
Q3	Solar System	Prediction of outcome showing different Statechanges.
Q4	Solar System	Prediction of outcome with different Statechanges and Conditions.
Q5	Industrial Machine	Prediction of outcome showing different Statechanges.

The purpose of the questions was to assess participants' comprehension of the visual models and determine the predictability of the model outcomes. Table 3 shows the categories of questions related to model understanding, including the use case represented and the purpose of each category[6]. A total of three use cases were included. The first use case guides potential users through the assembly of different colored bricks. The second use case, the solar system use case, provides a learning opportunity by displaying the different planets and moons in our solar system. The third use case, the industrial machine use case, guides users through a working process, indicating which buttons to press.

Additionally, participants were presented with statements about the *ARWFML* modeling language and asked to identify all correct statements in five

[6] The survey is available on: https://doi.org/10.5281/zenodo.13219036.

separate questions (see general questions GQ1–GQ5 in Table 4). The purpose of the general questions was to gather information about the specific concepts of the modeling method. GQ1 had the goal of determining if participants could recall the different *ARWFML SceneTypes* presented in a selection of unrelated other *SceneTypes*. GQ2 aimed to determine whether participants were able to recall the purpose of the three different *SceneTypes* by selecting true statements about each one. Questions GQ3 to GQ5 were presented separately for each *SceneType* of *ARWFML*. The participants were presented with different choices of different concepts. They had to select only the concepts that are part of the *SceneType* to which the question refers. The purpose of these questions was to evaluate the participant's understanding of the *SceneTypes* of the *ARWFML*.

Table 4. General questions (GQ1–GQ5) for evaluating *ARWFML* method understanding.

GQ	Question	Purpose
GQ1	Which are the 3 different types of models that can be created with ARWFML?	SceneTypes
GQ2	ARWFML defines the three types ObjectSpace, Statechange, and FlowScene. Choose the three right statements.	SceneType Purpose
GQ3	Which concepts are available in an ObjectSpace model? Choose the two available modeling concepts of an ObjectSpace model.	ObjectSpace Understanding
GQ4	Which concepts are available in a Statechange model? Choose the only available modeling concepts of a Statechange model.	Statechange Understanding
GQ5	Which concepts are available in a FlowScene model? Choose the seven introduced modeling concepts of a FlowScene model.	FlowScene Understanding

The sections that follow will cover the experimental subjects, evaluation metrics, and questionnaire results in quantitative terms.

Experimental Subjects: To ensure that the subjects had at least a basic understanding of modeling, we recruited them from university courses in "Introduction to Business Informatics" and "Databases" at the University of Fribourg, where various modeling methods are taught. Our sample consisted of 35 students, aged between 18 and 44 years, the majority of whom were under 24 years of age. The study involved participants with varying levels of education, including high school graduates (25), individuals with Bachelor's degrees (7), Master's degrees (2), and Doctoral degrees (1).

To evaluate the participants' familiarity with *conceptual modeling* and *augmented reality*, we gathered data using five-point Likert scales [13]. Responses are categorized as "Very Familiar", "Familiar", "Somewhat familiar", "Somewhat unfamiliar", and "Very unfamiliar", with corresponding participant counts for each category. The data indicate a range of exposure and understanding among the participants in these two domains. Of the 35 respondents, 18 rated their familiarity with *conceptual modeling* as "Somewhat familiar" or higher, and four considered themselves "Familiar". In the context of *augmented reality*, 25 participants stated that they are "Somewhat unfamiliar" or "Very unfamiliar".

Evaluation Metrics: Measuring the comprehensibility of a modeling method is difficult, given that modeling is typically performed using a modeling tool, making it challenging to separate the method from the tool for evaluation. Moody's *Methods Evaluation Model* [14] defines four measures to considered when evaluating information systems design methods in general: *Performance*, *Perceptions*, *Intentions*, and *Behavior*. Since we wanted to objectively evaluate only the modeling language that is not yet used in practice, we only evaluated *Performance*, which is composed by the measures *Actual Efficiency* and *Actual Effectiveness* [10]. The efficiency of a method is determined by the amount of effort required to apply it. The effectiveness of a method is determined by how well it reaches its objectives. To evaluate the performance of an unproductive method, we have simplified the assessment to determine whether participants can distinguish between different model scenarios and understand the different language concepts. This is achieved by presenting them with various models for validation and asking general questions about the methodology (see Table 4).

Results: This section presents the results of the empirical comprehensibility study. The results for Q1–Q5 are discussed first, followed by the results of GQ1–GQ5. Additionally, a correlation analysis for Q1–Q5 and GQ1–GQ5 in regard to familiarity with conceptual modeling and augmented reality is presented.
Q1–Q5: Table 5 shows the percentage of correct answers for each of the five questions on *ARWFML* model understanding (Q1 to Q5) in the two studies. The data is presented to show the percentage of participants choosing the right answer out of three given possibilities. A "Total" row aggregates the performance of both studies, providing an overall success rate for each question.

The results show a high overall percentage of correct responses for Q1 (0.94), Q4 (0.94), and Q5 (0.97) on average, indicating a robust understanding of the models. Q2 had moderate accuracy (0.91) with a notable increase in study group two. Q3 had the lowest average accuracy (0.83), which is still moderate. These findings indicate that the participants understand the models presented and the intended AR application scenario derived from these models.

GQ1–GQ5: Table 6 shows the average accuracy of responses across the two studies for the five general question on *ARWFML* method understanding (GQ1–GQ5) – refer to Table 4. The questions were formatted as multiple-choice, with different amounts of possible answers and correct responses. The bottom row displays the total average value for correct answers over all study participants. These five questions provide insights into the relative difficulty or clarity of the different concept of the modeling language (see *Purpose* column in Table 4).

The results of both studies indicated that question GQ3 (*ObjectSpace* Understanding) consistently achieved the highest and second-highest average scores for correct responses (scores of 0.90 and 0.92), suggesting that it was possibly the

Table 5. Percentage of correct responses across studies for questions on model understanding (Q1 to Q5).

	Study 1	Study 2	Total
Q1	0.94	0.95	0.94
Q2	0.88	0.95	0.91
Q3	0.81	0.84	0.83
Q4	0.94	0.95	0.94
Q5	1.00	0.95	0.97

Table 6. Average correct answer rate for questions on *ARWFML* method understanding (GQ1 to GQ5).

	Study 1	Study 2	Total
GQ1	0.91	0.88	0.89
GQ2	0.78	0.87	0.83
GQ3	0.90	0.92	0.91
GQ4	0.92	0.86	0.89
GQ5	0.84	0.79	0.81

simplest or most comprehensible language concept. The lowest average correct answer rate in the first study was observed for GQ2 (SceneType Purpose) at 0.78, while in study two it was observed for GQ5 (*FlowScene* Understanding) at 0.79. This suggests that these concepts were the most difficult or least clear. In the second group, the mean correct answer rates for questions GQ2 and GQ3 were generally higher than in the first group, but lower for questions GQ1, GQ4, and GQ5. The total average correct answer rate across both groups for each question shows that, overall, GQ3 (Object Space model) had the highest average correct answer rate (0.91), while GQ2 (SceneType Purpose) had the lowest (0.83). This indicates that the *ObjectSpace* concept was the best understood or easiest language concept (GQ2), while it is more challenging for participants to distinguish the general purpose of the different *SceneTypes* (GQ3).

Correlation: To investigate the performance disparities related to varying degrees of familiarity with conceptual modeling or AR, we calculated the Pearson correlation coefficients between the measures of familiarity and the rates of correct answers for various *ARWFML* questions, based on a five-point Likert scale. Age and education level were not included in the correlation analysis because most of the participants fell into the same categories. The correlation coefficients were all in the range between -0.12 and 0.39 (see Table 7). A t-test was performed to assess the statistical significance of the observed results. The analysis revealed that none of the values tested exhibited a significant correlation at the significance level $\alpha = 0.01$. However, GQ1 was the only question that demonstrated a significant correlation between familiarity with conceptual modeling and the correct answer rate at the significance level $\alpha = 0.05$. It is important to highlight that the study involved only 35 participants, which could affect the robustness and generalizability of the correlation analysis results.

These findings provide insight on aspects of the *ARWFML* method that could benefit from more detailed explanations or improved educational resources. The perceived level of difficulty or ease by the participants in responding to the questions highlights the areas requiring improvement. In summary, the language concepts and models created with *ARWFML* are highly comprehensible. For model understanding, responses were accurate in more than 80% of instances, with an average correctness exceeding 80% across eight of ten domains, and sur-

Table 7. Correlation coefficients between correct answer rates for *ARWFML* questions and familiarity measures for conceptual modeling or augmented reality. (*) Significant correlation at $\alpha = 0.05$.

	Q1–Q5	GQ1	GQ2	GQ3	GQ4	GQ5
Conceptual Modeling	0.02	0.39*	0.32	−0.12	0.07	0.33
Augmented Reality	−0.11	0.31	0.08	0.11	0.22	0.19

passing 90% in four domains regarding general language comprehension. There were no discernible differences in the number of correct answers considering different levels of familiarity with augmented reality or conceptual modeling. This suggests that deep knowledge in these areas is not necessary for understanding *ARWFML* models created on the basis of the improved 3D notation.

Summary: In summary, the newly introduced 3D notation of *ARWFML* and its associated language concepts are in general highly comprehensible for users with various levels of knowledge in augmented reality and conceptual modeling.

Threats to Validity: To assess the comprehensibility of *ARWFML*, a controlled experiment was conducted with the objective of ensuring both internal and external validity. In order to ensure external validity, participants with at least minimal modeling knowledge were recruited. However, the university course setting and predefined use cases may limit the generalizability of the results to real-world contexts. Moreover, the evaluation of the methodology through the use of screenshots rather than hands-on interaction with *M2AR* may result in a limitation of the level of comprehension that could be obtained through active engagement. Furthermore, the emphasis on simple scenarios raises concerns about the applicability of the methodology to complex situations.

With regard to internal validity, the use of screenshots to test model understanding may not fully measure *ARWFML*'s performance. Direct interaction with models could provide authenticity, but also introduce biases in terms of comprehensibility. Furthermore, participant selection may introduce bias due to varying proficiency levels. Finally, sequencing the prototype introduction before administering the questionnaire could influence perceptions, but the interdependence between the language and the application may mitigate this.

4 Conclusion and Outlook

In this paper, we explore how modeling languages for the domain of augmented reality can be evaluated from multiple perspectives. By using the example of the recently developed *ARWFML* language for modeling AR workflows, we could illustrate how such an evaluation can be conducted in practice. One of the key insights that can be derived is that the empirical evaluation of such languages requires the availability of adequate tool support. This principle also applies to the assessment of a language's comprehensibility. The reason is that modeling languages for augmented reality typically require the specification of spatial information in three-dimensional space, which cannot be accomplished in 2D modeling environments. The introduction of a new 3D-enabled modeling platform allows for the creation of formally correct models that were subsequently utilized as input for an empirical user study. The study showed that the concepts of the *ARWFML* language are well comprehensible even by non-experts in the domain of augmented reality.

The next step in a subsequent design cycle will be the extension of the *ARWFML* language towards supporting further workflow patterns. Furthermore, we plan to advance the usability of the *M2AR* modeling platform so that further empirical studies can be conducted with it. This will permit, for example, to assess whether the interaction with *ARWFML* models helps to even better understand the working of such a language.

References

1. van der Aalst, W.M.P., ter Hofstede, A.H.M.: Workflow patterns: on the expressive power of (petri-net-based) workflow languages. DAIMI/PB **560**, 1–20 (2002). https://doi.org/10.7146/dpb.v31i560.7117
2. van der Aalst, W.M.P., ter Hofstede, A.H.M., Kiepuszewski, B., Barros, A.P.: Workflow patterns. Distrib. Parall. Datab. **14**(1), 5–51 (2003). https://doi.org/10.1023/A:1022883727209
3. Bork, D., Schrüffer, C., Karagiannis, D.: Intuitive understanding of domain-specific modeling languages: proposition and application of an evaluation technique. In: Laender, A.H.F., Pernici, B., Lim, E., de Oliveira, J.P.M. (eds.) ER 2019. LNCS, vol. 11788, pp. 311–319. Springer, Cham (2019).https://doi.org/10.1007/978-3-030-33223-5_26
4. Buchmann, R.A., Karagiannis, D.: Agile modelling method engineering: lessons learned in the ComVantage research project. In: Ralyté, J., España, S., Pastor, Ó. (eds.) PoEM 2015. LNBIP, vol. 235, pp. 356–373. Springer, Cham (2015). https://doi.org/10.1007/978-3-319-25897-3_23
5. Campos-López, R., Guerra, E., de Lara, J., Colantoni, A., Garmendia, A.: Model-driven engineering for augmented reality. J. Object Technol. **22**(2), 1–15 (2023). https://doi.org/10.5381/JOT.2023.22.2.A7
6. Charness, G., Gneezy, U., Kuhn, M.A.: Experimental methods: between-subject and within-subject design. J. Econ. Behav. Organiz. **81**(1), 1–8 (2012). https://doi.org/10.1016/j.jebo.2011.08.009
7. Fill, H., Karagiannis, D.: On the conceptualisation of modelling methods using the ADOxx meta modelling platform. Enterp. Model. Inf. Syst. Archit. Int. J. Concept. Model. **8**(1), 4–25 (2013). https://doi.org/10.18417/emisa.8.1.1
8. Grambow, G., Hieber, D., Oberhauser, R., Pogolski, C.: A context and augmented reality BPMN and BPMS extension for industrial internet of things processes. In: Marrella, A., Weber, B. (eds.) BPM 2021. LNCS, vol. 436, pp. 379–390. Springer, Cham (2021). https://doi.org/10.1007/978-3-030-94343-1_29
9. Jones, B., Goregaokar, M., Cabanier, R.: Webxr device API. In: W3C Candidate Recommendation Draft, work in progress. World Wide Web Consortium (2023). https://www.w3.org/TR/2023/CRD-webxr-20230303/

10. Kekes, J.: The pragmatic idealism of Nicholas Rescher. Philos. Phenomenol. Res. **54**(2), 391–394 (1994). http://www.jstor.org/stable/2108498
11. Lechner, M.: ARML 2.0 in the context of existing AR data formats. In: Latoschik, M.E., Reiners, D., Blach, R., Figueroa, P.A., Wingrave, C.A. (eds.) 6th Workshop on Software Engineering and Architectures for Realtime Interactive Systems, SEARIS 2013, Orlando, 17 March 2013, pp. 41–47. IEEE Computer Society (2013). https://doi.org/10.1109/SEARIS.2013.6798107
12. Lenk, M., Vitzthum, A., Jung, B.: Model-driven iterative development of 3d web-applications using SSIML, X3D and Javascript. In: Mouton, C., Posada, J., Jung, Y., Cabral, M. (eds.) The 17th International Symposium on Web3D Technology (Web3D 2012), Los Angeles, 4–5 August 2012, pp. 161–169. ACM (2012). https://doi.org/10.1145/2338714.2338742
13. Likert, R.: A technique for the measurement of attitudes. In: Archives of Psychology; no. 140, [s.n.]. New York (1932)
14. Moody, D.L.: The method evaluation model: a theoretical model for validating information systems design methods. In: European Conference on Information Systems (2003). https://api.semanticscholar.org/CorpusID:11092142
15. Morana, S., Kroenung, J., Maedche, A., Schacht, S.: Designing process guidance systems. J. Assoc. Inf. Syst. **20**(5), 6 (2019). https://doi.org/10.17705/1jais.00542
16. Muff, F., Fill, H.: A domain-specific visual modeling language for augmented reality applications using WebXR. In: Almeida, J.P.A., Borbinha, J., Guizzardi, G., Link, S., Zdravkovic, J. (eds.) ER 2023. LNCS, vol. 14320, pp. 334–353. Springer, Heidelberg (2023). https://doi.org/10.1007/978-3-031-47262-6_18
17. Muff, F., Fill, H.: M2AR: a web-based modeling environment for the augmented reality workflow modeling language. In: Proceedings of the ACM/IEEE 27th International Conference on Model Driven Engineering Languages and Systems (MODELS Companion 2024). ACM (2024). https://doi.org/10.1145/3652620.3687779
18. Petri, C., Reisig, W.: Petri net. Scholarpedia **3**(4), 6477 (2008). https://doi.org/10.4249/scholarpedia.6477
19. Ruiz-Rube, I., Baena-Pérez, R., Mota, J.M., Sánchez, I.A.: Model-driven development of augmented reality-based editors for domain specific languages. IxD&A **45**, 246–263 (2020). https://doi.org/10.55612/s-5002-045-011
20. Ruminski, D., Walczak, K.: Dynamic composition of interactive AR scenes with the carl language. In: Bourbakis, N.G., Tsihrintzis, G.A., Virvou, M. (eds.) IISA 2014, The 5th International Conference on Information, Intelligence, Systems and Applications, pp. 329–334. IEEE, Chania (2014). https://doi.org/10.1109/IISA.2014.6878808
21. Wild, F., Perey, C., Hensen, B., Klamma, R.: IEEE standard for augmented reality learning experience models. In: Mitsuhara, H., et al. (eds.) IEEE International Conference on Teaching, Assessment, and Learning for Engineering, TALE 2020, Takamatsu, 8–11 December 2020, pp. 1–3. IEEE (2020). https://doi.org/10.1109/TALE48869.2020.9368405

22. Wild, F., et al.: Towards data exchange formats for learning experiences in manufacturing workplaces. In: Kravcik, M., Mikroyannidis, A., Pammer, V., Prilla, M., Ullmann, T.D., Wild, F. (eds.) Proceedings of the 4th Workshop on Awareness and Reflection in Technology-Enhanced Learning In conjunction with the 9th European Conference on Technology Enhanced Learning: Open Learning and Teaching in Educational Communities, ARTEL@EC-TEL 2014, Graz, 16 Septembe 2014. CEUR Workshop Proceedings, vol. 1238, pp. 23–33. CEUR-WS.org (2014). http://ceur-ws.org/Vol-1238/paper2.pdf
23. Xue, L., Parker, C.J., McCormick, H.: A virtual reality and retailing literature review: current focus, underlying themes and future directions, pp. 27–41. Springer, Cham (2019). https://doi.org/10.1007/978-3-030-06246-0_3

Application of the Tree-of-Thoughts Framework to LLM-Enabled Domain Modeling

Jonathan Silva[1(✉)], Qin Ma[1], Jordi Cabot[1,2], Pierre Kelsen[1], and Henderik A. Proper[3]

[1] University of Luxembourg, Esch-sur-Alzette, Luxembourg
{jonathan.silva,qin.ma,jordi.cabot,pierre.kelsen}@uni.lu
[2] Luxembourg Institute of Science and Technology, Esch-sur-Alzette, Luxembourg
jordi.cabot@list.lu
[3] TU Wien, Vienna, Austria
henderik.proper@tuwien.ac.at

Abstract. Domain modeling is typically an iterative process where modeling experts interact with domain experts to complete and refine the model. Recently, we have seen several attempts to assist, or even replace, the modeler with a Large Language Model (LLM). Several LLM prompting strategies have been attempted, but with limited success. In this paper, we advocate for the adoption of a Tree-of-Thoughts (ToT) strategy to overcome the limitations of current approaches based on simpler prompting strategies. With a ToT strategy, we can decompose the modeling process into several sub-steps using for each step a specialized set of generators and evaluators prompts to optimize the quality of the LLM output. As part of our adaptation, we provide a Domain-Specific Language (DSL) to facilitate the formalization of the ToT process for domain modeling. Our approach is implemented as part of an open source tool available on GitHub.

Keywords: Domain Modeling · Large Language Models · Tree of thoughts

1 Introduction

Domain modeling is the process of creating conceptual models of a specific domain to serve a particular purpose. This process typically involves a collaborative effort [12] between domain experts, who provide insights and knowledge about the domain, and modeling experts, who are skilled in abstracting the relevant aspects of the domain and expressing such an abstraction using a modeling notation, which can be either textual or graphical. Executing the domain modeling process is cognitively demanding due to many factors [16]. This includes the inherent complexity of the problem domain, the involvement and coordination of various stakeholders, and the need for the modeling abstraction to be constrained

W. Maass et al. (Eds.): ER 2024, LNCS 15238, pp. 94–111, 2025.
https://doi.org/10.1007/978-3-031-75872-0_6

by the modeling purpose [13]. Further evidence of this cognitive demand is provided by Feltus et al. [10], where they suggested that modeling experts should simultaneously manage at least four conceptions in their mind to successfully create a domain model. These are: (1) a comprehensive understanding of the domain, (2) a clear conception of the modeling purpose, (3) an abstraction of the domain that aligns with the modeling purpose, and (4) a conception of the domain model as an artifact that represents the abstracted domain in terms of a modeling language.

Manifold modeling languages exist, including both General-Purpose Modeling Language (GPML) and Domain-Specific Modeling Languages (DSML), to capture different aspects of a domain [2]. For example, in the context of Model-Driven Software Engineering (MDSE), an Entity Relationship (ER) model [7] or an UML class diagram [1] can be used to capture the static data and information structure of the system, while an UML sequence diagram to illustrate the dynamic behavior of the system. To enable structural modeling of systems, both ER and UML class diagram provide a similar set of key modeling elements. These include entity types (or classes in UML terminology), inheritance relation between entity types, and relationship types (equivalent of UML associations). Furthermore, entity types (classes) can have attributes (properties), and both attributes and relationships may be constrained by cardinality specifications. Beyond ER, UML class diagram also supports more sophisticated modeling elements as first-class citizens, such as defining containment as a special kind of association to represent the whole-part relationships, and the use of association classes to further specify properties uniquely associated to relationships.

Research to facilitate the domain modeling process and consequently alleviate the cognitive demand associated to it has been proposed in different approaches, focusing on different modeling activities during the process, such as creating domain models from textual requirements, completing partially created models, and repairing inconsistencies in models [2]. For example, an approach to support human modelers is to implement Natural Language Processing (NLP) techniques to process textual requirements. These techniques have existed for a long time, and recent research has used heuristic rules to identify model elements [3], and Machine Learning models to classify them [14].

The recent advancements in generative AI such as Large Language Models (LLMs) has triggered a new trend in research towards supporting domain modeling, by leveraging the language processing capabilities of LLMs to create domain models. Both the domain description and the modeling purpose, articulated in natural language, are provided as input to an LLM, referred to as "prompts". The LLM then generates outputs, also in natural language, which define the elements of the domain models in a specified notation [11]. Among others, two factors play a crucial role in the success of LLMs for the domain modeling task: the inherent trained capability of the LLM and the choice of prompting techniques, i.e., how the prompts are designed. A range of prompting techniques have been tested with two LLMs: GPT-3.5 and GPT-4 [5,6,8,11], spanning from the simplest input-output (IO) prompting (aka. zero-shot prompting), to IO prompting enhanced with in-context learning [4] (aka. few-shot prompting), and finally to Chain-of-Thought (CoT) prompting [15]. Despite their promising performance in recognizing classes and relationships, these prompting techniques all have shown limitations in (1) correctly classifying relationships [6], (2) identifying complex modeling constructs such as association classes [8], and (3) leveraging best modeling practices (i.e., applying design patterns) [6].

Meanwhile, a new prompting technique: the Tree-of-Thoughts (ToT) framework, has been proposed [17]. This technique guides LLMs to solve a problem by explicitly decomposing it into a series of intermediate steps and considering multiple reasoning paths at each step, thus forming a tree of thoughts. LLMs are then instructed to explore the tree and heuristically evaluate intermediate thoughts towards the final solution. The ToT framework outperforms all existing prompting techniques in solving complex reasoning-based problems, a category to which our domain modeling problem belongs.

In this paper, we investigate the potential of this new prompting technique for domain modeling. More specifically:

- We propose a way to decompose domain modeling tasks using UML class diagram modeling as an example;
- We recommend our choice of the strategies for generator prompts and the evaluator prompts, as well as the search algorithm, among the options offered by the ToT framework;
- We develop a domain-specific language (DSL) to facilitate the configuration of the ToT framework for domain modeling tasks, and to automate their execution with LLMs;
- We validate our work by conducting experiments with GPT-4.

The rest of the paper is organized as follows. In Sect. 2 we review related work. Then, in Sect. 3, we review the ToT framework and design considerations. Next, in Sect. 4, we will present our approach to designing the ToT with domain modeling tasks. In Sect. 5 we propose the implementation of a DSL to configure the ToT framework for domain modeling. Then, in Sect. 6, we present experiments to validate our implementation. Section 7 reports on the experiments conducted using the ToT framework for domain modeling. Before concluding, Sect. 8 provides information about the support to our DSL.

2 SOTA: LLM-Enabled Domain Modeling

The LLMs have the ability to recognize the task requested by the context provided in the prompt, this is known as In-context learning [4]. The IO prompting technique uses this ability combining task instructions and examples. The zero-shot prompting is an IO prompting that relies on the ability developed by the LLM during the training to recognize the task [4]. The performance of LLMs can improve using another variant of IO prompting named Few-shot, this technique combines the task instructions with examples of the problem and the desired solution [4]. Another prompting technique is Chain-of-Thought (CoT); it is used in challenging tasks for LLMs, such as complex arithmetic problems, by adding examples that include intermediate reasoning steps [15].

Research conducted in [5,8,11] evaluated the potential to create domain models from textual descriptions using IO prompting. Camara et al. used zero-shot prompting to create UML class diagrams with few syntactic errors, however, the worst results were found when the model required abstractions, such as using inheritance instead of attributes or creating association classes [8]. Fill et al. used GPT-4 to create domain models for Entity Relationship diagrams for conceptual modeling, BPMN diagrams for business processes, and Heraklit models for embedded systems by providing one example of the desired output [11]. Another research experimented with the Few-shot technique using between 2 and 4 examples for the recommendation of concepts for different domain contexts, and to assist with static and dynamic domain modeling [5]. Additionally, Chen et al. compared the performance of suggested model elementes compared to a reference solution using the Few-shot technique with one or two examples to generate domain models, and concluded that adding two examples does not improve the performance in comparison with one example [6]. These experiments also used the CoT prompting with one example that illustrates the intermediate reasoning steps where the domain description was divided into sentences, and for each sentence the model elements are recognized. These experiments compared IO prompting with CoT prompting, and surprisingly, the use of the intermediate reasoning steps in CoT showed no improvement in performance to recommend model elements [6]. Using prompt techniques has shown that the recommendation of domain model elements has some limitations because LLMs struggle to classify relationships [6], to recommend complex constructs such as association classes [8], and using more examples in the prompts does not increase the performance of the elements suggested [6].

3 Background: Tree-of-Thoughts Framework

The Tree of Thoughts (ToT) is "a paradigm that allows LMs to explore multiple reasoning paths over thoughts" [17]. The thoughts are used as intermediate steps towards a problem solution. The tree representation is given because in each intermediate step there are alternative thoughts as shown in Fig. 1 that are evaluated to select the most promising to continue with the problem solution. To implement the framework, first the LLM acts as a Thought generator to create a set of thoughts that correspond to a partial solution of the problem. Then, the LLM is used as State evaluator to self-evaluate the thoughts and choose the most promising option to solve the problem [17]. The following four questions are to be analyzed in the problem to apply the ToT framework:
(1) *How to decompose the intermediate process into thought steps*: The thought decomposition requires us to design the intermediate thought steps. These should be promising and diverse, in order to evaluate the best prospects to achieve a solution. Some recommendations for the thoughts are that it is not too 'small' (e.g. a word or sentence) that cause it lack of diversity, and it is not too 'big' (e.g. a book) that makes it difficult to evaluate the coherence [17].

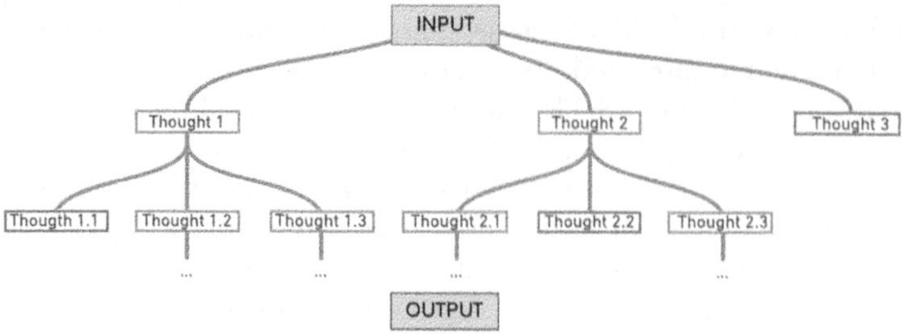

Fig. 1. Representation of ToT approach, the green boxes are the intermediate thoughts used for the problem solution. The number of thoughts is k=3 and the number of promising thoughts to explore is b=2. The red boxes indicate the thoughts not explored. (Color figure online)

(2) *How to generate potential thoughts from each state*: There are two possible strategies to generate the intermediate thoughts, and the best option will depend on the problem to be resolved.

- Sample: The same prompt creates diverse outputs, and each one can be used independent thoughts. This strategy is preferred when the thought is a paragraph, and the samples are diverse [17].
- Propose: The prompt proposes multiple thoughts in the same output, and we require to avoid duplicated thoughts in the same context. This is used when the thought is constrained to word or phrase. For example, in the Crosswords game, we require with one prompt multiple words, and each word is a thought towards a solution [17].

(3) *How to heuristically evaluate states*: The evaluation of states determines which thoughts are the best prospects to continue with the solution of the problem. For evaluation, two strategies are suggested:

- Value: The LLM prompt evaluates the thought with a scalar value (e.g., 1–5) or classification (e.g., complete/partial/incomplete) [17]. It is suggested when the valuation helps to decide the best choice.
- Vote: The prompt compares the different thought options and votes for the best promising one. This strategy is preferred to use when comparing partial solutions [17].

(4) *What search algorithm to use*: The search algorithm is used to explore promising thoughts identified by the state evaluator. The algorithms used in the experiments in [17] are as follows:

- Breadth-first search (BFS): In every step of the algorithm, the b most promising thoughts in each tree level are maintained to continue exploring in the next level. The number of k generated thoughts is reduced to b most promising thoughts, as shown in Fig. 1. Both k and b are configurable parameters in the algorithm defined in [17].

- Depth-first search (DFS): In this algorithm, the most promising thought among the k thoughts proposed is explored until either a final result of the problem is achieved, or we reach an intermediate state that is deemed impossible to achieve a solution by the state evaluator[1]. In the latter case, the state is pruned and the algorithm backtracks to the parent state to explore the next most promising thought.

4 A ToT Framework Setup for Domain Modeling

In this section, we review our approach to implement the Tree of Thoughts for task decomposition in domain modeling, selection of thought generator and evaluator strategies, and search algorithm. We illustrate this section with an example to create UML class diagrams.

4.1 Domain Modeling Task Decomposition

Figure 2 represents the tree structure identified to create a UML class diagram with five modeling tasks: (1) identifying classes and attributes, (2) identifying associations among classes, (3) refining associations to containments, (4) identifying inheritance, and (5) refining associations to association classes.

Proposals to create UML class diagrams from natural language texts use two steps as implemented in [3] and [14]. The selection of model elements is applied sentence by sentence in the domain descriptions and starts with class identification, then continues with relationship classification. Our proposal will use these two intuitive steps to separate classes from relationships; however, we will preserve the entire domain description as input for ToT because previous experiments using CoT with sentence decomposition [6] did not show improvements in performance for suggestion of model elements.

Furthermore, in the rule-based NLP approach [3], relationships are classified using different extraction rules per relationship type. Moreover, the performance of LLMs on the relationship identification task is the worst compared to class identification [6]. For those reasons, our approach starts with the identification of classes and attributes, then uses this intermediate thought to identify and classify the relationships for those classes. We propose to divide it into three tasks: association, containment, and inheritance. We identify that recognition of relationships performed by human modelers follows this intuitive approach starting by recognizing associations and then classifying containment or inheritance.

The thought decomposition will be completed by the identification of the association classes. As reviewed in the previous section, the association class is an abstraction in the UML class diagram where GPT does not produce good results [8]. The UML specification states that this abstraction is a class and an association. For that reason, we choose to separate it in a step after these two thoughts are completed.

[1] The state evaluator evaluates the progress made towards solving the problem, serving as a heuristic for the search algorithm to determine which states to keep exploring and in which order [17].

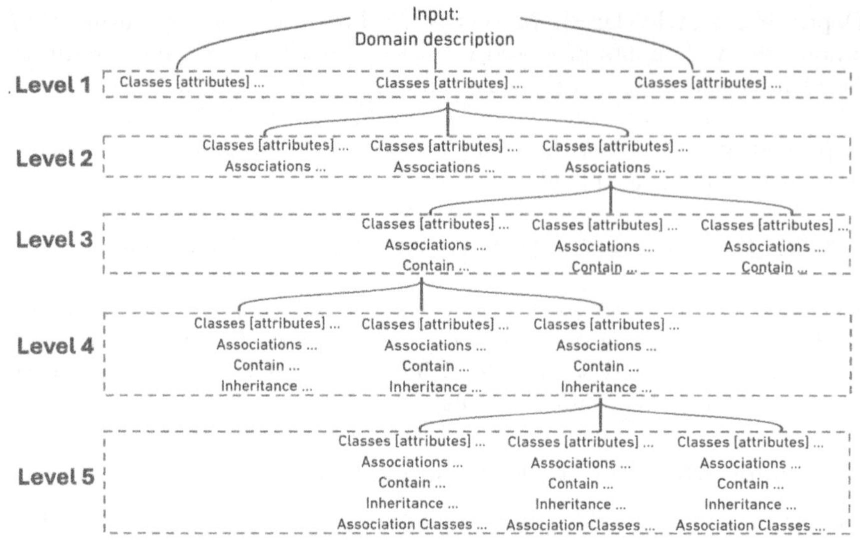

Fig. 2. Representation of the thought decomposition in the tree of thoughts. The root node represents the domain description as the input to generate the thoughts. The thoughts are alternatives of model elements. The blue boxes represent all the thoughts in the same level, and the best thought selected is used to continue with the model creation. (Color figure online)

4.2 Generator Strategy

After defining the task decomposition, we evaluated the generator strategy. The purpose of the generator prompt is to create diverse and promising thoughts. As discussed earlier, two strategies are possible: the sample strategy is used when the problem space is rich (e.g. the LLM provides diverse responses for the same prompt); and the propose strategy is better when the problem space is more constrained (e.g. the thought is a word or a line) [17]. We choose the sample strategy for the generator prompt because we have experimented that diverse model elements are suggested even with the same prompt. The reason for this behavior is that LLMs are not deterministic and different domain models are generated for the same prompt [8]. Our proposal is to generate k=3 thoughts per tree level as shown in Fig. 2, so that the evaluator has a sufficient variety of options to select from.

4.3 Evaluator Strategy

In the case of the evaluator prompt, our purpose is to assess the proposed modeling elements and choose the best options to continue with the domain model creation. In this scenario, we discarded the value strategy because it requires to score each individual thought with a scalar value, which is difficult to obtain objectively even for human modelers [6]. Therefore, the vote strategy [17] is selected, where we ask the LLM to act as a domain modeler expert and select the best proposal among the generated options. The LLM votes 5 times, and the option with the highest number of votes is maintained at each level. Having a higher number of votes (i.e., 5) compared to the number of thoughts (i.e., 3) reduces the chance of ties.

4.4 Search Algorithm

To complete the definition of the ToT framework, we evaluated the BFS and DFS algorithms. The BFS algorithm self-evaluates the thoughts and maintains the b most promising ones at each level. Then, it continues the exploration with the best thoughts identified. In the case of DFS, the most promising thought is explored until a final solution is achieved. When such a solution is not possible to achieve, the algorithm backtracks to the next most promising thought [17]. In our proposal, we select the BFS algorithm with $b = 1$. Namely, for each level, we always select the best proposal and continue with it for the creation of the domain model afterwards, as shown in Fig. 2. BFS allows us to build upon the best previous thoughts without the need to backtrack.

5 A DSL to Configure ToT Framework Setups

The decomposition of the modeling tasks defined in Sect. 4 is an example that modelers could modify based on the purpose, size, and complexity of their modeling process. Using a DSL for complex techniques is advised [11] because it simplifies running experiments without the need to modify the ToT underlying code. The role of the DSL is to facilitate the configuration and automate the execution of the ToT, based on the task decomposition identified by the modeler.

5.1 DSL Abstract Syntax

Figure 3 presents the metamodel of the DSL, comprising two packages: the problem space package that contains concepts pertinent to the domain modeling problem, and the solution space package mainly to setup the ToT configuration as a solution to the domain modeling problem.

The problem space is characterized by the modeling problem with a description of the domain being modeled and a purpose of modeling, e.g., to create a UML class diagram. The modeling problem is then decomposed into a sequence of tasks, each of which is identified by a name and a task description. Moreover, each task contains one or more assessment criteria against which model elements proposed by the task should be evaluated. Finally, one also needs to specify the modeling notation to use for representing the final domain model.

The ToT configuration is set up using concepts from the solution space. Basically, one instantiates a tree by specifying the number of levels, the number of samples (thoughts) to create at each level, and the number of vote to cast at each level to select a winning thought. The problem space specification informs such

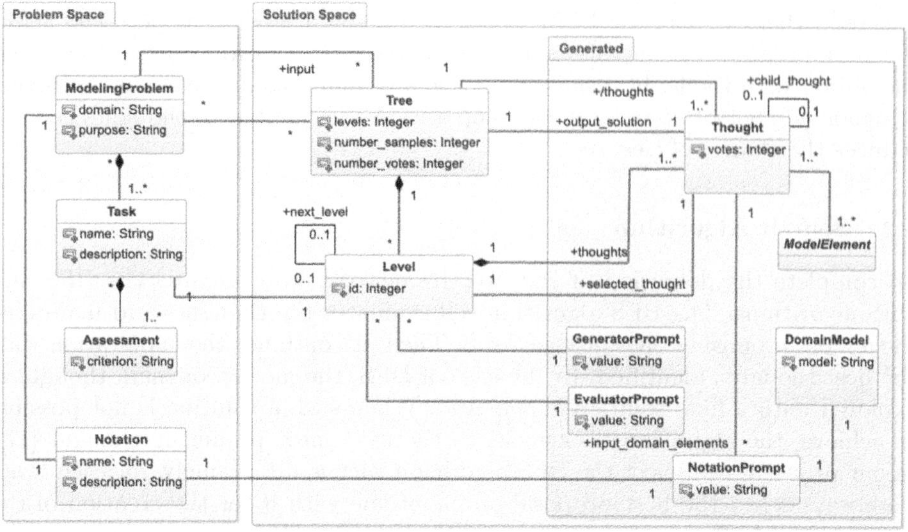

Fig. 3. DSL to facilitate the configuration and automate the execution of the ToT framework for domain modeling tasks.

a tree configuration. For example, the levels of the tree should be in accordance with the tasks, whereby the task description constitutes an integral input for designing the generator prompt of the level, and the assessment criteria are to be incorporated in the evaluator prompt. Moreover, both the domain description and the modeling purpose are repeated throughout all the generator prompts.

A part of the solution space concepts, grouped in the generated sub-package, are generated during the ToT execution (instead of instantiated by the user). These include the thoughts, i.e. intermediate (partial) domain models, created by the LLM, and the selected winning thought of each level as evaluated by the LLM. Moreover, all prompts, including those for generating the thoughts, for evaluating the thoughts, and for transforming the final thought into the modeling notation of choice, are also generated following predefined templates. More specifically, the generator prompt of a level incorporates the description of the task tackled by the level and the winning thought of the previous level, the evaluator prompt enumerates the assessment criteria specified for the corresponding task, and the notation prompt refers to the named notation and its description.

For example, Fig. 4 shows the prompt templates (in the first row) and the corresponding generated prompts for the task to identify association classes, the fifth level of the tree presented in Fig. 2. The prompts are available on GitHub[2].

[2] https://github.com/BESSER-PEARL/dsl-tot-dm/blob/main/dsl/prompts.py.

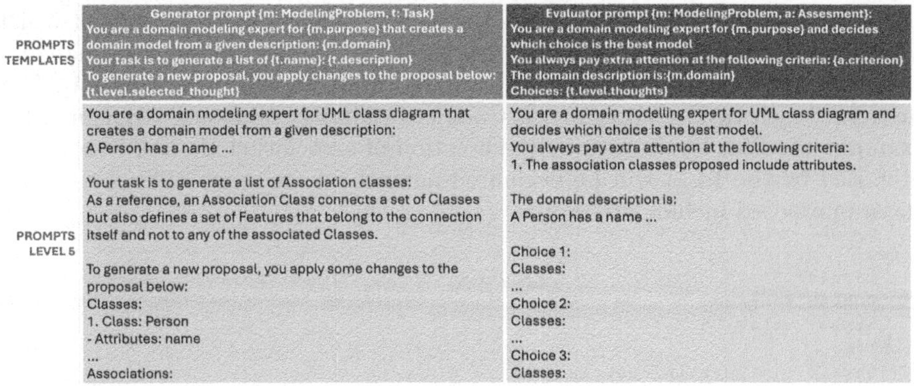

Fig. 4. Templates of generator and evaluator prompts, and example prompts for fifth level of the ToT.

5.2 DSL Concrete Syntax

We provide the concrete syntax designed with the grammar of TextX [9] for the metamodel defined in Sect. 5.1. The grammar shown in Listing 1.1 allows customization of the ToT for modeling tasks.

```
Model: tree=Tree  problem=Problem
tasks=Task+ notation=Notation;
Tree: ''tree:
  ''levels:'' levels=INT
  ''number_samples:'' number_samples=INT
  ''number_votes:'' number_votes=INT;
Problem: ''problem:''
  ''domain:'' domain=STRING  ''purpose:'' purpose=STRING;
Task: ''task:''
  ''level:'' level=INT  ''name:'' name=STRING
  ''description:'' description=STRING
''assessments:'' assessments=STRING+;
Notation: ''notation:''
  ''name:'' name=STRING  ''description:'' description=STRING;
```

Listing 1.1. Grammar for the concrete syntax definition

We illustrate the concrete syntax using the example ToT configuration presented in Fig. 2. As can be seen in Listing 1.2, the tree consists of 5 levels. For each level, the generator prompt is executed 3 times to create 3 sample thoughts, and the evaluator prompt is executed 5 times to vote for the most promising thought. The next step is to describe the modeling problem by specifying the purpose of the modeling process and the textual description of the domain. The latter can be provided by either a string or through a path to a text file that contains the domain description. In our example, the description is given by a text file.

After that, intermediate modeling tasks are specified, with the level at which a task is, the task name, and the task description that defines the modeling knowledge relevant to the task, for example, what an association class is. Furthermore, each task requires at least one criterion to evaluate its thoughts. For example, the fifth level concerns the creation of association classes. The classes proposed by the LLM will be evaluated against one criteria: "The association classes proposed include attributes.".

```
tree:
    levels: 5
    number_samples: 3
    number_votes: 5
problem:
    domain: ''./domain/exercise1.txt''
    purpose: ''UML class diagram''
task:
    level: 1
    name: ''Classes''
    ...
task:
    level: 2
    name: ''Association''
    ...
task:
    level: 3
    name: ''Containment''
    ...
task:
    level: 4
    name: ''Inheritance''
    ...
task:
    level: 5
    name: ''Association classes''
    description: ''As a reference, an Association Class connects
    a set of Classes but also defines a set of Features that belong
    to the connection itself and not to any of the associated Classes.''
    assessments:
        ''The association classes proposed include attributes.''
notation:
    name: ''Plantuml code''
    description: ''Create the PlantUML ...
association classes use the format: (<Source_Class> ,
    <Target_Class>) .. <Association_Class>''
```

Listing 1.2. Concrete syntax for Tree, Problem, Tasks, and notation

Listing 1.2 describes that the first task is to identify classes. Then, the tasks from level 2 to 4 are to identify the relationships divided into three tasks: Association, containment, and inheritance. In level 5, the task is specified for association classes. Our purpose using this approach is to influence the association class identification with two key thoughts: 1) the prompt has information about classes and associations identified in the upper level and 2) by adding modeling knowledge with the description of association classes.

The last step is to specify the modeling notation (e.g., PlantUML), in which the thoughts created in the tree should be represented. We describe the syntactic representation of association classes in PlantUML in the description.

6 Validation

In this section, our aim is to experiment with the ToT prompting technique to create UML class diagrams that include association classes, which LLMs struggle to recommend. The use of the DSL, based on our own experience, has helped reduce the complexity of setting up the ToT configuration and automating the testing process to a great extent.

6.1 Experiment Setup

Our experiment dataset is composed of five domain descriptions and five corresponding reference solution domain models expressed as UML class diagrams. They are collected from various sources: the Theaters and Robots domains used by Camara et al. [8], the Person and Resources domains from a university modeling course, and the e-Commerce and Courses proposed by us. The reference models contain 35 classes, 40 attributes, 24 relationships (including both association, containment, and inheritance), and 9 association classes in total.

To run the experiments, we use GPT-4 as the example LLM, which is the model with the best results for the creation of domain models according to [6]. We use the five-level ToT configuration presented in Sect. 4 in our experiments, namely to identify classes and attributes, associations, containment relationships, inheritance relationships, and association classes.

6.2 Evaluation Criteria

For the evaluation of the models, we compare the output in PlantUML notation and consider a correct prediction if the element of the suggested model is semantic equivalent to the reference model, including elements with different names. An example of similarity is shown in Fig. 5b, the association class and attributes names are different from the reference model; however, it is equivalent because the source class, target class, association class and attributes have the same meaning in the domain model. In contrast, in Fig. 5c, the association class is incorrect because the class session is used as the target class and has a different meaning in the domain model compared to the reference model.

The criteria for the evaluation of classes and attributes are similar; we consider a correct prediction the use of equivalent names. For attributes, we are not evaluating the data types. In the case of relationships, the correct prediction should match the lower and upper cardinality; if the lower cardinality is not specified in the reference model, we consider only the upper cardinality.

```
@startuml
...
class Session{
  int timeBegin
  int timeEnd
}
...
(Play, Participant) .. Session
...

@enduml
```

(a) Reference solution

```
@startuml
...
class Play_Session_Participant {
    +Session start time
    +Session end time
}
...
(Play , Participant) ..
Play_Session_Participant
...
@enduml
```

(b) Equivalent

```
@startuml
...
class Act {
    - role: string
}
...

(Participant, Session) .. Act
...

@enduml
```

(c) Not equivalent

Fig. 5. Comparison of association classes in PlantUML syntax

To evaluate the experiments, we used precision, recall, and the F1 score. For precision, we consider equivalent predictions as true positives (*TP*), and not equivalent predictions as false positives (*FP*). The formula for precision is:

$$Precision = \frac{TP}{TP + FP} \tag{1}$$

For recall, we use the *TP* and the elements not predicted as false negatives (*FN*). The calculation is performed using the following formula:

$$Recall = \frac{TP}{TP + FN} \tag{2}$$

Finally, we use the F1-score formula below:

$$F1 = 2 \times \frac{Precision \times Recall}{Precision + Recall} \tag{3}$$

6.3 Experiment Results

Our aim with these experiments is to compare the performance of the ToT framework to recommend model elements with the reference solutions. Table 1 shows that the performance is better to suggest classes and association classes between all the model elements. For attributes and relationships, the performance of the recommendations decreases. Although we have specific intermediate steps for association, containment, and inheritance, the result for relationships is the worst among all the model elements. The issue with relationship recommendation is a well-known issue that was reviewed in the previous sections. Finally, the attribute elements are not an intermediate step and are suggested with the classes, which appears to cause lower performance using ToT.

The results reported in Table 1 show that ToT has the best performance for recommendation of classes and association classes with 0.895 and 0.824 for the F1 score, respectively. The precision and recall performance in these elements are very similar, and no major gap is identified. However, when comparing the performance of the attribute element recommendation, there is a major difference

Table 1. Result of the performance of ToT for UML class model elements

	Precision	Recall	F1-score
Class	0.829	0.971	0.895
Attribute	0.545	0.900	0.679
Relationship	0,227	0,417	0,294
Association Class	0.875	0.778	0.824

between precision and recall, specifically with a low precision score of 0.545 compared to the recall of 0.9. This result indicates that various suggested attributes are not included in the reference model. In Fig. 6a, we have an example of a model that contains two association classes: access and ancestor. These classes are correctly recommended at the fifth level and are included in the model shown in Fig. 6b. We found that both elements were suggested for the 3 thoughts at that level, but with slight name differences, such as genealogy.

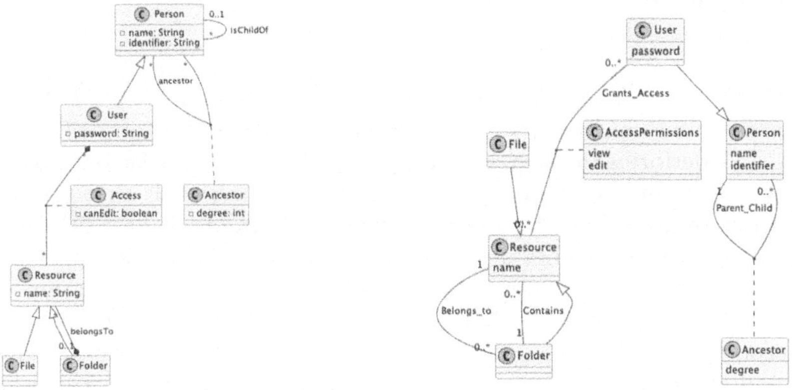

(a) Reference solution (b) ToT with 5 levels

Fig. 6. Person and Resource domain model used in the experiments

Regarding relationship recommendations, the performance of the F1 score is lower compared to the other model elements with 0.294. The performance for both precision and recall are the lowest compared with the other model elements. Similarly to attributes, the lower precision indicates that the relationships recommended are not part of the reference model, and the lower recall indicates that various relationships are not recommended. The reference solution in Fig. 6a has a containment relationship between the folder and resource classes; however, the ToT suggests two associations, as shown in Fig. 6b. We found that in the third level of the ToT, duplicated relationships are suggested between Resource and Folder for all the thoughts, which cause the error in the final model.

6.4 Threats to Validity

Equivalent Model Elements for Association Classes. It is possible to represent association classes in a syntactically distinct but semantically equivalent way replacing them with one class and two associations for the source and target classes. We are not considering these equivalent representations in the evaluation of our experiments.

LLMs are not Deterministic. LLMs are generative models that produce different results with similar prompts. Because it is not deterministic, we can generate different thoughts using the same generator prompt; however, this also affects the evaluator votes that can choose two different thoughts as the best option with the same prompt.

Reference Models in the Dataset. Due to the lack of data with domain description and reference models, we have used exercises from different sources: previous papers, a university modeling course, and created by us.

7 Discussion

Performance. Our experiments show that using ToT enables GPT-4 to create complex modeling constructs (e.g., association classes) as part of the final domain models. ToT performs the best at identifying classes and association classes, compared to identifying other model elements. Our conjecture is that the intermediate results of preceding steps, namely identification of the best fit classes and associations, provide insights that extends beyond the domain description, which ToT was able to leverage towards recommending suitable association classes. This result is encouraging to explore more configurations in future research for task decomposition for other modeling processes, such as behavioral diagrams.

To address the performance of ToT to recommend attributes, we envision that extending the task decomposition with an additional level dedicated to attribute generation and evaluation would help. Regarding the relationships, we confirm that GPT-4 recommendations are not reliable and ToT technique alone can not resolve this issue. As a consequence, a combination of ToT with other prompt techniques, such as using few-shots at the levels regarding relationship generation would be the next target of investigation, especially for identifying associations and containment relationships where LLMs do not differentiate properly.

Generator Prompts. We have reviewed the diversity of the thoughts created by the generator prompt, and observed that fewer diversity exists for thoughts related to inheritance in comparison with association and containment. For those model elements that have less diverse thoughts, we recommend using the Few-shot or CoT prompting techniques for the recommendation of model elements.

Evaluator Prompts. The number of votes selected was 5 to avoid ties while evaluating thoughts; however, we have observed that ties occur for some thoughts in association classes that have two different proposals. This result indicates that in certain domains the result of the evaluator prompt does not recognize the difference between two different thoughts, and the assistance of a human expert will be useful to choose the best option. For future research, we suggest including human modeling experts in the evaluator role to select the best thoughts.

Costs. Use of the ToT framework involves a higher cost because more prompts are used compared to other techniques. We suggest to experiment with this framework for complex modeling tasks where other prompting techniques do not achieve good results. Moreover, the DSL is an open source tool that can be extended to experiment with open-source LLMs to reduce such cost.

8 Tool Support

We implemented an open-source DSL tool on GitHub[3]. It allows the definition of ToT configurations for domain modeling and the execution of them to generate and evaluate thoughts, as detailed in Sect. 5. The dataset and results of the experiments are included in the same repository. Additionally, the repository includes additional examples that use ToT configurations with other modeling languages, such as Entity-Relationship and UML activity diagrams.

The DSL is defined in Python using TextX [9]. The Python template shown below is used for the code generation that instantiates the classes from our DSL, these classes use the ToT framework library [17] to execute the generator and evaluator strategy with the BFS algorithm. To use the DSL, it is required a subscription to OpenAI API or Azure OpenAI API; however, it is possible to extend the DSL to use it with other LLMs.

```
...
def run():
    problem = ModelingProblem(levels = {{tree.levels}}, purpose = ‘‘{{problem.
    purpose}}’’, description = ‘‘‘‘‘‘{{ problem.domain }}’’’’’’)
    tree = Tree(number_levels = {{tree.levels}}, generator_samples = {{tree.
    number_samples}}, evaluator_votes %= {{tree.number_votes}})
    ...
    output = tree.execute(logName)
    ...
```

Listing 1.3. Python template used for code generation

9 Conclusion and Further Work

Creating domain models is a complex task that demands domain experts and modelers a profound understanding of the domain to conceptualize the elements that will be included in the model. The creation of domain models with prompting strategies has limitations, and we support the idea of decomposing the process into tasks and use the ToT framework to improve the recommendation of

[3] https://github.com/BESSER-PEARL/dsl-tot-dm.

model elements. Furthermore, we propose the use of a DSL that orchestrate and executes the prompts needed to generate and evaluate model elements in various thoughts. Using GPT-4, our ToT approach obtained better results for class and association classes; however, for attributes and relationships, some recommendations are not accurate for the domain (low precision).

The potential of our ToT approach resides in its design to generate model recommendations by recommending alternatives of model elements in intermediate thoughts and self-evaluate them with specific criteria. As future work, we plan to combine the prompting techniques for domain modeling, e.g. using Few-shot examples for the generator prompts. Moreover, to facilitate the use of the DSL, we will add configuration templates to represent different modeling processes that modelers can use as basis to define their own configurations.

References

1. UML Specifications. (2015). https://www.omg.org/spec/UML/2.5/PDF/. Accessed 3 May 2024
2. Almonte, L., Guerra, E., Cantador, I., De Lara, J.: Recommender systems in model-driven engineering: a systematic mapping review. Softw. Syst. Model. **21**(1), 249–280 (2022) https://doi.org/10.1007/s10270-021-00905-x
3. Arora, C., Sabetzadeh, M., Briand, L., Zimmer, F.: Extracting domain models from natural-language requirements: approach and industrial evaluation. In: Proceedings of the ACM/IEEE 19th International Conference on Model Driven Engineering Languages and Systems, pp. 250–260. ACM, Saint-Malo (2016). https://doi.org/10.1145/2976767.2976769
4. Brown, T., et al.: Language models are few-shot learners. In: Larochelle, H., Ranzato, M., Hadsell, R., Balcan, M., Lin, H. (eds.) Advances in Neural Information Processing Systems, vol. 33, pp. 1877–1901. Curran Associates, Inc. (2020). https://proceedings.neurips.cc/paper_files/paper/2020/file/1457c0d6bfcb4967418bfb8ac142f64a-Paper.pdf
5. Chaaben, M.B., Burgueño, L., Sahraoui, H.: Towards using few-shot prompt learning for automating model completion. In: 2023 IEEE/ACM 45th International Conference on Software Engineering: New Ideas and Emerging Results (ICSE-NIER), pp. 7–12. IEEE, Melbourne (2023). https://doi.org/10.1109/ICSE-NIER58687.2023.00008
6. Chen, K., Yang, Y., Chen, B., Hernández López, J.A., Mussbacher, G., Varró, D.: Automated domain modeling with large language models: a comparative study. In: 2023 ACM/IEEE 26th International Conference on Model Driven Engineering Languages and Systems (MODELS), pp. 162–172. IEEE, Västerås (2023). https://doi.org/10.1109/MODELS58315.2023.00037
7. Chen, P.P.S.: The entity-relationship model-toward a unified view of data. ACM Trans. Datab. Syst. **1**(1), 9–36 (1976). https://doi.org/10.1145/320434.320440
8. Cámara, J., Troya, J., Burgueño, L., Vallecillo, A.: On the assessment of generative AI in modeling tasks: an experience report with ChatGPT and UML. Softw. Syst. Model. **22**(3), 781–793 (2023). https://doi.org/10.1007/s10270-023-01105-5
9. Dejanović, I., Vaderna, R., Milosavljević, G.: Vuković,: Textx: a python tool for domain-specific languages implementation. Knowl.-Based Syst. **115**, 1–4 (2017). https://doi.org/10.1016/j.knosys.2016.10.023

10. Feltus, C., Ma, Q., Proper, H.A., Kelsen, P.: Towards AI assisted domain modeling. In: Reinhartz-Berger, I., Sadiq, S. (eds.) Advances in Conceptual Modeling. LNCS, vol. 13012, pp. 75–89. Springer, Cham (2021). https://doi.org/10.1007/978-3-030-88358-4_7
11. Fill, H.G., Fettke, P., Köpke, J.: Conceptual modeling and large language models: impressions from first experiments with ChatGPT. In: Enterprise Modelling and Information Systems Architectures (EMISAJ), pp. 3:1-:15 (2023). https://doi.org/10.18417/EMISA.18.3, https://emisa-journal.org/emisa/article/view/318. Artwork Size: 3:1–15 Pages Publisher: Enterprise Modelling and Information Systems Architectures (EMISAJ)
12. Frederiks, P.J.M., van der Weide, T.P.: Information modeling: the process and the required competencies of its participants. Data Knowl. Eng. **58**(1), 4–20 (2006). https://doi.org/10.1016/j.datak.2005.05.007
13. Mussbacher, G., et al.: Opportunities in intelligent modeling assistance. Softw. Syst. Model. **19**(5), 1045–1053 (2020). https://doi.org/10.1007/s10270-020-00814-5
14. Saini, R., Mussbacher, G., Guo, J.L.C., Kienzle, J.: DoMoBOT: a bot for automated and interactive domain modelling. In: Proceedings of the 23rd ACM/IEEE International Conference on Model Driven Engineering Languages and Systems: Companion Proceedings, pp. 1–10. ACM, Virtual Event Canada (2020). https://doi.org/10.1145/3417990.3421385
15. Wei, J., et al.: Chain-of-thought prompting elicits reasoning in large language models. In: Koyejo, S., Mohamed, S., Agarwal, A., Belgrave, D., Cho, K., Oh, A. (eds.) Advances in Neural Information Processing Systems, vol. 35, pp. 24824–24837. Curran Associates, Inc. (2022). https://proceedings.neurips.cc/paper_files/paper/2022/file/9d5609613524ecf4f15af0f7b31abca4-Paper-Conference.pdf
16. Wilmont, I., Hengeveld, S., Barendsen, E., Hoppenbrouwers, S.: Cognitive mechanisms of conceptual modelling. In: Ng, W., Storey, V.C., Trujillo, J.C. (eds.) Conceptual Modeling, pp. 74–87. Springer, Heidelberg (2013). https://doi.org/10.1007/978-3-642-41924-9_7
17. Yao, S., et al.: Tree of thoughts: deliberate problem solving with large language models. In: Oh, A., Naumann, T., Globerson, A., Saenko, K., Hardt, M., Levine, S. (eds.) Advances in Neural Information Processing Systems, vol. 36, pp. 11809–11822. Curran Associates, Inc. (2023). https://proceedings.neurips.cc/paper_files/paper/2023/file/271db9922b8d1f4dd7aaef84ed5ac703-Paper-Conference.pdf

ECQL: Towards Succinct and Extensible Modeling of Multi-model Query Results

Gengyuan Shi, Chaokun Wang(✉), and Yabin Liu

School of Software, BNRist, Tsinghua University, Beijing 100084, China
{shigy19,liu-yb23}@mails.tsinghua.edu.cn, chaokun@tsinghua.edu.cn

Abstract. The field of database technology has expanded to include diverse data models, leading to the exploration of the polystore concept, which aims to provide unified management for heterogeneous data. However, the development of multi-model query languages, which serve as the primary interface for polystores, remains a significant challenge. Existing multi-model query languages face limitations, such as restricted expressiveness in query representation and inflexibility imposed by predefined data models. To address these problems, this paper introduces the Equivalent Combinations of Query Languages (ECQL) as a holistic representation of multi-model queries. We first establish foundational abstractions for the query results across various data models. Subsequently, we construct a novel multi-model query language called ECQL that naturally combines sub-queries of different data models through expression interfaces based on these abstractions. The expressiveness of ECQL lies in its capability to support both single-model and cross-model query operations. Comparative evaluations against existing multi-model query languages on polystore benchmarks underscore the succinctness of ECQL. Finally, we illustrate the extensibility of ECQL by demonstrating its compatibility with the incorporation of query languages that are not initially included in ECQL's grammar.

Keywords: Multi-model query language · Polystore · ECQL

1 Introduction

With the development of conceptual modeling and data management technologies, modern applications often engage with multi-model data simultaneously. In response to this demand, the concept of polystores has been proposed and studied [10]. Polystores not only support the characteristics of native database engines (DBEs) but also enable efficient execution of cross-model queries. By leveraging polystores, users can universally manage heterogeneous data to support complex real-world applications.

Multi-model query languages serve as the major interface for manipulation of multi-model data in polystores. As single-model query languages fall short in multi-model contexts, existing polystores commonly design their own multi-model query languages. These languages can be classified into three categories:

W. Maass et al. (Eds.): ER 2024, LNCS 15238, pp. 112–130, 2025.
https://doi.org/10.1007/978-3-031-75872-0_7

1) those based on universal data models [6,14,30] and express the same semantics of those data models, 2) extensions of existing single-model query languages [10, 23,26], and 3) those based on specific hybrid data structures native to polystores [1,4]. Despite these advancements, existing query languages for polystores still encounter limitations. For instance, consider the multi-model query requirement R_1 which is based on the data schema discussed in Sect. 2: *To find all Peking Opera tracks featuring any apprentice of a given master named "Mei Lanfang".* This query requirement involves both graph and document data. Notably, R_1 cannot be adequately expressed through ArangoDB's AQL [1] or Polypheny-DB's query language [31] (PolyQL for short). Although both AQL and PolyQL accommodate graph and document queries, they lack support for complex query operations like induced sub-graph search and element-wise matching.

Table 1 overviews the characteristics of selected polystore-oriented multi-model query languages, which have a common issue in balancing expressiveness, succinctness, and extensibility.

Table 1. Comparison between ECQL and existing polystore query languages. Symbol ∘ denotes partial support. R, G, and D stand for relational, graph, and document data models respectively.

Query Language	Expressiveness				Extensibility
	R	G	D	Cross-model	
MyriaL [33]	√	∘	∘	√	×
CloudMdsQL [23]	√	√	∘	√	√
Polypheny-DB [31]	√	√	∘	×	√
ArangoDB AQL [1]	∘	√	√	√	×
OrientDB SQL [4]	√	√	∘	√	×
ECQL	√	√	√	√	√

Expressiveness. Multi-model query languages should be capable of fully representing both single-model and cross-model queries [16,29]. However, certain existing multi-model query languages are constrained by their adherence to specific unified data models, which may limit their expressiveness. This deficiency stems from the oversimplifications in these unified data models, which reduces the compatibility with the various single data models that they aim to cover.

Succinctness. Multi-model query languages are expected to insulate users from the complexity of unfamiliar query operations. However, some existing multi-model query languages adopt an imperative style, which resembles that of programming languages, thereby increasing the difficulty of query authoring.

Extensibility. The application scenarios of polystores demand the integration of new database engines and impose an expectation on multi-model query languages to be highly extensible. However, many existing multi-model query languages are constrained by fixed grammatical structures and have challenges in integration with single-model query languages that are not originally considered.

The major challenge stems from the significant difference among various data models. Unfortunately, it is difficult for existing universal data models to express the diverse characteristics inherent in these models. According to the "no one size fits all" principle [28], universal data models can hardly achieve a balance; they must not only provide comprehensive functionalities of different DBEs but also be adaptable to the demands of specific data models in various applications.

To address the problems above, this paper studies an innovative approach to the modeling of heterogeneous data. We first proposes a representation for the data format of the query results from various data models, without attempting to unify the diverse range of query operations. This representation keeps the inherent heterogeneity and allows each data model to retain its unique characteristics and capabilities. Second, this paper designs Equivalent Combinations of Query Languages (ECQL), a novel multi-model query language that combines the grammars of query languages from different data models through interface-based mechanisms. Therefore, the proposed query language has a flexible structure and can be adapted to incorporate new query languages. For instance, an ECQL query Q_1 corresponding to R_1 can be written as follows:

```
db.track.find({
  "players": {
    $elemMatch: { $in: {
      MATCH (master:Artist)-[r:Mentor*]->(apprentice:Artist)
      WHERE master.name = "Mei Lanfang"
      RETURN DISTINCT apprentice.name
    }}
}})
```

The query combines a Cypher sub-query with an MQL (MongoDB query language) sub-query to utilize the native query operations, such as the induced sub-graph search in Cypher and the element-match matching in MQL.

The main contributions of this paper are summarized as follows.

1. This paper proposes an abstract presentation for the query results from various data models.
2. This paper presents ECQL, a novel multi-model query language that combines different query languages based on the proposed abstract presentation.
3. We evaluate the succinctness of ECQL using polystore benchmarks and demonstrate its extensibility through a case study.

The rest of this paper is organized as follows. Section 2 illustrates the multi-model query requirements of polystores with an example. Section 3 gives the definitions relevant to our abstract representation. We propose the ECQL in Sect. 4. Experimental evaluation results are reported in Sect. 5. We review the related research efforts on multi-model query languages in Sect. 6. Section 7 concludes the paper.

2 Running Example

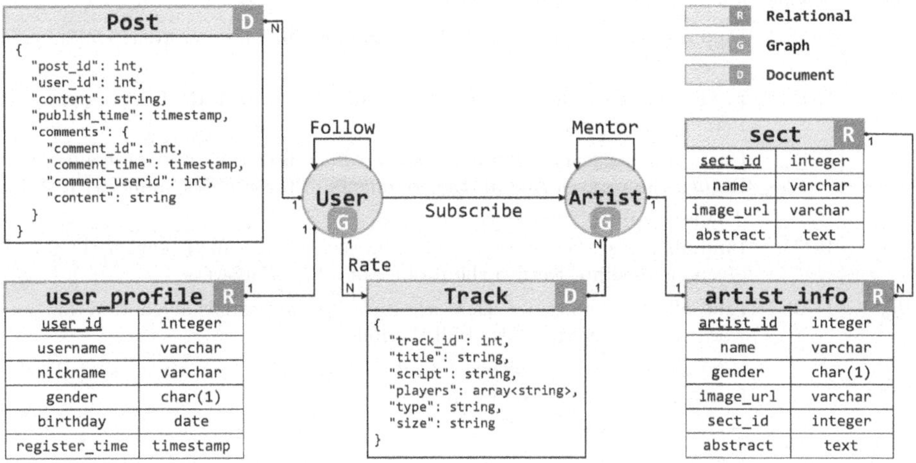

Fig. 1. The global multi-model data schema of the Peking Opera Web application.

This section introduces a running example that illustrates a multi-model data management scenario. This example is drawn from a real-world Peking Opera (a traditional Chinese opera format) Web application. The application involves heterogeneous data that span across diverse common data models such as relational, document, and graph. In Subsect. 2.1, we explain the global multi-model data schema. On top of this schema, Subsect. 2.2 presents a collection of multi-model query requirements.

2.1 Multi-model Data Schema

The global schema of the application involves both Peking Opera knowledge graph and social network scenarios, as depicted in Fig. 1.

Peking Opera. The Peking Opera knowledge graph includes correlations among Peking Opera artists and aria tracks. The `Artist` entity models Peking Opera artists. The structural `artist_information` is represented as relational data, with the `sect_id` attribute referring to the primary key of the `Sect` table. The `Mentor` relationships are represented as edges in the graph data, connecting the `Artist` vertices. The SPSVERBc7s of Peking Opera arias are detailed in document form containing cast lists, video metadata, and scripts with long text.

Table 2. Multi-model query requirements extracted from the Peking Opera scenario, with the data models indicated in the order of their nesting, from the most to the least nested.

Name	Models	Query requirement description
R_1	G-D	Find all Peking Opera tracks in which any multi-hop apprentice of a given artist participates.
R_2	G-R	Find the names and the abstracts of all multi-hop students of a given Peking Opera artist.
R_3	D-R	Find all posts whose comment number is greater than a given count. Return the content and all the comments of these posts, along with the nicknames of the authors.
R_4	R-G	Find all users who follow any user whose register time is earlier than a given timestamp. Return the profiles of all the followers.
R_5	D-G-R	Find all followers of the users who publish the posts that contain a given word. Return the profiles of all the followers.
R_6	G-D	Find all the posts published by the users followed by a given user. Return the posts and the authors' profiles.

Social Network. The social network aspect of the schema is derived from the interactions of social users on the application's forum. The `user_profile` is represented as relational data. The `Follow` relationships are modeled as graph edges between social `User` vertices. Social users contribute to the forum by authoring Web posts. Each `Post` is a document that comprises a title, content, the identity of the publishing user, and additional information. An array of SPSVERBc12s is nested within each post document, representing the replies to the original post. Users have the option to `Subscribe` Peking Opera artists, with these subscription modeled as graph edges.

2.2 Multi-model Query Requirements

Table 2 describes six representative multi-model analytical query requirements derived from the realistic workloads of the Peking Opera Web application. The selected query requirements incorporate query operations over different data models, including induced sub-graph queries on graph data for R_1 and R_2, as well as nested array filters on document data for R_1 and R_3. Furthermore, each query requirement includes one or more cross-model `Join` operations which are essential for polystores [20]. These operations demand the polystores to access multi-model data simultaneously, rather than merely merging execution results from isolated database engines.

For instance, query requirement R_1 aims to find multi-hop apprentices of a specific artist, such as *"Mei Lanfang,"* and then identifies all Peking Opera tracks featuring any of these apprentices. In order to represent R_1, a multi-model query language must be able to express native query operations within both graph and document DBEs.

3 Multi-model Query Result Abstraction

As previously discussed in Sect. 1, the diversity of data models poses a significant challenge in designing a unified representation for query operations. To address this challenge, we propose an interface-based abstract representation that focuses on the holistic representation of query results. This approach is based on the understanding that, despite the complexity and diversity of multi-model query operations, their outputs can be effectively harmonized through a comprehensive abstraction. Specifically, we define the Abstract Query Operation Tree (AQOT) as the abstract representation that captures the results of both single-model and cross-model queries. Both operands and outputs of AQOT nodes (i.e., query operations) are data collections. This design allows for the combination of single-model queries, which can also be represented as the combination of the corresponding single-model AQOTs.

We first give the definitions of foundational concepts related to data collections in Subsect. 3.1. Subsequently, Subsect. 3.2 gives the definition of the Abstract Query Operation Tree.

3.1 Representation of Data Collections

The proposed representation regards multi-model datasets as data collections. This subsection gives the formal definitions of Literal Value, Record, and Collection.

Definition 1 (Literal Value and Literal Type). *A* literal value *(*literal *for short) $l \in \mathbb{L}$ is a certain value in a multi-model query, where $\mathbb{L}$ denotes the set of all literals. The basic* literal types *constitute a set of labels, i.e.,* $\mathbb{T} = \{\texttt{INTEGER}, \texttt{NUMERIC}, \texttt{BOOLEAN}, \texttt{STRING}, \texttt{LIST}, \texttt{OBJECT}, \texttt{NULL}\}$. *The global type function* $\tau_\Omega : \mathbb{L} \rightarrow \mathbb{T}$ *maps each literal l to its corresponding literal type $\tau_\Omega(l)$.*

Definition 2 (Record). *A* record *r is a tuple $r = (\alpha, \tau, \varphi)$, where α is the set of* attribute names. *The* type function *$\tau : \alpha \rightarrow \mathbb{T}$ and the* value function *$\varphi : \alpha \rightarrow \mathbb{L}$ map each attribute $a \in \alpha$ to its respective literal type $\tau(a)$ and literal value $\varphi(a)$.*

Definition 3 (Collection). *A* collection *c is a list of records $c = (r_1, \cdots, r_{n_c})$, where n_c is the number of elements in c. Specifically, if every record $r \in c$ shares the same α and τ, then let $\alpha_c = \alpha$ and $\tau_c = \tau$ denote the attribute name set and the type function of c, respectively. The set of all collections is denoted by $\mathbb{C}$.*

It is noteworthy that we do not require an arbitrary collection to conform to the relational data model. For instance, the execution result of the Cypher subquery within query requirement R_2 can be represented as a collection c_{g2}. Each record $r_i \in c_{g2}$ comprises an attribute name set $\alpha_{g2} = \{apprentice\}$, a shared type function τ_{g2} that satisfies $\tau_{g2}(apprentice) = \texttt{OBJECT}$, and a value function φ_i that maps the attribute name *apprentice* to its corresponding graph nodes in r_i. The literal values of type OBJECT are complex objects whose attribute values can be accessed through attribute names.

Table 3. Definitions of fundamental multi-model query operations.

Required	Name	Symbol	# Operand(s)	Description
×	Project	Π	1	Return r preserving only the given attributes for each $r \in c_1$
√	Filter	σ	1	Return records $r \in c_1$ that satisfy the given conditions
√	Materialize	$\oplus$	1	Cache a collection c_1 to polystore query processor and return itself
×	Cartesian Product	$\times$	2	Obtain a collection c_t as the Cartesian product of two collections c_1 and c_2

3.2 Abstract Query Operation Tree

To address the limited expressiveness problem of the existing approaches based on universal data models, our approach minimizes the requirements for representing multi-model query results. Definition 4 formalizes the abstract query operation tree.

Definition 4 (Query Operation and Abstract Query Operation Tree). *An* abstract query operation tree *is a directed tree, where each node represents a query operation. The set of all AQOTs is denoted by* $\mathbb{G}$. *A* query operation *o is a tuple $o = (n, f, scope)$, where n is the number of operands of o, function $f : \mathbb{C}^n \rightarrow \mathbb{C}$ accepts n collections as operands and produces one collection, and scope denotes the physical location where the output collection of f is stored.*

Without loss of generality, we denote the i-th operand collection of f as c_i and the output collection of f as c_t. The domain of *scope*, represented by $\mathbb{S}$, consists of the identifiers of all data models, along with "`X`" which represents the polystore itself.

We predefine four fundamental multi-model query operations with scope `X`, as described in Table 3. The polystore `Join` query operation, denoted by the symbol $\Diamond$, is equivalent to `CartesianProduct` followed by `Filter`, i.e., $c_1 \Diamond_p c_2 = \sigma_p(c_1 \times c_2)$, where p is the join condition. Notably, the $\Diamond$ symbol distinguishes it from the traditional relational `Join` symbol.

1. The operation `Project` returns a collection c_t composed of each record r from the child c_1, preserving only the specified attributes, i.e., $c_t \leftarrow \Pi_\alpha(c_1)$, where α denotes the attribute name list.
2. The operation `Filter` returns a collection c_t composed of each record $r \in c_1$ that satisfies the filter condition, i.e., $c_t \leftarrow \sigma_p(c_1)$, where p denotes the specified condition.
3. The operation `Materialize` saves a collection c_1 to the polystore query processor and returns the same collection, i.e., $c_t = c_1$.
4. The operation `Cartesian Product` takes two operand collections c_1 and c_2 and returns their Cartesian Product as c_t. Formally, for each record $r_i \in c_1$ and $r_j \in c_2$, a record $r_{ij} \in c_t$ exists such that 1) $\alpha_{ij} = \alpha_i \cup \alpha_j$, 2) $\tau_{ij}(a_{ik}) = \tau_i(a_{ik})$ for each $a_{ik} \in \alpha_i$ and $\tau_{ij}(a_{jm}) = \tau_j(a_{jm})$ for each $a_{jm} \in \alpha_j$, and 3) $\varphi_{ij}(a_{ik}) = \varphi_i(a_{ik})$ for each $a_{ik} \in \alpha_i$ and $\varphi_{ij}(a_{jm}) = \varphi_j(a_{jm})$ for each $a_{jm} \in \alpha_j$.

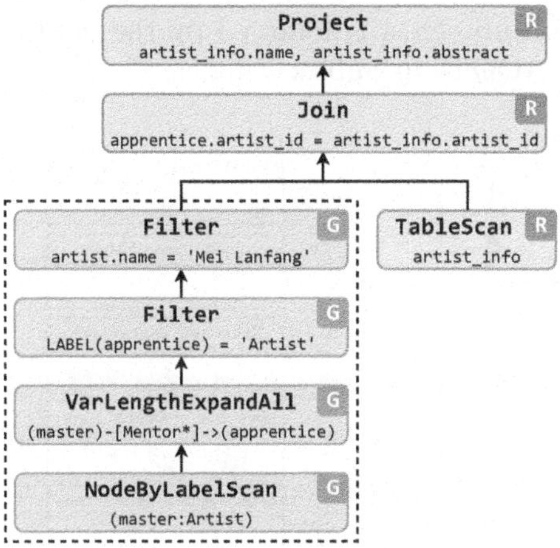

(a) The whole AQOT.

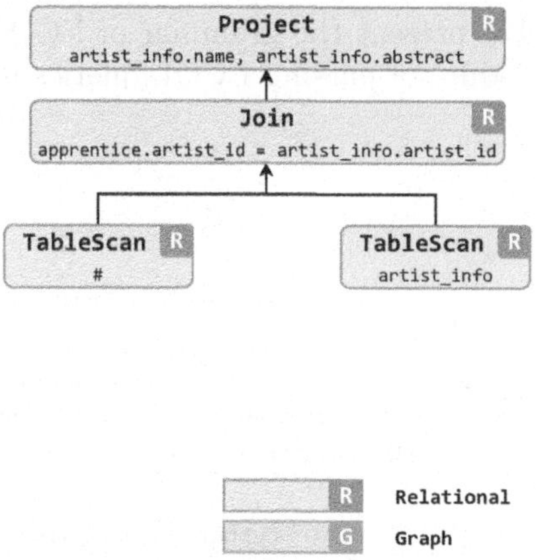

(b) Temporary AQOT during parsing.

Fig. 2. The abstract query operation trees corresponding to R_2.

One single AQOT can combine query operations from different data models. A combination of query operations of different data models in one AQOT is allowed. For instance, the AQOT depicted in Fig. 2a incorporates the relational query operations such as `TableScan` and the graph query operations like `NodeByLabelScan` and `VarLengthExpandAll`. Additionally, this AQOT involves polystore query operations including `Join` and `Project`.

4 Equivalent Combinations of Query Languages

This section describes the Equivalent Combinations of Query Languages, a novel query language designed to enable the natural and flexible combination of sub-queries written in various single-model query languages. As shown in Fig. 3, ECQL queries can be converted into AQOTs that ensure holisical representation of multi-model data. This conversion capability endows ECQL with the ability to nest an ECQL sub-query within one another, provided that the results of the inner sub-query are compatible with the operands of the outer sub-query. Leveraging this characteristic, the design of ECQL achieves the following key advantages.

Expressiveness: ECQL ensures that the native query operations of each individual single-model query language are fully preserved.

Succinctness: ECQL provides an intuitive way of authoring multi-model queries and avoids learning one new query language for polystore users.

Extensibility: ECQL allows for the integration of single-model query languages that are not initially included, as long as their query results conform to the proposed representation.

We present the grammar of ECQL in Subsect. 4.1, followed by the detailed procedure of parsing ECQL queries into AQOTs in Subsect. 4.2.

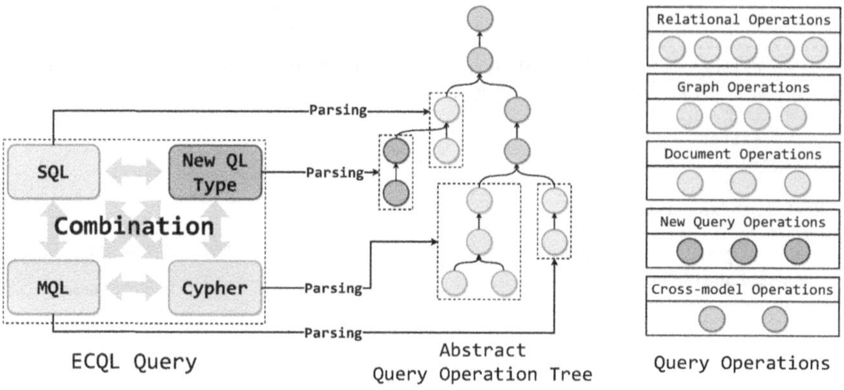

Fig. 3. ECQL query representation based on AQOT.

4.1 ECQL Grammar

Figure 4 shows a partial grammar of ECQL which at present incorporates SQL, Cypher, and MQL. It is noteworthy that the grammar of ECQL is flexible and can be integrated with production rules with respect to other single-model query languages, as demonstrated in Sect. 5. ECQL regards sub-queries from different query languages as structurally equivalent expressions. In detail, ECQL provides two ways of combinations of sub-queries, namely the *Entity Expression Interface* and the *Value Expression Interface*. This design not only maintains the full functionalities of the native single-model query languages but also ensures that the structure of the queries is preserved.

Entity Expression Interface (EEI). EEI facilitates the combination of sub-queries whose results are interpretable as entity data. Specifically, the non-terminal `sub_expr` denotes a sub-query expression that can produce any arbitrary single-model sub-query. Furthermore, a `sub_expr` can be nested within another `sub_expr` constructed in a different query language, in order to express cross-model `Join` queries. For instance, the ECQL query corresponding to R_2 can be written as follows:

```
SELECT ai.name, ai.abstract
FROM artist_info ai JOIN {
  MATCH (master:Artist)-[r:Mentor*]->(apprentice:Artist)
  WHERE master.name = "Mei Lanfang"
  RETURN apprentice
} ON ai.artist_id = apprentice.artist_id
```

```
expr              -> sub_expr
var_expr          -> var AS wrapped_sub_expr
wrapped_sub_expr -> L_BRACE sub_expr R_BRACE
sub_expr          -> sql_expr | cypher_expr | mql_expr
sql_expr          -> [WITH var_def]
                     SELECT sql_select_clause
                     [FROM sql_from_clause]
                     [WHERE sql_conditions]
                     [GROUP BY sql_group_by_clause]
                     [HAVING sql_having_clause]
                     [ORDER BY sql_order_by_clause]
                     [LIMIT sql_limit_clause]
                     [OFFSET sql_offset_clause]
var_def           -> var_expr {COMMA var_expr}
sql_from_clause   -> sql_from_item
                     [JOIN sql_from_item ON sql_conditions]
                     [COMMA sql_from_clause]

sql_from_item     -> var_expr | wrapped_sub_expr
sql_conditions    -> sql_cond_item
                     [ sql_cond_op sql_conditions]
sql_cond_item     -> item sql_predicate_op item
item              -> var | value | wrapped_sub_expr
```

Fig. 4. Partial grammar of ECQL.

The last non-terminal **sql_from_item** produces a **wrapped_sub_expr** and finally produces a **cypher_expr** enclosed in braces. The Cypher sub-query results contain an apprentice entity, whose attribute **artist_id** is accessed in the outer SQL sub-query.

To avoid ambiguity in queries involving EEI combinations, ECQL also supports explicit aliasing of sub-queries. For example, the above query can be reconstructed to include an explicit alias, as demonstrated below. In this revised query, the last non-terminal **sql_from_item** produces a **var_expr**, and the non-terminal **var** produces the alias **graph** of the sub-query.

```
SELECT ai.name, ai.abstract
FROM artist_info ai JOIN graph AS {
  MATCH (master:Artist)-[r:Mentor*]->(apprentice:Artist)
  WHERE master.name = "Mei Lanfang"
  RETURN apprentice
} ON ai.artist_id = graph.apprentice.artist_id
```

Value Expression Interface (VEI). VEI represents sub-query results as a flattened list of enumerable values, facilitating list operations on these results within the query combinations. For instance, the ECQL query corresponding to R_2 can also be written using VEI, as shown below. This query involves an IN predicate that operates on the results of an nested Cypher sub-query.

```
SELECT ai.name, ai.abstract
FROM artist_info ai
WHERE ai.artist_id IN {
  MATCH (master:Artist)-[r:Mentor*]->(apprentice:Artist)
  WHERE master.name = "Mei Lanfang"
  RETURN apprentice.artist_id
}
```

In this case, the second `item` in the production of the non-terminal `sql_cond_item` produces the Cypher sub-query. The results of the Cypher sub-query are regarded as a list, which is then utilized to satisfy the `IN` predicate condition.

DML. In addition to analytical query capabilities, ECQL also supports multi-model data manipulation, an important aspect of operating within polystores. ECQL supports single-model data manipulation operations, such as `INSERT`, `UPDATE`, and `DELETE`. These operations are facilitated by treating them as valid sub-queries that can be derived from the non-terminal `sub_expr`. Moreover, ECQL allows the combination of these operations with selection queries for multi-model data. For instance, the cross-model data manipulation query D_2, which aims to delete all artists from the table `artist_info` who are present in the results of R_2, can be expressed as follows:

```
DELETE FROM artist_info
WHERE artist_info.artist_id IN {
  MATCH (master:Artist)-[r:Mentor*]->(apprentice:Artist)
  WHERE master.name = "Mei Lanfang"
  RETURN apprentice.artist_id
}
```

4.2 Parsing ECQL Queries into AQOT

In this subsection, we explain Algorithm 1 that parses an ECQL query into an AQOT, which can serve as the general input of polystore query processors. The procedure takes the root node of an input ECQL abstract syntax tree (AST) $\mathcal{A}$ as input and invokes a recursive function to parse it into an AQOT. The `Parse` function initializes an empty AQOT root node T_{root} (Line 2) and an empty array $\mathcal{H}$ for storing AQOT nodes of different data models (Line 3). The function first infers the data model m of the outer query (Line 5) and tries to parse it in a single-model way (Lines 7–8). If the single-model parsing succeeds, which represents that A is actually a single-model AST, and then the loop is exited (Lines 9–10). Otherwise, there is some sub-query whose data model is different from m. The first AST node $e.A_{err}$ incurring the error is recursively parsed into an AQOT node and saved in $\mathcal{H}$ (Lines 11–12). The function creates a temporary AST node A_{temp}, whose tag is assigned the index of the error node (Lines 13–15). The error node is replaced by A_{temp} in order to modify $\mathcal{A}$ as a single-model

Algorithm 1: ECQL Query Parsing

```
   Input: ECQL abstract syntax tree 𝒜.
   Output: Parsed abstract query operation tree 𝒯.
1  Function Parse(A):
2      T_root ← NULL;
3      ℋ ← Empty array;
4      i ← 1;
5      m ← InferDataModel(A);
6      while TRUE do
7          try:
8              T_root ← ParseWithSingleModel(A, m);
9              T_root.tag ← 0;
10             break
11         catch Exception as e:
12             ℋ[i] ← Parse(e.A_err);
13             A_temp ← TemporaryASTNode(m);
14             A_temp.tag ← i;
15             i ← i + 1;
16             Replace(e.A_err, A_temp);
17         end
18     end
19     for T ∈ T_root.descendants do
20         if T.tag ≠ 0 then Replace(T, ℋ[T.tag]) ;
21     end
22     return T_root;
23 T_root ← Parse(𝒜.root) ;
24 𝒯 ← AQOT(T_root) ;
25 return 𝒯;
```

AST. After the AST root node A is parsed into T_{root}, the multi-model AQOT nodes in $\mathcal{H}$ are replaced back according to their tags (Lines 19–21). The AQOT $\mathcal{T}$ is finally constructed through the root node T_{root} returned from the `Parse` function (Lines 22–24).

Figure 2 shows an example of parsing the ECQL query corresponding to R_2 (using EEI). The `Parse` function first tries parsing the outer query according to SQL's parsing rules until the inner Cypher sub-query is reached. The Cypher sub-query is parsed into a sub-AQOT, illustrated as the dashed box in Fig. 2a. Besides, the `expr` node in the AST is replaced by a temporary node `Scan(#)` as shown in Fig. 2b, which enables the outer query to be parsed. Finally, the `Parse` function replaces the temporary node back with the root node in the graph sub-AQOT to obtain a whole AQOT in Fig. 2a.

5 Experimental Evaluation

To illustrate the succinctness of ECQL, we conduct experiments to evaluate the complexity of queries written in ECQL compared with other multi-model query languages. The results show that ECQL can express the same multi-model analytical query requirements with less effort to design. We present the details of the experiment environments in Subsect. 5.1 and report our evaluation results in Subsect. 5.2. We also study a case in Subsect. 5.3 to demonstrate the extensibility of ECQL.

5.1 Experimental Setup

This subsection explains the evaluation metrics, multi-model languages used for comparison, and polystore benchmarks adopted for evaluation in detail.

Metrics. We measure the volume (V), the difficulty (D), and the effort (E) metrics which are designed to evaluate query complexity [15]. Specifically for a multi-model query, 1) N_1 denotes the total number of multi-model operators, 2) η_1 denotes the number of distinct multi-model operators, 3) N_2 denotes the total number of operands, and 4) η_2 denotes the number of distinct operands. In the polystore scenario, multi-model operators in a multi-model query include the model-specific operators from different data models as well as the inter-model operators such as `CAST` functions. We measure the volume of a query as $V = (N_1 + N_2)\log_2(\eta_1 + \eta_2)$, the difficulty of a query as $D = \frac{\eta_1}{2} \cdot \frac{N_2}{\eta_2}$, and the effort of a query as $E = V \cdot D$. For example, the N_1, η_1, N_2, and η_2 values of ECQL query Q_1 are 28, 17, 13, and 10 respectively. Consequently, Q_1 has the volume value 169.22, the difficulty value 12.27, and the effort value 2077.59 respectively. We also adapt these metrics to the multi-model scenario. Specifically, operators in ECQL queries may share same symbols but belong to different data models. These operators are only considered same if they represent same functionalities. Taking Q_1 as example, the dot (`.`) operators in the inner Cypher sub-query and the outer MQL query are considered same, while the colon (`:`) operators are considered different, since the colon leads a filter predicate in MQL but marks vertex labels in Cypher.

Compared Multi-model Languages. We compare ECQL with two representative multi-model query languages, namely AQL and OrientDB SQL. AQL is the query language of ArangoDB [1]. AQL operates on ArangoDB's own data structure which cooperates both graph and document functionalities. We adopt the AQL grammar based on ArangoDB v3.10. OrientDB [4] designs its own query language (OSQL for short) as an extension of SQL++. OSQL operates on OrientDB's own data structure which cooperates both graph and document functionalities. We adopt the OSQL grammar based on OrientDB v3.2.12.

Benchmarks. We adopt the multi-model query requirements in the UniBench [34,35] polystore benchmark. UniBench is a benchmark for multi-model database systems. It designs ten multi-model analytical query requirements based on the social network scenario. UniBench is used for query processing performance evaluation between ArangoDB and OrientDB. We also take into account the multi-model query requirements shown in Sect. 2 as cases that involve complex single-model query operations. The set of these multi-model query requirements is named *Opera*.

Table 4. Query complexity comparison on UniBench and Opera query requirement sets.

UniBench								
Query Language	# Implemented Queries	Volume		Difficulty		Effort		
		Avg.	Max.	Avg.	Max.	Avg.	Max.	
AQL	10	554	1398	18	34	13272	48200	
OSQL	10	340	697	**13**	30	5989	21082	
ECQL	10	**297**	**409**	15	**22**	**4937**	**9354**	
Opera								
Query Language	# Implemented Queries	Volume		Difficulty		Effort		
		Avg.	Max.	Avg.	Max.	Avg.	Max.	
AQL	5	149	168	8	**9**	1194	**1257**	
OSQL	5	145	169	9	11	1456	1835	
ECQL	6	**104**	**148**	**7**	10	**847**	1486	

5.2 Query Complexity Evaluation Results

We implement the query requirements in UniBench and Opera with ECQL and baseline query languages. Since UniBench is utilized to evaluate ArangoDB and OrientDB, we use the AQL and the OSQL queries provided in their public repositories. We carefully write ECQL queries according to the query requirements.

Table 4 shows the query complexity evaluation results on the query requirements. We record the average and the maximum values of the volume, the difficulty, and the effort among all queries respectively. The results show that ECQL can express all tested multi-model query requirements. Besides, ECQL achieves lowest volume, difficulty, and effort values in average in most cases. The results indicate ECQL achieves succinctness in worst cases. Contrastively, the authoring effort values of AQL and OSQL increase in the situation where intermediate variables are needed.

ECQL also achieves the lowest average volume, difficulty, and effort values on the Opera dataset. AQL has the lowest maximum difficulty benefiting from its `For` loop syntax. AQL and OSQL do not provide a direct way to implement the multi-model query requirement R_1 which involves document element-wise matching queries.

5.3 Case Study

In this subsection, we utilize a case to illustrate the extensibility of ECQL. Specifically, the multi-model data workloads proposed in UniBench involve key-value queries which are not included in ECQL's native grammar. The query below shows an ECQL query corresponding to the multi-model query requirement Q_1 in UniBench workloads. In this query, we integrate a RedisSearch sub-query in the Redis store into ECQL. The sub-query is named with an alias `kv_feedback`.

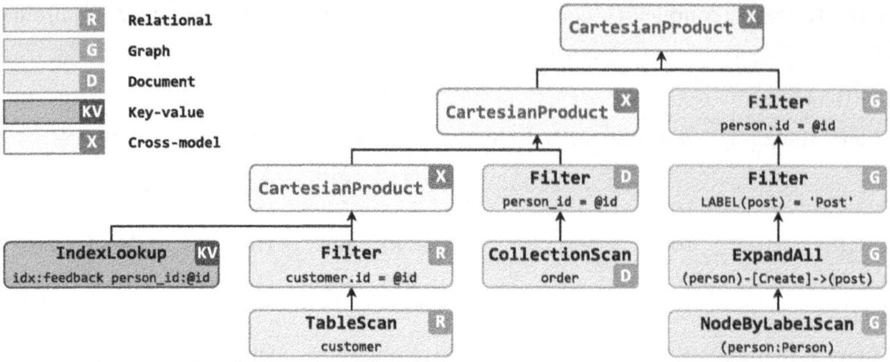

Fig. 5. The AQOT of the ECQL query corresponding to UniBench multi-model query requirement Q_1.

The returned documents can be modeled as a data collection such that the key-value query operations can be integrated into the original AQOT of this query, as illustrated in Fig. 5.

```
SELECT customer.*, order.*, kv_feedback.*, post.*
FROM customer,
  { db.order.find({ person_id: customer.id }) },
  kv_feedback AS { FT.SEARCH idx:feedback "@person_id:[@id]" },
  { MATCH (person:Person)-[:Create]->(post:Post)
    WHERE person.id = customer.id
    RETURN post }
WHERE customer.id = @id
```

6 Related Work

In this section, we briefly review related research efforts on multi-model query languages based on 1) universal data models derived from mathematical theories, 2) unified data structures, and 3) database interfaces.

There are universal data models proposed to represent multiple data types including relational, graph, documents, key-value, array, and so on [21], based on mathematical foundations. Researchers design multi-model query languages that implement these data models. The implementation of D4M [11,19,21] in Julia supports matrix calculation operations and basic relational algebra operations [22], while it lacks support for other data models. The type-safe implementation of TDM [14,24,25] in Scala provides tensor query operators, but does not support complex queries on graph or document data. Uotila et al. propose a query language based on category theory [7,18,30]. However, the proposed query language does not support composite data types including arrays and dictionaries.

Polystores and multi-model databases often develop their own unified data structures to management heterogeneous data. Consequently, they design multi-model query languages based on these data structures. These query languages are widely used in multi-model query representation in polystore evaluation and comparison studies [27,35]. ArangoDB [1] designs ArangoDB Query Language (AQL) that focuses on graph and document queries. However, AQL exhibits limitations in supporting sophisticated graph query operations, such as induced sub-graph search. The SQL++ query language [26] is proposed as an extension of SQL, aiming at a unified query interface for both relational and JSON data types. SQL++ is adopted by several multi-model databases such as OrientDB [4] and AsterixDB [2]. However, the expressiveness of SQL++ falls short in graph traversal queries.

There are also multi-model query languages that merge various single-model query languages through database interfaces. The MyriaL query language for the Myria [17,33] polystore is designed based on relational algebra. MyriaL represents graph traversal operations through a Do-While loop syntax. However, the syntax of MyriaL lacks simplicity compared with graph query languages. The Cloud Multidatastore Query Language (CloudMdsQL) [5,23] is proposed as an interface-based polystore query language, which supports Python UDFs to define sub-queries on relational, graph, document, and key-value data. Consequently, users have to manually implement complicated query operations in UDFs. To the best of our knowledge, the grammatical details of CloudMdsQL are not publically available. ADIL is a domain-specific query language for the AWESOME polystore [8,9]. ADIL provides interfaces for SQL and Cypher as well as text operations, while lacks support for document data models. XDB [12,13] utilizes SQL-like query language that involves relational and key-value database interfaces, but does not support declaration of graph or document operations natively. The query language of Polypheny-DB [31,32] includes the native query languages of the underlying data source, such as HSQLDB [3], Neo4j, MongoDB, and so on. However, the current version of Polypheny-DB does not support cross-model queries which span on different data sources.

ECQL distinguishes from the existing multi-model query languages based on database interfaces by the flexible grammar design. ECQL can be easily extended to include new query languages, which is an essential need in polystore scenario. Besides, ECQL does not require type cast functions between the sub-queries of different query languages.

7 Conclusion and Future Work

Conclusion. This paper proposes ECQL as a holistic representation of multi-model queries. We first propose the AQOT as an abstract representation of multi-model query results. On top of AQOT, we design the grammar of ECQL and the parsing method from an ECQL query into an AQOT. ECQL provides full functionalities of native query operations in different data models, as well as extensibility for integration of new query languages. The evaluation results show the expressiveness and the succinctness of ECQL.

Future Work. It is a challenging task to efficiently process multi-model queries in polystores. Our future work will implement ECQL in polystore query processors and optimize the execution plan based on AQOT holistically. We will further investigate the selection methods for data models under specific workloads to achieve more effective multi-model data management.

Acknowledgements. This work is supported in part by the National Natural Science Foundation of China (No. 62372264) and JD.com Inc. Chaokun Wang is the corresponding author.

References

1. ArangoDB. https://www.arangodb.com. Accessed 30 Aug 2024
2. AsterixDB. https://asterixdb.apache.org. Accessed 30 Aug 2024
3. HSQLDB. https://hsqldb.org. Accessed 30 Aug 2024
4. OrientDB. http://orientdb.org. Accessed 30 Aug 2024
5. Bondiombouy, C., Kolev, B., Levchenko, O., Valduriez, P.: Multistore big data integration with CloudMdsQL. In: Hameurlain, A., Küng, J., Wagner, R., Chen, Q. (eds.) Transactions on Large-Scale Data- and Knowledge-Centered Systems XXVIII. LNCS, vol. 9940, pp. 48–74. Springer, Heidelberg (2016). https://doi.org/10.1007/978-3-662-53455-7_3
6. Chen, A., Edelman, A., Kepner, J., Gadepally, V., Hutchison, D.: Julia implementation of the dynamic distributed dimensional data model. In: 2016 IEEE High Performance Extreme Computing Conference (HPEC), pp. 1–7. IEEE (2016)
7. Čontoš, P.: Abstract model for multi-model data. In: Jensen, C.S., et al. (eds.) DASFAA 2021. LNCS, vol. 12683, pp. 647–651. Springer, Cham (2021). https://doi.org/10.1007/978-3-030-73200-4_53
8. Dasgupta, S., Coakley, K., Gupta, A.: Analytics-driven data ingestion and derivation in the AWESOME polystore. In: 2016 IEEE International Conference on Big Data (Big Data), pp. 2555–2564. IEEE (2016)
9. Dasgupta, S., McKay, C., Gupta, A.: Generating polystore ingestion plans-a demonstration with the AWESOME system. In: 2017 IEEE International Conference on Big Data (Big Data), pp. 3177–3179. IEEE (2017)
10. Duggan, J., et al.: The BigDAWG polystore system. ACM SIGMOD Rec. **44**(2), 11–16 (2015)
11. Gadepally, V., et al.: D4M: bringing associative arrays to database engines. In: 2015 IEEE High Performance Extreme Computing Conference (HPEC), pp. 1–6. IEEE (2015)
12. Gavriilidis, H., Beedkar, K., Quiané-Ruiz, J., Markl, V.: In-situ cross-database query processing. In: 39th IEEE International Conference on Data Engineering, ICDE 2023, pp. 2794–2807. IEEE (2023)
13. Gavriilidis, H., Rose, L., Ziegler, J., Beedkar, K., Quiané-Ruiz, J., Markl, V.: XDB in action: decentralized cross-database query processing for black-box DBMSes. Proc. VLDB Endow. **16**(12), 4078–4081 (2023)
14. Gillet, A., Leclercq, É., Savonnet, M., Cullot, N.: Empowering big data analytics with polystore and strongly typed functional queries. In: IDEAS 2020: 24th International Database Engineering and Applications Symposium, Seoul, 12–14 August 2020, pp. 13:1–13:10. ACM (2020)

15. Glenn, G., Carey, M.J.: Graphix: "One user's JSON is another user's graph". In: 2024 IEEE 40th International Conference on Data Engineering (ICDE). IEEE (2024)
16. Guo, Q., Zhang, C., Zhang, S., Lu, J.: Multi-model query languages: taming the variety of big data. Distrib. Parall. Datab. **42**(1), 31–71 (2024)
17. Halperin, D., et al.: Demonstration of the Myria big data management service. In: Proceedings of the 2014 ACM SIGMOD International Conference on Management of Data, pp. 881–884 (2014)
18. Holubova, I., Contos, P., Svoboda, M.: Categorical management of multi-model data. In: 25th International Database Engineering and Applications Symposium, pp. 134–140 (2021)
19. Jananthan, H., Zhou, Z., Gadepally, V., Hutchison, D., Kim, S., Kepner, J.: Polystore mathematics of relational algebra. In: 2017 IEEE International Conference on Big Data (Big Data), pp. 3180–3189. IEEE (2017)
20. Karimov, J., Rabl, T., Markl, V.: PolyBench: the first benchmark for polystores. In: Nambiar, R., Poess, M. (eds.) TPCTC 2018. LNCS, vol. 11135, pp. 24–41. Springer, Cham (2019). https://doi.org/10.1007/978-3-030-11404-6_3
21. Kepner, J., et al.: Dynamic distributed dimensional data model (D4M) database and computation system. In: 2012 IEEE International Conference on Acoustics, Speech and Signal Processing (ICASSP), pp. 5349–5352. IEEE (2012)
22. Kepner, J., Gilbert, J.: Graph Algorithms in the Language of Linear Algebra. SIAM (2011)
23. Kolev, B., Bondiombouy, C., Valduriez, P., Jiménez-Peris, R., Pau, R., Pereira, J.: The CloudMdsQL multistore system. In: Proceedings of the 2016 International Conference on Management of Data, pp. 2113–2116 (2016)
24. Leclercq, É., Gillet, A., Grison, T., Savonnet, M.: Polystore and tensor data model for logical data independence and impedance mismatch in big data analytics. In: Hameurlain, A., Wagner, R. (eds.) Transactions on Large-Scale Data- and Knowledge-Centered Systems XLII. LNCS, vol. 11860, pp. 51–90. Springer, Heidelberg (2019). https://doi.org/10.1007/978-3-662-60531-8_3
25. Leclercq, E., Savonnet, M.: TDM: a tensor data model for logical data independence in polystore systems. In: Gadepally, V., Mattson, T., Stonebraker, M., Wang, F., Luo, G., Teodoro, G. (eds.) DMAH/Poly -2018. LNCS, vol. 11470, pp. 39–56. Springer, Cham (2019). https://doi.org/10.1007/978-3-030-14177-6_4
26. Ong, K.W., Papakonstantinou, Y., Vernoux, R.: The SQL++ unifying semi-structured query language, and an expressiveness benchmark of SQL-on-Hadoop, NoSQL and NewSQL databases. arXiv preprint arXiv:1405.3631 (2014)
27. Shi, G., Wang, C., Zhang, M., Wang, B.: FONT: a flexible polystore evaluation platform. In: 40th IEEE International Conference on Data Engineering, ICDE 2024, pp. 5489–5492. IEEE (2024)
28. Stonebraker, M., Çetintemel, U.: "One size fits all" An idea whose time has come and gone. In: Making Databases Work: the Pragmatic Wisdom of Michael Stonebraker, pp. 441–462 (2018)
29. Tan, R., Chirkova, R., Gadepally, V., Mattson, T.G.: Enabling query processing across heterogeneous data models: a survey. In: 2017 IEEE International Conference on Big Data (IEEE BigData 2017), Boston, 11–14 December 2017, pp. 3211–3220. IEEE Computer Society (2017)
30. Uotila, V., Lu, J., Gawlick, D., Liu, Z.H., Das, S., Pogossiants, G.: Multi-model query processing meets category theory and functional programming. In: SEA-Data@ VLDB, pp. 48–49 (2021)

31. Vogt, M., et al.: Polypheny-DB: towards bridging the gap between polystores and HTAP systems. In: Gadepally, V., et al. (eds.) DMAH/Poly -2020. LNCS, vol. 12633, pp. 25–36. Springer, Cham (2021). https://doi.org/10.1007/978-3-030-71055-2_2
32. Vogt, M., Stiemer, A., Schuldt, H.: Polypheny-DB: towards a distributed and self-adaptive polystore. In: 2018 IEEE International Conference on Big Data (Big Data), pp. 3364–3373. IEEE (2018)
33. Wang, J., et al.: The Myria big data management and analytics system and cloud services. In: CIDR (2017)
34. Zhang, C., Lu, J.: Holistic evaluation in multi-model databases benchmarking. Distrib. Parall. Datab. **39**(1), 1–33 (2021)
35. Zhang, C., Lu, J., Xu, P., Chen, Y.: UniBench: a benchmark for multi-model database management systems. In: Nambiar, R., Poess, M. (eds.) TPCTC 2018. LNCS, vol. 11135, pp. 7–23. Springer, Cham (2019). https://doi.org/10.1007/978-3-030-11404-6_2

Ontological Modeling

An Analysis of the Semantic Foundation of KerML and SysML v2

João Paulo A. Almeida[1(✉)], Luís Ferreira Pires[2], Giancarlo Guizzardi[2], and Gerd Wagner[3]

[1] Ontology and Conceptual Modeling Research Group (NEMO), Federal University of Espírito Santo (UFES), Vitória, Brazil
jpalmeida@ieee.org

[2] Semantics, Cybersecurity and Services (SCS) Group, University of Twente, Enschede, The Netherlands
{l.ferreirapires,g.guizzardi}@utwente.nl

[3] Institute of Informatics, Brandenburg University of Technology, Cottbus, Germany
wagnerg@b-tu.de

Abstract. In the last decades, Model-Based Systems Engineering (MBSE) has received significant attention, leading to standards such as SysML. SysML is due to a recent and radical update, breaking the dependence of its specification from UML, and leading to the development of two languages: KerML, which provides a top layer of general constructs, and SysML v2, which specializes KerML for systems engineering. In this paper, we analyze the formal and real-world semantics of the proposed KerML and SysML v2 specifications, and draw implications for their improvement and further development. Our attention is focused towards key constructs of the languages. We also examine the approach taken in the specifications to deal with dynamic aspects, which is inspired by the 'four-dimensionalist' view.

Keywords: Model-Based Systems Engineering · Semantics · Foundations · Kernel Modeling Language (KerML) · Systems Modeling Language (SysML) v2

1 Introduction

SysML is a systems modeling language developed in the scope of the Object Management Group (OMG) to facilitate systems engineering. The first major version of the language (SysML v1) [16] was defined as an extension of UML 2 [17] as a profile. This dependence on UML had negative effects on the language because it introduced artificial complexity (for UML compliance). SysML v2 [20] is a major redesign, removing the constraints imposed by UML dependence. SysML v2 also aims to address a significant limitation of SysML v1, namely, that—similarly to UML—it lacks an authoritative commonly accepted formal semantics. This has the consequence that SysML v1 constructs could be interpreted differently by

W. Maass et al. (Eds.): ER 2024, LNCS 15238, pp. 133–151, 2025.
https://doi.org/10.1007/978-3-031-75872-0_8

different people [18], including tool builders, posing a threat to model interoperability and reuse.

SysML v2 is expected to play a central role in Model-Based Systems Engineering (MBSE) by serving as a backbone for the development of digital threads that cover the whole system's lifecycle, from conception (requirements capturing) to operation, possibly including digital twins of the system [22]. In order to fulfill this role, SysML v2 should be able to provide a 'single source of truth' and be based on solid semantic notions, avoiding ambiguity.

In this paper, we investigate how the semantics of SysML v2 is being defined, aiming at assessing its suitability to support model interoperability. Ideally, the semantics definition should enable unambiguous interpretation of SysML v2 models and reliable automated processing. In particular, SysML v2 should be able to support model verification to assess whether the models are valid in accordance with the language rules, model checking to verify properties of the models, simulation, generation of valid instances (universes that are admitted by the models) and possibly code generation in the future.

An integral aspect of the development of SysML v2 is that the language is built as an extension of a more general language called KerML [19]. KerML provides basic (domain-independent) modeling constructs which are reused in the specification of SysML v2. KerML is intended for reuse in other specialized modeling languages in the future, with the ambition to form a family of semantically integrated modeling languages [19]. Hence, the quality of the (semantic) definition of KerML may have consequences reaching beyond SysML v2.

The complexity of the specifications makes our analysis a challenging task. At the time of writing, the main documents specifying KerML [19] and SysML [20] have 407 and 646 pages respectively. The abstract syntax of KerML has 79 classes and that of SysML has 172 classes (based on the present reference implementation in Ecore). Because of this, we focus our attention on key constructs that are required to understand the main design choices in language architecture and semantic foundations. We should also note that the specifications are being finalized at the time of writing, in what OMG calls a Finalization Task Force (FTF). This makes our effort timely, given that there is the possibility of influencing the development of the specifications prior to their main release. Hence, our main contribution is to provide some recommendations and identify alternatives in order to address some issues revealed in the analysis.

The remainder of this paper is structured as follows: Section 2 presents an overview of the KerML/SysML v2 language architecture, introducing the key constructs we analyze; Sect. 3 discusses how the semantics of these constructs is defined; Sect. 4 focuses on how dynamic aspects are represented in the languages, revealing implications of the 'four-dimensionalist' approach adopted; Sect. 5 provides some recommendations based on our analysis; Sect. 6 draws conclusions and outlines future work.

2 KerML/SysML v2 Architecture

SysML v2 has a complex language architecture. Its abstract syntax is defined in a large monolithic MOF metamodel, and two concrete syntaxes are provided: a textual notation (specified with an EBNF grammar) and an accompanying diagrammatic notation. Furthermore, the specification employs more than one strategy with the intent of providing semantics for its constructs. Given this complexity, we focus our attention here on the overall language architecture and on a couple of key constructs which are required to understand how the semantics of SysML v2 is defined, namely the *Classifier* and *Feature* metaclasses of KerML and the *Definition* and *Usage* metaclasses of SysML v2[1] itself. Throughout the paper, we strive to remain faithful to the way in which the languages are presented in the specifications (and indicate explicitly otherwise).

2.1 Overview

SysML v2 is specified as an extension of the *Kernel Modeling Language* (KerML [19]). KerML has been developed to be used as a base language for the definition of other modeling languages and has been specified in three layers:

1. the *Root layer*, which defines the "syntactic foundation" of the language: elements, relationships, dependencies, annotations and namespaces;
2. the *Core layer*, which defines the "semantic foundation" of the language: types, classifiers and features (attributes, parts, actions, etc.);
3. the *Kernel layer*, which defines the remaining elements of the language including classes, data types, structures, behaviors, functions.

In addition, KerML defines model libraries with elements that are to be reused across models. Particularly, the *Semantic Library* is meant to give semantics to the KerML metamodel.

SysML v2 reuses the KerML concepts and extends them to enable a more detailed representation of requirements, structure, and behavior of systems, aiming at supporting various system engineering methods and practices [20]. Similarly to KerML, SysML v2 also defines model libraries: (i) the *Systems Library*, which is intended to give semantics to the Systems metamodel, and (ii) the *Domain Library*, which defines fundamental concepts for systems engineering, such as, e.g., geometry, and quantities and units.

Figure 1 shows the SysML v2 language architecture, with MOF (M2) metamodels at the left-hand side defining the abstract syntax of KerML and SysML, and their instantiations (M1 models) at the right-hand side. KerML defines not only the basic elements of the SysML abstract syntax, but also the SysML (formal) semantics, as we discuss in Sect. 3. In addition to the abstract syntax, both languages are given specialized textual notations, and SysML is also given a diagrammatic notation.

[1] Henceforth, whenever we refer to 'SysML' with no version qualification, we mean SysML v2.

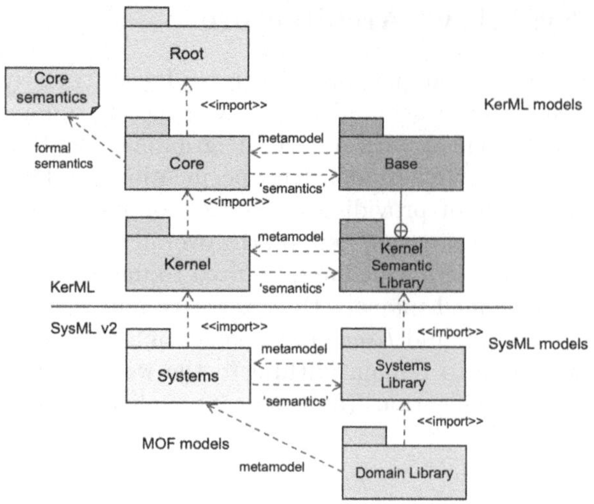

Fig. 1. KerML/SysML v2 language architecture.

2.2 KerML Classifier and Feature

The KerML Root and Core layers contain the basic language constructs necessary to define KerML models. The MOF language metamodel fragment in Fig. 2 shows some of these constructs, starting from `Element`, which represents any element of a model; `Namespace`, which represents containers for elements; and `Type`, which represents types classifying things in the modeled system. `Type` is specialized into `Classifier` and `Feature`, with the latter representing how things are related [19].

Elements in a model may be related through instances of subclasses of the `Relationship` metaclass. We show here only two of those subclasses for the sake of brevity: `Specialization` and `FeatureTyping`. Other relationships (omitted in the diagram) include subsetting and redefinition between features, which are similar to homonymous mechanisms in MOF/UML, as well as disjoining, unioning, intersecting and differencing between types.

`Specialization` relates two types, a *general* one and a *specific* one, requiring "all instances of the specific type to also be instances of the general Type" [19]. `FeatureTyping` is defined as a special kind of `Specialization` in which the specific type is a feature (the `typedFeature`) and, when the general `type` is a classifier, "the `typedFeature` has values that are instances of the Classifier." [19]. (We will turn our attention to this construction later, as we understand it departs from the standard conception for relations and for specialization, making the feature—a relational notion—a specialization of its *co-domain*.)

The KerML specification also defines a concrete textual notation for the language. Listing 1.1 shows a simple example in this notation, defining a classifier `Car` with a feature `driver` typed by `Person`, which relates a car to at most one person as its driver. Feature typing is represented with a colon '`:`', making in this

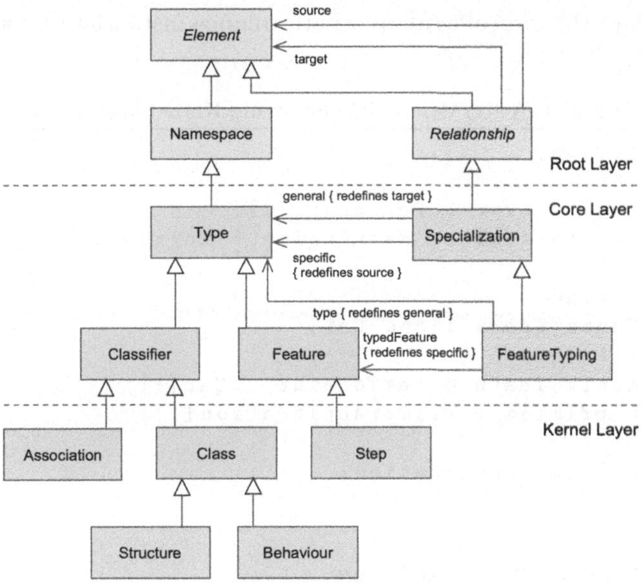

Fig. 2. Some important metaclasses of the KerML MOF metamodel.

case `Car::driver` specialize its range (`Person`). A feature `mainEngine` typed by `Engine` is specified as a 'composite' feature of `Car`. Finally, a classifier `Sedan` is defined to specialize `Car`.

Listing 1.1. A KerML model specifying persons, cars and engines with Core layer constructs.

```
classifier Person;
classifier Car {
    feature driver : Person[0..1];
    composite feature mainEngine : Engine[1];
}
classifier Engine;
classifier Sedan specializes Car;
```

The Core layer constructs are specialized in the Kernel layer (shown in the bottom of Fig. 2), which introduces the following kinds of classifiers: (i) *Classes*, whose instances are 'occurrences' (a semantic notion subsuming 'objects' and 'performances'), (ii) *Structures*, which are classes whose instances are 'objects', (iii) *Behaviors*, which are classes whose instances are 'performances'. A special kind of feature called *Step* is also introduced to model features which are typed by behaviors.

Listing 1.2 revisits Listing 1.1 using some of these Kernel layer constructs. It includes a behavior `PaintJob` that represents the performances which involve the painting of a particular car, including a `priming step`. The keyword `readonly` is used to indicate the **carToPaint** in a performance instantiating **PaintJob** does not change.

Listing 1.2. A KerML model employing Kernel layer constructs.

```
struct Person;
struct Car {
    feature driver : Person[0..1];
    composite feature mainEngine : Engine[1];
}
struct Engine;
struct Sedan specializes Car;
behavior PaintJob {
    readonly feature carToPaint : Car[1];
    step priming : PrimerApplication[1];
}
behavior PrimerApplication;
```

2.3 SysML Definition and Usage

The abstract syntax of SysML has been defined by specializing the KerML metamodel, as shown in Fig. 3 with KerML metaclasses in light blue and SysML metaclasses in light yellow. The **Definition** and **Usage** constructs specialize **Classifier** and **Feature**, respectively, inheriting their semantics. **Definition** and **Usage** are further specialized into **OccurrenceDefinition** and **OccurrenceUsage**, further specialized into **ItemDefinition** and **ItemUsage**, which in its turn is further specialized into **PartDefinition** and **PartUsage**. **OccurrenceDefinition** and **OccurrenceUsage** are also specialized into **ActionDefinition** and **ActionUsage**.

The concrete textual notation for SysML, although bearing some similarity with that of KerML, is fully redefined in the SysML specification. Listing 1.3 revisits the example in Listing 1.1 now with a SysML model. Differently from KerML, SysML also has a diagrammatic notation, but, given our focus on the semantic aspects of the language, we omit this diagrammatic notation in this paper for the sake of brevity. In Listing 1.3, **Person**, **Car**, **Engine** and **Sedan** are specified as *part definitions*. The term 'part' may sound strange when applied to persons and drivers. However, in SysML v2, the term is applied to all modular units of structure (previously called 'blocks' in SysML v1), regardless of whether they play a role in a parthood relation that is explicitly modeled. A car is related to a person through the *part usage* **driver**. Since the person is not a part of the car, it must be modeled as a *referential part usage*, indicated with the keywords **ref part**. The engine is also related to the car through a part usage, but in this case the engine is an actual part of the car and it was therefore described as a *composite part usage*, indicated simply with the keyword **part** (denoting a part usage, by default).

An *action definition* **PaintJob** is introduced with keyword **action def**. It includes a 'parameter' **carToPaint** of type **Car** with direction 'inout' and an

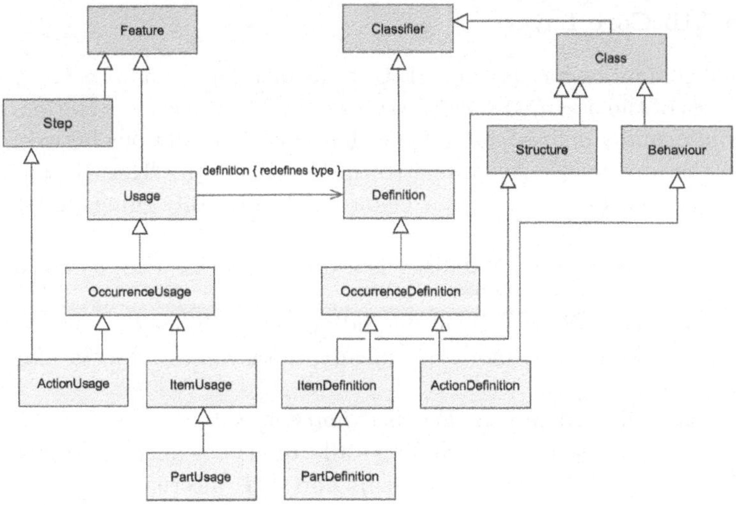

Fig. 3. Specialization of KerML metaclasses for definitions and usages in SysML.

action usage `priming`, with keyword `action`. Definitions and usages are defined for other concepts such as individuals, ports, connections, interfaces, control nodes, states, transitions, etc., so it is a predominant recurring pattern in the design of SysML.

Listing 1.3. A SysML v2 model specifying persons, cars, engines and paint jobs.

```
part def Person;
part def Car {
        ref part driver : Person [0..1];
        part engine : Engine[1];
}
part def Engine;
part def Sedan specializes Car;
action def PaintJob {
    inout carToPaint : Car;
    action priming : PrimerApplication[1];
}
action def PrimerApplication;
```

3 Semantics

A formal semantics, in the spirit of Tarski's model-theoretic semantics for predicate logic, is only defined for the KerML Core layer, discussed below. Furthermore, a model library written in KerML itself (the *Kernel Semantic Library*) is employed to provide semantics to the elements of the KerML Kernel layer. This library is then further specialized in the SysML *Systems Library*, adding system engineering-specific notions.

3.1 KerML Core Layer

The formal semantics for the KerML Core layer refers to a *vocabulary* provided by the names of the *classifiers* and *features* defined as *types* in a KerML model. A feature is informally defined as "a Type that classifies relations between multiple things (in the universe)". According to the specification, "KerML semantics are based on classification: a model has elements that classify things in the modeled system."

An *interpretation* of a vocabulary is a quadruple $\langle \Delta, P, S, I \rangle$ consisting of[2]:

1. a *universe* Δ containing "all actual and potential things the vocabulary could possibly be about" (or, more specifically, data values, objects, links, performances, etc.);
2. a strict partially ordered set P called *marking set*;
3. a set S of *sequences* including all unary sequences (consisting of a single element of the universe) and all alternating sequences like (d_1, p_1, d_2), $(d_1, p_1, d_2, p_2, d_3), \ldots$, where $d_i \in \Delta$ and $p_i \in P$;
4. an *interpretation function* I that maps each classifier and feature name of the vocabulary to a subset of S.

Consider the KerML model in Listing 1.1 defining the classifiers `Car` and `Person`, as well as the features `driver` and `mainEngine`. Imagine a situation with two persons (John and Mary), two cars (car1 and car2) and two engines (e1 and e1) such that car1 is driven by John, car2 does not have a driver, Mary is not driving any car, car1 has e1 as its main engine, and car2 has e2. Then, sequences like (john), (mary), (car1), (car2), (e1), (e2), (car1, p1, john), (car1, p2, e1), (car2, p3, e2) would be required in set of sequences S for the interpretation of `Car`, `Person`, `driver` and `mainEngine`.

Marking elements (p1, p2, p3, etc.) separate elements of the universe in sequences like (car1, p1, john) and are used to account for features that are 'non-unique' or 'ordered'. For non-unique features, the same pair of elements is separated with different markings, and hence the collection of entities in the feature's range for a particular entity of the domain can be conceived as a bag/-multiset. For ordered features, the markings used form a total order, such that the collection of entities in the feature's range for a particular entity of the domain can be conceived as a sequence.

The core semantics provides rules to interpret: the predefined top-level classifier `Anything`, which is present in all models and subsumes all other classifiers in the model, and the predefined top-level feature `things`, also present in all models, subsuming all other features; specialization between types; disjoining between types, when the interpretation of two types has no intersection; feature typing, where a feature is given a 'featuring type' corresponding to the domain, and a 'type', corresponding to the co-domain; feature redefinition, multiplicity, uniqueness, ordering, inverting and chaining.

---

[2] We deviate slightly from the specification here in an attempt to clarify the formal model structure, but this deviation is not substantive.

The semantics is defined in such a way that the interpretation function in our example would map `Car` to {(car1), (car2)}, `driver` to {(car1, p1, john)}, `mainEngine` to {(car1, p2, e1), (car2, p3, e2)} and `Person` to {(john), (mary), (car1, p1, john)} and `Engine` to {(e1), (e2), (car1, p2, e1), (car2, p3, e2)}. Note that all sequences in the interpretation of a feature are also included in the interpretation of the 'type' (or co-domain) of the feature, therefore, all sequences ending with a person, like (car1, p1, john), are included in the interpretation of `Person`, and all those ending with an engine, like {(car1, p2, e1), (car2, p3, e2)}, are included in the interpretation of `Engine`.

Discussion. KerML's model-theoretic semantics departs from the standard model-theoretic semantics for structural modeling languages such as RDF(s) [11], OWL [15], and Alloy [12], as well as from formalizations of UML class and ER diagrams in the following way:

1. In addition to a *universe* Δ, interpretations also include a *marking set* and the set of all *sequences* S formed with elements of Δ and of the marking set, to allow for non-unique and ordered features.
2. While in standard model-theoretic semantics unary and binary predicates (such as classes and properties) are interpreted as subsets of Δ and of $\Delta \times \Delta$, in KerML they are interpreted as special subsets of S.
3. Due to its peculiar *FeatureTyping* construct, in KerML, the interpretation of classifiers unusually also contains non-unary sequences.

Concerning the latter point, we believe it results from semantic overload, as the specification seems to conflate in features the notions of: (1) a *relation* between entities (car 'has main engine', 'has wheel'); (2) the *related entity* for a given entity of the domain (a car's 'mainEngine') or *the collection of related entities* (a car's 'wheels', each of which instantiates 'Wheel'); (3) a *function* that produces the related entity or collection; and, (4) the *type that an entity instantiates when in a relation* ('Main Engine', 'Attached Wheel', which in fact specialize 'Engine' and 'Wheel' respectively).

The specification of KerML seems to switch between each of these interpretations indistinctly, for various purposes. For example, to discuss the *specialization of features by other features (Subsetting)*, features are treated as relations (following sense (1) above), with the sequences in the extension of the specializing/subsetting feature included in the extension of the specialized feature.

To discuss the *multiplicity of features*, it becomes necessary to talk about the cardinality of the collection of related entities (in sense (2) above), such as the wheels of a particular car. The same is required to make sense of the *ordering of features*: what is *ordered* is the collection of "values of a feature for a given instance of its domain". We have observed that appeal to the notion of "value" or "values" of a feature is common throughout the specification.

The choice for semantics of features (as specializing classifiers) has the consequence that, while features are defined in the scope of their domain (e.g., `driver` as a feature of `Car` in Listing 1.1), they do not change the extension of their domain (`Car`), but rather the extension of their co-domain (in this example, `Person`). Consider the case of mandatory features (such as `mainEngine` in our example). The presence of this feature requires every car to have a main engine. This effectively changes the intension of `Car`, since now engineless cars are ruled out from the interpretation. However, formally in the proposed semantics, it is the extension of `Engine` that changes as a result, even if it is only optional for an engine to be part of a car.

In our view, it is the type that an entity of the co-domain instantiates when in a relation (in sense (4) above, such as 'Main Engine') that is a *bona fide* specialization of the 'featuring type' (such as 'Engine'). This corresponds to what is termed a 'role' in ontology-driven conceptual modeling [8].

There seems to be another issue with the semantics of features involving *FeatureTyping*, which concerns its interpretation when the general type is itself a feature. How would this interpretation be different from that of a *Subsetting* with the same general and specific features?

While features are given a formal semantics based on tuples, and hence most aligned with sense (1) above, the examples in the specification do not adopt relational terminology which is typically based on verbs (such as 'has driver', 'is married with', 'has engine', etc.), opting consistently instead for nouns written in lower case for features ('driver', 'spouse', 'engine')—suggesting sense (2) discussed above and corresponding to what is called *role name* in UML [17]. In the case of features with multiplicity upper bound greater than one, the specification uses nouns in the plural, e.g., 'wheels' of a car. In this case 'wheels' in the plural would specialize 'Wheel'. This convention does not match the 'is a' verbalization for specializations, i.e., 'wheels is a Wheel' does not parse.

Limitations of the Core Semantics. The semantics of type union, intersection and difference are not defined at present, although we expect that to be a relatively easy fix. The semantics for 'abstract' types (classifiers and features) is not provided either, and would likely require a more involved solution. It is not clear whether coextensional types, i.e., types that have the same extension, are considered identical, as there is no notion of type identity in the specification.

Some properties of features such as 'directionality' (in, out, inout) are discussed informally in the text, but not given a formal semantics, and would certainly require more involved structures in the formalization, as they evoke notions of 'externality' to an instance. The same can be said of the notion of *conjugation of types*, in which a "type inherits visible and protected memberships from the original type, except the direction of input and output features is reversed".

The `all` qualifier for types determines that a type includes in its definition not only the necessary conditions for type application (the default interpretation) but also the sufficient conditions; no formal semantics is provided for the corresponding metaproperty of type (`isSufficient`).

Mereological qualifiers for features such as `composite` and `portion` are only defined informally, along with `end` qualifiers and visibility qualifiers (`public`, `private`, `protected`). This means that the semantics is largely underspecified; nothing is present in the formal structure to guarantee the informal interpretation provided for these notions is respected. For example, nothing would prevent an entity from being a `composite` part of itself, or to enforce that "the values of the [composite] Feature cannot exist after its featuring instance no longer does" as required in the specification.

Finally, there is an issue concerning 'variation' of the extent of classifiers and features in time. The interpretation function maps a vocabulary element to a fixed set of entities in the universe. Hence, it cannot account for change in the population of classifiers or in features. This makes it impossible to distinguish `readonly` features from features that are not thus qualified (and that could change in time), such as `driver` in our example. Considering the current specification, all possible tuples involving cars and drivers would be in the interpretation of `driver`. This poses a challenge for the semantics of multiplicities for non-read-only features in the present specification.

No validation and verification efforts for the formalization are reported. As far as we are aware, the formalization does not support the verification and validation of properties of models expressed in the language. A machine-readable version of the Core semantics is not made available.

3.2 Kernel Model 'Semantic' Library

The 'Core layer' whose semantics was reviewed in the previous section is specialized by a 'Kernel layer'. This layer introduces the following metaclasses specializing the (Core layer) `Classifier` metaclass: `Class`, `Datatype`, `Structure`, `Behavior` and `Association`. The specification defines rules for these metaclasses such that their instances in a KerML model are required to specialize certain elements of the Kernel Semantic Library. For example, all *structures* (such as `Car` in Listing 1.2) specialize the `Object` top-level structure in the Kernel Semantic Library, either with explicit specialization declarations or implicitly by default. All *behaviors* (such as `PaintJob` in Listing 1.2) specialize the `Performance` top-level behavior in the Kernel Semantic Library. All *datatypes* specialize `DataValue`, all *classes* specialize `Occurrence` and all *associations* specialize `Link`. We omit the treatment of associations further in this paper, noting solely that there is some semantic overlap with features.

The Kernel Semantic Library is written in KerML itself, using also constructs from the Kernel layer. A fragment of the library is shown in Listing 1.4, which omits package structures and features for brevity. The library defines a taxonomy for all entities in the model's semantic domain. The top-level classifier `Anything` is included explicitly, and is then specialized into `Datavalue`, `Occurrence` and `Link`. `Datavalue` is the top-level *datatype*, `Occurrence` the top-level *class*, and `Link` the top-level *association*. `Occurrence` is specialized into `Object` and `Performance`, where performances are disjoint from objects. All of these types are declared `abstract`, revealing the intention that they should be further specialized in KerML models.

Listing 1.4. A fragment of the Kernel Semantic Library in KerML

```
abstract classifier Anything;
abstract datatype DataValue specializes Anything;
abstract class Occurrence specializes Anything
                          disjoint from DataValue;
abstract assoc Link specializes Anything;
abstract struct Object specializes Occurrence;
abstract behavior Performance specializes Occurrence
                          disjoint from Object;
```

Most of the content of the Kernel Semantic Library is in the form of taxonomic constraints, more specifically specialization and disjoining declarations as seen in the listing above, as well as feature typing. A few classes have redefinitions for features of their supertypes in order to determine specific admissible values. For example, the *struct* `Body` is defined as a specialization of `Object` with feature `innerSpaceDimension=3` (a feature defined originally for `Occurrence` that represents "the number of variables needed to identify space points in this Occurrence" [19]). Some elements in the Kernel Semantic Library are given invariants (presently 46 invariants in total) written in an expression language that is also part of the Kernel layer. Some elements are given so-called 'binding connectors' which "require their source and target features to have the same values on each instance of their domain." This is a simplified form of invariant specification, and there are presently 21 of such invariants in the library.

Limitations of the Kernel Semantics. The semantics of the expression language is only defined informally. This means ultimately that the formal semantic content of a KerML model is constricted to: (i) what is represented with the use of constructs that specialize the Core layer fragment as discussed in the previous sub-section (specialization and disjoining between types, feature typing, multiplicity, redefinition, uniqueness, ordering, inverting and chaining), and (ii) what is inherited from the elements of the Kernel Semantic Library that use the formalized Core layer constructs, e.g., that all *structs* are disjoint from *behaviors* that all *behaviors* are disjoint from *datatypes.* A consequence of this is that the semantics of KerML is largely underspecified.

We have observed that the mapping of constructs of the expression language to the formal mathematical structure of the Core is unclear, due to the choices concerning the interpretation function (to have tuples in the interpretation of classifiers). For example, consider the case of an 'extent expression' in the expression language that is introduced with the unary `all` operator that takes a type as argument (as in `all Person`). It is defined as evaluating "to a sequence of all instances of the named type." If we are to follow the formal interpretation, in the case of classifiers, these would include not only sequences of one element (such as (john) and (mary)), but also sequences in the interpretation of features typed by the classifier (such as (car1, p1, john)). This is most likely not the intended semantics for the expression language. Further, what would happen if an extent expression is applied to a feature? What would count as an 'instance' of the feature? According to the formal interpretation function, these would be tuples (or even sequences with markings). We believe informal expressions such as 'instances of a type' in the specification do not correspond to the entities in the co-domain of the corresponding interpretation function. This creates a barrier for the precise interpretation of natural language statements that employ the term 'instances' throughout the text.

3.3 SysML Systems Library

The semantics of KerML is inherited by SysML as its abstract syntax is defined by specializing the KerML MOF metamodel. SysML *definitions* are KerML *classifiers* and SysML *usages* are KerML *features*. The SysML System Library extends the KerML Kernel Semantic Library, with the abstract item definition `Item` specializing Kernel System Library's `Object` and abstract action definition `Action` specializing `Performance`. A fragment of the Systems Library, which is specified in SysML itself is shown in Listing 1.5; again, we omit package structures and features for brevity.

Listing 1.5. A fragment of the System Library in SysML

```
// Object, Performance imported from
// KerML Kernel Semantic Library
abstract item def Item specializes Object;
abstract part def Part specializes Item;
abstract action def Action specializes Performance;
```

The specification defines rules for the SysML metaclasses, such that instances of `ItemDefinition` specialize `Item`, instances of `PartDefinition` specialize `Part`, and instances of `ActionDefinition` specialize `Action`. The KerML expression language is reused in SysML; in the Systems Library, it is used for a few assertions (5 in total).

4 Time Matters

As discussed above, KerML introduces the notion of *occurrence* in order to generalize both *objects* and *performances*. While we would normally say that *objects exist* and *performances happen*, the specification defines occurrences as "things existing in space and time" [19, 9.2.4.1], and also as anything that "happens over time and space" [19, 9.2.4.2.13]. There is no clear commitment to a particular foundational ontology in the specification, but the foundational choices can be traced back to the work of some of the contributors of the specification. More specifically, in [1], Bock and Galey (henceforth, B&G) explicitly position their contribution in the camp of "four-dimensional ontology". In this section, we briefly position the four-dimensionalist and three-dimensionalist views in the philosophical literature in order to analyse the foundations of KerML/SysML v2 from the perspective of temporal ontology.

In the philosophical literature, the distinction between objects (also called continuants or endurants), on one hand, and occurrences (also called perdurants, happenings, events), on the other, is a hallmark of what is called a *three-dimensionalist (3D) view*. A 3D framework typically distinguishes *abstract* and *concrete* individuals, with the former being outside space and time, and the latter having a spatiotemporal existence. Concrete individuals are them normally specialized into objects and occurrences. Objects *exist* in time with all their parts and can change qualitatively while maintaining their identity, provided that certain *essential* properties (including essential parts) are preserved. Occurrences, in contrast, *happen* in time, being composed of temporal parts. Objects participate in occurrences, and the latter *are the changes* that happen to these objects. For example, a particular person, say John, can undergo several qualitative changes throughout his life including changes in mass, height, a tragic loss of a limb, etc. However, it is the very same individual that remains the same across these changes.

In contrast, in a *four-dimensionalist (4D)* view (aka'perdurantist' view) [10], one aims at unifying (what we would ordinarily perceive as) objects as well as performances as four-dimensional entities, also termed 'space-time worms' in the philosophical literature. In this view, all concrete individuals can be 'sliced' into 'portions' in time, i.e., they have temporal parts. A defining feature of the four-dimensional approach, as opposed to the three-dimensional approach, is that there is no genuine change in entities: instead, they have temporal parts with different properties. Consider an example in which a car (car_1) is initially painted red. Later, the owner of car_1 decides to paint it black. What is the color of car_1 in the four-dimensional account? In that view, car_1 does not have a single color; instead, its temporal slices, say car_1*BeforePaintJob* and car_1*AfterPaintJob*, which are temporal parts of car_1, exhibit different properties; the color of car_1*BeforePaintJob* is red, and the color of car_1*AfterPaintJob* is black. This leads to a massive multiplication of entities in the face of changes [25]. Furthermore, all occurrences (not only performances) are "frozen" in the time interval they occupy, i.e., they cannot be different from what they are in any aspect (a notion termed *modal fragility*) and, hence, all their parts and all their properties are essential. So, although different temporal slices of the same occurrence can exhibit different properties, the set of time slices composing an occurrence is fixed. This is because occurrences only exist in the past, i.e., technically speaking, there are neither future nor ongoing occurrences [4, 9][3].

Despite being centered around this notion of occurrence, B&G are never clear on what is exactly meant by an occurrence there (and the same applies to the specifications). At first, the reader has the impression that their main interest is on dealing uniformly with entities that exist in time (i.e., a notion of *concrete individual* mentioned above, which is not an exclusive feature of a 4D view). But do they mean by occurrences really occurrences in an ontological sense,

[3] An exception comes from very recent work in formal ontology [6] that proposes a special category of occurrences to deal with *ongoing-ness* and possible temporal change of occurrences.

i.e., perdurants? If so, what exactly is the theory of occurrences adopted? What is the mereological theory adopted for connecting occurrences to their parts? Does their 4D approach depart from a classical theory of occurrences and allow ongoing, future, possibly changing occurrences?

Adopting a truly 4D approach has its ontological and conceptual costs. For starters, there are several mature 3D frameworks [2,8,21], some of which have been successfully employed to ground conceptual modeling languages (e.g., [8]). Additionally, there is evidence that 3D approaches are pragmatically more efficient than their 4D counterparts in supporting the users of models in problem-solving tasks [24]. The authors seem to brush off these difficulties by proposing to hide the ontological complexity of the framework behind a 3D terminology and way of speaking, while claiming that users could be shielded from that complexity by the development of sophisticated tools. It is not presently clear how this can be achieved; for example, how would occurrences in a 4D approach have mutable (non-readonly) features? Even if mutable features were given a formal semantics in the KerML Core, they would remain in principle inconsistent with the 4D approach. The adoption of a 4D approach should be carefully and explicitly motivated, as well as fully developed, as it has far reaching (and often subtle) consequences. For example, the 4D approach taken in the Kernel causes havoc on the Core notion of multiplicity for classes and features. This is because it requires that portions "must be classified the same way as the Occurrences they are portionsOf." Therefore the extent of a *Class* always includes all portions of instances of that Class.

The specification leaves open several questions regarding occurrences and their parts. We will address two of these here. Firstly, the difference between objects and performances is made in the following way: objects are "occurrences that take up a single region of time and space"; performances are "occurrences that can be spread out in disconnected portions of space and time". However, the distinction as such is not adequate, as there are scattered objects (e.g., ranging from bikinis to archipelagos and constellations), which break that rule. Secondly, the authors are not clear about which kind of mereology is adopted for relating occurrences and their parts. Typically, perdurants follow what is called an extensional mereology: a partial-order relation plus the *weak supplementation* axiom (if an occurrence x has a proper part y then there is at least another part z of x that is disjoint from y), as well as the extensionality axiom (two occurrences are the same iff they have the same parts). On top of that, object parthood also requires some modal mereological notions to distinguish between optional parts (e.g., the radio on a car), mandatory parts (e.g., the engine – which is necessary but replaceable by other engines), and essential parts (e.g., the chassis – which is both necessary and irreplaceable). Despite the importance of parts and their composition in systems engineering, it is unclear how these mereological issues would be treated in B&G's framework and in the KerML/SysML v2 specifications.

5 Recommendations

In this section, we provide some recommendations considering the issues we have identified in this paper, covering the language's semantic definition and treatment of temporal aspects/variation in time. We also identify opportunities to improve on the choice of terminology employed in KerML and SysML v2.

Semantics of the Core Layer. There are a number of constructs in the Core layer that have not yet been given a formal semantics. So, either a more comprehensive semantic definition or a simplification of the Core layer constructs is required. A more comprehensive semantic definition following the current choice of Core layer constructs seems a daunting task, given that it would require an account of directionality of features (in, out, inout), variation of features in time (readonly versus non-readonly), mereology of features (composite vs. portion features), among others. We believe a simplification of the Core layer would be desirable. A formalization of the semantics of the expression language (currently part of the Kernel layer) would be required to establish a minimal formal basis to be explored further in the semantic libraries.

Formal Semantics for Features. As we have discussed in Sect. 3.1, there are some negative consequences of the present treatment of features, with tuples included in the interpretation of classifiers. We hold that maintaining the standard separation between monadic and relational types would simplify and clarify the semantic definition. This move would only require to revise the conceptualization of *FeatureTyping* moving away from its current definition as a form of *Specialization*. Whenever a contextualized specialization of a type is required, roles can be employed, in line with ontology-driven conceptual modeling [7]. Alignment with a more standard treatment of relations/properties could contribute to providing a translation of Core layer constructs into existing formal languages for automated processing, such as OWL [15], Alloy [12] and the TPTP First-Order Logics (FOL) syntax [23].

Time Matters. We would recommend factoring out of the Core layer all considerations of temporal ontology. This would simplify the Core's formal semantics, and, importantly, free language designers reusing KerML from the commitment to a 4D ontology, which has far-reaching consequences for the models produced. Libraries adopting either a 3D or a 4D approach would be able to adopt KerML, contributing to realizing its ambition of forming a family of semantically integrated modeling languages. Also in this case, factoring out of the Core layer considerations of temporal ontology simplifies the formalization, and enables a simpler transformation to languages which do not have a native treatment of time or modality (such as OWL and TPTP FOL).

Terminology Matters. A revision of terminological choices is also warranted to make the semantics of the various constructs more transparent. Consider the following set of key constructs in the metamodel that are related by specialization: (a) an *ActionUsage* is a *Step* which is a *Feature*; and (b) a *PartDefinition* is a *Structure* which is a *Class*. There are two choices which obscure both taxonomies (a) and (b): first, the shifts between KerML *Classifier* and *Definition* to SysML *Feature* and *Usage*; and, second, the dropping of general *Class* and *Feature* terminology which occurs in the KerML Kernel layer. Using modifiers could improve ease of use of the standard by making sure the inherited semantics of the constructs becomes transparent from their labels. This could lead to revisited taxonomies such as (a) *ActionFeature*, *BehavioralFeature* and *Feature*; (b) *PartClass*, *ObjectClass*, and *Class*. In this proposal, *ObjectClass* would replace the opaque term *Structure*, appealing to the notion of 'object' which is key to understand the semantics of the construct. Likewise, *PerformanceClass* would clarify the semantics for *Behavior*, also revealing the 'object'–'performance' semantic dichotomy. We observe further that the problems in the taxonomies are compounded with the use of words which have a relational connotation (such as 'part') for non-relational notions. Given the focus of the language on systems modeling, term 'part' could easily be switched for the more accurate term 'system'. So, taxonomy (b) would read *SystemClass*, *ObjectClass*, and *Class*. These revised choices consistently improve the similarity between the labels of metaclasses in each taxonomy. We have used LLM embeddings (of OpenAI's `text-embedding-3-large` model) to assess the cosine similarity in the original and in the recommended metaclass taxonomy labels. For taxonomy (a), we have an improvement of similarities from 0.34 ('action usage'–'step') to 0.48 ('action feature'–'behavioral feature'), and from 0.43 ('step'–'feature') to 0.54 ('behavioral feature'–'feature'). For taxonomy (b), we have an improvement of similarities from 0.33 ('part definition'–'structure') to 0.58 ('system class'–'object class'), and from 0.42 ('structure'–'class') to 0.59 ('object class'–'class').

6 Final Considerations

In this paper, we have studied central aspects of the semantic foundation proposed for KerML and SysML v2. We have observed that there are a number of aspects that deserve improvement and proposed recommendations which can be summarized as follows. First, we propose a complete formalization should be provided for the Core layer semantics, preferably in a standard technique; we believe this can be achieved by simplifying the layer's constructs and by revising the formal structure for the interpretation of features. Second, we propose all temporal ontology matters to be factored out of the Core layer; the Core layer then becomes reusable in 3D and 4D approaches. This is particularly important given the conceptual objections to the 4D approach and the empirical evidence of its cognitive cost for users [24]. Third, we propose terminological choices which have the potential to improve semantic transparency of the constructs.

Concerning related work focusing on SysML v2, Jansen et al. [13] have performed an assessment of how the language adheres to some general language engineering guidelines and best practices. They have emphasized the need for SysML v2 to be given a formal semantics, which was not available at the time the paper was published (2022). Given the evolution of the specification, our work complements the analysis they have performed, now with an in-depth perspective on the language's proposed semantic definition. Although there have been a number of efforts to provide a formal semantics for SysML v1 [3,5,14], we are unaware of other efforts devoted to the semantics of the current KerML/SysML v2 specifications.

Further work is required in order to study the behavioral aspects of KerML/SysML v2 in detail. This requires delving into the Kernel Semantic Library and into the Systems Library. Given the complexity of these libraries, we believe a reconstruction of key parts of this library in a technique amenable to automated processing is required to make sense of the implications of the library contents.

Acknowledgments. This study was financed in part by the Coordenação de Aperfeiçoamento de Pessoal de Nível Superior - Brasil (CAPES) - Finance Code 001, CNPq (443130/2023-0, 313412/2023-5) and FAPES (2021-GL60J, 2022-NGKM5, 1022/2022). We would like to thank Jim Logan and Ed Seidewitz who provided us with some clarifications during the writing of this paper. Any errors or omissions are ours alone.

References

1. Bock, C., Galey, C.: Integrating four-dimensional ontology and systems requirements modelling. J. Eng. Des. **30**(10–12), 477–522 (2019). https://doi.org/10.1080/09544828.2019.1642461
2. Borgo, S., et al.: DOLCE: a descriptive ontology for linguistic and cognitive engineering. Appl. Ontol. **17**(1), 45–69 (2022). https://doi.org/10.3233/ao-210259
3. Bougacha, R., Laleau, R., Collart-Dutilleul, S., Ayed, R.B.: Extending SysML with refinement and decomposition mechanisms to generate Event-B specifications. In: Theoretical Aspects of Software Engineering, pp. 256–273. Springer, Cham (2022). https://doi.org/10.1007/978-3-031-10363-6_18
4. Diekemper, J.: The existence of the past. Synthese **191**(6), 1085–1104 (2014). https://doi.org/10.1007/s11229-013-0311-3
5. Graves, H., Bijan, Y.: Using formal methods with SysML in aerospace design and engineering. Ann. Math. Artif. Intell. **63**(1), 53–102 (2011). https://doi.org/10.1007/s10472-011-9267-5
6. Guarino, N., Guizzardi, G.: Processes as variable embodiments. Synthese **203**(4) (2024). https://doi.org/10.1007/s11229-024-04505-2
7. Guizzardi, G., Fonseca, C.M., Benevides, A.B., Almeida, J.P.A., Porello, D., Sales, T.P.: Endurant types in ontology-driven conceptual modeling: yowards OntoUML 2.0. In: Trujillo, J.C., et al. (eds.) ER 2018. LNCS, vol. 11157, pp. 136–150. Springer, Cham (2018). https://doi.org/10.1007/978-3-030-00847-5_12
8. Guizzardi, G., Botti Benevides, A., Fonseca, C.M., Porello, D., Almeida, J.P.A., Sales, T.P.: UFO: unified foundational ontology. Appl. Ontol. **17**(1), 167–210 (2022). https://doi.org/10.3233/AO-210256
9. Guizzardi, G., Guarino, N., Almeida, J.P.A.: Ontological considerations about the representation of events and endurants in business models. In: La Rosa, M., Loos,

P., Pastor, O. (eds.) BPM 2016. LNCS, vol. 9850, pp. 20–36. Springer, Cham (2016). https://doi.org/10.1007/978-3-319-45348-4_2
10. Hawley, K.: Temporal parts. In: Zalta, E.N., Nodelman, U. (eds.) The Stanford Encyclopedia of Philosophy, Spring 2023 edn. Metaphysics Research Lab, Stanford University (2023). https://plato.stanford.edu/archives/spr2023/entries/temporal-parts/
11. Hayes, P.J., Patel-Schneider, P.F.: RDF 1.1 Semantics W3C Recommendation 25 February 2014 (2014). https://www.w3.org/TR/rdf11-mt/
12. Jackson, D.: Software Abstractions: Logic, Language, and Analysis. MIT Press (2012)
13. Jansen, N., Pfeiffer, J., Rumpe, B., Schmalzing, D., Wortmann, A.: The language of SysML v2 under the magnifying glass. J. Object Technol. **21**(3), 3–1 (2022). https://doi.org/10.5381/jot.2022.21.3.a11
14. Lima, L., et al.: An integrated semantics for reasoning about SysML design models using refinement. Softw. Syst. Model. **16**(3), 875–902 (2015). https://doi.org/10.1007/s10270-015-0492-y
15. Motik, B., Patel-Schneider, P.F., Grau, B.C.: OWL 2 Web Ontology Language Direct Semantics (Second Edition) W3C Recommendation 11 December 2012 (2012). https://www.w3.org/TR/owl2-direct-semantics/
16. Object Management Group. OMG Systems Modeling Language (SysML) Version 1.5 (2017). https://www.omg.org/spec/SysML/1.5
17. Object Management Group: OMG Unified Modeling Language (OMG UML) Version 2.5.1 (2017). https://www.omg.org/spec/UML/2.5.1. OMG formal/17-12-05
18. Object Management Group. Systems Modeling Language (SysML) v2 Request for Proposal (RFP) (2017). https://www.omg.org/cgi-bin/doc.cgi?ad/2017-12-2. OMG RFP ad/17-12-02
19. Object Management Group. Kernel Modeling Language (KerML) version 1.0 beta 2 (release 2024-03) (2024). https://github.com/Systems-Modeling/SysML-v2-Release
20. Object Management Group. OMG Systems Modeling Language (SysML) Version 2.0 Beta 2 (Release 2024-03) (2024). https://github.com/Systems-Modeling/SysML-v2-Release
21. Otte, J.N., Beverley, J., Ruttenberg, A.: BFO: basic formal ontology. Appl. Ontol. **17**(1), 17–43 (2022). https://doi.org/10.3233/ao-220262
22. Pessoa, M.V.P., Pires, L.F., Moreira, J.L.R., Wu, C.: Model-based digital threads for socio-technical systems. In: Marques, G., González-Briones, A., Molina López, J.M. (eds.) Machine Learning for Smart Environments/Cities. ISRL, vol. 121, pp. 27–52. Springer, Cham (2022). https://doi.org/10.1007/978-3-030-97516-6_2
23. Sutcliffe, G.: The TPTP problem library and associated infrastructure. From CNF to TH0, TPTP v6.4.0. J. Automat. Reason. **59**(4), 483–502 (2017). https://doi.org/10.1007/s10817-017-9407-7
24. Verdonck, M., Gailly, F., de Cesare, S.: Comprehending 3D and 4D ontology-driven conceptual models: an empirical study. Inf. Syst. **93**, 101568 (2020). https://www.sciencedirect.com/science/article/pii/S0306437920300582
25. Zamborlini, V., Guizzardi, G.: On the representation of temporally changing information in OWL. In: Workshops Proceedings of the 14th IEEE International Enterprise Distributed Object Computing Conference, EDOCW 2010, Vitória, 25–29 October 2010, pp. 283–292. IEEE Computer Society (2010). https://doi.org/10.1109/EDOCW.2010.50

Portions of Matter and Their Existential Events: An Ontology-Based Conceptual Model

Lucas Valadares Vieira[1,2](✉), Fabricio Henrique Rodrigues[2], and Mara Abel[2]

[1] E&P, Petroleo Brasileiro S/A, Rio de Janeiro, Brazil
lucasvaladares@petrobras.com.br
[2] Universidade Federal do Rio Grande do Sul, Porto Alegre, Brazil
{fabricio.rodrigues,marabel}@inf.ufrgs.br

Abstract. In this work, we propose a conceptual model for existential events that involve portions of matter. Portions of matter are entities that constitute most of the physical entities, for instance, water, oil, gold, and blood. Existential events are events that create or destroy entities. The proposed conceptual model is intended to support the design of information systems that capture the dynamic changes of portions of matter in natural and industrial settings. First, we propose a taxonomy for *collections of objects* (the entities that constitute portions of matter) and define the phase transitions that create and terminate the circumstances for a portion of matter to exist (*i.e.*, for a collection of objects to come to constitute a new portion of matter). Second, we define three existential events that affect portions of matter: (i) *Forming Stuff*, in which a portion of matter is created when a collection of objects becomes connected; (ii) *Terminating Stuff*, in which a portion of matter is terminated when a collection of granules becomes scattered; (iii) *Changing Stuff Type*, in which a portion of matter of one kind is created and a portion of matter of another kind is terminated. Lastly, we present an application example that uses the condensation of a portion of water and its freezing into a portion of ice to illustrate how to use the conceptual model in concrete cases.

Keywords: Ontology · Ontologies · Events · Portions of Matter · Material Constitution · Unified Foundational Ontology · UFO · Earth Materials

1 Introduction

Portions of matter are key entities in any knowledge domain dealing with the physical world. They are *stuff* that most other entities are made of. Among the types of events that might involve portions of matter, existential events are those that consist in the creation or destruction of such entities. They might be used to explain, for example, how a portion of petroleum or a portion of rock is created.

W. Maass et al. (Eds.): ER 2024, LNCS 15238, pp. 152–169, 2025.
https://doi.org/10.1007/978-3-031-75872-0_9

A conceptual model of existential events that affect portions of matter has several possible applications. For example, it can be used to develop simulation systems for the industry, or to extend information systems, allowing not only a representation of the current status of entities in the real world but also their history.

In this context, we propose an ontology-based conceptual model for existential events that involve portions of matter. We adopt the Unified Foundational Ontology (UFO) [7,11] as the top-level reference ontology, and use the OntoUML language [1,4,5,7], whose meta-model was designed to comply with UFO's formal theories.

This work aims to answer the following **research question**: *What are the types of existential events that can affect a portion of matter?* To achieve this objective, we complement the endurant taxonomy of the *Ontology of Portions of Matter* [17] by including the notion of *collection of objects* and some special cases of that. Then, we analyze the main types of events that create and destroy portions of matter as well as their underlying dynamics at the immediate lower granularity level, in which portions of matter are made of a collection of objects.

We have formulated this conceptual model with the intention of representing the behavior of Earth materials (*e.g.*, rocks, petroleum, water) within a sedimentary environment for the purpose of constructing simulation systems or extending databases in the Oil & Gas industry. However, to enhance clarity for a broader audience, we demonstrate our approach using a simpler example: the phase transitions of water.

The remainder of this work is organized as follows. Section 2 provides an overview of UFO and other relevant theories. Section 3 extends the taxonomies of collections of objects and portions of matter and defines phase transition events. Section 4 presents the existential events that affects portions of matter. Section 5 places our contribution among the related work. Section 6 discusses the findings of this work. Lastly, Sect. 7 presents the concluding remarks of this paper.

2 Background

This work is designed under the UFO top-level ontology, which is summarized below, however we also relied on some additional theoretical work. We adopted the material constitution view [2,6], which further restricts the constitution relation. We adopt the upper-level types of events proposed by [16], which fits with UFO and the material constitution view. Lastly, we use and extend the ontology of portions of matter proposed by [17].

2.1 The Unified Foundational Ontology (UFO)

The Unified Foundational Ontology (UFO) is a formal reference ontology that consists of a set of theories on the fundamental conceptual modeling notions [11]. It is organized in three fragments: *UFO-A* is an ontology of endurants,

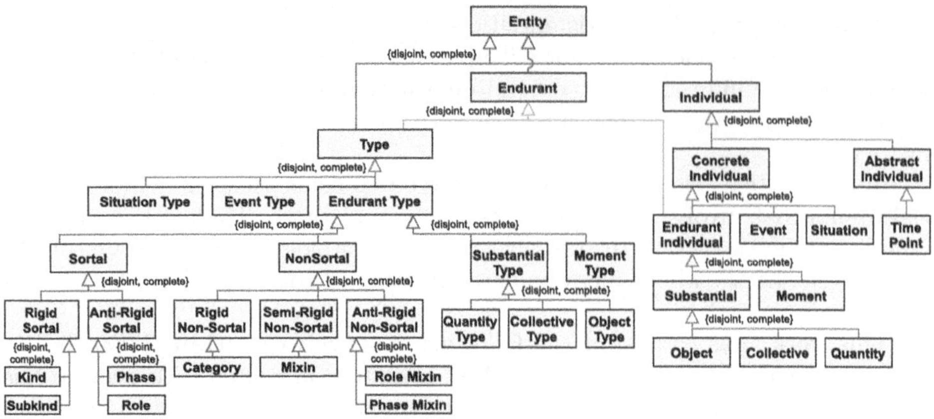

Fig. 1. Fragment of UFO taxonomy, based on [4,11]. Line colors are only an aid to visualize the distinct branches of the taxonomy.

UFO-B is an ontology of perdurants, and *UFO-C* is an ontology of social and intentional entities [11]. In this work, we will use mainly UFO-A and UFO-B, and we review the main concepts necessary following and refer to [1,4,11] for a more comprehensive overview of the current status of UFO.

Everything in UFO is an UFO:Entity (also named UFO:Thing), and there are two major partitions of entities (Fig. 1). First, an UFO:Entity is an UFO:Individual or a UFO:Type. An UFO:Individual (or particular) is something that exists in the real world. A UFO:Type (or universal) is an entity that collects patterns of properties found in entities. While a UFO:Type has instances, an UFO:Individual does not. In the second major partition, entities are either an UFO:Endurant, an UFO:Event, an Situation, or an UFO:Abstract Individual.

An UFO:Endurant is an entity that is completely present at any particular time they are present. They are specialized in UFO:Type and UFO:Endurant Individual, and the latter in UFO:Substantial and UFO:Moment. A UFO:Moment is an existentially dependent entity that exists by *inhering* in other entities [11]. A UFO:Substantial can be either a UFO:Object (functional complex), UFO:Collective, or UFO:Quantity.

An UFO:Object is an entity in which its parts play different functional roles in relation to the whole [8]. A UFO:Collective is an entity whose parts play a uniform whole concerning the whole and are unified by a characteristic relation [10]. A UFO:Collective, as a whole, is related to some UFO:Object parts through the memberOf parthood relation. A UFO:Quantity is a portion of matter, which means that it is a maximally topologically self-connected *amount of matter* [9]. A UFO:Quantity is mereologically invariant, that is, all their parts are essential.

A UFO:Situation is a particular state of things in the world that can be understood as a whole [12]. A UFO:Situation can be very small, for instance, an individual instantiating a non-rigid type, or an individual having a particular quality value. Situations can also be complex with several smaller situations as parts. Lastly, a UFO:Situation is bound to a specific time point, therefore, even if a particular arrangement of entities persists for an interval of time, at each time instant there is a distinct individual situation [12].

An UFO:Event is viewed both as a manifestation of the dispositions of objects and as a mapping between two situations [12]. In this work, we focus on the latter view of events. As an event is the transition between two situations, there are two types of relations used to link them. First, the triggers relation holds between a situation preceding an event if that situation is a necessary condition for the manifestation of the event [12]. Second, the bringsAbout relation holds between the event and the following situations that resulted from the event.

Furthermore, events are interval-based in UFO. They have a beginning and an end UFO:Time Point, and the former precedes the latter [3]. The situation that triggers an UFO:Event is obtained in the same UFO:TimePoint in which the event begins. And the event brings about a situation that is obtained in the same UFO:TimePoint in which the event ends.

UFO adopts a *historical model of description* view of events [1]. That means that particular events are described as finished occurrences that are rigid and immutable. Furthermore, by including past events in a model, there is a shift to historical semantics that is aligned with the *growing block* view of the world [1]. A consequence of these decisions is that entities, even if terminated by an event, do not leave the universe of discourse, and their termination is treated as a change in phase [1].

2.2 Material Constitution

We adopt the *constitution view*, as proposed in [2], restricted to material objects [6]. Constitution is a relationship between entities of different kinds (ultimate sortals) that share the same physical matter [6]. For example, the relation between a *collection of Mud Particles* and a *Portion of Mud*, and between the latter and a Statue of Davi.

There are some conditions necessary for the constitution relation to hold [2,6], first the constituent and constituted must be of distinct kinds (we assume that *kind* is *sensu* UFO). Second, constituent and constituted entities must be spatially co-located, therefore, the constitution relation has one-to-one cardinality. Third, the constituent entity must be in some favorable circumstances that are required for the existence of the constituted. Fourth, if *favorable circumstances* are met, then the constitution relation must exist. Fifth, being a constituent must be a contingent property. Lastly, the constitution is restricted between entities of the same ontological nature, *e.g.*, material things constitute and are constituted by material things.

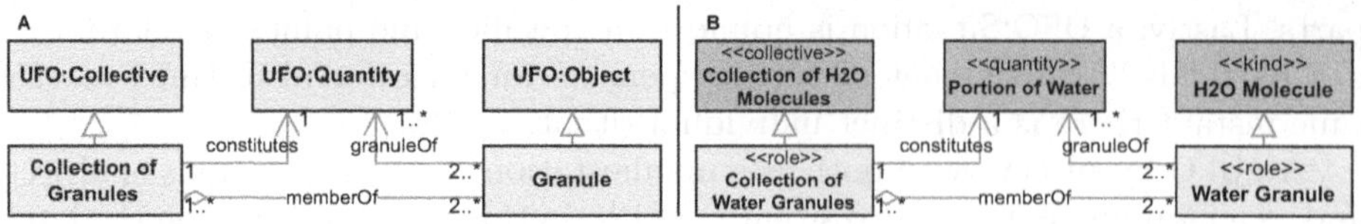

Fig. 2. (A) Fragment of the OPM ontology showing the relation between quantities, granules and collections of granules (modified from [17]). (B) The water constitution and granule pattern (modified from [17]).

2.3 Upper-Level Types of Event

In this work, we classify events into four types based on which properties are changed [16]. A *State* (a.k.a. *stasis*) is an event that does not change any of the properties of the entities involved, except their temporal position. A *Simple Change* event alters *ordinary properties* of the entities, so the same entities exist before and after, but with different qualities. A *Transformation* event changes *identity-related properties*, resulting in different individuals before and after the event.

Lastly, an *Existential Event* changes *favorable properties*, leading to the creation or termination of an entity associated with that property [16]. For instance, the shaping of a *portion of mud* in a particular way may change a *favorable property* that enables the creation of a *statue.*

2.4 The Ontology of Portions of Matter (OPM)

The Ontology of Portions of Matter (OPM) [17] is grounded in UFO ontology. It adds a layer of ontological analysis on how a UFO:Quantity is related to the other substantials in UFO (Fig. 2A). A core notion in OPM is that every UFO:Quantity is constituted by a Collection of Granules (a UFO:Collective) [17]. In addition, members of the constituent collection assume the role of a Granule and hold the granuleOf parthood relation with the portion of matter [17] (Fig. 2A).

For instance, a *Portion of Water* is constituted by a *collection of H_2O molecules*, which instantiates the Collection of Water Granules role while in the constitution relation (Fig. 2B). A single H_2O Molecule, member of the Collection of H_2O Molecules. It is a *granule of* a Portion of Water, and it instantiates the Water Granule role (Fig. 2B).

3 Collections of Objects and Quantities

As OPM focus is on a core level, most of the types proposed are non-sortal, *i.e.*, their instances do not have uniform identity criteria. These types are meant to be specialized in domain ontologies. To illustrate how OPM might be used in a specific case, we will use Portion of Water and related entities and events. As a UFO:Quantity (*i.e.*, a portion of matter) is constituted by a Collection of Granules, we will first discuss the underlying changes in the latter.

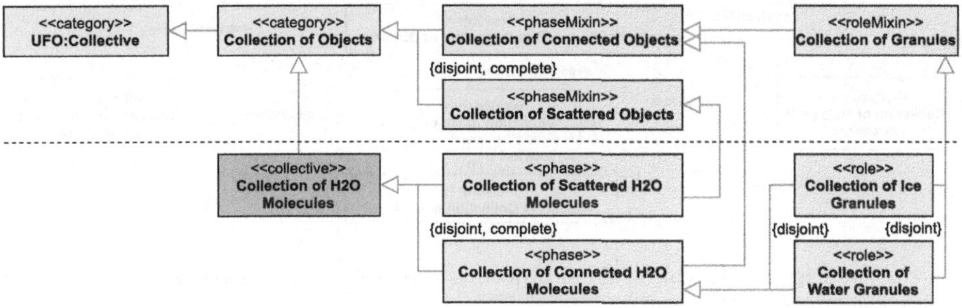

Fig. 3. Class diagram with the proposed taxonomy specializing Collection of Objects, extending the Ontology of Portions of Matter (OPM). The dashed line separates OPM classes above from the examples below.

We also propose some extra axioms using first-order logic to complement the OntUML model, especially for temporal aspects, since OntoUML is designed to describe only the current state of a world. The domain of discourse comprises individuals, represented by lowercase letters. Where possible, we use the letters c for collections, q for quantities, s for situations and e for events followed by a number in case there is more than one individual of the same type in the axiom. We also include non-rigid types in the domain of discourse, to include instantiating relations between them and individuals at specific time points (Eq. 1)[1].

$$\mathsf{iof}(x, y, t) \rightarrow \mathsf{UFO{:}Individual}(x) \wedge \mathsf{UFO{:}Non\text{-}RigidType}(y) \wedge \mathsf{UFO{:}TimePoint}(t) \quad (1)$$

3.1 Collection of Objects

A Collection of Objects is a type that specializes UFO:Collective that has members that are spatially contained in some volume of space, and they have a disposition to interact and bond. Collection of Objects is a non-sortal rigid type, therefore an instance of UFO:Category (Fig. 3).

The members of a Collection of Objects can be spatially related in two distinct manners. First, they can be scattered, *i.e.*, they are not in contact with each other. Second, these members can be spatially connected, *e.g.*, touching each other. These two spatial relations that are possibly observed between the members of Collection of Objects are contingent on the whole.

Therefore, we propose a phase partition of Collection of Objects. First, a Collection of Scattered Objects has members that are scattered inside their defining area. For example, loose sedimentary grains in a river. Second, a Collection of Connected Objects has physically connected members. For example, sedimentary

[1] iof stands for instance of.

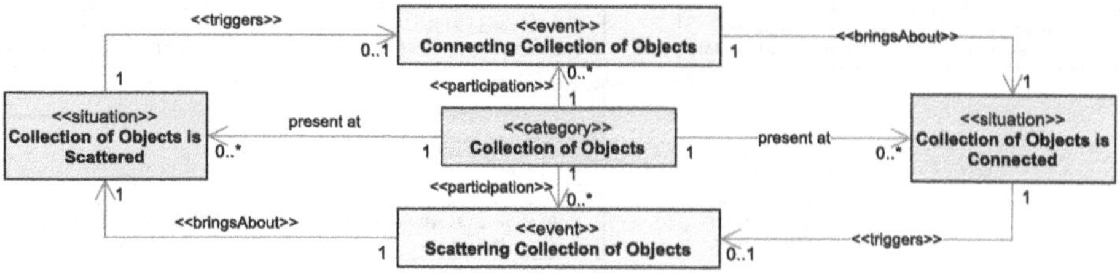

Fig. 4. The collection of objects scattered/connected pattern.

grains that form a rock portion. Both Collection of Scattered Objects and Collection of Connected Objects are non-rigid non-sortal types that depend on intrinsic properties of its instances, consequently they are instances of UFO:Phase Mixin.

A Collection of Granules is a specialization of Collection of Connected Objects, whose instances are constituents of a UFO:Quantity. As Collection of Granules is relational dependent and non-sortal, it is an instance of UFO:RoleMixin. Collection of Granules is among the types proposed by [17], and is now placed in a more general taxonomy (Fig. 3).

In our examples, we will use Collection of H_2O Molecules and its specializations. A Collection of H_2O Molecules is a Collection of Objects whose members are all H_2O Molecules (a functional complex). A Collection of H_2O Molecules is a rigid sortal type that provides identity criteria for its instances; therefore, an instance of UFO:Kind. Furthermore, Collection of H_2O Molecules is partitioned in Collection of Scattered H_2O Molecules andCollection of Connected H_2O Molecules (Fig. 3), following the pattern of phase mixins of Collection of Objects described above.

Collection of Scattered H_2O Molecules specializes Collection of H_2O Molecules and Collection of Scattered Objects. Collection of Connected H_2O Molecules specializes Collection of H_2O Molecules and Collection of Connected Objects. Both types are non-rigid sortals that are instances of UFO:Phase.

A Collection of Connected H_2O Molecules can constitute different kinds of portion of matter. To reflect this, it is specialized in Collection of Water Granules if it *constitutes* a Portion of Water, and in Collection of Ice Granules if it *constitutes* a Portion of Ice. As Collection of Water Granules and Collection of Ice Granules are non-rigid sortal types that are relational dependent, they are instances of UFO:Role.

Phase Transitions. As presented in Sect. 2.3, an existential event occurs when the *favorable circumstances* for the existence of a particular kind are created or terminated [16]. In the case of portions of matter, the *favorable circumstances* are related to the topological connection of the members of their constituent Collection of Objects.

As presented in Sect. 3.1, a Collection of Objects can instantiate Collection of Scattered Object or Collection of Connected Object. An entity instantiating a non-rigid type configures a UFO:Situation. Consequently, there are two different types of UFO:Situation as a Collection of Object instantiates the two above-mentioned phases. Those are the Collection of Objects is Scattered situation and the Collection of Objects is Connected situation (Fig. 4).

A Collection of Objects is Scattered is a UFO:Situation in which a UFO:Collection of Objects is instantiating the Collection of Scattered Objects phase mixin in a particular UFO:Time Point (Eq. 2). Likewise, a Collection of Objects is Connected is a UFO:Situation in which a UFO:Collection of Objects is contingently instantiating the Collection of Connected Objects phase mixin in a particular UFO:Time Point (Eq. 3).

$$\forall s(\mathsf{CollectionObjectsIsScattered}(s) \rightarrow \exists! c, !t(\mathsf{presentAt}(c, s) \wedge \mathsf{CollectionObjects}(c) \wedge \mathsf{UFO{:}TimePoint}(t) \wedge \mathsf{obtainsIn}(s, t) \wedge \mathsf{iof}(c, \mathsf{CollectionScatteredObjects}, t))) \tag{2}$$

$$\forall s(\mathsf{CollectionObjectsIsConnected}(s) \rightarrow \exists! c, !t(\mathsf{presentAt}(c, s) \wedge \mathsf{CollectionObjects}(c) \wedge \mathsf{UFO{:}TimePoint}(t) \wedge \mathsf{obtainsIn}(s, t) \wedge \mathsf{iof}(c, \mathsf{CollectionConnectedObjects}, t))) \tag{3}$$

According to the view of events as transitions between situations [12], the passage from instances of one of the two above types of situations to the other is an event[2]. The two types of events are Connecting Collection of Objects and Scattering Collection of Objects. In instances of both types of events, there is a single participant: a Collection of Objects.

It is important to note that these situations are necessary but not sufficient conditions to trigger the events, which is reflected in the cardinality of the OntoUML diagrams (Fig. 4).

A Connecting Collection of Objects is an UFO:Event in which a Collection of Objects changes its phase from Collection of Scattered Objects to Collection of Connected Objects, as its members become spatially connected. It is *triggered by* a Collection of Objects is Scattered situation and *brings about* a Collection of Objects is Connected situation (Fig. 4).

A Scattering Collection of Objects is an event in which a Collection of Objects changes its phase from Collection of Connected Objects to Collection of Scattered Objects, as its members become scattered, *i.e.*, spatially disconnected. It is *triggered by* a Collection of Objects is Scattered situation and *brings about* a Collection of Objects is Connected (Fig. 4).

The situations and events described above focus on a single Collection of Objects, the same individual Collection of Objects that participates in a Connecting Collection of Objects event or in a Scattering Collection of Objects event must be the same individual present in the situation that triggers and in the situation brought about by the event (Eqs. 4 and 5).

[2] There is a *stasis* event between situations of the same type. However, we will not discuss those events in this work.

$$\forall e, s1, s2(\mathsf{ConnectingCollectionObjects}(e) \wedge \mathsf{CollectionObjectsIsScattered}(s1) \wedge \mathsf{CollectionObjectsIsConnected}(s2) \wedge \mathsf{triggers}(s1, e) \wedge \mathsf{bringsAbout}(e, s2) \rightarrow \exists! c(\mathsf{CollectionOfObjects}(c) \wedge \mathsf{participatesIn}(c, e) \wedge \mathsf{presentAt}(c, s1) \wedge \mathsf{presentAt}(c, s2))) \tag{4}$$

$$\forall e, s1, s2(\mathsf{ScatteringCollectionObjects}(e) \wedge \mathsf{CollectionObjectsIsConnected}(s1) \wedge \mathsf{CollectionObjectsIsScattered}(s2) \wedge \mathsf{triggers}(s1, e) \wedge \mathsf{bringsAbout}(e, s2) \rightarrow \exists! c(\mathsf{CollectionOfObjects}(c) \wedge \mathsf{participatesIn}(c, e) \wedge \mathsf{presentAt}(c, s1) \wedge \mathsf{presentAt}(c, s2))) \tag{5}$$

3.2 Quantities

As discussed in Sect. 2.1, by adopting a *growing block universe* view in a conceptual model, entities that are terminated by events do not leave the domain of discourse. And, as recommended by [1], the termination of entities is modeled as a phase transition. To capture this notion, we propose a complete and disjoint partition of UFO:Quantity into two types, Existing Quantity and Terminated Quantity.

An Existing Quantity is a UFO:Quantity that was created by some UFO:Event (Eq. 6) and is not yet terminated by any UFO:Event (Eq. 7). A Terminated Quantity is a UFO: Quantity that was terminated by some UFO:Event (Eq. 8). A Terminated Quantity must have been an Existing Quantity at some time before (Eq. 9). Both Existing Quantity and Terminated Quantity are anti-rigid non-sortal types that instantiate UFO:PhaseMixin.

$$\forall q, t2(\mathsf{iof}(q, \mathsf{ExistingQuantity}, t2) \rightarrow \exists e, t1(\mathsf{UFO{:}Event}(e) \wedge \mathsf{endPoint}(t1, e) \wedge \mathsf{createdBy}(q, e) \wedge t2 \geq t1))) \tag{6}$$

$$\forall q, t2(\mathsf{iof}(q, \mathsf{ExistingQuantity}, t2) \rightarrow \neg\exists e, t1(\mathsf{UFO{:}Event}(e) \wedge \mathsf{endPoint}(t1, e) \wedge \mathsf{terminatedBy}(q, e) \wedge t2 \geq t1))) \tag{7}$$

$$\forall q, t2(\mathsf{iof}(q, \mathsf{TerminatedQuantity}, t2) \rightarrow \exists e, t1(\mathsf{UFO{:}Event}(e) \wedge \mathsf{endPoint}(t1, e) \wedge \mathsf{terminatedBy}(q, e) \wedge t2 \geq t1))) \tag{8}$$

$$\forall q, t2(\mathsf{iof}(q, \mathsf{TerminatedQuantity}, t2) \rightarrow \exists t1(\mathsf{iof}(q, \mathsf{ExistingQuantity}, t1) \wedge t2 \geq t1))) \tag{9}$$

Phase Transitions. Similarly to the situation types defined in Sect. 3.1, there are two situation types depending on whether a UFO:Quantity instantiates Existing Quantity or Terminated Quantity. Those situations are Quantity is existing and Quantity is terminated.

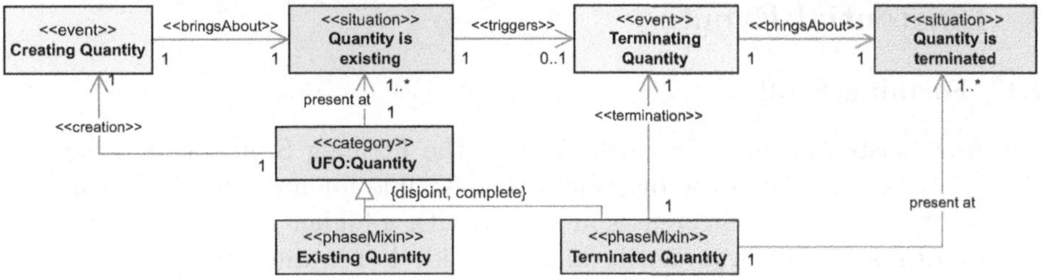

Fig. 5. The quantity existing/terminated pattern.

In a situation Quantity is existing, a unique UFO:Quantity is present and instantiates the Existing Quantity phase at the time the situation obtains (Eq. 11). As a UFO:Situation can reflect a configuration of reality in the past, every UFO:Quantity was present, at some time, in a Quantity is existing situation, even quantities that are currently terminated (Fig. 5).

$$\forall s(\text{QuantityIsExisting}(s) \rightarrow \exists! q! t(\text{UFO:Quantity}(q) \wedge \text{UFO:Time Point}(t) \wedge \text{obtainsIn}(s,t) \wedge \text{presentAt}(q,s) \wedge \text{iof}(q, \text{ExistingQuantity}, t))) \tag{10}$$

A Quantity is terminated situation also has a unique Terminated Quantity present. An Existing Quantity cannot be present at any time in a Quantity is terminated situation.

As OntoUML is intended to model the current state of a world. A Terminated Quantity can be present at a Quantity is existing situation that is obtained in a time point preceding its termination.

The same UFO:Quantity can be present at many Quantity is existing and Quantity is terminated situations. Situations in UFO are bound to specific time points, and a UFO:Quantity exists or is terminated during an interval of time.

$$\forall s(\text{QuantityIsTerminated}(s) \rightarrow \exists! q! t(\text{UFO:Quantity}(q) \wedge \text{UFO:Time Point}(t) \wedge \text{obtainsIn}(s,t) \wedge \text{presentAt}(q,s) \wedge \text{iof}(q, \text{TerminatedQuantity}, t))) \tag{11}$$

Two events can transition in and between the situations described above (Fig. 5). The Creating Quantity is an UFO:Event that *brings about* a Quantity is existing situation. This event is *participational* by nature (*sensu* [1]) and focuses on the participation of a Quantity that is created in the event.

A Terminating Quantity is an UFO:Event in which a UFO:Quantity is terminated and changes from an Existing Quantity to a Terminated Quantity phase. A Quantity is existing situation contributes to trigger a Terminating Quantity and brings about a Quantity is terminated situation.

As a UFO:Quantity in the Terminated Quantity phase cannot be reverted to a Existing Quantity phase, there is no possible event that transitions between a Quantity is terminated situation and a Quantity is existing.

4 Existential Events

4.1 Forming Stuff

The first existential event we will discuss, the Forming Stuff, occur when new *stuff*[3] is created. This type of event is responsible for an increase in the complexity of the world, as it creates an entity with a higher level of granularity (a portion of matter) from an entity in a lower level of granularity (a collection of objects). In this event, a *favorable circumstance* for a kind of UFO:Quantity is created from a situation in which no favorable circumstances existed for any kind of Quantity.

A Forming Stuff is an UFO:Event in which a UFO:Quantity is created from a previously scattered Collection of Objects. The Quantity becomes constituted by the collection after the event. A Forming Stuff event is *triggered by* a Collection of Objects is Scattered situation and *brings about* a Collection of Objects constituting a Quantity situation (Fig. 6).

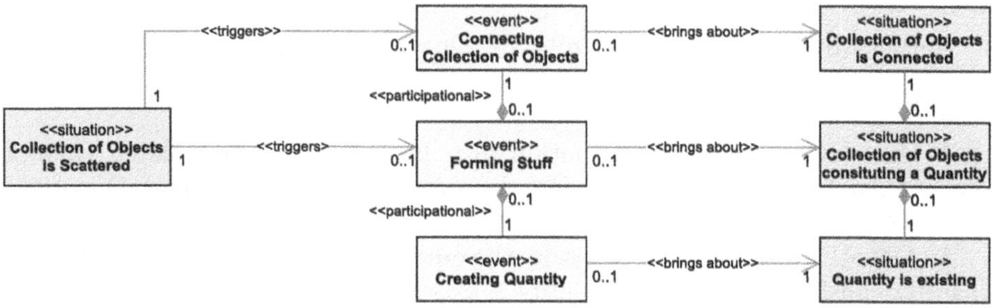

Fig. 6. Class diagram of the *Forming Stuff* event, related situations, and participational events.

A Collection of Objects constituting a Quantity is a situation in which a Collection of Objects has the constitutes relation to a Quantity. For this situation to be configured, a Collection of Objects must instantiate Collection of Connected Objects and Collection of Granules at the time the situation is obtained.

Therefore, a Collection of Objects constituting a Quantity has a Collection of Objects Connected (Sect. 3.1) as its part. Likewise, a UFO:Quantity must instantiate Existing Quantity, so a Quantity is existing is also part of Collection of Objects constituting a Quantity.

A Forming Stuff event is composed, through participations (*sensu* [1]), of a Connecting Collection of Objects event (Sect. 3.1) and of a Creating Quantity event (Sect. 3.2) 6).

An example of a Forming Stuff is the Water Condensation event (Fig. 7), in which a Collection of H_2O Molecules is scattered before and becomes connected

[3] We use the term *stuff* to refer to matter formed by atoms (in the physical and chemical sense).

after the event. During the event, a Portion of Water is created and is constituted by the participant Collection of H_2O Molecules.

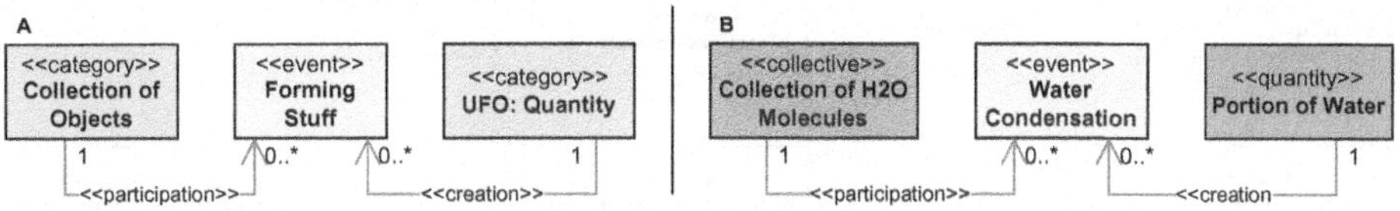

Fig. 7. (A) The *Forming Stuff* event has a participation of a *Collection of Objects* and the creation of a portion of matter (*UFO: Quantity*). The *Water Condensation* event is an example of a *Forming Stuff* event.

4.2 Terminating Stuff

The Terminating Stuff is an event in which *stuff* is destroyed, which means that a *portion of matter* ceases to exist and no other is created. During this event, the *favorable circumstances* present at the beginning cease to exist.

A Terminating Stuff is an UFO:Event in which a UFO:Quantity is terminated and the Collection of Objects that previously constituted it becomes scattered. A Collection of Objects constituting a Quantity situation *triggers* a Terminating Stuff event, which *brings about* both a Quantity is terminated situation and a Collection of Objects is Scattered situation.

Regarding the Quantity individual, which is terminated by the Terminating Stuff event, it changes its phase from Existing Quantity to Terminated Quantity. This is in accordance with the *growing block universe* as terminated entities remain in the universe of discourse after termination [1] (Sect. 2.1).

The Collection of Objects which is connected and constituting a Quantity before the Terminating Stuff event instantiates the Collection of Connected Objects and Collection of Granules at that time. After the event, the same Collection of Objects instantiates Collection of Scattered Objects. This phase transition occurs in a Scattering Collection of Objects event that is a participation part of the Terminating Stuff event (Fig. 8).

An example of a Terminating Stuff is the Water Evaporating event in which a Portion of Water is terminated. The Collection of H_2O Molecules that constituted the Portion of Water prior to the Water Evaporating, becomes scattered and instantiates Collection of Scattered Objects after the event. The created Portion of Water changes its phase from Existing Quantity to Quantity Terminated.

4.3 Changing Stuff Type

The last existential event that might affect a Quantity is the Changing Stuff Type event. This type of existential event is a composite existential event (Sect. 2.3) in the sense that it involves the destruction of *favorable circumstances* for a certain

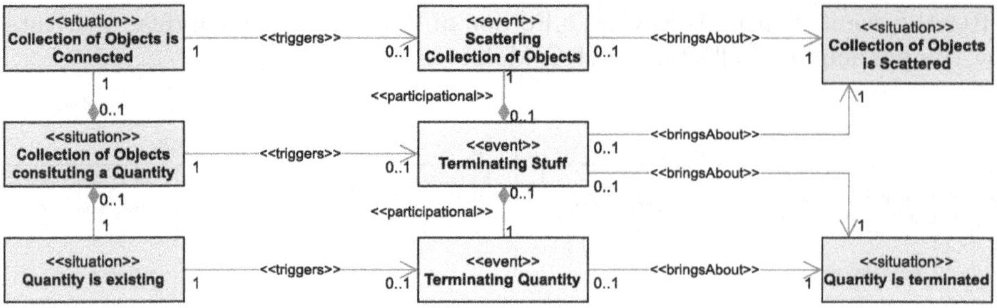

Fig. 8. Class diagram of the *Terminating Stuff* event, its related situations, and participational events.

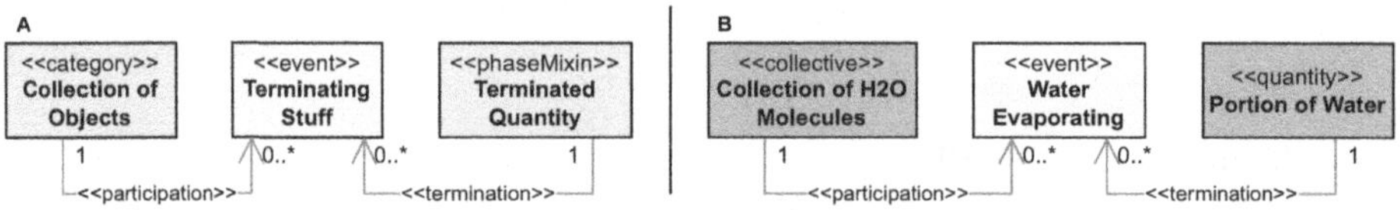

Fig. 9. (A) The *Terminating Stuff* event has a participation of a *Collection of Objects* and the termination of a portion of matter (*UFO: Quantity*). The *Water Evaporating* event is an example of a *Terminating Stuff* event.

kind of *portion of matter*, and the immediate creation of *favorable circumstances* for a distinct kind of *portion of matter*.

A Changing Stuff Type is an UFO:Event in which an instance of UFO:Quantity is terminated and another is created, and the two are instances of different kinds. A Collection of Objects constituting a Quantity *triggers* a Changing Stuff Type event that *brings about* another Collection of Objects constituting a Quantity situation and a Quantity is terminated situation (Fig. 10).

A Changing Stuff Type is composed of three participational events. A Creating Quantity is the participation of the Quantity created. A Terminating Quantity is the participation of the Quantity that is terminated. And a Change Connection Persistence is the participation of the Collection of Objects.

A Changing Connection Persistence is an UFO:Event in which there is a change in the persistence of the connection between the members of a Collection of Objects, while they are still connected. For instance, a Collection of Objects might have a temporary or persistent connection between its members.

The Collection of Objects that participates in a Changing Stuff Type constitutes the Terminated Quantity during the Collection of Objects constituting a Quantity that triggered the event, and constitutes the created UFO:Quantity.

An example of Changing Stuff Type is the Water Freezing event in which a Portion of Water is terminated and a Portion of Ice is created (Fig. 11). The Collection of H_2O Molecules changes the persistence of the connection of its members from a temporary connection, that are part of the *favorable circumstances* for Portion

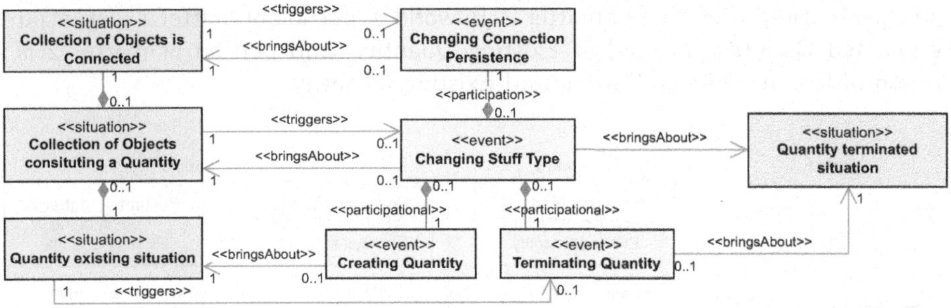

Fig. 10. Class diagram showing the *Changing Stuff Type* event, its three participational sub-events and the situations triggered and brought about by them.

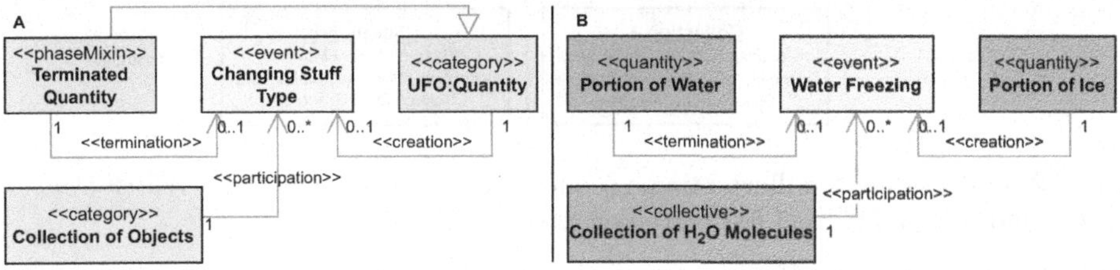

Fig. 11. (A) Class diagram showing the endurants that participate in a *Changing Stuff Type* event. (B) The *Water Freezing* event is an example of a *Changing Stuff Type* event.

of Water to a persistent connection, which is part of the *favorable circumstances* for Portion of Ice.

4.4 A Simple Example

To illustrate how the existential events proposed above can be used to model instances of the world, we will use two events in which a Collection of H_2O Molecules participates. In Fig. 12, we represented three possible worlds in which these events occur, and that illustrate a scenario in which some scattered molecules of H_2O are condensed in a portion of water and then frozen into a portion of ice.

In world 1, the collection 1 is present, and it instantiates Collection of H_2O Molecules, its kind, and it also instantiates Collection of Scattered Objects, a phase mixin. In world 2, event 1 happened, which is a Water Condensation, with the participation of collection 1 and resulting in the creation of portion of matter 1.

In world 2, collection 1 instantiates Collection of Granules, and by consequence Collection of Connected Objects, as it constitutes portion of matter 1, which is a Portion of Water, an Original Portion and an Existing Quantity.

In world 3, event 1 and event 2 occurred, the latter being a Water Freezing with the participation of collection 1 and the termination of portion of matter 1 and the creation of portion of matter 2. In world 3, portion of matter 1 instantiates Terminated Quantity, instead of Existing Quantity; and portion of matter 2 is a Portion of Ice, an Original Portion and Existing Quantity.

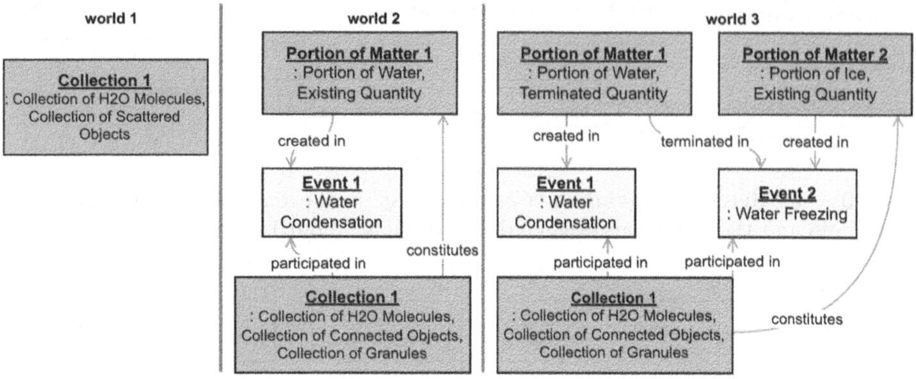

Fig. 12. Object diagram illustrating a sequence of worlds in which the *Water Condensation* and *Water Freezing* existential events occurred.

5 Related Work

[13] uses material constitution to model the different levels of granularity in Earth materials in a similar manner to this work. However, they focus on a static and descriptive view, while our work focuses on the dynamic of creation and termination of portions of matter.

[14] proposes a core ontology of macroscopic stuff (portions of matter). One of the highlights of this ontology is using the granular nature of portions of matter to propose a taxonomy of stuff. Their work also focus on a static descriptive view of portions of matter.

[15] proposes an ontology of blood, its components and the laboratory processes that manipulate these entities by changing or creating them. Although their work recognize the granular components of a portion of blood, they use a generic parthood relation to associate these entities. The processes are modeled in a simply manner that tracks what are the inputs and products of each event.

[18] classify events in the geology domain in deformation, transformation, creation and destruction. The latter two are closely related to the existential events proposed here. However, they do not separate events that create the portions of matter from their constituent collections or constituted objects.

6 Discussion

In Sect. 3, we presented two phase transitions that form reusable patterns. The first pattern shows how a Collection of Objects could transition from being a

Collection of Connected Objects to being a Collection of Scattered Objects (Fig. 4). In this pattern, the same instance might change between two phases in any direction at any number of times. The other reusable phase transition pattern is shown in Fig. 5, in which a Quantity might transition from Existing Quantity to a Terminated Quantity, but the inverse transition is not possible. These two types of pattern are evidence that there are metaproperties of phase partitions that, while out of the scope of this work, can be defined in the future and will help build conceptual models that include phase partitions.

This work also highlights the importance of defining the material constitution of portions of matter (UFO:Quantity) to better model their existential events. Using the conceptualization that a UFO:Quantity is *constituted by* a Collection of Objects, we can better explain what existed before and after the Forming Stuff and Terminating Stuff events.

In the existential events proposed in this work, we used a pattern of decomposing the main event into the participation of each of the involved substantials. Using this view allows one to detail the main event by describing what happens with each participant. However, it is still necessary to investigate how the participations are related to each other in cases of entities that are related through constitution. Although the constitution relationship between events is discussed in UFO [11], there are still some theoretical issues that need to be addressed, for instance, if the modal fragility would allow constitution between events to exist and if there must be a temporal co-location between events.

The classification of Changing Stuff Type as an existential event might sound counter-intuitive, as there is a portion of matter before and after the event, which are constituted by the same Collection of Objects at those times. However, UFO's classification of endurants aids in revealing that the portions of matter are of different kinds, and that, in fact, the Changing Stuff Type event is existential, as there is an essential difference between the causal powers and identity criteria of the entities before and after the event.

Finally, our work is based on the idea that portions of matter are constituted by collections of spatially connected objects. Although this view can account for portions of condensed matter, *i.e.*, solids or liquids, it does not fit well the case of other forms of matter composed of particles that are not necessarily in contact with each other, *e.g.*, gas or plasma. This is evidence that there may exist other favorable circumstances for the constitution of portions of matter, which we intend to investigate in future works.

7 Conclusion

The main contribution of this work is the proposition of three types of existential events that create or terminate portions of matter. We ground the proposed ontology in UFO top level ontology and used the OntoUML language, which implements UFO's theories.

First, we define two phases of a Collection of Objects, depending on whether their members are spatially connected or scattered, and the phase transition events that can happen between them. Then, we define the phases of existence of a UFO:Quantity (portion of matter), and the phase transition between them. Lastly, the main contribution is the definition of the Forming Stuff, the Terminating Stuff and the Changing Stuff Type existential events. Furthermore, we detail the existential events by using the previously defined phase transitions as participational sub-division of the main event.

Although we used the simple case of *portion of water* to exemplify our conceptual model of existential events, there are several applications that will benefit from it. For instance, in the Oil & Gas industry, this conceptual model can be used to simulate scenarios of the creation and termination of petroleum. It can also be used to help describe and infer past existential events related to rocks in the subsurface.

In future work, we will define a full set of axioms and validate them through theorem provers. In addition, we will implement the ontology in a semantic web language (OWL) that will aid in further evaluation of the ontology in real-case application in the empirical simulation of reservoir properties. Finally, we will also investigate how to extend our model to accommodate additional states of matter, such as gas or plasma.

Acknowledgements. The authors thank the three anonymous reviewers for their corrections and insights. Lucas Vieira thanks Petrobras for supporting this work. Mara Abel acknowledges CAPES-Brazil Finance Code 001, the Brazilian Agency CNPq, and The Georeservoir project supported by Petrobras. Fabricio Rodrigues thanks the Petwin Project, supported by FINEP, Libra Consortium (Petrobras, Shell Brasil, Total Energies, CNOOC, CNPC).

References

1. Almeida, J.P.A., Falbo, R.A., Guizzardi, G.: Events as entities in ontology-driven conceptual modeling. In: Laender, A.H.F., Pernici, B., Lim, E.-P., de Oliveira, J.P.M. (eds.) ER 2019. LNCS, vol. 11788, pp. 469–483. Springer, Cham (2019). https://doi.org/10.1007/978-3-030-33223-5_39
2. Baker, L.R.: Persons and bodies: A constitution view. Cambridge University Press (2000)
3. Botti Benevides, A., Bourguet, J.R., Guizzardi, G., Peñaloza, R., Almeida, J.P.A.: Representing a reference foundational ontology of events in sroiq. Appli. Ontol. **14**(3), 293–334 (2019)
4. Fonseca, C.M., Guizzardi, G., Almeida, J.P.A., Sales, T.P., Porello, D.: Incorporating types of types in ontology-driven conceptual modeling. In: International Conference on Conceptual Modeling, pp. 18–34. Springer (2022). https://doi.org/10.1007/978-3-031-17995-2_2
5. Fonseca, C.M., Porello, D., Guizzardi, G., Almeida, J.P.A., Guarino, N.: Relations in ontology-driven conceptual modeling. In: Laender, A.H.F., Pernici, B., Lim, E.-P., de Oliveira, J.P.M. (eds.) ER 2019. LNCS, vol. 11788, pp. 28–42. Springer, Cham (2019). https://doi.org/10.1007/978-3-030-33223-5_4
6. Fonseca Garcia, L., Carbonera, J.L., Rodrigues, F.H., Roca Antunes, C., Abel, M.: What rocks are made of: towards an ontological pattern for material constitution

in the geological domain. In: Laender, A.H.F., Pernici, B., Lim, E.-P., de Oliveira, J.P.M. (eds.) ER 2019. LNCS, vol. 11788, pp. 275–286. Springer, Cham (2019). https://doi.org/10.1007/978-3-030-33223-5_23
7. Guizzardi, G.: Ontological foundations for structural conceptual models (2005)
8. Guizzardi, G.: The problem of transitivity of part-whole relations in conceptual modeling revisited. In: van Eck, P., Gordijn, J., Wieringa, R. (eds.) CAiSE 2009. LNCS, vol. 5565, pp. 94–109. Springer, Heidelberg (2009). https://doi.org/10.1007/978-3-642-02144-2_12
9. Guizzardi, G.: On the representation of quantities and their parts in conceptual modeling. In: FOIS, pp. 103–116 (2010)
10. Guizzardi, G.: Ontological foundations for conceptual part-whole relations: the case of collectives and their parts. In: Mouratidis, H., Rolland, C. (eds.) CAiSE 2011. LNCS, vol. 6741, pp. 138–153. Springer, Heidelberg (2011). https://doi.org/10.1007/978-3-642-21640-4_12
11. Guizzardi, G., Botti Benevides, A., Fonseca, C.M., Porello, D., Almeida, J.P.A., Prince Sales, T.: Ufo: unified foundational ontology. Appli. Ontol. **17**(1), 167–210 (2022)
12. Guizzardi, G., Wagner, G., de Almeida Falbo, R., Guizzardi, R.S.S., Almeida, J.P.A.: Towards ontological foundations for the conceptual modeling of events. In: Ng, W., Storey, V.C., Trujillo, J.C. (eds.) ER 2013. LNCS, vol. 8217, pp. 327–341. Springer, Heidelberg (2013). https://doi.org/10.1007/978-3-642-41924-9_27
13. Hahmann, T., Brodaric, B., Grüninger, M.: Interdependence among material objects and voids. In: Formal Ontology in Information Systems, pp. 37–50. IOS Press (2014)
14. Keet, C.M.: A core ontology of macroscopic stuff. In: Janowicz, K., Schlobach, S., Lambrix, P., Hyvönen, E. (eds.) EKAW 2014. LNCS (LNAI), vol. 8876, pp. 209–224. Springer, Cham (2014). https://doi.org/10.1007/978-3-319-13704-9_17
15. Mendonça, F., Almeida, M.B.: Hemocomponents and hemoderivatives ontology (hemonto): an ontology about blood components. In: ONTOBRAS, pp. 11–22 (2013)
16. Rodrigues, F.H., Carbonera, J.L., Abel, M.: Upper-level types of occurrent based on the principle of ontological conservation. In: Dobbie, G., Frank, U., Kappel, G., Liddle, S.W., Mayr, H.C. (eds.) ER 2020. LNCS, vol. 12400, pp. 353–363. Springer, Cham (2020). https://doi.org/10.1007/978-3-030-62522-1_26
17. Vieira, L.V., Abel, M., Rodrigues, F.H., Sales, T.P., Fonseca, C.M.: Towards an ontology of portions of matter to support multi-scale analysis and provenance tracking (2024), [Manuscript submitted for publication]
18. Zhan, X., Lu, C., Hu, G.: Event sequence interpretation of structural geological models: a knowledge-based approach. Earth Sci. Inf. **14**(1), 99–118 (2021)

Model-Driven Design and Generation of Training Simulators for Reinforcement Learning

Sotirios Liaskos[1](✉), Shakil M. Khan[2], John Mylopoulos[3], and Reza Golipour[1]

[1] School of Information Technology, York University, Toronto, Canada
{liaskos,golipour}@yorku.ca
[2] Department of Computer Science, University of Regina, Regina, Canada
shakil.khan@uregina.ca
[3] Department of Computer Science, University of Toronto, Toronto, Canada
jm@cs.toronto.edu

Abstract. Reinforcement learning (RL) is an important class of machine learning techniques, in which intelligent agents optimize their behavior by observing and evaluating the outcomes of their repeated interactions with their environment. A key to successfully engineering such agents is to provide them with the opportunity to engage in a large number of such interactions safely and at a low cost. This is often achieved through developing simulators of such interactions, in which the agents can be trained while also different training strategies and parameters are explored. However, specifying and implementing such simulators can be a complex endeavor requiring a systematic process for capturing and analyzing both the goals and actions of the agents and the characteristics of the target environment. We propose a framework for model-driven goal-oriented development of RL simulation environments. The framework utilizes a set of extensions to a standard goal modeling notation that allows concise modeling of a large number of ways by which an intelligent agent can interact with its environment. Though subsequent formalization, the model is used by a specially constructed simulation engine to simulate agent behavior, such that off-the-shelf RL algorithms can use it as a training environment. We present the extension of the goal modeling language, sketch its semantics, and show how models built with it can be made executable.

Keywords: Goal Modeling · Reinforcement Learning · DT-Golog

1 Introduction

Over the past years, the demand for Artificial Intelligence (AI) systems has been on the rise. Such systems perform tasks requiring autonomy and complex decision making, such as driving vehicles, controlling devices, or making trading

W. Maass et al. (Eds.): ER 2024, LNCS 15238, pp. 170–191, 2025.
https://doi.org/10.1007/978-3-031-75872-0_10

decisions. Some of these AI systems are based on Reinforcement Learning (RL), whereby intelligent software agents learn to optimize their behavior by continuously interacting with their environment [62]. RL has been studied in a variety of application domains including energy [5], traffic control [64], finance [58], and healthcare [26]. Software *RL agents* engage in goal-oriented activity, whereby they perform actions to fulfill functional goals (e.g., administer a therapy, trade securities, control a heating device), while maximizing the satisfaction of higher level quality objectives (respectively, health outcome, profit, occupant comfort) based on experience.

Key to successfully engineering an RL agent is the ability to subject it to a large number of training interactions with the target environment. Using a *simulator* based on a model of the latter allows a large number of such interactions to take place safely and at a low cost. When such a model is accurate, the trained agent is readily deployable to the target environment. When the model is provisional, approximate, or imprecise, simulator-based training is useful for exploring the performance of different learning algorithms under alternative problem formulations and parameter settings.

We propose a framework for model-driven goal-oriented development of training simulators for RL. The framework is based on developing goal models that describe the required intentional structure of RL agents through representing how high-level agent goals are refined into low level actions, how the latter, upon their performance, give raise to stochastic outcomes, and how such outcomes, in turn, affect a variety of quality variables of interest, an aggregate of which is used to represent outcome rewards. The requirements model is then translated into an action- and decision-theoretic formal specification, which, through a set of proposed querying and simulation components, can be directly used by RL algorithms as a training workbench. In this way, the training simulator is the result of a principled requirements-based approach that fully embraces modeling both for facilitating analysis and communication of the RL agent design and for generating its training simulator.

Our main contributions include the extensions to an existing decision-theoretic goal-modeling language to allow RL agent modeling, the corresponding formalization rules, and the architecture and implementation of components that make the models executable and usable by RL algorithms. To demonstrate feasibility, a set of experiments with a selection of popular RL algorithms is performed.

The paper is organized as follows. We describe the modeling language and its semantics in Sects. 2 and 3 and the generation of simulators in Sect. 4. In Sect. 5 we discuss related work and we conclude in Sect. 6.

2 Modeling RL Domains

2.1 Motivating Example

Consider a large-scale woodwork manufacturer who builds custom furniture and cabinetry in a make-to-order fashion. For every order they receive, they need to

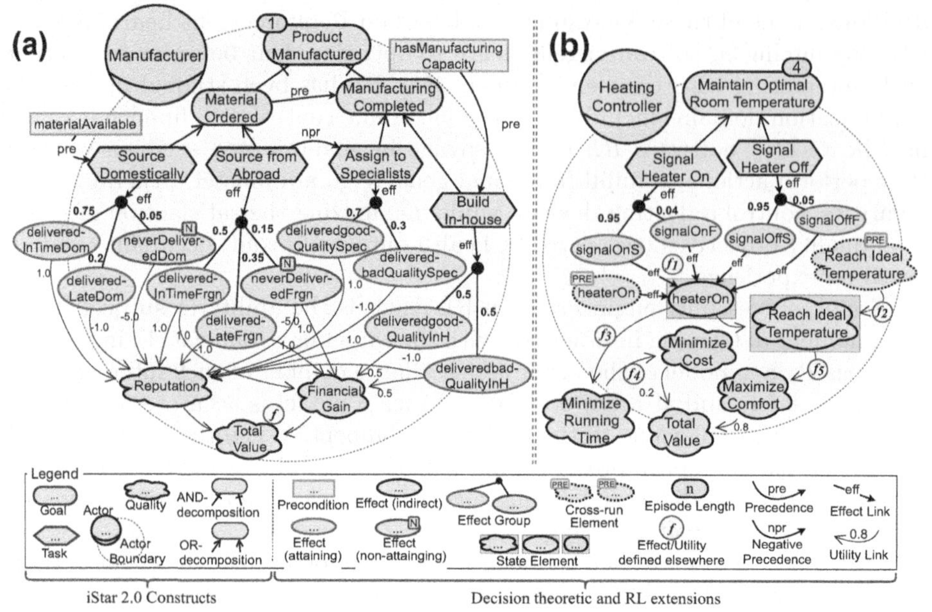

Fig. 1. An extended goal model – a (partial) meta-model can be found in [40].

source the material and manufacture the requested product – among many other activities omitted here for simplicity. They have options as to how they perform these two steps. The material can be sourced from domestic or foreign sources. In the first case, the cost is higher, but in the latter case there are delay risks. Once the material is acquired, they can engage their in-house craftspersons to build the product or subcontract to a more specialized group, who use precise manufacturing techniques but cost more and only work with domestic material. Importantly, a decision outcome of one step of the process, may affect what decision is best in a subsequent step. For example, a delay in sourcing may necessitate expedience in manufacturing to meet deadlines. In addition, choices have non-deterministic outcomes. For example, sourcing material from abroad may or may not result in a delay, and the in-house craftspersons may or may not produce a lower quality product.

The question for the manufacturer as they engage in this sequential decision making process for every incoming order is what decision they should be making at each step so that their goals are, on average, maximally satisfied in the end. Reinforcement learning (RL) refers to a set of techniques that has been proposed for addressing this problem via learning through experience [62]. Specifically, an RL agent actively engages with the environment by repeatedly performing *actions* which have the effect of (a) changing the *state* of the environment, typically in a non-deterministic way, and (b) offering to the agent a (positive or negative) *reward* reflecting the desirability of the action outcome or state change. This is repeated until a goal state is reached. The agent then restarts with a new effort to achieve the same goal. In our example, an RL agent would, for each order, chose and take a sourcing action, observe the outcome (delayed or not), proceed with a manufacturing action, observe that result (good quality or not), and move on to the next order. Various RL algorithms exist for turning these repeated decision making sequences into a *policy*, which maps each state to an action to be taken at that state so that the total expected reward is maximized.

As RL agents need to first process a potentially large number of cases before they can start making safe and good quality decisions, it is preferable that their training is not taking place in the actual environment but an executable model thereof, i.e., a simulator. Such a model should capture the decision points that are available to the RL agent, the corresponding alternative actions, the possible effects that these actions bring about, as well as the reward structure reflecting the preferability of these effects. The latter can be challenging in RL applications within socio-technical systems, such as the one of our example, where reward structures are abstract and multi-dimensional. We next describe an extension to a standard goal modeling language that aims at developing such models.

2.2 Extending iStar for Reinforcement Learning: iStar-RL

The proposed language, which we will refer to as *iStar-RL*, extends iStar 2.0 [17], a state-of-the-art goal-oriented requirements modeling language for socio-technical systems. Two example models can be viewed in Fig. 1. The one on the left (a) shows the goals of our hypothetical woodwork manufacturer.

As per the iStar 2.0 ontology, *actors*, such as *Manufacturer*, have *goals*, such as *(Have) Material Ordered*, which represent states of affairs that actors want to achieve and/or maintain. Through *AND-* and *OR-decompositions*, high-level goals are refined into lower-level ones, whereby satisfaction of all or, respectively, one subgoal(s) is necessary (resp., sufficient) for fulfilling the parent goal. At the leaf level, *tasks* signify concrete actions to be taken for fulfilling goals – e.g. *Source Domestically.* Quality goals (*qualities*) describe attributes for which actors desire some level of achievement, without the requirement that such level is precisely defined. *Contribution links* are used to signify that achievement of a goal/task affects a quality in a way that is described using an annotation on the link.

Models such as that of Fig. 1(a) can encode a great number of subsets of leaf-level tasks and temporal orderings thereof that can fulfill top-level goals. Various ways for formalizing goal models for purposes similar to identifying such task sequences have been introduced – e.g. [23,30,36,42,53]. We adopt here a decision-theoretic extension to iStar for reasoning in the presence of probabilistic task effects [40,41] and further extend it with constructs that facilitate RL.

The baseline extensions are showcased in Fig. 1. A set of *domain propositions* are, firstly, introduced for describing the state of the environment at different points in time – for example, *hasManufacturingCapacity* and *materialAvailable.* Domain propositions are used in *precondition* and *effect* elements. A precondition contains a Boolean formula of domain propositions, whereas an effect contains one such predicate. Preconditions are connected to tasks through *precedence links*

$\xrightarrow{pre}$ and, respectively, *negative precedence links* $\xrightarrow{npr}$ which denote that performance of the task is not possible unless (resp., if) the formula in the precondition is satisfied. Precedence (resp., negative precedence) links can also originate from goals meaning that the task cannot be performed unless (resp., if) the origin goal has been satisfied (resp., has been attempted, i.e. at least one of its descendant tasks has been successfully performed).

Further, tasks are connected with effects through the use of *effect links* $\xrightarrow{eff}$, denoting that performance of the task from where the link originates can cause the effect which the link points at to occur, i.e., make the domain proposition contained in it true. As tasks may have several possible effects, they may be connected to *effect groups* which represent a collection of effects, each carrying a distinct probability to occur once the task is performed. The probability is added as a label on the corresponding link on the diagram. Effects are marked as *task satisfying* if their occurrence implies successful performance of the task, and *non-satisfying* otherwise. For example, an attempt to submit an order may be deemed successful (task satisfying) if it is finally delivered, despite delays, errors, etc., and non-satisfying if it is never delivered. Moreover, *indirect effects*, such as *heaterOn* in Fig. 1(b), are effects whose truth status depends on other effects in a way that is defined outside the diagram – noted through an ⓕ annotation. Effect links are used to connect regular effects with indirect effects.

Further, effects, including indirect ones, are connected to qualities through *utility links*, a specialization of iStar 2.0 contribution links. These are annotated either with a number representing the amount of satisfaction that the effect, if it occurs, adds to the quality or with the ⓕ icon indicating that a more complex formula describes the relationship. Using utility links, qualities also form an hierarchy whose root o_{top} represents the overall quality – in Fig. 1, this is *Total Value*. Each quality in iStar-RL is considered to be a continuous variable whose value represents the level of satisfaction of the quality at a given state.

2.3 Task Histories, Goal Runs, and Episodes

Let us now focus on tasks. Let *task (performance) history* be a sequence $tH^{|I} = [t_1, t_2, \ldots]^{|I}$ of leaf-level tasks that (a) starts from an initial state in which propositions and qualities have a value configuration I, and (b) is feasible with respect to the precondition and effect constraints, i.e., t_1 is feasible under I and each subsequent t_i is possible given the state that t_{i-1} brought about. Attempt of each task results in the occurrence of an effect. Hence, a task history is mapped to a set of possible *effect (occurrence) histories*, $eH^{|I} = [e_1, e_2, \ldots]^{|I}$ – we will henceforth omit the initial state superscript I unless needed. Further, let $\mathcal{H}$ be the set of all goals and $\mathcal{O}$ the set of all qualities in a model. The mappings $satG : \mathcal{H} \times \mathbf{eH} \mapsto \{true, false\}$ and $satQ : \mathcal{O} \times \mathbf{eH} \mapsto \mathbb{R}$, describe the satisfaction or not of a goal, and, respectively, the level of satisfaction of a quality, given an effect history eH from the set $\mathbf{eH}$ of all such. The former mapping reflects the AND/OR decomposition structure and the latter the structure of utility links; precisely how is discussed in a subsequent section.

To make effect histories meaningful for RL, we need constructs additional to the original extension [40]. Let $\mathcal{G}$ be a goal model with root goal $r_{\mathcal{G}}$. A *goal run* for goal $r_{\mathcal{G}}$ is an effect history $eH = [e_1, e_2, \ldots]$ such that (a) $satG(r_{\mathcal{G}}, eH)$, i.e. the root goal is satisfied, (*successful run*) *or* (b) no other task can be performed at eH, due to precondition constraints, a situation we will call a *deadlock*.

Back in Fig. 1(a), consider effect histories *[deliveredInTimeDom, delivered-BadQualityInH]* (materials sourced domestically and in-house production was of bad quality) and *[neverDeliveredFrgn]* (materials ordered from foreign sources and were never delivered). Both histories are goal runs: the former satisfies the root goal, whereas the latter cannot be continued due to the precedence link between *Material Ordered* and *Manufacturing Completed.* However, neither *[deliveredLateDom]* nor *[deliveredInTimeFrgn]* are goal runs: in both cases, the root goal is not satisfied and there are actions that are still possible. The level of satisfaction *satQ* of quality *Reputation* for each of the aforementioned four (partial) histories is +1.0 –1.0 = 0, –5.0, –1.0, 1.0, respectively, calculated by adding up the annotations of utility links originating from effects included in the history.

We further define an *episode* to be a concatenation of n goal runs $eP^{|I} = [eH_1^{|I}, eH_2^{|I}, ..., eH_n^{|I}]$ such that for all $eH_i^{|I}$, $i < n$ the root goal is satisfied. In other words, an episode describes a history of repeated goal runs all of which successful except for the last one, which may be either successful or a deadlock. For $n > 1$ the episode is a *multi-run episode* and for $n = 1$ a *single-run episode.* We can specify the maximum number of runs that comprise an episode (*episode length*) as an annotation next to the root goal - see Fig. 1. In multi-run episodes, each run is, by default, assumed to start from the same initial configuration I. We may however wish to designate elements that carry their values across goal runs. We accomplish this through *cross-run elements.*

To appreciate the rationale for multi-run episodes and the role of cross-run elements in such episodes, consider the model of Fig. 1(b). It describes the function of a heating device controller, contrived here to showcase additional features of the language. The controller periodically signals wirelessly to the device to turn *on* or *off.* This *on* or *off* signal can be lost with a probability. The overall quality accrued from a sequence of signaling tasks is a function of the distance of the temperature to an ideal one and the amount of time heating is on, which represents cost and environmental impact. To make meaningful optimal decisions we need to look at the quality value accumulated over a sequence of goal runs. In the diagram this is set to four (4). Hence, if the controller makes a decision every, e.g., 5 min, which constitutes one goal run, an entire episode spans 20 min and overall quality is calculated for all 4 decisions made.

In Fig. 1(b), cross-run elements (dashed outline and with a "PRE" annotation) represent the (truth) value of the enclosed proposition or quality in the previous state. The previous state is the configuration of truth values before the latest action was performed within the episode, irrespective of goal run boundaries. Thus, the truth status of the proposition within indirect effect *heaterOn* (solid line effect), depends on its truth status at the end of the previous state (dashed line effect) and the current state of four regular effects in the second run, represented through the remaining four incoming effects. The symbol f_1 denotes that the exact formula that translates the truth value of these five propositions into the new truth value for *heaterOn* is specified outside the diagram. Likewise, the current value of *Reach Ideal Temperature* depends on its previous value and the current value of *heaterOn*. Again, a symbol f_2 denotes that the formula for combining the two values is specified outside the diagram. Note that whether an element is discrete or continuous is orthogonal to its status as cross-run.

We finally designate the *exported state set* to be the set of propositions and qualities to be used for the calculation of policies. By default, we assume that the problem is modeled as a *discrete-state* one, i.e., the exported state set is the configuration of values of all propositions – the *discrete (exported) state set*. However, in some cases it is useful to use qualities as part of the set. In the heating controller example, whether the heater should turn on or off more obviously depends on the satisfaction level of *Reach Ideal Temperature* than the history of *on/off* actions. In Fig. 1 we put a shaded rectangle at the background of an indirect effect or a quality, to mark its inclusion in the exported state. When the exported state contains at least one non-propositional element, we model the problem as a *continuous-state* one. In Fig. 1(b) we designate variables *heaterOn* and *Reach Ideal Temperature* to exclusively comprise the exported state set – a *continuous exported state set*. Note that such designation does not affect how validity of effect histories is established, which is based solely on the discrete state set; hence the clarifying "exported" qualification. Further, the cross-run status of an element is orthogonal to its inclusion in the exported set.

2.4 iStar-RL and Reinforcement Learning

Let us now sketch how iStar-RL models can be used by an RL agent to allow for optimal decision making. Recall that RL-agents observe the state of the environment, perform an action from a set of available ones, and sense the state that results from the action along with the reward that the action yields. In our case, the state of the environment is, as we saw, the exported state, i.e., a combination of values of designated domain propositions and/or qualities. Upon sensing that state, the RL agent performs a task, which brings about one of the corresponding effects, which, in turn, augments the current episode eP with one more effect, and may also imply updated $satG$ and $satQ$ values. The RL agent will sense the new state and perceive the total value $satQ(o_{top}, eH_i)$ as the reward of the latest action. It will then repeatedly proceed with the next action until the episode is over, i.e., it reaches the maximum number of successful runs or a deadlock. During training, the RL agent will attempt a great number of such episodes, aimed at identifying a policy, i.e., a mapping from state to tasks that, when repeatedly followed, maximizes the average total value.

For the RL agent to accomplish such training using the iStar-RL model, the latter needs to be executable. In the next section, we describe how iStar-RL models can be formalized, aiming at both clarifying their semantics and paving the way for generating executable simulations of such models.

3 Semantics

3.1 DT-Golog

The semantics of iStar-RL are defined by means of its translation to DT-Golog, a high-level agent programming language [12,61] based on the Situation Calculus [59]. The basic constructs of DT-Golog are fluents, stochastic (or agent) actions, nature actions, and situations. *Fluents* play the role of state features and have different truth values in different situations. They are represented through predicates such as *materialDelivered(s)*, with the situation s as one of the parameters. *Stochastic actions* a are first-order terms signifying specific activity initiated by agents and may have several alternative outcomes, each occurring with a different probability. These outcomes are modeled through a set of *nature actions* $\hat{A} = \{\hat{a}_1, \hat{a}_2, ...\}$ associated with a through predicate $choice(a, \hat{A})$. The corresponding probabilities are represented using $prob(\hat{a}, v, s)$, where v is the probability of the occurrence of $\hat{a}$. Further, a *situation* s denotes a sequence of actions. The function $do(\hat{a}, s)$ denotes the situation which results from the performance of nature action $\hat{a}$ in situation s. A special constant S_0 denotes the initial situation, where no action has been performed.

A DT-Golog specification contains axioms that prescribe what actions are possible in different situations and how the truth value of fluents is affected by the performance of actions. The former, *precondition axioms*, are of the form:

$$\forall s.poss(a, s) \leftrightarrow \Pi_a(s)$$

where $\Pi_a(s)$ is a fluent formula and special predicate $poss(a, s)$ states that action a is executable in situation s. The latter, *successor state axioms*, are of the form:

$$\forall \hat{a}, \mathbf{x}, s. f(\mathbf{x}, do(\hat{a}, s)) \leftrightarrow \Phi_f(\mathbf{x}, \hat{a}, s)$$

where $\mathbf{x}$ signifies a list of arguments, f a fluent symbol and $\Phi_f(\mathbf{x}, \hat{a}, s)$ a formula whose truth value depends on the parameters, the current situation, and the nature action in question. Finally, by defining:

$$reward(v, s) \leftrightarrow \Psi_r(v, s)$$

where $\Psi_r(v, s)$ is a formula grounded on fluents, it is possible to assign a reward value v to any situation or action.

3.2 From iStar-RL Models to DT-Golog Specifications

The DT-Golog-based semantics of iStar-RL is based on a treatment offered by Liaskos et al. [40], with the necessary additions for supporting RL. In what follows, let a goal model $\mathcal{G}$ contain a set $\mathcal{H}$ of goals, a set $\mathcal{T}$ of tasks, a set $\mathcal{E}$ of effects, a set $\mathcal{Q}$ of domain predicates, and a set $\mathcal{O}$ of qualities.

Primitives. Each element in the set is translated to a DT-Golog primitive as follows. For each domain proposition $q \in \mathcal{Q}$ introduce a fluent $\phi_q(s)$. For each task $t \in \mathcal{T}$ associated with an effect group $\mathcal{E}_t \subseteq \mathcal{E}$ introduce the following: a stochastic agent action a_t and a set of nature actions N_t each $\hat{a}_t \in N_t$ associated with an effect in $\mathcal{E}_t$. For each task $t \in \mathcal{T}$ and goal $h \in \mathcal{H}$, introduce fluents $\phi_t(s)$ and $\phi_h(s)$. For each quality $o \in \mathcal{O}$ introduce two fluents $\phi_o^{(r)}(v, s)$ and $\phi_o^{(m)}(v, s)$,

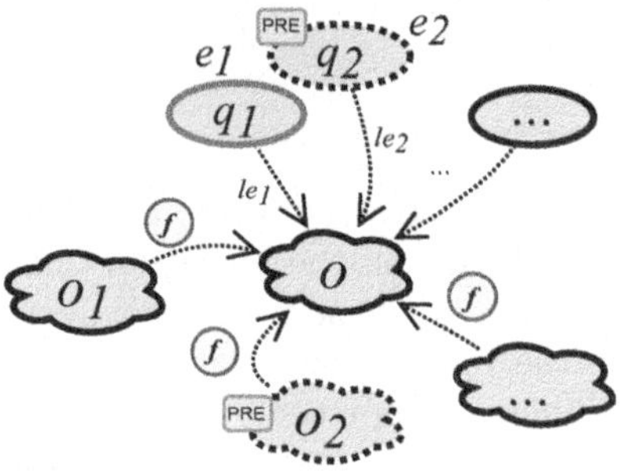

$$
\begin{aligned}
&\phi_o^{(r)}(v_{init}, S_0)\\
&\phi_o^{(r)}(v, do(a,s)) \leftrightarrow\\
&\quad (\phi_{o_1}^{(r)}(v_{o_1}, do(a,s)) \wedge \phi_{o_2}^{(r)}(v_{o_2}, s) \wedge \ldots)\wedge\\
&\quad (a = \hat{a}_1 \wedge v_{e_1} = l_{e_1} \vee a \neq \hat{a}_1 \wedge v_{e_1} = 0)\wedge\\
&\quad (\phi_{q_2}(s) \wedge v_{e_2} = l_{e_2} \vee \neg\phi_{q_2}(s) \wedge v_{e_2} = 0)\wedge\\
&\quad (\ldots) \wedge v = f(v_{o_1}, v_{o_2}, \ldots, v_{e_1}, v_{e_1}, \ldots)\\
&\phi_o^{(m)}(v, S_0) \leftrightarrow \phi_o^{(r)}(v, S_0)\\
&\phi_o^{(m)}(v, do(a,s)) \leftrightarrow\\
&\quad \phi_o^{(m)}(v_p, s) \wedge \phi_o^{(r)}(v_a, do(a,s)) \wedge (v = v_p + v_a)
\end{aligned}
$$

Fig. 2. Constructing quality formulae

respectively called *current satisfaction fluent* and *cumulative satisfaction fluent*; for both fluents, parameter $v \in \mathbb{R}$ represents the satisfaction value of o.

Given the 1–1 correspondence between iStar-RL effects and situation calculus nature actions, effect histories $eH = [e_{t_1}, e_{t_2}, \ldots]$ also map 1–1 to situations $s = do(\ldots do(\hat{a}_{t_2}, do(\hat{a}_{t_1}, s_0))\ldots)$, where $\hat{a}_{t_i}$ is the nature action corresponding to effect e_{t_i}. For a goal h and quality o: $satG(h, eH)$ iff $\phi_h(s)$ and $satQ(o, eH) = v$ iff $\phi_o^{(r)}(v, s)$, where s is the situation corresponding to effect history eH.

Successor State Axioms. For each domain predicate q, collect all effects $e_1, e_2, \ldots$ that mention it and consider the corresponding $\hat{a}_1, \hat{a}_2, \ldots$ nature actions. Introduce the following successor state axiom:

$$\phi_q(do(a,s)) \leftrightarrow (a = \hat{a}_1 \vee a = \hat{a}_2 \vee \ldots) \vee \phi_q(s).$$

Attempt and Attainment Formulae. Consider each task t connected with an effect group $\mathcal{E}_t$. Consider *all* the effects of $\mathcal{E}_t$, and the domain predicates $q_1^{(t)}, q_2^{(t)}, \ldots$ contained in them. Generate the following *task attempt formula* for t:

$$\phi_t^{(att)}(s) \leftrightarrow \phi_{q_1^{(t)}}(s) \vee \phi_{q_2^{(t)}}(s) \vee \ldots$$

A *task attainment formula* $\phi_t(s)$ is defined similarly with the only difference being that it excludes non-satisfying effects. Introduce also a *goal attainment formula* for each goal h as follows:

$$\phi_h(s) \leftrightarrow f_{\text{AND/OR}}(\phi_{t_1}(s), \phi_{t_2}(s), \ldots)$$

where $t_1, t_2, \ldots$ are the tasks that are descendants of h in the goal hierarchy, $\phi_{t_1}(s), \phi_{t_2}(s), \ldots$ their corresponding task attainment formulae, and $f_{\text{AND/OR}}$ an AND/OR formula reflecting the corresponding goal decomposition structure. A *goal attempt formula* for h, $\phi_h^{(att)}(s)$, is similarly defined but grounded on task attempt, rather than attainment, formulae.

Quality Formulae. Consider each quality or domain variable $o \in \mathcal{O}$, all the contribution links toward it coming from effects $e_1, e_2, \ldots$ labeled with values $l_{e_1}, l_{e_2}, \ldots$, and all contribution links coming from other qualities $o_1, o_2, \ldots$ – see Fig. 2 left side. Recalling that o is associated with fluents $\phi_o^{(r)}$ and $\phi_o^{(m)}$, the value of each is defined by the formulae at the right side of Fig. 2. In the formulae, $\hat{a}_i$ are the nature actions associated with effects e_i. Intuitively, the value v of quality o is a function f of the corresponding current or previous (depending on cross-run status) values of the other qualities and the labels of utility links coming from effects that are(/were) currently(/previously) true.

Action Precondition Axioms. For each task t which receives precedence links from a precondition element, a set of tasks $\{t_1, t_2, \ldots\}$, a set of goals $\{h_1, h_2, \ldots\}$ and a set of effects containing predicates $\{q_1, q_2, \ldots\}$ introduce:

$$poss(a_t, s) \leftrightarrow \phi_{q_1}(s) \wedge \phi_{q_2}(s) \wedge \ldots \wedge \phi_{t_1}(s) \wedge \phi_{t_2}(s) \wedge \ldots$$
$$\wedge \phi_{h_1}(s) \wedge \phi_{h_2}(s) \wedge \ldots \wedge g_{prec}(s) \wedge \neg\phi_t^{(att)}(s)$$

where $g_{prec}(s)$ is the formula inside the precondition element, grounded on fluents of type $\phi_q(s)$, and $\phi_t^{(att)}(s)$ is the attempt formula for the task in question itself. As will become apparent below, the latter addition prevents the RL learning agent from selecting the same task more than once in a given goal run. The above formula can be extended to include $\xrightarrow{npr}$ incoming links, omitted here for brevity; however it must be noted that for these links specifically, we utilize task and goal *attempt* formulae rather than *attainment* ones.

Reward. The total reward calculated for each situation is simply the *current* quality value of what has been designated as o_{top} as per the quality formula:

$$reward(v, s) \leftrightarrow \phi_{o_{top}}^{(r)}(v, s)$$

Probabilities. For each link that connects an effect e with its effect group, introduce $prob(\hat{a}, p, \cdot)$, where $\hat{a}$ is the nature action associated with e, and p is the probability label of the link – independent of situation, hence $\cdot$ instead of s.

OR-Decomposition Exclusivity. We finally demand that all children of OR-decompositions are connected in pairs with $\xrightarrow{npr}$ links. More formally, let $g_1, g_2, \ldots$ be children (goals or tasks) of an OR-decomposition. Then, assume $g_i \xrightarrow{npr} g_j$ for all $i \neq j$. The additions appear in action precondition axioms for the involved goals, following from the semantics of $\xrightarrow{npr}$.

The above translation process is automatable. A first prototype we have built to demonstrate this is capable of automatically generating the bulk of DT-Golog specification, leaving currently only a minimum of finishes to users [37].

4 Making Models Executable

4.1 The RL Simulation Components and Their Function

So far we have discussed the iStar-RL modeling language and how it can be formalized into a DT-Golog specification. We now describe how the latter specification can serve as a domain simulator usable by software agents implementing arbitrary RL algorithms. We adopt a widely used interface specification for RL simulators, Open AI's Gym framework [1], called *gym.Env*, which offers a small collection of functions that satisfy the RL observe-decide-act interaction pattern. Specifically, the most important of *gym.Env*'s functions is:

$$observation,\ reward,\ terminated,\ info \leftarrow step(action)$$

The function requests the simulator to perform *action*, identified as an integer within a range, and return: (a) the state which results from the performance of *action*, which is encoded in variable *observation* as a state-identifying integer for discrete-space problems or as an array of real values for continuous-space problems, (b) the *reward* obtained for performing the action, and (c) whether the current episode is *terminated*, and (d) other miscellaneous *info*. Our goal is, hence, to implement *step* (along with other auxiliary functions) such that it behaves in a way that is compliant to iStar-RL models of our choice.

To achieve this we introduce two software components. The *Query Engine* (*QE*) offers a number of functions that answer queries about the domain relative to a given history of actions, such as what fluents are true and what actions are possible. These services are used by *GMEnv*, a second component which implements the *gym.Env* standard. *GMEnv* maintains information about the current state of execution of a simulated episode, and executes actions or relays information as per the requests of the client environment. The latter is an arbitrary RL agent, implementing some RL learning algorithm (e.g., A2C [46], Deep Q Network (DQN) [47], etc.) and requiring the *gym.Env* interface for its training. We examine the development of *QE* and *GMEnv* in sequence.

4.2 The Query Engine (QE)

QE offers a set of functions whereby the iStar-RL model can be queried with respect to an effect history *eH*. The supported functions are listed in Table 1 and are implemented as logic programs in Prolog and in accordance to DT-Golog semantics also seen in the table. Below we present these semantics in more detail.

Extracting State Information. Consider the set $\mathcal{Q} = q_1, q_2, \ldots$ of domain predicates in the goal model and an effect history $eH = [e_1, e_2, \ldots]$. Define also list $L_{\mathcal{Q}} = [ql_1, ql_2, \ldots]$ where $ql_i = 1$ if the predicate q_i is satisfied after effect history eH has been observed, and $ql_i = 0$ otherwise. For discrete-state problems, $L_{\mathcal{Q}}$ offers a representation of discrete exported state and it is easily translatable to an integer identifier. For continuous-state problems, list $L_{\mathcal{O}} = [ol_1, ol_2, \ldots]$, where $ol_i = satQ(o_i, eH)$, represents continuous exported state for the goal model after eH for continuous exported state set $\{o_1, o_2, \ldots\} \subseteq \mathcal{O}$.

The semantics of $L_{\mathcal{Q}}$ and $L_{\mathcal{O}}$ in DT-Golog terms are understood as follows. Recall that there is a 1–1 correspondence between domain predicates $\mathcal{Q} = \{q_1, q_2, \ldots\}$ and DT-Golog fluents $\Phi_{\mathcal{Q}} = \{\phi_{q_1}, \phi_{q_2}, \ldots\}$, as well as between an effect history eH and a DT-Golog situation s. The following rule then defines $L_{\mathcal{Q}}$ in terms of situation s:

$getState(s, L_{\mathcal{Q}}) \leftrightarrow (\phi_{q_1}(s) \wedge (ql_1 = 1) \vee \neg\phi_{q_1}(s) \wedge (ql_1 = 0)) \wedge$
$(\phi_{q_2}(s) \wedge (ql_2 = 1) \vee \neg\phi_{q_2}(s) \wedge (ql_2 = 0)) \wedge \ldots$

Thus, $getState(s, L_{\mathcal{Q}})$ holds when binary list $L_{\mathcal{Q}}$ captures the truth value of every fluent in situation s. The predicate is the semantics of *QE* function `getState(eH): bit[]` seen in entry 5 of Table 1. For continuous exported states, recall that qualities $o \in \mathcal{O}$ in the goal model are associated with fluents of the

Table 1. Query Engine (QE) functions and their semantics. The functions assume a mapping of nature and stochastic actions to integers, hence `t` and `eH` are respectively an integer and an array thereof.

	QE Function	Semantics		QE Function	Semantics
1	`possibleAt(t,eH): bool`	$poss(a_t, s)$	7	`done(eH):bool`	$done(s) \equiv \phi_{rg} \vee deadlock(s)$
2	`getOutcomes(t): integer[]`	$choice(a_t, \{\hat{a}_t^{(1)}, \hat{a}_t^{(2)}, ...\})$	8	`deadlock(eH): bool`	$\forall \hat{a} \in \mathcal{N}_\mathcal{G}. \neg poss(\hat{a}, s)$
3	`getProbs(t,eH): float[]`	$getProbs(a_t, \{p_t^{(1)}, p_t^{(2)}, ...\}, s)$	9	`getCrState(eH): float/bool[]`	$crossState(L_{CR}, s)$
4	`reward(eH): float`	$reward(s, r)$	10	`setCrState(X)` (`X`: *initializations*)	assert(X)
5	`getState(eH):bit[]`	$getState(s, L_\mathcal{Q})$	11	`rootAchieved(eH): bool`	$\phi_{rg}(s)$
6	`getContState(eH): float[]`	$getConState (s, L_\mathcal{O})$			

form $\phi_o^{(r)}(v, s)$ in which v is a real value representing o's satisfaction $satQ(o, eH)$. Hence, for continuous exported state set $\{o_1, o_2, \ldots\} \subseteq \mathcal{O}$:

$$getContState(s, L_\mathcal{O}) \leftrightarrow \phi_{o_1}^{(r)}(v_1, s) \wedge (ol_1 = v_1) \wedge \phi_{o_2}^{(r)}(v_2, s) \wedge (ol_2 = v_2) \wedge ...$$

The predicate effectively maps a situation s with the value of fluents representing the qualities included in the exported state set, and constitutes the semantics of QE function `getContState(eH):float[]` – entry 6 of Table 1.

Episodes and Goal Runs. We now express the semantics of goal runs in terms of DT-Golog constructs. Recall that a task history is a goal run iff the root goal is satisfied or it leads to a deadlock. Recall also that for goal h, $satG(h, eH)$ iff $\phi_h(s)$, where s is the situation corresponding to history eH. Thus, root goal $r_\mathcal{G}$ is satisfied iff $\phi_{r_\mathcal{G}}(s)$. Secondly, to decide if a situation s is a deadlock we examine if any of the action precondition axioms allow the performance of any task at s. Let $\mathcal{N}_\mathcal{G}$ to be the set of all nature actions $\hat{a}$ (each corresponding to an effect $e \in \mathcal{E}_\mathcal{G}$), a situation s is a deadlock according to the following definition:

$$deadlock(s) \equiv \forall \hat{a} \in \mathcal{N}_\mathcal{G}. \neg poss(\hat{a}, s)$$

where $poss(\hat{a}, s)$ are, as we saw, the left-hand sides of action precondition axioms. Given the above, we can now define predicate $done(s)$ (entry 7 of Table 1) that holds when a situation s is a complete run with respect to root goal $r_\mathcal{G}$:

$$done(s) \equiv \phi_{r_\mathcal{G}}(s) \vee deadlock(s)$$

Cross-Run Elements. Recall from Fig. 2 that in the initial situation S_0, qualities are assigned an initial value v_{init}, while all other predicates/fluents are assumed to be false. QE allows the client environment to both assert these initial values and to read the values at a given situation s. This is useful for implementing cross-run elements within multi-run episodes. Let $L_{CR} = \{ol_1, ol_2, ..., ql_1, ql_2, ...\}$ represent the values of all cross-run qualities $o_1, o_2, \ldots$ and propositions

Algorithm 1. Implementation of the Step function of GMEnv.

```
GLOBAL: eH,tH = []                                      ▷ run-wide effect and task history
        eH_Ep,tH_Ep =[]                                 ▷ episode-wide effect and task history
        curRun = 0                                      ▷ the goal run under current consideration
        penaltyReward                                   ▷ default penalty for infeasible actions
        qe                                              ▷ reference to a QE implementing object
function STEP(t)
    if qe.possibleAt(t,eH) then
        Et = qe.getOutcomes(t)                          ▷ Et : list of effects
        Pt = qe.getProbs(t,eH)                          ▷ Pt: list of effect probabilities
        et = pickRndAction(Et,Pt)                       ▷ randomly pick effect
        eH = append(eH,et)                              ▷ append effect to history
        tH = append(tH,t)                               ▷ append task to history
        reward = qe.reward(eH)                          ▷ retrieve reward
        state = qe.getState(eH)                         ▷ retrieve new discrete state
        c_state = qe.getConState(eH)                    ▷ optional: retrieve
         new continuous state
        n_state = bitToInt(state)                       ▷ bit array to int
    else
        reward = penatlyReward                          ▷ penalize infeasible action
    end if
    if qe.rootAchieved(eH) then
        X = constructInitClauses(qe.getCrState(eH))
        qe.setCrState(X)
        eH_Ep.append(eH),tH_Ep.append(tH)
        eH,tH = []
        curRun = curRun + 1
    end if
    return n_state, reward, DONE, [c_state]
end function

function DONE
    return ((curRun == N) or qe.deadlock(eH))
end function
```

$q_1, q_2, \ldots$, where $ol_i = v$ iff $\phi_{o_i}(v, s)$ and $ql_i = 1$ iff $\phi_q(s)$, 0 otherwise. Predicate $crossState(s, L_{CR})$ (the semantics of *QE*'s `getCrState` – see entry 9 of Table 1) allows extraction of cross-state information given situation s corresponding to effect history eH:

$crossState(s, L_{CR}) \leftrightarrow \phi_{o_1}^{(m)}(v_1, s) \wedge (ol_1 = v_1) \wedge \phi_{o_2}^{(m)}(v_2, s) \wedge (ol_2 = v_2) \wedge \ldots$ $[\phi_{q_1}(s) \wedge (ql_1 = 1) \vee \neg\phi_{q_1}(s) \wedge (ql_1 = 0)] \wedge [\phi_{q_2}(s) \wedge (ql_2 = 1) \vee \neg\phi_{q_2}(s) \wedge (ql_2 = 0)] \wedge \ldots$

Dynamically defining initial states is a matter of asserting in the specification, using `setCrState`, the list of initializations $\{\phi_{o_1}(v_1', s_0), \phi_{o_2}(v_2', s_0), \ldots, \Phi_q^T(s_0)\}$, where v_i' are the desired initial values, $\Phi_q^T(s_0)$ the subset of fluents representing propositions that are true in s_0 – see entry 10 of Table 1. Thanks to the above two functions, *GMEnv* can implement multi-run episodes by reading the values of cross-run elements $o_1, o_2, \ldots, q_1, q_2, \ldots$ at the end of a run using `getCrState` and setting these as the initial values of the next episode using `setCrState`.

Other Predicates. The query engine offers additional functions, which can be viewed in Table 1, along with their DT-Golog semantics. One of them:

$$getProbs(a_t, \{p_1, p_2, \ldots\}, s) \leftrightarrow choice(a_t, \{\hat{a}_t^{(1)}, \hat{a}_t^{(2)}, \ldots\}) \wedge$$
$$prob(\hat{a}_t^{(1)}, p_1, s) \wedge prob(\hat{a}_t^{(2)}, p_2, s) \wedge \ldots$$

uses $choice(a_t, \hat{A})$ to collect probabilities $\{p_1, p_2, \ldots\}$ for all nature actions $\hat{A} = \{\hat{a}_t^{(1)}, \hat{a}_t^{(2)}, \ldots\}$ associated with task t's stochastic action a_t.

4.3 The GMEnv Component

GMEnv implements *gym.Env* through utilizing *QE*'s services. While *QE* is stateless, *GMEnv* maintains episode information including the history of tasks that have been attempted from the beginning of an episode, the effect history that has resulted from these attempts, the run count since the episode's beginning, as well as the state after the performance of the latest action.

Of the *gym.Env* functions that *GMEnv* implements, the most important is, as we saw, `step(task): state, reward, terminate, info`. Algorithm 1 sketches the implementation of the function. The function is iteratively called by the RL agent, with parameter a task `t` of its choosing. Upon its call, `step` checks first if the task is feasible given the current history of effect occurrences, stored in `eH`, through the use of *QE*'s `possibleAt(t,eH)`. If yes, it uses `getOutcomes(t)` to retrieve a list of possible effects `Et` that `t` may have and through `getProbs(t,eH)` their probabilities `Pt`. A random choice on the basis of the probabilities is made and both task `t` and the chosen effect `et` are appended to the corresponding lists, `tH` and `eH` respectively. The state resulting from the performance of `t` is calculated through `getState(eH)`, which translates a history of effect occurrences to an array of bits representing the truth values of domain propositions. An integer representation of the bit array, `n_state`, is, in turn, returned to the calling environment as per the *gym.Env* requirements. Likewise, `getConState(eH)` is called to retrieve any continuous exported state set.

If task `t` is not feasible at `eH`, `step` does not proceed with any changes to history lists and state, but may, based on user configuration, result in a negative reward to bias the learning procedure against performance of the task in the specific state. On the other hand, if the goal is achieved, the current run has concluded at `eH`. Consequently (a) the cross-run elements at `eH` are retrieved and reasserted as initial state for the next run, (b) the action and effect lists are added to the episode-wide record and (c) reset, and (d) the run counter increases by one. As we saw above, the episode is `done` if the root of the Nth goal run has been achieved or a deadlock has been detected.

Finally, the second important *gym.Env* function to be implemented by *GMEnv* `reset()`, simply empties the history lists and resets state to its initial values.

Table 2. Training with off-the-shelf RL agents. Times in CPU seconds. (*) next to an **Rnd.** reward signifies inclusion of deadlock penalty. Model size n, m: n is total # of OR-nodes, m total # of elements.

	Model Characteristics				Learning Tests									
	Model	Size	Run #	State Space	Learning Reward			Rnd.	Training Steps			Training Time (s)		
					A2C	DQN	PPO		A2C	DQN	PPO	A2C	DQN	PPO
Discrete	Material Ordered	1,12	1	2^6	0.924	0.924	0.924	0.773	10K	10K	10K	6.813	5.000	24.00
			2	2^{12}	1.711	1.712	1.715	1.466	10K	10K	10K	106.2	4.469	113.9
	Product Manuf.	2,20	1	2^{10}	0.477	0.480	0.465	0.058	10K	150K	20K	81.97	848	147.8
			2	2^{20}	0.946	0.705	0.710	0.065	10K	80K	20K	8,123	23.49K	20.32K
	Organize Travel	3,29	1	2^{14}	0.789	0.694	0.788	0.059	20K	150K	10K	400.3	1,957	436.7
	HVAC Control	1,13	4	2^{16}	-1.36	-1.37	-1.36	-5.041	10K	70K	10K	585	702.4	724.2
Conts.	Product Manuf.	2,20	1	$\mathbb{R}^2$	0.456	0.472	0.048	-78.42*	50K	80K	50K	778.4	972.9	181.3
			2	$\mathbb{R}^2$	0.286	0.667	0.325	-90.95*	70K	4.5M	70K	62.59	30,379	343.5
	HVAC Control	1,13	4	$\mathbb{R}^2$	-1.36	-1.36	-1.37	-5.00*	10K	110K	10K	709.5	390.1	769.8

4.4 In Action

The proposed components *QE* and *GMEnv* can be used by off-the-shelf algorithms for learning optimal policies for any appropriately formalized iStar-RL model. We performed tests with three such implementations, namely, Advantage Actor Critic (A2C) [46], Deep Q Network (DQN) [47] and Proximal Policy Optimization (PPO) [60], which are part of the Stable-Baselines3 RL package [57]. For the experiments, we used discrete and continuous versions of models such as those of Fig. 1. As a benchmark, for discrete-space problems, we also calculated optimal policies and their expected rewards using the DT-Golog interpreter. An Intel(R) Core(TM) i7-8650U CPU @ 1.90 GHz, 4 Core(s), 16 Gb RAM computer was used. As shown in Table 2, in all cases, using default hyper-parameters, the RL agents converged close to the optimal reward and away from the reward of the random policy. The tool and a reproducibility package can be found at [38].

Note, that, while the formalized iStar-RL models can be used by DT-Golog for exact, search-based identification of optimal policies as presented in our earlier work [40], that option is restricted to discrete-state problems and requires accurate probabilities. In the absence of accurate probabilities, where neither exact [40] nor learning-based methods (enabled in this paper) can calculate the true optimal, generating simulators as described here can still be useful for exploring the behavior of different RL algorithms using provisional probabilities. The utility of the toolset for such exploratory/feasibility analysis work is hinted at by the experimental results of Table 2 in which the three algorithms performed differently both in terms of optimization outcome and in terms of numbers of steps and time required.

5 Related Work

Substantial interest has developed over the past few years in studying the intersection of conceptual modeling (CM) with artificial intelligence (AI), a space referred to as CMAI [10,11]. The latter describes both the application of AI to support CM tasks (AI4CM), and reversely, the application of CM to systematize and support various qualities of AI-intensive systems (CM4AI). In the CM4AI space, where our work naturally fits, the use of models to organize and support the ML development pipeline from input collection and preparation to training and inference is explored [18]. The use of models has specifically been proposed for quality assuring the AI/ML process [33], detecting bias [66], supporting meta-learning [28], chatbot generation [56], or generation of neural architectures [35].

The problem of systematically devising AI-intensive systems has also been studied from the RE point of view. A major theme in that context is the quality of the end-result [27], with an emphasis on explainability [13–15], how such systems can be specified [9,63], and how the RE process can be organized [55]. In search for a solution to the RE4AI [3] problem, Nalchigar et al. [51,52] propose a goal-oriented conceptual framework for expressing machine learning requirements and designs organized around three main modeling views (business, analytics design, and data preparation). Ahmad et al. [3] review, among other things, modeling approaches for conducting RE for AI, to find that Goal Oriented RE languages, along with UML/SySML, are the most popular for modeling in that space.

Goal models have indeed been known to be effective vehicles for allowing formal reasoning about requirements and designs in various ways [19,20,23, 30,36,43]. This capability of goal models has been utilized also in the area of adaptive systems [6,8,22] and multi-agent systems [25]. The modeling approach proposed here, iStar-RL, is heavily based on an iStar dialect proposed for modeling decision-theoretic domains and, through formalization, perform search-based reasoning thereof [40,41]. The strength of the modeling approach we adopt, compared to common approaches for modeling probabilistic transition systems (e.g., [32]) lies in the combined ability of goal models both to concisely encode high-variability processes and behaviors, stemming from overarching stakeholder goals, and to compare variants vis-à-vis intricate, multi-dimensional quality requirements structures [50]. Hence, efforts such as on probabilistic logic shields [65] using ProbLog [34], or on using DT-Golog for Q-learning [7], indicate promising destinations of iStar-RL transformations. Probabilistic reasoning using conceptual models other than goal models, such as BPMN [54], has also been proposed [21,31], with no clear connection to RL however.

6 Concluding Remarks and Future Work

We presented a framework for goal-oriented modeling and generation of simulators for training RL agents. Through an extension to a standard goal modeling language, designers capture the goals, action space, and reward structure of the desired RL agents, along with the state and effect model of the environment the agents are meant to interact with. The resulting models are subsequently translated to a formal specification, which is used by a set of interpreting components to allow step-wise model execution, which is, in turn, directly usable by a variety of RL algorithms. The framework is aimed at supporting feasibility and performance analyses of training techniques against different action, reward, and probability models, and even at identifying a directly usable optimal policy when reward and probability models are deemed accurate but search-based methods are computationally forbidding or otherwise inapplicable.

Future research can focus on applications, tool support, and exploration of how goal models can support learning quality. Case studies can be helpful in assessing the utility of our approach in various domains, such as behavioral customization [39] and adaptive systems [24,48] with an emphasis on adaptive business processes [16], whose socio-technical nature fits naturally our $i*$-based approach. Enhancing our translation tool [37] to allow full automation will facilitate such studies. Further, while iStar 2.0 is a natural choice for agent modeling, extending the work to other languages, both goal-modeling ones, e.g., URN [4], and others, such as business process modeling ones [54], may be of value for the respective user communities. In addition, given the richness of the proposed extensions, studying approaches for dealing with diagrammatic complexity [44], including text-based modeling [2,45] or various forms of intelligent assistance [49] is high in our future work agenda. Potential may also exist in using our approach to address AI safety and explainability, via recognizing that the behavior of an RL agent that is trained exclusively based on an iStar-RL model is both constrained and explainable by information contained in that model. Finally, adapting our implementation to support multi-objective RL [29] is a logical step toward fully exploiting iStar-RL's ability to represent complex structures of quality criteria.

References

1. Open AI Gym (2022). https://github.com/openai/gym
2. Abdelzad, V., Amyot, D., Alwidian, S., Lethbridge, T.: A textual syntax with tool support for the goal-oriented requirement language. In: Proceedings of the 8th International i* Workshop (iStar 2015) (2015).https://ceur-ws.org/Vol-1402/paper6.pdf
3. Ahmad, K., Bano, M., Abdelrazek, M., Arora, C., Grundy, J.: What's up with requirements engineering for artificial intelligence systems? In: Proceedigns of the 29th IEEE International Requirements Engineering Conference (R 2021), pp. 1–12 (2021). https://doi.org/10.1109/RE51729.2021.00008
4. Amyot, D., Mussbacher, G.: User requirements notation: the first ten years, the next ten years (invited paper). J. Softw. (JSW) **6**(5), 747–768 (2011)
5. Anderson, R.N., Boulanger, A., Powell, W.B., Scott, W.: Adaptive stochastic control for the smart grid. Proc. IEEE **99**(6), 1098–1115 (2011). https://doi.org/10.1109/JPROC.2011.2109671
6. Angelopoulos, K., Papadopoulos, A.V., Silva Souza, V.E., Mylopoulos, J.: Model predictive control for software systems with CobRA. In: Proceedings of the 11th International Symposium on Software Engineering for Adaptive and Self-Managing Systems (SEAMS 2016), pp. 35–46. Association for Computing Machinery, New York (2016). https://doi.org/10.1145/2897053.2897054
7. Beck, D., Lakemeyer, G.: Reinforcement learning for Golog programs with first-order state-abstraction. Logic J. IGPL **20**(5), 909–942 (2012). https://doi.org/10.1093/jigpal/jzs011

8. Bencomo, N., Belaggoun, A.: Supporting decision-making for self-adaptive systems: from goal models to dynamic decision networks. In: Doerr, J., Opdahl, A.L. (eds.) REFSQ 2013. LNCS, vol. 7830, pp. 221–236. Springer, Heidelberg (2013). https://doi.org/10.1007/978-3-642-37422-7_16
9. Berry, D.M.: Requirements engineering for artificial intelligence: what is a requirements specification for an artificial intelligence? In: Gervasi, V., Vogelsang, A. (eds.) REFSQ 2022. LNCS, vol. 13216, pp. 19–25. Springer, Cham (2022). https://doi.org/10.1007/978-3-030-98464-9_2
10. Bork, D., Ali, S.J., Roelens, B.: Conceptual modeling and artificial intelligence: A systematic mapping study. The Computing Research Repository (CoRR) abs/2303.0 (2023). https://doi.org/10.48550/arXiv.2303.06758
11. Bork, D., et al.: 1st workshop on conceptual modeling meets artificial intelligence and data-driven decision making (CMAI 2020). In: Grossmann, G., Ram, S. (eds.) Advances in Conceptual Modeling. ER 2020 Workshops CMAI, CMLS, CMOMM4FAIR, CoMoNoS, EmpER. Vienna, Austria (2020), https://doi.org/10.1007/978-3-030-65847-213
12. Boutilier, C., Reiter, R., Soutchanski, M., Thrun, S.: Decision-theoretic, high-level agent programming in the situation calculus. In: Proceedings of the 17th Conference on Artificial Intelligence (AAAI 2000), pp. 355–362. AAAI Press, Austin, TX (2000). https://dl.acm.org/doi/10.5555/647288.721273
13. Brunotte, W., Chazette, L., Klös, V., Speith, T.: Quo vadis, explainability? – a research roadmap for explainability engineering. In: Gervasi, V., Vogelsang, A. (eds.) REFSQ 2022. LNCS, vol. 13216, pp. 26–32. Springer, Cham (2022). https://doi.org/10.1007/978-3-030-98464-9_3
14. Chazette, L., Brunotte, W., Speith, T.: Exploring explainability: a definition, a model, and a knowledge catalogue. In: Proceedings fo the 29th IEEE International Requirements Engineering Conference (RE 2021), pp. 197–208 (2021). https://doi.org/10.1109/RE51729.2021.00025
15. Chazette, L., Schneider, K.: Explainability as a non-functional requirement: challenges and recommendations. Requirements Eng. **25**(4), 493–514 (2020). https://doi.org/10.1007/s00766-020-00333-1
16. Cognini, R., Corradini, F., Gnesi, S., Polini, A., Re, B.: Business process flexibility - a systematic literature review with a software systems perspective. Inf. Syst. Front. **20**(2), 343–371 (2018). https://doi.org/10.1007/s10796-016-9678-2
17. Dalpiaz, F., Franch, X., Horkoff, J.: iStar 2.0 Language Guide. The Computing Research Repository (CoRR) abs/1605.0 (2016). http://arxiv.org/abs/1605.07767
18. Damiani, E., Frati, F.: Towards conceptual models for machine learning computations. In: Trujillo, J.C., et al. (eds.) ER 2018. LNCS, vol. 11157, pp. 3–9. Springer, Cham (2018). https://doi.org/10.1007/978-3-030-00847-5_1
19. Dell'Anna, D., Dalpiaz, F., Dastani, M.: Validating goal models via bayesian networks. In: Proceedings of the 5th International Workshop on Artificial Intelligence for Requirements Engineering (AIRE 2018), pp. 39–46 (2018). https://doi.org/10.1109/AIRE.2018.00012
20. Dell'Anna, D., Dalpiaz, F., Dastani, M.: Requirements-driven evolution of sociotechnical systems via probabilistic reasoning and hill climbing. Autom. Softw. Eng. **26**(3), 513–557 (2019). https://doi.org/10.1007/s10515-019-00255-5
21. Durán, F., Rocha, C., Salaün, G.: Stochastic analysis of BPMN with time in rewriting logic. Sci. Comput. Program. **168**, 1–17 (2018). https://doi.org/10.1016/j.scico.2018.08.007

22. Félix Solano, G., Diniz Caldas, R., Nunes Rodrigues, G., Vogel, T., Pelliccione, P.: Taming uncertainty in the assurance process of self-adaptive systems: a goal-oriented approach. In: Proceedings of the 14th IEEE/ACM International Symposium on Software Engineering for Adaptive and Self-Managing Systems (SEAMS 2019), pp. 89–99 (May 2019). https://doi.org/10.1109/SEAMS.2019.00020
23. Giorgini, P., Mylopoulos, J., Nicchiarelli, E., Sebastiani, R.: Formal reasoning techniques for goal models. In: Spaccapietra, S., March, S., Aberer, K. (eds.) Journal on Data Semantics I. LNCS, vol. 2800, pp. 1–20. Springer, Heidelberg (2003). https://doi.org/10.1007/978-3-540-39733-5_1
24. Goldsby, H.J., Sawyer, P., Bencomo, N., Cheng, B.H.C., Hughes, D.: Goal-based modeling of dynamically adaptive system requirements. In: 15th Annual IEEE International Conference and Workshop on the Engineering of Computer Based Systems (ecbs 2008), pp. 36–45 (200). https://doi.org/10.1109/ECBS.2008.22
25. Gonçalves, E., Araujo, J., Castro, J.: iStar4RationalAgents: modeling requirements of multi-agent systems with rational agents. In: Laender, A.H.F., Pernici, B., Lim, E.-P., de Oliveira, J.P.M. (eds.) ER 2019. LNCS, vol. 11788, pp. 558–566. Springer, Cham (2019). https://doi.org/10.1007/978-3-030-33223-5_46
26. Gottesman, O., et al.: Guidelines for reinforcement learning in healthcare. Nat. Med. **25**(1), 16–18 (2019). https://doi.org/10.1038/s41591-018-0310-5
27. Habibullah, K.M., Horkoff, J.: Non-functional requirements for machine learning: understanding current use and challenges in industry. In: Proceedings of the 29th IEEE International Requirements Engineering Conference (RE 2021), pp. 13–23 (2021). https://doi.org/10.1109/RE51729.2021.00009
28. Hartmann, T., Moawad, A., Schockaert, C., Fouquet, F., Le Traon, Y.: Meta-modelling meta-learning. In: Proceedings of the 2019 ACM/IEEE 22nd International Conference on Model Driven Engineering Languages and Systems (MODELS 2019), pp. 300–305 (2019). https://doi.org/10.1109/MODELS.2019.00014
29. Hayes, C.F., et al.: A practical guide to multi-objective reinforcement learning and planning. Auton. Agent. Multi-Agent Syst. **36**(1), 26 (2022). https://doi.org/10.1007/s10458-022-09552-y
30. Heaven, W., Letier, E.: Simulating and optimising design decisions in quantitative goal models. In: Proceedings of the 19th IEEE International Requirements Engineering Conference (RE 2011), pp. 79–88. Trento, Italy (2011). https://doi.org/10.1109/RE.2011.6051653
31. Herbert, L.T., Hansen, Z.N.L., Jacobsen, P.: SBOAT: a stochastic BPMN analysis and optimisation tool. In: Karlaftis, M.G., Lagaros, N.D., Papadrakakis, M. (eds.) Proceedings of the 1st International Conference on Engineering and Applied Sciences Optimization (OPT-i), pp. 1136–1152. National Technical University of Athens (2014). http://www.opti2014.org/
32. Hinton, A., Kwiatkowska, M., Norman, G., Parker, D.: PRISM: A tool for automatic verification of probabilistic systems. In: Hermanns, H., Palsberg, J. (eds.) TACAS 2006. LNCS, vol. 3920, pp. 441–444. Springer, Heidelberg (2006). https://doi.org/10.1007/11691372_29
33. Ishikawa, F.: Concepts in quality assessment for machine learning - from test data to arguments. In: Trujillo, J.C., et al. (eds.) ER 2018. LNCS, vol. 11157, pp. 536–544. Springer, Cham (2018). https://doi.org/10.1007/978-3-030-00847-5_39
34. Kimmig, A., Demoen, B., De Raedt, L., Costa, V.S., Rocha, R.: On the implementation of the probabilistic logic programming language ProbLog. Theory Pract. Logic Program. **11**(2–3), 235–262 (2011). https://doi.org/10.1017/S1471068410000566

35. Kusmenko, E., Nickels, S., Pavlitskaya, S., Rumpe, B., Timmermanns, T.: Modeling and training of neural processing systems. In: Proceedings of the ACM/IEEE 22nd International Conference on Model Driven Engineering Languages and Systems (MODELS 2019), pp. 283–293 (2019). https://doi.org/10.1109/MODELS.2019.00012
36. Letier, E., van Lamsweerde, A.: Reasoning about partial goal satisfaction for requirements and design engineering. In: Proceedings of the 12th International Symposium on the Foundation of Software Engineering (FSE 2004), pp. 53–62. ACM Press, Newport Beach, CA (Nov 2004). https://doi.org/10.1145/1041685.1029905
37. Liaskos, S.: Tool support for modeling and reasoning with decision theoretic goal models. CEUR Workshop Proceedings **3618** (2023). https://ceur-ws.org/Vol-3618/pd_paper_2.pdf
38. Liaskos, S., Golipour, R.: Tool and reproducibility package for: Model-driven design and generation of training simulators for reinforcement learning (2024). https://github.com/cmg-york/RLGen
39. Liaskos, S., Khan, S.M., Litoiu, M., Jungblut, M.D., Rogozhkin, V., Mylopoulos, J.: Behavioral adaptation of information systems through goal models. Inform. Syst. (IS) **37**(8), 767–783 (2012). https://doi.org/10.1016/j.is.2012.05.006
40. Liaskos, S., Khan, S.M., Mylopoulos, J.: Modeling and reasoning about uncertainty in goal models: a decision-theoretic approach. Softw. Syst. Model. **21**, 1–24 (2022). https://doi.org/10.1007/s10270-021-00968-w
41. Liaskos, S., Khan, S.M., Soutchanski, M., Mylopoulos, J.: Modeling and Reasoning with Decision-Theoretic Goals. In: Proceedings of the 32th International Conference on Conceptual Modeling, (ER 2013), Hong-Kong, China, pp. 19–32 (2013). https://doi.org/10.1007/978-3-642-41924-9_3
42. Liaskos, S., McIlraith, S.A., Mylopoulos, J.: Towards augmenting requirements models with preferences. In: Proceedings of the 24th IEEE/ACM International Conference on Automated Software Engineering (ASE 2009), pp. 565–569 (2009). https://doi.org/10.1109/ASE.2009.91
43. Liaskos, S., McIlraith, S.A., Sohrabi, S., Mylopoulos, J.: Integrating preferences into goal models for requirements engineering. In: Proceedings of the 10th IEEE International Requirements Engineering Conference (RE 2010), Sydney, Australia (2010). https://doi.org/10.1109/RE.2010.26
44. Lima, P., et al.: Scalability of istar: a systematic mapping study. In: Workshop em Engenharia de Requisitos (WER 2016) (2016). https://api.semanticscholar.org/CorpusID:59248836
45. Liu, W., Wang, Y., Zhou, Q., Li, T.: Graphical modeling vs. textual modeling: an experimental comparison based on istar models. In: Proceedings of the 45th IEEE Annual Computers, Software, and Applications Conference (COMPSAC 2021), pp. 844–853 (2021). https://doi.org/10.1109/COMPSAC51774.2021.00117
46. Mnih, V., et al.: Asynchronous methods for deep reinforcement learning. In: Proceedings of the 33rd International Conference on Machine Learning (ICML 2016), pp. 1928–1937. JMLR.org (2016). https://dl.acm.org/doi/10.5555/3045390.3045594
47. Mnih, V., et al.: Human-level control through deep reinforcement learning. Nature **518**(7540), 529–533 (2015). https://doi.org/10.1038/nature14236
48. Morandini, M., Penserini, L., Perini, A.: Towards goal-oriented development of self-adaptive systems. In: Proceedings of the 2008 International Workshop on Software Engineering for Adaptive and Self-Managing Systems, SEAMS 2008, pp. 9–16.

Association for Computing Machinery, New York (2008). https://doi.org/10.1145/1370018.1370021
49. Mussbacher, G., et al.: Opportunities in intelligent modeling assistance. Softw. Syst. Model. **19**(5), 1045–1053 (2020). https://doi.org/10.1007/s10270-020-00814-5
50. Mylopoulos, J., Chung, L., Liao, S., Wang, H., Yu, E.: Exploring alternatives during requirements analysis. IEEE Softw. **18**(1), 92–96 (2001). https://doi.org/10.1109/52.903174
51. Nalchigar, S., Yu, E.: Business-driven data analytics: a conceptual modeling framework. Data Knowl. Eng. **117**, 359–372 (2018). https://doi.org/10.1016/j.datak.2018.04.006
52. Nalchigar, S., Yu, E., Keshavjee, K.: Modeling machine learning requirements from three perspectives: a case report from the healthcare domain. Requirements Eng. **26**(2), 237–254 (2021). https://doi.org/10.1007/s00766-020-00343-z
53. Nguyen, C.M., Sebastiani, R., Giorgini, P., Mylopoulos, J.: Multi-objective reasoning with constrained goal models. Requirements Eng. **23**(2), 189–225 (2018). https://doi.org/10.1007/s00766-016-0263-5
54. Object Management Group: Business Process Model And Notation (v2.0). Tech. rep. (2011). https://www.omg.org/spec/BPMN/2.0.2/PDF
55. Pei, Z., Liu, L., Wang, C., Wang, J.: Requirements engineering for machine learning: a review and reflection. In: Proceedings of the 30th IEEE International Requirements Engineering Conference Workshops (REW 2022), pp. 166–175 (2022). https://doi.org/10.1109/REW56159.2022.00039
56. Pérez-Soler, S., Guerra, E., de Lara, J.: Model-driven chatbot development. In: Dobbie, G., Frank, U., Kappel, G., Liddle, S.W., Mayr, H.C. (eds.) ER 2020. LNCS, vol. 12400, pp. 207–222. Springer, Cham (2020). https://doi.org/10.1007/978-3-030-62522-1_15
57. Raffin, A., Hill, A., Gleave, A., Kanervisto, A., Ernestus, M., Dormann, N.: Stable-baselines3: reliable reinforcement learning implementations. J. Mach. Learn. Res. **22**(268), 1–8 (2021). http://jmlr.org/papers/v22/20-1364.html
58. Rao, A., Jelvis, T.: Foundations of Reinforcement Learning with Applications in Finance. Chapman and Hall/CRC (2022)
59. Reiter, R.: Knowledge in Action. MIT Press, Logical Foundations for Specifying and Implementing Dynamical Systems (2001)
60. Schulman, J., Wolski, F., Dhariwal, P., Radford, A., Klimov, O.: Proximal Policy Optimization Algorithms. The Computing Research Repository (CoRR) (201). https://doi.org/10.48550/arxiv.1707.06347
61. Soutchanski, M.: High-Level Robot Programming in Dynamic and Incompletely Known Environments. Ph.D. thesis, Department of Computer Science, University of Toronto (2003)
62. Sutton, R.S., Barto, A.G.: Reinforcement Learning: An Introduction. The MIT Press (2018)
63. Vogelsang, A., Borg, M.: Requirements engineering for machine learning: perspectives from data scientists. In: Proceedigns of the 6th International Workshop on Artificial Intelligence for Requirements Engineering (AIRE 2019), pp. 245–251 (2019). https://doi.org/10.1109/REW.2019.00050
64. Wei, H., Zheng, G., Yao, H., Li, Z.: IntelliLight: a reinforcement learning approach for intelligent traffic light control. In: Proceedings of the 24th ACM SIGKDD International Conference on Knowledge Discovery & Data Mining (KDD 2018), pp. 2496–2505. Association for Computing Machinery, New York (2018). https://doi.org/10.1145/3219819.3220096

65. Yang, W.C., Marra, G., Rens, G., De Raedt, L.: Safe Reinforcement learning via probabilistic logic shields. In: Proceedings of the 32nd International Joint Conference on Artificial Intelligence (IJCAI 2023), pp. 5739–5749 (2023). https://doi.org/10.24963/ijcai.2023/637
66. Yohannis, A., Kolovos, D.: Towards model-based bias mitigation in machine learning. Proceedings of the 25th ACM/IEEE International Conference on Model Driven Engineering Languages and Systems (MODELS 2022), pp. 143–153 (2022). https://doi.org/10.1145/3550355.3552401

Domain and Goal Modeling

Generating Secure Workflow Designs from Requirements Goal Models Using Patterns

Sotirios Liaskos[1](✉), Ibrahim Jaouhar[1], Syed Muhammad Danish[1], and Shakil M. Khan[2]

[1] School of Information Technology, York University, Toronto, Canada
{liaskos,jaouhar,smdanish}@yorku.ca
[2] Department of Computer Science, University of Regina, Regina, Canada
shakil.khan@uregina.ca

Abstract. Identifying and analyzing security requirements is an essential part of the information systems engineering lifecycle. Several techniques have been introduced for comprehensively modeling such requirements. Once identified, security requirements must be translated into designs that allow domain actors to securely accomplish business tasks under given risk assumptions and contexts. Correctly translating requirements to such designs, however, can be challenging when considering both the complexity and specialized nature of security mechanisms, such as cryptography, and the role of varying practical and contextual aspects of the problem at hand in correctly applying such mechanisms. We propose a model-driven pattern-based approach for supporting the implementation of security requirements. Security requirements models, augmented with descriptions of contextual and threat assumptions, are combined with reusable domain-agnostic workflow patterns which model established ways for securely performing common business tasks. The combined models are compiled into a formal specification, whereby automated reasoning is applied for generating domain-appropriate workflows that satisfy the security requirements. Using the technique, analysts can efficiently explore the impact of different threat assumptions and pragmatic constraints to candidate security designs, while ensuring that the latter are consistent with tried-and-tested community knowledge.

Keywords: Goal Modeling · Security Requirements · AI Planning

1 Introduction

Identifying and analyzing security requirements is considered to be an essential part of the early stages of the software development lifecycle [9,10,19,36]. Specifying such requirements upfront allows the security components that implement them to become an organic part of the resulting system [11,14,23]. A wealth of techniques for modeling security requirements have been proposed, aimed at

W. Maass et al. (Eds.): ER 2024, LNCS 15238, pp. 195–214, 2025.
https://doi.org/10.1007/978-3-031-75872-0_11

allowing precise description of both such requirements and their relationship to other dimensions of the problem at hand [29,33,39].

However, developing models of security requirements is only the first step towards a secure system. A design must be produced that appropriately implements such requirements in accordance to widely accepted security standards. For example, to support secure exchange of information, cryptographic primitives [32] of the right kind vis-à-vis the required security guarantees need to be introduced and correctly [15] applied. Furthermore, there may be multiple options with regards to the choice and practical application of these primitives based on varying perceptions about the key threats, vulnerabilities, and practical constraints in the domain. Effectively capturing and combining these different problem aspects to devise a well-fitted solution, that also includes the correct choice and use of security mechanisms, can be challenging without support.

We propose a model-driven framework for supporting the implementation of security requirements according to recommended best practices and consistent with pragmatic constraints and threat assumptions of the problem at hand. The framework is based on encoding such best practices as patterns that compactly describe a large number of alternative workflows for fulfilling common business tasks. Each such workflow includes or does not include different kinds of security-enhancing steps, and is accompanied by a set of attack models, which encode alternative attacks against security properties of the processes modeled by the pattern. To address a specific problem, goal-oriented requirements analysis is performed using a combination of general-purpose and security-centered goal models. Patterns that constitute appropriate implementations of security-relevant goals in those models are adopted and infused into the models. The result is subsequently augmented with a threat model, that describes the level of sophistication of the attacks to be defended against, as well as other pertinent domain constraints. It is then compiled into a formal specification that can be used for automatically identifying workflows that indicate what security steps domain actors need to take while pursuing their domain-specific business tasks.

The approach allows systematic exploration and derivation of security designs that comply with requirements, community best practices, and constraints of the problem at hand. Among its contributions are the use of high-variability goal decompositions as best practice-encoding models for security and the utilization of planners for high-level reasoning about both the security mechanisms and the socio-technical processes in which these are embedded. To demonstrate the technique, we apply it to a common inter-organizational order fulfillment scenario, using a prototypical inter-actor information exchange pattern.

The paper is organized as follows. We present the modeling process in Sect. 2 and the formalization and analysis details in Sect. 3. We offer related work in Sect. 4 and conclude in Sect. 5.

2 Developing Security-Enhanced Goal Models

2.1 Motivating Example and Framework Overview

Consider the example of a medium-sized residential building contractor requesting quotes, submitting orders, and sending payments to various material suppliers. Typically, the contractor submits orders for materials and, once the materials have been delivered, an invoice is sent with a payment information, often in the form of a bank account number for sending a wire transfer. The contractor performs such interactions via email, which, however, introduces several threats, including the submission and fulfillment of unauthorized orders through spoofing, and invoice fraud, i.e., submission of a tampered invoice, where the payment information has been replaced with the attacker's account numbers.

If our contractor were a large company, a holistic B2B solution may have been devised by experts, acquired, and integrated with, e.g., the company's enterprise resource planning system. However, such solutions may not be accessible by smaller organizations that use common communication and productivity software such as word processors, emails, and shared drives to arrange common business transactions. Nevertheless, such systems offer security functions that could offer protection to at least some level. In the contractor example, simple encryption of the exchanged order and invoice documents from within their authoring software [2,35] could protect against certain kinds of attacks. However, without guidance, improper application of those tools and functions is possible. For example, sending a symmetrically encrypted invoice by email followed by a second email with the encryption key in plaintext does not protect against attack scenarios in which the email accounts are compromised. How the encryption key can be shared otherwise depends on what communication channels are available and how secure these are perceived to be, given an assessment of how motivated and capable potential attackers are. Contextual and practical aspects, such as the willingness and skill of actors across organizations to utilize specific software or take extra security steps may also affect the recommended solution.

The proposed framework is aimed at assisting analysts of cases such as the above in systematically generating secure workflow designs – i.e., sequences of steps that domain actors can take to accomplish business tasks in a secure way. The framework is based on the development and gradual refinement of a series of models of various aspects of the problem, the selection and adoption of authoritative patterns that encode multiple ways to implement security requirements, and the fusion of these developed and adopted artifacts into a formal specification that allows automated identification of solutions.

An overview can be seen in Fig. 1. The analysts begin by developing goal models that describe the domain-specific functional and non-functional goals of stakeholders of the socio-technical system in question (Step 1). Subsequently, goals and dependencies that entail security-relevant actor activity are identified and the security requirements vis-à-vis those goals are specified (Step 2). For each of the security-relevant goals, analysts identify matching security decomposition patterns from a collection of such developed and supported by the community of

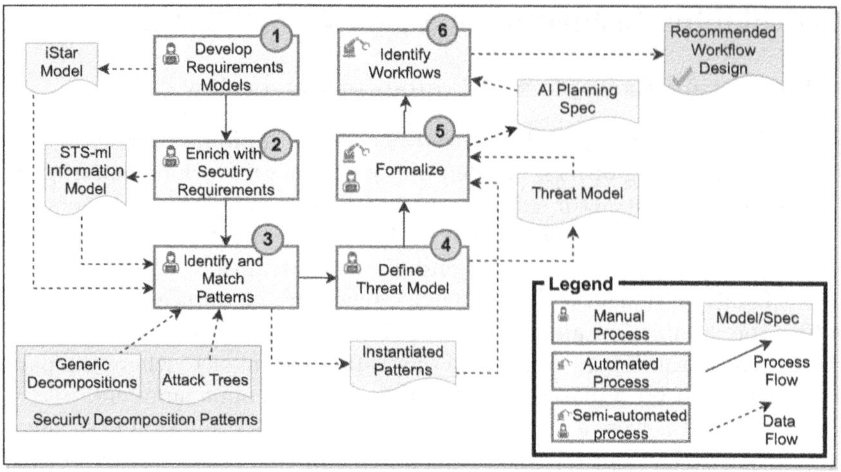

Fig. 1. Framework overview.

experts. They adopt the identified patterns by instantiating them with domain specific information, and linking them to the matching security-relevant goals (Step 3). Subsequently, they develop a threat model that reflects the specific business context (Step 4). The subsequent tasks aim at identifying secure workflows, i.e., solutions of the instantiated patterns that describe actor activity to satisfy the domain goals of interest in a secure way. Specifically, the instantiated decomposition patterns are first transformed into a formal specification (Step 5) and the latter is used by an automated reasoner to generate the required solutions (Step 6). In the following we describe each of these steps.

2.2 Extending iStar 2.0: iStar T

The main modeling language we use in our proposal is based on an extension of the goal modeling standard iStar 2.0 [8], which we will here refer to as *iStar T*. An example of an iStar T model can be viewed in Fig. 3. The model features most typical iStar 2.0 elements, such as *goals* (states of affairs that an actor wants to achieve) and *tasks* (actions that an actor can execute to achieve goals). For simplicity, the specific example omits additional iStar 2.0 elements such as *actors* and *qualities*, the latter being attributes for which an actor wants some level of achievement [8]. When a goal is AND-refined (resp., OR-refined) into a set of other goals and/or tasks, all (resp., exactly one) of the goals in that set needs to be satisfied for the parent goal to be considered satisfied.

The additional elements of *iStar T* are aimed at modeling temporal and causal constraints. Firstly, a vocabulary of *domain predicates* and *domain objects* is introduced to be used for constructing first-order *domain literals*, to, in turn, represent the state of the environment and how state changes as tasks are performed. Thus, *Has(john, encryptedDoc(invoice, publicKey(bill))* is a domain literal, constructed from predicate *Has* and objects *john*, *bill*, *encryptedDoc*(·,·), and *publicKey*(·) – henceforth predicates and variables start with capital and individuals/functions with small letter. Two added visual elements contain domain predicates: *preconditions* and *effects*. Preconditions contain Boolean formulae of domain literals and effects contain lists of such. In both cases, arguments are either objects or variables. Three additional kinds of links are also introduced in *iStar T*: *precedence links* $\xrightarrow{pre}$, *negative precedence links* $\xrightarrow{npr}$ and *effect links* $\xrightarrow{eff}$. Precedence (resp., negative precedence) links can be drawn from preconditions, goals, or tasks and can target goals or tasks, and mean that performance of the latter is not possible unless (resp., if), the origin is satisfied. Effect links are drawn from tasks to effects and signify that performance of the task makes the non-negated domain predicates listed in the effect true, and the negated false.

In addition, iStar T models may contain an *initialization template*. This element contains a list of patterns that describe what kinds of domain predicates need to be introduced to allow instance-level analysis. The patterns are of the form $\{P_1, P_2, \ldots : Pred(P_1, P_2, \ldots)\}$ and mean that instances of $Pred(P_1, P_2, \ldots)$ can be produced for various bindings of the corresponding variables with objects. For example, based on domain information, template {*S,R: HasEmailAddress(S, R)*}, may be instantiated to predicates *HasEmailAddress(contractor,supplier)* and *HasEmailAddress(accountant,contractor)* – or to no predicates at all.

Finally, the content of goals and tasks in iStar T are also first-order literals – e.g., *Encrypt(Sender, Recipient, Document)*. Replacing the parameters with domain objects signifies a specific instance of a goal or task, e.g., *Encrypt(john, bill, invoice)*. A subgoal, task, or effect can contain a subset of the parameters contained by the parent goal and every enabling precondition. Likewise, the parameters of literals in effects are a subset of those in the task that is associated with the effect. Typically, the leaf level elements of an iStar T decomposition model within the scope of an actor are tasks. However, it is possible that the decomposition is terminated at a predicate-containing goal.

Given a complete iStar T model there is variability in the ways by which tasks can be sequentially executed for fulfilling a root goal. A *task trajectory* $tH = \{a_1, a_2, \ldots\}$ (also: *solution* to the root goal) represents one such sequence that satisfies the added temporal constraints. It is, furthermore, *goal-satisfying* if the tasks included in tH satisfy the root goal. The term *workflow* as discussed in this paper refers to such trajectories.

2.3 Modeling Domain and Security Requirements

We now turn our focus to how we use iStar T, in conjunction with other kinds of models, to generate security designs based on high-level security requirements.

Firstly, a goal-oriented analysis of the requirements of the problem at hand is performed using iStar T. In Fig. 2, top diagram, the interaction between *Contractor* and *Supplier* is shown in the form of a hybrid strategic rationale / strategic dependency diagram [8]. The resulting model (here using only the iStar 2.0 subset

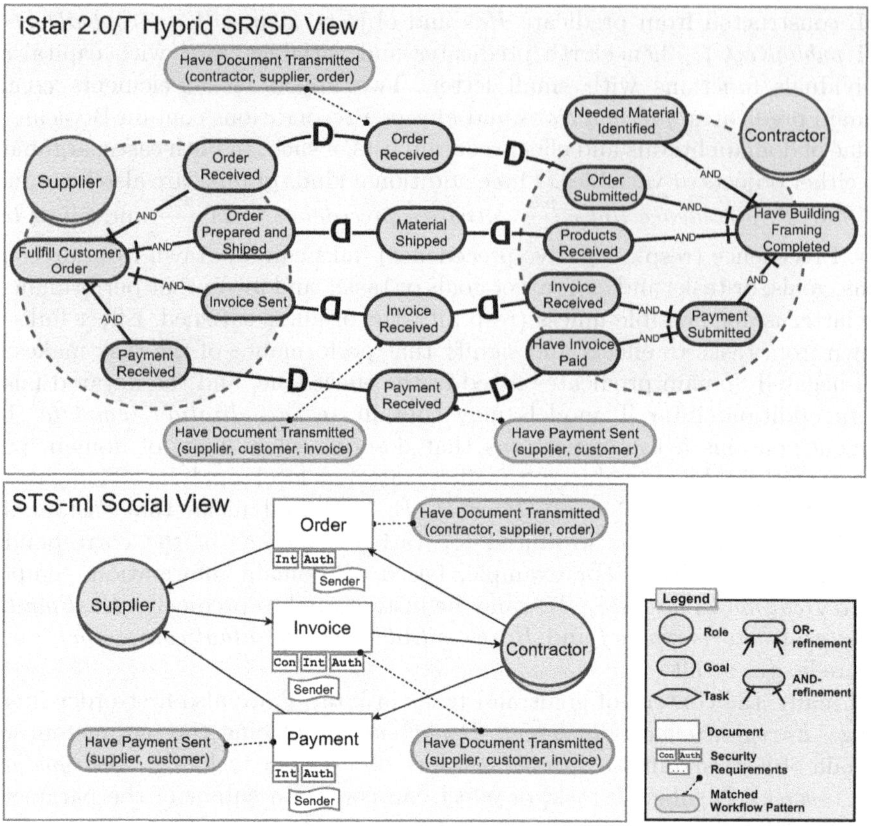

Fig. 2. iStar and STS-ml requirements models.

for simplicity) offers the rationale and context in which security-relevant activity between the two actors needs to take place. To further identify such activity and specify the exact security associated with it we use STS-ml (Socio-Technical Security modeling language [9]). In STS-ml, a variety of views are defined for describing security requirements within a socio-technical context. We are here interested in the *social view* in which, among other things, the exchange of information between domain actors is displayed, along with security requirements that such exchange should satisfy. In Fig. 2, bottom diagram, an *Invoice* document needs to be submitted to the *Contractor* containing the amount owed and a bank account in which the amount is to be deposited. The sender is to ensure that security requirements are to be met in such transmission. In our case, we require that the document needs to remain confidential (marked with the label `Con`), that it shall not be tampered with (marked with `Int`), and that the recipient shall be able to verify that the document was indeed prepared by the supplier (marked with `Auth`). This kind of analysis is performed for all dependencies identified in the iStar model that entail some form of exchange of an informational asset.

2.4 Decomposition Patterns

The models resulting from the above process describe the business context and rationale of security-relevant actor activity and the specific security requirements associated with the latter. However, although they describe what security is needed they do not say *how* it can be attained. For example, the models describe a need to transfer an invoice document from the supplier to the contractor with specific security requirements (`Con`, `Int`, etc.), but no concrete steps are offered to fulfill those requirements. For example, should the supplier just email the invoice as-is? Or should they encrypt it first? Maybe also sign it? If yes, with what tools and configurations?

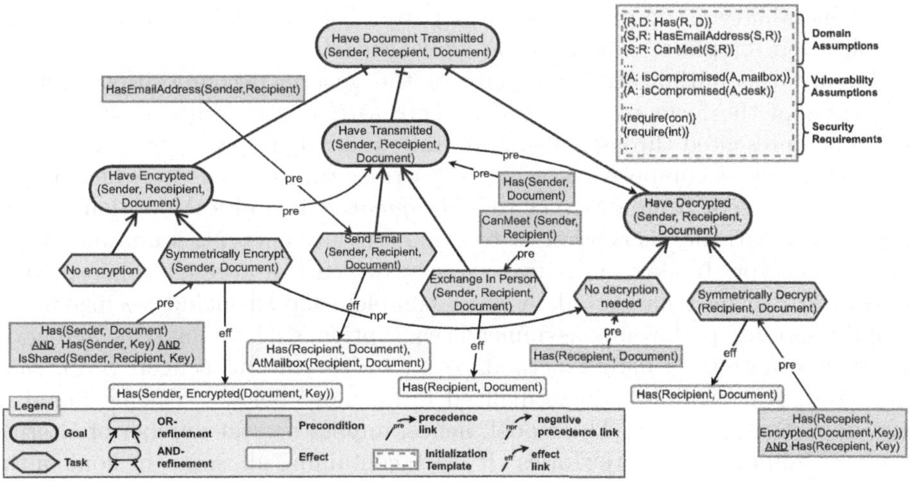

Fig. 3. The Transmit Information decomposition pattern (simplified).

To capture authoritative ways by which such questions can be answered, a number of *security decomposition patterns* embodying best practices for fulfilling common business tasks are maintained and available for adoption and use. Each pattern consists of (a) a goal decomposition model in iStar T with a mandatory initialization template, together called the *generic decomposition*, and (b) a set of *attack trees* and *satisfaction conditions* to be discussed below. The pattern is identified by the root of the generic decomposition. Figure 3 shows a (partial for brevity) generic decomposition for pattern *Have Document Transmitted(Sender, Recipient, Document)*. The model encodes various ways by which the goal can be executed in secure or less secure ways. Further, its initialization template seen at the top right of Fig. 3, offers a vocabulary of predicates to be used to define instance-level: (a) *domain assumptions*, (b) *vulnerability assumptions* and (c) pertinent *security requirements*.

Domain assumptions are practical aspects of the domain at hand that may affect the applicability of security controls and/or attacks against them. Examples of instances of such assumptions include whether the involved parties have each other's handles (email address, phone number, etc.), e.g., *HasEmailAddress (contractor, supplier)*, or statements about the format and size of the information to be exchanged, e.g., *DigitalFile(invoice)*. Vulnerability assumptions, on the other hand, represent a state of affairs in which possible attacks have been successfully carried out. For instance, we may assume that the email account of either party has been compromised, that their PCs or phones run a rootkit, or that their physical space is compromised, using predicates such as *IsCompromised (supplier, emailAccount)*, *IsHacked(contractor, cellphone)*, or *IsCompromised (supplier, desk)*. Asserting a vulnerability assumption indicates that an attacker is motivated enough to bear the cost of the corresponding attack, given the business context and anticipated benefit. The set of concrete domain and vulnerability assumptions that result from instantiating the corresponding initialization templates constitute the *threat model*.

Finally, the initialization template of the generic decomposition contains predicates of the form *requires([SR])*, where *[SR]* is a security requirement of interest, represented through the appropriate individual (e.g., *con* or *int*).

The generic decomposition of Fig. 3 describes various ways by which a *Document* can be sent from a *Sender* to a *Recipient*. It includes the option to send in plaintext with no encryption or to symmetrically encrypt, send, and subsequently decrypt. It also shows two ways by which the message (encrypted or otherwise) can be transmitted. A more complete model includes subgoals for digitally signing, performing asymmetric encryption, exchanging keys, and additional information exchange methods (e.g., by specific messenger, SMS, snail mail etc.). An example – in formalized form, more below – can be found in our supporting page [30]. The model, hence, implies a great number of alternative goal-fulfilling task trajectories tH, each containing all, some, or none of the security enabling tasks in the model. Which one of the implied trajectories is recommended for the problem at hand will depend on the specific threat model and security requirements, i.e., how the initialization template is instantiated, as well as a model of possible attacks. We discuss the latter next.

2.5 Attack Trees and Satisfaction Conditions

While decomposition patterns capture a family of workflows by which goals of domain actors can be fulfilled, associated *attack trees* [43] present a family of ways by which an attacker can compromise such workflows from a point of view of a specific security requirement. We model attack trees using iStar T as seen in Fig. 4. The model contains a quality goal whose breach is the root goal of the attack tree. Each decomposition pattern is associated with a number of attack trees, each showing how a specific security requirement (e.g., confidentiality, integrity, or authentication) can be breached.

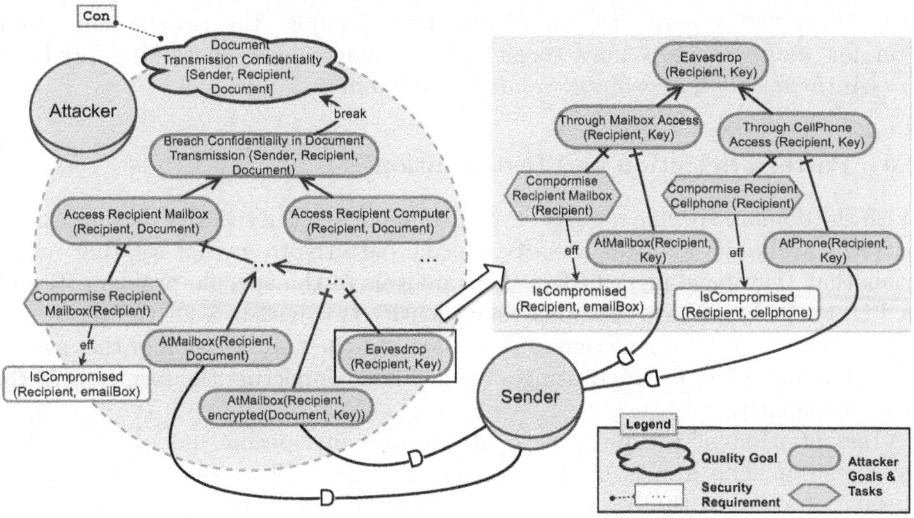

Fig. 4. An attack tree. Ellipses ("...") signify decomposition parts omitted for brevity.

The attack tree contains several steps (and alternatives thereof) an attacker needs to take in order to achieve that root goal. In the case of document transmission, the attacker can compromise the recipient's mailbox (e.g., crack their email password) in order to retrieve the document itself or the key to its decryption, if it has been encrypted. Alternatively, they can gain physical access to the computer of the recipient and install tracking devices (e.g., keyloggers or cameras). Importantly, for some attacks to be successful, the victim must have performed enabling actions. For example, for the encryption key to be retrieved from the recipient's mailbox following successful cracking of their password, the recipient must have received such keys in plaintext by email. These are represented as goals at the leaf level of the attack tree, containing domain predicates that appear in the associated generic decomposition (Fig. 2).

From the attacker's standpoint, each attack tree reduces to an AND/OR formula that reflects the decomposition structure and is grounded on domain literals that are either contained in effects of attacker's actions (e.g., *IsCompromised(Recepient, emailBox)*) or are included as the content of the leaf level goals delegated to other actors (e.g., *AtMailbox(Recepient, Document)*). Depending on the truth values of the domain literals, the formula is true or false, signifying that the attack can be successful or not, respectively. The goal, hence, is to identify task trajectories tH in the decomposition pattern such that, given an initialization instantiation of the generic decomposition, the root(s) of one or more attack trees relating to desired security qualities is/are not satisfied.

In addition to attack trees, patterns may contain *satisfaction conditions* that describe necessary conditions that must be true for a specific security requirement to be satisfied. These are also AND/OR decompositions whose leaf level is exclusively goals containing domain predicates from the generic decomposition. For example, the satisfaction condition for *authentication* may consist of the single goal containing predicate $HasAuthenticated(Recepient, Sender, Document)$.

2.6 Pattern Selection and Instantiation

With the domain specific models developed and the set of security decomposition patterns available, analysts identify specific patterns from that set that match goals that they have identified in their analysis of the specific problem (Step 3 in Fig. 1). In Fig. 2, for example, they identify two instances of the pattern of Fig. 3, namely the transmission of the order and the transmission of the invoice. The matching is represented using a dashed line connecting the former with the root of the latter.

Instantiation of the pattern to fit the domain specific model takes place in two steps. The first is binding the parameters of the root goal to domain-specific objects. In the invoice transmission example, *Sender* is bound to *supplier*, *Recipient* to *contractor*, and *Document* to *invoice*. The second step involves appropriately instantiating the initialization template of the generic decomposition to encode the desired threat model and specific security requirements. In our example, the initialization template can be instantiated with the threat model *isCompromised(contract,mailbox)* (vuln. assumption) and *CanMeet(contractor,supplier)* (dom. assumption), and concrete security requirements *require(con)*, *require(int)*, and *require(auth)* as per the STS-ml model of Fig. 2.

The result of the above process is that domain-specific goals are now linked with generic decompositions, appropriately instantiated to information specific with the problem at hand. This linkage can be seen as supplying authoritative decomposition trees to security-relevant goals of the domain-specific model, instead of developing these decompositions from scratch for every problem instance. However, the adopted authoritative decompositions continue to be generic in a sense that they support all possible ways, secure or otherwise, to fulfill the security-relevant goals. The final step is to identify solutions tH of each decomposition that satisfy the threat model and the security requirements, the latter via denying and enabling, respectively, the corresponding attack trees and satisfaction conditions. To do so, we formalize the instantiated patterns (Step 4 of Fig. 1) and utilize an automated reasoner to find such solutions (Step 5).

3 Generating Secure Workflows

To identify security requirements-satisfying solutions of the instantiated patterns we translate the latter into an AI planning specification, according to translation rules we sketch in this section. We start by presenting the constituents of an AI planning specification and proceed to present the rules.

3.1 HTN Planning

AI planners are automated reasoners which receive a *domain specification* and a *problem specification* as input and generate a solution to the planning problem as output. We will here focus on Hierarchical Task Network (HTN) Planners, specifically SHOP2 [37] and its specification language.

A domain specification consists of: a set of domain predicates, a set of *tasks*, a set of *operators*, a set of *methods*, and a set of *axioms* [37]. Domain predicates are first-order predicate symbols used for representing state features, as, e.g., in literal `Encrypted(Document, Key)`. Tasks represent activity to be performed and consist of a task symbol and its parameters, as in `Encrypt(Document, Key)`. Tasks can be *primitive*, in which case they can be accomplished through an operator, or they can be *compound*, in which case they are broken down into smaller tasks according to one or more alternative method specifications. Operators describe how primitive tasks can be performed and consist of a head $\mathtt{t}$, which is the primitive task that the operator specifies and its parameters, a *precondition* $\mathtt{t}^{pre}$ containing a formula specifying what needs to be true in order for the operator to be applicable, a *delete list* $\mathtt{t}^{del}$, and an *add list* $\mathtt{t}^{add}$, listing predicates that turn, respectively, false or true, upon application of the operator. Operators can also carry a *cost* value $\mathtt{t}^{c}$. In a well-formed operator, the parameters of the predicates of $\mathtt{t}^{del}$ and $\mathtt{t}^{add}$ are the subset of the union of parameters of $\mathtt{t}$ and $\mathtt{t}^{pre}$. Methods consist of a compound task $\mathtt{m}$ that the method decomposes, a precondition $\mathtt{m}^{pre}$ which needs to be true before the method can be considered, and a list of tasks $\mathtt{m}^{t} = \{\mathtt{m}_1, \mathtt{m}_2, \ldots, \mathtt{t}_1, \mathtt{t}_2\}$ (marked *ordered* or *unordered*), to which the method decomposes the head task. Finally, axioms are clauses of the form $\mathtt{h} \leftarrow \mathtt{l}$, signifying that predicate $\mathtt{h}$ is true if formula $\mathtt{l}$ is true.

The planning problem specification includes an initial state, i.e., a list of literals initially true, and a set of tasks to be accomplished. Given a domain and a problem specification, an HTN planner recursively attempts different method applications, aimed at finding sequences of primitive tasks $\mathtt{t}_1, \mathtt{t}_2, \ldots, \mathtt{t}_n$ (a *plan*) that can be performed using operators, such that $\mathtt{t}_1$ is possible given the initial state and $\mathtt{t}_{i+1}$ is possible given the state after t_i. In searching for such plans, the planner will also bias towards plans that minimize cost $\sum_{i=1}^{n} \mathtt{t}_i^c$.

3.2 Transforming to Planning Specifications

We now sketch how the instantiated decomposition patterns, which are iStar T models, translate into HTN domain and problem specifications to allow reasoning. The domain specification includes translations of: (a) the generic decomposition model of the matched pattern (Fig. 3), (b) attack trees related to the matched pattern (e.g., Fig. 4), and (c) security requirements as initialization instances of the generic decomposition. The following are the key components of the translation of the generic decomposition model to the domain specification.

Primitives. Primitive elements of the iStar T models are translated as follows: (a) every iStar T domain predicate into an HTN domain predicate, (b) every iStar T goal g into (b-i) a compound task $\mathtt{m}_g$, and (b-ii) a predicate $\mathtt{sat}_g$ (c) every iStar T task a into (c-i) an HTN primitive task $\mathtt{t}_a$, (c-ii) an operator with the same head, (c-iii) an HTN predicate $\mathtt{sat}_a$, (d) every iStar T precondition into an HTN formula representing the corresponding precondition formula, and (e) every iStar T effect into a list of HTN literals corresponding to the iStar T literals contained in the effect.

AND/OR Decompositions. For each AND-decomposition of a goal g into subgoals $g_1, g_2, \ldots$, and subtasks $a_1, a_2, \ldots$, introduce a method whose head $\mathtt{m}_g$ is the compound task corresponding to g, and its task list $\mathtt{m}_g^t$ contains an unordered set $\{\mathtt{m}_1,\ \mathtt{m}_2,\ \ldots,\ \mathtt{t}_1,\ \mathtt{t}_2\}$ of compound and primitive tasks corresponding to the subgoals and the subtasks, respectively. For each OR-decomposition of a goal g, introduce a method for *each* subgoal or subtask to which g is decomposed. Each method's head is $\mathtt{m}_g$ is the compound task corresponding to goal g and the task list contains exactly one element: the compound task $\mathtt{m}$ or primitive task $\mathtt{t}$ corresponding to the subgoal or subtask, respectively. In addition, create an axiom of the form $\mathtt{sat}_g \leftarrow \mathtt{sat}_{g_1}$ $\mathtt{[op]}$ $\mathtt{sat}_{g_2}$ $\mathtt{[op]}$ $\ldots$ $\mathtt{[op]}$ $\mathtt{sat}_{a_1}$ $\mathtt{[op]}$ $\mathtt{sat}_{a_2}$ $\mathtt{[op]}\ldots$ where $\mathtt{[op]}$ is $\wedge$ or $\vee$ for AND and OR decompositions, respectively.

Effect Links. For each effect link, identify the operator whose head $\mathtt{t}_a$ is the primitive task corresponding to the iStar T task a from where the effect link originates. Set $\mathtt{t}_a^{del}$ to be the list of predicates (translated to their HTN counterparts) that are negated in the effect (if any), and $\mathtt{t}_a^{add}$ to the remaining predicates (if any). Further, add predicate $\mathtt{sat}_a$ to the $\mathtt{t}_a^{add}$.

Precedence Links. Firstly, for every $\xrightarrow{pre}$ and $\xrightarrow{npr}$ link that targets a goal, replace the link with links of the same origin that target each leaf level task that is a descendant of the goal. As a result, only tasks are now recipients of such links. Subsequently, for each task a, first, collect predicates $\mathtt{sat}_{g_i}$, $\mathtt{sat}_{a_i}$, and formulae ϕ_{p_i} corresponding to goals g_i, tasks a_i and preconditions p_i that are origins of a $\xrightarrow{pre}$ link targeting the task. Create formula $\phi^{pre} = \mathtt{sat}_{g_1} \wedge \mathtt{sat}_{g_2} \ldots \wedge\ \mathtt{sat}_{a_1} \wedge \mathtt{sat}_{a_2} \ldots \wedge\ \phi_{p_1} \wedge \phi_{p_2} \ldots$. Next, for the same task a, collect the corresponding elements that are origins of a $\xrightarrow{npr}$ link that targets the task, and create formula $\phi^{npr} = \mathtt{sat}_{g_1} \vee \ldots \vee \mathtt{sat}_{a_1} \ldots \vee \phi_{p_1} \ldots$. Set the precondition $\mathtt{t}_a^{pre}$ of the operator corresponding to task a to $\phi^{pre} \wedge \neg\phi^{npr}$.

Costs. As a final step, the costs $\mathtt{t}^c$ of primitive tasks are set in a way that reflects the delay, cognitive load, or actor dissatisfaction that performing the task entails. Tasks such as *No encryption* have a cost of zero, and tasks such as *Generate Keys* (not seen in the diagrams) have a cost greater than zero.

The above rules concern the translation of the generic decomposition trees of a pattern. A different approach is followed for attack trees.

Attack Trees. Recall that an attack tree is an AND/OR formula grounded on iStar T domain literals, originating from effects or goals that reside at the leaf of the tree. Construct first the corresponding HTN formula ϕ^{atk}, in which the list of domain literals in the effects translate to a conjunction of the corresponding HTN literals, and leaf level goals g translate to the corresponding HTN predicates $\mathtt{sat}_g$. Then, for each attack tree, create an axiom of the form `[SR]Breached`

$\leftarrow \phi^{atk}_{[SR]}$, where `[SR]` is the security requirement the tree attempts to breach. The tree of Fig. 4 for example is translated into an *attack axiom* `ConBreached` $\leftarrow \phi^{atk}_{Con}$, where ϕ^{atk}_{Con} corresponds to the formula representing the specific tree. If satisfaction conditions are defined for a security requirement `[SR]`, a *success axiom* of the form `[SR]Successful` $\leftarrow \phi^{succ}_{[SR]}$ is also introduced, where formula $\phi^{succ}_{[SR]}$ corresponds to `[SR]`'s satisfaction condition.

The above constitutes a translation of the decomposition pattern that is reusable in any analysis instance. The security requirements and the threat model need to be generated separately for every problem instance, as follows.

Security Requirements. Introduce a dummy primitive task $\mathtt{t}_d$ and a dummy compound task $\mathtt{m}_d$. The former will play the role of a necessary final task and the latter will be the new root task. To accomplish that, introduce a method with head $\mathtt{m}_d$ and ordered task list $\mathtt{m}^t_d = \{\mathtt{m}_{root}, \mathtt{t}_d\}$, where $\mathtt{m}_{root}$ is the task that corresponds to the root goal of the decomposition pattern. Notice that task $\mathtt{m}^t_d$ is not solvable unless $\mathtt{t}_d$ is feasible after $\mathtt{m}_{root}$ is attained. For each security requirement SR mentioned in the pattern instantiation (through *require(SR)*), introduce a conjunct to the $\mathtt{t}^{pre}_d$ that is itself a conjunction of the head of the success axiom with the negation of the head of the attack axiom. For example, if `Auth` is required, ¬AuthBreached∧`AuthSuccessful` is added as a conjunct in $\mathtt{t}^{pre}_d$. The intuition is that the solver will ignore plans which produce effects that satisfy the attack model or deny the satisfaction conditions, as the precondition of the last mandatory action $\mathtt{t}_d$ would not be satisfied in that case.

Threat Model. The threat model informs the construction of the HTN problem specification. Specifically, recall that a pattern instantiation includes an instantiation of the initalization associated with the pattern's generic decomposition with literals grounded on objects from the specific domain. Of these, collect the domain and vulnerability assumptions and form formulae ϕ_{dom} and ϕ_{vln}, respectively, which are conjunctions of corresponding predicates. Set the initial state of the problem specification to be $\phi_{init} = \phi_{dom} \wedge \phi_{vuln}$.

3.3 Identifying Secure Workflows

With the instantiated patterns translated we can now use the planner to identify secure workflows. The process involves selecting a domain-specific goal of interest, and use the HTN specification of the associated decomposition instance to generate plans. Each generated plan corresponds to a trajectory tH in the corresponding iStar T decomposition.

Let us return to our running example and assume we are interested in a workflow for goal *Invoice Received.* The goal is associated with an instantiated decomposition pattern *Have Document Transmitted (supplier, customer, invoice).* We can calculate different workflows for accomplishing invoice transmission for different threat models and security requirements, effectively cycling through Steps 2-6 (noting that Step 3 is performed once) in an exploratory mood. Let us consider a scenario in which no security requirements are given. This means that, in the translation, the dummy final task $\mathtt{t}_d$ has no preconditions. In such case,

the planner will not be constrained in any way to produce the cheapest possible plan, which involves a simple plaintext transmission of the invoice:
{`0: email(supplier, contractor, invoice)`}

Assume now confidentiality requirements for invoice transmission, as per the STS-ml model of Fig. 2. Then, plans will depend on the threat model. If no vulnerability assumptions are made, meaning that attackers are not assumed to be capable/motivated to perform any of the tasks in their attack tree, emailing plaintext is again the best plan: none of the workflows satisfies the attack tree.

Assume subsequently that `IsCompromised (mailbox, contractor)` is true, i.e., we assume that, in the worst scenario, the attackers can actually gain access to the mailbox of the contractor. This can make the attack tree formula satisfied if the domain actors perform certain tasks. Indeed the emailing of plaintext no longer returns as part of a recommended plan. The planner will propose sending the plaintext invoice via SMS attachment. At this point the analysts may decide that either SMS is an inappropriate means of exchange of the document itself or that cellphones are also assumed to be compromised. These are expressed as an additional domain or vulnerability assumption, respectively. Under the new assumption, the planner will now output plans that involve encryption, e.g.:

```
{1: genSharedKey(supplier,contractor)
2: exchangeViaPhoneCall(supplier,contractor,key),
3: symmetricEncrypt(supplier,invoice,key),
4: email(supplier,contractor,invoice),
5: symmetricDecrypt(contractor,invoice,key)}
```

Thus, the plan involves symmetric encryption of the invoice preceded by key generation and exchange through a channel not assumed to be compromised according to the vulnerability assumptions, in our case via a voice call.

Assume, finally, that confidentiality is not an issue but invoice authenticity is, i.e., the contractor must verify that the invoice was prepared by the supplier (`Auth`) and has not been tampered with along the way (`Int`). Thus initialization will instantiate with *require(auth)* and *require(int)* which will be translated into the appropriate preconditions to $\mathtt{t}_d$. For the same vulnerability assumptions (compromised email accounts), the solution includes asymmetric public key exchange (`pKey`) and digitally signing the document, but excludes encryption:

```
{1: installEncSoftware (supplier),
2: installEncSoftware(contractor),
3: genAsymKeys (supplier),
4: email (supplier, contractor, pKey),
5: sign (supplier, invoice, sKey),
6: email (supplier, contractor, invoice),
7: verify (contractor,supplier, invoice)}
```

Note that the above plans have been simplified for the interest of space; readers can find full examples and commentary in our accompanying page [30]. Analysts can repeat this exploratory process for all security-relevant information exchange tasks of the initial domain-specific model. With relatively minor adaptations to the translation rules, omitted here for simplicity, global analysis can be performed on the basis of a higher level domain-specific goal, such as *Have Building Framing Completed*, following fusion of pattern instances into a now expanded domain-specific model. The generated workflows then encompass activities that aim to satisfy all relevant goals including order exchange, receipt of invoice, and submission of payment.

4 Related Work

Several approaches to model security requirements have been proposed. The SI* security language and the Secure Tropos methodology, for example, allow modeling and reasoning with permission delegations in the presence or absence of trust among agents [18,33,36]. Reasoners such as ASP [33], or, closer to our approach, planners [6] have been used for reasoning about such models. These early proposals appear to have inspired the Socio-Technical Security (STS) approach and modeling language we utilize here [9,39]. However, these approaches largely stay at the requirements level, naturally leaving implementation details, such as use of cryptographic primitives, outside of their scope. Work that does address utilization of cryptographic primitives has been introduced within the UMLSec context [24,25,42] where architectural security patterns are used for informing the design problem, supported by theorem proving techniques.

Many threat modeling frameworks have also been proposed – [44,49] for surveys. Our approach is based on attack trees [43,45] implemented here as goal decomposition models; an idea introduced and explored within the KAOS [10] goal modeling framework [46]. Among the differences of our work to the KAOS-based approach is the focus on run-time agent decisions (vs. design-time analysis) and on the generation of concrete secure sequences of actions.

Pattern systems have also been introduced [13,17,21,38,48] including for modeling attack types and using them to test an STS specification [29]. Rather than patterns of attack, we here envision design patterns (e.g., as in [47]) that specifically describe workflows for correctly utilizing cryptographic and other security primitives. Li et al. do adopt such a pattern system [27,28] based on contextual goal models and a matching, adoption, and instantiation approach similar to the one we propose. Among several differences, however, our proposal exploits iStar T's ability to model the temporal and causal aspect, allowing the generation of concrete solution workflows. Our approach is, further, distinct in scope from the broad literature on formalizing and verifying security protocols, (e.g., [3,4,7,22,31]) – [34] and [40] for surveys. This also applies vis-à-vis efforts for using AI planners specifically [5,20], which, in addition, focus on generating attack plans rather than security designs. Rather than verifying the nuts-and-bolts of security protocols against elaborate attacks [12], our goal is to abstract away the details of both protocols and attacks and recommend high-level designs that take into account practical aspects of the underlying socio-technical processes while remaining aligned with the specific security requirements of stakeholders.

5 Concluding Remarks

We presented a model-driven technique for automated generation of secure workflow designs based on identified security requirements. The technique is based on the availability of patterns, in the form of high-variability goal decomposition models, that encode authoritative best practices for performing common business tasks. The patterns also include attack trees that describe alternative attacks against these authoritative models with respect to different security properties, as well as templates for modeling security goals and threat assumptions of specific problems. When solving a specific problem, analysts adopt and instantiate the patterns within their domain-specific models, and through automated reasoning identify workflows whereby domain actors can fulfill business tasks in compliance with security requirements. The benefits of the approach include: (i) assisting analysts with no deep security expertise to produce high-level designs that make coherent use of security primitives, (ii) ensuring that the necessary and only the necessary security-related steps are included in the resulting designs, and (iii) offering a mechanism for exploring solutions under alternative security requirements and threat assumptions, informing thereby the risk management process at an early requirements stage. Our contribution is centered in the modeling techniques introduced to accomplish the above: the use of high-variability goal models to concisely represent multiple workflows involving different levels of security-related actions (including none), the use of attack models to test the appropriateness of candidate workflows, and the automated generation of compliant workflows using an off-the-shelf reasoning tool.

The patterns we have developed so far employ basic cryptographic primitives for information exchange using common channels, such as email, text messaging, or in-person exchange [30]. A set of proof-of-concept attack trees that we have built encode examples of compromising these exchange media as well as the physical contexts in which they are utilized. For the framework to be directly applicable in practice vis-à-vis information exchange, more comprehensive attack trees and digital communication process models will be needed. Security pattern development is generally known to be non-trivial [41]. Development of a useful and reliable pattern base for our framework would require consultation with experts and the literature, followed by extensive testing of the reasoning outputs.

While our current application scope, secure information exchange, by no means exhausts the range of advanced threats and sophisticated attacks against organizations and citizens, seemingly solvable problems within that scope such as email compromise due to user oversight continue to be a major societal problem [26]. Our modeling and reasoning architecture is aimed at being applicable for different business activities, such as storing and archiving data, accessing system functions and resources, handling payments (see Fig. 2), or even handling physical security and privacy in, e.g., transporting goods and people, or storing materials. These can, moreover, be analyzed with respect to a variety of security or privacy concerns via development of the corresponding attack trees. In general, the approach is particularly applicable when complex sequences of steps are required by both the domain actors to perform a business task and the attackers for compromising said task with respect to a specific security requirement.

Moreover, substantial empirical work will be needed to evaluate the usability and utility of the proposed modeling process, and to identify ways to optimize it. For example, our so far experimentation with building patterns has revealed that identifying the right level of model detail while keeping automated reasoning tractable can be challenging. Examples are deciding the level of detail to include when modeling primitives, and choosing whether to explicate exemplar workflows or leave the reasoner to construct such. Further, case studies in different domains will help us to better understand the scope of applicability of our technique.

Finally, tool support is essential for performing meaningful user and case studies. Thanks to the translation rules (Sect. 3.2), the core of the formalization process is automatable. Nevertheless, an interactive visual tool in support of the end-to-end modeling and analysis process requires substantial interaction design and evaluation. Alternatively, a textual representations (e.g., [1]) could be explored for performance of said tasks through scripting.

References

1. Abdelzad, V., Amyot, D., Alwidian, S., Lethbridge, T.: A textual syntax with tool support for the goal-oriented requirement language. In: Proceedings of The 8th International i* Workshop (2015). https://ceur-ws.org/Vol-1402/paper6.pdf
2. Adobe: Choosing a security method for PDFs (2024). https://helpx.adobe.com/ca/acrobat/using/choosing-security-method-pdfs.html, Accessed 19 Aug 2024
3. Armando, A., Carbone, R., Compagna, L.: LTL model checking for security protocols. J. Appl. Non-Classical Logics **19**(4), 403–429 (2009). https://doi.org/10.3166/jancl.19.403-429
4. Blanchet, B.: A computationally sound mechanized prover for security protocols. IEEE Trans. Dependable Secure Comput. **5**(4), 193–207 (2008). https://doi.org/10.1109/TDSC.2007.1005
5. Boddy, M.S., Gohde, J., Haigh, T., Harp, S.A.: Course of action generation for cyber security using classical planning. In: Proceedings of the 15th International Conference on Automated Planning and Scheduling (ICAPS 2005), pp. 12–21. AAAI, Monterey, California, USA (2005). https://dl.acm.org/doi/10.5555/3037062.3037065
6. Bryl, V., Massacci, F., Mylopoulos, J., Zannone, N.: Designing security requirements models through planning. In: Proceedings of the 18th International Conference on Advanced Information Systems Engineering (CAiSE 2006). Luxembourg, Luxembourg (2006). https://doi.org/10.1007/11767138_4
7. Burrows, M., Abadi, M., Needham, R.: A logic of authentication. ACM Trans. Comput. Syst. **8**(1), 18–36 (1990). https://doi.org/10.1145/77648.77649
8. Dalpiaz, F., Franch, X., Horkoff, J.: iStar 2.0 Language Guide. The Computing Research Repository (CoRR) (2016). http://arxiv.org/abs/1605.07767
9. Dalpiaz, F., Paja, E., Giorgini, P.: Security Requirements Engineering: Designing Secure Socio-Technical Systems. MIT Press (2016)
10. Dardenne, A., van Lamsweerde, A., Fickas, S.: Goal-directed requirements acquisition. Sci. Comput. Program. **20**(1-2), 3–50 (1993). https://doi.org/10.1016/0167-6423(93)90021-G

11. Devanbu, P.T., Stubblebine, S.: Software engineering for security: a roadmap. In: Proceedings of the 22nd International Conference on on Software Engineering, Future of Software Engineering Track (ICSE 2000), pp. 227–239. Association for Computing Machinery, New York (2000). https://doi.org/10.1145/336512.336559
12. Dolev, D., Yao, A.: On the security of public key protocols. IEEE Trans. Inf. Theory **29**(2), 198–208 (1983). https://doi.org/10.1109/TIT.1983.1056650
13. Dougherty, C.R., Sayre, K., Seacord, R., Svoboda, D., Togashi, K.: Secure Design Patterns. Tech. rep., Carnegie Mellon University (2018). https://doi.org/10.1184/R1/6583640.v1
14. Dubois, E., Mouratidis, H.: Guest editorial: security requirements engineering: past, present and future. Requirements Eng. **15**(1), 1–5 (2010). https://doi.org/10.1007/s00766-009-0094-8
15. Egele, M., Brumley, D., Fratantonio, Y., Kruegel, C.: An empirical study of cryptographic misuse in Android applications. In: Proceedings of the 2013 ACM SIGSAC Conference on Computer & Communications Security, CCS 2013, pp. 73–84. Association for Computing Machinery, New York (2013). https://doi.org/10.1145/2508859.2516693
16. Fabian, B., Gürses, S., Heisel, M., Santen, T., Schmidt, H.: A comparison of security requirements engineering methods. Requirements Eng. **15**(1), 7–40 (2010). https://doi.org/10.1007/s00766-009-0092-x
17. Fernandez, E.B., Yoshioka, N., Washizaki, H., Yoder, J.: Abstract security patterns and the design of secure systems. Cybersecurity **5**(1), 7 (2022). https://doi.org/10.1186/s42400-022-00109-w
18. Giorgini, P., Massacci, F., Zannone, N.: Security and trust requirements engineering. In: International School on Foundations of Security Analysis and Design III (FOSAD 2005, FOSAD 2004), LNCS, vol. 3655, pp. 237–272 (2005). https://doi.org/10.1007/11554578_8
19. Haley, C., Laney, R., Moffett, J., Nuseibeh, B.: Security requirements engineering: a framework for representation and analysis. IEEE Trans. Software Eng. **34**(1), 133–153 (2008). https://doi.org/10.1109/TSE.2007.70754
20. Harp, S.A., Gohde, J., Haigh, T., Boddy, M.S.: Automated vulnerability analysis using AI planning. In: AI Technologies for Homeland Security, Papers from the 2005 AAAI, Spring Symposium, pp. 46–53. AAAI (2005)
21. Hatebur, D., Heisel, M., Schmidt, H.: A pattern system for security requirements engineering. Proceedings of the Second International Conference on Availability, Reliability and Security (ARES 2007), pp. 356–365 (2007). https://doi.org/10.1109/ARES.2007.12
22. Hommersom, A., Meyer, J.j., De vink, E.: Update semantics of security protocols. Synthese **142**(2), 229–267 (2004). https://doi.org/10.1007/s11229-004-2247-0
23. Howard, M., Lipner, S.: The Security Development Lifecycle. Microsoft Press (2006)
24. Jürjens, J.: Sound methods and effective tools for model-based security engineering with UML. In: Proceedings of the 27th International Conference on Software Engineering (ICSE 2005), pp. 322–331 (2005).https://doi.org/10.1145/1062455.1062519
25. Jürjens, J., Yu, Y.: Tools for model-based security engineering: Models vs. code. In: Proceedings of the 22nd ACM/IEEE International Conference on Automated Software Engineering (ASE 2007), Atlanta, Georgia, pp. 545–546 (2007). https://doi.org/10.1145/1321631.1321736
26. Langan, T.: Internet Crime Report 2023. Tech. rep., Federal Bureau of Investigation (2023). https://www.ic3.gov/Media/PDF/AnnualReport/2023_IC3Report.pdf

27. Li, T., Horkoff, J., Mylopoulos, J.: Integrating security patterns with security requirements analysis using contextual goal models. In: Frank, U., Loucopoulos, P., Pastor, Ó., Petrounias, I. (eds.) Proceedings of the 7th IFIP Working Conference on The Practice of Enterprise Modeling, PoEM 2014, pp. 208–223. Springer, Heidelberg (2014). https://doi.org/10.1007/978-3-662-45501-2_15
28. Li, T., Horkoff, J., Mylopoulos, J.: Analyzing and enforcing security mechanisms on requirements specifications. In: Fricker, S.A., Schneider, K. (eds.) Proceedings of the 21nd International Working Conference on Requirements Engineering: Foundation for Software Quality, REFSQ 2015, pp. 115–131. Springer, Cham (2015). https://doi.org/10.1007/978-3-319-16101-3_8
29. Li, T., Paja, E., Mylopoulos, J., Horkoff, J., Beckers, K.: Security attack analysis using attack patterns. In: Proceedings of the 10th IEEE International Conference on Research Challenges in Information Science (RCIS 2016), pp. 1–13. Grenoble, France (2016). https://doi.org/10.1109/RCIS.2016.7549303
30. Liaskos, S.: Model-driven implementation of security requirements using patterns - Supplementary Material. https://github.com/cmg-york/sFuse
31. Lomuscio, A., Woźna, B.: A complete and decidable security-specialised logic and its application to the TESLA protocol. In: Proceedings of the Fifth International Joint Conference on Autonomous Agents and Multiagent Systems (AAMAS 2006), pp. 145–152. Association for Computing Machinery, New York (2006). https://doi.org/10.1145/1160633.1160658
32. Martin, K.M.: Everyday Cryptography: Fundamental Principles and Applications. Oxford University Press (2012). https://doi.org/10.1093/acprof:oso/9780199695591.001.0001
33. Massacci, F., Mylopoulos, J., Zannone, N.: Security requirements engineering: the SI* modeling language and the Secure Tropos methodology. In: Studies in Computational Intelligence (SCI), vol. 265, pp. 147–174 (2010). https://doi.org/10.1007/978-3-642-05183-8_6
34. Meadows, C.: Formal methods for cryptographic protocol analysis: emerging issues and trends. IEEE J. Selected Areas Commun. **21**(1), 44–54 (2003). https://doi.org/10.1109/JSAC.2002.806125
35. Microsoft: How to password protect your Word documents (2024). https://www.microsoft.com/en-us/microsoft-365-life-hacks/privacy-and-safety/how-to-password-protect-word-documents, Accessed 19 Aug 2024
36. Mouratidis, H., Giorgini, P.: Secure Tropos: a security-oriented extension of the tropos methodology. Int. J. Software Eng. Knowl. Eng. **17**(02), 285–309 (2007). https://doi.org/10.1142/S0218194007003240
37. Nau, D.S., et al.: SHOP2: An HTN planning system. J. Artifi. Intell. Res. (JAIR) **20**, 379–404 (2003). https://dl.acm.org/doi/abs/10.5555/1622452.1622465
38. Nguyen, P.H., Yskout, K., Heyman, T., Klein, J., Scandariato, R., Traon, Y.L.: SoSPa: a system of security design patterns for systematically engineering secure systems. In: Proceedings of the 18th ACM/IEEE International Conference on Model Driven Engineering Languages and Systems (MODELS 2015), pp. 246–255 (2015). https://doi.org/10.1109/MODELS.2015.7338255
39. Paja, E., Dalpiaz, F., Giorgini, P.: Modelling and reasoning about security requirements in socio-technical systems. Data Knowl. Eng. **98**, 123–143 (2015). https://doi.org/10.1016/j.datak.2015.07.007
40. Pucella, R.: Knowledge and security. In: van Ditmarsch, H., Halpern, J.Y., van der Hoek, W., Kooi, B. (eds.) Handbook of Epistemic Logic, chap. 12, pp. 591–565. College Publications (2015)

41. Riaz, M., Williams, L.: Security requirements patterns: understanding the science behind the art of pattern writing. In: Proceedings of the 2nd IEEE International Workshop on Requirements Patterns (RePa 2012), pp. 29–34 (2012). https://doi.org/10.1109/RePa.2012.6359977
42. Schmidt, H., Jürjens, J.: Connecting security requirements analysis and secure design using patterns and UMLsec. In: Proceedings of the 23rd International Conference on Advanced Information Systems Engineering, CAiSE 2011, LNCS, vol. 6741, pp. 367–382. Springer, Heidelberg (2011). https://doi.org/10.1007/978-3-642-21640-4_28
43. Schneier, B.: Attack Trees: Modelling Security Threats. Dr. Dobb's J. (1999). https://www.schneier.com/academic/archives/1999/12/attack_trees.html
44. Shevchenko, N., Chick, T.A., O'riordan, P., Scanlon, T.P., Woody, C.: Threat Modeling: A Summary Of Available Methods, Carnegie Mellon University: Software Engineering. Tech. Rep. July (2018). https://insights.sei.cmu.edu/documents/569/2018_019_001_524597.pdf
45. Tøndel, I.A., Jensen, J., Røstad, L.: Combining misuse cases with attack trees and security activity models. In: Proceedings of the 5th International Conference on Availability, Reliability, and Security (ARES 2010), Krakow, Poland, pp. 438–445 (2010). https://doi.org/10.1109/ARES.2010.101
46. van Lamsweerde, A.: Elaborating security requirements by construction of intentional anti-models. In: Proceedings of the 26th International Conference on Software Engineering (ICSE 2004), pp. 148–157 (2004). https://doi.org/10.1109/ICSE.2004.1317437
47. Weiss, M., Mouratidis, H.: Selecting security patterns that fulfill security requirements. In: Proceedings of the 16th IEEE International Requirements Engineering Conference (RE 2008), Barcelona, Spain, pp. 169–172 (2008)
48. Wen, Y., Haihong Zhao, Liu, L.: Analysing security requirements patterns based on problems decomposition and composition. In: Proceedings of the 1st International Workshop on Requirements Patterns, RePa 2011, pp. 11–20. IEEE (2011). https://doi.org/10.1109/RePa.2011.6046726
49. Xiong, W., Lagerström, R.: Threat modeling - A systematic literature review. Comput. Sec. **84**, 53–69 (2019). https://doi.org/10.1016/j.cose.2019.03.010

Modeling and Reasoning About Explanation Requirements Using Goal Models

Sotirios Liaskos[1(✉)], John Mylopoulos[2], Alex Borgida[3], and Shakil M. Khan[4]

[1] School of Information Technology, York University, Toronto, Canada
liaskos@yorku.ca
[2] Department of Computer Science, University of Toronto, Toronto, Canada
jm@cs.toronto.edu
[3] Department of Computer Science, Rutgers University, Burnswick, USA
borgida@cs.rutgers.edu
[4] Department of Computer Science, University of Regina, Regina, Canada
shakil.khan@uregina.ca

Abstract. As modern software-intensive systems grow in complexity and autonomy there is a demand for them to incorporate services that explain their actions. Such explanation services allow stakeholders, especially end-users, to develop trust that the corresponding system complies with its objectives and limitations. Before such explanation services can be designed, their requirements need to be analyzed, in terms of both the kinds of stakeholder questions such services can entertain and the content of the answers they respond with. We propose a framework for goal-oriented modeling and analysis of explanation requirements. Explanation requirements are captured as stakeholder goals and are subsequently analyzed into specific explanation tasks and explanation interaction templates. By further extending the models with temporal and causal constraints, the resulting conceptual model can be used to generate answers to certain families of stakeholder questions. Formalization of the model allows both simulations of the explanation service and, under restrictive assumptions, a working prototype thereof.

Keywords: Goal Modeling · Software Systems Explainability · Golog

1 Introduction

We are interested in software systems that can explain their actions. Such systems include an autonomous vehicle (AV) that can explain its driving actions to its passengers, such as *"Why did you turn?" "Because I need to get gas"*, or a meeting scheduler (MS) that answers *"Why was I invited to this meeting?"* with *"Because of your expertise on the topics to be discussed"*. Explainability as a quality of software systems came to prominence with the advent of AI-intensive systems that play an important role in our daily lives and need to be

W. Maass et al. (Eds.): ER 2024, LNCS 15238, pp. 215–234, 2025.
https://doi.org/10.1007/978-3-031-75872-0_12

transparent about their actions so that they can be justifiably [23] trusted by their stakeholders, and particularly their end-users [4,25]. The concern, however, extends to any socio-technical system – AI-powered or not – whose size and complexity makes the rationale of actions performed within its context difficult to comprehend without assistance.

Explanations are aimed at allowing an explainee to understand how and why an aspect of a system is as it is in a given context [4,21]. In one of their common forms, explanations are assignments of causal responsibility for a phenomenon [22] (as cited in [33]) [41]. In our case, the phenomenon is an action that a system has performed. For such phenomena, causes can be goals the system is trying to achieve. In the AV example, the overarching goal *"Be at Pittsburgh by 6pm"* is viewed as the cause of the corresponding system subgoals such as g_1 = *"Enter the highway"* and g_2 = *"Drive towards Pittsburgh"* and, as such, constitutes an explanation for the pursuit of these subgoals. We call such causes *teleological* [33], [10] (as cited in [20]). Alternatively, causes can be found in system design rules, such as that g_2 is enabled by g_1, so the question *"Why did you enter the highway?"* may be answered with *"Because that allows me to Drive towards Pittsburgh"*. We call these causes *canonical* as they are derived from design rules.

For a system to be capable of providing such explanations, the requirements for the corresponding explanation functionality need to first be identified and modeled. Such functional requirements can be captured as *explanation goals* which express what domain *explainees* want to have explained. Explanation goals are, in turn, analyzed into explanation tasks. The latter describe the textual format and content of explanation interactions with explainees in order to fulfill the explanation goals. At the same time, when a model of the domain in question is present, it can serve as a basis for constructing certain additional explanations.

Based on these ideas, we present a goal-oriented framework for analyzing, modeling, simulating, and implementing explanation requirements. Functional and non-functional system requirements are captured using the *i** goal-modeling language [13,42], appropriately extended to capture temporal and causal relationships between goals and actions. Then, explanation requirements are captured in the form of explanation goals, assigned to various explainee roles. These explanation goals are operationalized into actions that capture run-time explanation information or render explanation interactions. The textual format of the latter is described through templates. In addition, a set of axioms are introduced that utilize the information of the extended model to construct responses to ad hoc explainee questions. Subsequent formalization of said templates and axioms allows design-time simulation of the envisioned explanation interactions, supporting its early assessment and improvement. Further, when the envisioned system is implemented in accordance to the goal model and its actions are logged, our formalization can serve as the basis of the run-time explanation engine.

The main contribution of our work is a model-driven approach for systematically discovering and specifying explanation requirements within an established goal-oriented requirements framework, while at the same time, thanks to the pro-

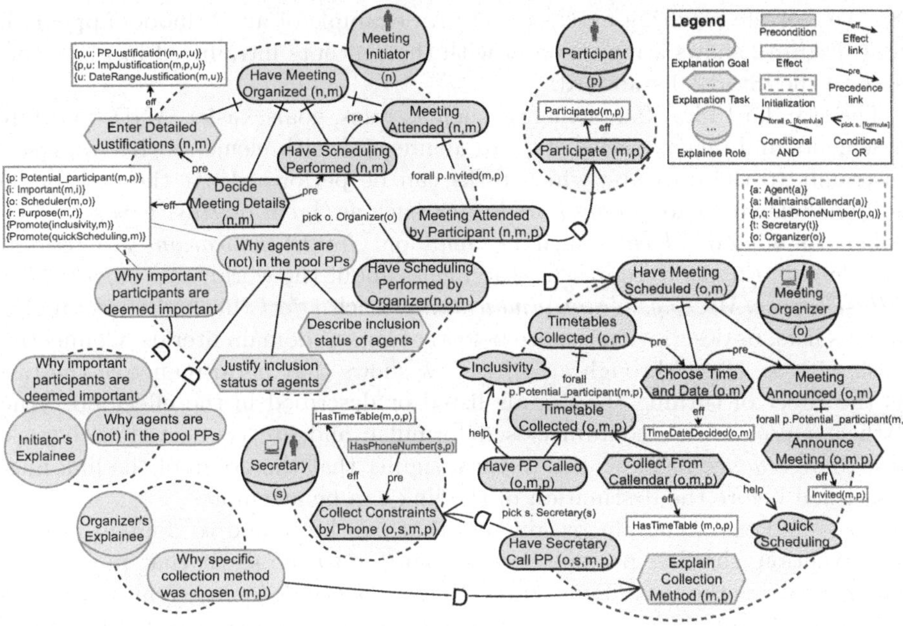

Fig. 1. Augmented Goal Model (for meaning of baseline iStar 2.0 elements see [13])

posed formalization and axiomatization, allowing simulation and prototyping of the specified explainability service.

The rest of the paper is organized as follows. In Sect. 2 we describe the extensions to i^* that are needed for capturing explanations. In Sects. 3 and 4 we describe explanation templates and explanation axioms for custom and generic explanations, respectively. In Sect. 5 we sketch how the above are formalized to allow for design-time and run-time reasoning, described in Sect. 6. We present related work in Sect. 7 and conclude in Sect. 8.

2 Capturing Requirements in i^+

The i^* requirements modeling language [42] captures requirements in terms of *goals* that actors (stakeholders) need to fulfill and the actions (aka *tasks* in i^*) through which their goals can be fulfilled. Given an i^* model of stakeholder requirements, we are interested in extracting explanations that stem from *teleological causes* of actions, that is, what goal the action serves, as well as *canonical causes* of actions, that is, what rules or constraints lead the actor to perform a specific action. Teleological causes are readily captured in i^* through modeling tasks as the result of recursive goal refinement. However, to capture canonical causes, we need to extend i^* with the appropriate constructs for representing temporal and causal constraints. We adopt and extend a recent derivative of i^*'s successor *iStar 2.0* [13] for representing action theoretic aspects of goal models

[28]. We call the resulting extension i^+. An example of an i^+ model appears in Fig. 1. Figure 2 shows a meta-model with the concepts introduced in i^+ as they relate to the iStar 2.0 standard.

The standard iStar 2.0 elements, such as roles, goals, tasks, AND- and OR-refinements and dependencies [13] are augmented with elements that represent constraints to the order by which tasks can be performed. At the core of the additional elements are *domain predicates*, such as *Agent* or *HasPurpose*, which, applied to *domain objects*, such as *John* or *GrantAdjudication*, are used to build *domain literals* to represent statements about the world, e.g., *Agent(John)* or *HasPurpose(Meeting, GrantAdjudication)*. Each *effect* (unshaded rectangles) contains lists, or descriptions (more below) of lists of domain literals. Connecting a task with an effect through an *effect link* shows that performance of the task has the effect of turning the literals listed or described in the effect box true. Further, *preconditions* contain closed formulae and are connected with tasks through *precedence* links, which, in turn, signify that the origin of the link must be satisfied before the destination of the link can be attempted.

Goals and tasks contain parameters that can be bound to domain objects. By convention, the first parameter is a reference to the agent that pursues the goal or performs the task. Thus, *Have Meeting Scheduled(o,m)* signifies that the goal *Have Meeting Scheduled* is pursued by an agent *o* for a distinct meeting *m*. This way i^+ allows us to reason with multiple *instances* of goals and tasks, each uniquely identified by its parameter instantiations. When a goal is (unconditionally) *refined* into a subgoal or *operationalized* into a task, the parameters of the subgoal/subtask must be a subset of the parameters of the parent goal. An exception is *conditional AND* and *conditional OR* refinements, which allow extension of an AND- or OR-refinement respectively to all objects that fulfill a stated condition (a formula of domain literals), and may result in an additional parameter for the subgoal or subtask. In Fig. 1, *Timetables Collected (o,m)* is refined into as many instances of the goal *TimeTable Collected (o,m,p)* as the known potential participants *p* for meeting *m*. We signify this through the formula *forall p. Potential_participant(m,p)* on the refinement link. Likewise, goal *Have PP Called (o,m,p)* (*PP* is, henceforth, shorthand for *Potential Participant*) is OR-refined into an instance of task *Ask Secretary to Call PP (o,s,m,p)*, whose performance for some *s* that is a secretary suffices for the fulfillment of the goal. This is indicated by formula *pick s. Secretary(s)* on the refinement link.

The parameters of the literals listed in an effect must be a subset of the parameters found in the task that is connected to the effect. Often, however, tasks such as *Decide Meeting Details (n,m)* generate new instance-level information and we wish to represent this generation process. We use *assertion descriptions* for the purpose. They come in the form {*params: Predicate(params)*} which is a shorthand for the list of literals $Predicate(Param_1)$, $Predicate(Param_2)$, ..., where $Param_i$ are objects of the domain. Thus, the description {*p: Potential_participant(m,p)*} found in the effect of task *Decide Meeting Details (n,m)*, can be instantiated to list *Potential_participant (m, Alice)*, *Potential_participant (m, John)*. The description denotes that, as a result of performing the task, the

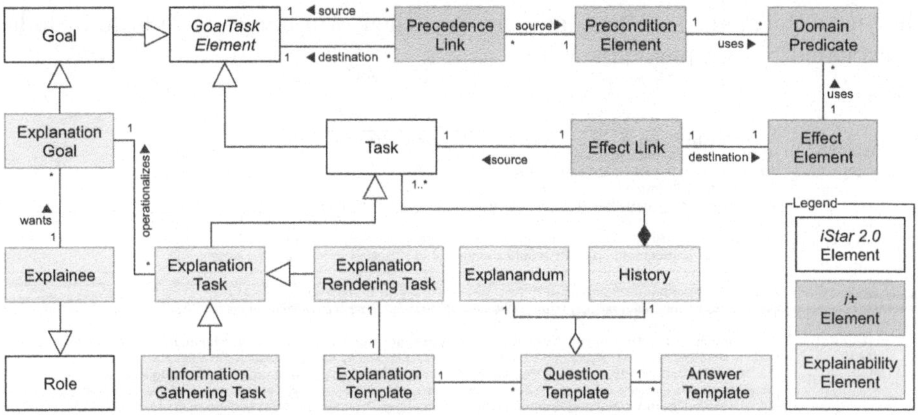

Fig. 2. Meta-model of *i+* and explainability extensions

meeting initiator will come up with instances of potential participants (Alice, John, etc.), that are unknown at the time of the analysis.

Further, we define *(task) histories tH* to be sequences of leaf level tasks, which have all their parameters bound to domain objects, and which can be executed in the given sequence in compliance with the precedence constraints of the model. A history is, further, *goal satisfying* with respect to a goal g, if after all tasks are executed, g is satisfied according to the AND/OR decomposition structure. Finally, *initialization elements* containing assertion descriptions are added to the model to describe what domain literals need to be asserted as true or false prior to calculating task histories.

3 Modeling Explanation Requirements

The i^+ extension is used for developing models of stakeholder goals pertinent to a requirements problem at hand. When we are interested to also model stakeholder requirements for acquiring explanations on why actor actions are chosen and performed, i.e., *explanation requirements*, the models need to be augmented accordingly. We propose to approach explanation requirements as functional ones, stemming from explanation needs of *explainees* in the domain. Explainees are actors that inquire about the performance of tasks by other actors. We model explainees as *i* roles*. Depending on the application, explainee roles may reflect specific organizational roles and positions, e.g., mandated regulatory, quality control, or customer advocacy officers, or they may be generic roles that any actor in the domain may play. Explainee roles may also be dedicated to explaining the actions of one particular other actor. In the example of Fig. 1, two explainee roles are included, one concerned with the actions of the initiator (Initiator's Explainee) and one concerned with the actions of the organizer (Organizer's Explainee). Thus, a participant may play the initiator's explainee role when they have the goal to understand why, e.g., their own names have been included or excluded from a participant list.

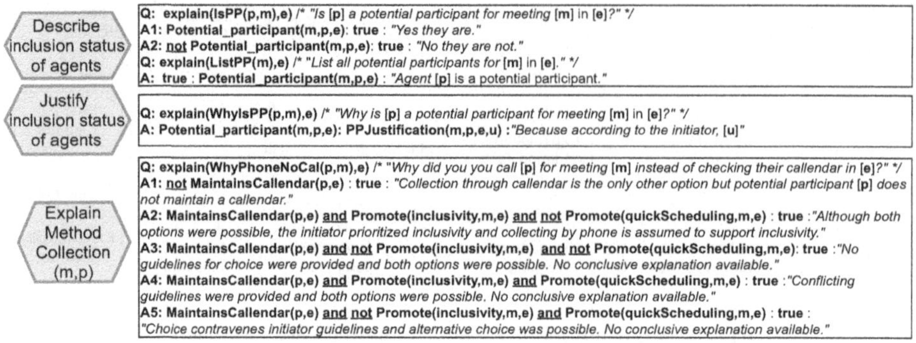

Fig. 3. Explanation Rendering Tasks and the associated Explanation Templates.

Explainees have *explanation goals*. These goals reflect states of the world in which a desired explanation about the actions of an actor has been acquired. For example, the initiator's explainee has the explanation goal to *"[Have] why important participants are deemed important [explained]."* – we omit the first and last word when writing such goals. Top level explanation goals like this are delegated or refined like any other $i*$ goal. In our example, the explanation goal *"Why agents are (not) in the pool of potential participants"*, is delegated to the initiator, as she is the one who makes the corresponding decisions. The delegated goal is further analyzed into specific tasks that are required for satisfying the corresponding explanation goal. This includes verifying the inclusion status of various agents in the list of potential participants and offering an explanation as to why the status is as such. We call such tasks that gather or render explanation information *explanation tasks*. In our example, to be able to perform the explanation task that explains the potential participant status of each agent, explanations must be registered by the meeting initiator at an earlier time. Thus, the *information gathering task Enter Detailed Justifications (n,m)* with the corresponding effect is added as one of the initiator's tasks. According to the effect, at run time, the task results in a number of literals of the form *PPJustification(m,p,u)* to be generated, each assigning a message u as justification for inclusion of an agent p in the PP list for meeting m. This informs the designers that a facility for adding message u for each p when deciding meeting details for m must be available to the initiator. Thus, the analysis of explanation goals leads to the discovery of additional requirements for functions that are necessary for capturing explanation information. Such information capture is the first of two aspects of operationalizing explanation goals. The second aspect is the rendering of explanations which is described using explanation templates.

3.1 Explanation Templates

Explanations are offered in response to appropriately formulated explanation questions posed by the explainees. Part of the requirements specification process is to precisely describe the required format of both the question and the answer to the question, as well as the content of the answer based on information available in the system, including information acquired through other tasks in the model. Each *explanation rendering task* is, hence, associated with an *explanation template* to describe the format of question and answer that the task entails as well as how the content of the answer can be retrieved or constructed.

Three explanation templates can be seen in Fig. 3, each corresponding to one of the explanation tasks for Fig. 1. An explanation template consists of a set of *question templates* and, for each such, one or more alternative *answer templates*. Question templates are of the form:

$explain(explanandum(q_1,q_2,\ldots),e)$

where $explanandum(q_1,q_2,\ldots)$ is a goal or task whose parameters are to be bound at the time that the question is posed, and e is a task history offering the context within which the explanation is required. For example, consider the scenario in which an explainee studies the task history that unfolded for the scheduling of a meeting in a university setting. A question they may ask is of the form:

$explain(WhyIsPP(p,m),\ldots,e)$

which, in plain language, asks why agent object m is treated as a potential participant for meeting m in history e. At the time of posing the question, examples of specific objects are used, such as p = *"Anita"* and m = *"the promotion adjudication meeting"*. The answer templates are of the form:

$guard/(q_1,q_2,\ldots,e) : query/(q_1,q_2,\ldots,a_1,a_2,\ldots,e) : render/(a_1,a_2,\ldots)$

The *guard* is a logical expression grounded on domain literals that must be true for the answer to be provided. Variables $q_1,q_2,\ldots$ are a subset of those contained in the question. The *query* part consists of a logical expression that is grounded on domain literals and that contains parameters $q_1,q_2,\ldots,e$ that are, again a subset of those of the question, as well as free parameters $a_1,a_2,\ldots$. The *render* part is a function that presents the output parameters $a_1,a_2,\ldots$ in a human readable format through, e.g., instantiating parameterizable text templates as seen below. For example, the following can be an answer template to the above question:

Potential_participant(m,p,e) : PPJustification(m,p,u,e) : "Because, according to the initiator, [u]."/(u)

At run time the answer is instantiated as follows. First the guard condition is instantiated using the parameters of the question. In the example above, the guard condition is *Potential_participant("the promotion adjudication meeting", "Anita", e)*. If the guard is true, an answer can be rendered. Firstly, a value for u will be sought such that the following holds:

PPJustification("the promotion adjudication meeting", "Anita",u,e)

Recall that, as a result of analysing explanation goals, the model contains task *Decide Meeting Details (n,m)* in which initiator n creates such literals. In our case, u = *"Anita has been elected as recording secretary"* may have been entered by the initiator and, as such, satisfy the query expression. The final response instance is simply a human-friendly rendering of the query results. If multiple u's satisfy the query, multiple answers will be provided. Notice also that a specific task history e is present in all relevant literals.

In Fig. 3, additional examples of explanation templates are provided. The one addressing explanation task *Explain Method Collection (m,p)* tackles the question why a certain child of an OR-decomposition is chosen. The explainability analyst designs various alternatives based on different guard conditions. The first answer observes that the alternative is not feasible. The second answer suggests that the choice is compliant to quality guidelines offered by the initiator and does not contradict any other guidelines. The remaining choices contextualize the choice but do not offer a definitive explanation. In the particular case, the analyst does not fully determine how variability is bound at the cost of being able to only provide plausible and not definite explanations.

4 Ad Hoc Explanations and Explanation Axioms

Explanation goals, tasks, and templates help analysts to identify and represent specific explanation requirements and designs thereof (templates) that can be known at the requirements stage. This analysis ensures that the requirements specification includes requirements for explanation information tracking and answer-rendering functions that are specific to the domain in question.

However, there may be explanation requirements that evade capture during analysis. In that case, we may still be able to exploit information embedded in the i^+ model – in the form of intentional (refinements, operationalizations, contributions) and canonical (precedences, effects) relationships – to provide *ad hoc explanations*, that is, explanations not captured during requirements analysis. Given an observed action to be explained, such ad hoc explanations can render (a) the motivation for the action's performance in terms of actor goals they may support, (b) the action's potential role in enabling subsequent necessary steps, (c) the possible absence of feasible alternatives for the action, or (d) compliance of the action with certain preferences over quality goals.

For generating such explanations, we utilize a set of general *explanation axioms* that describe how such relationships can be combined to explain performance of tasks. Axioms are of the form:

$$explains(y, x, e) \longleftarrow f(y, x, e)$$

where y is an explanation, x is an explanandum (what needs to be explained), e the history relative to which the explanation is sought, and $f(y, x, e)$ is a formula based on structural characteristics of the i^+ model and, where applicable, the content of e. The explanandum x is a task that appears in e and the explainee desires to have explained, or a goal that has been rendered as an explanation to an earlier query. Likewise, explanations y are other goals or tasks. In a typical application of the axioms, the explainee will start by asking what explains a task within a history, which will return various other tasks or goals, which are, in turn, the explananda of follow-up queries. Below we present the axioms in detail and in later sections we show how they can be used.

Operationalizations. The first axiom is based on the observation that in an operationalization relationship, i.e., the (AND- or OR-) refinement of a goal into a task, the goal being operationalized constitutes a possible explanation as to why the task was performed. Hence, in Fig. 1 task *Collect From Calendar (o,m,p)* is one of the tasks that operationalize goal *Timetable Collected (o,m,p)*. Clearly, question *"Why did organizer [o] collect [p]'s constraints from their calendar for meeting [m]?"* can be answered with *"Because [o] wanted to collect [p]'s timetable for [m]"*. Hence our first axiom can be as follows, where x is a task, y is a goal, and e is a task history:

$$explains(y, x, e) \longleftarrow occurredIn(x, e) \wedge operationalizedBy(y, x) \qquad \text{(Axiom 1)}$$

where $occuredIn(x, e)$ holds if task x is included in e.

Refinements. The above can be extended to refinements between goals. In the example, *"Timetables Collected (o,m)"* is a subgoal of *"Have Meeting Scheduled(o,m)"*, hence the latter explains the former. The axiom is then as follows, where both x and y are goals and $satisfiedIn(x, e)$ holds iff task occurrences in e satisfy x according to AND/OR structure.

$$explains(y, x, e) \longleftarrow satisfiedIn(x, e) \wedge refinedBy(y, x) \qquad \text{(Axiom 2)}$$

Dependencies. The initiator for a meeting is the original actor who wants to schedule it. However, the scheduling is delegated to the meeting organizer. Accordingly, a question about meeting organizer o, *"Why did [o] want to have meeting [m] scheduled?"* can be reasonably answered with *"Because the initiator [n] asked [o] to"*. In reference to Fig. 1, *Have Scheduling Performed by Organizer(n,o,m)* explains why *Have Meeting Scheduled (o,m)*, where n is the initiator, o is the chosen organizer, and m is the meeting.

Let $dependency(r, d, y, x)$ denote a dependency between actors, whereby a depender actor r depends on a dependee actor d to fulfill depender goal y which becomes dependee goal or task x. Then:

$$explains(y, x, e) \longleftarrow \exists(r, d).dependency(r, d, y, x) \wedge delegated(r, d, y, x, e) \quad \text{(Axiom 3)}$$

where $delegated(r, d, y, x, e)$ holds if, in history e, actor r delegated goal y to actor d, which goal became goal or task x for d.

Enablement. Consider the question *"Why did [o] collect timetables for meeting [m]?"*, now answered with *"Because [o] needed to choose a time and a date for meeting [m]"*. The specific answer constitutes a canonical explanation rather than a teleological one. It explains performance of a task on the basis of it being necessary for allowing some other task to be executed later in the history of tasks. In the example, this is established by the precedence link that prevents performance of task *"Choose Time and Date (o,m)"* unless *"Timetables Collected (o,m)"* is first fulfilled. We formulate the above with the axiom:

$$explains(y, x, e) \longleftarrow enables(x, y) \wedge includedIn(y, e) \wedge includedIn(x, e) \qquad \text{(Axiom 4)}$$

In the above, y and x are goals or tasks and $includedIn\ (z, e) \longleftrightarrow occuredIn\ (z, e) \vee satisfiedIn(z, e)$. Furthermore, $enables(x, y)$ means that there is an explicit or implicit precedence constraint between x and y, such that prior performance, achievement, or satisfaction of x is necessary (but not necessarily sufficient) for performance (task) or satisfaction (goal) of y to be possible.

An explicit constraint exists when there is a direct precedence link from x to y. Implicit constraints emerge when precedence links originate from high-level goals and are, hence, inherited by their successors in the refinement hierarchy. Specifically, if goal g_1 targets goal g_2 with a precedence link, every task that is a descendant of g_1 can be seen as an enabler of g_2. This is formalized as follows:

$enables(x, y) \longleftarrow pre(x, y)$ (Axiom 4.1)

$enables(x, y) \longleftarrow ancestorOf(w, x) \wedge enables(w, y)$ (Axiom 4.2)

In the above, $ancestorOf(w, x)$ denotes that there is a chain of refinements and/or operationalizations from high-level goal w down to goal or task x. In Fig. 1, for example, a precedence link is drawn from goal *"Timetables Collected (o,m)"* to task *"Choose Time and Date (o,m)"*. According to the axiom, satisfaction or performance of any descendant of *"Timetables Collected (o,m)"* contributes to the enablement of *"Choose Time and Date (o,m)"*. As such, goal *"Have Secretary Call PP (o,s,m,p)"* enables *"Choose Time and Date (o,m)"*.

OR-refinements. A final set of axioms offers explanations on why a child of an OR-refined goal, henceforth: OR-sibling, is chosen over some other child, as evident in a history e. In goal analysis, identifying optimal choices for OR-refinements is typically done by a global optimization process whose details are not part of the model (e.g., [28,29]). Even if the optimization algorithm is known, explaining local decisions within the context of a complex global optimization task can be hard. Nevertheless, in our case, *plausible* explanations for OR-sibling choices made by the external optimizer can be possible. Specifically, a plausible explanation can be produced when (a) at the time of the choice of an OR-sibling no other sibling was possible, or when (b) in the presence of more than one possible alternatives, the alternative chosen is the only one that contributes to qualities for which express statement(s) of preference exist. To produce the corresponding axioms we first define the following auxilary predicates:

$onlyFeasibleIn(x, e) \leftrightarrow \forall y_i.[\textsc{or\_}sibling(y_i, x) \rightarrow \neg poss(y_i, e)]$ (Aux. 1)

$preferred(x) \leftrightarrow \exists q1.[contr(x, q_1, plus) \wedge promote(q_1)] \wedge \neg \exists q_2.[contr(x, q_2, minus) \wedge promote(q_2)]$ (Aux. 2)

$onlyPreferredIn(x, e) \leftrightarrow \forall y_i.[\textsc{or\_}sibling(y_i, x) \rightarrow \neg(prefered(y_i) \wedge poss(y_i, e))]$ (Aux. 3)

The first predicate, $onlyFeasibleIn(x, e)$, holds if none of x's OR-siblings y_i are possible ($poss(y_i, e)$) at the end of e. Predicate $preferred(x)$ holds if x sends a positive contribution to some quality q_1 ($contr(x, q_1)$) and that quality has been declared to be a preferred quality ($promote(q_1)$), while x does not contribute negatively to some other preferred quality. Predicate $onlyPreferredIn(x, e)$ holds when there is no alternative y_i to x that is both feasible in history e and preferred. We note that $\textsc{or\_}sibling(y, x)$ holds both for direct OR-siblings and for cases in which, e.g., y is an OR-sibling of an ancestor of x, which also makes y and x alternatives. For example, *Collect Constraints by Phone (o,s,m,p)* is an alternative to *Collect From Calendar (o,m,p)*. We omit here the exact definition for brevity. The explanation axioms are then as follows:

$explains(x, e) \longleftarrow onlyFeasibleIn(x, e_{sel})$ (Axiom 5)

$explains(x, e) \longleftarrow onlyPreferredIn(x, e_{sel})$ (Axiom 6)

where e_{sel} is a prefix $t_1, t_2, \ldots, t_n$ of e such that t_{n+1} is either x or, if x is a goal, a leaf-level successor of x but no t_i is any of the two for $i \leq n$. Thus, e_{sel} marks the moment in e where the choice to perform/satisfy x is made.

According to Axiom 5 selection of an OR-sibling is explained if none of its other siblings was possible at the time e_{sel} when goal or task x was selected. Axiom 6, on the other hand, explains OR-child selection on the basis that none of the competing alternatives is possible and preferred with respect some quality.

5 Semantics

So far we have introduced an extension to the standard i^+ notation, explanation templates, as well as axioms for ad-hoc explanations. We now offer a brief overview of the semantics of these extensions that pave the way for automatically calculating run-time explanations in a simulated or real environment. A complete presentation can be found in the long version of this paper [30].

Golog. The semantics is based on Golog [27], a Situation Calculus-based [26] language for specifying dynamic domains. Its main concepts are *fluents*, which are first-order predicates describing what is true in a given situation `s` and *situations*, which represent a sequence of *actions* from an initial situation `S0`. Function symbol `do(a,s)` denotes the situation that results from performing action `a` in situation `s`, and atomic formula `Poss(a,s)` denotes that it is possible to perform action `a` in situation `s`. In a complete Golog specification, a set of *successor state axioms* and *action precondition axioms* are defined. The former, specified for each fluent, describe if and how the truth value of the fluent changes from one situation to the next. The second, defined for each action, characterize `Poss(a,s)` and describe what conditions must be true for action `a` to be executable in situation `s`. Golog further allows the definition of *procedures*, written as `proc([name],[body])`, where `[body]` can be, among other common programming constructs (e.g., loops, conditionals), a *sequence* or a *nondeterministic choice* of other actions or procedures. When asked to perform a procedure `[name]`, the Golog interpreter attempts ways to perform the content of `[body]` in compliance to the aforementioned axioms.

The semantics is grounded in Golog via three kinds of translations: (i) of the i^+ model into a Golog specification that encodes the domain structure and allows generating simulated task histories, (ii) of the explanation templates into formulae that can yield custom explanations, and (iii) of the ad-hoc explanation axioms into formulae and routines for, likewise, yielding ad-hoc explanations.

i^+ Translation - Primitives. Every actor in the goal model is mapped to an individual in the Golog domain. Every goal is translated into a fluent (*satisfaction fluent*) and a Golog procedure. Every task is translated into a fluent (*performance fluent*) and a primitive action. Every effect is translated into as many fluents (*effect fluents*) as the atomic formulae that are listed in the effect.

i^+ Translation - Structure. Consider each goal in the i^+ model and the Golog procedure it associates with. If the goal is OR-refined (resp., AND-refined), the procedure's body contains a non-deterministic choice of the procedures/actions corresponding to each sub-goal/task (resp., of all permutations of said procedures/actions). For conditional OR- and AND-refinements, procedures involve constructs for, respectively, non-deterministically picking an object that satisfies the condition and calling the sub-goal/sub-task with it (OR-refinement) or doing the same for every object that satisfies the condition (AND-refinement). The satisfaction fluent of goal is defined to be the disjunction (OR-refinement) or conjunction (AND-refinement) of satisfaction/performance fluents of the sub-goals, sub-tasks. Further, when the goal is the depender goal of a dependency, a reserved `delegates` action is introduced as the body of the procedure, followed by invocation of the procedure of the dependee goal.

Successor state axioms are added for every effect and performance fluent, which make the fluent true in a situation if it already was true in the previous situation or the latest action is the task the fluent associates with – through an effect link in effect fluents. For each task, an action precondition axiom is constructed based on the conjunction of all satisfaction/performance fluents that correspond to the goals/tasks that target the task with a a precedence link.

Given the above, a situation $\texttt{do(a}_n\texttt{,do(a}_{n-1}\texttt{, ...,do(a}_1\texttt{,S}_0\texttt{)...)))}$ in Golog terms corresponds to a history $[t_1,t_2, ...,t_n]$ in the i^+ ontology, where each task t_i corresponds to Golog action a_i, and the initial situation $\texttt{S}_0$ corresponds to a state in which no task has been performed.

Explanation Templates. Recall that explanation templates are of the form *guard : query : render* and are relativised to histories e. The latter map to situations `s`, according to the above. The guard condition corresponds to a Boolean expression constructed with fluents relativized to that situation `s`. The parameters in the expression are all bound by the user to specific objects. The query is then another such expression with free parameters to be bound to values that make the expression true in `s`. For human readability, these parameters are then used to construct the answer through the `render` predicate which concatenates constant text with parameter instantiations to construct the answer.

Explanation Axioms. Of the explanation axioms introduced, translation of the first Axioms 1–4 are straightforward rules which depend on predicates reflecting structural characteristics of the i^+ model. The challenge in translating of Axioms 5 and 6 reduces to constructing atomic formula $\texttt{getPrefix(x,s,s}_{sel}\texttt{)}$ for extracting situation $\texttt{s}_{sel}$ corresponding to history prefix e_{sel} (see Sect. 4). The formula holds if (a) `x` holds in $\texttt{S}_0$, in which case $\texttt{s} = \texttt{s}_{sel} = \texttt{S}_0$ or (b) $\texttt{s}_{sel}$ is a prefix of `s` such that if $\texttt{do(a,s}_{sel}\texttt{)}$ is also a prefix for `s`, then `x` does not hold in

s_{sel} but holds in do(a,s_{sel}) – i,e., performance of a turns x from false to true. To implement this, a simple logic program replays s from initial situation S_0 until the first a is found that brings about this transition to the truth value of x and the corresponding prefix s_{sel} is returned [30].

6 Simulation Analysis and Implementation

The formalized models are useful for both simulating the explanation services of the system-to-be in order to support the process of discovering and specifying explanation requirements and, assuming a compliant implementation of the required system, forming the backbone of an explanation service prototype. A prototypical implementation of the explanation engine and the example of Fig. 1 is available at the associated online code repository [31].

Exploring Explanations via Simulation. Simulation is based on generating possible action histories and asking explanation questions based on them. Specifically, Golog's predicate FindSit(p(...),S_0,s) renders situations s which result from executing procedure p(...), starting from the initial situation S_0. By setting p(...) to be the procedure that maps to the top-level goal, the resulting situation s maps to an i^+ history that captures one way of fulfilling the corresponding goal. The situations can be subsequently passed as the input situation of the explanation templates and rules. To allow such simulations, analysts will need to instantiate assertion descriptions – including these in the intialization element – with concrete objects (see Sect. 2).

Returning to our example of Fig. 1, let us hypothesize that *Abdul*, the meeting initiator, wants to ask organizer, *Matilda*, to schedule a meeting with three participants, *Xing*, *Amr*, and *Naya*. The first two have their on-line calendars up-to-date, and *Alex*, the executive secretary, has the phone numbers of the last two. We further know that the organizer wants to promote *Quick Scheduling*.

After having Golog generate a hypothetical history e1, as seen in the top frame of Fig. 4, we observe that Alex collected (at the behest of Matilda) Naya's constraints by phone (task #07). We request an ad-hoc explanation for this action, in the first question (Q1) at the bottom frame of Fig. 4. As ad-hoc explanations are agnostic to the purpose or context of the sought explanation, predicate explain will consider all possible ways by which axioms can be instantiated to provide a response. The outcomes are answers A1.1 - A1.3. The first (A1.1) is a teleological explanation making use of dependency Axiom #3 to inform that said action took place at the request of the organizer, Matilda. The second explanation (A1.2) is a canonical one, and points to a subsequent task (#08 in the upper frame) whose performance requires prior performance of the task in question. The third (A1.3) informs that this is the only possible alternative; indeed Naya does not maintain an on-line calendar and there is no other way to collect constraints. Out of these answers, the explainee may focus on the one they intended with their question. Note also that the natural language in the answer is due to simple templates translating the atomic formulae in parentheses into more accessible descriptions.

Simulated History e1

```
– 01: s0
– 02: decideMeetingDetails(abdul)
– 03: delegate(abdul,matilda,haveSchedulingPerformedByOrganizer(abdul,matilda)
                                  haveMeetingScheduled(matilda))
– 04: collectFromCallendar(matilda,xing)
– 05: collectFromCallendar(matilda,amr)
– 06: delegate(matilda,alex,haveSecretaryCallPP(matilda,alex,naya),
                        collectConstraintsByPhone(matilda,alex,naya))
– 07: collectConstraintsByPhone(matilda,alex,naya)
– 08: chooseTimeandDate(matilda)
– 09: announceMeeting(matilda,xing)
– ...
```

Explanations

```
Q1: explain(collectConstraintsByPhone(matilda,xing,naya), e1)
 – A1.1: Teleological Explanation: Because organizer matilda wanted to
   have secretary alex call participant naya to collect their constraints.
   (haveSecretaryCallPP(matilda,alex,naya)) [dependency (axiom 3)]
 – A1.2: Canonical Explanation: Because organizer matilda wanted to choose time and
   date for the meeting. (chooseTimeandDate(matilda)) [enablement (axiom 4)]
 – A1.3: Choice mandatory, no other feasible alternative. (...) [only feasible
   (axiom 5)]

Q2: explain(collectFromCallendar(matilda,amr), e1).
 – A2.1: Teleological Explanation: Because organizer matilda wanted to collect
   amr's timetable. (timetableCollected(matilda,amr)) [operationalization (axiom
   1)]
 – A2.2: Canonical Explanation: Because organizer matilda wanted to choose time and
   date for the meeting. (chooseTimeandDate(matilda)) [enablement (axiom 4)]
 – A2.3: Canonical Explanation: Because organizer abdul wanted to have the meeting
   attended. (meetingAttended(abdul)) [enablement (axiom 4)]
 – A2.4: From the available choices this is the only preferred one. (...) [only
   preferred from feasible (axiom 6)]

Q3: explain(whyisPP(amr), e1).
 – A3.1: Because amr needs to report on agenda items 3 and 4.
```

Fig. 4. Simulated history and ad-hoc explanations.

The second question (`Q2`) of Fig. 4 offers similar answers for the question why Amr's constraints were collected from the calendar. In this case, we have an additional canonical explanation `A2.3` stemming from the precedence between an ancestor of the task in question, namely *Have Scheduling Performed(Abdul)*, to goal *Meeting Attended(Abdul)*. In other words, collecting constraints – in the case of Amr from his calendar – is necessary for the meeting to be eventually attended. This explanation is likely too distant from the explanandum to be of interest. In general, since ad-hoc questions lack context, they may include several uninteresting explanations in response. For canonical explanations, specifically, the level of ancestry at which explanation producing precedence constraints are sought (see Axiom 4.2) can be limited to avoid explanations that are unlikely to be of interest or even comprehensible. This limit is exceeded in `Q1` hence the additional canonical explanation does not show up. The final answer for `Q2`, `A2.4.`, shows that while for collecting Amr's constraints both options are available, the one that aligns with the promotion of the *Quick Scheduling* quality appears to have been chosen. Note that this is not a definite but a plausible explanation, as how exactly the variability-binding decision is made is, as we saw, subject to optimization procedures outside of the model. Finally, the third question `Q3` is not ad-hoc but based on a pre-designed template from Fig. 3.

As part of the explanation requirements exploration process, analysts may add or remove constraints and initialization clauses from/to the model, and further steer the interpreter to generate situations which satisfy certain properties, e.g., omit or necessarily include a specific action/task. The exercise allows testing the efficacy of the explanation axioms to the given domain and, when the latter fall short, triggers development of custom templates. To facilitate exploration, in our prototypical implementation [30] the possibility of interactive ad-hoc explanation exploration is also available. Following the initial explanation question, the possible answer literals are listed prompting the explainee to choose one of them for adoption as the explanandum of the next round.

Implementing the Explanation Service. Let us further assume that the systems supporting the socio-technical structure captured in i^+ are implemented (a) in full compliance with the i^+ model, (b) such that performance of every i^+ task is captured and logged, (c) instances of top-level goal fulfillment have concrete identifiers, such that different instances of top-level goal fulfillment can be extracted from logs. In that case, the formalization of the axioms and templates can be used as-is for the generation of explanations. Thus, in the meeting scheduling example of Fig. 1, the name and parameter instances of leaf-level tasks are appended to the log upon their performance, and, hence, in the order in which they are performed. By requiring the value of parameter `m` to identify a specific meeting of interest, a pre-processor can then extract the tasks that relate to that meeting and construct a history such as the one in Fig. 4, top frame. The history is then used according to the process sketched above.

7 Related Work

The topic of explanations spans multiple disciplines and a broad literature that stretches back to Aristotle and his seminal work on causality in Nature [17]. In the context of software-intensive systems and their actions, we consider an explanation to be about a set of phenomena (*explananda*) (e.g., the actions of an autonomous vehicle (AV)) that needs to be generated by an explainer (the explanation service of the AV), and help an explainee (e.g., passenger, owner, auditor) to understand the phenomena. Our proposal for the form of explanation requirements was inspired by *competency questions* used for scoping and evaluating formal ontologies (e.g., [18]).

In the Requirements Engineering (RE) literature, explainability has been largely studied as a non-functional requirement [3–7,15,25]. Through literature [4], survey [3], and case study research [5,6], Chazette et al. devise a definition of explainability – consistent with our approach – and highlight the desire for and value of embedding explanation services within software-intensive systems [5]. In other studies [15,25], the focus is how explainability interacts with other non-functional requirements, such as transparency [11,12], understandability, and usability using Softgoal Interdependency Graphs (SIGs) [8]. Sterz et al. use the umbrella term *perspicuity* to refer to this class of qualities [40], Speith focuses on categories that enable evaluation of explainability of a system, while Berani et al. [2] propose a framework for organizing such concepts at different granularity levels. At the same time, the motivation for seeking explanations has been studied by Sadeghi et al. [36], and includes training, validation, and interaction; all of which are suitable application areas of our proposal. Consistent with our $i*$-based approach, an explainee-oriented elicitation practice has been proposed through the use of personas [16]. Elsewhere, Mann et al. [32] offer categories of opacity that explainability aims at addressing, of which complexity (in our case: variability of system outputs/behaviors) and epistemic dependency (actors possessing different pieces of the explanation puzzle) can be seen as particularly suitable targets of our approach. In general, rather than studying explainability as a quality, our effort is oriented towards developing tools and techniques for systematic elicitation, modeling, analysis, and implementation of explanation requirements of specific kinds, namely, observed system actions.

The problem of explainable AI (XAI) was first discussed in the AI community in the context of expert systems [9], and has been regularly studied ever since. For instance, Shanahan [37] proposes a deductive and an abductive approach in the situation calculus, while, more recently, Dennis and Oren [14] proposed an interactive Belief-Desire-Intention (BDI) agent system to explain agent actions. Structural Equation Models (SEM)-based models have also been proposed to address causal notions of explanation [1] and applied to explain the behavior of model-free reinforcement learning agents. Causal models are also utilized for enabling contrastive explanations [34], while elsewhere, non-monotonic reasoning, probabilistic planning, and interactive learning are combined to develop an explainable robotic architecture [38,39]. Finally, Khan and Rostamigiv [24] appeal to theory of mind, causal analysis of agents' knowledge, and goal recognition to explain agent behaviour in communicative multiagent contexts. Comparatively, we aim at supporting the requirements analysis and design of explanation services within an established requirements modeling framework, and generating explanations based on information within the specific kind of models.

8 Conclusions

We presented a goal-oriented framework for modeling, analyzing, simulating, and prototyping explanation requirements for actions of software-intensive systems. We utilize i^+, an extension of $i*$ that allows temporal and causal relationships among intentional elements. Subsequently, explanation requirements are captured through explanation goals, are assigned to various explainee roles, and are operationalized into actions that capture run-time explanation information or render explanation interactions, the format of which is described through templates. Further, a set of axioms exploits information embedded in the i^+ models to offer possible answers to ad-hoc explanation questions. By appropriately formalizing the model, both simulations and, under certain assumptions, prototyping of the envisioned explanation interactions are possible.

Future work aims at empirically evaluating both the proposed analysis approach and the quality of explanations produced by our axioms through case studies and experiments. We, further, plan to broaden the kinds of explanations our system can offer, including explanations for exceptional system actions, action failures, and, generally, expected actions that did not occur, such as counterfactual explanations [19] – our current axioms are restricted to explaining actions that have occurred. In addition, we are interested in refining our axiomatization to include ad hoc explanations that are context- and explainee-sensitive [35]. We, finally, wish to study how systems can be engineered in full compliance with the explanation requirements model, especially in the context of learning-based systems, whose decision-making rules are known to be opaque.

References

1. Beckers, S.: Causal explanations and XAI. In: Schölkopf, B., Uhler, C., Zhang, K. (eds.) Proceedings of the 1st Conference on Causal Learning and Reasoning, (CLeaR 2022), vol. 177, pp. 90–109. PMLR (2022). https://openreview.net/forum?id=pJuO-5QEKa
2. Bersani, M.M., Camilli, M., Lestingi, L., Mirandola, R., Rossi, M., Scandurra, P.: A conceptual framework for explainability requirements in software-intensive systems. In: Proceedings of the 31st IEEE International Requirements Engineering Conference Workshops (REW 2023), pp. 309–315 (2023). https://doi.org/10.1109/REW57809.2023.00059
3. Chazette, L., Karras, O., Schneider, K.: Do end-users want explanations? analyzing the role of explainability as an emerging aspect of non-functional requirements. In: Proceedings of the 27th IEEE International Requirements Engineering Conference (RE'19), pp. 223–233 (2019). https://doi.org/10.1109/RE.2019.00032
4. Chazette, L., Brunotte, W., Speith, T.: Exploring explainability: a definition, a model, and a knowledge catalogue. In: Proceedings of the 29th IEEE International Requirements Engineering Conference (RE'21), pp. 197–208 (2021https://doi.org/10.1109/RE51729.2021.00025
5. Chazette, L., Brunotte, W., Speith, T.: Explainable software systems: from requirements analysis to system evaluation. Requirements Eng. **27**(4), 457–487 (2022). https://doi.org/10.1007/s00766-022-00393-5
6. Chazette, L., Klös, V., Herzog, F., Schneider, K.: Requirements on explanations: a quality framework for explainability. In: Proceedings of the 30th IEEE International Requirements Engineering Conference (RE'22), pp. 140–152 (2022). https://doi.org/10.1109/RE54965.2022.00019
7. Chazette, L., Schneider, K.: Explainability as a non-functional requirement: challenges and recommendations. Requirements Eng. **25**(4), 493–514 (2020). https://doi.org/10.1007/s00766-020-00333-1
8. Chung, Lawrence, Nixon, Brian A.., Yu, Eric, Mylopoulos, John: Non-Functional Requirements in Software Engineering. Springer US, Boston, MA (2000). https://doi.org/10.1007/978-1-4615-5269-7

9. Clancey, W.J.: An antibiotic therapy selector which provides for explanations. In: Proceedings of the 5th International Joint Conference on Artificial Intelligence (IJCAI'77), p. 858 (1977)
10. Cohen, J.: Teleological explanation. Proc. Aristotelian Society **51**, 255–292 (1950). http://www.jstor.org/stable/4544486
11. Cysneiros, L.M.: Using i* to elicit and model transparency in the presence of other non-functional requirements: a position paper. In: Proceedings of the 6th International i* Workshop (iStar 2013), CEUR Vol-978. vol. 978, pp. 19–24 (2013). https://ceur-ws.org/Vol-978/paper_4.pdf
12. Cysneiros, L.M., Raffi, M., Leite, J.C.S.D.P.: Software transparency as a key requirement for self-driving cars. In: Proceedings of the 26th IEEE International Requirements Engineering Conference (RE'18), pp. 382–387. IEEE (2018). https://doi.org/10.1109/RE.2018.00-21
13. Dalpiaz, F., Franch, X., Horkoff, J.: iStar 2.0 Language Guide. The Computing Research Repository (CoRR) **abs/1605.0** (2016). http://arxiv.org/abs/1605.07767
14. Dennis, L.A., Oren, N.: Explaining BDI agent behaviour through dialogue. Autonomous Agents Multi Agent Syst. **36**(1), 29 (2022). https://doi.org/10.1007/s10458-022-09556-8
15. Deters, H., Droste, J., Obaidi, M., Schneider, K.: How explainable is your system? towards a quality model for explainability. In: Mendez, D., Moreira, A. (eds.) Proceedings of the 30th International Working Conference on Requirements Engineering: Foundation for Software Quality (REFSQ 2024). pp. 3–19. Springer Nature Switzerland, Cham (2024).https://doi.org/10.1007/978-3-031-57327-9_1
16. Droste, J., Deters, H., Puglisi, J., Klunder, J.: Designing End-User Personas for Explainability Requirements Using Mixed Methods Research, pp. 129–135 (2023). https://doi.org/10.1109/REW57809.2023.00028
17. Falcon, A.: Aristotle on Causality. In: Zalta, E.N., Nodelman, U. (eds.) The Stanford Encyclopedia of Philosophy. Metaphysics Research Lab, Stanford University, Spring 2 edn. (2023). https://plato.stanford.edu/archives/spr2023/entries/aristotle-causality/
18. Grüninger, M., Fox, M.S.: The role of competency questions in enterprise engineering. In: Rolstadås, A. (ed.) Benchmarking — Theory and Practice. IAICT, pp. 22–31. Springer, Boston, MA (1995). https://doi.org/10.1007/978-0-387-34847-6_3
19. Guidotti, R.: Counterfactual explanations and how to find them: literature review and benchmarking. Data Min. Knowl. Disc. (2022). https://doi.org/10.1007/s10618-022-00831-6
20. Guizzardi, G., Guarino, N.: Explanation, semantics, and ontology. Data Knowl. Eng. **153**, 102325 (2024). https://doi.org/10.1016/j.datak.2024.102325, https://www.sciencedirect.com/science/article/pii/S0169023X24000491
21. Honderich, T.E.: Explanation (2005). https://www.oxfordreference.com/display/10.1093/acref/9780199264797.001.0001/acref-9780199264797-e-838
22. Josephson, J.R., Josephson, S.G. (eds.): Abductive Inference: Computation, Philosophy, Technology. Cambridge University Press, New York, NY, US (1996)
23. Kastner, L., Langer, M., Lazar, V., Schomacker, A., Speith, T., Sterz, S.: On the Relation of trust and explainability: why to engineer for trustworthiness. In: Proceedings of the 29th IEEE International Conference on Requirements Engineering Workshops (REW'21), pp. 169–175 (2021). https://doi.org/10.1109/REW53955.2021.00031

24. Khan, S.M., Rostamigiv, M.: On Explaining agent behaviour via root cause analysis: a formal account grounded in theory of mind. In: Gal, K., Nowé, A., Nalepa, G.J., Fairstein, R., Radulescu, R. (eds.) Proceedings of the 26th European Conference on Artificial Intelligence (ECAI 2023). Frontiers in Artificial Intelligence and Applications, vol. 372, pp. 1239–1247. IOS Press (2023). https://doi.org/10.3233/FAIA230401
25. Köhl, M.A., Baum, K., Langer, M., Oster, D., Speith, T., Bohlender, D.: Explainability as a Non-Functional Requirement. In: Proceedings of the 27th IEEE International Requirements Engineering Conference (RE'19), pp. 363–368 (2019). https://doi.org/10.1109/RE.2019.00046
26. Levesque, H., Pirri, F., Reiter, R.: Foundations for a Calculus of Situations. Electron. Trans. AI (ETAI) **2**(3–4), 159–178 (1998). https://ep.liu.se/ej/etai/1998/005/
27. Levesque, H.J., Reiter, R., Lespérance, Y., Lin, F., Scherl, R.B.: GOLOG: a logic programming language for dynamic domains. J. Logic Programm. **31**(1–3), 59–83 (1997). https://doi.org/10.1016/S0743-1066(96)00121-5
28. Liaskos, S., Khan, S.M., Mylopoulos, J.: Modeling and reasoning about uncertainty in goal models: a decision-theoretic approach. Softw. Syst. Model. **21**, 1–24 (2022). https://doi.org/10.1007/s10270-021-00968-w
29. Liaskos, S., McIlraith, S., Sohrabi, S., Mylopoulos, J.: Representing and reasoning about preferences in requirements engineering. Requirements Eng. J. (REJ) **16**, 227–249 (2011). https://doi.org/10.1007/s00766-011-0129-9
30. Liaskos, S., Mylopoulos, J., Borgida, A., Khan, S.M.: Model-driven analysis and design of explanation services (long technical report). Tech. rep., York University (2024). https://hdl.handle.net/10315/42239
31. Liaskos, S., Mylopoulos, J., Borgida, A., Khan, S.M.: Xp-i: extracting explanations from models (2024). https://github.com/cmg-york/xp-i
32. Mann, S., Crook, B., Kastner, L., Schomacker, A., Speith, T.: Sources of opacity in computer systems: towards a comprehensive taxonomy. In: Proceedings of the 31st IEEE International Requirements Engineering Conference Workshops (REW 2023), pp. 337–342 (2023). https://doi.org/10.1109/REW57809.2023.00063
33. Miller, T.: Explanation in artificial intelligence: Insights from the social sciences. Artif. Intell. **267**, 1–38 (2019). https://doi.org/10.1016/j.artint.2018.07.007
34. Miller, T.: Contrastive explanation: a structural-model approach. Knowl. Eng. Rev. **36**, e14 (2021). https://doi.org/10.1017/S0269888921000102
35. Sadeghi, M., Herbold, L., Unterbusch, M., Vogelsang, A.: SmartEx: a framework for generating user-centric explanations in smart environments. In: 2024 IEEE International Conference on Pervasive Computing and Communications (PerCom), pp. 106–113. IEEE Computer Society, Los Alamitos, CA, USA (2024). https://doi.org/10.1109/PerCom59722.2024.10494449
36. Sadeghi, M., Klos, V., Vogelsang, A.: Cases for explainable software systems: characteristics and examples. In: Proceedings of the IEEE International Conference on Requirements Engineering Workshops (REW'21), pp. 181–187 (2021https://doi.org/10.1109/REW53955.2021.00033
37. Shanahan, M.: Explanation in the situation calculus. In: Bajcsy, R. (ed.) Proceedings of the 13th International Joint Conference on Artificial Intelligence (IJCAI'93), pp. 160–165. Morgan Kaufmann (1993). https://dl.acm.org/doi/abs/10.5555/1624025.1624048
38. Sridharan, M.: REBA-KRL: Refinement-based architecture for knowledge representation, explainable reasoning and interactive learning in robotics. In: Giacomo,

G.D., Catalá, A., Dilkina, B., Milano, M., Barro, S., Bugarin, A., Lang, J. (eds.) Proceedings of the 24th European Conference on Artificial Intelligence (ECAI 2020). Frontiers in Artificial Intelligence and Applications, vol. 325, pp. 2935–2936. IOS Press (2020). https://doi.org/10.3233/FAIA200461
39. Sridharan, M., Meadows, B.: Towards a theory of explanations for human-robot collaboration. Künstliche Intelligenz **33**(4), 331–342 (2019). https://doi.org/10.1007/s13218-019-00616-y
40. Sterz, S., Baum, K., Lauber-Ronsberg, A., Hermanns, H.: Towards perspicuity requirements. In: Proceedings of the 29th IEEE International Conference on Requirements Engineering Workshops (REW'21), pp. 159–163 (2021). https://doi.org/10.1109/REW53955.2021.00029
41. The Editors of Encyclopedia: Explanation (2017). https://www.britannica.com/topic/explanation
42. Yu, E.S.K., Mylopoulos, J.: Understanding "Why" in software process modelling, analysis, and design. In: Proceedings of the 16th International Conference on Software Engineering (ICSE'94), pp. 159–168. Sorrento, Italy (1994). https://dl.acm.org/doi/10.5555/257734.257757

Enhancing Domain Modeling with Pre-trained Large Language Models: An Automated Assistant for Domain Modelers

Dominik Prokop, Štěpán Stenchlák, Petr Škoda, Jakub Klímek, and Martin Nečaský(✉)

Faculty of Mathematics and Physics, Charles University, Prague, Czechia
martin.necasky@matfyz.cuni.cz

Abstract. Domain modeling involves creating abstract representations of information within a specific domain using techniques such as conceptual modeling and ontology engineering. Traditionally, manual creation and maintenance of domain models are labor intensive and require modeling expertise. This paper explores the automation of domain modeling using pre-trained large language models (LLMs), presenting an experimental LLM-based conceptual modeling assistant that collaborates with a human expert. The assistant provides modeling suggestions based on a given textual description of the domain of interest, aiding in the design of classes, attributes, and associations. We present a generic framework for domain modeling assistants that consists of class, attribute, and association generators, and show how they can be implemented using an LLM. We demonstrate a concrete configuration of this framework and its prototype implementation. We evaluated the effectiveness of the framework configuration across various domains. Our findings indicate that the assistant significantly enhances the efficiency of modeling while maintaining reasonable quality of the outputs.

Keywords: Domain Modeling · Conceptual Modeling · Large Language Models · Domain Modeling Automation

1 Introduction

Domain modeling is fundamental in data and software engineering. Domain modeling techniques, such as conceptual modeling techniques, where a domain model is expressed as an ER or UML class diagram, or ontology engineering techniques, which define a domain model as a domain ontology, are well established in academia and industry [19]. However, manual modeling is time consuming and requires trained experts [19]. Therefore, various modeling automation techniques have been proposed [31]. Recently, researchers began to experiment with pre-trained large language models (LLMs) for possible automation [17,25].

W. Maass et al. (Eds.): ER 2024, LNCS 15238, pp. 235–253, 2025.
https://doi.org/10.1007/978-3-031-75872-0_13

In this paper, we introduce an LLM-based domain modeling assistant that cooperates with a human modeling expert. We do not aim at full modeling process automation since the human participation is crucial for the accuracy of the final model. We envision an assistant that provides suggestions of possible modeling steps. Our starting point is an unstructured domain description that the expert uses as input into the domain modeling process. We focus only on the basic modeling constructs of classes, their attributes, and binary associations. We introduce a generic framework based on class, attribute and association suggestion generators, its concrete configuration, and a prototype implementation. Despite being only a baseline configuration, it demonstrates an interesting level of performance in our thorough evaluation with real-world domains and users.

The paper is structured as follows. Section 2 introduces the necessary formalization of a simplified modeling process. Section 3 describes the framework for building automated modeling assistants. Section 4 describes a concrete configuration of the framework and briefly demonstrates our prototype software implementation. Section 5 presents the detailed evaluation. Section 6 presents the related work. Section 7 concludes.

2 Domain Modeling Process

In this paper, a *domain model* $M = (\mathcal{C}, \mathcal{P})$ consists of a set of *classes* $\mathcal{C}$ and *properties* $\mathcal{P}$. A class $C \in \mathcal{C}$ has its $name(C)$ which identifies C in M and briefly characterizes the semantics of C. A property $P \in \mathcal{P}$ has also $name(P)$ used for the same purposes. It has a *source class*, $source(P) \in \mathcal{C}$, and it can have a *target class*, $target(P) \in \mathcal{C}$. P is a *binary association* if $target(P)$ is defined. Otherwise, P is an *attribute*. These basic modeling constructs are prevalent in real conceptual models [16], so their automation could have a significant impact. We leave other modeling constructs such as cardinalities or ISA hierarchies, and the more advanced constructs and patterns [13] for future work.

We consider a *modeling process* starting with a textual domain description T. T can be a well-curated text, but may encompass varied interpretations articulated by different stakeholders at various levels of detail. A modeling expert translates T into a domain model M in a sequence of steps:

Design a class For a concept in T, create a class C with a designated $name(C)$.

Design a class attribute For a class C and a concept in T that characterizes C, create an attribute P, where $C = source(P)$, and define its $name(P)$.

Design an association for a class For a class C and a concept in T that describes a relationship of C with another concept, create an association P such that $C = source(P)$ or $target(P)$, and define its $name(P)$. If not yet represented, create a class D for the other concept and specify its $name(D)$.

3 LLM-Based Modeling Assistant Framework

We propose solving the automation of these steps as *text generation problems* similarly to [17], where the authors consider a domain description T with an underlying ground truth model M, and approach the problem of model generation as the problem of defining a text generator f with $M' = f(T)$, where M' is the generated model similar to M. The generator f is an LLM-based operator defined by a predesigned prompt that instructs an LLM to return a structured textual representation of M' for the input T. We consider more fine-grained text generation problems solved by the following generators:

Class generator gen_c that for T suggests classes $\{C_1, \ldots, C_n\}$ each with a suggested $name(C_i)$.

Attribute generator gen_a that for T and a class C suggests attributes $\{P_1, \ldots, P_n\}$, each with $source(P_i) = C$, suggested $name(P_i)$, and original text $orig(P_i)$ that is part of T on which base gen_a suggested P_i.

Association generator gen_r that for T and a class C suggests associations $\{P_1, \ldots, P_n\}$, each with $source(P_i) = C$ (or $target(P_i) = C$), suggested $name(P_i)$, and with the original text $orig(P_i)$ that is part of T on which base gen_r suggested P_i. It also suggests the other class D_i, with $target(P_i) = D_i$ (or $source(P_i) = D_i$), and suggested $name(D_i)$.

```
01 Solely based on the given context {main control instruction}
02 {modeling procedure}
03 {output specification}
04 EXAMPLE START
05 Solely based on the given context {example main control instruction}
06 This is the given context: {example context specification}
07 Output: "{example output}"
08 EXAMPLE END
09 Solely based on the given context {main control instruction}
10 This is the given context: {context specification}
11 Output:
```

Fig. 1. Prompt meta-template for concept generators

A generator is defined with a prompt template. The template should instruct the LLM to work within the domain description context, to provide the required task-specific suggestions, and to output them in a predefined format for easy parsing. It should support techniques that provably improve LLM outputs, such as Chain-of-Thoughts [32] (CoT, instructing the LLM to generate intermediate reasoning steps) or N-shot prompting [8] (inserting N examples in the prompt).

Based on these generic requirements, we propose a prompt meta-template shown in Fig. 1. A generator template is constructed by replacing the placeholders in the meta-template with generator-specific instructions. The meta-template has the following structure. The `main control instruction` (line `01`) summarizes the given task, which is to suggest classes/attributes/associations, based solely on the given context. The context is specified in the `context specification` (line `10`). Basically, it is the domain description T but it is possible to implement various text processing and filtering techniques here. The `modeling procedure` (line `02`) instructs the LLM on how to proceed before

Table 1. Our configuration of the meta-template for the generators

	`main control instruction`	`modeling procedure`	`output specification`
gen_c	extract all class names		Output each class name in JSON object like this: `{''name'': ''class name''}`
gen_a	generate all attributes for the class: "{source_class}"	For each attribute copy the part of the given context describing this attribute	and then output this attribute in JSON object like this: `{''originalText'': ''copy the part of the given context containing this attribute'', ''name'': ''attribute name''}`
gen_r	which associations does the class: "{source_class}" have?	For each association, output its name and source class and target class and copy the part of the given context containing this association	in JSON object like this: `{''originalText'': ''copy the part of the given context containing this association'', ''name'': ''association name'', ''source'': ''source class name'', ''target'': ''target class name''}`

generating the final suggestions. Here, various prompt design strategies, such as CoT, can be implemented. The `output specification` (line 03) defines the required output format. Lines 04-08 represent optional examples. Here, an N-shot prompt design strategy can be implemented, where the prompts contain expected output samples based on a sample context. Each example starts with the `example main control instruction` (line 05) which is the same as the `main control instruction` but with a concrete class C if the task is class-specific. The `example context specification` (line 06) is the concrete context specification for the example and `example output` (line 07) is the expected output for the given context. Line 09 repeats the task definition to request the LLM for suggestions. We use it to reduce leaks of the examples in the LLM's responses.

4 Implementation of Domain Modeling Assistant

Let us now use the framework to implement a concrete modeling assistant. At its core are concrete implementations of the generators. A generator takes the domain description and a class (for property generators) as input and constructs the final prompt based on its template. Then it prompts the underlying LLM and tries to parse the output in the specified format. We do not restrict the choice of the underlying LLM but we suppose that a given implementation is based on one chosen LLM. If successful, it presents the suggestions to the user who accepts or rejects the suggestions. In the remainder of this section, we describe our concrete configuration of the generators and also our software prototype.

4.1 Configurations of the Generators

The generator configuration includes defining (1) the main control instruction, modeling procedure specifications, and output specifications to construct the prompt template, (2) examples (N-shot prompting), and (3) a context specification technique. Moreover, a concrete LLM must be chosen.

Generator Templates. Table 1 summarizes the configurations of the meta-template for the generators. gen_c incorporates the main control instruction that directs the LLM to *extract all class names* from the input provided. The output is specified to be a list of suggested class names structured as JSON objects. A modeling procedure is empty, so we do not provide any instruction on how to discover the classes. gen_a and gen_r incorporate similar main control instructions. Because they are parametrized with an input class C, the instructions contain a placeholder `source class` which is replaced by $name(C)$ for each generator call. The output is specified to be a list of suggestions structured as JSON objects. The suggestions also contain the original text. The generators incorporate the modeling procedure specification, which introduces a simple CoT strategy that first instructs the LLM to generate some preliminary descriptions of the suggestions before providing the final output.

N-Shot Prompting. The study [17] shows that inserting one example significantly improves the output domain model. Adding more examples did not provide clear evidence of improvements, but the authors still observed some. We use examples based on the domain description and its domain model shown in Fig. 2. For gen_c, we use the three classes as examples. For gen_a, we use the colored attributes, each with the colored part of the text as examples of the corresponding original texts. For gen_r, we proceed similarly, but we provide each sample association twice – for the source class and for the target class.

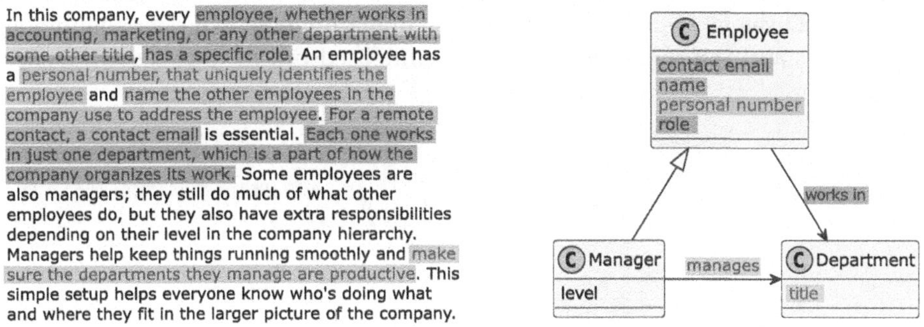

Fig. 2. The simple company employees domain description and its corresponding domain model used for N-shot prompting in our generator templates.

Context Specification Technique. The context specification part of the templates restricts an LLM to work in a specified domain context. Instead of providing the original T as a context, we can preprocess it to make it clearer or more focused. We use Retrieval Augmented Generation (RAG) [34], which selectively enhances the prompts with contextually relevant information from T. This emulates modeling experts, who refer to only parts of T relevant to their current task, and abbreviates the prompts in the case of long descriptions. We implement RAG for gen_a and gen_r that provide suggestions for a given class C. We aim to retrieve the sentences from T that are relevant for C. Given the inherent complexity of natural language, where references to C may not always be direct and could appear as pronouns or through other indirect means, achieving high levels of specificity can be challenging. Various NLP techniques, such as anaphora and coreference resolution [24], are available that could make indirect means of concepts explicit. We employ a straightforward technique that enriches a sentence starting with a pronoun with a link back to the previous sentence. If a sentence in T directly mentions C, it is retrieved primarily. In addition, we retrieve sentences that refer to this primary sentence transitively. For the retrieval of the primary sentences, we implemented a syntactic technique that lemmatizes T and retrieves all sentences that contain the lemmatized $name(C)$. We also implemented a semantic retrieval technique for which we vectorize individual sentences of T. For the given attribute or association generation task, we primarily retrieve all sentences whose vector is close to the vector of $name(C)$. The Top-K strategy could negatively impact recall if C has a large set of properties described in T. Therefore, we retrieve all sentences above a given threshold that can be parametrized in our implementation.

4.2 Software Prototype

We developed a software prototype[1] to demonstrate the viability of the approach. Its back-end implements the generators and provides them via an API. Its browser front-end provides a text area to insert a domain description and a modeling canvas where the user creates the domain model using manual modeling features and the suggestion features highlighted by the *magic wand* icon.

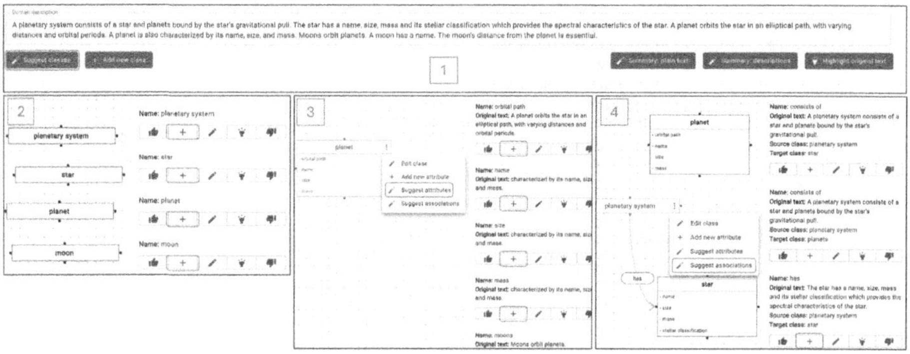

Fig. 3. Screenshots of the main functionalities of the prototype application.

Figure 3 demonstrates these features. Screenshot 1 shows the text area for the domain description and action buttons. The highlighted button *Suggest classes* calls the gen_c operator with the inserted domain description. Screenshot 2 shows the list of suggested classes. The user can use the highlighted + buttons to insert

[1] https://github.com/dataspecer/llm-assistant.

suggested classes into the modeling canvas. The other buttons are used for *liking* and *disliking* a suggestion, its editing before inserting the suggested class into the canvas, and highlighting the suggestion in the original domain description. For the selected class, the user can ask for attribute and association suggestions, i.e. gen_a and gen_r operators for the class and domain description. Screenshots 3 and 4 show the attribute and association suggestions. For the suggested attributes and associations, the tool also shows the original text returned by the generators.

5 Experimental Evaluation

This section explores the effectiveness of our approach in real-life domains. We measured the precision, recall, and F1 scores based on our manual evaluation of the suggestions. Domain descriptions, manual evaluation of individual suggestions, detailed measured values of precision, recall, and F1 scores, and also detailed data from user-based evaluation are available in our evaluation repository[2]. In the paper, we describe the evaluation methodology and only the summary of the measurements due to space limitation.

5.1 Generator Evaluation Methodology

Evaluation Domains. To assess the quality of the generators, we used six domains with their domain description and manually created reference domain models. We used the reference models to evaluate the suggestions generated based on the domain descriptions. Table 2 summarizes the size of these reference models. We categorize the domains into two groups. The first group contains three domains: *aircraft manufacturing*, *conference papers*, and *farming*. They are characterized by simpler descriptions with a limited scope of concepts. For each domain, we manually created three semantically equivalent domain descriptions in three different styles. *Analytical* descriptions are written with analytical precision, describing each concept rigorously, unambiguously, and preferably with a consistent sequence of sentences. *Eclectic* are written as a collection of less structured knowledge from different stakeholders, each describing the domain from a different point of view. *Educational* emphasize the most important concepts at the beginning, where only essential aspects are described, followed by adding more details about the concepts later in the description.

The second group contains 3 more complex domains: *zoological gardens*, *public colleges*, and *vehicle registration*. We experiment with one domain description per domain that we sourced externally and its reference domain model that we created manually based on the description. The domain of zoological gardens is the simplest of the three. We retrieved its description from a bachelor student in our research group who works on a software application for zoological gardens. For the domain of public colleges, we combined the English translation

[2] https://github.com/dataspecer/domain-modeling-benchmark.

Table 2. The size of the reference domain models

	Aircrafts	Papers	Farming	Zoos	Colleges	Vehicles
# classes	8	7	14	14	63	66
# attributes	10	12	15	26	14	72
# associations	8	9	9	24	67	46

of the Czech Higher Education Act[3] and the Code of study and examination of our university[4]. For the domain of vehicle registrations, we combined the English translation of the Czech Act on the Conditions of Operation of Vehicles on Roads and the corresponding Directive of the European Council[5].

Generator Evaluation Tasks. For the given domain D, its domain description T, and a reference conceptual model $M = (\mathcal{C}, \mathcal{P})$ manually created based on T, we consider the following sequence of evaluation tasks.

- $gen_c(T)$ to generate class suggestions based on T,
- $gen_a(C, T)$ to generate attribute suggestions based on T for each reference class C in the reference model M that has at least one attribute in M,
- $gen_r(C, T)$ to generate association suggestions based on T for each reference class C in the reference model M that has at least one association in M.

For each domain description T, this results in one evaluation task gen_c, m evaluation tasks gen_a and n evaluation tasks gen_r where m is the number of classes with some attributes in M, and n is the number of classes with some associations in M. For each generator configuration evaluated (see Sect. 5.2 for their description), the suggestions generated by the evaluation tasks are recorded in three evaluation tables (for classes, attributes, and associations) for manual evaluation by a human evaluator. The evaluation tables contain the suggested $name(X')$ for each suggested class, attribute, and association X'. For each property suggested, the tables contain $name(source(X'))$ and $orig(X')$. For each suggested association, we also contain $name(target(X'))$.

Manual Assessment of Generated Suggestions. Each generated suggestion must be manually evaluated by a human evaluator who records the evaluation in the evaluation tables in columns *Matches class*, *Matches attribute*, and *Matches association*. *Semantic correspondence* between a suggested X' and a reference $X \in M$ is essential for the evaluation. If the question *"Can we model X also as X'?"* can be answered positively, *X' semantically corresponds to X*.

To limit subjectivity, we requested that the manual evaluation be carried out according to the rules summarized in Table 3. If the class X' suggested by

[3] https://www.msmt.cz/areas-of-work/tertiary-education/national-accreditation-bureau-for-higher-education?highlightWords=higher+education+act.

[4] Code of study and examination of the BLINDED, https://BLINDED.com.

[5] European Council Directive 1999/37/EC of 29 April 1999 on the registration documents for vehicles, https://eur-lex.europa.eu/eli/dir/1999/37/oj.

Table 3. Summary of manual evaluation rules

	Matches class	*Matches attribute*	*Matches association*
$gen_c(T)$	$name(X)$ | * | $name(X_1)$;...	N/A N/A	N/A N/A
$gen_a(T, C)$ $gen_r(T, C)$	$name(D)$ | *	$name(X)$ | * | :$name(X)$ | :* | $name(X_1)$;...	$name(X)$ | * | :$name(X)$ | :* | $name(X_1)$;...

$gen_c(T)$ corresponds to a single class X, we record $name(X)$ in *Matches class.* The assessment considers both the occurrences of $name(X')$ within T and how X is structured within M. If X' does not correspond to any class in M, but the evaluator considers it valid from the semantic point of view based on T, we record an asterisk (*) in *Matches class.* This scenario can arise especially in more complex domains where not all concepts described in the domain description are modeled, or a concept can be modeled with an attribute instead of an association and a class. If X' does not correspond to any single class in M', but its $name(X')$ corresponds to a list of classes $X_1, \ldots, X_n \in M$, their names are concatenated to $name(X_1); \ldots; name(X_n)$ which we record in *Matches classes.* This corresponds to scenarios where domain models are more coarse-grained.

For a property X' suggested by $gen_a(T, C)$ and $gen_r(T, C)$, we consider similar rules with some differences. If X' is a suggested attribute, it can also correspond to an association X and vice versa. This scenario arises in practice, where properties can be modeled as attributes or associations interchangably based on the desired level of semantic and structural detail of the resulting domain model. Therefore, $name(X)$ is recorded in *Matches attribute* if X is a reference attribute or *Matches association* if X is a reference association. Moreover, X' must correspond to X also in its source class and, if X' is an association, in its target class. X' can be suggested in the reverse direction of X. The asterisk (*) and the lists are used in the same way as for the classes. In addition, when X' corresponds to an association X then $name(D)$ of the class at the other end of X than the end with C is recorded in *Matches class.* This corresponds to a scenario where a domain modeler models D not in the step of identifying classes in T, but when modeling X starting in C. When X' corresponds to an association that is not in M, the class at the other end of this association is a class D in M, which we record again with $name(D)$ in *Matches class.* Last but not least, it might happen that X' corresponds to X only when the correspondence requirement in the source/target class is relaxed so that the classes at the ends of X' can be subclasses or superclasses of the corresponding classes at the ends of X. In that case, we write a colon(:) followed by $name(X)$ to *Matches attribute* or *Matches class.* We write a colon followed by an asterisk (:*) if X' makes sense, but should be modeled for a subclass or superclass of C. We provide several examples of the evaluation rules in our online evaluation repository.

Precision and Recall Measures Definition. For the given domain description T and its reference model $M = (\mathcal{C}, \mathcal{P})$, let $\mathcal{C}' = gen_c(T)$ be the set of all suggested classes, $\mathcal{P}' = \bigcup_{C \in \mathcal{C}} gen_a(C, T) \cup \bigcup_{C \in \mathcal{C}} gen_r(C, T)$ the set of all suggested properties, and $M' = (\mathcal{C}', \mathcal{P}')$ the suggested model. Let $eval_c(X')$, $eval_a(X')$, and $eval_r(X')$ denote the assessment recorded for X' in columns *Matches class/attribute/association*, respectively. We distinguish the following matching functions $\mathcal{C}' \cup \mathcal{P}' \times \mathcal{C} \cup \mathcal{P} \to \{\texttt{True}, \texttt{False}\}$:

- $matches_{strict}(X', X)$ iff X is a class, X' is a suggested class, and $eval_c(X') = name(X)$ (similarly for attributes and associations),
- $matches_{constr}(X', X)$ iff $eval_{c|a|r}(X') = name(X)$ for a suggestion X'.
- $matches_{isa}(X', X)$ iff $matches_{constr}(X', X)$, or $eval_{a|r}(X') = {:}name(X)$ for a property X,
- $matches_{list}(X', X)$ iff $matches_{isa}(X', X)$, or $eval_{c|a|r}(X')$ is a list containing $name(X)$ or ${:}name(X)$.

These functions allow us to distinguish different levels of strictness in determining how much the suggestions must conform to the reference model M. The variant *strict* (shortcut *strict*) requires that the suggestion X' exactly corresponds to X, including the correspondence of the suggested modeling construct to the construct actually used in M. The variant *modeling construct agnostic* (shortcut *constr*) relaxes the need to use the exact modeling constructs. It supports situations where an attribute is suggested instead of association or vice versa and where a class is suggested as a part of an attribute or association suggestion. The variant *ISA agnostic* (shortcut *isa*) relaxes the exact match in the inheritance hierarchy where a property is suggested for a subclass or superclass of the class in M. The variant *list agnostic* (shortcut *list*) relaxes the need to identify individual properties instead of an umbrella property. The last two variants *isa* and *list* add relaxations only for properties, not for classes.

With these matching functions, we define different recall and precision variants. Recall measures to what extent M' covers M considering the different levels of strictness. For classes, it is expressed as

$$R^{\mathcal{C}}_{\square}(M', M) = \frac{|\{X \in \mathcal{C} : (\exists X' \in M')(matches_{\square}(X', X))\}|}{|\mathcal{C}|}$$

which is the number of reference classes for which there exists a matching suggestion based on manual evaluation compared to the total number of reference classes. The strictness of the matching is given by the chosen matching function. Similarly, we define the recall for attributes and associations.

Precision measures the correctness of M'. M' is correct if each $X' \in M'$ is correct. X' is correct if it matches some $X \in M$ or if it does not match any $X \in M$ but it is still meaningful compared to T which is recorded in the evaluation tables with the * symbol. For this, we introduce the following auxiliary functions $\mathcal{C}' \cup \mathcal{P}' \to \{\texttt{True}, \texttt{False}\}$ to consider also the asterisk symbols in the evaluation:

- $matches^{*}_{strict}(X')$ iff X' is a suggested class, and $eval_c(X') = *$ (similarly for attributes and associations)

- $matches^*_{constr}(X')$ iff $eval_{c|a|r}(X') = *$
- $matches^*_{isa}(X')$ iff $matches^*_{constr}(X')$, or $eval_{c|a|r}(X') = :*$
- $matches^*_{list}(X')$ iff $matches^*_{isa}(X')$, or $eval_{c|a|r}(X')$ is a list with * or :*

For classes, the precision is expressed as

$$P^{c}_{\square}(M', M) = \frac{|\{X' \in \mathcal{C}' : (\exists X \in \mathcal{C})(matches_{\square}(X', X)) \vee matches^*_{\square}(X')\}|}{|\mathcal{C}'|}$$

which is the number of generated class suggestions that match some reference class or any meaningful element that does not exist in the reference model compared to the total number of suggested classes. The precision of the attributes and associations is defined similarly with the condition that the suggested X' is matched with X being a reference property from $\mathcal{P}$.

5.2 Generator Evaluation Results and Their Discussion

We performed the evaluation tasks for all evaluation domain descriptions with two different LLMs, Mixtral-8x7B[6] [15] (medium-sized LLM) and Llama-3-70B[7] (large-size LLM). We used quantized representations of the models (on average 5 bits per parameter). Our goal is to experimentally demonstrate the difference between them and whether it is appropriate to use the larger model despite its higher resource consumption. For each LLM, we consider two different generator configurations in our evaluation – with and without RAG. The configuration without RAG puts the whole T in the prompts as context. The configuration with RAG uses T filtered with syntactical filtering. As described in Sect. 4.1, we also implemented semantic filtering. Our preliminary experiments showed that syntactical filtering performs better than semantic filtering. Due to space limitations, we present evaluation only for syntactical filtering and leave the evaluation with semantic filtering for our future work.

This results in 4 different evaluated configurations: Mixtral-8x7B w/wo syntactic RAG and Llama-3-70B w/wo syntactic RAG. All 4 configurations use the same prompt templates for the generators described in Sect. 4.1.

Figures 4 and 5 summarize the evaluation results with the average F1 score for the analytical, eclectic, and educational domain descriptions and the average precision, recall, and F1 score for the complex domain descriptions separately for classes, attributes, and associations at the four levels of strictness of the matching. For individual measures, see our evaluation repository.

Overall Performance. The results indicate that Llama generally performs better than Mixtral. This difference is clearly visible for the simpler evaluation domains in all description styles (Fig. 4). In contrast, for complex domains with intricate descriptions, the performance gap narrows (Fig. 5). In particular, Mixtral with RAG surpasses Llama without RAG in suggesting attributes and

[6] https://tinyurl.com/3pd79tdw, q. m. Q5_K_M.
[7] https://tinyurl.com/ywam3tva, q. m. Q5_K_M.

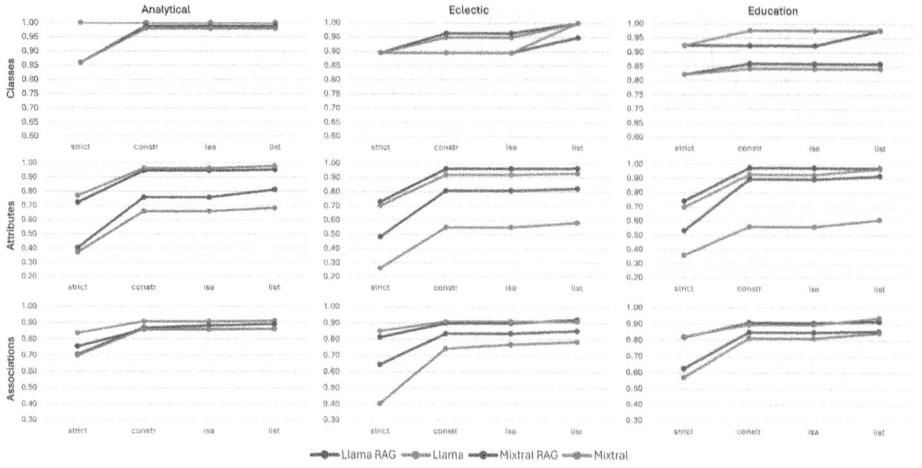

Fig. 4. Average F1 score for the analytical, eclectic, and educational domain descriptions at the four levels of matching strictness

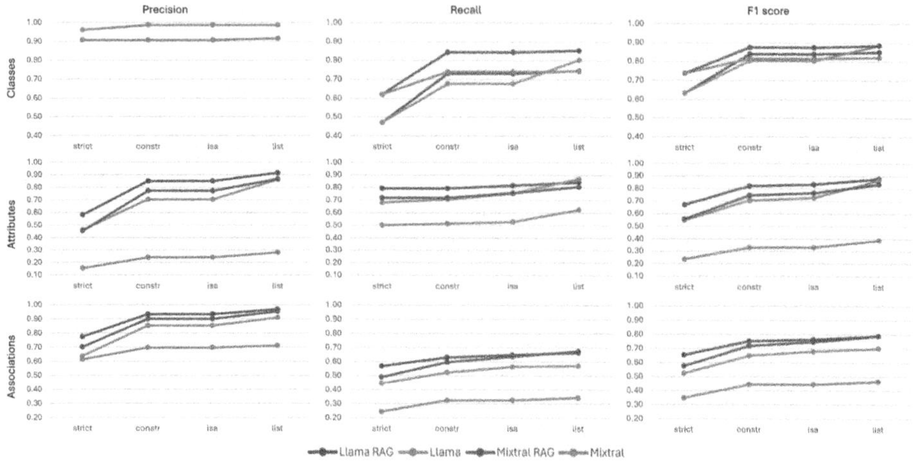

Fig. 5. Average Precision, recall and F1 scores for the complex domain descriptions at the four levels of matching strictness

associations within complex domain descriptions. Both models show the highest performance in suggesting classes. They are comparable in suggesting attributes and associations, which is given by the duality in their manual evaluation. The average precision for classes on complex domains is the same with and without RAG, as RAG is not used for classes.

Impact of RAG. Introducing RAG with syntactic filtering of domain descriptions improves the performance of both models compared to using unfiltered domain descriptions. Syntactic filtering did not lead to loss of important information, and both LLMs returned better suggestions when provided with the filtered descriptions. For Mixtral, syntactic filtering RAG significantly improves F1 scores for attributes and associations across all domains, making its performance almost comparable to Llama without RAG and even slightly better for complex domains. This suggests that RAG can compensate for the smaller size of the Mixtral model. This finding is crucial for implementing the generators, since using a large LLM like Llama-3-70B in the generators is very resource-demanding. **Even a simple RAG technique makes a less demanding LLM comparable to the larger one for generator implementation.** For Llama, the improvement with RAG is less pronounced but still noticeable, particularly for complex domains. For classes, the impact of RAG is minimal, because the class generator always works with the entire domain description. We can see some improvements in recall for the less strict levels of matching that also consider classes suggested as part of property suggestions, where RAG brings improvements.

Domain and Style Specific Performance. Both LLMs perform better in analytical and educational descriptions, probably due to the shorter, more structured, and consistent nature of these descriptions. The eclectic and complex domain descriptions show more variability in performance. Both benefit from introducing syntactic filtering RAG. Therefore, **implementing RAG syntactic filtering helps to handle the diverse and less structured domain descriptions that frequently occur in practice.**

Limitations of LLMs. The well-known problem of LLM hallucinations could lead to low precision if LLMs were too creative and provided false positive suggestions. Although the results indicate relatively high precision for syntactical RAG configurations (more than 0.8 for looser levels of matching strictness), there is still room for improvement, as the precision below 1 means that the evaluated LLMs still provided suggestions that were outside of or incorrect in the given domain description. Recall is lower even for the loosest level of matching strictness. This means that some important concepts modeled in the reference models were not suggested. This leaves open research questions on how to further improve the generators. The improvements can be in various directions, e.g., experimenting with future better performing LLMs or more advanced domain filtering strategies. Because the performance of the assistant is better on smaller domain descriptions, the modeling process can be extended with additional steps where the human expert instructs the assistant tool to focus its attention only to a specific part of the text. Performance also increases for more structured domain descriptions. Therefore, we could use LLMs to first restructure the original description to a more structured analytical description.

5.3 User-Based Evaluation of the Software Prototype

In addition to the measurements of the performance of the generators, we also evaluated how real domain modelers accept suggestions from the assistant. We prepared two domain descriptions, a summary of the main features of the prototype, and three 2-minute video tutorials[8]. We instructed real users to model the two domains using our prototype assistant tool and then asked them to assign a number between 0 (fully disagree) and 4 (fully agree) to express their agreement with five different claims about using the prototype. They also classified themselves as university teachers (who teach conceptual modeling in their courses), university students (who had a database course with conceptual modeling lessons), modeling experts (who create conceptual models in their everyday work and projects), database experts (who work at the logical level of database querying), application programmers (who develop application code on top of a database), or managers (who manage software development teams) with multiple options allowed. We received responses from 18 users.

Table 4 shows for each type of users the number of responses that picked this type and the average marks received for that type. The last line shows the average of all users. As we can see, the users agree that using the assistant providing modeling suggestions is better than pure manual modeling without any suggestions (C1) and found it intuitive (C2). The suggestions provided by the assistant are subjectively not always appropriate (C3), which is also supported by our measurements presented in the previous part, and manual modeling is still necessary (C5). Despite these imperfections, users claimed that the assistant made them more productive (C4).

Table 4. Summary of the user-based evaluation. 0 = fully disagree, 4 = fully agree. C1: I find it better to model with such an assistant compared to just manual modelling. C2: I found the assistant intuitive to use. C3: The assistant suggested appropriate classes, attributes and associations. C4: The assistant helped me to solve the given tasks faster compared to just manual modelling. C5: I was able to solve all the tasks using only the assistant and manual modelling was not needed.

	#	C1	C2	C3	C4	C5
Teacher	11	3.09	3.27	2.27	2.64	**1.64**
Student	5	3.20	2.80	2.60	**3.40**	1.40
Modeling expert	5	3.20	**3.40**	2.40	3.00	1.80
Database expert	5	3.00	**3.40**	1.80	2.80	0.80
Programmer	9	**3.22**	3.22	2.44	3.00	1.44
Manager	1	2.00	2.00	**3.00**	2.00	1.00
All	*18*	*3.11*	*3.00*	*2.61*	*2.89*	*1.67*

6 Related Work

We can observe two research directions, one exploring the methodological possibilities of allowing domain experts to create domain models without requiring

[8] See https://forms.gle/xZWb224x9pRSg2gC6 for the evaluation form.

modeling expertise [7,14,23], the other focusing on domain modeling automation [4,9,18,25]. In previous research on domain modeling automation, we can identify rule-based and machine learning methods. In the rule-based field, [4] studied rule-based methods for the extraction of models from the specification of requirements in the natural language (NL) and provided a comprehensive overview of the existing rule-based methods up to date. The paper also introduced novel extraction rules that better exploit linguistic dependency information from NLP parsers. The focus on complex NLP rules was later criticized in [18] where the authors proposed a simpler approach to extract domain models from user requirements expressed as user stories (requirements in the form of *As a <who>, I want <what>, so that <why>.*) Later works elaborated further on this approach, e.g. [30], with more recent [1] that considers so-called Behavior-Driven Development scenarios that extend user stories but they are still simpler than NL. The recent [9] focused on assisting modeling experts by generating potential new model elements to be added to an existing one instead of generating full models. Recent field surveys are available for further details [22,31].

The paper [9] complements the rule-based approach by identifying relevant parts of NL descriptions using word embeddings. This leads to domain model extraction techniques based on machine learning (ML). [26,28,29] introduced a technique that extends the NLP rule-based techniques with ML classifiers such as Linear Discriminant Analysis and Logistic Regression to predict concept categories and types, and Bidirectional Long Short-Term Memory (BiLSTM) neural network model to determine relationships, cardinalities, and patterns among domain concepts in clusters of sentences describing semantic concepts in domain descriptions. The authors then extended this approach in [27] with a bot-assisted approach that provides interactive support to domain modelers by generating multiple possible solutions for the given descriptions and incrementally adapting to the domain modeler's decisions. [33] describes another approach that combines NLP, rule-based concept extraction, and ML to label sentences as describing a class or a relationship and parsing the concepts out of these sentences.

Recent advances have directed the attention of researchers towards exploring the possibilities of using LLMs to automate domain modeling. [12] conducted early experiments using ChatGPT based on GPT-4 models [21] to show how to generate domain models. They show basic prompt templates and demonstrate on simple domain description examples that the model is able to generate ER and UML class diagrams in a structured JSON format. They also experiment with process models. [10] also analyze the possible use of ChatGPT as a domain modeling assistant. The analysis is based on two experiments. The first was based on individual interaction of the authors with ChatGPT who wrote prompts asking ChatGPT to create models of different size (10 to 40 classes+associations) based on short domain descriptions. The second was based on comparing the domain models generated by ChatGPT with predesigned domain models. The authors showed that the performance of the ChatGPT (in Feb 2023 version) was not as good as it was observed in the field of programming code generation.

The experiments demonstrated the ability of ChatGPT to correctly generate only models with fewer than 8–10 classes. However, they also demonstrated that the interaction with the ChatGPT to build the model incrementally improves the results which is a motivation for our approach. [11] provided the first systematic analysis of the capabilities of LLMs to generate domain models from textual descriptions using different prompting strategies. The authors focused on the task of generating a domain model from the given domain description without interaction with the user. They describe a versatile architecture that supports different prompt engineering techniques, LLMs, and domain modeling constructs on the output. The paper also presents an experimental evaluation of the proposed architecture, concluding that LLMs are still impractical for fully automated modeling because of low F1 scores (only 0.34 for associations).

The field of domain modeling automation is related to the field of *ontology learning* (OL) [2,3], which includes not only the automated extraction of domain models from unstructured text, but also from other sources, such as structured data [6]. In [20], the authors conclude that LLMs can be helpful to ontology engineers when designing their domain models as ontologies. However, we should not expect the output of an LLM to reflect a logically consistent and sound view of any given domain, because the training data of any LLM likely contain a variety of divergent views on any given subject matter. Recently, [5] explored the potential of LLMs for OL through three partial OL tasks – suggesting conceptual types for a given term, identifying ISA hierarchies between two types, and identifying non-ISA associations between two types. [25] investigated the potential of LLMs to help ontology engineers by generating OWL ontologies from ontological requirements. The evaluation involved comparing the ontologies generated by the LLMs with student solutions based on their ability to address the given CQs. The study concluded that only GPT-3.5 and GPT-4 produced reasonable OWL outputs. However, the evaluation was performed on simple domain descriptions with short narratives in a single paragraph each with 15 competency questions.

7 Conclusions

In this paper, we presented an approach to designing conceptual modeling assistants based on pre-trained Large Language Models (LLMs) that help human modeling experts discover classes, their attributes, and binary associations in the given textual domain description. Compared with recent pioneering work that utilizes LLMs for domain modeling automation, we proposed a generic framework comprising class, attribute, and association generators that focuses on assisting human modelers during the modeling process instead of suggesting the whole domain model. We defined the generators as prompt templates that can be configured in different and comparable ways. On the other hand, we did not focus on more complex ontological constructs such as the most recent [25]. We presented concrete baseline configurations of the generic generators and demonstrated their practical applicability. We also introduced a methodology for detailed experimental evaluation of the performance of the generators. The precision, recall and F1 scores measured on various real-life domain descriptions written in different styles and with different levels of complexity showed that even our baseline configuration with a middle-sized LLM is applicable for practical modeling. We further supported this conclusion through our user-based evaluation using the prototype tool that showed a high level of acceptance among real users with different specializations and levels of seniority. Our work can be further extended with more advanced generator configurations and future LLMs.

Acknowledgements. This research was supported by the Charles University project GAUK no. 262823 and SVV project number 260 698.

References

1. Gupta, A., Poels, G., Bera, P.: Generating multiple conceptual models from behavior-driven development scenarios. Data Knowl. Eng. **145**, 102141 (2023). https://doi.org/10.1016/j.datak.2023.102141
2. Konys, A.: Knowledge repository of ontology learning tools from text. In: Knowledge-Based and Intelligent Information & Engineering Systems: Proceedings of the 23rd International Conference, KES 2019, vol. 159, pp. 1614–1628 (2019). https://doi.org/10.1016/j.procs.2019.09.332
3. Khadir, A.C., Aliane, H., Guessoum, A.: Ontology learning: grand tour and challenges. Comput. Sci. Rev. **39**, 100339 (2021). https://doi.org/10.1016/j.cosrev.2020.100339
4. Arora, C., Sabetzadeh, M., Briand, L., Zimmer, F.: Extracting domain models from natural-language requirements: approach and industrial evaluation. In: Proceedings of the ACM/IEEE 19th International Conference on Model Driven Engineering Languages and Systems, MODELS 2016, pp. 250–260. Association for Computing Machinery, New York (2016). https://doi.org/10.1145/2976767.2976769
5. Babaei Giglou, H., D'Souza, J., Auer, S.: LLMs4OL: large language models for ontology learning. In: Payne, T.R., et al. (eds.) ISWC 2023. LNCS, vol. 14265, pp. 408–427. Springer, Cham (2023). https://doi.org/10.1007/978-3-031-47240-4_22
6. Lakzaei, B., Shamsfard, M.: Ontology learning from relational databases. Inf. Sci. **577**, 280–297 (2021). https://doi.org/10.1016/j.ins.2021.06.074
7. Bossung, S., Sehring, H.-W., Carl, H., Schmidt, J.W.: An agile process for the creation of conceptual models from content descriptions. In: Ioannidis, Y., Novikov, B., Rachev, B. (eds.) ADBIS 2007. LNCS, vol. 4690, pp. 114–129. Springer, Heidelberg (2007). https://doi.org/10.1007/978-3-540-75185-4_10
8. Brown, T., et al.: Language models are few-shot learners. In: Larochelle, H., Ranzato, M., Hadsell, R., Balcan, M.F., Lin, H. (eds.) Advances in Neural Information Processing Systems, vol. 33, pp. 1877–1901. Curran Associates, Inc. (2020)
9. Burgueño, L., Clarisó, R., Gérard, S., Li, S., Cabot, J.: An NLP-based architecture for the autocompletion of partial domain models. In: La Rosa, M., Sadiq, S., Teniente, E. (eds.) CAiSE 2021. LNCS, vol. 12751, pp. 91–106. Springer, Cham (2021). https://doi.org/10.1007/978-3-030-79382-1_6
10. Cámara, J., Troya, J., Burgueño, L., Vallecillo, A.: On the assessment of generative AI in modeling tasks: an experience report with ChatGPT and UML. Softw. Syst. Model. **22**(3), 781–793 (2023)

11. Chen, K., et al.: Automated domain modeling with large language models: a comparative study. In: 2023 ACM/IEEE 26th International Conference on Model Driven Engineering Languages and Systems (MODELS), pp. 162–172 (2023). https://doi.org/10.1109/MODELS58315.2023.00037
12. Fill, H.-G., Fettke, P., Köpke, J.: Conceptual modeling and large language models: impressions from first experiments with ChatGPT. Enterp. Model. Inf. Syst. Architect. (EMISAJ) **18**, 1–15 (2023)
13. Guizzardi, G., Wagner, G., Almeida, J.P.A., Guizzardi, R.S.S.: Towards ontological foundations for conceptual modeling: the unified foundational ontology (UFO) story. Appl. Ontol. **10**(3–4), 259–271 (2015). https://doi.org/10.3233/AO-150157
14. Ionita, D., Wieringa, R., Bullee, J.-W., Vasenev, A.: Tangible modelling to elicit domain knowledge: an experiment and focus group. In: Johannesson, P., Lee, M.L., Liddle, S.W., Opdahl, A.L., López, Ó.P. (eds.) ER 2015. LNCS, vol. 9381, pp. 558–565. Springer, Cham (2015). https://doi.org/10.1007/978-3-319-25264-3_42
15. Jiang, A.Q., et al.: Mixtral of experts. arXiv preprint arXiv:2401.04088 (2024)
16. Keet, C.M., Fillottrani, P.R.: An analysis and characterisation of publicly available conceptual models. In: Johannesson, P., Lee, M.L., Liddle, S.W., Opdahl, A.L., López, Ó.P. (eds.) ER 2015. LNCS, vol. 9381, pp. 585–593. Springer, Cham (2015). https://doi.org/10.1007/978-3-319-25264-3_45
17. Chen, K., Yang, Y., Chen, B., López, J.A.H., Mussbacher, G., Varró, D.: Automated domain modeling with large language models: a comparative study. In: 26th ACM/IEEE International Conference on Model Driven Engineering Languages and Systems, MODELS 2023, Vásterås, Sweden, 1–6 October 2023 (2023)
18. Lucassen, G., Robeer, M., Dalpiaz, F., Van Der Werf, J.M.E.M., Brinkkemper, S.: Extracting conceptual models from user stories with visual narrator. Requirements Eng. **22**, 339–358 (2017)
19. Verdonck, M., Gailly, F., Pergl, R., Guizzardi, G., Martins, B., Pastor, O.: Comparing traditional conceptual modeling with ontology-driven conceptual modeling: an empirical study. Inf. Syst. **81**, 92–103 (2019). https://doi.org/10.1016/j.is.2018.11.009
20. Neuhaus, F.: Ontologies in the era of large language models-a perspective. Appl. Ontol. **18**(4), 399–407 (2023)
21. OpenAI: GPT-4 Technical Report (2024). https://doi.org/10.48550/arXiv.2303.08774
22. Raharjana, I.K., Siahaan, D., Fatichah, C.: User stories and natural language processing: a systematic literature review. IEEE Access **9**, 53811–53826 (2021). https://doi.org/10.1109/ACCESS.2021.3070606
23. Denaux, R., Dolbear, C., Hart, G., Dimitrova, V., Cohn, A.G.: Supporting domain experts to construct conceptual ontologies: a holistic approach. J. Web Semant. **9**(2), 113–127 (2011). https://doi.org/10.1016/j.websem.2011.02.001
24. Mao, R., et al.: A survey on semantic processing techniques. Inf. Fusion **101**, 101988 (2024). https://doi.org/10.1016/j.inffus.2023.101988
25. Saeedizade, M.J., Blomqvist, E.: Navigating ontology development with large language models. In: Meroño Peñuela, A., et al. (eds.) ESWC 2024. LNCS, vol. 14664, pp. 143–161. Springer, Cham (2024). https://doi.org/10.1007/978-3-031-60626-7_8
26. Saini, R., Mussbacher, G., Guo, J.L.C., Kienzle, J.: DoMoBOT: a bot for automated and interactive domain modelling. In: Proceedings of the 23rd ACM/IEEE International Conference on Model Driven Engineering Languages and Systems: Companion Proceedings. MODELS 2020. Association for Computing Machinery, New York (2020). https://doi.org/10.1145/3417990.3421385

27. Saini, R., Mussbacher, G., Guo, J.L.C., Kienzle, J.: Machine learning-based incremental learning in interactive domain modelling. In: Proceedings of the 25th International Conference on Model Driven Engineering Languages and Systems, MODELS 2022, pp. 176–186. Association for Computing Machinery, New York (2022). https://doi.org/10.1145/3550355.3552421
28. Saini, R., Mussbacher, G., Guo, J.L.C., Kienzle, J.: A neural network based approach to domain modelling relationships and patterns recognition. In: 2020 IEEE Tenth International Model-Driven Requirements Engineering (MoDRE), pp. 78–82 (2020). https://doi.org/10.1109/MoDRE51215.2020.00016
29. Saini, R., Mussbacher, G., Guo, J.L.C., Kienzle, J.: Towards queryable and traceable domain models. In: 2020 IEEE 28th International Requirements Engineering Conference (RE), pp. 334–339 (2020). https://doi.org/10.1109/RE48521.2020.00044
30. Nasiri, S., Rhazali, Y., Lahmer, M., Chenfour, N.: Towards a generation of class diagram from user stories in agile methods. In: The 11th International Conference on Ambient Systems, Networks and Technologies (ANT), vol. 170, pp. 831–837 (2020). https://doi.org/10.1016/j.procs.2020.03.148
31. Sonbol, R., Rebdawi, G., Ghneim, N.: The use of NLP-based text representation techniques to support requirement engineering tasks: a systematic mapping review. IEEE Access **10**, 62811–62830 (2022). https://doi.org/10.1109/ACCESS.2022.3182372
32. Wei, J., et al.: Chain-of-thought prompting elicits reasoning in large language models. In: Koyejo, S., Mohamed, S., Agarwal, A., Belgrave, D., Cho, K., Oh, A. (ed.) Advances in Neural Information Processing Systems, vol. 35, pp. 24824–24837. Curran Associates, Inc. (2022)
33. Yang, S., Sahraoui, H.: Towards automatically extracting UML class diagrams from natural language specifications. In: Proceedings of the 25th International Conference on Model Driven Engineering Languages and Systems: Companion Proceedings, MODELS 2022, pp. 396–403. Association for Computing Machinery, New York (2022). https://doi.org/10.1145/3550356.3561592
34. Gao, Y., et al.: Retrieval-Augmented Generation for Large Language Models: A Survey (2024)

Language Models and Conceptual Modeling

How are LLMs Used for Conceptual Modeling? An Exploratory Study on Interaction Behavior and User Perception

Syed Juned Ali[1](✉), Iris Reinhartz-Berger[2], and Dominik Bork[1]

[1] TU Wien, Business Informatics Group, Vienna, Austria
{syed.juned.ali,dominik.bork}@tuwien.ac.at
[2] University of Haifa, Haifa, Israel
iris@is.haifa.ac.il

Abstract. Large Language Models (LLMs) have opened new opportunities in modeling in general, and conceptual modeling in particular. With their advanced reasoning capabilities, accessible through natural language interfaces, LLMs enable humans to deepen their understanding of different application domains and enhance their modeling skills. However, the open-ended nature of these interfaces results in diverse interaction behaviors, which may also affect the perceived usefulness of LLM-assisted conceptual modeling. Existing works focus on various quality metrics of LLM outcomes, yet limited attention is given to *how users interact with LLMs* for such modeling tasks. To address this gap, we present the design and findings of an empirical study conducted with information systems students. After labeling the interactions according to their intentions (e.g., Create Model, Discuss, or Present), and representing them as an event log, we applied process mining techniques to discover process models. These models vividly capture the interaction behaviors and reveal recurrent patterns. We explored the differences in interacting with two LLMs (GPT 4.0 and Code Llama) for two modeling tasks (use case and domain modeling) across three application domains. Additionally, we analyzed user perceptions regarding the usefulness and ease of use of LLM-assisted conceptual modeling.

Keywords: Large Language Model · Domain Modeling · UML · Process Mining

1 Introduction

In recent years, the advent of Large Language Models (LLMs) has revolutionized the landscape of natural language processing and machine learning. Trained on vast amounts of text data, LLMs exhibit remarkable proficiency in understanding and generating human-like text. They have proven to be effective tools across various tasks [29], including translation [18,27], text summarization [24,28], sentiment analysis [2,9,21] and recommender systems [15,19]. Particularly noteworthy is their significant impact on software engineering, where they excel in tasks

W. Maass et al. (Eds.): ER 2024, LNCS 15238, pp. 257–275, 2025.
https://doi.org/10.1007/978-3-031-75872-0_14

such as program synthesis from natural language specifications, code completion, debugging, and documentation generation [11,16].

The exploration of LLMs' potential to enhance modeling tasks has only recently gained attention, as evidenced by emerging research, e.g., [3,5–8,12,17]. Most of these works focus on the accuracy, utility and other quality metrics of the LLM-produced models. However, to the best of our knowledge, no study has investigated how modelers interact and perceive their interactions with LLMs for conceptual modeling tasks. These interactions can be influenced by factors such as the specific LLM used, the application domain, and the nature of the modeling task itself. Thus, our objective is to discover the process of interacting with LLMs and identify recurrent patterns that can inform 'best practices' for LLM-assisted conceptual modeling.

In this paper, we report on the design and results of an empirical study with 76 undergraduate information systems students. The students submitted the course assignments in 39 groups (of one or two students). The assignment used for the study required use case modeling with UML use case diagrams and domain modeling with UML class diagrams. The groups were first expected to interact with an LLM and then, if needed, to manually improve their models. Groups were randomly assigned to interact with either GPT 4.0 or Code Llama 34B Instruct in one of three application domains. To facilitate data collection without disclosing the LLM's identity, we developed a dedicated web application capable of logging all interactions between the groups and the LLMs. Finally, the students' perceptions were collected via a standard usefulness and ease of use questionnaire, in which the students were also requested to list the main positive and negative aspects they experienced.

The rest of the paper is structured as follows. Sections 2 and 3 elaborate on the experimental design and analysis procedure, respectively. Sections 4 and 5 present and discuss the results. Finally, Sect. 6 reviews related work, and Sect. 7 concludes and refers to future research directions.

2 Experimental Design

2.1 Goals, Research Questions, and Independent Variables

The goal of this study is to analyze modeler interactions with LLMs, for the purpose of identifying the underlying intentions and patterns, as well as exploring user perceptions on interacting with LLMs for conceptual modeling tasks. To this end, we identified the following two main research questions:

[RQ1] How do users interact with LLMs for conceptual modeling tasks?
[RQ2] How do users perceive the usefulness and ease of use of those interactions?

Considering that responses to these questions can be influenced by various factors, we identify three independent variables that potentially impact the modeling process and experience. These variables are:

- **LLM** –We investigate GPT-4 and Code-Llama 34B Instruct;

- **Application Domain** – We investigate NPA (Nature & Park Authority) for nature & archaeological sites management, R4A (Rating for All) for viewership data analytics, and PTr (Perfect Trip) for tourism management;
- **Task** – We investigate UCD (use case modeling with Use Case Diagrams) and CD (domain modeling with Class Diagrams).

Accordingly, we divided the first research question into the following sub-questions:

[RQ1.1] What are the recurrent interaction behaviors (i.e., intentions and patterns)?
[RQ1.2] To what extent do the recurrent interaction behaviors vary across different LLMs?
[RQ1.3] To what extent do the recurrent interaction behaviors vary across different application domains?
[RQ1.4] To what extent do the recurrent interaction behaviors vary across different modeling tasks?

We further refined the second research question into the following sub-questions[1]:

[RQ2.1] What are the overall perceived usefulness and ease of use users experience when utilizing LLMs for conceptual modeling?
[RQ2.2] To what extent do the perceived usefulness and ease of use vary across different LLMs?
[RQ2.3] To what extent do the perceived usefulness and ease of use vary across different application domains?

2.2 Settings and Objects

The rationale behind selecting GPT-4 and Code-Llama (referred to as Llama henceforth) lies in their distinct capabilities and performance metrics. GPT-4, a large multi-modal, general-purpose model capable of processing both image and text inputs, has demonstrated remarkable performance across various human-designed benchmarks [23]. Studies, such as [1], have highlighted GPT-4's superior performance, often outscoring a significant majority of human test takers. Llama, on the other hand, encompasses a range of LLMs of varying sizes developed by Meta AI[2], specifically designed for coding tasks. Llama stands out for its state-of-the-art performance among open models, robust infilling capabilities, support for extensive input contexts, and the ability to execute programming instructions without the need for prior training [14]. Notably, its fine-tuned 70 billion parameters variant has shown exceptional performance in coding tasks, outperforming GPT-4 in benchmarks such as HumanEval [23][3].

[1] We have no dedicated sub-question regarding differences related to the modeling tasks, as the participants could work on them interwinedly.
[2] https://www.meta.ai/.
[3] https://llama.meta.com/code-llama/.

Table 1. Descriptive statistics of application domains

Artifact	Element	NPA	R4A	PTr	Avg	Std
UCD	Use Case	11	14	12	12.33	1.25
	Actor	6	6	6	6.00	0.00
	Association	9	12	12	11.00	1.41
	Dependency	3	4	5	4.00	0.82
CD	Class	14	13	12	13.00	0.82
	Enumeration	2	2	1	1.67	0.47
	Attribute	36	26	30	30.67	4.11
	Operation	2	2	2	2.00	0.00
	Generalization	2	2	2	2.00	0.00
	Association	8	7	8	7.67	0.47
	Association Class	2	2	3	2.33	0.47
Description	Length in GPT-4 tokens	846	856	855	852.33	4.49
	Length in Llama tokens	943	945	943	943.66	0.94

Although GPT-4 features a larger context window of 32,000 tokens[4] compared to Llama's 16,000 tokens, allowing it to retain more information across interactions, our decision to include both models in the study is driven by their respective strengths - GPT-4's versatility in general-purpose tasks and Llama's specialization in coding-related tasks.

We further selected three application domains that are likely familiar to humans and LLMs: nature & archaeological sites management (NPA), viewership data analytics (R4A), and tourism management (PTr). Despite their differences, we took care to ensure that their expected models were of comparable size and complexity, as depicted by the descriptive statistics in Table 1. The entire experimental material is provided in our online supplementary material[5].

2.3 Modeling Tasks

The participants were asked to perform two modeling tasks using UML notation: use case modeling employing UCD and domain modeling utilizing CD. This choice is supported by their widespread adoption as well as their representation of distinct yet complementary aspects. The participants were instructed to engage with the LLM until they were satisfied with the results or opted to skip further refinement. Subsequently, they had the opportunity to enhance the models within a modeling tool. This process resulted in two distinct outcomes for each task: a *'DRAFT'* model, solely derived from interactions with the LLM, and a *'FINAL'* model, refined through additional manual adjustments in a modeling tool. Grading primarily focused on the 'FINAL' outcomes (85%). To incentivize engagement, interactions with LLMs accounted for 15% of the grade. Notably, the 'DRAFT' models did not factor into the grading.

[4] 1 token $\approx$ 0.75 words.

[5] Online supplementary material: https://zenodo.org/records/13513891.

2.4 Instrumentation and Data Collection

In order to collect the participants' interactions without revealing the LLM they are using, we designed a web application built using Streamlit[6], which is an open-source Python library for creating web applications. Our application permits up to 100 prompts per user (who can include one or two participants, see Sect. 2.5 for more details). This limit aimed to encourage participants to generate meaningful prompts for their tasks.

The interface design is similar to those of existing chatbots, allowing users to input their prompts and receive modeling artifacts in response. A screenshot of the interface is included in the experimental material (see footnote 5). The application also presents users with the number of prompts they have used and the number of remaining prompts. Additionally, it enables the research team to download an *interaction log* with the following fields: User ID, Input (the user prompt), Response (the modeling artifacts), and the Prompt Number (within user ID).

2.5 Participants and Experimental Design

The experiment took place in the academic year of 2024 in a second-year undergraduate course on 'Design and Implementation of Information Systems'. The course focused on object-oriented modeling with UML. The students were enrolled in a three-year BSc program in Information Systems. They were already knowledgeable in programming in general and in object-oriented programming with Java in particular. The tasks were part of the course assignments and were mostly submitted in groups of two students, with only two exceptions where students submitted individually. Table 2 summarizes the experiment design and the division of the 39 groups along the LLMs and the application domains. Each group was assigned to a single application domain and a single LLM, and had to perform both modeling tasks.

The experiment comprised three stages: (*i*) a 30-min tutorial providing a brief introduction to LLMs, prompt engineering, and a demonstration of the application the students were required to use for their assignment; (*ii*) a two-week window during which the students were asked to complete and submit the artifacts of the two modeling tasks; and (*iii*) a questionnaire (see Sect. 4.2 for the questions) aimed at assessing each student's perceived usefulness and ease of use when interacting with the LLM for both modeling tasks.

Table 2. Number of groups per experimental category

Domain↓ LLM →	Llama	GPT-4	Total
NPA	8	7	15
R4A	7	6	13
PTr	5	6	11
Total	**20**	**19**	**39**

[6] https://docs.streamlit.io/.

Table 3. Intentions used for labeling interaction prompts

Intention	Description
Create Model	Relates to the creation of a (potentially partial) model. This prompt does not refer to previous responses
Update Model	Relates to the update of a (potentially partial) model. This prompt refers to previous responses, e.g., for correcting or clarifying previous outcomes
Create List	Relates to the creation of a list of modeling elements, such as classes, use cases and associations. This prompt does not refer to previous responses
Update List	Relates to the update of a list of modeling elements. This prompt refers to previous responses
Present	Relates to the presentation of the response in a given format (e.g., XMI)
Explain	Asks the LLM to explain certain parts of previous responses. The purpose of Explain prompts is to understand and not update an outcome
Discuss	Asks the LLM to discuss possible solutions (presented either explicitly or implicitly), appearing in previous prompts or responses. Differently from Explain, Discuss has an implicit intention for updating an outcome

3 Analysis Procedure

Interaction Labeling. After downloading the log with 541 interactions in total, we explored the user prompts and identified seven intention types. Table 3 describes and explains the identified intentions in detail. They refer to model development operations (*'Create Model'*, *'Update Model'*, *'Create List'*, *'Update List'*), model presentation operations (*'Present'*), and explanatory operations (*'Explain'*, *'Discuss'*). Each interaction underwent manual labeling by two of the three conducting researchers, with each researcher responsible for labeling two-thirds of the interactions. While doing so, we also identified the task type (UCD or CD) of each interaction. Initially, our agreement level for intention labeling stood at 64.3%. To ensure consistency and accuracy, we engaged in multiple discussion sessions to refine the definitions of the various labels, eventually achieving full agreement on the labeling outcome.

Following the labeling phase, we encountered prompts that combined multiple intentions, requiring the splitting of rows in the log file. Additionally, we identified eight prompts lacking clear intentions, comprising only descriptions without actionable requests, which we consequently omitted. After these preprocessing steps, we were left with 566 interactions for analysis.

Behavior Extraction. We treated the interactions log as an event log and employed the process mining tool Disco[7] to: (*i*) discover the interaction process; and (*ii*) extract recurrent interaction patterns. We considered the combination of the user ID (corresponding to groups 1 to 39) and the task type (UCD or CD) as the case ID. We further added information on the LLM (GPT-4, Llama) and the application domains (NPA, R4A, PTr) of each group to check differences in the interaction behavior based on the independent variables.

[7] https://fluxicon.com/disco/.

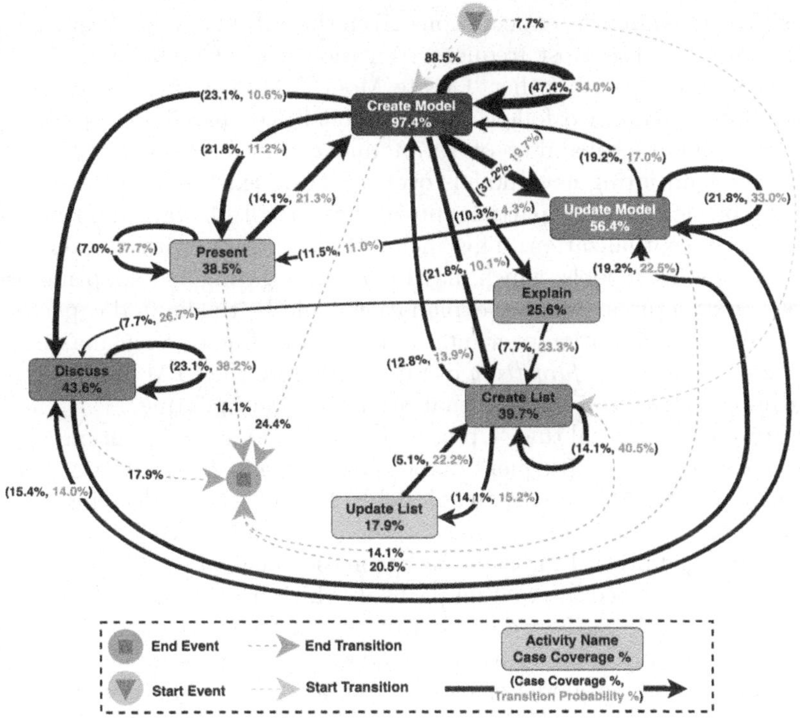

Fig. 1. Discovered interaction process model

4 Results

Next, we elaborate on the results of our study and answer the research questions.

4.1 Results for RQ1: Interaction Behavior

Overall Behavior Results (RQ1.1). In the discovered interaction process model (see Fig. 1), nodes depict intentions while edges depict transitions between intentions, i.e., appearance in sequential prompts. The percentages displayed on the nodes indicate case coverage, i.e., the proportion of cases employing an intention. On the edges, the black value on the left indicates the case coverage of transitions, while the orange value on the right refers to individual intention instances (rather than grouped by cases), showing the probability of proceeding with that transition from the source intention. Less traversed paths with a case coverage of $\leq$ 10% and a probability of $\leq$ 20% are omitted for the sake of comprehensibility. The interaction log is provided with the experimental material (see footnote 5).

Model Development Operations. In nearly all cases (97.4%), 'Create Model' was employed, and in 88.5% of cases, it initiated the interaction with the LLM.

These statistics align with expectations given the nature of tasks requiring model creation. Notably, the most frequent transition from 'Create Model', observed in 47.4% of cases, is to another 'Create Model.' Moreover, 'Create Model' has a probability of 34.0% to follow 'Create Model', compared to 'Update Model' which has a lower probability of 19.7% and covers fewer cases (37.2%). This preference for initiating new models over updating existing ones in specific scenarios can be attributed to participants' desire for a fresh start and the potential for clearer conceptualization. This inclination contrasts with the operation of modifying existing models, which may involve navigating and adapting previous decisions or structures. Another explanation could be the limited capacity of the LLMs to retain information over interactions depending on their maximum context window, leading to *forgetting* of information by the LLM and consequently generating unsatisfactory models that are not worth updating.

The results also reveal that 'Update Model' is a common intention, appearing in 56.4% of cases, with subsequent updates occurring in 21.8% of cases (vs. 19.2% cases that start over with 'Create Model'). This observed behavior implies an iterative process of model refinement, potentially influenced by feedback from the LLM or as additional information becomes available.

We further observed interaction paths in which lists are used, before or after using models. These paths were less frequent, accounting for 39.7% case coverage for 'Create List' and 17.9% for 'Update List.' These intentions primarily revolved around listing model elements, such as classes, associations, use cases, and actors. In some cases (7.7%), 'Create List' was the initial intention. However, it typically followed 'Create Model' (in 21.8% of the cases), potentially to assess the suggested model by listing certain modeling elements. Once lists were established, they were re-created, modified, or utilized to (re)create a model. List re-creating and modification had the same case coverage of 14.1%, yet the first exhibited a higher probability of 40.5% compared to list modification with a probability of 15.2%. In 12.8% of the cases, list creation was followed by a subsequent model creation with a transition probability of 13.9%.

Explanatory Operations. We observed that the use of explanatory operations was moderate, with 'Discuss' at case coverage of 43.6% and 'Explain' at 25.6%. Discussions embody a collaborative aspect, where modelers utilize the LLM outputs for deep exploration or decision-making between alternatives. The repeated use of 'Discuss' (with a case coverage of 23.1% and a probability of 38.2%) reflects ongoing clarification and negotiation of ideas, further indicating an active dialogue-based interaction with the LLM. A closer examination of the prompts reveals dissatisfaction with the LLM's responses in some cases. In about one-fifth of cases (19.2%), the discussion results or insights are integrated into the model through performing 'Update Model.'

'Explain' intentions aim to provide detailed insights into previous LLM responses. Through explanations, participants shed light on the reasoning behind specific outcomes, foster comprehension, and reach informed decision-making in subsequent interactions. Given that LLMs frequently offer explanations in their responses, the occurrence of 'Explain' is less frequent. Interestingly, in 23.3% of

Table 4. Five most recurring interaction patterns

Code	Pattern	Overall	No. of Groups (out of 39)	No. of Cases (out of 78)
P_1	Model Evolution Create Model+; Update Model+	37	20	29
P_2	Partial Model Visualization Create Model+; Present+	21	14	17
P_3	Partial Model Discussion Create Model+; Discuss+	20	14	18
P_4	Discussion-based Model Updating Discuss+; Update Model+	20	12	15
P_5	Partial Model Listing Create Model+; Create List+	19	13	17

the instances, 'Explain' preceded 'Create List,' which may serve to formalize the explanation results as lists of modeling elements. In 26.7% of instances, 'Explain' is followed by 'Discuss,' potentially indicating a desire for deeper insights into the suggested options.

Presentation Operations. 'Present' involves visualizing or representing outcomes in importable formats. This intention was observed in 38.5% of the cases where participants sought to visualize or import the results of their modeling efforts into a modeling environment to, e.g., continue manual modeling there. The repeated sequential uses of this intention (with a probability of 37.7%) may indicate dissatisfaction with the results. Indeed, both LLMs faced difficulties in generating outcomes that could be directly imported to the modeling environment used in the course (Visual Paradigm). Additionally, in 14.1% of cases (a probability of 21.3%), 'Present' is followed by 'Create Model,' suggesting a need to (re)create a model after reviewing the previous outcomes in a specific format.

Recurrent Patterns. The process model in Fig. 1 does not cover interaction patterns, i.e., paths that go beyond immediate transitions. Hence, in Table 4, we show the top five patterns with their overall instance frequencies, group coverage, and case coverage. The '+' sign indicates potential repetitive occurrences of an intention. Note, that since it is important to relate the recurrent patterns to the quality of the created models, we also examined the top recurrent patterns of cases achieving a passing grade. Despite a slight difference in their ordering, the patterns remained the same. We leave the analysis of the impact of specific interaction behaviors on the quality of models to future research.

As expected, the most frequent pattern is *'Model Evolution'* (P_1). This pattern starts with a sequence of 'Create Model' prompts followed by a sequence of 'Update Model' prompts. This pattern captures the iterative nature of conceptual modeling where refinement and progressive enhancement are key.

Table 5. Intention distribution categorized by independent variables. Significant results are in bold with an asterisk.

Intention	LLM (%)		Application Domain (%)			Task (%)	
	GPT-4	Llama	NPA	PTr	R4A	UCD	CD
Create Model	28.92	35.73	37.68	33.81	28.76	32.86	33.68
Update Model	**26.47***	**12.74***	**24.63***	19.42	**10.04***	15.90	19.50
Create List	**4.41***	**19.39***	**6.28***	12.95	**21.91***	13.78	14.18
Update List	1.96	3.87	1.93	3.59	4.07	2.12	4.25
Present	7.35	12.74	**5.31***	8.63	**17.35***	12.01	9.57
Explain	7.84	3.87	2.89	7.19	6.39	4.94	5.34
Discuss	**23.03***	**11.63***	**21.25***	14.38	**11.41***	18.37	13.12
Prompts Per Case	5.36	9.05	6.90	6.31	8.4	6.90	7.23

Table 6. Ranking of top five interaction patterns across independent variables

Code	LLM		Application Domain			Task	
	GPT-4	Llama	NPA	PTr	R4A	UCD	CD
P_1	Top 2	Top 1	Top 1	Top 1	Top 3	Top 1	Top 1
P_2	Top 6	Top 3	Top 7	Top 2	Top 3	Top 4	Top 2
P_3	Top 3	Top 8	Top 6	Top 7	Top 2	Top 4	Top 4
P_4	Top 1	Top 28	Top 3	Top 7	Top 6	Top 7	Top 2
P_5	Top 21	Top 2	Top 10	Top 4	Top 1	Top 2	Top 6

The second most recurrent pattern, *'Partial Model Visualization'* (P_2), also starts with a sequence of 'Create Model' prompts, but this is followed by 'Present' prompts, which aim at visualizing the modeling outcomes in certain formats. This step precedes decision-making on subsequent actions such as updating the outcomes, completing the task, seeking for explanations, or initiating the task.

The third pattern *'Partial Model Discussion'* (P_4) indicates pauses in the model creation process to explore and discuss potential alternatives, which may be subsequently implemented in the model (e.g., using pattern P_4). The fourth pattern *'Discussion-based Model Updating'* (P_3) empowers participants to distill discussion insights into actionable items for updating the model. Finally, *'Partial Model Listing'* (P_5), illustrates a shift in the modeling approach where participants move from working directly with models to using lists. This is used to explore specific aspects of the model, such as structural components by listing all classes and associations. Unlike the iterative process observed in 'Model Evolution' (P_1), participants following this pattern aim to systematically break down and analyze individual elements of the model to gain a more detailed understanding and enhance their modeling outcomes.

Behavior Results by Independent Variables (RQ1.2–RQ1.4). Next, we analyzed the results according to the independent variables – LLM, domain, and task. Tables 5 and 6 present the intention distribution and the ranking of the top five patterns across the independent variables, respectively. We further conducted pairwise comparisons of intention probabilities using Z-tests to compare proportions of independent populations. For reporting the statistical significance, we applied the Bonferroni adjustment [4] to control for multiple comparisons, reducing the likelihood of false positives by providing a more rigorous criterion for significance.

Interaction Behavior with Respect to LLM (RQ1.2). Overall, we noted a significantly higher average number of interactions when engaging with Llama compared to GPT-4 (9.03 vs. 5.37 per case). This observation aligns with the fact that GPT-4 currently ranks as the most proficient LLM[8]. Our findings further revealed significant differences in the use of three intentions. Specifically, 'Create List' emerged as significantly more prevalent in Llama prompts compared to those with GPT-4 (19.39% versus 4.41%, respectively). This observation can be attributed to Llama's specialization in coding tasks, which emphasizes breaking down problems into structured lists or steps, thereby encouraging users to approach tasks in a similar manner. On the other hand, 'Update Model' and 'Discuss' were significantly more common in GPT-4 interactions than in those with Llama (26.47% versus 12.74% for 'Update Model' and 23.03% versus 11.63% for 'Discuss'). This discrepancy may stem from GPT-4's broader language understanding and its tendency to facilitate dynamic exchanges and conceptual refinement, thus encouraging users to update existing models or engage in discussions more frequently.

As seen in Table 6, three of the top-five patterns appear on the top-five lists for both GPT-4 and Llama, i.e., 'Model Evolution' (P_1), 'Partial Model Discussion' (P_3), 'Discussion-based Model Updating' (P_4) for GPT-4; and 'Model Evolution' (P_1), 'Partial Model Visualization' (P_2), 'Partial Model Listing' (P_5) for Llama. In other words, GPT-4 seems to encourage more interactive and collaborative dialogues, while Llama nudges users to follow a try-and-fix approach, involving the listing of model elements and presenting partial models before continuing with model updating and refinement.

Interaction Behavior with respect to Application Domain (RQ1.3). In terms of the application domain, we conducted pairwise comparisons and discovered four significant differences, particularly between NPA and R4A: 'Create List' and 'Present' were more frequently utilized in R4A, while 'Discuss' and 'Update Model' were more common in NPA. Although the descriptive statistics in Table 1 do not offer an immediate explanation for this observation, it is possible that the participants were less familiar with the NPA domain compared to R4A, leading to more frequent discussions and model updates. In R4A tasks, the emphasis was on organizing and systematically presenting already known data.

[8] https://www.vellum.ai/llm-leaderboard, last accessed: 25.05.2024.

Moreover, the top five patterns appear on the top ten lists of all three domains. This is not surprising given that the application domains are of comparable size and complexity. These findings imply that LLM-assisted modeling tools do not necessarily need to be fine-tuned for different application domains. Further research is needed to study whether and how the size and complexity of application domains affect the distribution of intentions and the most recurrent interaction patterns. This is particularly relevant for large domain descriptions exceeding the LLM's context window, as participants often used the entire textual domain description in their interactions.

Interaction Behavior with Respect to Task (RQ1.4). The results further indicate that there are no statistically significant differences in the distribution of intentions or the most recurrent interaction patterns between use case modeling with UCD and domain modeling with CD. This suggests that the underlying processes and patterns of interaction remain consistent across different modeling tasks, implying that tools and techniques used for LLM-assisted modeling may be broadly applicable and versatile. However, further research is needed to validate this hypothesis and explore its implications.

Summary of RQ1 Results. From the analyses conducted, we conclude that interactions with LLMs for conceptual modeling primarily involve prompts aimed at creating and updating models, generating and modifying lists of model elements, explaining and discussing modeling alternatives or decisions, and presenting models (RQ1.1). Several recurrent patterns have emerged, supporting model evolution, partial model visualization and listing, and discussion-based model development (RQ1.1). Notably, no statistically significant differences have been observed in terms of interaction behavior across modeling tasks (RQ1.4), while a few explained differences have been noted in the frequency of certain intentions across LLMs (RQ1.2) and application domains (RQ1.3).

4.2 Response to RQ2: User Perception

Table 7 shows the perceived usefulness and ease of use of LLM-assisted modeling both overall and segmented by LLMs and application domains. Due to the iterative work on the modeling tasks, the results reflect the participants' feedback at the end of the assignment, after submitting both modeling artifacts.

Our questionnaire comprised 14 questions: six closed questions assessing *perceived usefulness*, six closed questions evaluating *perceived ease of use*, and two open-ended questions. Responses to closed questions were rated on a Likert scale from 1 (unlikely) to 7 (likely). The open-ended questions asked to list the most *negative* and *positive* aspects the participants faced while utilizing LLMs for modeling tasks. We employed GPT-4 to analyze and categorize the participants' feedback to these open questions. Furthermore, to evaluate the statistical significance of LLM and Application Domain, we performed the Kruskal-Wallis H-test [20] and show the p-values in Table 7.

Table 7. Perceived usefulness and ease of use, overall and categorized according to LLMs and application domains. Significant results are in bold with an asterisk.

	Overall		LLM		Application Domain	
	Mean [SD]	p-value	Mean [SD][a]	p-value	Mean [SD][b]	p-value
Perceived Usefulness						
Using LLMs for modeling would enable me to accomplish tasks more quickly	4.2 1.9	0.425	(4.7, 3.6) (1.9, 1.7)	**0.017***	(4.0, 4.0, 4.7) (2.0, 1.9, 1.6)	0.367
Using LLMs would improve my modeling performance	3.9 1.8	0.475	(4.3, 3.4) (1.8, 1.7)	**0.027***	(3.7, 3.5, 4.5) (2.0, 1.3, 1.8)	0.133
Using LLMs for modeling would increase my productivity	4.0 1.8	0.900	(4.2, 3.8) (1.9, 1.7)	0.303	(3.7, 4.0, 4.3) (1.9, 1.5, 2.0)	0.523
Using LLMs would enhance my modeling effectiveness	3.8 1.8	0.327	(4.0, 3.6) (1.8, 1.7)	0.324	(3.5, 3.8, 4.1) (2.0, 1.3, 1.8)	0.374
Using LLMs would make it easier to model	4.0 1.8	0.897	(4.4, 3.7) (1.9, 1.6)	**0.061***	(3.9, 4.0, 4.3) (1.8, 1.6, 2.0)	0.745
I would find LLMs useful for modeling	4.0 1.8	0.948	(4.4, 3.6) (1.8, 1.6)	**0.027***	(3.9, 3.8, 4.3) (1.8, 1.6, 1.9)	0.726
Perceived Ease of Use						
Learning to operate LLMs would be easy for me	4.8 1.7	**<0.001***	(5.0, 4.5) (1.6, 1.7)	0.171	(4.5, 4.9, 5.0) (1.6, 1.5, 1.9)	0.249
I would find it easy to get LLMs to do what I want it to do	3.9 1.7	0.469	(4.1, 3.6) (1.8, 1.7)	0.260	(3.4, 3.8, 4.4) (1.7, 1.6, 1.8)	0.090
My interaction with LLMs would be clear and understandable	4.2 1.5	0.300	(4.5, 3.9) (1.5, 1.5)	0.070	(4.0, 3.9, 4.9) (1.6, 1.4, 1.6)	**0.022***
I would find LLMs to be flexible to interact with	3.9 1.6	0.621	(4.2, 3.6) (1.7, 1.5)	0.086	(3.6, 3.7, 4.6) (1.6, 1.3, 1.8)	**0.039***
It would be easy for me to become skillful at using LLMs	4.4 1.7	**0.051***	(4.9, 3.9) (1.5, 1.7)	**0.012***	(4.2, 4.2, 4.9) (1.8, 1.4, 1.8)	0.147
I would find LLMs easy to use	4.4 1.7	**0.167***	(4.5, 4.1) (1.7, 1.6)	0.217	(4.2, 3.9, 4.8) (1.5, 1.4, 1.9)	0.083

[a] (GPT-4, Llama), [b] (NPA, R4A, PTr), * Significant

Overall User Perception (RQ2.1). Overall, the results show moderate user experiences, with an average of 4.0 for perceived usefulness and 4.4 for perceived ease of use. The only statistically significant result relates to the ease of learning to operate LLMs, suggesting the potential for steep learning curves associated with LLM-assisted modeling. The borderline significant result concerning the ease of becoming skillful at using LLMs further supports this observation.

To gain a deeper understanding of user perception, we analyzed their textual feedback. The positive feedback mainly referred to: (*i*) Efficiency and speed – "it is very responsive and quick," "Fast response, response explanation;" (*ii*) Guidance and direction – "it give[s] you a way to start your solution," "Helped me build something basic to start from;" and (*iii*) Supports Creativity – "it has a unique thinking about the problem," "provides too much aspects of certain topics which help generate new ideas." The negative aspects that were widely mentioned referred to: (*i*) Lack of contextual memory and continuity – "it gives answers to the question that was just asked and does not give answers that combine all the requirements of the question," "its answers aren't based on previous answers, could easily go off topic, make up things;" (*ii*) Inaccuracy and unreliability – "The answers provided to me were not close to what I was looking for," "it doesn't understand complex questions," "every time we tried to fix it or improve the diagram it made it worse;" (*iii*) Reliance on precise inputs – "Over caution, I kept fearing that my inputs needed to be extremely precise," "need to explain everything like he is a little kid, every single aspect and point;" and (*iv*) Difficulty in visualization – "When asked to visualize/demonstrate something using drawing or some sort of UML diagram, it is not done in alignment and is somewhat messy, although there is potential and it can improve drastically." This feedback may indicate the need for the development of concrete guidelines, such as prompt templates, for interacting with LLMs in conceptual modeling tasks. In our study, participants utilized entirely free-form text, which at times proved insufficient for eliciting the desired responses.

User Perception by Independent Variables (RQ2.2-RQ2.3). In Table 7, the results indicate a significant difference in perceived usefulness between GPT-4 and Llama, in favor of GPT-4, and no significant differences in perceived ease of use. This latter result aligns with the fact that students were provided with the same interface and were unaware of the specific LLM they were using, thus not expected to encounter different challenges in usage. Nevertheless, we observe a significant difference in the assessment of ease of becoming skillful at using LLMs, favoring GPT-4. This can be explained by the more advanced capabilities of GPT-4, which may facilitate a better experience of use. The usefulness of the application, on the other hand, could depend on the utilized LLM. We see that the choice of LLM not only affects the overall perceived usefulness but also impacts perceived efficiency (quickness) and perceived effectiveness (performance). This suggests that more advanced LLMs like GPT-4 provide a better user experience by delivering faster and more accurate responses.

Table 7 further shows that, with respect to application domains, there are no significant differences in either perceived usefulness or ease of use. This may be attributed to the relatively low number of participants per application domain (ranging from 21 to 27). However, two significant differences were observed in terms of ease of use: understandability and flexibility. These results are surprising, considering that the application domains are comparable in terms of size and complexity, and LLMs are not biased toward any particular domain. Further research is required to explore the reasons for this result.

Summary of RQ2 Results. Based on the analyses conducted, we conclude that overall, the user experience was moderate (RQ2.1). The perceived usefulness of GPT-4 was found to be better than that of Llama, while there were no statistically significant differences in terms of perceived ease of use across LLMs (RQ2.2). Finally, there were no statistically significant differences in terms of perceived usefulness and perceived ease of use across application domains (RQ2.3).

5 Discussion

In the subsequent discussion, we outline the key practical implications derived from our results, along with an analysis of the potential threats to validity.

Practical Implications. Overall, the results suggest the potential of LLM-assisted conceptual modeling. However, the current way of interaction, relying solely on completely free-form text, presents limitations and can lead to frustration. Therefore, the first implication of our findings is the *development of prompt templates* for conceptual modeling, derived from the observed intention distribution. Expert modelers or domain experts can offer general, domain-, or language-specific templates for various modeling tasks. These templates should break down the overall task into smaller units, aiding modelers in clarifying their intentions and facilitating an iterative and incremental modeling process. As an example, consider the intention 'Discuss': "Discuss `<variants>` [in the setting of `<setting>`] [considering `<metric>` measures]," where `<variants>` specifies the variants to be discussed, `<setting>` is optional and specifies the setting in which the variants should be discussed, and `<metric>` suggests the metrics for assessing the variants, such as correctness or comprehensibility.

The second implication involves the *development of a recommender* to guide modelers regarding their next steps in the modeling process. This recommender would utilize our findings regarding the top recurrent interaction patterns observed in the study. By analyzing these patterns, the recommender could suggest relevant prompts or actions to users based on the current state of their modeling session. This approach aims to enhance the efficiency and effectiveness of the modeling process by providing modelers with tailored guidance. Moreover, by offering personalized recommendations based on the user's current modeling context and the identified interaction patterns, the recommender would seek to improve the user experience and perceived usefulness of LLM-assisted modeling.

The final implication underscores the importance of a *thorough tool selection*. With GPT-4 demonstrating superior perceived effectiveness and efficiency, it may significantly influence decisions regarding which LLM to employ for conceptual modeling. Further research needs to explore updated versions of these LLMs, alongside other alternatives. Moreover, analyzing the impact of prompt templates and recommenders on interaction behavior and user perception is crucial for a comprehensive understanding of LLM-assisted conceptual modeling.

Threats to Validity. In the discussion of the validity threats encountered in our study and the corresponding mitigation strategies, several key considerations emerged. To tackle concerns regarding *conclusion validity*, particularly concerning sample size, as our study encompassed 39 groups, we opted to assign each group two modeling tasks. This decision yielded a total of 566 interactions, thus enhancing the robustness of our conclusions. Concerning *construct validity*, particularly regarding the selection of intentions, we adopted a data-driven approach, carefully analyzing all prompts within the research team, with each prompt analyzed by two researchers to reconcile any inconsistencies and establish consensus. Addressing *internal validity*, the potential impact of variations in participants' capabilities and LLM assignment on the study's integrity was mitigated by randomly assigning tasks, ensuring equitable distribution, and minimizing bias. Furthermore, in addressing *external validity* regarding the generalizability of our findings across application domains, we selected three distinct domains familiar to both students and LLMs, thereby enhancing the potential transferability of our conclusions. Notably, we do not see a threat in having students participate in our experiments as our research focuses on intuitive LLM interactions, therefore there was no prerequisite to involve modeling experts [10].

6 Related Work

In recent studies, researchers have explored the application of LLMs in conceptual model generation. Chaaben et al. [6] demonstrated the effectiveness of few-shot prompt learning in completing static and dynamic domain models, emphasizing its versatility across various modeling activities. Giglou et al. [13] demonstrated the suitability of LLMs as assistants when fine-tuned for specific tasks. Chen et al. [8] conducted a comprehensive comparative study on using LLMs for fully automated domain modeling, revealing impressive domain understanding capabilities while emphasizing the need for careful consideration due to practical limitations. They observed that while LLMs provide reliable domain elements, there are often missing elements. Arul et al. [3] investigated how LLMs can be used to extract domain models from agile product backlogs. Kanuka et al. [17] explored the bidirectional traceability problem between design models and code, and they demonstrated the proficiency of ChatGPT in understanding and integrating specific requirements into design models and code. Ruan et al. [22] presented an automated framework for requirement model generation that incorporates ChatGPT-based zero-shot learning to extract requirement models from textual requirements and subsequently compose them using predefined rules. All these works concentrate on the LLM outcomes and their evaluation. Differently, our study concentrates on the human-LLM interaction and provides unique insights into interaction behavior and user perception.

Several works address prompt engineering, either generally or within the modeling context. White et al. [26] curated a catalog of prompt patterns that can be applied collaboratively throughout the software life-cycle, encompassing requirements elicitation, system design and simulation, code quality, and refactoring. In another paper, White et al. [25] suggest initial classifications for the catalog of prompt patterns tailored for use with ChatGPT, covering input semantics, output customization, error identification, prompt improvement, interaction, and context control. Fill et al. [12] explored how to generate and interpret ER, business process, UML class diagrams, and Heraklit models.

Notably, these interactions were conducted by the researchers themselves with the LLM (GPT-4). While these works adopt a top-down approach for prompt catalog creation, we employed a data-driven approach that analyzes the intuitive interaction of humans with LLMs to extract interaction intentions. Moreover, we analyzed patterns of interactions rather than individual prompts.

7 Conclusion

In this paper, we conducted an empirical study to explore the interaction behavior and user perception of LLM-assisted conceptual modeling. Utilizing two LLMs (GPT-4 and Code-Llama), two modeling tasks (use case modeling with use case diagrams and domain modeling with class diagrams), and three application domains, we identified seven interaction intentions (create model, update model, create list, update list, present, explain and discuss) and five recurrent interaction patterns (model evolution, partial model visualization, partial model discussion, discussion-based model updating, and partial model listing).

In the future, we aim to expand our study by implementing a template-based approach designed to facilitate the interaction intentions and patterns identified in this research. Such an approach would offer a structured framework for users engaging with LLMs, enhancing efficiency and effectiveness in conceptual modeling. Additionally, we plan to broaden our investigation to encompass newer versions of various LLMs, allowing for a comprehensive assessment of their evolving capabilities. Finally, we will explore the impact of different interaction types on the quality metrics of the generated conceptual models, thereby providing deeper insights into enhancing LLM-assisted modeling processes.

References

1. Achiam, J., et al.: GPT-4 technical report. arXiv preprint arXiv:2303.08774 (2023)
2. Alex, N., et al.: Raft: a real-world few-shot text classification benchmark. arXiv preprint arXiv:2109.14076 (2021)
3. Arulmohan, S., Meurs, M.J., Mosser, S.: Extracting domain models from textual requirements in the era of large language models. In: 2023 ACM/IEEE International Conference on Model Driven Engineering Languages and Systems Companion (MODELS-C), pp. 580–587. IEEE (2023)
4. Brown, J.D.: The bonferroni adjustment. Statistics **12**(1), 23–27 (2008)
5. Cámara, J., Troya, J., Burgueño, L., Vallecillo, A.: On the assessment of generative AI in modeling tasks: an experience report with ChatGPT and UML. Softw. Syst. Model. **22**(3), 781–793 (2023)
6. Chaaben, M.B., Burgueño, L., Sahraoui, H.A.: Towards using few-shot prompt learning for automating model completion. In: 45th IEEE/ACM International Conference on Software Engineering: New Ideas and Emerging Results, NIER@ICSE, pp. 7–12. IEEE (2023)
7. Chen, B., et al.: On the use of GPT-4 for creating goal models: an exploratory study. In: 2023 IEEE 31st International Requirements Engineering Conference Workshops (REW), pp. 262–271. IEEE (2023)

8. Chen, K., Yang, Y., Chen, B., López, J.A.H., Mussbacher, G., Varró, D.: Automated domain modeling with large language models: a comparative study. In: 2023 ACM/IEEE 26th International Conference on Model Driven Engineering Languages and Systems (MODELS), pp. 162–172. IEEE (2023)
9. Chen, X., et al.: How robust is GPT-3.5 to predecessors? A comprehensive study on language understanding tasks. arXiv preprint arXiv:2303.00293 (2023)
10. Druckman, J.N., Kam, C.D.: Students as experimental participants. In: Cambridge Handbook of Experimental Political Science, vol. 1, pp. 41–57 (2011)
11. Du, X., et al.: Evaluating large language models in class-level code generation. In: 2024 IEEE/ACM 46th International Conference on Software Engineering (ICSE), pp. 865–865. IEEE Computer Society (2024)
12. Fill, H.G., Fettke, P., Köpke, J.: Conceptual modeling and large language models: impressions from first experiments with ChatGPT. Enterp. Model. Inf. Syst. Architect. (EMISAJ) **18**, 1–15 (2023)
13. Giglou, H.B., D'Souza, J., Auer, S.: LLMs4OL: large language models for ontology learning. In: Payne, T.R., et al. (eds.) ISWC 2023, Part I. LNCS, vol. 14265, pp. 408–427. Springer, Cham (2023). https://doi.org/10.1007/978-3-031-47240-4_22
14. Grattafiori, W.X., et al.: Code llama: open foundation models for code. arXiv preprint arXiv:2308.12950 (2023)
15. Hou, Y., et al.: Large language models are zero-shot rankers for recommender systems. In: Goharian, N., et al. (eds.) ECIR 2024. LNCS, vol. 14609, pp. 364–381. Springer, Cham (2024). https://doi.org/10.1007/978-3-031-56060-6_24
16. Izadi, M., Katzy, J., van Dam, T., Otten, M., Popescu, R.M., van Deursen, A.: Language models for code completion: a practical evaluation. arXiv preprint arXiv:2402.16197 (2024)
17. Kanuka, H., Koreki, G., Soga, R., Nishikawa, K.: Exploring the chatgpt approach for bidirectional traceability problem between design models and code. arXiv preprint arXiv:2309.14992 (2023)
18. Kocmi, T., Federmann, C.: Large language models are state-of-the-art evaluators of translation quality. arXiv preprint arXiv:2302.14520 (2023)
19. Liu, J., Liu, C., Lv, R., Zhou, K., Zhang, Y.: Is chatgpt a good recommender? A preliminary study. arXiv preprint arXiv:2304.10149 (2023)
20. MacFarland, T.W., Yates, J.M.: Kruskal–Wallis H-test for oneway analysis of variance (ANOVA) by ranks. In: Introduction to Nonparametric Statistics for the Biological Sciences Using R, pp. 177–211. Springer, Cham (2016). https://doi.org/10.1007/978-3-319-30634-6_6
21. Qin, C., Zhang, A., Zhang, Z., Chen, J., Yasunaga, M., Yang, D.: Is chatgpt a general-purpose natural language processing task solver? arXiv preprint arXiv:2302.06476 (2023)
22. Ruan, K., Chen, X., Jin, Z.: Requirements modeling aided by chatgpt: an experience in embedded systems. In: 31st IEEE International Requirements Engineering Conference, RE 2023 - Workshops, pp. 170–177. IEEE (2023)
23. Touvron, H., et al.: Llama 2: open foundation and fine-tuned chat models. arXiv preprint arXiv:2307.09288 (2023)
24. Van Veen, D., et al.: Clinical text summarization: adapting large language models can outperform human experts. Research Square (2023). https://doi.org/10.48550/ARXIV.2309.07430
25. White, J., et al.: A prompt pattern catalog to enhance prompt engineering with chatgpt. arXiv preprint arXiv:2302.11382 (2023)

26. White, J., Hays, S., Fu, Q., Spencer-Smith, J., Schmidt, D.C.: Chatgpt prompt patterns for improving code quality, refactoring, requirements elicitation, and software design. arXiv preprint arXiv:2303.07839 (2023)
27. Zhang, B., Haddow, B., Birch, A.: Prompting large language model for machine translation: a case study. In: International Conference on Machine Learning, pp. 41092–41110. PMLR (2023)
28. Zhang, T., Ladhak, F., Durmus, E., Liang, P., McKeown, K., Hashimoto, T.B.: Benchmarking large language models for news summarization. Trans. Assoc. Comput. Linguist. **12**, 39–57 (2024)
29. Zhao, W.X., et al.: A survey of large language models. arXiv preprint arXiv:2303.18223 (2023)

Small, Medium, and Large Language Models for Text-to-SQL

Aiko Oliveira[1,2], Eduardo Nascimento[1], João Pinheiro[2], Caio Viktor S. Avila[4], Gustavo Coelho[1], Lucas Feijó[1], Yenier Izquierdo[1], Grettel García[1], Luiz André P. Paes Leme[3], Melissa Lemos[1,2], and Marco A. Casanova[1,2](✉)

[1] Tecgraf Institute, PUC-Rio, Rio de Janeiro, RJ 22451-900, Brazil
{aikoramalho,rogerrsn,gustavocoelho,lucasfeijo,ytorres,ggarcia, melissa}@tecgraf.puc-rio.br

[2] Department of Informatics, PUC-Rio, Rio de Janeiro, RJ 22451-900, Brazil
{jpinheiro,casanova}@inf.puc-rio.br

[3] Instituto de Computação, UFF, Niterói, RJ 24210-310, Brazil
lapaesleme@ic.uff.br

[4] Federal University of Ceará, UFC, Fortaleza, CE 60440-900, Brazil
caioviktor@alu.ufc.br

Abstract. This paper investigates how the model size affects the ability of a Generative AI Language Model, or briefly a GLM, to support the text-to-SQL task for databases with large schemas typical of real-world applications. The paper first introduces a text-to-SQL framework that combines a prompt strategy and a Retrieval-Augmented Generation (RAG) technique, leaving as flexibilization points the GLM and the database. Then, it describes a benchmark based on an open-source database featuring a schema much larger than the schemas of most of the databases in familiar text-to-SQL benchmarks. The paper proceeds with experiments to assess the performance of the text-to-SQL framework instantiated with the benchmark database and GLMs of different sizes. The paper concludes with recommendations to help select which GLM size is appropriate for a text-to-SQL scenario, characterized by the difficulty of the expected NL questions and the data privacy requirements, among other characteristics.

Keywords: text-to-SQL · Generative AI Language Model · Retrieval-Augmented Generation · Prompt engineering · Real-World Databases

1 Introduction

Natural language database interfaces allow users to access databases using questions formulated in natural language (NL) [2]. A strategy for constructing such interfaces is to use a Generative AI Language Model, or briefly a GLM, to translate the NL questions into SQL queries. Such interfaces will be called *GLM-based text-to-SQL tools.*

W. Maass et al. (Eds.): ER 2024, LNCS 15238, pp. 276–294, 2025.
https://doi.org/10.1007/978-3-031-75872-0_15

Real-world databases, that is, databases that support real-world applications, are especially challenging for GLM-based text-to-SQL tools. Among other characteristics, their schema is typically large and complex, may not fit in the prompt area, and may lead to queries with many joins, which are difficult to synthesize. Furthermore, the data stored in such databases may have complex semantics, which must be passed to the GLM. The primary motivation of this paper is the design of GLM-based text-to-SQL tools for real-world databases.

Considering the relevance for the construction of text-to-SQL tools, a GLM may be characterized by: the *licensing mode*, where proprietary models run only on vendors' platforms versus open-source models that can be downloaded and run on a private platform; the *context length*, that is, the number of tokens accepted as input/output, which limits the database metadata and data that can be passed to the GLM in the text-to-SQL task; and the *model size* in billions of parameters, which mostly determines the hardware requirements. The *release date* of the model is also important since more recent models tend to have better performance. Smaller GLMs are attractive from the point of view of hardware requirements, but their performance for a given NL task must be assessed.

The research question addressed in this paper is then: "How does the model size affect the ability of a GLM to support the text-to-SQL task for databases with large, complex schemas?". This question is of tantamount importance for implementing GLM-based Natural Language database interfaces.

To address this question, the paper first introduces a prototype text-to-SQL framework based on a prompt strategy, SQLQueryChain[1], combined with a Retrieval-Augmented Generation (RAG) technique, leaving as flexibilization points the GLM adopted and the database. SQLQueryChain proved effective for real-world databases [5,19], vis-a-vis the strategies at the top of the benchmark leaderboards. The RAG technique adopted injects knowledge of the database schema and the data semantics into a GLM, and led to a considerable improvement of the accuracy of text-to-SQL Prompt strategies [5]. The retrieval step of the technique incorporates an NL question decomposition strategy to improve accuracy, not addressed in [5]. An assessment of the RAG technique with question decomposition is the first contribution of the paper.

Then, the paper describes a benchmark based on the Mondial database[2] which features a relational schema much larger than the schemas of most of the databases in familiar text-to-SQL benchmarks. The Mondial database is an open-source suitable proxy for the proprietary industrial database that motivated this paper but could not be made openly available. The benchmark includes 100 NL questions, with balanced difficulty, and their translation to SQL. The benchmark also includes a synthetic dataset with 60,000 entries to help apply RAG. It should be stressed that the benchmark is not meant to train a model for the text-to-SQL task but rather to test the model in a challenging scenario. The Mondial benchmark, prepared for RAG, is the second contribution of the paper.

---

[1] https://python.langchain.com/docs/use_cases/sql/prompting.

[2] Available at https://github.com/dudursn/text_to_sql_chatgpt_real_world/.

The paper proceeds with experiments to assess the performance of the text-to-SQL framework instantiated with the Mondial database and GLMs of different sizes. The experiments suggest recommendations that help select which GLM size is appropriate for the text-to-SQL task in a given context, characterized by the difficulty of the expected NL questions and the data privacy requirements, among other characteristics. The experiments and the derived recommendations are the third contribution of the paper.

The paper is organized as follows. Section 2 summarizes the required background concepts and related work. Section 3 presents the prototype NL database interface framework and the RAG technique. Section 4 describes the Mondial benchmark. Section 5 covers the experiments and derived recommendations. Section 6 contains the concluding remarks.

2 Background Concepts and Related Work

2.1 Generative AI Language Models

The approaches involved in Natural Language Processing (NLP) tasks have undergone profound changes over the past decade, converging to generalized language models that represent words with dense vectors [17]. The first Large Language Model (LLM) was successfully trained in 2018 by exposing a model to a vast quantity of text, representing an enormous amount of language knowledge.

The term *Generative AI Language Model - GLM* is used in this paper, rather than *Large Language Model - LLM*, to call attention to the fact that, recently, several language models have been made available that are, by comparison, smaller than LLMs published in the past and yet achieve excellent performance.

Different sets of attributes may characterize a GLM. The Open LLM Leaderboard[3] uses: *model type* – pretrained, continuously trained, fine-tuned on domain-specific datasets, chat models, etc.; *precision* – float16, bfloat16, 8bit, etc.; and *model size* in billions of parameters. Since models may not activate all parameters for a given request, the model size has to be qualified; for example, DBRX uses a fine-grained mixture-of-experts (MoE) architecture with a total of 132B parameters, of which 36B parameters are active on a given request [6].

The Independent Analysis of AI-Language Models and API Providers Web site[4] considers: *context length*, *model quality*, *price*, *throughput*, and *latency*. Context length refers to the number of tokens accepted as input/output, and limits the database metadata and data that can be passed to the GLM in the text-to-SQL task. Among the quality features, the Web site lists the *coding ability* of the model, which may be indicative of the text-to-SQL ability.

One may also list: *licensing mode*, where *proprietary* models run only on vendors' platforms, versus *open-source* models that can be downloaded and run on a private platform, and the *release date* of the model, where more recent models are expected to have better performance.

Using just the model size, a classification of GLMs would be:

[3] https://huggingface.co/spaces/HuggingFaceH4/open_llm_leaderboard.

[4] https://artificialanalysis.ai.

- *Small Language Model (SLM)*: the model typically has 10B parameters or less; an open-source small model can be downloaded and executed on a small server or a PC running a language model platform, such as LM Studio[5].
- *Medium Language Model (MLM)*: the model typically has more than 10B parameters, and at most 100B parameters; an open-source medium model can be downloaded and executed on a mid-range server, usually equipped with one or more GPUs; the server can be locally available or allocated as a cloud resource.
- *Large Language Model (LLM)*: the model typically has more than 100B parameters; a large model usually runs on a large-scale cloud-based infrastructure.

The licensing mode, model size, and context length stand out as relevant characteristics for the construction of natural language database interfaces based on text-to-SQL (see Table 1 for examples of recent GLMs). Indeed, the licensing mode determines where the model can be run, and a proprietary model running on the vendor's platform may raise data privacy concerns; the size directly influences the infrastructure requirements to run the model and achieve the desirable throughput and latency; and the context length has direct implications for the implementation of a text-to-SQL strategy since it limits the database metadata and data that can be passed to the GLM.

As mentioned in the introduction, the central question addressed in this paper is to assess how the model size affects the ability of a GLM to support the text-to-SQL task. This question is of tantamount importance for implementing GLM-based Natural Language database interfaces.

2.2 Text-to-SQL Benchmarks

The Spider – Yale Semantic Parsing and Text-to-SQL Challenge [25] defines 200 datasets, covering 138 domains, for training and testing text-to-SQL tools. For each database, Spider lists 20–50 hand-written NL questions and their SQL translations. An NL question Q_N, with an SQL translation Q_S, is classified as easy, medium, hard, and extra-hard, where the difficulty is based on the number of SQL constructs of Q_S – `GROUP BY`, `ORDER BY`, `INTERSECT`, nested sub-queries, column selections, and aggregators – so that an NL query whose translation Q contains more SQL constructs is considered harder. The set of NL questions introduced in Sect. 4 follows this classification.

Most databases in Spider have small schemas: the largest five databases have between 16 and 25 tables, and about half of the databases have schemas with five or fewer tables. Also, all Spider NL questions are phrased in terms used in the database schemas. These two features simplify the text-to-SQL task. Therefore, the results reported in the Spider leaderboard are biased toward databases with small schemas, and NL questions written in the schema vocabulary, which is not what one finds in real-world applications.

[5] https://lmstudio.ai.

Table 1. Examples of recent GLMs.

Owner	Model	License	Size	Context Length	Release Date	Reference
Meta	LLaMA-3-8B-instruct	Open	8B	8.18K	Apr 18, 2024	[3]
	LLaMA-3-70B-instruct	Open	70B	8.18K		
MS	Phi-3-mini	Open	3.8B	4K and 128K	Apr 23, 2024	[1]
	Phi-3-small	Open	7B	4K and 128K		
	Phi-3-medium	Open	14B	8K		
DataBricks	DBRX	Open	132B	32K	Mar 27, 2024	[6]
Google	Gemma 7B	Open	7B	8.19K	Feb 21, 2024	[12]
	Gemma 2	Open	27B	–	May 14, 2024	[24]
	Gemini 1.5 Pro	Proprietary	N/A	1.0M	Mar 08, 2024	[11]
Anthropic	Claude 3 Haiku	Proprietary	N/A	200K	Mar 04, 2024	[4]
	Claude 3 Sonnet	Proprietary	N/A	200K		
	Claude 3 Opus	Proprietary	N/A	200K		
OpenAI	GPT-4o	Proprietary	N/A	128K	May 13, 2024	[21]
	GPT-4-turbo	Proprietary	N/A	128K	Apr 09, 2024	
	GPT-3.5-turbo-0125	Proprietary	N/A	16K	Jan 25, 2024	

Spider has two interesting variations. Spider-Syn [8] is used to test how well text-to-SQL tools handle synonym, and Spider-DK [9] addresses testing how well text-to-SQL tools deal with domain knowledge.

BIRD – BIg Bench for LaRge-scale Database Grounded Text-to-SQL Evaluation [16] is a large-scale cross-domain text-to-SQL benchmark in English. The dataset contains 12,751 text-to-SQL data pairs and 95 databases with a total size of 33.4 GB across 37 domains. BIRD addresses real-world applications by exploring three additional challenges: dealing with large and messy database values, external knowledge inference, and optimizing SQL execution efficiency. However, BIRD still does not have many databases with large schemas: of the 73 databases in the training dataset, only two have more than 25 tables, and, of the 11 databases used for development, the largest one has only 13 tables. Again, all NL questions are phrased based on terms used in the database schemas.

WikiSQL [26] has 80,654 NL sentences and SQL annotations of 24,241 tables. Each query in WikiSQL is limited to the same table and does not contain complex operations such as sorting and grouping.

Despite the availability of these benchmarks for text-to-SQL, and inspired by them, Sect. 4 describes a benchmark based on the Mondial database, a set of 100 test NL questions, with their gold-standard SQL translations, and a synthetic dataset (see Sect. 3). The reasons for introducing the Mondial benchmark are threefold. Mondial features a relational schema which is much larger than the schemas of most of the databases in Spider and BIRD, which poses significant challenges to text-to-SQL strategies. The Mondial database is populated with real data, which allows using an RAG technique that proved effective (see

Sect. 3). Lastly, the test NL questions mimic those posed by real users and cover a wide range of SQL constructs.

2.3 Prompt Strategies for Text-to-SQL

The Spider Web site[6] publishes a leaderboard with the best-performing text-to-SQL tools. The top 5 tools listed in the published leaderboard are based on Prompt strategies and achieve an accuracy that range from an impressive 85.3% to 91.2% (two of the tools are not openly documented). Four tools use GPT-4, as their names imply. The three tools that provide detailed documentation have an elaborate first prompt that tries to select the tables and columns that best matches the NL question.

The BIRD Web site[7] also publishes a leaderboard with the best-performing tools. At the time of writing, the topmost two tools use GPT-4.

The Awesome Text2SQL Web site[8] lists the best-performing text-to-SQL tools on WikiSQL, Spider (Exact Match and Exact Execution) and BIRD (Valid Efficiency Score and Execution Accuracy). The "60 Top AI Text To SQL Bot Tools" Web site[9] lists other AI tools for text-to-SQL.

Finally, LangChain is a generic framework that offers several predefined Prompt strategies for text-to-SQL. Section 3 provides a few more details about the LangChain's SQLQueryChain, which proved to be cost-effective in [19], vis-a-vis the strategies at the top of the Spider leaderboard. Choosing a single text-to-SQL strategy, with the GLM as a flexibilization point, reduces the number of experiments, and permits concentrating on comparing the ability of different GLMs to generate SQL code.

2.4 Fine-Tuning LLMs for Text-to-SQL

Attempts to fine-tune open-source LLMs for the text-to-SQL task using NL question/SQL query pairs were reported in [10]. However, until recently, the fine-tuned models did not achieve a performance on Spider comparable to the zero-shot (i.e., with no examples) performance of GPT-3.5-turbo.

The Defog SQLCoder[10] is based on models fine-tuned for the text-to-SQL task. The latest version, sqlcoder-70b-alpha, features 70B parameters and was fine-tuned on a base StarCoder model on more than 20,000 human-curated questions, classified as in Spider, based on ten different schemas. The training dataset[11] consisted of prompt-completion pairs, encompassing several schemas with varying difficulty levels, whereas the evaluation dataset featured questions from novel schemas. The use of complex schemas, with 4–20 tables, challenged

6 https://yale-lily.github.io/spider.
7 https://bird-bench.github.io.
8 https://github.com/eosphoros-ai/Awesome-Text2SQL.
9 https://topai.tools/s/Text-to-SQL-bot.
10 https://github.com/defog-ai/sqlcoder?tab=readme-ov-file.
11 https://defog.ai/blog/open-sourcing-sqlcoder/.

the model. The fine-tuning process occurred in two stages: the base model was first refined using easy and medium questions and then further fine-tuned on hard and extra-hard questions to yield the final model. The accuracy of the sqlcoder-70b-alpha model on the Defog's dataset achieved 93.0%, whereas GPT-4 (Feb. 5, 2024) achieved 86%. Still, the experiments were based on databases with very small schemas.

DTS-SQL [23] is a two-stage fine-tuning process that separates schema linking and SQL generation. The authors first applied DTS-SQL to fine-tune Mistral-7B [14] and DeepSeek-7B [7] for text-to-SQL. Then, they evaluated the fine-tuned models on Spider and Spider-Syn and showed that the execution accuracy was improved by 3% to 7%. The fine-tuned DeepSeek-7B performed comparably to the best strategies in the Spider leaderboard. However, these results reflect the limitations of Spider, namely, that the databases have simple schemas.

Natural-SQL-7B by ChatDB[12] was fine-tuned for text-to-SQL from deepseek-coder-6.7b-instruct, using 8,000 pairs of NL questions/SQL queries (for PostgreSQL). It is part of the NaturalSQL by ChatDB[13] collection of models.

Using a proprietary, real-world database with a large schema, early experiments showed that Mistral-7B frequently hallucinated, and Code Llama 2-13B-instruct-text2-sql[14] had poor performance, even using RAG (see Sect. 2.5). This may reflect the fact that Code Llama 2-13B-instruct-text2-sql was trained on Spider and WikiSQL, again on databases with small schemas.

Finally, these last experiments, including the DTS-SQL fine-tuning, required only modest hardware, and showed that it is feasible to run SLMs on small local servers and yet achieve state-of-the-art performance on Spider. But, fine-tuned tools proved to be less than satisfactory for databases with larger schemas [19].

2.5 Retrieval-Augmented Generation (RAG) for Text-to-SQL

Retrieval-Augmented Generation (RAG), introduced in [15], is a strategy to incorporate data from external sources. This process ensures that the responses are grounded in retrieved evidence, thereby significantly enhancing the accuracy and relevance of the output.

In the context of text-to-SQL, recent RAG references include a technique for an LLM-based Text-to-SQL framework involving sample-aware prompting and a dynamic revision chain [13]. A RAG technique is used in [22] to retrieve the table and column descriptions from a metadata store to ensure that the NL question is related to the right tables and columns.

Section 3 outlines an approach that, given a relational database D_R, its schema D_S, and associated documentation D_{doc}, generates a synthetic dataset E of pairs (Q_N, Q_S), where Q_N is an NL question and Q_S is its SQL translation, using D_R, D_S and D_{doc}. The synthetic dataset E is then used in a RAG

[12] https://huggingface.co/chatdb/natural-sql-7b-GGUF.
[13] https://github.com/cfahlgren1/natural-sql.
[14] https://huggingface.co/support-pvelocity/Code-Llama-2-13B-instruct-text2sql-GGUF.

technique to improve the accuracy of text-to-SQL strategies on D_R. This approach is independent of the GLM adopted, that is, it can be combined with any GLM. The approach contrasts with the model fine-tuning strategy outlined in Sect. 2.4, which is model-specific but independent of the database. Also, the RAG technique may be combined with different text-to-SQL prompt strategies; the experiments in Sect. 5 combine SQLQueryChain with this RAG technique.

3 A Prototype Text-to-SQL Framework

This section outlines a prototype text-to-SQL framework based on a prompt strategy, SQLQueryChain[15], combined with a Retrieval-Augmented Generation (RAG) technique, leaving as flexibilization points the GLM and the database (the synthetic dataset is constructed from the database and is not considered as a flexibilization point here).

Figure 1 depicts the text-to-SQL framework, with the flexibilization points indicated in light grey. The framework has roughly the following steps:

Pre-processing

P1. (Sample Generation) Generate pairs (Q_i, S_i) from the database DB, where Q_i is an NL question and S_i is the corresponding SQL query.
P2. (Embedding) Embed each NL question Q_i into a vector V_i and store V_i along with the pair (Q_i, S_i) in a *synthetic dataset* SD.

Processing

S1. (Sample Retrieval) Given an NL question Q_0, embed Q_0 in a vector V_{Q_0}; retrieve from DS the top-k vectors V_i, $i \in [1, k]$, most similar to V_{Q_0}; create a context C with the pairs (Q_i, S_i), $i \in [1, k]$.
S2. (Schema Linking) Retrieve from DB a description of the tables and columns required to process Q_0; add these descriptions to C.
S3. (SQL Translation) Ask the GLM to translate Q_0 into an SQL query S_0 under the context C.

SQLQueryChain, adopted in this paper, is the simplest LangChain text-to-SQL chain and is adapted in the framework to care for Steps S2 and S3. It trivializes the Schema Linking step by adding to the context C a description of all tables in the database schema. SQLQueryChain proved effective for real-world databases [5,19], vis-a-vis much more complex text-to-SQL strategies listed at the top of the Spider and BIRD leaderboards.

The RAG technique adopted injects knowledge of the database schema and the data semantics into the SQL Translation step, and led to a considerable improvement of the accuracy of text-to-SQL Prompt strategies [5].

Steps P1 and P2 must be run only once for each database to generate the synthetic dataset SD in such a way as to improve the performance of the Schema

[15] https://python.langchain.com/docs/use_cases/sql/prompting.

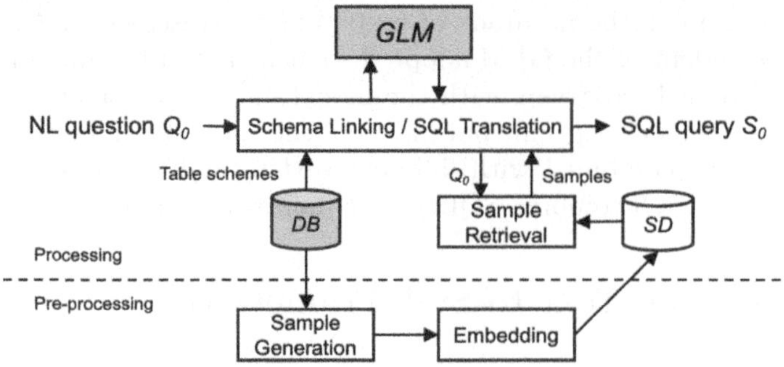

Fig. 1. The architecture of a prototype text-to-SQL framework.

Linking and SQL Translation steps. The technique introduced in [5] provides a robust strategy to construct database-specific synthetic datasets, especially when it comes to conveying the data semantics of the database to the GLM. The generation of SD is based on an algorithm that samples the database DB, its schema, and associated documentation, and calls a GLM to create an NL question Q_i from the sampled data and to translate Q_i into an SQL query S_i. Roughly, by varying how the sampling works, the pairs in SD provide SQL examples illustrating how the database schema is structured, how the user's language maps to the database schema, and how NL language constructions map to data values. Therefore, the synthetic dataset SD is specific to the database, but the algorithm is generic and applicable to any database. Table 3, discussed in Sect. 4.2, shows a sample of the synthetic dataset for Mondial.

This basic RAG technique has a limitation, though, since the Retrieval Step often returns pairs (Q_i, S_i) whose SQL queries are similar. The net effect is that the examples passed in the context C have little diversity. The *RAG technique with Question Decomposition* tries to remedy this limitation by decomposing the NL question into sub-questions, which are used in the Sample Retrieval step.

This paper then introduces a revised version of the Sample Retrieval step, not addressed in [5], and implemented using LangChain Question Decomposition:

S0. (Question Decomposition) Given an NL question Q_0, decompose Q_0 into sub-questions $Q_1, ..., Q_n$.

S1. (Sample Retrieval) Embed $Q_1, ..., Q_n$ into vectors $V_{Q_1}, ..., V_{Q_n}$. $m = \lceil k/n \rceil$. Retrieve from DS the top-m vectors $V_{i,j}$ most similar to V_{Q_i}, and create a list L_i in decreasing order of similarity to V_{Q_i}, $i \in [1, n]$, $j \in [1, m]$; intercalate the lists L_i and retain the top-k vectors U_p, $p \in [1, k]$. each $p \in [1, k]$, add to the context C the pair (Q_p, S_p) in DS associated with U_p.

4 The Mondial Benchmark

The Mondial benchmark[16] is based on the openly-available Mondial database, a set of 100 NL questions, and a synthetic dataset.

4.1 The Mondial Database and the Set of NL Questions

The Mondial database stores geographic data and is an open-source suitable proxy for the proprietary industrial database that motivated this paper, but could not be made openly available. The relational version, adopted in this paper, has a total of 47,699 instances and features a schema with 46 tables, a total of 184 columns, and 49 foreign keys (some of which are multi-column)[17]. The Mondial schema is sophisticated but uses familiar terms, such as countries, cities, rivers, etc. A Mondial version with 34 tables is also part of the BIRD benchmark.

As introduced in [19], the benchmark contains a set of 100 NL questions and their gold-standard SQL queries, collected from the Internet or defined manually over the Mondial relational schema; the execution of a gold-standard SQL query returns the expected answer to the corresponding NL question. The NL questions are manually classified into *simple*, *medium*, and *complex*, that correspond to the easy, medium, and hard classes of the Spider benchmark. The difficulty of an NL question Q is based on the number of constructs of the corresponding gold-standard SQL query S, so that Q is considered harder, if S contains more constructs (GROUP BY, ORDER BY, INTERSECT, nested subqueries, column selections, and aggregators). The list of NL questions contains 33 simple, 33 medium, and 34 complex.

Table 2 shows an example of each type of NL question Q and its gold-standard SQL translation S. Note that, in the examples, S has just a restriction, when Q is simple, S has a join and a restriction, when Q is medium, and S has two joins and an aggregation, when Q is complex.

4.2 The Mondial Synthetic Dataset

The Mondial benchmark also includes a synthetic dataset with 60,000 pairs, obtained using the technique outlined in Sect. 3 and adopting GPT-4. The construction of the synthetic dataset does not take into account the list of test NL questions. As such, the synthetic dataset should be useful to process any NL question the user submits to Mondial.

Table 3 shows examples of the synthetic dataset for Mondial. Table 3(a) corresponds to the sampled pair (“`MONDIAL_LAKE.AREA`”, `500`), that is, to the `AREA` column of table `MONDIAL_LAKE`, sampled from the database schema, and the value `500`, sampled from the set of the `AREA` column values. The technique generated

[16] Available at https://github.com/dudursn/text_to_sql_chatgpt_real_world/.
[17] https://relational.fit.cvut.cz/dataset/Mondial.

Table 2. A sample of the benchmark NL questions and their translations to SQL.

Type	NL Question	Gold-standard SQL Query	ID
simple	Show the Airports with elevation more than 3000	SELECT NAME FROM MONDIAL_AIRPORT WHERE ELEVATION > 3000.0	33
medium	What type of government does Iran have?	SELECT p.GOVERNMENT FROM MONDIAL_COUNTRY c INNER JOIN MONDIAL_POLITICS p ON p.COUNTRY = c.CODE WHERE c.NAME ="Iran"	99
complex	How much area do the countries that are adjacent to (or encompassed by) the Caribbean Sea cover in total?	SELECT SUM(DISTINCT c.area) AS total_area FROM mondial_Country c JOIN mondial_encompasses e ON c.code = e.country JOIN mondial_geo_sea gs ON e.country = gs.country WHERE gs.sea = "Caribbean Sea"	24

three different NL questions, which are paraphrases of each other, and mapped them to the same SQL query (repeated in the last column).

Table 3(b) shows a second example generated by sampling two columns: ESTABLISHED of MONDIAL_ORGANIZATION and ELEVATION of MONDIAL_CITY. Sampling two columns leads to a join between the two tables, reflected in the SQL query in the last column of the table.

The rest of this section uses the Mondial benchmark to briefly illustrate the effect of Question Decomposition on Sample Retrieval.

Consider the following NL question in the Mondial benchmark:

Q_{17} : "Select cities whose population is greater than 100000, altitude greater than 2500, and the countries they belong to have population growth greater than 1."

Question Decomposition produces the following sub-questions for Q_{17}:

$Q_{17.A}$: "What are the cities with a population greater than 100000?"
$Q_{17.B}$: "What are the cities with an altitude greater than 2500?"
$Q_{17.C}$: "What are the countries with a population growth greater than 1?"

Table 4 shows some examples of NL Question/SQL Query pairs retrieved from the synthetic dataset for these sub-questions.

Table 5 presents the gold-standard SQL query corresponding to Q_{17}, and the SQL queries generated with and without Question Decomposition using GPT-4. Without Question Decomposition, GPT-4 joined just tables CITY and COUNTRY, and hallucinated, creating a restriction on column population_growth of table COUNTRY, which does not exist. With Question Decomposition, the NL question was broken into three simpler sub-questions, one for each restriction, and Sample Retrieval returned examples that helped GPT-4 correctly synthesize the required joins and restrictions.

Table 3. Examples of the synthetic dataset for Mondial.

(a) A simple example generated from sampling a single column.

#	NL question	SQL query
1	What are the lakes in the MONDIAL_LAKE table with an area greater than 500?	`SELECT NAME, AREA FROM MONDIAL_LAKE WHERE AREA >500`
2	Which lakes have an area larger than 500?	`SELECT NAME, AREA FROM MONDIAL_LAKE WHERE AREA >500`
3	lakes area larger than 500	`SELECT NAME, AREA FROM MONDIAL_LAKE WHERE AREA >500`

(b) A more complex example generated from sampling two columns.

#	NL question	SQL query
1	What is the time range of ESTABLISHED for organizations in the MONDIAL_ORGANIZATION table where the corresponding cities in the MONDIAL_CITY table have a non-null ELEVATION value?	`SELECT MIN(MO.ESTABLISHED), MAX(MO.ESTABLISHED) FROM MONDIAL_ORGANIZATION MO JOIN MONDIAL_CITY MC ON MO.CITY = MC.NAME WHERE MC.ELEVATION IS NOT NULL`
2	What is the time period when organizations were established in cities with known elevation values?	`SELECT MIN(MO.ESTABLISHED), MAX(MO.ESTABLISHED) FROM MONDIAL_ORGANIZATION MO JOIN MONDIAL_CITY MC ON MO.CITY = MC.NAME WHERE MC.ELEVATION IS NOT NULL`
3	time period organizations established cities known elevation values	`SELECT MIN(MO.ESTABLISHED), MAX(MO.ESTABLISHED) FROM MONDIAL_ORGANIZATION MO JOIN MONDIAL_CITY MC ON MO.CITY = MC.NAME WHERE MC.ELEVATION IS NOT NULL`

Table 4. Some examples retrieved for the sub-questions of Q_{17}.

Sub-Question	Examples Retrieved	
	NL Question	SQL Query
$Q_{17.A}$	countries cities population more than 100,000	SELECT DISTINCT MC.NAME FROM MONDIAL_COUNTRY MC JOIN MONDIAL_CITY MCI ON MC.CODE = MCI.COUNTRY WHERE MCI.POPULATION > 100000
$Q_{17.B}$	countries GDP higher than 100,000 and cities elevation greater than 1000 meters	SELECT E.COUNTRY, E.GDP, C.NAME, C.ELEVATION FROM MONDIAL_ECONOMY E JOIN MONDIAL_CITY C ON E.COUNTRY = C.COUNTRY WHERE E.GDP > 100000 AND C.ELEVATION > 1000
$Q_{17.C}$	Which countries have a status of 'member' and a population growth rate higher than 0.5?	SELECT MC.NAME FROM MONDIAL_ISMEMBER MI JOIN MONDIAL_COUNTRY MC ON MI.COUNTRY = MC.CODE JOIN MONDIAL_POPULATION MP ON MI.COUNTRY = MP.COUNTRY WHERE MI.TYPE = 'member' ANDMP.POPULATION_GROWTH > 0.5

Table 5. Comparison of SQL queries for Q_{17}.

NL Question	Gold-standard SQL Query	SQL Query generated without decomposition	SQL Query generated with decomposition
Select cities whose population is greater than 100000, altitude greater than 2500, and the countries they belong to have population growth greater than 1.	SELECT ci.name FROM mondial_city ci INNER JOIN mondial_country c ON c.code = ci.country INNER JOIN mondial_population p ON p.country = c.code WHERE ci.population > 100000 AND ci.elevation > 2500 AND p.population_growth > 1	SELECT city.name, city.population, city.elevation, country.population_growth FROM city JOIN country ON city.country = country.code WHERE city.population > 100000 AND city.elevation > 2500 AND country.population_growth > 1	SELECT c.name, c.population, c.elevation, p.population_growth FROM MONDIAL_CITY c JOIN MONDIAL_COUNTRY co ON c.country = co.code JOIN MONDIAL_POPULATION p ON co.code = p.country WHERE c.population > 100000 AND c.elevation > 2500 AND p.population_growth > 1

5 Experiments

Setup Configurations. All experiments used the text-to-SQL framework, described in Sect. 3, instantiated with the Mondial database. The experiments ran three versions of the framework, identified as:

- *SQLQueryChain*: just Steps S2 and S3 of the framework, that is, the standard SQLQueryChain. This is the baseline strategy.
- *SQLQueryChain with RAG*: Steps S1, S2, and S3, using the synthetic dataset with 60,000 pairs pre-computed for Mondial, defined in Sect. 4. The usual cosine similarity function was adopted to compare the user's NL question and the NL questions in the dataset. These experiments assess whether RAG improves accuracy for a given model.
- *SQLQueryChain with RAG and Question Decomposition*: Step S0, the modified Step S1, and Steps S2 and S3. These experiments assess whether Question Decomposition further improves accuracy for a given model, as proposed in this paper.

The final SQL queries were then run on the Mondial database. In all three versions, the GLM remains the only open flexibilization point of the framework since the experiments aimed to test different GLMs under the same conditions.

The experiments then instantiated the framework with the following models, running on different platforms:

- *Proprietary Large Language Models:* GPT-3.5-turbo-16K and GPT-4, running on the OpenAI (paid) platform.
- *Open-source Medium Language Models:* LLaMA-3-70B-instruct and DBRX, running on a server configured on the Azure platform.
- *Open-source Small Language Models:* Gemma 7B and Natural-SQL-7B by ChatDB, running locally on LM Studio.

Natural-SQL-7B by ChatDB was selected because it was fine-tuned for text-to-SQL and had good results. Gemma 7B was just released at the time of writing. The other models were chosen because they performed well on a coding task.

Performance Indicator. The experiments tested the *accuracy*, defined as the number of correct predicted SQL queries divided by the total number of SQL queries, as usual.

The experiments used an automated procedure to compare the *predicted* and the *gold-standard* SQL queries, entirely based on column and table values, and not just column and table names. The results of the automated procedure were manually checked to eliminate false negatives, caused mainly by mismatches in the target clause when there were multiple alternatives to identify entities.

Results. Recall that the Mondial benchmark has 100 NL questions, where 33 are simple, 33 are medium, and 34 are complex.

Table 6 summarizes the results for the selected models. Note that the lines are grouped according to the alternative of the framework used. Also, note that the experiments ran the SQLQueryChain with RAG and Question Decomposition alternative only for each of the small, medium, and large models that had the best accuracy in the SQLQueryChain with the RAG alternative. The results in Table 6 are contributions of this paper, except for Lines 1 and 2, published in [19], and Lines 7 and 8, published in [5].

Results for the Large Language Models. Lines 1 and 7 show the results for the framework instantiated with GPT-3.5-turbo-16K without RAG (Line 1) and with RAG (Line 7). The configuration with RAG achieved a total accuracy of 72%, surpassing all previous strategies tested in [18], except for the RAG-based technique with GPT-4 and C3 with GPT-4.

Lines 2, 8, and 13 show that, in all three alternatives, the framework instantiated with GPT-4 obtained the best total accuracy. The Query Decomposition technique led to a total accuracy (Line 13) comparable to the state-of-the-art tools reported in the Spider and BIRD leaderboards, recalling again that the Mondial benchmark is far more challenging than any of the databases used in Spider or BIRD. In particular, this configuration correctly translated 97% of the simple and medium NL questions, which is a remarkable achievement. However, GPT-4 is proprietary and runs on the OpenAI (paid) platform.

Results for the Medium Language Models. Lines 3, 9, and 14 correspond to the results of the framework instantiated with LLaMA-3-70B-instruct. Comparing LaMA-3-70B-instruct (Line 9) and GPT-3.5-turbo-16K (Line 7), the former

Table 6. Results for the different models - Mondial Benchmark.

#	Size	Strategy / Model	#Correct Predicted Queries				Accuracy			
			Simple	Medium	Complex	Total	Simple	Medium	Complex	Total
		SQLQueryChain								
1	L	GPT-3.5-turbo-16k	25	22	13	60	0,76	0,67	0,38	0,60
2	L	GPT-4	27	28	15	70	0,82	0,85	0,44	0,70
3	M	LLaMA-3-70B-instruct	22	21	23	66	0,67	0,64	0,68	0,66
4	M	DBRX	4	2	6	11	0,12	0,06	0,15	0,11
5	S	Natural-SQL-7B by ChatDB	28	25	11	64	0,85	0,76	0,32	0,64
6	S	Gemma 7B	12	7	2	21	0,36	0,21	0,06	0,21
		SQLQueryChain with RAG								
7	L	GPT-3.5-turbo-16K	28	23	21	72	0,85	0,70	0,62	0,72
8	L	GPT-4	28	31	27	86	0,85	0,94	**0,79**	0,86
9	M	LLaMA-3-70B-instruct	29	29	22	80	0,88	0,88	0,65	0,80
10	M	DBRX	21	15	10	46	0,64	0,45	0,29	0,46
11	S	Natural-SQL-7B by ChatDB	29	18	11	58	0,88	0,55	0,32	0,58
12	S	Gemma 7B	14	6	5	25	0,42	0,18	0,15	0,25
		SQLQueryChain with RAG and Question Decomposition								
13	L	GPT-4	32	32	25	89	**0,97**	**0,97**	0,74	**0,89**
14	M	LLaMA-3-70B-instruct	28	27	25	80	0,85	0,81	0,73	0,80
15	S	Natural-SQL-7B by ChatDB	27	19	16	62	0,82	0,58	0,47	0,62

achieved a better total accuracy (80%) and better accuracies in all types of NL questions. When comparing the RAG-only (Line 9) and the RAG with Query Decomposition techniques (Line 14), the total accuracy remained the same, but Query Decomposition improved the accuracy for the complex NL questions.

By contrast, Lines 4 and 10 indicate that DBRX had poor accuracy, which suggests that this model is not suited for text-to-SQL, although it performed well on a coding task.

These results suggest that an open-source, medium-sized model may replace a proprietary large-sized model. They imply that an NL database interface may run, with comparable accuracy, on a private platform, rather than on a proprietary platform, which may mitigate data privacy concerns.

Results for the Small Language Models. Lines 5, 11, and 15 show the results for the framework instantiated with Natural-SQL-7B by ChatDB. The model achieved the second-best accuracy (88%) among all models and alternatives for simple NL queries, surpassed only by GPT-4 with RAG with Query Decomposition. However, note that the use of the RAG technique substantially decreased the accuracy for medium NL questions and did not increase the accuracy for complex NL queries. By inspecting the sample SQL queries retrieved, one observes that the examples were of poor quality and referred to tables not directly related to input the NL question, which presumably confused the model and led it to generate incorrect SQL queries.

Lines 6 and 12 show the results for the text-to-SQL framework instantiated with Gemma 7B without RAG (Line 6) and with RAG (Line 12). The performance of the model was significantly less than that of Natural-SQL-7B by ChatDB. The Phi-3-mini-128K, Mistral-7B-Instruct-text2sql, and Code Llama

2-13B-instruct-text2-sql models were also tested, but had very poor performance, which indicates that these models are not a suitable choice.

These results suggest that a Small Language Model fine-tuned for text-to-SQL, running on a local small server, is a competitive option when the NL questions are mostly simple.

Additional Comments. The RAG technique of Sect. 3 injects knowledge of the database schema and the data semantics into a GLM. Overall, the results suggest that accuracy is improved for large and medium models but not necessarily for small ones. This is an effect that has to be further investigated. Apparently, the Sample Retrieval step fetched pairs whose SQL queries had tables unrelated to the user NL question, which confused the GLM.

In general, an analysis of the incorrect predicted SQL queries uncovered that the GLMs had difficulties interpreting the Mondial schema, which indicates that the database designer should revise the schema to facilitate the Schema Linking step given the expected NL questions. The designer should also consider creating views that introduce some redundancies to reduce the number of joins required to translate the user NL questions. For example, quite a few of the incorrect predicted SQL queries reflect a simple problem – several Mondial tables, such as

```
MONDIAL_CITY(NAME, COUNTRY, PROVINCE, POPULATION, LATITUDE,
             LONGITUDE, ELEVATION)
```

have a column named `COUNTRY` that is populated with the Country code, not the Country name. By contrast, the user NL questions refer to Countries by their names, not by their codes. This can be easily fixed by creating a view that includes a predefined column, `COUNTRY_NAME`, such as

```
MONDIAL_CITY_VIEW(NAME, COUNTRY_NAME, COUNTRY_CODE, PROVINCE,
                  POPULATION, ...)
```

This simple solution proved quite effective for a real-world private database with a large schema that was not considered *LLM-friendly* [20].

6 Conclusions and Directions for Future Work

This paper investigated how the model size affects the ability of a Generative AI Language Model (GLM) to support the text-to-SQL task for databases with sophisticated schemas typical of real-world applications. The paper described experiments using a text-to-SQL framework, instantiated with the Mondial database and a synthetic dataset with 60,000 pairs, pre-computed for Mondial. The experiments tested GLMs of different sizes under the same conditions.

The results suggest that, for a database with a sophisticated schema and a set of 100 challenging NL questions:

1. The text-to-SQL framework obtained the best results with GPT-4, as expected from previous results [5,19].

2. When compared with SQLQueryChain, the baseline, the RAG technique with Question Decomposition led to a significant improvement of the total accuracy for large and medium models, but not necessarily for small models.
3. An open-source medium-sized model may achieve an accuracy similar to a proprietary large-sized model.
4. An open-source small-sized model fine-tuned for text-to-SQL, running on a small local server, is a competitive option when the NL questions are simple.

The results reported in the paper, therefore, suggest that an open-source medium-sized model, coupled with a RAG technique with Question Decomposition, can achieve sufficient performance to provide the basis for an NL interface for a real-world database that may run on a private platform rather than on a proprietary platform, which may mitigate data privacy concerns.

When dealing with a Natural Language database interface based on a language model, a database designer should also worry about the design of a synthetic dataset for the database in question, as outlined in Sects. 3 and 4.2, to pass knowledge of the database schema and the data semantics to the language model. That is, the database designer should be concerned with exposing the database metadata and the data semantics to the language model, and not just to the programmers or end-users, which is a task different from traditional database design. However, when the problem is a mismatch between the vocabulary of the user NL questions and the vocabulary induced by the database schema, simply renaming the tables and columns or introducing views would be a viable solution, as illustrated at the end of Sect. 5.

There are multiple paths for future work. New, more powerful language models emerge with a high frequency. These models should be considered for the text-to-SQL task on real-world databases, using the Mondial benchmark and the framework introduced in this paper as a testbed. In another direction, the technique to create a synthetic dataset for a given database can be enhanced to generate more accurate samples. Lastly, the ambiguity problem, inherent to NL questions, must be addressed, perhaps using a disambiguation dialog.

Acknowledgement. This work was partly funded by FAPERJ under grants E-26/ 200.834/ 2021, by CAPES under grant 88881.134081/2016-01 and 88882.164913/2010-01, and by CNPq under grant 305.587/2021-8.

References

1. Abdin, M.I., et al.: Phi-3 technical report: a highly capable language model locally on your phone. Technical report MSR-TR-2024-12, Microsoft (2024). https://www.microsoft.com/en-us/research/publication/phi-3-technical-report-a-highly-capable-language-model-locally-on-your-phone/
2. Affolter, K., Stockinger, K., Bernstein, A.: A comparative survey of recent natural language interfaces for databases. VLDB J. **28** (2019). https://doi.org/10.1007/s00778-019-00567-8
3. AI@Meta: Llama 3 model card. Technical report, Meta (2024). https://github.com/meta-llama/llama3/blob/main/MODEL_CARD.md

4. Anthropic: Introducing the next generation of claude (2024). https://www.anthropic.com/news/claude-3-family
5. Coelho, G., et al.: Improving the accuracy of text-to-SQL tools based on large language models for real-world relational databases. In: Strauss, C., et al. (eds.) DEXA 2024. LNCS, vol. 14910, pp. 1–25. Springer, Cham (2024). https://doi.org/10.1007/978-3-031-68309-1_8
6. DataBricks: Introducing DBRX: a new state-of-the-art open LLM (2024). https://platform.openai.com/docs/models/overview
7. DeepSeek-AI, et al.: Deepseek LLM: scaling open-source language models with longtermism (2024). https://doi.org/10.48550/arXiv.2401.02954
8. Gan, Y., et al.: Towards robustness of text-to-SQL models against synonym substitution. CoRR abs/2106.01065 (2021). https://doi.org/10.48550/arXiv.2106.01065
9. Gan, Y., Chen, X., Purver, M.: Exploring underexplored limitations of cross-domain text-to-SQL generalization. In: Proceedings of 2021 Conference on Empirical Methods in Natural Language Processing, pp. 8926–8931 (2021). https://doi.org/10.18653/v1/2021.emnlp-main.702
10. Gao, D., et al.: Text-to-SQL empowered by large language models: a benchmark evaluation. Proc. VLDB Endow. **17**(5), 1132-1145 (2023). https://doi.org/10.14778/3641204.3641221
11. GeminiTeam: Gemini 1.5: Unlocking multimodal understanding across millions of tokens of context (2024). https://storage.googleapis.com/deepmind-media/gemini/gemini_v1_5_report.pdf
12. GemmaTeam: Gemma: Open models based on gemini research and technology. arXiv preprint (2024). https://doi.org/10.48550/arXiv.2403.08295
13. Guo, C., et al.: Retrieval-augmented GPT-3.5-based text-to-SQL framework with sample-aware prompting and dynamic revision chain. In: Luo, B., Cheng, L., Wu, Z.G., Li, H., Li, C. (eds.) ICONIP 2023. LNCS, vol. 14452, pp. 341–356. Springer, Singapore (2024). https://doi.org/10.1007/978-981-99-8076-5_25
14. Jiang, A.Q., et al.: Mistral 7b. arXiv preprint (2023). https://doi.org/10.48550/arXiv.2310.06825
15. Lewis, P., et al.: Retrieval-augmented generation for knowledge-intensive NLP tasks. In: Larochelle, H., Ranzato, M., Hadsell, R., Balcan, M., Lin, H. (eds.) Advances in Neural Information Processing Systems, vol. 33, pp. 9459–9474. Curran Associates, Inc. (2020). https://api.semanticscholar.org/CorpusID:218869575
16. Li, J., et al.: Can LLM already serve as a database interface? A big bench for large-scale database grounded text-to-SQLs. In: Proceedings of the 37th International Conference on Neural Information Processing Systems. NIPS 2023. Curran Associates Inc., Red Hook (2024)
17. Manning, C.D.: Human language understanding & reasoning. Daedalus **151**(2), 127–138 (2022). https://doi.org/10.1162/daed_a_01905
18. Nascimento, E.R.: Querying databases with natural language: the use of large language models for text-to-SQL tasks. Master's thesis, Dissertation presented to the Graduate Program in Informatics, PUC-Rio (2024)
19. Nascimento, E.R., et al.: Text-to-SQL meets the real-world. In: Proceedings of the 26th International Conference on Enterprise Information Systems, vol. 1, pp. 61–72 (2024)
20. Nascimento, E.R., et al.: My database user is a large language model. In: Proceedings of the 26th International Conference on Enterprise Information Systems, vol. 1, pp. 800–806 (2024)
21. OpenAI: Openai models (2024). https://platform.openai.com/docs/models

22. Panda, S., Gozluklu, B.: Build a robust text-to-SQL solution generating complex queries, self-correcting, and querying diverse data sources. AWS Machine Learning Blog (2024)
23. Pourreza, M., Rafiei, D.: DTS-SQL: decomposed text-to-SQL with small large language models. arXiv preprint (2024). https://doi.org/10.48550/arXiv.2402.01117
24. Warkentin, T., Zhai, X., Peran, L.: Introducing paligemma, gemma 2, and an upgraded responsible AI toolkit. Technical report, Google (2024). https://developers.googleblog.com/en/gemma-family-and-toolkit-expansion-io-2024/
25. Yu, T., et al.: Spider: a large-scale human-labeled dataset for complex and cross-domain semantic parsing and text-to-SQL task. In: Proceedings of 2018 Conference on Empirical Methods in Natural Language Processing, pp. 3911–3921 (2018). https://doi.org/10.18653/v1/D18-1425
26. Zhong, V., Xiong, C., Socher, R.: Seq2sql: generating structured queries from natural language using reinforcement learning. CoRR abs/1709.00103 (2017). https://doi.org/10.48550/arXiv.1709.00103

Establishing Traceability Between Natural Language Requirements and Software Artifacts by Combining RAG and LLMs

Syed Juned Ali[1(✉)], Varun Naganathan[2], and Dominik Bork[1]

[1] TU Wien, Business Informatics Group, Vienna, Austria
{syed.juned.ali,dominik.bork}@tuwien.ac.at
[2] Microsoft, Hyderabad, India
varun.naganathan@microsoft.com

Abstract. Software Engineering aims to effectively translate stakeholders' requirements into executable code to fulfill their needs. Traceability from natural language use case requirements to classes in a UML class diagram, subsequently translated into code implementation, is essential in systems development and maintenance. Tasks such as assessing the impact of changes and enhancing software reusability require a clear link between these requirements and their software implementation. However, establishing such links manually across extensive codebases is prohibitively challenging. Requirements, typically articulated in natural language, embody semantics that clarify the purpose of the codebase. Conventional traceability methods, relying on textual similarities between requirements and code, often suffer from low precision due to the semantic gap between high-level natural language requirements and the syntactic nature of code. The advent of Large Language Models (LLMs) provides new methods to address this challenge through their advanced capability to interpret both natural language and code syntax. Furthermore, representing code as a knowledge graph facilitates the use of graph structural information to enhance traceability links. This paper introduces an LLM-supported retrieval augmented generation approach for enhancing requirements traceability to the class diagram of the code, incorporating keyword, vector, and graph indexing techniques, and their integrated application. We present a comparative analysis against conventional methods and among different indexing strategies and parameterizations on the performance. Our results demonstrate how this methodology significantly improves the efficiency and accuracy of establishing traceability links in software development processes.

Keywords: Large Language Models · LLM · Requirements Traceability · Retrieval Augmented Generation · Requirements Engineering

W. Maass et al. (Eds.): ER 2024, LNCS 15238, pp. 295–314, 2025.
https://doi.org/10.1007/978-3-031-75872-0_16

1 Introduction

Traceability information is a fundamental prerequisite for many essential software maintenance and evolution tasks, such as change impact and software reusability analyses. Traceability can also help validate that the right system is being built, effectively meeting user and business needs as specified in the use case. A traceable relationship between requirements, conceptual design, and implementation helps effective communication about the software across stakeholders. However, manually maintaining traceability is costly and error-prone [14].

Unified Modeling Language (UML) class diagrams are a de-facto standard for the static structural representation of a system's design [3]. However, there can be several reasons for employing traceability from use case requirements to the classes in source code rather than UML class diagrams and then subsequently update the UML class diagram such as—*i*) Readily available and regularly updated source code particularly those involving legacy systems or open-source projects whereas UML class diagrams may not be regularly updated or might not exist at all, especially in agile development settings where documentation might lag behind code changes, *ii*) Richness of information in source code especially the availability of the business logic that the UML class diagram might lack, *iii*) Automatic generation of UML diagrams from source code using modern tools and IDEs (Integrated Development Environments)[1] and *iv*) Dynamic adaptation to system changes, thereby keeping the code to UML class diagrams synchronous with the latest system state.

Given that source code changes more frequently than most other artifacts during software development, traceability from source code ensures that the derived UML diagrams are kept synchronous with the latest system state and thereby helps maintain the relevance and usefulness of the UML diagrams as conceptual models of the system. Figure 1 illustrates the support that traceability from requirements to classes in source code provides for the evolution of UML class diagrams. Therefore, in this work, our approach focuses on improving the state-of-the-art of use case requirements to source code classes traceability, as a prerequisite for the approach in Fig. 1.

Automated approaches that utilize textual similarities between artifacts to establish trace links exist, however, these approaches tend to achieve low precision at reasonable recall levels, as they are not able to bridge the semantic gap between high-level NL requirements and code [14]. Recent advancements in Large Language Models (LLM) have marked a substantial progression in software engineering. The utilization of LLMs in software engineering can be effectively reframed into data, code, or text analysis tasks. The applicability of LLMs is particularly pronounced in tasks such as code summarization [35], which involves yielding an abstract NL depiction of a code's functionality, as well as the generation of well-structured code [40] and code artifacts like annotations [22].

[1] https://staruml.io/, https://pypi.org/project/pyreverse/.

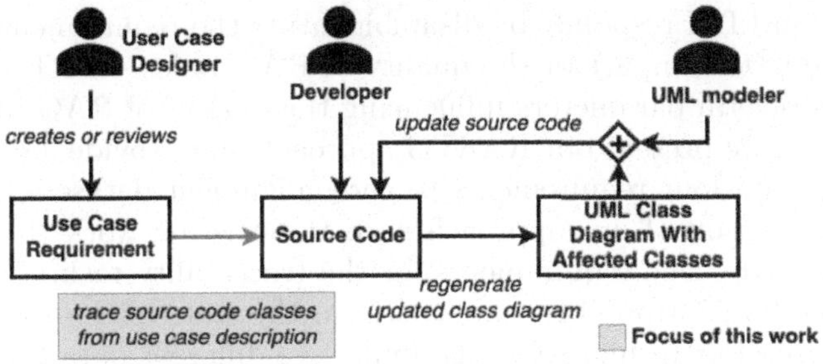

Fig. 1. Requirements to Code Traceability-based UML Classes Evolution

Despite their ability to interpret the syntax and logic of programming languages, LLMs face huge challenges in applying this technical understanding to non-technical, use case-driven code descriptions. Documentation like code comments, while informative, often remains incomplete, overly technical, and detached from the actual code structure, and fails to consider the broader use case and context of the code's application. A recent survey on the use of LLMs in software engineering [15] highlights that LLMs often produce syntactically correct but functionally inadequate code, compromising the reliability and efficacy of LLM-based code generation. The survey reveals that LLMs are employed in software development in 58.37% of cases but only in 4.72% of requirements engineering scenarios. This discrepancy underscores LLMs' efficiency in generating syntactically accurate solutions when provided with clear requirements, yet indicates a gap in addressing ambiguities within requirements engineering.

LLMs are trained on extensive data, limiting their efficacy on tasks requiring specialized domain knowledge. Retrieval Augmented Generation (RAG) techniques enhance LLM's performance by utilizing external knowledge sources to augment the LLM's inherent data representation. This approach offers notable advantages over purely generative models: 1) knowledge is not merely encoded within model parameters but is dynamically incorporated in a scalable, plug-and-play fashion; and 2) it leverages human-authored texts for response generation, which simplifies the generation process and may improve output quality. As highlighted in the survey by Hou (2023) [15], the increasing complexity of tasks in this field necessitates more advanced, tailored computational strategies.

To address these crucial challenges, we introduce a novel **R**etrieval **A**ugmented **G**eneration (RAG)-based approach for code repository-specific **R**equirements **T**raceability (**RARTG**). Our approach is designed to bridge the gap between abstract, high-level use-case requirements and their corresponding source code. By leveraging code comments and the class functions dependency graph as contextual anchors for the RAG model, our solution provides an alignment of code with use-case requirements. The performance of an LLM with RAG depends on the quality of the RAG index. The RAG index acts as a contextual bridge between the query and the response from an LLM. The better the context provided by a RAG index for given requirements in natural language as a query is, the better an LLM responds by disambiguating the requirements. Therefore, we aim to study the impact of the quality of RAG index on RT by evaluating the impact of several parameters influencing the quality of RAG indexes.

In summary, we present our RARTG approach and provide a comprehensive evaluation of it on four requirements to code alignment datasets from [14] and provide a comparison of our approach with the existing work [14] (cf. Sect. 5) for the natural language requirements for the traceability task. The evaluation reveals our method's capability to outperform the state-of-the-art on the given datasets. Further our results show the impact of different data sources and the constructed RAG indexes for traceability, thereby showing that an improvement in the semantic quality of the RAG index leads to an improvement in requirements to code traceability. Finally, we provide the entire source code for the implementation of our approach.

In the remainder of this paper, Sect. 2 introduces relevant foundations to our approach. We present the related work in Sect. 3. In Sect. 4, we present the architecture and details of our RAG-based approach. In Sect. 5, we provide the evaluation of our approach. In Sect. 6 we discuss our results and findings and provide some insights and finally, we conclude in Sect. 7.

2 Background

Traceability in software engineering refers to the ability to link and trace the life of a requirement, forward and backward, throughout the stages of the Software Development Life Cycle. By establishing a clear and coherent connection between requirements and their corresponding implementation in the code, traceability not only supports effective project management but also provides a roadmap for future maintenance and upgrades. This end-to-end visibility is crucial in complex software projects, where understanding how each piece of code reflects specific requirements can significantly improve the efficiency and effectiveness of the software development process, e.g., connecting requirements to source code elements provides insight into what has been implemented and where [14].

Large Language Models - In the field of language processing, traditional Language Models (LMs) have been foundational elements, establishing a basis for text generation and understanding [28]. Increased computational power, advanced machine learning techniques, and access to very large-scale data have led to a significant transition into the emergence of LLMs. Equipped with expansive and diverse training data, these models have demonstrated an impressive ability to simulate human linguistic capabilities [15]. The training of LLMs involves learning patterns and structures in language by analyzing and predicting text sequences, which enable LLMs to generate coherent and contextually relevant responses. Their applications are diverse and impactful, ranging from natural language processing tasks like translation, summarization, and question-answering, to more creative uses such as content generation and dialogue systems [13,15]. LLMs have become integral in enhancing user experiences in virtual assistants, providing support in customer service through chatbots, and even assisting in writing and educational tools [19].

Retrieval Augmented Generation (RAG) is an approach in natural language processing that combines the strengths of information retrieval and language generation. In this methodology, a system first retrieves relevant information from a large dataset, like a database or the internet, and then uses this information to generate a response or output. RAG leverages a combination of information retrieval and neural network-based natural language generation to vectorize documents. The process involves two main components i.e., a *retriever* and a *generator*. The retriever is responsible for fetching relevant context from a large corpus of documents. The retrieval can be based on classical information retrieval techniques such as TF-IDF best matching (BM) algorithm [32], which is a ranking function used by search engines to estimate the relevance of documents to a given search query, or advanced vector embeddings-based similarity techniques. Vector-embedding-based retrieval techniques vectorize both the query and the documents as points in a shared continuous high-dimensional vector space. The embeddings are typically produced by models such as BERT [7] (Bidirectional Encoder Representations from Transformers) or its variants. These embeddings aim to capture deep semantic meaning of words and phrases in the context of the entire document, rather than inisolation. The generator, often an LLM, then takes the retrieved documents and the original query to generate a coherent response. The generator has been trained on a vast amount of text and thus has learned to predict the next word in a sequence, generating human-like text based on the context it is given. RAG allows the model to access a wide range of information beyond its training data, enabling it to provide more accurate, detailed, and contextually relevant responses.

3 Related Work

There has been significant work conducted in the area of applying natural language processing (NLP) and machine learning (ML) techniques for software requirements traceability. Several existing systematic literature reviews and mapping studies elaborate on the intersection of the RT and NLP or ML [31,38]. Hou et al. [15] provide a systematic mapping study at the intersection of LLMs and Software Engineering (LLM4SE). In the following, we first discuss the works involving traceability in UML models and source code, and then the role of LLMs in the context of RT. Finally, we discuss the role of context enrichment in improving RT.

3.1 Requirements Traceability in Models

Mills et al. [26] present an approach that supports the maintenance of traceability relations between requirements, analysis and design models of a software systems expressed in UML. Eyl et al. [9] present a metamodel expressing relationships between requirements and the UML model at the meta-level. For each meta-requirement, the author adds a 'REQTYPE' attribute to decide which UML diagram shall be used for the traceability. Netaji et al. [30] present a graph-based information retrieval approach to identify the requirement change impact on design models. Yazawa et al. [39] present an approach to derive a functional model from a use case diagram, a structure diagram, and a transition diagram. By decomposing the existing functional model into model components, traceability links are recovered based on guidelines that allow a mapping of model components to requirements. Divya et al. [8] present an approach to calculate the semantic traceability between the use case documentation and the sequence diagram. Khlif et al. [20] present an approach to support traceability between design, requirements, and code. Their approach extracts an expanded textual description from a natural language text available in UML models in order to trace between related elements belonging to requirements, design, and code while using an information retrieval technique.

3.2 Requirements Traceability in Source Code

Hey et al. [14] propose an approach for traceability link recovery by leveraging fine-grained, method-, and sentence-level similarities between the artifacts using word embeddings. Guerrouj et al. [12] present a solution that uses deep learning to incorporate requirements semantics and domain knowledge into the tracing solution. Tian et al. [34] adapt the word embeddings for traceability recovery tasks, and handle the out-of-vocabulary words involved in tracing words the artifacts that might not be in the vocabulary of an embedding model.

3.3 LLM-Based Requirements Traceability in Source Code

Anaphoric ambiguity in software requirements arises when a single reader can interpret a natural language requirement in multiple ways, or different readers have varying understandings of the same requirement. Unclear and ambiguous software requirements can lead to suboptimal or even invalid software artifacts during later development stages. Moharil et al. [27] and Ezzini et al. [10] have empirically demonstrated the significant role of LLMs such as BERT [7] and SpanBERT [18] in effectively addressing anaphoric ambiguity. Lin et al. [23] found that T-BERT can effectively migrate knowledge from code search to NL artifacts to programming language artifacts traceability, even with limited training instances. It outperforms existing techniques in accuracy and can be adapted to different domains without intermediate training for each project, offering a promising step toward practical, trustworthy traceability. Sridhara et al. [33] revealed that ChatGPT excels in addressing anaphoric ambiguity in software requirements. ChatGPT consistently demonstrated its capability to accurately identify antecedents. These studies assert the valuable role of LLMs like GPT-4 [2] or the most capable open source LLMs like Llama 3[2] can play in enhancing

[2] https://ai.meta.com/blog/meta-llama-3/.

the clarity and precision of software requirements, thereby contributing to more effective software development with minimal interpretational uncertainties.

3.4 Context Enrichment for Requirements Traceability

Chen et al. [5] propose a self-enhanced automatic traceability link recovery approach based on structure knowledge mining for small-scale labeled data. This work enhances the semantic representations of artifacts by mining context information from the code structure. Lin et al. [24] exploit the idea that software source code contains a large amount of software-specific conceptual knowledge and semantic relatedness between queries and documents could be measured according to software-specific concepts involved in them. Iyer et al. [17] present a data-driven approach for generating high-level summaries of source code which can later be used as a semantic representation of the code for RT.

3.5 Synopsis

A limitation of existing works in RT for models and source code include the fact that such works employ syntactical methods and guidelines for RT. Even the semantic approaches involve *shallow* semantics, i.e., semantics derived from textual similarity and therefore miss out on capturing the 'purpose' of the UML model or the code of the class and thereby cannot bridge the semantic gap between the UML model/code and the corresponding NL requirement.

In summary, we believe that none of the presented works use the benefits of RAG-based approaches for software RT. To the best of our knowledge, ours is the first work that combines RAG with LLM-based code summarization and combined (keyword, vector, and graph) indexing for RT. Our research contributes to the growing body of work seeking to bridge the gap between high-level requirements and executable code. By integrating the advances in LLMs with RAG techniques and exploiting the latent knowledge within codebases and the knowledge graph-based structural representation of software code, we provide a novel solution that tackles the challenges outlined by previous research while paving the way for more improvements in requirement-to-code traceability.

4 Retrieval Augmented Requirements Traceability Generation

Next, we present the details of our RAG-based approach for code repository-specific traceability. We present a novel architecture for enhancing traceability from natural language requirements to code through the utilization of Llama 3 and a suite of indexing and retrieval mechanisms. Our methodology is structured into several interconnected stages, as depicted in Fig. 2. The approach involves an *indexing stage* (steps 1 and 2) and a *querying stage* (steps 3, 4, and 5).

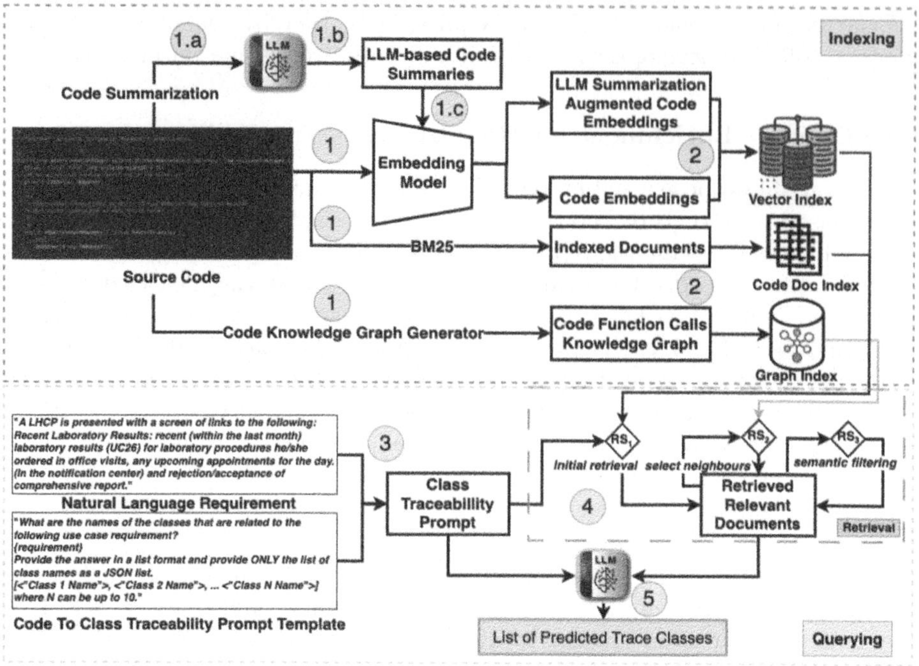

Fig. 2. Retrieval Augmented Requirements Traceability Generation

4.1 Indexing Stage

The indexing stage involves LLM-based code summary generation and the subsequent storage indexes creation from the available codebase for efficient storage and retrieval of code documents, thereby facilitating quick and relevant matches, given a specific use-case requirement.

Code Summary Generation - There are cases where the classes *i)* do not have any docstrings; *ii)* the docstrings are incomplete; or *iii)* the docstrings are generic and do not capture the high-level purpose in the codebase and the relationship to other classes. To circumvent these issues, we use an LLM to generate the class docstring using the source code of the whole class. Note that all the subsequent prompts used in this paper are a result of rigorous prompt engineering, i.e., constructing different prompts and evaluating which prompt provides the best results. This task was entirely manual, and we chose the prompt that provided the best results. Below we show the code summarization prompt. The ⟨CODE_EXAMPLE⟩ and ⟨DOC_TEMPLATE⟩ are examples of code and structure of the document that are used to provide some contextual information for code summarization.

> You are an expert in summarizing code. Given a class in a Java code file, generate a class summary that can be used to map the code to a given use case requirement of the provided java code. The summary should capture the purpose of the class and its attributes and methods. Given a doc with the following structure that will be useful for use case requirements with code elements traceability: ⟨DOC_TEMPLATE⟩. Code example: ⟨CODE_EXAMPLE⟩ Provide the summary in simple abstract use case scenario language in the following format: Class Name: ¡Class Summary¿ Method Name: ¡Method Summary¿ . . Method Name N: ¡Method Summary N¿ Here is the code - ⟨code⟩

After LLM-based code summary generation, we create several code indexes.

Code Documents Keyword Index - We create a keyword-based index (KI) that treats the code documents as natural language documents and applies standard text preprocessing steps of stemming and stopwords, i.e., common frequent words removal from the code. We use the PorterStemmer [36] to stem the words. We store the generated index in a vector database. We create separate keyword indexes with and without code summaries in the code files.

Vector Index. In this step, we use a multi-lingual embedding model [4]which is well suited for its versatility in Multi-Linguality to generate the text embeddings of the code documents and subsequently construct a vector index (VI). It can support more than 100 working languages, leading to new state-of-the-art performances on multi-lingual and cross-lingual retrieval tasks. We chose a multi-lingual embedding model because our dataset contains source code in two languages i.e., English and Italian. We store the generated embeddings of the code documents in a vector database. We create separate vector indexes with and without code summaries in the code files.

Knowledge Graph Index. A knowledge graph index (KGI) is constructed from the dependency graph of the modules in the codebase. We refer to this knowledge graph as *Function Dependency Graph* (FDG). Each node of the FDG stores class names and the existing code documentation of the class as the class content. Next, we generate triples of subject, object, and a predicate where the subject is the calling method's class and the object is the called method's class. Finally, we store the created FDG in a Neo4j database to support querying.

Index Creation. Subsequently, in step two, the system generates three specialized indexes as shown in Fig. 2. The first index is constructed using only the code comments and the names of the classes, class attributes and method names in the codebase. The second index is constructed using docstrings generated from an LLM as a code summarization response in the data embedding step and finally, the last index is for indexing the node embeddings from the FDG. The indexes generated using only the code docstrings do not consider any external sources of information or structural semantics from the code via interconnections from the code and only focus on the available semantics of the code from the code's textual content. The LLM-based indexes aim to improve on the first indexes by augmenting the documentation by an LLM-generated docstring, thereby including the LLM's knowledge as an external source of knowledge. However, this index still does not involve the structural semantics of the codebase. Therefore, the knowledge graph index aims to capture the structural semantics from the code. Furthermore, as performed in [14], we can optionally add the method call triples of a given class in the knowledge graph during the creation of the VIs and KIs. This step adds the structural connections explicitly to the indexes. However, as the authors in [14] showed, the effect of this addition on the traceability depends on the semantic quality of the connections with respect to the purpose of the class, which can result in an improved or worsened index quality. We investigate the impact of this step in our evaluation.

4.2 Querying Stage

In this stage, we use the constructed indexes of the indexing stage to first retrieve a set of documents relevant to the use case requirements and then subsequently using the contents of these documents as context to the LLM for predicting the classes relevant to the given requirement.

Requirement Traceability Prompt Generation. Upon receiving a NL requirement, in step three the system first uses a prompt template to construct a prompt that will be used to fetch the documents relevant to the query. The generated prompt is subsequently provided, along with the contents of the retrieved documents as context to the LLM to generate the final answer. For the purpose of requirements to code traceability, we constructed the following template where the use-case requirements is filled in the place of the 'requirements' placeholder.

> What are the names of the classes that are related to the following use case requirement? ⟨requirement⟩
>
> Provide the answer in a list format and provide ONLY the list of class names as a JSON list. [¡"Class 1 Name"¿, ¡"Class 2 Name"¿, ... ¡"Class N Name"¿] where N can be up to 10.

Furthermore, a requirement that is too brief and lacks sufficient detail can result in poor recall of initial document retrieval. Therefore, to enhance the semantic quality of the initial requirements, we employ query expansion by generating semantically similar requirements. We use LLM to generate these similar requirements, which are then added as context to the prompt. However, this step does not guarantee improved traceability, as its effectiveness depends on the quality of the generated requirements. We investigate the impact of this step in our evaluation. After formulating the requirement-specific prompt, our system proceeds to fetch the relevant documents using various indexes from the indexing stage.

Relevant Documents Retrieval. The retrieval step takes place in step four in three stages denoted by retrieval stages RS_i in Fig. 2. In RS_1, the keyword and vector indexes are queries to give a combined set (union) of the relevant documents. In case of the VI, the retrieval is achieved by querying the indexes for vectors closest to the vector representation of the requirement. Note that the requirement is transformed into a vector using the same embedding model which is used to generate the code structural and semantic embeddings in step 1 so that the requirement shares the same vector space as the vector representation of the existing docstrings and LLM-generated docstrings. This initial selection using the keyword and vector indexes can retrieve semantically similar documents, however this approach may miss out on the structurally connected relevant documents, thereby reducing the recall of the approach. Therefore, in RS_2, the structurally connected neighbouring documents of the retrieved relevant documents in the knowledge graph are added to the list of relevant documents. This forms the content of all candidate documents that can be given as a context to the LLM. However, this further has few limitations. Firstly, retrieving a higher number of nodes (all the neighbours in this case) can affect the precision of our approach by retrieving false positives. Secondly, a context created from a large number of documents does not fit the maximum prompt size allowed for the LLM. To mitigate these limitations, in RS_3, we add a semantic filter that selects only the documents with a semantic similarity higher than a predefined threshold. Note, that this threshold is more relaxed than the threshold for document retrieval in RS_1 to allow keeping the documents that were not selected in RS_1 but not entirely semantically unrelated. In summary, our retrieval mechanism combines multiple indexes to construct a unified context and provide that as input to the LLM for preparing the response.

Response Generation. In the final step, the LLM receives the contextualized prompt, which includes the query, i.e., the natural language requirement and the relevant code elements and documentation. The LLM utilizes this enriched context to formulate a response that aims to predict the classes relevant to the requirement.

5 Evaluation

Now, we elaborate on an extensive evaluation of our approach. First, we provide the description of the experimental setup involving the investigated research questions, the datasets description and evalution metrics, and finally the results.

5.1 Research Questions

We aim to investigate the following research question with our approach:

[**RQ.1**] How does RARTG perform compared to the state-of-the-art?
[**RQ.2**] How do various parameterizations influence the traceability performance?

- [**RQ.2.1**] How does incorporating the LLM generated summaries influence traceability?
- [**RQ.2.2**] How does incorporating the structural knowledge graph index influence traceability?
- [**RQ.2.3**] How does query expansion by adding similar requirements to the initial requirements influence traceability?
- [**RQ.2.4**] How does incorporating method calls explicitly to the VI and KI influence traceability?
- [**RQ.2.5**] How does incorporating combining all the three indexes influence traceability compared to a single index (VI or KI)?

Table 1. Datasets

Project	Domain	Language			Codebase description		
		Use-case	Code	Docstrings	# Usecases	#Classes	#Links
eTour	Tourism	EN	Java-EN	EN	58	116	308
iTrust	Healthcare	EN	Java-EN	EN	131	226	286
SMOS	Education	IT	Java-IT	IT	67	100	1044
eAnci	Governance	IT	Java-IT	IT	139	55	567

5.2 Experimental Setup

Datasets: We use the datasets with the descriptions given in Table 1. The table shows the language of the use-case descriptions and the code artifacts. EN and IT indicate if the language of the artifact is English or Italian. The programming language for all the datasets is Java, however, the identifiers, such as class and method names can be in Italian as well. We see that for two datasets, eTour and iTrust, the artifacts are in English and for the remaining two datasets, the artifacts are in Italian. These datasets are provided by the Center of Excellence for Software & Systems Traceability (CoEST) [1] and are commonly used in automated traceability link recovery [14,25,29]. These datasets are suitable for our study as they provide trace links between NL requirements and source code. Note that iTrust is composed of Java and JSP target artifacts. However, we only consider the Java target artifacts and links here.

RARTG Configuration Parameters: There are five controlling parameters that can affect the performance of RARTG: *i*) Use Generated Summary (GS) - which controls if the indexes use the LLM-generated summaries during indexing, *ii*) Use KG Index (KGI) - which controls if document retrieval from KGI using RS_2 and RS_3 is performed or not during RAG context generation, *iii*) Use Method Calls (MC) - which controls if method calls are explicitly added as strings in the documents during indexing stage, *iv*) Use Query Expansion (QE) - which controls if extra semantically similar requirements are generated and added to the context before response generation using LLM and *v*) Combine Indexes (CI) - which controls if all the three indexes are used together or not. These five parameters are used to respond to the five sub-RQs of RQ2. We execute the experiments on all the combinations of the values of these five parameters to evaluate the impact of these parameters. We term a single combination of values of all the parameters a single *configuration*.

Evaluation Metrics: In all our experiments we use the precision, recall and F1-score to evaluate our approach. The F1-score is the preferred metric for classification tasks and is commonly used for traceability link recovery [14]. It is defined as the harmonic mean of precision and recall. In case of traceability link recovery, precision reveals how accurate an approach proposes correct trace

Table 2. Traceability comparison across evaluation datasets

Dataset	iTrust			eANCI			SMOS			eTour		
Approach	Prc	Rec	F1	Prc	Rec	F1	Prc	Rec	F1	Prc	Rec	F1
Baseline	0.176	0.353	0.235	0.294	0.220	0.252	0.443	0.297	**0.356**	0.411	0.623	**0.495**
RARTG-C2	0.284	0.286	0.285	0.737	0.178	0.287	0.526	0.118	0.192	0.488	0.239	0.321
RARTG-C1	**0.289**	0.292	**0.290**	**0.779**	0.199	**0.317**	**0.608**	0.126	0.209	**0.543**	0.242	0.334

Prc: Precision, Rec: Recall

links. It measures the ratio of correctly proposed links to all proposed links. Recall shows the ability of an approach to propose all correct links. It measures the share of expected trace links that were actually found by an approach. High F1-scores should be the goal for all automated traceability link recovery approaches [11], as they indicate the approaches' ability to produce the expected results without missing links and producing many false positives. In our work, we not only focus on the F1-score but also on precision individually due to the research gap that indicates that existing approaches perform poorly, specifically in precision (cf. [14]).

5.3 Results

In the following, we provide the results of our experimental evaluation and respond to the RQs.

Response to RQ1: In order to respond to RQ1, we show the performance of our approach regarding the selected evaluation metrics in Table 2. Out of all the different configurations, we selected the *configuration* that gives the best F1-scores. We consider the results from [14] on the same four datasets as the baseline. The results in Table 2 show, that the top two performing configurations of RARTG outperform the baseline for iTrust and eANCI datasets for F1-scores. Our approach improved the state-of-the-art F1-scores by almost 6% for both datasets. In case of the SMOS and eTour dataset, our approach underperforms with respect to the F1-score due to insufficient recall scores. Moreover, given that our approach focused on improving the precision scores for traceability based on the research gap, it is important to note that our approach consistently sufficiently outperforms the baseline with respect to precision. Furthermore, given that we used a single multi-lingual embedding model, it is important to note that our approach is robust to the language of the artifacts. This makes our approach independent of any translation step to English. In summary, these results clearly show the feasibility and value of our approach to support precise natural language to code traceability.

Response to RQ2: We performed a statistical evaluation of the F1-scores for different configurations. We had five controlling RARTG configuration parameters i.e., GS, MC, QE, KGI, and CI. To evaluate the impact of each of these

Table 3. Impact of parameter change on the F1-score

Parameter	iTrust			eANCI			SMOS			eTour		
	TS	P	Effect	TS	P	Effect	TS	P	Effect	TS	P	Effect
GS	2.60	0.02	**SP**	5.48	<0.05	**SP**	0.40	0.70	-	1.60	0.13	-
MC	−2.36	0.03	**SN**	2.24	0.04	**SP**	3.22	<0.05	**SP**	1.78	0.09	Pos.
QE	−4.77	<0.05	**SN**	1.72	0.10	-	0.29	0.77	-	-3.14	0.01	**SN**
KGI to VI	25.84	0.02	**SP**	−0.31	0.77	-	0.36	0.73	-	15.75	<0.05	**SP**
KGI to KI	0.18	0.87	-	0.40	0.70	-	12.24	<0.05	**SP**	3.08	0.02	**SP**
CI to VI	6.34	0.00	**SP**	0.58	0.58	-	1.74	0.12	-	7.96	<0.05	**SP**
CI to KI	−0.19	0.86	-	3.42	0.01	**SP**	16.32	<0.05	**SP**	3.06	0.02	**SP**

SP: Significant Positive, SN: Significant Negative, -: Inconclusive, Pos. - Positive
TS: T-statistic, P: p-value

parameters, we evaluate the change in F1-score by changing the value of the parameter in question and keeping the remaining parameters fixed. We do this exercise for all the combinations of the fixed values for each parameter. For e.g., to evaluate the impact of using LLM generated summaries, we calculated the change in F1-scores with and without using GS by keeping a particular combination of the values of other parameters fixed. We calculate the change in F1-scores for all possible combinations and calculate the T-statistic and P-values [21] to determine the significance of change in F1-scores. A p-value of less than 0.05 indicates a significant impact on the F1-score. The t-statistic indicates a significant positive or negative impact depending upon the sign of the t-statistic. Table 3 shows the impact of all five parameters on the F1-scores. The KGI and CI parameters have two rows because we evaluate the impact of using KGI on top of an already existing VI in one case, and an already existing KI in another. Similarly, we evaluate the impact of using CI compared to configurations using single VI or single KI.

Impact of GS: The p-values for GS in Table 3 show a significant positive impact of adding LLM generated summaries to the F1-scores for iTrust and eANCI dataset. Note that our approach also outperforms for these two datasets. This indicates using LLM-generated summaries that capture the high-level purpose can be a very useful contrary to using the technical code docstrings. Adding LLM summaries do not have a significant impact on SMOS and eTour datasets, however the t-statistic still shows a slight positive impact which indicates an overall positive potential of adding LLM generated summaries.

Impact of MC: The p-values for the impact of adding method calls directly to indexes show a mixed result, i.e., for iTrust we see a significantly negative impact and for eANCI and SMOS, we see a significantly positive result. This indicates that using method calls information directly in the document indexes may or may not be beneficial depending on the dataset and the relatedness of the semantic quality of the function calls with the purpose or the associated use-cases of the classes.

Impact of QE: The p-values for the impact of QE are significantly negative on two out four datasets. This is an interesting result because intuitively we would expect that adding semantically related information to an already existing document would improve the retrieval of semantically related documents, however, our results indicate a negative impact on the performance. This indicates that query expansion by adding more questions may add more noise to the data that reduces the semantic similarity of a NL use-case requirement with code. Furthermore, the impact of QE may be dataset dependent as well. A dataset may require use-case language to be even syntactically close to the code. For e.g., a use-case requirement extract from the eTour dataset - "Use case name: DeleteCulturalHeritage. View the list of CulturalHeritage as a result of the use case SearchCulturalHeritage" directly hints towards a match with code with class names based on the keywords. In such cases keyword-based retrieval methods may outperform retrieval methods based on vector-based methods, therefore, adding extra information may act as noise.

Impact of KGI: The p-values for the impact of using KGI with VI and KI show, that KGI can have a positive impact as can be seen for iTrust, SMOS and eTour datasets. This result is quite expected because our RAG-based approach gave lower recall scores because of its strict semantic or even keyword-based similarity threshold, whereas a knowledge graph index adds structurally connected documents to the list of relevant documents that may not necessarily be related based on the semantic or keyword similarity and thereby missed by VI or KI.

Impact of CI: The p-values for the impact of using a combined index comprising of all three indices shows an overall positive impact. Using a CI with VI shows a significant improvement in iTrust and eTour datasets and using CI with KI shows a significant improvement for three out of four datasets. This result underpins the value of our approach that combines the different indexes for relevant documents retrieval and subsequent querying the LLM for extracting the requirement-specific classes from the retrieved documents.

6 Discussion

In the following, we discuss our results regarding both of our research questions and provide some meta-insights that we learned from our experiments.

Our results showed, that LLMs can be used to enrich the existing documentations which lack the contextual semantics to fill the abstraction gaps as pointed out in [16]. In our work, we exploited LLM's code summarization capabilities to associate high-level descriptions and tasks related to the abstract description of the source code thereby creating a contextual summary of the code which enabled improved traceability. This is particularly useful in cases where the code is not well documented and hence the semantic gap between the technical and business layers is high. We note that LLMs have shown a remarkable expertise in code generation from natural language descriptions [41]. However, semantically ambiguous descriptions can lead to incorrect code generation. Using our approach to incorporate contextual, semantically enriched summaries with a high-level description can enable an unambiguous natural language description to code generation. Finally, we note that combining a structural and a semantic index is beneficial and we learnt that a knowledge graph representation of the code provides significant value toward requirements to code traceability.

While investigating the reason for low recall scores, we analysed the RAG pipeline. The effectiveness of RAG-based applications heavily relies on the quality of RAG index such that for a given query, all the information relevant for answering the query should not only be retrieved but also fit into the maximum allowed prompt length for an LLM (e.g., 4096 tokens for Llama 3). This limits the number of documents that can be retrieved and hence it becomes imperative for the RAG-based approach to have a strict relevance check on the indexed documents. Due to this, a number of moderately relevant documents are missed. However, this also means that the document that are retrieved have a higher relevance accuracy. This can be preferable over higher recall in a setting like RT which ensures that the links established between requirements and code are accurate and reliable, reducing the likelihood of irrelevant connections that can mislead developers and complicate maintenance and verification processes [6].

Nevertheless, the lower recall underscores potential areas for future research and refinement of our model, indicating a clear path for progressive enhancements. As part of our future work, we aim to improve the recall scores by relaxing the initial documents retrieval constraints to retrieve more documents and then employing domain-specific criteria to perform a relevant information retrieval from the retrieved documents itself. This approach involves a layered documents retrieval that incrementally builds a more relevant, requirement-specific context from a larger set of documents, thereby not compromising with recall. We aim to make our approach accessible by making the source code openly available on GitHub[3]. Our tool provides support for creating indexes, code summarization, text embddings, setting up multiple retrieval mechanism including vector, keyword and knowledge graph index so that users can simply extend our implementation for their solution.

Lastly, assessing threats to validity is essential to ensure the reliability and generalizability of your findings. We use the four different types of validity threats as defined by Wohlin et al. [37]. If the generated code summaries or indexed documents miss information critical to traceability, then the construct validity is threatened. We mitigated this threat by manually refining prompts and examining the generated code summaries and their alignment with the code purpose. We mitigated the construct validity threats on the indexes by evaluating the different indexes on four datasets for the traceability quality. The dataset quality of the initial traceability requirements dataset threatens the internal validity of our work. We mitigated this threat by choosing quality evaluated datasets used in literature [1]. If the datasets are not diverse enough (e.g., all from similar types of software or similar domains), the results might not be widely applicable. Our work mitigates this threat by choosing all the datasets from different

[3] https://github.com/junaidiiith/nl2codeTrace

domains. The precision, recall, and F1 metrics need to be reliably measured to ensure that the observed effects are real and not due to measurement errors or randomness. We mitigated this error by repeating the experiments by making the index creation reproducible and fixing a seed and temperature value for an LLM to make the results reproducible.

7 Conclusion

In this work, we presented a novel RAG-based approach that enhances traceability from natural language use-case requirements to code repositories. We leveraged the synergy between code comments and the code dependency tree within the RAG framework, coupled with a technique to generate improved code summarizations. After an empirical evaluation of our approach, we have demonstrated an effective method for bridging the divide between high-level business requirements and the corresponding technical code constructs. The empirical evaluation reveals that a configuration that integrates class names and LLM-generated code summaries with the KGI created from class function calls improves tracing code from natural language requirements. Further, we evaluated the impact of using different indexes and their combination thereof and provided a statistical evaluation to analyze the impact of each parameter on RT. In the future, we aim to extend our solution to develop a tool for tracking a UML class diagrams evolution and impact analysis with changing requirements, thereby providing an feedback during design time about the history and impact of the requirement on the software artifacts.

References

1. Center of excellence for software & systems traceability (COEST) (2024). http://sarec.nd.edu/coest/datasets.html. Accessed 3 June 2024
2. Achiam, J., et al.: GPT-4 technical report. arXiv preprint arXiv:2303.08774 (2023)
3. Booch, G., Rumbaugh, J.E., Jacobson, I.: The Unified Modeling Language User Guide - Covers UML 2.0. 2nd edn. Addison Wesley Object Technology Series. Addison-Wesley (2005)
4. Chen, J., Xiao, S., Zhang, P., Luo, K., Lian, D., Liu, Z.: M3-embedding: multi-linguality, multi-functionality, multi-granularity text embeddings through self-knowledge distillation. In: Findings of the Association for Computational Linguistics ACL 2024, pp. 2318–2335 (2024)
5. Chen, L., Wang, D., Shi, L., Wang, Q.: A self-enhanced automatic traceability link recovery via structure knowledge mining for small-scale labeled data. In: 2021 IEEE 45th Annual Computers, Software, and Applications Conference (COMPSAC), pp. 904–913. IEEE (2021)
6. De La Vara, J.L., Wnuk, K., Berntsson-Svensson, R., Sánchez, J., Regnell, B.: An empirical study on the importance of quality requirements in industry. In: SEKE, pp. 438–443 (2011)

7. Devlin, J., Chang, M., Lee, K., Toutanova, K.: BERT: pre-training of deep bidirectional transformers for language understanding. In: Proceedings of the 2019 Conference of the North American Chapter of the Association for Computational Linguistics: Human Language Technologies, NAACL-HLT 2019, Minneapolis, pp. 4171–4186. Association for Computational Linguistics (2019). https://doi.org/10.18653/V1/N19-1423
8. Divya, K., Subha, R., Palaniswami, S.: Similar words identification using Naive and TF-IDF method. Int. J. Inf. Technol. Comput. Sci. (IJITCS) **6**(11), 42 (2014)
9. Eyl, M., Reichmann, C., Müller-Glaser, K.: Traceability in a fine grained software configuration management system. In: Winkler, D., Biffl, S., Bergsmann, J. (eds.) SWQD 2017. LNBIP, vol. 269, pp. 15–29. Springer, Cham (2017). https://doi.org/10.1007/978-3-319-49421-0_2
10. Ezzini, S., Abualhaija, S., Arora, C., Sabetzadeh, M.: Automated handling of anaphoric ambiguity in requirements: a multi-solution study. In: Proceedings of the 44th International Conference on Software Engineering, pp. 187–199 (2022)
11. Gotel, O., et al.: The grand challenge of traceability (v1. 0). In: Software Systems Traceability, pp. 343–409 (2012)
12. Guerrouj, L., Bourque, D., Rigby, P.C.: Leveraging informal documentation to summarize classes and methods in context. In: 2015 IEEE/ACM 37th IEEE International Conference on Software Engineering, vol. 2, pp. 639–642. IEEE (2015)
13. Hadi, M.U., et al.: A survey on large language models: applications, challenges, limitations, and practical usage. Authorea Preprints (2023)
14. Hey, T., Chen, F., Weigelt, S., Tichy, W.F.: Improving traceability link recovery using fine-grained requirements-to-code relations. In: 2021 IEEE International Conference on Software Maintenance and Evolution (ICSME), pp. 12–22. IEEE (2021)
15. Hou, X., et al.: Large language models for software engineering: a systematic literature review. CoRR abs/2308.10620 (2023). https://doi.org/10.48550/ARXIV.2308.10620
16. Huang, Y., Liu, Z., Chen, X., Luo, X.: Automatic matching release notes and source code by generating summary for software change. In: 2016 6th International Conference on Digital Home (ICDH), pp. 104–109. IEEE (2016)
17. Iyer, S., Konstas, I., Cheung, A., Zettlemoyer, L.: Summarizing source code using a neural attention model. In: 54th Annual Meeting of the Association for Computational Linguistics 2016, pp. 2073–2083. Association for Computational Linguistics (2016)
18. Joshi, M., Chen, D., Liu, Y., Weld, D.S., Zettlemoyer, L., Levy, O.: Spanbert: improving pre-training by representing and predicting spans. Trans. Assoc. Comput. Linguist. **8**, 64–77 (2020)
19. Kasneci, E., et al.: Chatgpt for good? On opportunities and challenges of large language models for education. Learn. Individ. Differ. **103**, 102274 (2023)
20. Khlif, W., Kchaou, D., Bouassida, N.: A complete traceability methodology between UML diagrams and source code based on enriched use case textual description. Informatica **46**(1) (2022)
21. Kim, T.K.: T test as a parametric statistic. Korean J. Anesthesiol. **68**(6), 540 (2015)
22. Liang, Y., Zhu, K.: Automatic generation of text descriptive comments for code blocks. In: Proceedings of the AAAI Conference on Artificial Intelligence, vol. 32 (2018)

23. Lin, J., Liu, Y., Zeng, Q., Jiang, M., Cleland-Huang, J.: Traceability transformed: generating more accurate links with pre-trained BERT models. In: 2021 IEEE/ACM 43rd International Conference on Software Engineering (ICSE), pp. 324–335. IEEE (2021)
24. Lin, Z., Zou, Y., Zhao, J., Xie, B.: Improving software text retrieval using conceptual knowledge in source code. In: 2017 32nd IEEE/ACM International Conference on Automated Software Engineering (ASE), pp. 123–134. IEEE (2017)
25. Lohar, S., Amornborvornwong, S., Zisman, A., Cleland-Huang, J.: Improving trace accuracy through data-driven configuration and composition of tracing features. In: Proceedings of the 2013 9th Joint Meeting on Foundations of Software Engineering, pp. 378–388 (2013)
26. Mills, C., Escobar-Avila, J., Haiduc, S.: Automatic traceability maintenance via machine learning classification. In: 2018 IEEE International Conference on Software Maintenance and Evolution (ICSME), pp. 369–380. IEEE (2018)
27. Moharil, A., Sharma, A.: Tabasco: a transformer based contextualization toolkit. Sci. Comput. Program. **230**, 102994 (2023)
28. Moore, R.C., Lewis, W.: Intelligent selection of language model training data. In: Proceedings of the ACL 2010 Conference Short Papers, pp. 220–224 (2010)
29. Moran, K., et al.: Improving the effectiveness of traceability link recovery using hierarchical Bayesian networks. In: Proceedings of the ACM/IEEE 42nd International Conference on Software Engineering, pp. 873–885 (2020)
30. Nejati, S., Sabetzadeh, M., Arora, C., Briand, L.C., Mandoux, F.: Automated change impact analysis between sysml models of requirements and design. In: Proceedings of the 2016 24th ACM SIGSOFT International Symposium on Foundations of Software Engineering, pp. 242–253 (2016)
31. Pauzi, Z., Capiluppi, A.: Applications of natural language processing in software traceability: a systematic mapping study. J. Syst. Softw. **198**, 111616 (2023)
32. Robertson, S., Zaragoza, H., et al.: The probabilistic relevance framework: BM25 and beyond. Found. Trends®Inf. Retrieval **3**(4), 333–389 (2009)
33. Sridhara, G., Mazumdar, S., et al.: Chatgpt: a study on its utility for ubiquitous software engineering tasks. arXiv preprint arXiv:2305.16837 (2023)
34. Tian, Q., Cao, Q., Sun, Q.: Adapting word embeddings to traceability recovery. In: 2018 International Conference on Information Systems and Computer Aided Education (ICISCAE), pp. 255–261. IEEE (2018)
35. Wan, Y., et al.: Improving automatic source code summarization via deep reinforcement learning. In: Proceedings of the 33rd ACM/IEEE International Conference on Automated Software Engineering, pp. 397–407 (2018)
36. Willett, P.: The porter stemming algorithm: then and now. Program **40**(3), 219–223 (2006)
37. Wohlin, C., Runeson, P., Höst, M., Ohlsson, M.C., Regnell, B., Wesslén, A.: Experimentation in Software Engineering. Springer, Heidelberg (2012)
38. Xu, C., Li, Y., Wang, B., Dong, S.: A systematic mapping study on machine learning methodologies for requirements management. IET Software **17**(4), 405–423 (2023)
39. Yazawa, Y., Ogata, S., Okano, K., Kaiya, H., Washizaki, H.: Traceability link mining - focusing on usability. In: 41st IEEE Annual Computer Software and Applications Conference, COMPSAC 2017, vol. 2, pp. 286–287. IEEE Computer Society (2017). https://doi.org/10.1109/COMPSAC.2017.254

40. Yin, P., Neubig, G.: A syntactic neural model for general-purpose code generation. arXiv preprint arXiv:1704.01696 (2017)
41. Zan, D., et al.: Large language models meet NL2Code: a survey. In: Proceedings of the 61st Annual Meeting of the Association for Computational Linguistics (Volume 1: Long Papers), pp. 7443–7464 (2023)

Applications of Conceptual Modeling

GenACT: An Ontology-Based Temporal Web Data Generator

Gunjan Singh[1(✉)], Udit Arora[1], Shashikant Kumar[1], Riccardo Tommasini[2,5], Pieter Bonte[3], Sumit Bhatia[4], and Raghava Mutharaju[1]

[1] Knowledgeable Computing and Reasoning Lab, IIIT, Delhi, India
{gunjans,udit18417,shashikant18096,raghava.mutharaju}@iiitd.ac.in
[2] LIRIS Lab, INSA, Lyon, France
riccardo.tommasini@insa-lyon.fr
[3] University of Tartu, Tartu, Estonia
riccardo.tommasini@ut.ee
[4] KU Leuven Campus Kulak, Kortrijk, Belgium
pieter.bonte@kuleuven.be
[5] MDSR, Adobe Inc., Delhi, India
sumit.bhatia@adobe.com

Abstract. Time is a fundamental concept in data processing. The growth of social media (SM) data and the rise of the Internet of Things (IoT) underscores the necessity for studying temporal data on the Web. However, accessing realistic temporal data poses significant challenges across data collection, knowledge representation, and real-time provisioning, with no comprehensive solution available yet. To tackle these challenges, we introduce GenACT, a novel data generator rooted in the dynamics of Academic Conference Tweets (ACT), which serves as an ideal domain for eliciting application scenarios spanning temporality, dynamicity, and timeliness. The foundation of GenACT is a domain-specific ontology crafted to conceptualize tweets around an Academic Conference Event (ACE) realistically. The ACE ontology is available in all four OWL 2 profiles. Additionally, RDF instantiation allows for real-time simulation of ongoing academic discussions on Twitter. GenACT stands out for its ability to configure different data segments using SPARQL-based partitioning strategies. This versatility makes it adaptable to various analytical tasks, enabling researchers to focus on specific aspects of the data for their studies. GenACT is designed to seamlessly provide temporal and static data in a streaming format, tailored specifically for applications in studying knowledge graph evolution, temporal reasoning, and stream reasoning. The ontology, code, and documentation are available under the Apache 2.0 License at https://github.com/kracr/temporal-data-generator.

Keywords: Data Generation · Stream Reasoning · Knowledge Representation

W. Maass et al. (Eds.): ER 2024, LNCS 15238, pp. 317–336, 2025.
https://doi.org/10.1007/978-3-031-75872-0_17

1 Introduction

The domain of knowledge representation and reasoning has evolved significantly with the rise of knowledge-intensive temporal data, largely influenced by social media and the Internet of Things, which resemble dynamic knowledge graphs (KGs) due to their structure and the ever-evolving nature of data. Although KGs are becoming more prevalent, there remains a lack of exploration in analyzing and managing their evolution. In their recent survey, Polleres et al. [26] encouraged a closer look at KG evolution. However, to study KG evolution effectively, we need more control over the construction and maintenance of the KGs. Even when KG changelogs and versions are available, e.g., in the case of Wikidata[1] or DBpedia [21], the existing real-world datasets fall short in three crucial aspects required to capture real-world activities in data [26]: (a) *temporality*, i.e., the ability of the KG to capture the order and duration of the events, is often incomplete or enforced in RDF via reification; (b) *dynamicity*, i.e., the ability of the KG to capture progressive variation, is usually implemented using versioning and is not well documented; (c) *timeliness*, i.e., the ability of the KG to stay up to date, is neglected, especially when the velocity of change meets streaming scenarios [7].

While the previously discussed aspects are crucial, KGs must also exhibit additional characteristics to capture the dynamic and complex nature of real-world activities accurately: (a) *diverse graph patterns*: real-world data rarely follows a single, rigid structure, and KGs that support a variety of graph patterns can better represent the intricate relationships between entities. (b) *temporal granularity*: real-world events often consist of subevents occurring over different timeframes, and KGs should accommodate these varying timescales. This enables the modeling and analysis of relationships with different complexities. (c) *scalability and data fluctuations*: information density can fluctuate with sudden data bursts during significant events, and KGs that incorporate these fluctuations accurately represent diverse data volumes. (d) *segmented by attributes*: different entities possess unique characteristics, and KGs segmented by attributes can capture these variations, allowing for more nuanced analysis and exploration of specific entity types. KGs endowed with these characteristics offer a significant advantage: *the ability to tailor data to simulate several application scenarios.*

Unfortunately, real-world KGs with these comprehensive capabilities are currently rare. Incorporating this flexibility is crucial for KGs to become more suitable for applications like temporal web data generation and analysis, where capturing the dynamic intricacies of real-world activities is paramount. *Synthetic data generation* [3] offers the flexibility to explore all these features, possibly enhancing evaluation accuracy and enabling realistic simulation of dynamic KG evolution. However, existing works in the area are limited in scope (cf. Section 6).

To address these gaps, this work introduces GenACT, a synthetic data generator for the Web. GenACT data are modeled after realistic data from a knowledge-intensive yet interpretable domain, i.e., Academic Conference Tweets (ACT). From a comprehensive study, we found that ACT is the ideal domain to elicit application scenarios that span temporality, dynamicity, and timeliness.

[1] https://www.wikidata.org/wiki/Wikidata:Main_Page.

We built an OWL 2 [13] ontology based on tweets related to academic conferences. This ontology is available in four flavors corresponding to each of the four OWL 2 profiles (EL, QL, RL, DL) [13]. This extends the utility of GenACT for applications modeled using any of these profiles. Furthermore, GenACT generates data that can be partitioned into segments based on specific graph patterns and attributes (e.g., conferences, users). These partitions exhibit varying data peaks and intricate relationships, allowing researchers and developers to conduct insightful analyses.

Outline. Section 2, first elaborates on the rationale behind selecting this domain, domain analysis, and different application scenarios that illustrate the practical applications of GenACT. Section 3 discusses the knowledge representation efforts, i.e., an overview of the construction of the ontologies involved. The data generation process is discussed in Sect. 4, while Sect. 5 engages in a discussion regarding the generated data, evaluating its effectiveness on two reasoners, CSparql2[2] and RDFox [22], thereby demonstrating the potential of the generated data. Additionally, we address limitations and outline potential avenues for future development. Section 6 provides a comprehensive review of related work, followed by conclusions in Sect. 7.

2 Academic Conference Tweets (ACT)

Indeed, drawing upon the principles outlined in [20], a critical step in the development of ontologies is defining a well-scoped domain. The domain needs rich temporality (timestamps, durations, versions) to model evolving knowledge. It should also be dynamic and timely, with continuous information flow and real-time interactions. Ideally, the domain should resonate with the target research community, be representable using ontological modeling frameworks like OWL 2, and allow simulated data generation. Social media platforms like Twitter or Reddit provide an excellent source for such temporally rich data due to their continuous streams of user-generated content, which capture evolving trends, events, and discussions in real-time. However, collecting real data from these platforms has become increasingly challenging due to their stringent terms of service, limited API access, and the high costs associated with data extraction. Beyond the technical hurdles, there are also significant legal and ethical barriers, such as data privacy regulations which impose strict restrictions on how data can be collected and used. These factors make it difficult to obtain large-scale, real-world datasets from these sources.

Twitter stood out as an ideal data source for our synthetic data generation approach due to its event-driven nature and medium to high rate of data generation [24,29]. Within Twitter, we specifically target tweets surrounding academic conferences. This focus offers two advantages: first, ACT inherently captures the detailed sequence of events (rich temporality) surrounding the conference, which is crucial for knowledge modeling. Second, event-related tweets exhibit extended engagement (Fig. 1), aligning with our modeling goals.

[2] https://github.com/streamreasoning/csparql2.

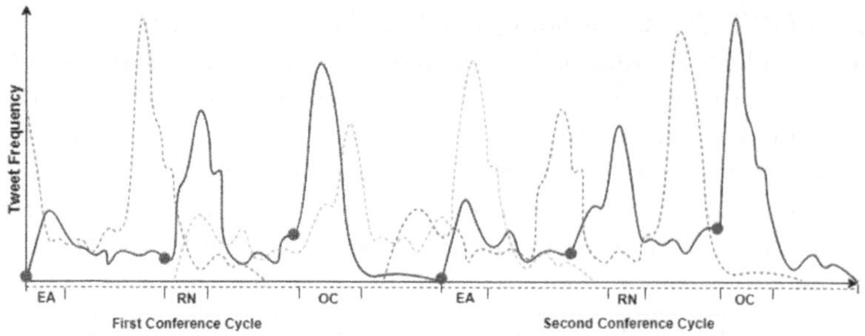

Fig. 1. Conference Lifecycle: dots represent Absolute Events. **Legend:** [E]arly [A] announcements, [R]review [N]otifications, or the currently [O]ngoing [C]conference. Colours and strokes differentiate the conferences, running simultaneously yet in different phases, animating the temporal landscape.

The ACT domain accurately captures the "when" (temporality), "what is new" (dynamicity), and "staying informed" (timeliness) aspects crucial for representing real-world activities. Temporality guarantees the precise sequencing and duration of events, enabling queries like "What happened before the call for papers?" It accurately represents the chronological order of events, such as announcements, submissions, and notifications. Furthermore, ACT incorporates simple ordering, e.g. order (conference announcements precede call for papers), and all forms of temporality [26]: timestamped event data (Tweets), versioned data (conference series and user bios updates), and intervals (conference duration). Dynamicity ensures real-time adaptation to new tweets, updates, and schedule changes, providing users with the most current information. ACT encompasses continuous information flow (real-time schedule updates), interactions (social media engagement), and progressive data changes (user profiles and conference details). Timeliness includes prompt notifications and reminders, enabling effective user participation in the conference process. ACT involves prompt notifications (session starts and submission deadlines), timely data updates (new information reflection), and responsive adjustments (adaptive scheduling). Moreover, ACT offers a rich context to explore and model different language constructs from the OWL 2 profile (discussed in Sect. 3), facilitating diverse reasoning challenges, which are reflected in the scenarios provided in the next section that can be used as CQs.

Furthermore, the domain's accessibility and familiarity within the academic community make it highly suitable for research and analytical purposes. Moreover, since Twitter data is not openly accessible, enabling data generation is valuable for stimulating research, underscoring its relevance and impact in knowledge representation and reasoning domains.

Competency Questions (CQs). We explored the domain's suitability in simulating real-world temporal applications by formulating scenarios that can be used as CQs [30], listed in Table 1. Due to space constraints, these scenarios are

Table 1. Scenarios for Competency Questions.

	Scenario	Temporality	Dynamicity	Timeliness
1	Trending Topics Across Conferences *Keeps users posted on topics trending across conferences*	✓	✗	✓
2	Active Research Groups *Monitor key players and their collaborators in given fields*	✓	✓	✗
3	Publication Activities of Organizations *Analyse researchers' interdisciplinary work*	✓	✓	✗
4	Conference Match by Research Interests *Identifies conferences that match users' research interests*	✗	✓	✗
5	Interdisciplinary Authors *Identify potential interdisciplinary collaborations*	✓	✓	✗
6	Session Popularity *Identify the most popular topics and speakers*	✓	✓	✗
7	Global Research Focus *Identifies countries most active in a given research field*	✓	✓	✓
8	Funding Organizations *Identifies organizations financing researchers*	✗	✓	✗
9	Networking Opportunities *Identifies researchers interested in the same given areas*	✓	✓	✗
10	Collaboration Networks *Monitors academic collaboration networks to understand research dynamics*	✓	✓	✗
11	Non-academic Collaborators *Monitors industry-academia relations to highlight knowledge transfer*	✗	✓	✗
12	Geographical Distribution *Identifies active countries in given research fields*	✓	✓	✗
13	Platform Impact *Analyse conference trends on various platforms*	✓	✗	✓

presented concisely, yet each entry effectively captures the essence of its corresponding query. The queries corresponding to the competency questions can be found in our GitHub repository[3]. The table also further emphasizes opportunities for modeling temporality, dynamicity, and timeliness, thus addressing the dynamic nature of academic research.

The following conceptualization is required to understand the ontology modeling efforts presented later. In particular, we introduce the notion of Temporal and Continuous Queries for the unfamiliar reader that are needed to address notions such as temporality, dynamicity, and timeliness that push the envelope of the standard Semantic Web stack [13]. We use the CQ 3: "Monitoring Publication Activities of Organizations" as an example.

[3] https://github.com/kracr/temporal-data-generator.

Definition 1. *Temporal queries offer native support for retrieving and manipulating time-referenced data, such as timestamps, durations, and time intervals..*

Listing 1.1 shows an example query implemented using a temporal extension of SPARQL (T-SPARQL). The query execution leverages the `INTERSECT` clause to exploit data temporality in RDF, in this case, the year 2023.

```
SELECT ?organization ?domain (COUNT(?paper) AS ?publications)
INTERSECT(?t,"[2023-01-01,2023-12-31]")
WHERE {
  ?paper :hasAuthor ?author; ?author :hasAffiliation ?
    organization. | t.
  ?paper :hasDomain ?domain.
}
GROUP BY ?organization ?domain
```

Listing 1.1. Counting papers published in 2023 with T-SPARQL.

Definition 2. *A continuous query is a query whose evaluation is repeated at regular time intervals and whose results are the union of results [6].*

Listing 1.2 shows an example query implemented using a streaming extension of SPARQL (RSP-QL). The query execution leverages the `Named Window` class to chunk the input stream into finite portions and continuously updates the results every 10 min over a 1-hour window. RSP-QL allows static and streaming data to join for enrichment and reasoning.

```
REGISTER STREAM <http://example.org/stream/publications>
FROM NAMED WINDOW :W1 ON <stream1> [RANGE PT1H STEP PT10M]
SELECT ?organization ?domain (COUNT(?paper) AS ?publications)
WHERE {
    WINDOW :W1 {
  ?paper :hasAuthor ?author; ?author :hasAffiliation ?
    organization. | t.
  ?paper :hasDomain ?domain.
    }
}
GROUP BY ?organization ?domain
```

Listing 1.2. RSP-QL Query to continuously monitor publication activities of organizations over a window of 1 hour.

3 Ontology Modeling

This section presents our efforts in capturing the knowledge for the ACT domain. The conceptualization is based on a comprehensive study of academic conferences conducted on Twitter. The study aimed to gain insights into the temporal patterns and content categories associated with tweets about conference events.

Domain Understanding. The tweets on an academic conference span several months, commencing with early announcements encompassing conference announcements and the calls for papers. The process then navigates through distinct phases such as submission reminders, review notifications, and post-paper acceptance tweets, culminating in the conference period marked by active sharing of presentations and experiences. Post-conference engagement also occurs as the community reflects on the event's impact, while random tweets inject diversity, including keynote announcements, discussions on trends, and user insights. The tweets around an Academic Conference Event (ACE) span over several months with different data peaks at different time intervals, similar to real-world scenarios. Moreover, the cyclic nature of conferences, occurring regularly every year, further helps simulate real-world scenarios.

Table 2. Overview of Tweet Categories. The shape indicates the category.

Tweet Category	Before Conference	During Conference	After Conference
Announcements	Main Conference ▲ Call for Papers ▲ Keynotes, Panelists and Sponsors ▲	-	Best Paper Awards ▲ Next Conference ▲
Reminders	Submission ● Registration ●	Upcoming Sessions ●	-
Notifications	Accepted Papers ■ Schedule Changes ■	Ongoing Sessions ■	-
Insights	Based on Accepted Papers or Schedule Changes ☆	Based on Presentations ☆	Recap and Reflections ☆
Others	Excitement for the Conference ◆ Gratitude for the Grants and Volunteer Opportunities ◆	Job Postings ◆	Acknowledgement and Gratitude ◆

We categorized tweets into five main types: Announcements, Reminders, Notifications, Insights, and Others. Table 2 indicates different categorizations and the types of tweets that fall into each category. Announcements, reminders, notifications, and insights follow a structured sequence, while the Others category encompasses tweets that may occur randomly. Such a categorization clarifies the data generation algorithm's flow. Moreover, it sets a basis for extensibility, allowing easy integration of new categories or templates in the future.

Note that this list is not a comprehensive list of tweet types, and there may be additional categories, such as tweets expressing disappointment after rejections or complaints, among others. However, we have included a significant number of tweet templates that replicate the real-world scenarios described earlier. Our data generation algorithm is adaptable and can incorporate new templates or categories (see Sect. 4) in the future.

We can correlate the tweeting pattern with the concept of 'Absolute Events', as depicted in Fig. 1. Three distinct data peaks, each signifying an absolute event,

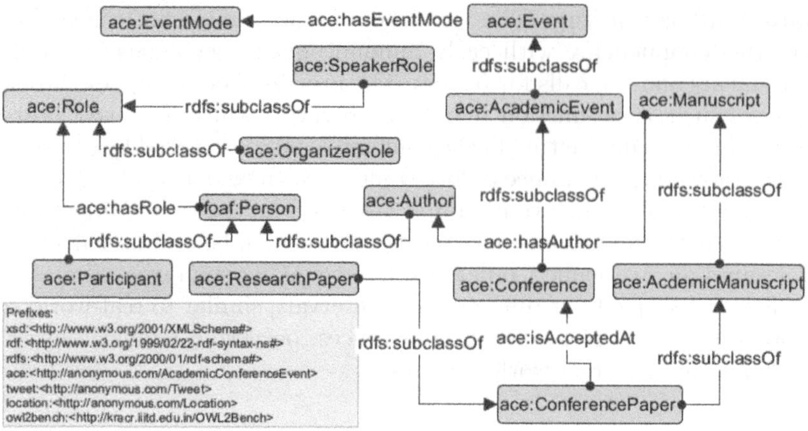

Fig. 2. Partial class/relationship hierarchy in ACE Ontology.

mark critical junctures like 1) the Early Announcement (EA) encompassing the main Conference Announcement (CA) and the first Call for Papers (CfP), 2) Review Notifications (RN), and 3) the ongoing conference (OC). Notably, peaks rise significantly during notification periods, show a small increase just before the conference, reach their highest point during the event, and gradually decline in the post-conference phase.

Domain Conceptualisation. Our ontologies address temporality by representing order, eventful timestamps, and duration intervals [26].
<u>The Ordered Time Model</u> captures the relation between absolute events. Indeed, we can ask CQs such as "*Was the call for paper announced before the conference?*" to have a negative (or positive) answer and can be leveraged to test the temporal consistency of the data.
<u>The Absolute Time Model</u> adds to the previous model the notion of timestamps and allows a finer grain comparison. In particular, it is possible to ask questions about trends (cf Sect. 1), quantify time windows, or compute historical queries like "*How many times, on average, authors write during a conference*?"
<u>The Interval Time Model</u>. We adopted this model for the conference (and its sessions). They are described by start and end dates and duration (e.g., five days). Such modeling enables asking questions such as "*What happened during ESWC 2024?*", and "*What is the session that overlaps with session 3, and is having the most participation*?".

ACE Ontology. We developed four moderate-sized ontologies describing an ACE, one for each OWL 2 profile (EL, QL, RL, and DL). The ontologies can be accessed from the GitHub repository (see Footnote 3). Each ontology consists of concepts and properties describing various aspects of academic conferences. The hierarchy among some classes, including the relations between them, is shown in Fig. 2.

Every ontology includes the classes `Conference`, `Organizer`, `Talks`, `Manuscript`, `Author`, `Role`, `EventMode` and `Attendee`, object properties such

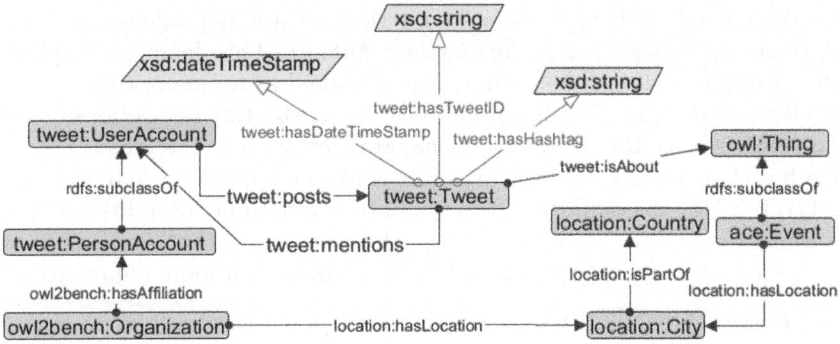

Fig. 3. Other Schemas

as `hasAuthor`, `attends`, and `hasCollaborator` and data properties such as `hasTitle`, `hasLocation`, and `givesTalkOn`. We ensure that the axioms cover all the constructs corresponding to a particular OWL 2 profile. In Table 3, we include a few examples of the axioms in description logics [14] from ACE ontology.

To expedite development, the ACE ontology reuses concepts such as `foaf:Person` and `foaf:Organization`. We also incorporate concepts such as `Student`, and `Organization`, from OWL2Bench [31], a benchmark based on a university domain designed for evaluating OWL 2 reasoners.

To demonstrate the syntactic and semantic limitations imposed on different constructs in each OWL 2 profile, we use the example, *Every manuscript has at least one author.* The class `Manuscript` is added to all the profiles, and the definition varies slightly (provided below) depending on the OWL 2 profile.

- In OWL 2 EL, $\texttt{Manuscript} \equiv \exists\texttt{hasAuthor.Author}$, indicating that every manuscript must have at least one author.

Table 3. Examples of TBox axioms from GenACT. OWL Constructs are in Manchester syntax, and the axioms are written in Description Logics Syntax.

OWL Construct Involved	Axiom
ObjectSomeValuesFrom	$\texttt{KeynoteSpeaker} \equiv \exists\texttt{hasRole.KeynoteSpeakerRole}$
ObjectAllValuesFrom	$\texttt{OrganizingCommittee} \equiv \forall\texttt{hasOrganizingCommitteeMember.Organizer}$
ObjectExactCardinality	$\texttt{SingleAuthorPaper} \equiv =1\texttt{hasAuthor.Author}$
ObjectMaxCardinality	$\texttt{ConferencePaper} \equiv \leq 1\ \texttt{isAcceptedAt.Conference}$
ObjectMinCardinality	$\texttt{Manuscript} \equiv \geq 1\ \texttt{hasAuthor.Author}$
ObjectIntersectionOf	$\texttt{StudentAuthor} \equiv \texttt{Student} \sqcap \texttt{Author}$
ObjectComplementOf	$\texttt{NonAuthor} \equiv \neg\texttt{Author}$
SubClassOf	$\texttt{Volunteer} \sqsubseteq \texttt{Participant}$
EquivalentClasses	$\texttt{Attendee} \equiv \texttt{Participant}$
ObjectPropertyChain	$\texttt{hasAcceptedPaper} \circ \texttt{hasAuthor} \sqsubseteq \texttt{hasCoAuthor}$

- In OWL 2 QL, where existential restrictions are not allowed in subclass expressions, $\texttt{Manuscript} \sqsubseteq \exists\texttt{hasAuthor.Author}$. This definition implies that when there is at least one author, it is classified as a manuscript.
- In OWL 2 RL, due to the prohibition of existential restrictions in superclass expressions, the definition is $\exists\texttt{hasAuthor.Author} \sqsubseteq \texttt{Manuscript}$, which signifies that when an author exists, it is associated with a manuscript.
- In OWL 2 DL, the definition uses qualified minimum cardinalities, expressed as $\texttt{Manuscript} \equiv\, \geq 1\ \texttt{hasAuthor.Author}$, ensuring that every manuscript must have at least one author and making the axiom more expressive.

Tweet Ontology. Our ontology development prioritizes modularity for future scalability and integration. Hence, the ontology that captures the tweet metadata is kept separate from the ACE ontology. This allows for future expansions, potentially incorporating other social media platforms. The core classes in the Tweet ontology include `UserAccount` and `Tweet`, which are connected via the object property `posts`. Each `Tweet` includes attributes such as `dateTimeStamp`, `hasHashtags`, and `mentions` of other Twitter users. To capture the relatively stable but occasionally changing nature of the user's bio information, we added the object property `hasAffiliation`. Additionally, entities from the Tweet and ACE ontology are linked with OWL2Bench and Location ontologies, such as `Organizations` and `City`, which are considered static background knowledge for the generated data. Figure 3 illustrates this integration. Note that the location of `Organizations` is defined as `City` for simplicity, but this will be refined in the future for more detailed location information.

4 Data Generation

The data generation is based on several key observations. Firstly, given the inherent diversity in natural language expressions within tweets, multiple variations of a particular tweet type can exist. For example, when a paper is accepted, the co-authors might post about it. Despite language differences, the meaning of the tweet from each of the co-authors would, most likely, remain consistent. Secondly, despite the brevity of the tweets, each tweet encapsulates significant implicit information related to the conference, covering multiple entities from the ontologies. Figure 4 illustrates how multiple tweets of the same type are mapped to the same RDF Graph, involving several entities, regardless of how short the tweet is. This mapping approach was leveraged to generate the data.

As shown in Fig. 5, the data generation pipeline consists of two steps: Event Data Generation and Sequence Data Generation. The first step generates data for the specified number of conference instances. The second step allows users to create segments of the generated data to simulate different scenarios.

4.1 Event Data Generation

In the first step, we defined several realistic templates for different categories of tweets (Table 2). These templates act as structured formats for building RDF

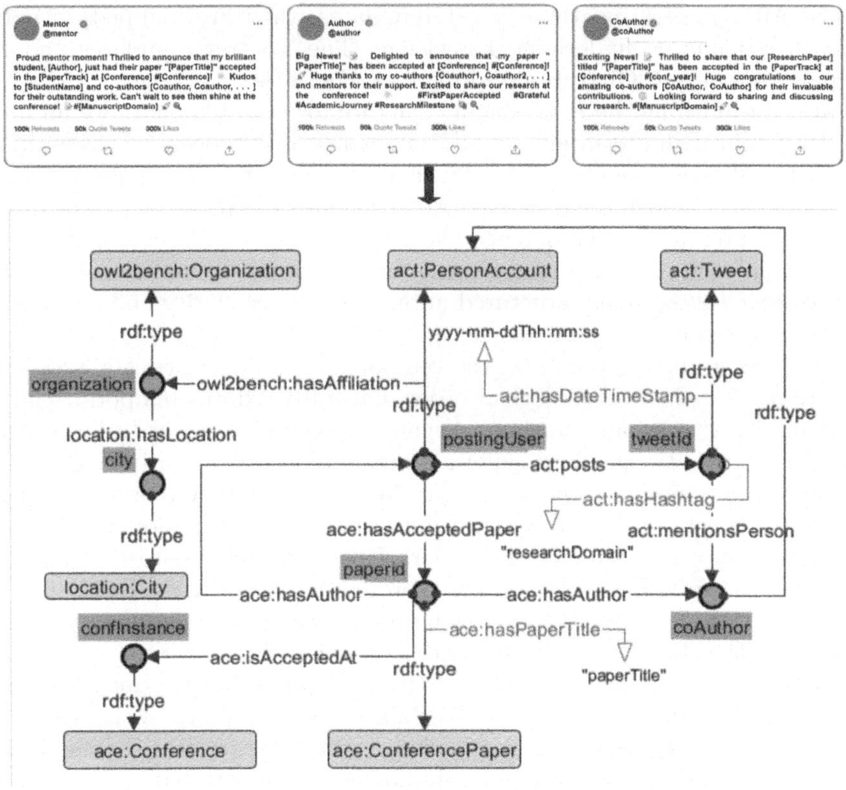

Fig. 4. Mapping of tweets generated after paper acceptance to RDF Graph

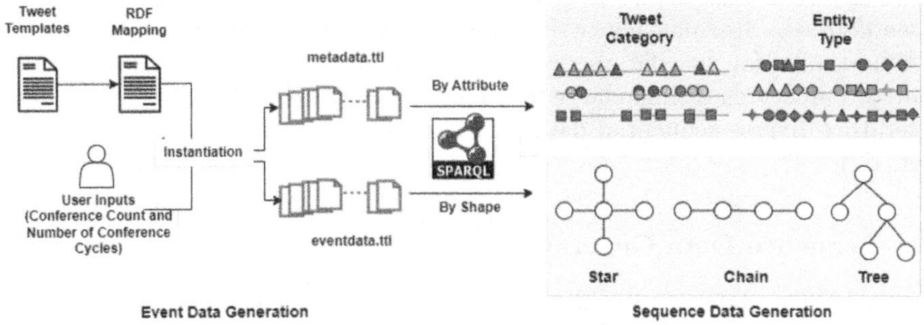

Fig. 5. Data Generation Pipeline. Identical shapes in a sequence denote partitioning by tweet categories (Table 2), while identical colors denote partitioning by the same type of entity (e.g., Conference, User).

graphs. After generating these tweet templates, they are mapped with RDF triples based on the underlying knowledge. The Twitter templates and their mappings are on our GitHub repository (see Footnote 3).

After establishing the RDF graph structure for each template, we fill in specific details through instantiation. The data generation process begins with user-specified conference counts and cycles. For example, if a user requests data for two conferences and ten cycles, GenACT generates two distinct data directories, each representing a conference like *ER2024* and *ISWC2024*. Data is organized within each directory to represent ten cycles, for example, spanning from *ER2014* to *ER2024*. This structured approach ensures clarity and organization in the generated dataset.

For realistic data generation, the temporal modeling of tweets is essential. Tweets, generated in chronological order, naturally exhibit temporal relations. For example, a tweet announcing a keynote speech or a paper to be presented typically precedes tweets discussing its content. When instantiating RDF graphs, we ensure the temporal sequence in our data generation. While we maintain a sequence in tweet generation, we introduce an element of randomness by generating tweets in a non-sequential manner. This adds richness to the dataset by simulating the spontaneity and diversity in real-world social media interactions. To allow flexibility in generating varying peaks, we use random number generators to vary the start times of conferences, durations between events, and tweets within these conferences. It is noteworthy that, akin to users modifying their bios on Twitter, we also ensure that certain users can update their bios.

We have adopted an approach to enhance efficiency to meet the requirement of tunable streaming rates for temporal web data. As illustrated in Fig. 5, instead of having all tweets represented as RDF triples in a single file, we have organized them into separate files for each tweet instance. Specifically, we store RDF triples corresponding to each tweet in two files, one for the metadata corresponding to the tweet *(metadata.ttl)* and another for the conference-related information *(eventdata.ttl)*. Storing each tweet's data in separate files facilitates quick access to timestamps for specific observations and helps avoid the performance issues related to querying a single large file. This method is especially advantageous for generating diverse sequential data that can be streamed at the desired rate (see Sect. 4.2).

4.2 Sequence Data Generation

The generated data can be divided into multiple segments through strategic partitioning using SPARQL[4] queries. This customization enhances the dataset's utility for diverse research and analysis purposes.

Partitioning by Attribute. The generated event data offers flexibility by allowing partitioning based on various attributes. Each tweet metadata file created in the previous step contains relevant information that can be used to generate attribute-specific datasets. These attributes include different entities

[4] https://www.w3.org/TR/sparql11-overview/.

involved in the ACT domain, such as conferences, persons, organizations, research domains, and conference phases. For instance, querying `?tweetid :isAbout ?conferenceInstance. ?conferenceInstance rdf:type :Conference` on the metadata files, the triples in the corresponding event data file are used to create dedicated `Conference` segments for each `?conferenceInstance`. Similarly, querying the metadata files for `?tweetid :mentions ?userAccount` will create different `User` segments. Figure 6 shows these two partitions: `Conference` and `User`. The former creates segments for each conference. This facilitates analysis of a conference's temporal evolution, from the initial announcement to its conclusion. While these segments are fewer, they encompass a variety of users, organizations, and related data. Figure 6 shows the mix of tweets within each conference stream. Partitioning by users results in segments representing the activities of individual users. Although individual user tweet frequency might be low, user-based segments offer a multitude of interconnections, leading to potentially complex reasoning tasks. Here, the number of partitions equals the number of users involved in the conference tweets. It is important to note that a single user might be involved in multiple conferences and have different roles within those conferences. Similarly, a single tweet might involve multiple users. Figure 6 also depicts this user-based partitioning with its inherent challenges due to the high number of streams and interconnected entities.

Partitioning by Shape. Our data partitioning strategies extend beyond specific attributes such as conferences and users. The data can also be partitioned based on its inherent structure, revealing valuable relationships within the event data. Here, we define and enforce specific structural patterns within data segments, ensuring that all events within a segment adhere to a consistent form. This fosters a structured approach to data modeling and analysis [8].

Figure 7 illustrates three common shapes (out of a variety of possible graph patterns) in our generated data: tree, star, and chain. Tree structures represent hierarchical relationships, useful for analyzing nested dependencies. Chain structures model linear events or interactions, ideal for chronological analysis. Star structures centralize around a single node with multiple connected entities. This is useful for hub-and-spoke models like social media interactions where a central user connects with many others.

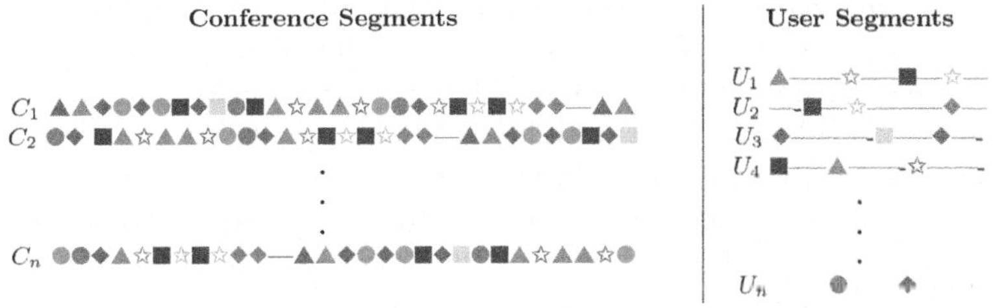

Fig. 6. Partitioning by Attributes. Different shapes and colors represent different tweet categories as outlined in Table 2.

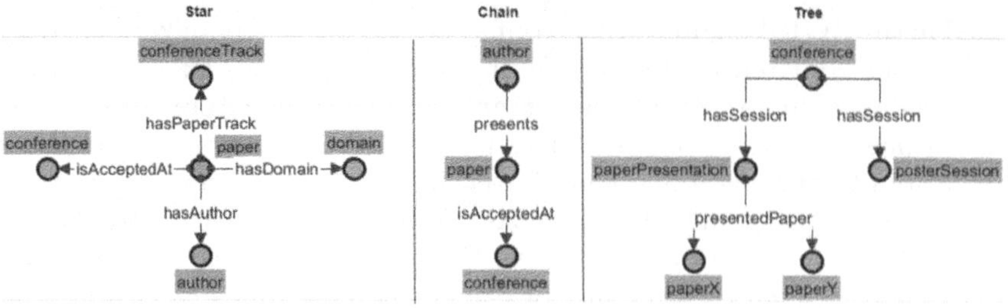

Fig. 7. Partitioning by Shapes

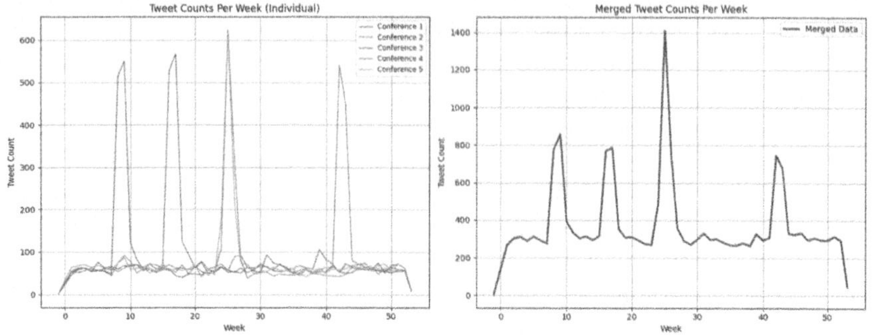

Fig. 8. Tweet volume patterns and peaks for five conferences: individual conference streams (left) and merged stream (right).

5 Discussion

Patterns and Peaks Analysis. Figure 8 illustrates an example of the tweet volume patterns and peaks generated per week for five conferences. It demonstrates that even if each conference displays three distinct peaks individually, merging the data into a single stream leads to diverse peaks and volumes. Thus providing insights into the dynamic nature of the events and their usefulness in mimicking different real-world activities for various analytical purposes.

Functional Utility. To demonstrate GenACT's utility in evaluating reasoning systems, we executed two queries corresponding to CQ 3: *Monitoring Publication Activities* and CQ 7: *Global Research Focus* (cf. Table 1), on two reasoners: CSparql2 (see Footnote 2) and RDFox[22]. CSparql2 is a stream reasoner based on RSP4J [33], while RDFox is a highly scalable, parallelized, in-memory RDF store supporting incremental reasoning. We employed pre-existing code available at[5]. Our evaluations were conducted on a system equipped with an Intel(R) Core(TM) i7-8550U CPU @ 1.80 GHz and 8 GB RAM. CQ 7 is a variant of CQ 3 (refer to Listings 1.1 and 1.2) with an additional basic graph pattern in the query: `?organization :hasLocation ?location`. This query utilizes static

[5] https://github.com/SRrepo.

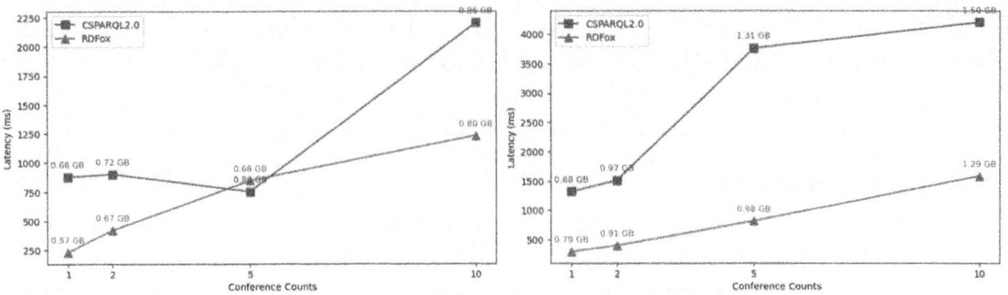

(a) Varying number of parallel streams without background data
(b) Single stream with static (increasing) background data

Fig. 9. KPIs: Latency (ms) and Memory Consumed (GB), for the queries corresponding to CQs 3 and 7, for different numbers of conferences.

background data about locations to respond. The evaluation outcomes, as illustrated in Fig. 9, reveal that the generated data effectively identifies variations in performance. It is important to note that our focus here is not on performance evaluation but on demonstrating the utility of the generated data in evaluating reasoning systems. Detailed results will be added to the GitHub repository (see Footnote 3).

6 Related Work

Bonifati et al. [5] discuss the efforts related to graph data generation in detail. They identified 35 data generators classified based on the domain (Social Media, Academic, e-commerce, or User Defined), their generation capabilities (fixed, schema-driven, extracted), and data distribution (and other dimensions out of the scope of this work). Being GenAct, a fixed, academic, and social media-based RDF data generator that follows realistic Twitter data, we discuss its relation with the closest ones selected by such survey and additional works published afterward. To this extent, we divide the selected generators into the following sub-areas: (Knowledge) Graph Generation and time-related data generation.

Linked Data. In the Semantic Web context, data generation is commonly associated with benchmarking. **WatDiv** [2] focuses on stress testing, i.e., it is workload-oriented. It provides a data generator that generates scalable datasets according to the provided schema. Temporality, dynamicity, and timeliness are not considered in the dataset or the workload. The **SP^{2}Bench** [28] is based on the DBLP dataset. The generated RDF graph follows the same data distribution as the original DBLP dataset, mimicking entity relations and correlations. A fixed seed ensures that the data generation process is deterministic. The final data contains a temporal dimension related to the publication date. However, this is not prioritized in the generation of related queries. **LinkGen** [16] can generate data in RDF for a given vocabulary. It supports Zipf's power-law and Gaussian distributions for entity generation. Being agnostic to the vocabulary,

LinkGen could be tuned to generate temporal data. Moreover, the generation can be performed in streaming. Nevertheless, it does not support stream partitioning, nor can it describe absolute events in the vocabulary. In future work, we plan to compare the efficiency of GenAct generation with LinkGen.

Streaming Linked Data. Among the numerous benchmarks [1,9,10,17,23, 25,32,35], only LSBench, SLUBM, and LASS provide a way to stress stream reasoning systems and data generators. The former two approach the generation process naively, considering a single data stream. While LSBench shares GenAct's domain of social media and the static-streaming data duality, it lacks accurate Twitter templates and realistic data distribution. On the other hand, SLUBM streams LUBM [12] individuals without considering data distribution or partitioning. Additionally, RSPLab [34], a framework for testing RDF stream processing systems, incorporates a solution for generating data based on TripleWave [19]. Although RSPLab claims the ability to study the RSP response to change in the input frequency, such a feature does not appear in the code.

Reasoning. The benchmarks designed for highly expressive ontology reasoners [12,18,31] are limited to static data, making them unsuitable for mimicking domains that require reasoning over temporality, dynamicity, and timeliness. This latter gap was attempted to be bridged by RSP benchmarks, like LASS 1.0 [32], but its adoption seems minimal. **PyGraft** [15] is a tool for KG generation written in Python. It is domain-agnostic but supports a subset of OWL 2 and RDF language features. Data generation is pipelined with a DL reasoner to ensure consistency. Although PyGraft allows users to implement their own conceptualization, it does not include any explicit temporal feature nor consider dynamicity and timeliness, making it unsuitable for studying evolving Knowledge Graphs. **GDD**$_x$ [11] is a schema-driven graph generator based on Extended Graph Differential Dependencies, i.e., an extension of graph entity/differential dependencies that represent formal constraints for graph data. However, it cannot generate domain-agnostic schemas and requires an existing schema as input.

7 Conclusion

This paper presents GenACT, a temporal web data generator based on ACE that can generate data that has temporal, dynamic, and timeliness characteristics. These are critical for evaluating systems on KG evolution and stream reasoning, two areas that do not have realistic and large, publicly available data. GenACT comes with a novel ontology for each of the OWL 2 profiles, allowing it to stress different reasoning systems. The generation process allows for the creation of different data segments using SPARQL-based partitioning strategies, allowing users to define custom partitioning strategies.

Our synthetic data generation approach emphasizes adaptability across multiple dimensions. Future plans include expanding to platforms like Reddit and LinkedIn, incorporating the Shapes Constraint Language (SHACL)[6] for enforcing temporal constraints and data validation and extending data generation beyond RDF, e.g., Property Graphs or Datalog, to encourage the benchmarking of expressive reasoners [4] and graph stream processing languages [27].

Acknowledgement. Gunjan Singh and Raghava Mutharaju acknowledge the partial support of the Infosys Centre for Artificial Intelligence (CAI), IIIT-Delhi, in this work. We also thank Nandika Jain and Jishnu Raj Parashar for their contributions during the early discussions in modelling the ACE ontology. The French Research Agency supports Tommasini under grant agreement nr. ANR-22-CE23-0001 Polyflow. He also acknowledges the support of Prof. Andrea Mauri from Lyon 1.

References

1. Ali, M.I., Gao, F., Mileo, A.: CityBench: a configurable benchmark to evaluate rsp engines using smart city datasets. In: Arenas, M., Corcho, O., Simperl, E., Strohmaier, M., d'Aquin, M., Srinivas, K., Groth, P., Dumontier, M., Heflin, J., Thirunarayan, K., Staab, S. (eds.) ISWC 2015. LNCS, vol. 9367, pp. 374–389. Springer, Cham (2015). https://doi.org/10.1007/978-3-319-25010-6_25
2. Aluç, G., Hartig, O., Özsu, M.T., Daudjee, K.: Diversified stress testing of RDF data management systems. In: Mika, P., Tudorache, T., Bernstein, A., Welty, C., Knoblock, C., Vrandečić, D., Groth, P., Noy, N., Janowicz, K., Goble, C. (eds.) The Semantic Web – ISWC 2014: 13th International Semantic Web Conference, Riva del Garda, Italy, October 19-23, 2014. Proceedings, Part I, pp. 197–212. Springer International Publishing, Cham (2014). https://doi.org/10.1007/978-3-319-11964-9_13
3. Bauer, A., et al.: Comprehensive exploration of synthetic data generation: a survey. CoRR **abs/2401.02524** (2024). https://doi.org/10.48550/arXiv.2401.02524
4. Beck, H., Dao-Tran, M., Eiter, T.: LARS: a logic-based framework for analytic reasoning over streams. Artif. Intell. **261**, 16–70 (2018). https://doi.org/10.1016/J.ARTINT.2018.04.003
5. Bonifati, A., Holubová, I., Prat-Pérez, A., Sakr, S.: Graph generators: state of the art and open challenges. ACM Comput. Surv. **53**(2), 36:1–36:30 (2021). https://doi.org/10.1145/3379445
6. Bonifati, A., Tommasini, R.: An overview of continuous querying in (modern) data systems. In: Barceló, P., Sánchez-Pi, N., Meliou, A., Sudarshan, S. (eds.) Companion of the 2024 International Conference on Management of Data, SIGMOD/PODS 2024, Santiago AA, Chile, June 9-15, 2024, pp. 605–612. ACM (2024). https://doi.org/10.1145/3626246.3654679
7. Bonte, P., et al.: Grounding stream reasoning research. TGDK **2**(1), 2:1–2:47 (2024). https://doi.org/10.4230/TGDK.2.1.2
8. Bonte, P., Ongenae, F., Tommasini, R.: A holistic view over ontologies for streaming linked data. Semantic Web (To Appear) (2024)
9. Verborgh, R., et al. (eds.): The Semantic Web: ESWC 2021 Satellite Events: Virtual Event, June 6–10, 2021, Revised Selected Papers. Springer International Publishing, Cham (2021)

[6] https://www.w3.org/TR/shacl/.

10. Dell'Aglio, D., Calbimonte, J.-P., Balduini, M., Corcho, O., Della Valle, E.: On correctness in RDF stream processor benchmarking. In: Salinesi, C., Norrie, M.C., Pastor, Ó. (eds.) Advanced Information Systems Engineering: 25th International Conference, CAiSE 2013, Valencia, Spain, June 17-21, 2013. Proceedings, pp. 326–342. Springer Berlin Heidelberg, Berlin, Heidelberg (2013). https://doi.org/10.1007/978-3-642-41338-4_21
11. Feng, Z., et al.: A schema-driven synthetic knowledge graph generation approach with extended graph differential dependencies (gdd^{x}s). IEEE Access **9**, 5609–5639 (2021)
12. Guo, Y., Pan, Z., Heflin, J.: LUBM: a benchmark for OWL knowledge base systems. J. Web Semant. **3**(2–3), 158–182 (2005)
13. Hitzler, P., Krötzsch, M., Rudolph, S.: Foundations of Semantic Web Technologies. Chapman & Hall/CRC (2009)
14. Horrocks, I.: OWL: a description logic based ontology language. In: van Beek, P. (ed.) CP 2005. LNCS, vol. 3709, pp. 5–8. Springer, Heidelberg (2005). https://doi.org/10.1007/11564751_2
15. Hubert, N., Monnin, P., d'Aquin, M., Brun, A., Monticolo, D.: Pygraft: configurable generation of schemas and knowledge graphs at your fingertips. CoRR **abs/2309.03685** (2023). https://doi.org/10.48550/arXiv.2309.03685
16. Joshi, A.K., Hitzler, P., Dong, G.: Linkgen: Multipurpose linked data generator. In: Groth, P., Simperl, E., Gray, A.J.G., Sabou, M., Krötzsch, M., Lécué, F., Flöck, F., Gil, Y. (eds.) The Semantic Web - ISWC 2016 - 15th International Semantic Web Conference, Kobe, Japan, October 17-21, 2016, Proceedings, Part II. Lecture Notes in Computer Science, vol. 9982, pp. 113–121 (2016). https://doi.org/10.1007/978-3-319-46547-0_12
17. Bozzon, A., Cudre-Maroux, P., Pautasso, C. (eds.): Web Engineering: 16th International Conference, ICWE 2016, Lugano, Switzerland, June 6-9, 2016. Proceedings. Springer International Publishing, Cham (2016)
18. Sure, Y., Domingue, J. (eds.): The Semantic Web: Research and Applications. Springer Berlin Heidelberg, Berlin, Heidelberg (2006)
19. Groth, P., et al. (eds.): The Semantic Web – ISWC 2016: 15th International Semantic Web Conference, Kobe, Japan, October 17–21, 2016, Proceedings, Part II. Springer International Publishing, Cham (2016)
20. Monfardini, G.K.Q., Salamon, J.S., Barcellos, M.P.: Use of competency questions in ontology engineering: a survey. In: Almeida, J.P.A., Borbinha, J., Guizzardi, G., Link, S., Zdravkovic, J. (eds.) Conceptual Modeling, pp. 45–64. Springer Nature Switzerland, Cham (2023)
21. Morsey, M., Lehmann, J., Auer, S., Ngomo, A.C.: DBpedia SPARQL benchmark–performance assessment with real queries on real data. In: The Semantic Web – ISWC 2011, pp. 454–469 (2011)
22. Arenas, M., et al. (eds.): The Semantic Web - ISWC 2015: 14th International Semantic Web Conference, Bethlehem, PA, USA, October 11-15, 2015, Proceedings, Part II. Springer International Publishing, Cham (2015)
23. Nguyen, T.N., Siberski, W.: SLUBM: an extended LUBM benchmark for stream reasoning. In: Celino, I., Della Valle, E., Krötzsch, M., Schlobach, S. (eds.) Proceedings of the 2nd International Workshop on Ordering and Reasoning, OrdRing 2013, Co-located with the 12th International Semantic Web Conference (ISWC 2013), Sydney, Australia, October 22nd, 2013. CEUR Workshop Proceedings, vol. 1059, pp. 43–54. CEUR-WS.org (2013). https://ceur-ws.org/Vol-1059/ordring2013-paper6.pdf

24. Parra, D., Trattner, C., Gómez, D., Hurtado, M., Wen, X., Lin, Y.: Twitter in academic events: a study of temporal usage, communication, sentimental and topical patterns in 16 computer science conferences. Comput. Commun. **73**, 301–314 (2016). https://doi.org/10.1016/j.comcom.2015.07.001
25. Cudré-Mau, P., et al. (eds.): The Semantic Web – ISWC 2012. Springer Berlin Heidelberg, Berlin, Heidelberg (2012)
26. Polleres, A., et al.: How does knowledge evolve in open knowledge graphs? TGDK **1**(1), 11:1–11:59 (2023). https://doi.org/10.4230/TGDK.1.1.11
27. Rost, C., et al.: Seraph: Continuous queries on property graph streams. In: Tanca, L., Luo, Q., Polese, G., Caruccio, L., Oriol, X., Firmani, D. (eds.) Proceedings 27th International Conference on Extending Database Technology, EDBT 2024, Paestum, Italy, March 25 - March 28, pp. 234–247. OpenProceedings.org (2024). https://doi.org/10.48786/EDBT.2024.21
28. Schmidt, M., Hornung, T., Meier, M., Pinkel, C., Lausen, G.: SP2Bench: a SPARQL performance benchmark. In: de Virgilio, R., Giunchiglia, F., Tanca, L. (eds.) Semantic Web Information Management: A Model-Based Perspective, pp. 371–393. Springer Berlin Heidelberg, Berlin, Heidelberg (2010). https://doi.org/10.1007/978-3-642-04329-1_16
29. Shin, J., Jian, L., Driscoll, K., Bar, F.: The diffusion of misinformation on social media: Temporal pattern, message, and source. Comput. Hum. Behav. **83**, 278–287 (2018). https://doi.org/10.1016/j.chb.2018.02.008
30. Almeida, João Paulo A.., Borbinha, José, Guizzardi, Giancarlo, Link, Sebastian, Zdravkovic, Jelena (eds.): Conceptual Modeling: 42nd International Conference, ER 2023, Lisbon, Portugal, November 6–9, 2023, Proceedings. Springer Nature Switzerland, Cham (2023)
31. Singh, G., Bhatia, S., Mutharaju, R.: Owl2bench: a benchmark for OWL 2 reasoners. In: Pan, J.Z., et al. (eds.) The Semantic Web - ISWC 2020 - 19th International Semantic Web Conference, Athens, Greece, November 2-6, 2020, Proceedings, Part II. Lecture Notes in Computer Science, vol. 12507, pp. 81–96. Springer (2020). https://doi.org/10.1007/978-3-030-62466-8_6
32. Tommasini, R., Balduini, M., Della Valle, E.: Towards a benchmark for expressive stream reasoning. In: Calbimonte, J., Dao-Tran, M., Dell'Aglio, D., Phuoc, D.L., Saleem, M., Usbeck, R., Verborgh, R., Ngomo, A.N. (eds.) Joint Proceedings of the 2nd RDF Stream Processing (RSP 2017) and the Querying the Web of Data (QuWeDa 2017) Workshops co-located with 14th ESWC 2017 (ESWC 2017), Portoroz, Slovenia, May 28th - to - 29th, 2017. CEUR Workshop Proceedings, vol. 1870, pp. 26–36. CEUR-WS.org (2017). https://ceur-ws.org/Vol-1870/paper-03.pdf
33. Tommasini, R., Bonte, P., Ongenae, F., Valle, E.D.: RSP4J: an API for RDF stream processing. In: Verborgh, R., Hose, K., Paulheim, H., Champin, P., Maleshkova, M., Corcho, Ó., Ristoski, P., Alam, M. (eds.) The Semantic Web - 18th International Conference, ESWC 2021, Virtual Event, June 6-10, 2021, Proceedings. Lecture Notes in Computer Science, vol. 12731, pp. 565–581. Springer (2021). https://doi.org/10.1007/978-3-030-77385-4_34

34. Tommasini, R., Della Valle, E., Mauri, A., Brambilla, M.: Rsplab: RDF stream processing benchmarking made easy. In: d'Amato, C., Fernández, M., Tamma, V.A.M., Lécué, F., Cudré-Mauroux, P., Sequeda, J.F., Lange, C., Heflin, J. (eds.) The Semantic Web - ISWC 2017 - 16th International Semantic Web Conference, Vienna, Austria, October 21-25, 2017, Proceedings, Part II. Lecture Notes in Computer Science, vol. 10588, pp. 202–209. Springer (2017). https://doi.org/10.1007/978-3-319-68204-4_21
35. Zhang, Y., Pham, M., Corcho, Ó., Calbimonte, J.: Srbench: a streaming RDF/SPARQL benchmark. In: Cudré-Mauroux, P., Heflin, J., Sirin, E., Tudorache, T., Euzenat, J., Hauswirth, M., Parreira, J.X., Hendler, J., Schreiber, G., Bernstein, A., Blomqvist, E. (eds.) The Semantic Web - ISWC 2012 - 11th International Semantic Web Conference, Boston, MA, USA, November 11-15, 2012, Proceedings, Part I. Lecture Notes in Computer Science, vol. 7649, pp. 641–657. Springer (2012). https://doi.org/10.1007/978-3-642-35176-1_40

SAQI: An Ontology Based Knowledge Graph Platform for Social Air Quality Index

Saad Ahmad[1], Sudhir Attri[1(✉)], Ruchi Dwivedi[2], Muzamil Yaqoob[3], Aasim Khan[1], Praveen Priyadarshi[1], and Raghava Mutharaju[1]

[1] IIIT-Delhi, Delhi, India
{saad18409,sudhir18267,aasim,praveen,raghava.mutharaju}@iiitd.ac.in
[2] Dr. B. R. Ambedkar University, Delhi, Delhi, India
[3] IIT Delhi, Delhi, India

Abstract. Air Quality Index (AQI) is a number aggregated from several air quality sensors deployed in an area. AQI is useful in communicating the air quality to the general public and in making governance decisions to tackle air pollution. However, our ethnographic surveys revealed the existence of a knowledge barrier in interpreting the AQI and data illiteracy in understanding AQI-related charts and trends commonly facilitated by government organizations. This knowledge gap is wider for the marginalized sections of society, who, it turns out, are more exposed to pollution. We use an ontological approach to homogenize the air quality data with social and spatial aspects. The Social Air Quality Index (SAQI) ontology integrates the data from local and central air quality monitoring sensors, meteorological data, and field surveys. This data is converted into a Knowledge Graph, which is used to build an application for civic engagement with the public on pollution to improve community participation of the local institutions and individuals. We evaluated this application through a user survey and received positive feedback. The ontologies, code, and datasets are available under the Apache 2.0 License at https://github.com/kracr/aq-structured-platform.

Keywords: Air Pollution · AQI · Ethnography · Community Participation · Data Integration · Ontology · Knowledge Graph · Social AQI

1 Introduction

Air pollution is a significant problem across the major cities of the World and is also a part of the sustainable development goals[1]. Tackling it, however, is a rather complex task as the solution lies at the intersection of society, politics, science and technology. Air pollution has a substantial spatial variance. Even within one city, air quality can vary greatly depending on the locality, proximity to industrial

[1] https://www.un.org/sustainabledevelopment/health/.

W. Maass et al. (Eds.): ER 2024, LNCS 15238, pp. 337–354, 2025.
https://doi.org/10.1007/978-3-031-75872-0_18

areas, population density, etc. To tackle air pollution, government agencies frame policies for mitigating the sources of pollution, increasing civic engagement and promoting standardized air quality indices such as the Air Quality Index (AQI). In this work, we delve into the latter two aspects, i.e., improving community engagement and studying AQI from the perspective of different social cohorts. This led to a socially relevant AQI, which we named Social AQI (SAQI).

We conducted an ethnographic survey at six different locations in Delhi, India, which is one of the most polluted cities in the World. At these six locations, we have also deployed air quality sensors to record the hyperlocal AQI. The details of the data collection and the survey results are discussed in Sect. 3. To model and integrate these disparate and heterogeneous datasets, we built a SAQI ontology. This ontology [7] captures the relationship between the seemingly unrelated concepts in the datasets, which in turn are used to construct a Knowledge Graph (KG) [9]. A SAQI app is built on top of the KG. This app considers the different social cohorts and their understanding of the AQI. The following are our contributions.

1. An ontology that models the data from the air quality sensors and the ethnographic survey. This is built using the Pollution ontology design pattern[2] [4] and is available at https://github.com/kracr/aq-structured-platform. The documentation is at https://w3id.org/saqi.
2. A SAQI KG that integrates the air pollution data from local and central sensors with the data from the ethnographic survey. YARRML[3] is used to convert the sensor and survey data into a KG. These mappings, along with the SHACL[4] constraints and SPARQL queries on the KG, are available at https://doi.org/10.5281/zenodo.10300235. The SPARQL endpoint over the KG is available at https://w3id.org/saqi/sparql.
3. An SAQI App that is built using the KG to encourage community engagement and response. This is available at https://w3id.org/saqi/app.
4. The two datasets – ethnographic survey questionnaire along with the responses and the hyperlocal air quality data from six different locations in Delhi. This is available at https://doi.org/10.5281/zenodo.10300235. These datasets will be helpful to social scientists, environmental scientists, biophysicists and biochemists.

2 Related Work

There are a few existing ontologies related to air pollution and air quality. Adeleke and Moodley, [1] built an ontology to model pollution as a part of a web of IoT sensors. Their ontology is used in an indoor air pollution monitoring and control application. Oprea and Mihaela, [14], developed an ontology to model air pollution. They used human experts and heuristic rules generated

[2] http://ontologydesignpatterns.org/wiki/Submissions:Pollution.
[3] https://rml.io/yarrrml/spec/.
[4] https://www.w3.org/TR/shacl/.

through machine learning techniques as knowledge sources. They use the ontology to monitor and control air pollution in urban regions. Riga et al., [15] use ontologies to make efficient environmental decision support systems. Ontologies are used to model the status of the environment and its impact on citizens' health and actions. Mertal et al., [13] use CityGML and aim to connect 3D city models with air pollution ontologies for sustainable urban development.

Some of the applications related to air pollution have focused on categorizing AQI value into good, poor and severe to generate recommendations on actions to be performed. Examples of such applications are CPCBcrr[5] by CPCB, AQICN[6], SAFAR[7] and European Air Quality Index[8]. The forecasting system developed by SAFAR predicts air quality and generates recommendations a few days ahead. Urban Emissions[9] analyses the contribution of components such as traffic, dust and wind on the AQI at a particular location. They use a chemical transport model system known as WRF-CAMx to integrate the data. All the applications discussed here do not generate spatiotemporally aware recommendations and do not consider a locality's social makeup. Instead, they rely on centrally located sensors that may not be able to capture the complete dynamics of air pollution at a location.

Air quality research generally involves analyzing pollution sources, government policies, and their adverse effect on public health. For example, Agarwala M. and Chandel A., explain the role of crop residue burning on Delhi's air quality [3] and Huang et al., studied the emission of pollutants from power generation plants [11]. We focus on social factors operating at the individual and institutional levels that affect the public's perception and awareness of pollution. We use an ontology based approach to integrate the air quality data with the ethnographic data of locations.

3 Requirements Analysis

We conducted a workshop on AQI and its social implications. The participants of this workshop include officials from the Central Pollution Control Board (CPCB)[10], social scientists, field workers and technologists. During the discussion, several issues were raised, such as the coverage of the centrally deployed sensors, the impact of air pollution on different social groups (students, daily wage workers, athletes, shopkeepers, etc.), the awareness about air pollution and AQI among the different social groups and the citizen participation to tackle the problem of air pollution. In order to get answers to these questions and to know the ground reality, two field workers were hired and asked to run a survey in two

[5] CPCBcrr https://cpcbccr.com/.
[6] https://aqicn.org/.
[7] http://safar.tropmet.res.in/.
[8] https://airindex.eea.europa.eu/AQI/index.html/.
[9] https://urbanemissions.info/.
[10] https://cpcb.nic.in/.

different regions of Delhi. These two regions were selected because they had variations in terms of demography and consisted of educational institutes, industries, dairy farms, sports academies and grocery stores. In each region, three different locations were selected to get a representation of the region's demography and social groups.

After identifying the six locations, a field survey was conducted in these locations inquiring people about their awareness of the air quality indexes, their perception of pollution, and their views on government response towards pollution. The survey targeted six social groups - teachers, students, mothers of young kids, local shopkeepers, sports academies, and social workers. At these six locations, air quality sensors were also deployed to study the hyperlocal AQI in the context of the social groups. Exposure to hyperlocal data[11] increases local participation, which can make local institutions respond effectively to their local pollution problems. We term this as socializing and localizing the AQI in the neighbourhood. The policies related to handling air pollution can be tuned by the local government bodies for each social group to address their specific needs. For example, the local school timings can be changed so that school children can avoid the time when the pollution is high.

The survey responses show that the AQI numbers and the data behind them are not interpretable to most people, even in Delhi, which has been one of the most polluted cities for consecutive years. Several survey respondents correctly identified the contributors to the air quality, which are crop burning, construction, and industries. However, except for the teachers and students social groups, others either did not have access to the AQI or could not draw any inferences from the AQI numbers. The local government bodies were also untrained to tackle the pollution locally and remained uninvolved. Details on the study methodology used, the workshops conducted, the interaction and the survey response from the people in the six locations are available at [6].

Given this context, we proposed building a mobile and Web friendly application that is available in the local language. This application can increase the awareness of AQI by explaining the relevant facts and recommending steps that can be taken locally to mitigate the problem of air pollution within a particular locality. To build such an application, the data from heterogeneous sources must be integrated and structured. So, an ontology that can satisfy all the requirements discussed here will be appropriate for this application.

3.1 Competency Questions

From the workshop and the survey results, we collected the following minimal set of questions, also referred to as *competency questions*, that should be answered by the ontology.

1. What is the air pollution literacy of a particular social group?

[11] Data relevant to a small geographical area or community. e.g. a bus stop, market or a village.

2. What is the major perception of people towards air quality in a region?
3. What is the average AQI value at a place over a period of time?
4. How do people expect the government to mitigate the effect of air pollution in a region?
5. What is the perception of people living in different regions towards air quality?

As can be observed from the competency questions, multiple data sources are required to answer them. They may have different structures and formats. These datasets include the AQI data, social data and meteorological data.

4 Methodology

The methodology of building the SAQI ontology revolved around continual iterative development. We developed the ontology in two phases – building a barebones ontology consisting of classes and properties that were minimally essential and, later on, iteratively extending it based on the feedback and the requirements of the SAQI application.

The barebones ontology is extended from Pollution ontology design pattern [4] In the latter phase, feedback on the ontology is obtained from the social scientists and the field workers in our team. An example of the importance of their feedback is the presence of the `Person` class. Since most of the survey responses are connected to the people living in a locality, the feedback was that it would be an important concept in the SAQI ontology. To build the SAQI ontology, we reused some of the concepts from foaf [5], WeatherOntology[12], schema.org[13], SOSA [12] and WGS84[14] ontologies (see Table 1).

Table 1. The ontologies and the concepts in those ontologies that were reused in the SAQI ontology.

Ontology reused	Concepts reused
WeatherOntology	AirPollution, Irridance, Precipitation
foaf schema.org	Person Organization, Place, Event
SOSA	FeatureOfInterest, Observation, Sensor, Result
WGS84	SpatialThing, Point

[12] https://www.auto.tuwien.ac.at/downloads/thinkhome/ontology/WeatherOntology.owl.
[13] https://schema.org/.
[14] https://www.w3.org/2003/01/geo/wgs84_pos.

4.1 FAIR Principles

SAQI ontology is designed by considering the Findability, Accessibility, Interoperability, and Reuse (FAIR) principles[15].

1. **Findable.** Metadata is well defined, and data is retrievable using global identifiers.
2. **Accessible.** Data is accessible using HTTP protocol which is free and open. When data is inaccessible, the metadata (ontology) will still be available.
3. **Interoperable.** Other ontologies/vocabularies are reused and linked to their IRIs. Representation is formal and acceptable, and related vocabularies follow FAIR principles.
4. **Reusable.** Along with the license, the ontologies and their serialization are also available.

5 Ontology Description

The SAQI ontology is divided into three sub-ontologies, which we refer to as modules – *Pollution* module, built using Pollution ODP[16], *Trajectory* module built from the Trajectory ODP [17] and *Ethnography* module for structural representation of field survey responses.

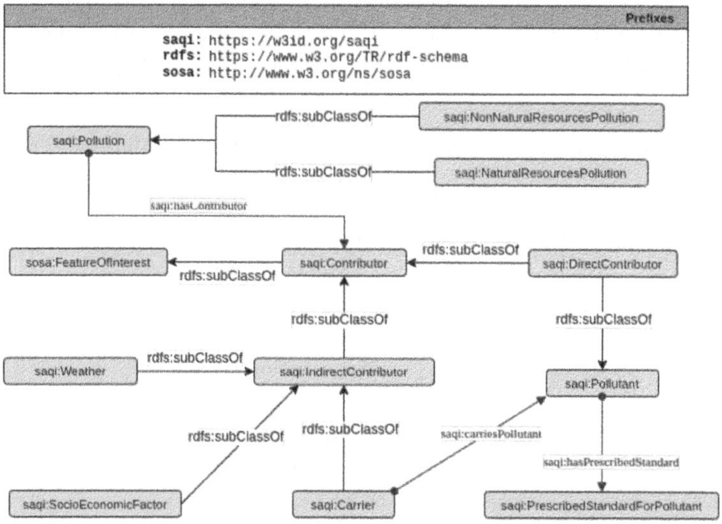

Fig. 1. Main concepts and properties of the Pollution module

[15] https://www.go-fair.org/fair-principles/.
[16] http://ontologydesignpatterns.org/wiki/Submissions:Pollution.
[17] http://ontologydesignpatterns.org/wiki/Submissions:Trajectory/Trajectory.

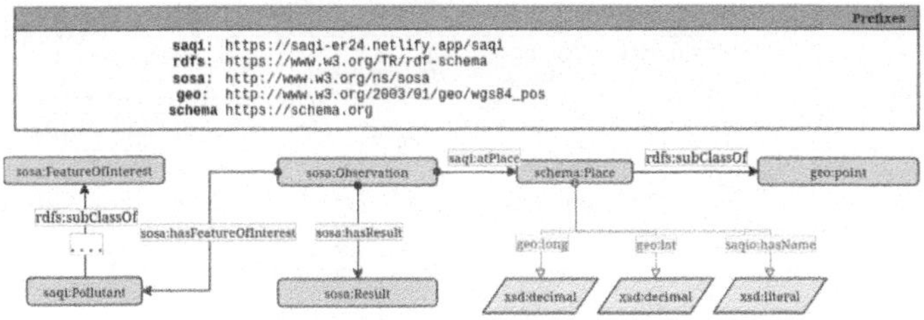

Fig. 2. Re-used concepts from WGS84 and SOSA

5.1 Pollution Ontology

The Pollution ontology is extended from the Pollution ODP as shown in Fig. 1. The ODP has been adapted to the air pollution domain by extending some of the classes. For example, the `Pollutant` class is extended to `PrimaryPollutant` and `SecondaryPollutant`. `PrimaryPollutant` is further extended to `GaseousPollutant` and `ParticulateMatter`. The sensors, observations, samples and actuator (SOSA) ontology includes concepts related to sensors and their observations. We derived `Contributor` from sosa:FeatureOfInterest. With this, we can describe sensor observations with time and spatial information. The WGS84 vocabulary provides SpatialThing for describing a spatial location on Earth. Figures 2, 3, and 4 capture these re-used concepts in SAQI ontology. Some important concepts and properties from the Pollution module are discussed here.

AirPollution. This class is extended from the `Pollution` class of the Pollution ODP. The `Pollution` class represents the different types of contaminants in the natural environment. `AirPollution` is linked to `Pollutant` through the `hasContributor` property (Axiom 1). The institutions working to mitigate the pollution sources through policies and awareness campaigns are linked by the object property `takesActionAgainst`. These properties and their connection with the `AirPollution` class are shown in Fig. 3.

$$\texttt{Pollution} \sqsubseteq \exists \texttt{hasContributor.Contributor} \tag{1}$$

hasContributor. This object property connects the `AirPollution` class to its direct and indirect contributors (pollutants).

takesActionAgainst. The institutions that are working to mitigate the effects of air pollution are connected through this object property. We considered two possible types of institutions – government and non-government institutions such as NGOs.

Contributor. It is a subclass of sosa:FeatureOfInterest, allowing us to record observations of the contributors. A contributor can either be a contaminant particle, i.e., `Pollutant` or it could be a `Carrier` that transports a `Pollutant`. The `Contributor` class and other related classes are shown in Fig. 4.

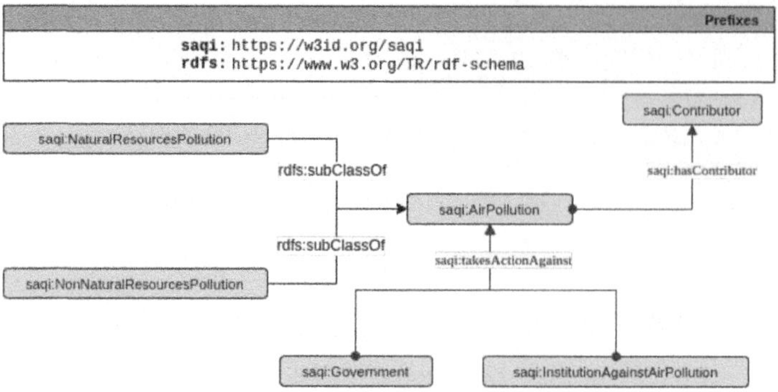

Fig. 3. AirPollution class and its connections

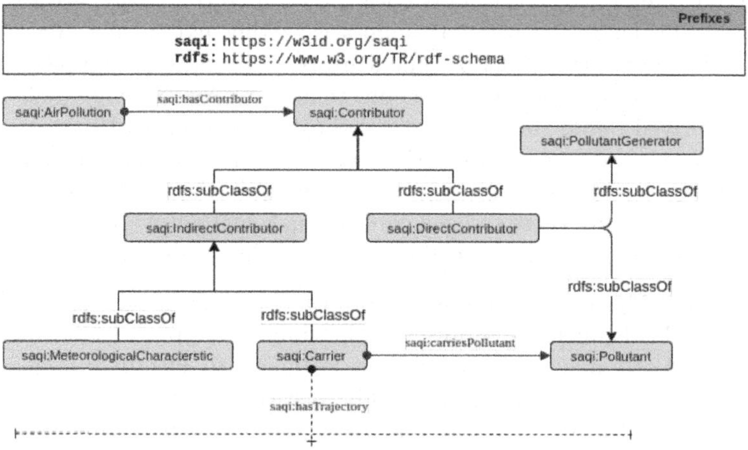

Fig. 4. Contributor class and its connections

carriesPollutant. This object property is used with an `IndirectContributor` that transports a `Pollutant` from one spatial location to another, for example, wind and water flow.

DirectContributor. This class represents the contributors that directly impact pollution. `Pollutant` is a subclass of `DirectContributor`. Some examples of pollutants include biological pollutants (viruses, pathogens, bacteria, etc.), chemical pollutants (toxic metal, radionuclides, organophosphorus compounds, gases, etc.) and physical pollutants (sound, thermal energy, space debris, etc.) present in the environment.

IndirectContributor. This represents the things that indirectly contribute to pollution at a particular spatiotemporal point. These include environmental factors like temperature, the air or water streams flowing into or out of a particular place, the socio-economic factors such as policies and demographics. We have modelled the `Carrier` concept as the subclass of `IndirectContributor` since other indirect contributors are specific to certain kinds of pollution.

Carrier. This concept is a subclass of the `IndirectContributor` concept and represents the air, water, and other kinds of streams flowing into or out of a particular place. It is linked to the `Trajectory` concept through the `hasTrajectory` property. Carriers are generally observed to affect the concentration of pollutants at a particular place and are important in modelling pollutants. To represent the pollutants that might be carried through a trajectory, the `Carrier` concept is linked to the `Pollutant` concept by the `carriesPollutant` property.

Pollutant. `Pollutant` is a central concept in the Pollution module. It is associated with the `Observation` class to keep a record of pollutant concentrations at any location and timestamp. Each pollutant has a prescribed standard that is defined by the government authorities. The `Pollutant` class and its connections are shown in Fig. 5.

hasPrescribedStandard. Links a pollutant with standard limits based on concentration/amount of that pollutant in the environment. For example, WHO prescribed standard for $PM_{2.5}$ is less than 5 $\mu g/m^3$ mean concentration in the air annually.

hasObservation. This is used to capture the concentration of a particular pollutant at a given time and spatial location.

PrescribedStandardForPollutants. This is a stub meta-pattern [2] that can be used to describe the prescribed ranges for pollutants. For a particular location, pollutants have a defined range of permissible concentrations that are specified by various global authorities. A standard for a pollutant may change with time and place. Hence the `PrescribedStandardForPollutant` concept is linked to the `Observation` concept by the `hasObservation` property.

PollutantGenerator. Pollutant generators are events that generate pollution, such as crop burning, power plants, waste burning and dusty weather. It is related to the `Perception` class in the *Ethnography* module, indicating the perception of people on the severity of pollution concentration in a specific area. The `PollutantGenerator` class and its connections are shown in Fig. 6.

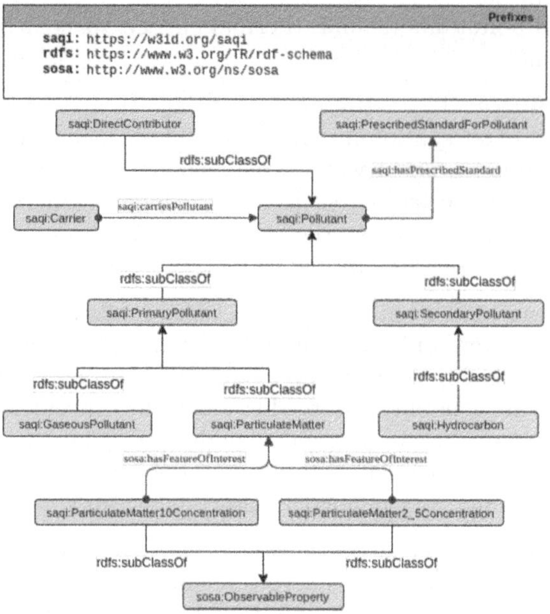

Fig. 5. Pollutant class and its connections

nearby. This property links a pollution generator to a carrier trajectory.

sourceResponsibleForLocalPollution. The perception of pollution is directly linked to observable pollution generators in a locality, resulting in the perception of pollution by the people in that locality.

5.2 Trajectory Ontology

Concepts in the *Trajectory* module use the concepts from the Pollution ODP (Fig. 7). It models the trajectories of pollution carriers. For example, a wind current passing through a crop burning site may carry carbon based pollutants to another destination. This displacement of pollutants needs to be accounted for to get a holistic understanding of air pollution. The trajectory component has been adapted from the Trajectory ODP [10]. A brief description of the *Trajectory* module concepts is as follows.

Trajectory. The `Trajectory` concept represents a set of ordered spatiotemporal points.

TrajectoryPoint and TrajectorySegment. The `Trajectory` concept is linked to the `TrajectoryPoint` and `TrajectorySegment` through the `hasPoint` and `hasSegment` properties. The `nextPoint` property links trajectory points

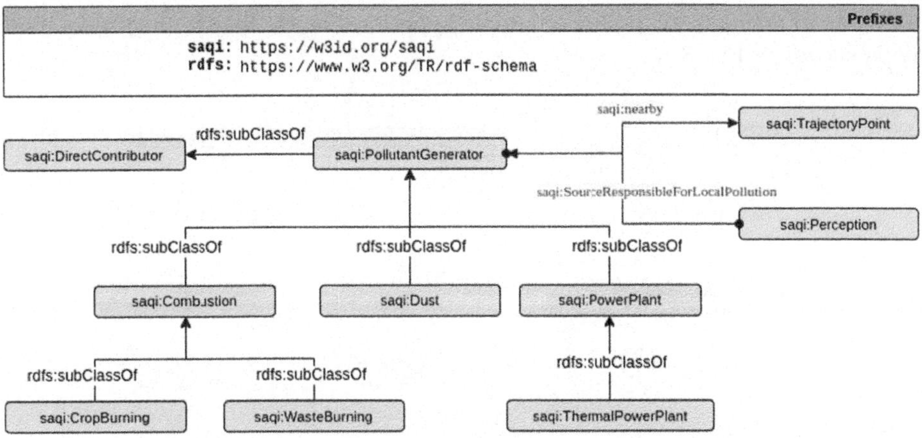

Fig. 6. PollutantGenerator class and its connections

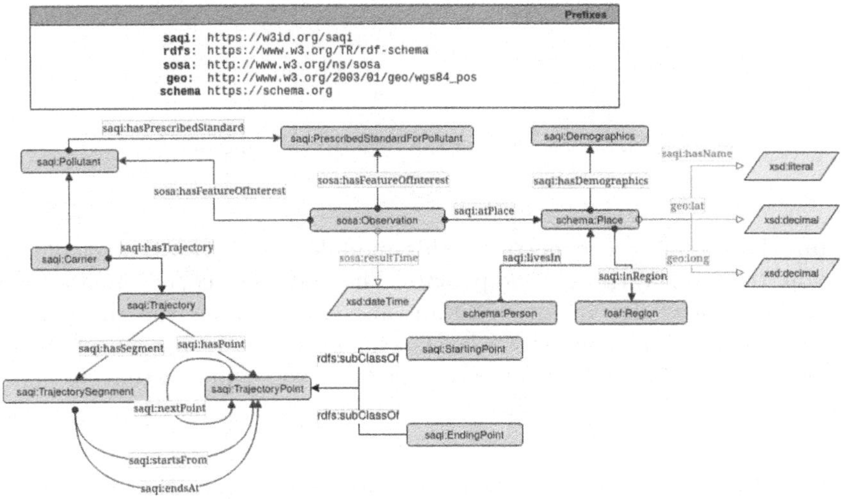

Fig. 7. Trajectory class and its connections

in the appropriate order within a trajectory. The segments in the trajectory are defined by a starting trajectory point $\{x_i, y_i, t_i\}$ and an ending trajectory point $\{x_j, y_j, t_j\}$ where t_i, t_j denote time points such that $t_i < t_j$. The `TrajectorySegment` concept represents this notion of a segment which is connected to two fixes through `startsFrom` and `endsAt` properties.

5.3 Ethnography Ontology

This ontology captures the ethnographic details of a location we obtained from the field survey. This data and the ontology can help frame policies and make decisions to mitigate air pollution at the hyperlocal level. The *Ethnography* module is shown in Fig. 8.

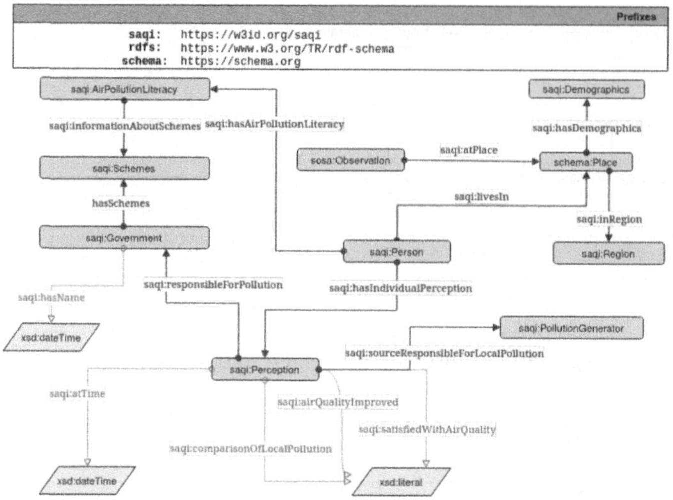

Fig. 8. Overview of the Ethnography module

Person. This is a core concept of this module since the ethnographic data relies on the observations of a person. The data we collect relates a person to their knowledge of air pollution and accounts for the social makeup through the aggregation of person-level data. This concept is connected to concepts such as `AirPollutionLiteracy`, `Perception` and `Region` through the `hasAirPollutionLiteracy`, `hasIndividualPerception` and `livesIn` properties.

AirPollutionLiteracy. This concept describes the air pollution literacy of the people in a locality. We assess this by asking questions[18] to the people related to their awareness of AQI and air pollution in general. The `AirPollutionLiteracy` concept has the data properties `hasAQILiteracy`, `hasAirPollutionGraphicLiteracy`, `hasParticulateMatterLiteracy` and `hasAQIColorLiteracy`.

Perception. This concept captures the perception of an individual with regard to the level of air pollution in their local neighbourhood and the city. It consists of data properties such as `howIsYourLocalityComparedToOtherAreas` (the literals that can be linked using this property are "equally polluted", "less polluted", "more polluted", "don't know"), `shouldPollutionIssuesBeRaisedInElections` and `localAirQualityRating`. An aggregation of people's perceptions in a particular region is expected to give the perception of that region.

[18] The questionnaire for collecting ethnographic data has been designed by social scientists in our team.

6 SHACL Shapes

SHACL[19] can be used to enforce constraints on the KG. The constraints are defined in shape graphs. KG must satisfy the condition specified in the shape graphs to be validated. Shapes for the classes were created, and the triples generated from the data using YARRRML mappings were validated using the SHACL constraints. A snippet of the SHACL shape for the `Person` class is given in Listing 1.1. It describes the constraint that a person can wear exactly one mask. The rest of the SHACL constraints are available at https://github.com/kracr/aq-structured-platform/tree/main/dataset/SHACL-shapes.

7 SAQI Application

We built a mobile and Web friendly SAQI application (Fig. 9)[20] that makes use of the KG to answer questions related to air quality. To mitigate the knowledge barrier in understanding AQI, increase awareness related to air pollution and improve citizen engagement, the app is designed to address all the sections of the community, including the tech ill-literate people. This is achieved using features such as support for local language – Hindi/English, heavy/large fonts, minimal user input, text-to-speech narration on every page and colourful graphics for AQI readings. The app consists of knowledge on air pollution and its effects which caters to specific social and spatial cohorts and also acts as AQI monitoring app that utilizes a KG built using SAQI ontology.

```
sh:property [
  rdf:type sh:PropertyShape ;
  sh:path saqi:wearsMask ;
  sh:datatype xsd:boolean ;
  sh:maxCount 1 ;
  sh:minCount 1 ;
  sh:name "wears mask" ;
] ;

sh:targetClass saqi:Person ;
sh:targetSubjectsOf saqi:hasAirPollutionLiteracy ;
sh:targetSubjectsOf saqi:hasIndividualPerception ;
sh:targetSubjectsOf saqi:livesIn ;
```

Listing 1.1. SHACL constraints snippet for the Person class

[19] https://www.w3.org/TR/shacl/.

[20] Web version of the app can be accessed live at https://w3id.org/saqi/app.

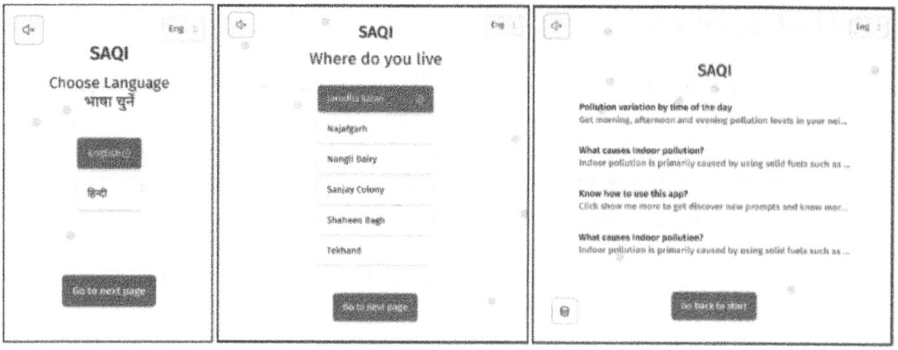

Fig. 9. User interface of the SAQI app. Each screen has only one clickable input with large, clear fonts with minimal content

A SPARQL endpoint is also embedded in the application with eight queries (an example is given in Listing 1.2 and its result in Fig. 10) on the pollution sensors data and the ethnography data from surveys. The ethnographic data and pollution data from local and central sensors are mapped to triples using YARRML[21] [8].

```
# The query returns average pollutants in specific time bands
  SELECT (AVG(?pm10Instance) AS ?pm_10)
  (AVG(?pm25Instance) AS ?pm_25) ?timesofday WHERE {
    ?obs_pm_25 a sosa:Observation .
    ?obs_pm_25 sosa:resultTime ?time .
    ?obs_pm_25 saqi:atPlace ?place .
    ?obs_pm_25 saqi:madeBySensor ?source .
    ?obs_pm_10 a sosa:Observation .
    ?obs_pm_25 sosa:observedProperty saqi:ParticulateMatter2_5Concentration .
    ?obs_pm_25 sosa:hasResult ?pm25Instance .
        ?place saqi:hasName ?placeName .
          ?source rdfs:label ?dataSource .
    BIND (hours(?time) AS ?hour)
    OPTIONAL { FILTER (?hour <= 8)
      BIND("Morning" AS ?timesofday)
    }
    OPTIONAL { FILTER (?hour > 8 && ?hour <= 16)
      BIND("Afternoon" AS ?timesofday)
    . . . ~(Filters for other time zones)
    }
  }
  GROUP BY ?timesofday
  LIMIT 10000
```

Listing 1.2. A sample SPARQL query used by SAQI

7.1 Evaluation

To evaluate the SAQI app, we conducted a user survey across the six locations where the local sensors were deployed. There were 60 participants spread across

[21] https://rml.io/yarrrml/.

PM 10	PM 2.5	Time of Day
331.96637	282.92276	Morning
381.802	332.8371	Night
302.69052	260.283	Afternoon
335.77588	285.6778	Evening

Fig. 10. Result of SPARQL Query from Listing 1.2

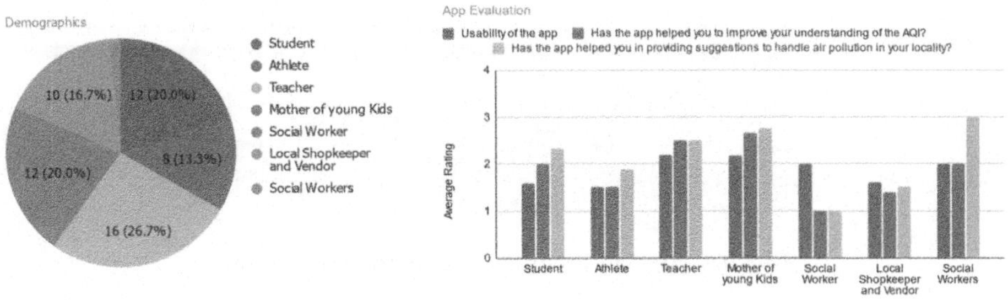

Fig. 11. Demographics and Evaluation scores

each of the six social cohorts. There were an equal number of male and female participants, and the age range of the participants was between 17 and 57 years. The questions to the participants were on media and digital literacy, AQI and air pollution awareness, the app's usability and utility, and community building after using the app. We used the Likert scale (1 to 5) for several questions, with 1 depicting the best case scenario and 5 the worst case. The feedback on the app was largely positive. The app got a usability score of ∼1.8, a utility score of ∼2.1 on the understanding of AQI and ∼2.25 on suggestions to handle air quality in a local region. This is shown in Fig. 11. The survey also captures feedback on the improvements to the app, which is available after anonymization at https://doi.org/10.5281/zenodo.10300235.

7.2 Triple Store Back-End

We deployed an instance of Apache Jena Fuseki[22] opting for the TDB2 database that provides efficient storage and query on RDF data. A lightweight cron job can be configured to periodically upload data to triple store using SPARQL Graph Store HTTP Protocol (GSP)[23] (Fig. 12). The uploaded data in KG consists of 3.4 million triples, mostly from sensor data collected over four months. The triple store is deployed on a server with 512MB RAM and a two core CPU. All of the SPARQL queries (https://github.com/kracr/aq-structured-platform/tree/main/sparql) embedded in the application run under 1 s.

[22] https://jena.apache.org/documentation/fuseki2/.
[23] https://www.w3.org/TR/sparql11-http-rdf-update/.

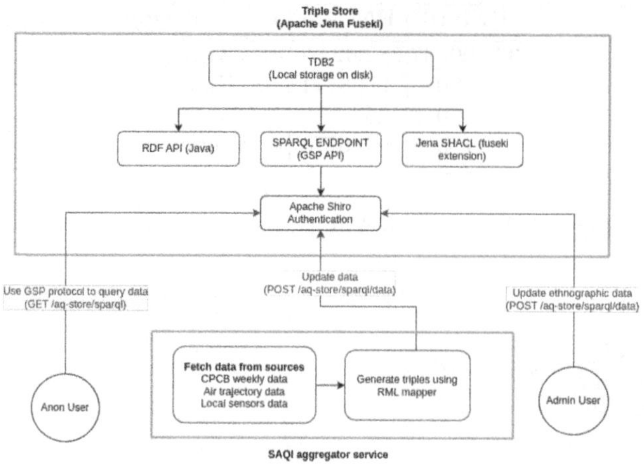

Fig. 12. System architecture for the triple store

8 Sustainability and Maintenance of Resources

Since the YARRRML mappings are used, generating KG from air quality sensor data and survey data is easy. This is scalable, i.e., we can expand to more regions and get more data. As long as the data format does not change, converting heterogeneous sensor and survey data to KG is sustainable. Over time, the SAQI ontology and the application may need changes. We will continue to work on the SAQI platform and make changes whenever required. We also hope the community will be interested and take this up. Since all the resources are publicly available, it is possible to make changes and share them with the community.

9 Conclusion and Future Work

We proposed Social Air Quality Index (SAQI), a new approach to increase awareness about air pollution, democratize AQI knowledge at the neighbourhood level and improve community participation. We developed a SAQI ontology to model the local and central air quality data and the ethnographic survey data from six localities in Delhi. The sensor and survey data are integrated into a KG using YARRRML mappings. We designed a neighbourhood pollution dashboard (SAQI app) that uses the KG to answer questions related to air pollution and the steps that each social cohort (students, teachers, mothers of young kids, athletes, etc.) can take to mitigate the effects of air pollution. The app has received positive feedback on its usability and utility. All these resources are publicly available under an Apache License 2.0 at https://github.com/kracr/aq-structured-platform and https://doi.org/10.5281/zenodo.10300235

In the future, we plan to incorporate more social characteristics from the neighbourhood into the ontology and the SAQI app, such as addresses and contacts of local government officials and the local pollution generating sources. We also plan to introduce graphical visualization in the app to explain the distribution and variation of AQI with respect to the time of the day, the seasonal variations, and their correlation to activities in the neighbourhood.

Acknowledgement. This work is partially supported by the Delhi Research Implementation and Innovation (DRIIV) program and The Infosys Centre for Artificial Intelligence (CAI), IIIT-Delhi, India.

References

1. Adeleke, J., Moodley, D.: An ontology for proactive indoor environmental quality monitoring and control. In: SAICSIT 2015: The 2015 Annual Research Conference of the South African Institute of Computer Scientists and Information Technologists, pp. 1–10. Association for Computing Machinery, New York (2015). https://doi.org/10.1145/2815782.2815816
2. Adila Krisnadhi, P.H.: Stub metapattern (2016). http://ontologydesignpatterns.org/wiki/Submissions:Stub_Metapattern
3. Agarwala, M., Chandel, A.: Temporal role of crop residue burning (CRB) in Delhi's air pollution temporal role of crop residue burning (CRB) in Delhi's air pollution. Environ. Res. Lett. **15**(11), 114020 (2020). https://doi.org/10.1088/1748-9326/abb854
4. Ahmad, S., Attri, S., Mutharaju, R.: An ontology design pattern for modeling pollution. In: Proceedings of the 12th Workshop on Ontology Design and Patterns (WOP 2021) co-located with 20th International Semantic Web Conference (ISWC 2021), Auckland, New Zealand, 24 October 2021. CEUR Workshop Proceedings, vol. 3011. CEUR-WS.org (2021). https://ceur-ws.org/Vol-3011/pattern3.pdf
5. Brickley, D., Miller, L.: FOAF Vocabulary Specification. Namespace Document 2 Sept 2004, FOAF Project (2004). http://xmlns.com/foaf/0.1/
6. Dwivedi, R., et al.: In search of a "Social-AQI"; democratic deficits in the air pollution data regime in Delhi. South Asia Multidiscip. Acad. J. **30**, 134–160 (2023). https://doi.org/10.4000/samaj.8768
7. Guarino, N., Oberle, D., Staab, S.: What is an ontology? In: Staab, S., Studer, R. (eds.) Handbook on Ontologies. IHIS, pp. 1–17. Springer, Heidelberg (2009). https://doi.org/10.1007/978-3-540-92673-3_0
8. Heyvaert, P., De Meester, B., Dimou, A., Verborgh, R.: Declarative rules for linked data generation at your fingertips! In: Proceedings of the 15th ESWC: Posters and Demos (2018)
9. Hogan, A., et al.: Knowledge graphs. ACM Comput. Surv. **54**(4) (2021). https://doi.org/10.1145/3447772
10. Hu, Y., et al.: A geo-ontology design pattern for semantic trajectories. In: Tenbrink, T., Stell, J., Galton, A., Wood, Z. (eds.) COSIT 2013. LNCS, vol. 8116, pp. 438–456. Springer, Cham (2013). https://doi.org/10.1007/978-3-319-01790-7_24
11. Huang, L., Hu, J., Chen, M., Zhang, H.: Impacts of power generation on air quality in china-part i: an overview. Resour. Conserv. Recycl. **121**, 103–114 (2017). https://doi.org/10.1016/j.resconrec.2016.04.010
12. Janowicz, K., Haller, A., Cox, S.J., Le Phuoc, D., Lefrançois, M.: Sosa: a lightweight ontology for sensors, observations, samples, and actuators. J. Web Semant. **56**, 1–10 (2019). https://doi.org/10.1016/j.websem.2018.06.003. https://www.sciencedirect.com/science/article/pii/S1570826818300295

13. Métral, C., Falquet, G., Karatzas, K.: Ontologies for the integration of air quality models and 3D city models. CoRR abs/1201.6511 (2012)
14. Oprea, M.M.: AIR_POLLUTION_Onto: an ontology for air pollution analysis and control. In: Iliadis, Maglogiann, Tsoumakasis, Vlahavas, Bramer (eds.) Artificial Intelligence Applications and Innovations III, pp. 135–143. Springer, Boston (2009). https://doi.org/10.1007/978-1-4419-0221-4_17
15. Riga, M., Kontopoulos, E., Karatzas, K., Vrochidis, S., Kompatsiaris, I.: An ontology-based decision support framework for personalized quality of life recommendations. In: Dargam, F., Delias, P., Linden, I., Mareschal, B. (eds.) ICDSST 2018. LNBIP, vol. 313, pp. 38–51. Springer, Cham (2018). https://doi.org/10.1007/978-3-319-90315-6_4

Conceptual Framework for Designing Hippocratic APIs

Sarmad Rezayat[1(✉)], Gerrit Burmester[1], Hui Ma[2], and Sven Hartmann[1]

[1] Clausthal University of Technology, Clausthal-Zellerfeld, Germany
sarmad.rezayat@tu-clausthal.de
[2] Victoria University of Wellington, Wellington, New Zealand

Abstract. The rapid proliferation of Application Programming Interfaces (APIs) enhances data exchange. Still, it introduces significant privacy and security risks, especially in the Internet of Things (IoT), where APIs often lack mechanisms to manage privacy and security, leading to vulnerabilities. Hippocratic Databases (HDBs) provide mechanisms, e.g., purpose-based access, to control database use. However, to effectively manage data access to the HDB, proper API design is crucial. This paper proposes a conceptual framework for a Hippocratic API (HAPI), revising traditional API design aiming to protect data subjects' rights and enhance security. By embedding data protection and ethical standards into API operations, HAPIs rectify inadequacies in consent mechanisms and mitigate privacy risks. We identify non-functional requirements, design objectives, and techniques through extensive research of recent literature, informed by the ethical principles of the GDPR, ISO/IEC 27001, and HDBs. We present our findings by knowledge graphs, providing a comprehensive conceptual view of the relevant design knowledge.

Keywords: API · GDPR · Non-functional requirements · Design objectives · Sensitive data · Privacy · Security · Transparency · Accountability

1 Introduction

The protection of privacy, recognized universally as a fundamental human right, faces escalating threats in our digital age [59]. This era is characterized by the rapid proliferation of digital data acquisition, processing, and distribution. Despite the presence of legal and ethical frameworks designed to safeguard individual privacy and data integrity [28,78], the challenge of implementing these principles on a technical level remains [70]. This is evident, for example, in the mechanisms of user consent [8], where traditional approaches often fall short in addressing user autonomy and informed decision-making under the prevailing conditions of digital interactions [49].

Originating in the early 2000s, HDB integrate privacy protection at their core, akin to the medical ethos of patient confidentiality underscored in the Hippocratic Oath [3]. They exemplify important steps towards privacy-aware data

W. Maass et al. (Eds.): ER 2024, LNCS 15238, pp. 355–376, 2025.
https://doi.org/10.1007/978-3-031-75872-0_19

management, setting the stage for further advancements in this field. Furthermore, the enactment of the General Data Protection Regulation (GDPR) by the European Union in 2018 marked a significant shift in legal frameworks governing data privacy [31]. It reinforces principles such as data minimization, purpose limitation, and the right to be forgotten. As the landscape of data management evolves and becomes more legally and ethically complex, it is crucial to consider the technological advancements that have paralleled these changes.

The widespread development and integration of APIs is a testament to this technological progression [38]. APIs, which have become ubiquitous in digital interactions, further complicate the challenges of maintaining privacy and security in an increasingly interconnected world [47].

This paper introduces the concept of HAPIs in an effort to respond to these developments. Drawing inspiration from the venerable Hippocratic Oath in medicine, which emphasizes 'first, do no harm' and upholds the confidentiality of patient information [62]. We propose HAPIs to bridge the gap between ethical frameworks and technical implementations, ensuring the privacy and integrity of user data are actively protected in the digital realm. By identifying the specific requirements needed to implement privacy and robust security measures, our initiative aims to protect data against misuse, collective data collection, forced consent, unauthorized access, breaches, and various cyber threats. These requirements encompass advanced encryption techniques, comprehensive authentication protocols, and continuous monitoring systems, fortifying the system's security and privacy framework. This integrated approach ensures that our API design aligns with GDPR compliance principles, effectively embedding ethical standards into technical practices [9,40,45,54,60,80].

Objectives of this Paper. We consider an API as Hippocratic if it is obliged to be designed with privacy in mind, safeguarding personal and sensitive data while being implemented by state-of-the-art security standards, maintaining transparency for users and accountability towards all involved parties, and incorporating the latest principles and laws of privacy regulations. The main contributions of this paper are the following:

1. We present a list of weaknesses of the current API design practice and introduce the concept of HAPIs;
2. We identify *non-functional requirements* from the literature, including the GDPR's principles, that are essential for HAPIs and provide knowledge graphs to link them to existing conceptual frameworks for general APIs; and
3. We identify a list of *design objectives* that address these essential non-functional requirements, integrate them in our knowledge graphs, and discuss state-of-the-art *design techniques* to customize them for HAPIs.

Requirements engineering has been a long-standing research direction of the conceptual modeling community, cf. [79]. Over the years, various methodologies have been proposed to support stakeholders in eliciting, understanding, analyzing, documenting, communicating, validating, or reasoning about software and information systems development requirements. Conceptual models help generate an abstract view of software and information systems that can be analyzed, developed, or maintained, thus facilitating shared understanding among stakeholders. Here, we focus on *non-functional requirements*, i.e., quality requirements of APIs. Our paper builds on prior work in the conceptual modeling community, in particular Sadi & Yu's WEBAPIK methodology [73] for handling requirements in API design but is also inspired by Gharib, Giorgini, & Mylopopouls [35] recent work on representing privacy requirements.

Organization of the Paper. This paper is organized as follows: Sect. 2 presents preliminaries and the background of our work. Section 3 discusses the observed shortcomings related to privacy, security, and transparency & accountability in APIs and provides an overview of the research methodology. Section 4 presents the non-functional requirements that are essential for extending API design towards HAPIs. Section 5 proposes design objectives and techniques to address these non-functional requirements as a first step towards practical implementation. In Sect. 6, we discuss the validation of our work. Section 7 is devoted to related work. Section 8 provides conclusions and suggestions for future research.

2 Preliminaries and Background

In this section, we present the background of our approach. We start with a brief overview of the GDPR and introduce terms and definitions to be used later on.

GDPR's Impact on Data Privacy and Security. The GDPR[1], introduced by the EU in 2018, marked a major shift in data privacy laws. It emphasizes principles like data minimization, purpose limitation, and the right to be forgotten [88], with strict penalties for non-compliance [18,58]. Defining key concepts like *personal data*, *processing*, and *data subject* is crucial for organizations [31]. Reflecting OECD (Organisation for Economic Co-operation and Development) principles, GDPR enacts specific laws rather than guidelines [66]. Its influence extends globally, as seen in the California Privacy Rights Act and the Federal Communications Commission Broadband Privacy Order, which may shape a future US privacy law [44]. GDPR's scope affects any organization processing EU residents' data, influencing global data practices [6].

Evolution and Impact of APIs in the Digital Era. APIs initially evolved as simple in-system code libraries to facilitate internal software communications. They serve as interfaces to reusable software components, integrated into libraries, frameworks, or web services [52]. With the Internet's rise, APIs became crucial for connecting disparate systems, enhanced by RESTful APIs leveraging

[1] https://gdpr-info.eu.

HTTP for client-server interactions [16]. Open APIs further revolutionized the digital landscape by allowing external developers to extend platform functionalities, marking APIs as significant technological advancements.

WEBAPIK knowledge base. [73] examines the design of web APIs with a focus on *non-functional requirements* by analyzing the relevant literature from March to August 2018 and in August 2022. Their work resulted in the development of WEBAPIK, a body of structured knowledge for the design of web APIs [73]. We adopted their conceptual model, see Fig. 1, as this is the basis for our work that aims at extending the WEBAPIK body of knowledge by incorporating the GDPR's goals and related principles. We aim at adding specific *non-functional requirements* for Hippocratic APIs and the adequate state-of-the-art design mechanisms to realize them.

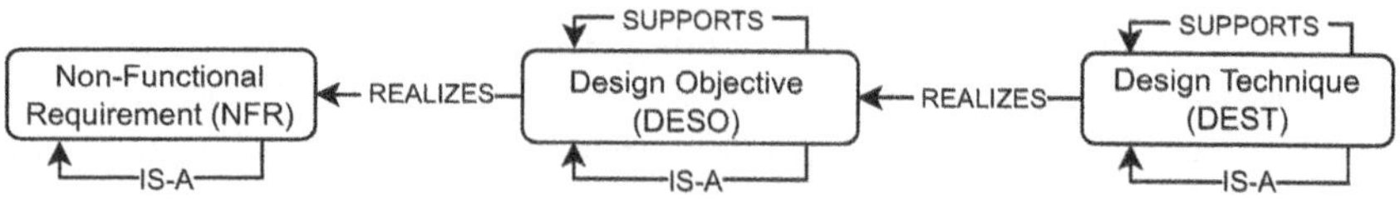

Fig. 1. The entity-relationship diagram that is used as the conceptual model for the WEBAPIK knowledge graphs adapted from [73] for our purposes here. We added the relationships "*SUPPORTS*" between two *design objectives* or *design techniques*, respectively, indicating that they have similar goals in which they support the other.

Knowledge Graphs. Following [73], we use knowledge graphs to display our findings. The nodes represent entities, such as *non-functional requirements*, *design objectives*, or *design techniques*. These are labeled as NFR, DESO, or DEST in this paper's knowledge graphs. The directed edges represent relationships and are labeled according to their type. Edges labeled with IS-A reflect hierarchical relationships between two *non-functional requirements*, *design objectives*, or *design techniques*, indicating specializations. Edges labeled with REALIZES indicate that a *non-functional requirement* is addressed by a *design objective* or that a *design objective* can be implemented by a *design technique*. We added the relationships of type SUPPORTS between two *design objectives* or *design techniques* and used them in our knowledge graphs to depict that these can still be realized without the other one and may not be a sub-class of the other one, but aim at a similar goal. It implies an overlap of the respective objectives of the child node and its parent, which enhances the parent's effectiveness and, therefore, supports the parent's objective.

3 Shortcomings and Research Methodology

With respect to the security of APIs, the Open Web Application Security Project (OWASP)[2] offers invaluable guidance. The OWASP API Security Top 10, a subset of the broader OWASP Top 10, specifically addresses common vulnerabilities within APIs, providing a roadmap for developers to secure their APIs against prevalent threats [10,51]. However, several gaps remain in OWASP's coverage in different domains. These include the lack of integration of security patterns and architectures, inadequate handling of OWASP IoT Top Ten vulnerabilities, insufficient domain-specific applicability and reusability, issues in dynamic and heterogeneous IoT environments, emerging IoT security threats not fully addressed, and incomplete consideration of privacy concerns [68].

The following weaknesses of API design practice are addressed by our proposed HAPIs: (W1) Traditional APIs often lack robust mechanisms to manage privacy and security, leading to significant vulnerabilities, especially in the IoT context. (W2) Also, such APIs typically have static rules for data handling and often face challenges in adapting to dynamically changing data and contextual requirements [57,67]. (W3) The integration of ethical and legal standards needs to be addressed as existing APIs do not adequately incorporate the GDPR and related ethical frameworks and legal standards into their design and operation. (W4) Another persistent challenge for APIs is ensuring data security across data transmission and storage stages. (W5) Lastly, APIs often lack transparency in data handling, making it difficult for users to understand how their data is collected, used, and shared. Insufficient accountability for data practices leads to potential misuse and results in a lack of trust.

Methodology of Research. The process to obtain the relevant information and literature as a basis for our work was done via systematic literature review, cf. [20,46]. Our research questions included the following: *RQ1*: Which *non-functional requirements* fulfill the definition of a HAPI. *RQ2*: Which *design objectives* and *design techniques* are needed to realize these requirements. For our search process, we used the search engines Google Scholar for scholarly articles and academic journals and Google to complement with other resources. Furthermore, we extended our search with databases like SpringerLink, ScienceDirect, ACM DL, and IEEE Xplore. We also consulted the survey paper [79] regarding recent conceptual modeling approaches for representing requirements. After we collected a wide amount of resources, we filtered those documents to gather requirements addressing *RQ1*. We derived 20 *non-functional requirements* that are essential for the design of HAPIs according to the GDPR's principles. We conducted further reviews to investigate *RQ2* to address all derived *non-functional requirements* and identified 28 *design objectives* and 13 *design techniques* to realize them

[2] https://owasp.org.

4 Non-functional Requirements of Hippocratic APIs

This section gives an overview of the *non-functional requirements* that we have derived from the principles in the GDPR and other related literature and identified as being essential for Hippocratic APIs. We have grouped them into three categories (API Privacy, API Security, and API Transparency & Accountability). The knowledge graph in Fig. 2 instantiates the entity-relationship diagram in Fig. 1 and shows all these non-functional requirements and their relationships.

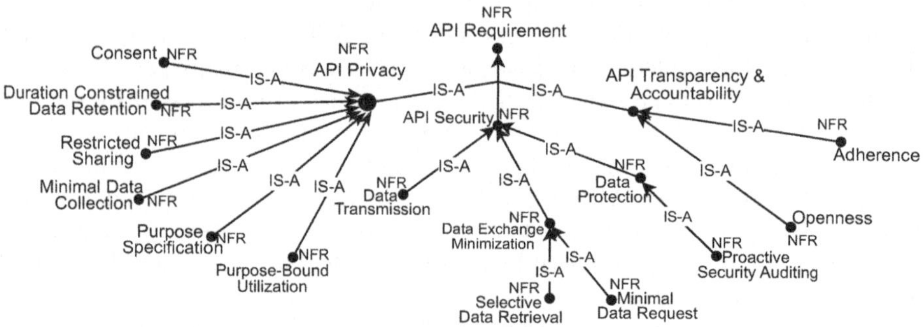

Fig. 2. Knowledge graph that incorporates the non-functional requirements that are essential for Hippocratic APIs and their relationships.

API Privacy (NFR). For Hippocratic APIs, the non-functional requirement API Privacy comprises of the following set of essential sub-requirements:

- *Consent (NFR):* The data subject must give explicit and specific consent for processing their data for a particular purpose and be able to withdraw it at any time. The consent must be freely given, informed, and unambiguous, and it must be given by a statement or a clear affirmative action, such as an opt-in [84]. The API controller, which we call the consent inspector, must demonstrate and observe that the consent was obtained lawfully and respect the data subject's rights under the GDPR.
- *Duration-Constrained Data Retention (NFR):* Ensures personal data is retained only as long as necessary for its intended purposes. This approach mandates a systematic review and deletion or anonymization of data beyond its utility, safeguarding privacy and minimizing data vulnerability.
- *Restricted Sharing (NFR):* The API should only disclose the data to parties who have the right and the need to access it and block any unauthorized or improper data sharing.
- *Minimal Data Collection (NFR):* The API and its clients must only collect the data essential for the intended tasks and refrain from collecting any unnecessary or irrelevant data; the data subject should be able to change what data is stored about the data subject.

- *Purpose Specification (NFR):* For personal information collected by the API clients, the collection purpose shall always be explicitly associated with the information in all applications that use the API.
- *Purpose-Bound Utilization (NFR):* The use of data must be tightly aligned with the purposes explicitly stated at the time of its collection. This ensures that each instance of data use is justified, ethical, and has received clear consent from the individual.

API Security (NFR). For Hippocratic APIs, the non-functional requirement API Security comprises of the following set of essential sub-requirements:

- *Data Transmission (NFR):* The API shall ensure that all personal information collected by the API clients is securely transferred and stored in the API's database and no third party can access or alter it. Authorized third-party access is permitted under strict conditions, ensuring alignment with consent and purpose specification principles.
- *Data Exchange Minimization (NFR)*: The data exchanged between the client and the API should be minimized. Only request and transmit the minimum necessary data to fulfill the client's request. Note that this non-functional requirement has the following sub-requirements:
  - *Selective Data Retrieval (NFR)*: Implement mechanisms to retrieve only the data needed for a specific operation, which allows clients to specify the exact data they need and reduces unnecessary data transfer [37].
  - *Minimal Data Request (NFR)*: Request and transmit only the minimum necessary data to fulfill client requests.
- *Data Protection (NFR):* (From Data Accuracy and Integrity) Ensures that all data handled by the API not only faithfully represents the truth in a precise and correct manner but is also safeguarded against unauthorized, unintended, or harmful alterations irrespective of its state. Note that this non-functional requirement has the following sub-requirement:
  - *Proactive Security Auditing (NFR)*: Automated tools are required to assess the API's security posture, identify potential weaknesses, and ensure data integrity and confidentiality.

API Transparency and Accountability (NFR). Lastly, for Hippocratic APIs to ensure transparency and accountability, the following sub-requirements are essential:

- *Openness (NFR):* The API shall clearly identify the organization responsible for data collection and processing, both in the API documentation and the application interface. This is crucial for user trust and accountability. Also, mechanisms to dynamically identify and communicate errors to users need to be implemented comprehensibly. This includes the effective detection of errors and translation of technical issues into user-friendly messages.
- *Adherence (NFR):* The API shall provide mechanisms to monitor and audit all API clients' adherence to the above principles.

5 Design Objectives for Hippocratic APIs

In this section, we present design objectives that we identified based on the principles in the GDPR and other related literature to address the essential non-functional requirements given in Sect. 4. Where suitable, we also indicate state-of-the-art design techniques and similar mechanisms that are recommended for implementation. This section is divided into three subsections: we start with the design mechanisms concerned with API Privacy, then API Security, and finally, API Transparency & Accountability.

5.1 HAPI Design Objectives for API Privacy

Article 25[3] of the GDPR introduces the principle of 'data protection by design and by default'. However, it has been observed that in most online interactions, data collection occurs before the user's awareness or consent, undermining the GDPR's principles of transparency, accountability, and timely informed consent [89]. The current practice deviates significantly from the GDPR's demands, keeping individuals ignorant without the opportunity to consent before their data is collected and used [65]. Given the gap between the GDPR's ideals and current practices, our proposed HAPI initiative seeks to comply with the GDPR's principles. The knowledge graph in Fig. 3 shows the design mechanisms related to API Privacy and its sub-requirements that are essential for HAPI design.

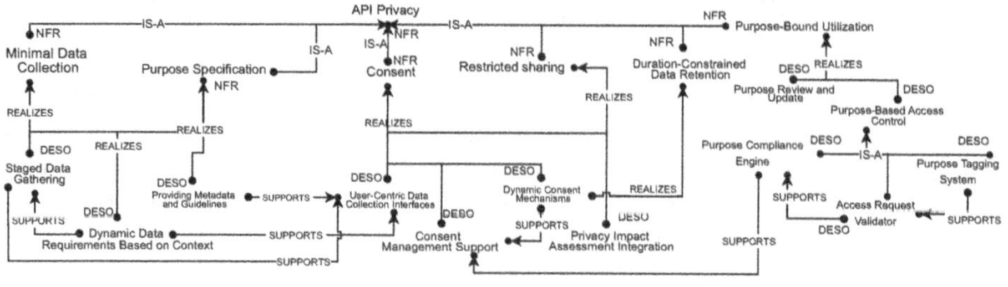

Fig. 3. Knowledge graph that shows the design objectives related to the non-functional requirement API Privacy and its sub-requirements that are essential for HAPI design.

Staged Data Gathering (DESO): Embodies a privacy-centric [43] approach to *Minimal Data Collection (NFR)*, employing a design objective where data is collected incrementally as needed. Initially, users are asked for minimal information, with additional data requested only when necessary. This improves user comprehension by providing concise explanations and requiring less review time. Implementing *User-centric Data Collection Interfaces (DESO)* in *Staged Data Gathering* ensures compliance with *Purpose Specifications (NFR)* and fosters a deeper understanding of data collection, enhancing the consent process and improving the quality of user *Consent (NFR)*.

[3] https://gdpr-info.eu/art-25-gdpr/.

Dynamic Data Requirements Based on Context (DESO): This approach allows the API and clients to dynamically determine which data fields are necessary for specific operations or under varying conditions. Consequently, client interfaces can adjust in real-time, requesting only the data crucial for the current interaction or process step [24]. This example can be seen in Fig. 6.

Providing Metadata and Guidelines (DESO): The API can offer metadata [91] about required data fields, including their purpose and significance. This can be implemented through an endpoint that returns descriptions detailing why each field is needed and how it is used. Providing guidelines for *Client developers* on presenting these data fields enhances transparency and facilitates understanding. By using *API Specifications (DEST)*, developers can better understand functionality [64,90] and specify the intended use of each data field, leading to intuitive and accessible interfaces.

User-Centric Data Collection Interfaces (DESO): Prioritizes privacy and empowers users by illustrating each data field's significance and potential uses, including conditions for data sharing. This approach helps users understand data collection and sharing, facilitating informed consent aligned with purpose specifications [71]. For example, users are informed that their data could be shared with research partners only with explicit consent. This design objective promotes a consent-based framework by linking data fields to their intended use and transparently communicating these details. This builds user trust through clear communication and explicit consent mechanisms. It complies with the GDPR's privacy-by-design principle and meets regulatory requirements for explicit communication of data use [85].

Consent Management Support (DESO): Offer endpoints for managing user consents tied to specific data fields or purposes. This allows the client to send user consent decisions back to the API, where they can be logged and adhered to. The API can manage a consent registry, keeping track of which users have consented to what data collection and usage, and provide this information back to the client as needed for verification or audit purposes.

Dynamic Consent Mechanisms (DESO): Integrating dynamic consent mechanisms into the API is crucial for enhancing ethical standards and ensuring regulatory compliance with evolving data protection laws [19] such as the GDPR and the changes in the purposes of data usage in the API. Dynamic consent empowers users to manage their data consent in real-time [27], adapting to changes in data use and personal preferences. Unlike one-time consent, which may become outdated or misaligned with user intentions-particularly in cases of coercion or undue influence-dynamic consent allows for the ongoing adjustment of consent settings, reflecting the fluid nature of digital interactions and user autonomy [48]. By adopting this design objective, the APIs is empowered to continuously update users' consent in line with informed decisions.

Privacy Impact Assessment Integration (DESO): Embed mechanisms within the API for efficiently conducting and managing Data Protection Impact Assessment (DPIA) [32,33]. This could be facilitated through API tools that help clients evaluate the privacy impact of their projects and share results seamlessly.

Purpose Review and Update (DESO): Conduct periodic reviews and updates of the purposes for which data is collected and used.

Purpose-Based Access Control (DESO): Ensure that any data access or processing request is checked against the stored purpose metadata to verify user consent compliance [23,63].

Purpose Tagging System (DESO): Tag each data element with the purpose metadata at the time of collection. This metadata should include the explicitly stated purpose for collecting the data.

Access Request Validator (DESO): Validate and log every data access request to ensure compliance with the purpose.

Purpose Compliance Engine (DESO): Verify data access and processing requests against stored purpose metadata.

5.2 HAPI Design Objectives for API Security

The security of an API plays an important role and guarantees protection against data breaches and unauthorized access. Figure 4 shows an overview of API Security and in the following, we explain it divided into API Data Transmission, API Data Exchange Minimization, and API Data Protection.

API Data Transmission (NFR): Data Transmission is realized by *Secure Communication Channels (DESO)* and *Message Encryption (DESO)*, which is based on the following design objective and design techniques.

Encrypting Data at Every Stage (DESO): The HAPI data transmission requirements employ targeted DESOs to safeguard against unauthorized access, breaches, and vulnerabilities. [72] analyzed different design techniques for requirements for API access authorization. Based on their analysis, they found hybrid encryption as a suitable design technique. Hybrid encryption generally showed to be the state-of-the-art and the most secure approach [1,92].

TSL Hybrid Encryption (DEST): We propose leveraging the Transport Layer Security (TLS) protocol's hybrid encryption model, which combines Advanced Encryption Standard (AES) for data encryption with public key cryptography for secure key exchange [41]. This dual-layer encryption strategy is suggested to enhance the security of data transmission, offering robust protection

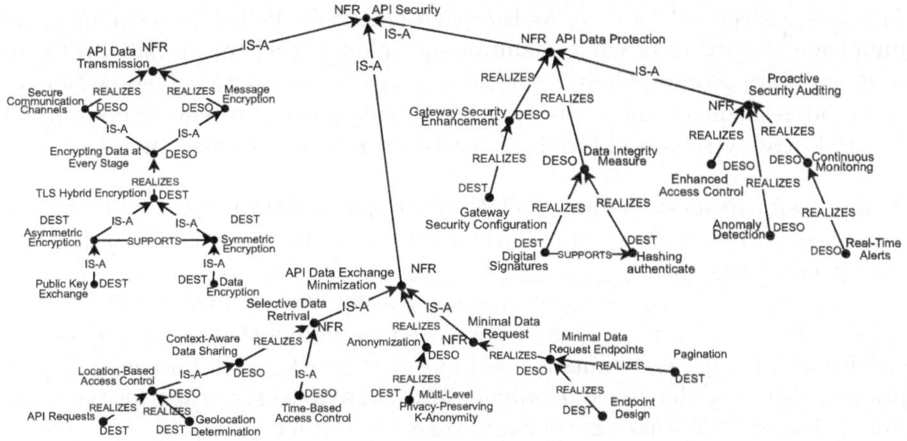

Fig. 4. Knowledge graph that shows the design objectives and design techniques for Hippocratic APIs related to the non-functional requirement API Security and its sub-requirements that are essential for HAPI design.

against unauthorized access, eavesdropping, tampering, and message forgery during transit and at rest. This approach aligns with our conceptual commitment to comprehensive security standards. Additionally, we studied homomorphic and quantum encryption as part of our investigation into advanced security measures.

Context-Aware Data Sharing (DESO): Adjust the data shared based on the specific context of the request to minimize exposure.

Location-Based Access Control (DESO): Use the user's IP address or GPS data to determine the location and adjust data sharing accordingly, e.g., only permit access to some dataset if the request comes from inside a certain country.

Geolocation Determination (DEST): Accurately determine the geographic location of the requester using their IP address or GPS data.

Location Checks in API Requests (DEST): Integrate location checks into the API request handling process to enforce access rules and modify the API request handling logic to include a geolocation check.

Time-Based Access Control (DESO): Use time constraints to control when data can be accessed, e.g., only allow access to certain financial reports during business hours.

Anonymization (DESO): To enhance privacy protections under our Decentralized Management and Auditing framework, we propose applying advanced anonymization techniques.

Multi-level Privacy-Preserving K-Anonymity (DEST) [87]: This technique could minimize exposure risks while maintaining tailored levels of privacy protection for diverse data groups. Though this necessitates precise data categorization and careful adjustment of anonymization levels, it is posited to effectively mitigate potential privacy risks and build a trust-based relationship with users.

Minimal Data Request Endpoints (DESO): Improve data privacy and efficiency by creating API endpoints that request and return only the essential data needed for a specific task.

Endpoint Design (DEST): Create specialized endpoints that serve minimal and specific data. Design endpoints focused on specific tasks, each returning only the data necessary for that task. *Example*: `GET /users/basic-info` for basic user information vs. `GET /users/contact-info` for contact details.

Pagination (DEST): Reduce the amount of data transferred in each request by implementing pagination for large datasets. A simple implementation can be using pagination parameters like page and size to break down data into manageable chunks. *Example:* `GET /products?page=2&size=10`

API Data Protection (NFR): This non-functional requirement is realized by two design objectives.

Gateway Security Enhancement (DESO): We suggest that API gateways could mitigate risks of security misconfigurations and injection attacks.

Gateway Security Configuration (DEST) : We propose implementing state-of-the-art mechanisms like Rate Limiting [77] or IP Whitelisting [7].

Data Integrity Measures (DESO): Digital Signatures (DEST) and *Hashing authenticate (DEST)* verify data integrity and prevent unauthorized alterations [11,40,60].

Implementing an effective Proactive Security Auditing requires a comprehensive, multi-layered design technique that includes the following key components:

- *Enhanced Access Control (DESO):* Strengthening Role-Based Access Control systems to ensure only authorized access to HAPI [76].
- *Anomaly Detection (DESO):* Specifically employing machine learning techniques to scrutinize API traffic and system behavior, detecting unusual patterns that may signal imminent security threats [29,74].
- *Continuous Monitoring (DESO):* Continuously scanning the entire IT infrastructure using advanced monitoring tools integrated with predictive analytics to identify and rectify misconfigurations and vulnerabilities promptly [55].
  Real-Time Alerts (DESO): Set up real-time alerting mechanisms that immediately notify administrators of potential security incidents, enhancing the ability to respond swiftly to threats [55].

5.3 HAPI Design Objectives for API Transparency and Accountability

Through transparency and accountability, it is possible to uphold ethical standards and foster trust between users, clients, and API. An overview of the knowledge graph can be seen in Fig. 5.

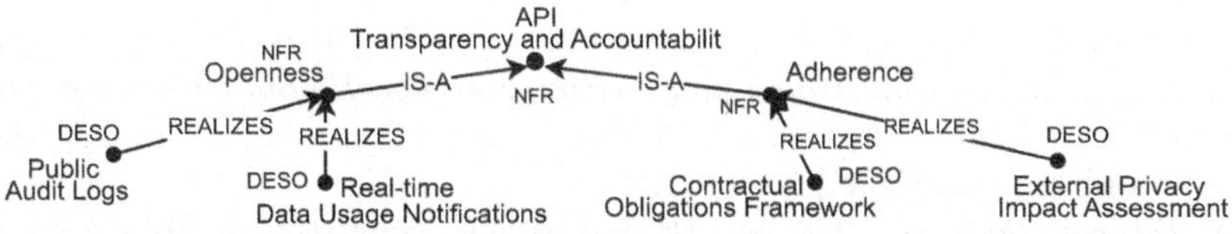

Fig. 5. Knowledge graph that shows the design objectives for Hippocratic APIs related to the non-functional requirement API Transparency & Accountability and its sub-requirements that we found essential for HAPIs.

Public Audit Logs (DESO): Implementing Public audit logs involves creating transparent logs of all data operations, such as access, modification, and deletion requests, which can be audited by authorized external auditors. This ensures that all actions are traceable and comply with the GDPR's principle of accountability.

Contractual Obligations Framework (DESO): Develop a standardized framework for Data Processing Agreements (DPAs) [86] that API clients must adhere to. This framework should detail both parties' responsibilities, including adherence to principles, compliance audits, and DPIAs.

Real-time Data Usage Notifications (DESO): To enhance transparency, HAPIs can implement real-time notifications that inform users whenever their data is accessed or used. This continuous feedback mechanism helps increase user trust and ensures that data usage is always transparent to the data-subject.

External Privacy Impact Assessments (DESO): Regularly conducting external privacy impact assessments and publishing the results can help ensure that HAPIs remain compliant with the relevant privacy laws and regulations such as the GDPR. These assessments help identify potential privacy risks and the effectiveness of existing privacy controls.

The design objectives and techniques described in Sect. 5 aim to ensure that HAPIs comply with legal requirements and set a higher standard for ethical data management, enhancing user trust and system integrity.

6 Validation of Our Approach

In Sect. 3, we summarized the weaknesses of the current API design practice in comparison to the GDPR principles. We now explain how our proposed HAPIs addresses each weakness. To tackle (W1), we developed a concept that integrates privacy, security, and transparency from the ground up. We use a systematic literature review approach to identify requirements and provide design objectives and techniques. Our findings indicate that embedding privacy considerations early in API design ensures compliance with API Privacy requirements by establishing *Minimal Data Collection (NFR)*, *Purpose-Bound Utilization (NFR)*, *Dynamic Consent Management (DESO)*, etc., resulting in a privacy-centric API design to address this issue [22,43,71,85].

To address (W2), our framework equips API with the flexibility to adapt to dynamically changing data and contextual requirements. We achieve this by implementing *context-aware data sharing (DESO)* and *dynamic data requirements based on context (DESO)*. By incorporating mechanisms like selective data retrieval and real-time data usage notifications, our APIs can adjust to varying conditions and requirements efficiently. This ensures that the data handled by the APIs is always relevant and used appropriately, thereby enhancing their adaptability and responsiveness to changing environments (see Sect. 5.1 for details). Appropriate privacy policies can be applied dynamically by using metadata and contextual information (such as location, time, user role, and data sensitivity).

Example. Figure 6 illustrates how HAPI design knowledge can be integrated into an API. Assume there is a health app that collects data for an API. The API uses this data to train and suggest exercise plans. The health app acts as a client in this scenario. Assume the health app monitors the user's exercise activity and overall health regime by utilizing heart rate data from their smartwatch and other data collected at earlier stages preceding the interactions depicted in this sequence diagram. Upon recognizing the commencement of an exercise session, the smartwatch informs the app (*Dynamic Data Requirements Based on Context (DESO)*). The app then requests to collect and process the user's data through the API (*Dynamic Consent Management (DESO)*). After verifying the user's consent, the app notifies the user about the ongoing monitoring. During the exercise, the smartwatch continuously monitors the user's heart rate and transmits the data to the mobile application in real-time. If an abnormality in the heart rate is detected, the app halts the monitoring and sends the data to the API to evaluate a potential change in the exercise plan. The API analyzes the heart rate data using a machine learning model trained to recommend exercises. If necessary, the user's exercise plan is updated accordingly. This streamlined process ensures that users receive personalized exercise recommendations while adhering to the highest standards of data privacy (i.e., staged, minimal, and context-aware data collection) and security (i.e., exchange minimization). □

In tackling the challenge (W3), we optimize our API framework by directly embedding comprehensive legal and ethical guidelines into its core, ensuring

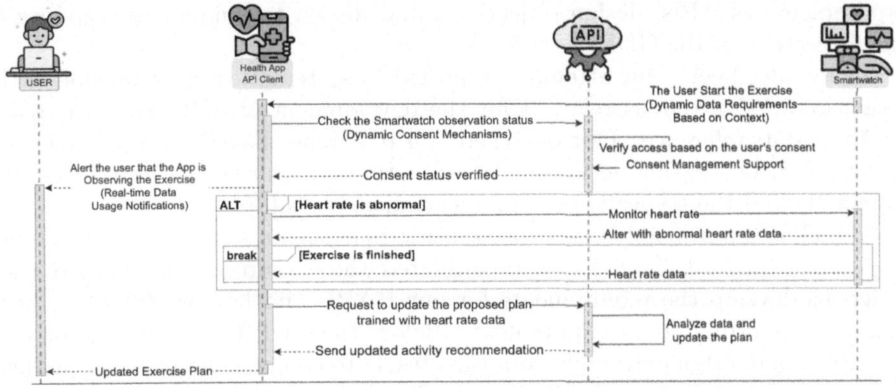

Fig. 6. Sequence diagram of a real-life scenario for the design objectives *Dynamic Data Collection Based on Context (DESO)* and *Dynamic Consent Management (DESO)*.

seamless GDPR compliance. Recognizing the existing gap between legal mandates and technical execution, we delved into GDPR and other ethical standards. For instance, our framework features *Purpose-Bound Data Utilization (NFR)*, *Dynamic Consent Mechanisms(DESO)*, and *External Privacy Impact Assessments (DESO)*, among other measures, meticulously designed to meet the requirements (see Sects. 5.1, 5.2, and 5.3).

To address (W4), we propose three main security requirements: API Data Transmission, API Data Exchange Minimization, and API Data Protection. These requirements include four sub-requirements and are operationalized through 14 *design objectives (DESO)* and 13 *design techniques (DEST)*, ensuring robust security at all stages of API interaction. As seen in Fig. 4, these measures collectively enhance the overall security framework, effectively mitigating vulnerabilities and ensuring compliance with data protection standards.

Lastly, regarding (W5) our framework implements comprehensive transparency measures to address this, including *Real-time Data Usage Notifications(DESO)* and *Public Audit Logs (DESO)*. These mechanisms ensure users are continuously informed about their data's status and usage, thereby enhancing accountability and fostering trust (see Sect. 5.3 for detailed methodologies). Furthermore, regular security audits and proactive monitoring can be incorporated to identify and mitigate potential security threats.

Additionally, using generative AI [30] to review error logs and present the errors more user-friendly will help increase transparency and gain users' trust, aligning with the *Openness (NFR)*.

7 Related Work

We have conducted an extensive literature review when writing this paper to find weaknesses of current API design practice, new or upgraded non-functional requirements of APIs, design objectives, and design techniques in response to the occurrence of the GDPR.

There have been some attempts to provide a systematic representation of the design knowledge that is relevant for the development of APIs; see in particular [73] and its references. Our work here was to extend the API design knowledge in [73] by incorporating additional non-functional requirements found essential for HAPIs and the respective design mechanisms to address them.

The GDPR's principles were discussed in many papers that we studied, such as [5,13,21,25,26,42,50,81]. We investigated these sources and adapted their design to develop the requirements for our HAPIs and how we translate principles into non-functional requirements. Before the GDPR was enacted, privacy principles were often extracted from the OECD to complement existing privacy-aware patterns found in the literature. See for example [81]. The emergence of the GDPR in 2018 stimulated a lot of new research since then. In [25], the interpretation of privacy by the design of GDPR is investigated with the aim of creating a conceptual model of privacy by design in compliance to the deducted requirements set by GDPR for processing personal data. [26] analyzed ontologies, policy languages, and vocabulary in the context of privacy-related rights and obligations regarding the GDPR. [4] analyzed five different laws, including the GDPR, to observe major challenges for the integration of privacy-preserving techniques in software development. [83] proposed a standard data protection model for GDPR compliance through structured technical and organizational measures. It analyzed data protection requirements and protection goals to suggest a versatile framework for organizations to safeguard personal data and meet legal obligations resulting from the GDPR. We investigated the observations in these works to obtain a fundamental basis for interpreting the GDPR principles into non-functional requirements we considered essential for HAPIs.

In the conceptual modeling community, there have been several works on representing requirements such as [17,34–36,39,53] that were relevant for our research here. Various works emphasized the need for conceptual models to support requirements engineering. [35] proposed a core ontology for privacy requirements (called *COPri v.2*) providing important core concepts like privacy requirement, privacy goal, privacy mechanism, and privacy policy. [39] proposed the Ontology-based Requirements Engineering (ObRE) method that advocates the initial development of a domain ontology, which can then be instantiated and used during requirements engineering. This method is then illustrated by analyzing ethical requirements like beneficence or explicability based on a case of driverless cars. While these works were not concerned with API design, the idea of using conceptual models to make the domain knowledge explicit in the form of knowledge graphs for the discussion between domain experts, API developers, and users stimulated our paper.

We extensively searched the literature for works related to design objectives and techniques regarding their ability to realize the identified non-functional requirements for HAPIs. We referenced the main sources for individual design objectives and design techniques when we described them in Sect. 5. Security and its aspects were discussed, e.g., in [2,14,56,61,69,93]. [69] presented a framework to support finding undetected conflicts between requirements in the privacy domain, especially data minimization, security, and fairness. [2] proposed a combined security ontology to bridge the gap between security and safety domains using core concepts like security risk, vulnerability, and threat. We analyzed these works and selected suitable design mechanisms for our HAPI design knowledge. We also consulted several works that aimed at incorporating transparency & accountability and its aspects into existing software and information systems, such as [12,15,22,75,82,94]. E.g. [15] analyzed clinical workflows to integrate privacy-awareness, motivated by GDPR principles. They developed an algorithm to add privacy checks into existing workflows, such as newborn hearing screening, which was a fitting use-case to demonstrate their approach. [22] developed a tool to increase transparency based on informed consent and data protection by design. The tool's core is a 'regulation-to-code process' that translates GDPR principles into software code in their workflow.

We used the design knowledge that we extracted from the consulted literature to select those non-functional requirements and design mechanisms that we considered essential for HAPIs in extension of the existing body of knowledge on API design, in particular [73], and developed knowledge graphs reflecting this extended understanding.

8 Conclusions

This paper presents a conceptual design of a Hippocratic API, an API that prioritizes privacy, security, transparency, and accountability and represents a significant advancement in ethical API design. By identifying essential non-functional requirements from general API frameworks, legal texts (e.g., GDPR or ISO/IEC 27001), and research literature, we were able to develop design objectives and techniques specialized for the concept of HAPIs. Requirements, design objectives, and techniques outlined in this paper provide a solid foundation for developing APIs that align with global data protection regulations, ensuring that APIs are designed with privacy in mind, safeguarding personal and sensitive data, and maintaining transparency for users and accountability towards all parties.

In [73], trade-offs between design techniques for APIs and the extent to which they effectively address their goals are studied. A similar discussion on HAPI design is crucial, but falls beyond the scope of this paper due to space constraints. We recommend this topic for future investigation, including a thorough examination of the validity and justification of the proposed conceptual framework.

References

1. Abroshan, H.: A hybrid encryption solution to improve cloud computing security using symmetric and asymmetric cryptography algorithms. Int. J. Adv. Comput. Sci. Appl. **12**, 31–37 (2021)

2. Adach, M., Hänninen, K., Lundqvist, K.: A combined security ontology based on the unified foundational ontology. In: IEEE International Conference on Semantic Computing (ICSC), pp. 187–194. IEEE (2022)
3. Agrawal, R., Kiernan, J., Srikant, R., Xu, Y.: Hippocratic databases. In: International Conference on Very Large Data Bases (VLDB), pp. 143–154. VLDB (2002)
4. Aljeraisy, A., Barati, M., Rana, O., Perera, C.: Privacy laws and privacy by design schemes for the internet of things: a developer's perspective. ACM Comput. Surv. **54**(5), 1–38 (2021)
5. Alkhariji, L., Alhirabi, N., Alraja, M.N., Barhamgi, M., Rana, O., Perera, C.: Synthesising privacy by design knowledge toward explainable internet of things application designing in healthcare. ACM Trans. Multimed. Comput. Commun. Appl. **17**, 1–29 (2021)
6. Amoo, O.O., Atadoga, A., Osasona, F., Abrahams, T.O., Ayinla, B.S., Farayola, O.A., et al.: GDPR's impact on cybersecurity: a review focusing on USA and European practices. Int. J. Sci. Res. Arch. **11**, 1338–1347 (2024)
7. Aryavalli, S.N.G., Kumar, H.: Top 12 layer-wise security challenges and a secure architectural solution for Internet of Things. Comput. Electr. Eng. **105**, 108487 (2023)
8. Askin, S., Burkhalter, D., Calado, G., El Dakrouni, S.: Artificial intelligence applied to clinical trials: opportunities and challenges. Heal. Technol. **13**, 203–213 (2023)
9. Atlidakis, V., Godefroid, P., Polishchuk, M.: Checking security properties of cloud service REST APIs. In: IEEE International Conference on Software Testing, Validation and Verification (ICST) (2020)
10. Bach-Nutman, M.: Understanding the top 10 OWASP vulnerabilities. arXiv preprint arXiv:2012.09960 (2020)
11. Badawy, M.: Security evaluation of different hashing functions with RSA for digital signature. Int. J. Comput. Inf. **10**, 99–116 (2023)
12. Barati, M., et al.: Privacy-aware cloud auditing for GDPR compliance verification in online healthcare. IEEE Trans. Industr. Inf. **18**, 4808–4819 (2021)
13. Barth, S., Ionita, D., Hartel, P.: Understanding online privacy - a systematic review of privacy visualizations and privacy by design guidelines. ACM Comput. Surv. **55**, 1–37 (2022)
14. Basdekis, I., et al.: Pseudonymisation in the context of GDPR-compliant medical research. In: International Conference on the Design of Reliable Communication Networks (DRCN), pp. 1–6. IEEE (2023)
15. Besik, S.I., Freytag, J.C.: A formal approach to build privacy-awareness into clinical workflows. SICS Softw. Intensive Cyber-Phys. Syst. **35**, 141–152 (2020)
16. Biehl, M.: RESTful Api Design, vol. 3. API-University Press (2016)
17. Bincoletto, G., et al.: Data protection by design in the E-health care sector: theoretical and applied perspectives, vol. 22. Nomos Verlagsgesellschaft (2021)
18. Bollinger, D., Kubicek, K., Cotrini, C., Basin, D.: Automating cookie consent and GDPR violation detection. In: USENIX Security Symposium, pp. 2893–2910 (2022)
19. Budin-Ljøsne, I., et al.: Dynamic consent: a potential solution to some of the challenges of modern biomedical research. BMC Med. Ethics **18**, 1–10 (2017)
20. Carrera-Rivera, A., Ochoa, W., Larrinaga, F., Lasa, G.: How-to conduct a systematic literature review: a quick guide for computer science research. MethodsX **9**, 101895 (2022)
21. de Chaves, S.A., Barreto Vavassori Benitti, F.: Privacy by design in software engineering: An update of a systematic mapping study. In: ACM/SIGAPP Symposium on Applied Computing (SAC), pp. 1362–1369 (2023)

22. Chhetri, T.R., Kurteva, A., DeLong, R.J., Hilscher, R., Korte, K., Fensel, A.: Data protection by design tool for automated GDPR compliance verification based on semantically modeled informed consent. Sensors **22**, 2763 (2022)
23. Colombo, P., Ferrari, E.: Enhancing MongoDB with purpose-based access control. IEEE Trans. Dependable Secure Comput. **14**, 591–604 (2017)
24. Diaz, R.A.C., Ghita, M., Copot, D., Birs, I.R., Muresan, C., Ionescu, C.: Context aware control systems: an engineering applications perspective. IEEE Access **8**, 215550–215569 (2020)
25. Drev, M., Delak, B.: Conceptual model of privacy by design. J. Comput. Inf. Syst. **62**, 888–895 (2022)
26. Esteves, B., Rodríguez-Doncel, V.: Analysis of ontologies and policy languages to represent information flows in GDPR. Semant. Web **15**, 709–743 (2024)
27. European Union: Art. 7 GDPR conditions for consent (2016). https://gdpr-info.eu/art-7-gdpr/
28. Faruque, M.O., Habibullah, S.M.: Privacy as a human right in the digital age: In quest of a safer protection regime in Bangladesh. ELCOP Yearbook of Human Rights, pp. 1–30 (2018)
29. Feroze, A., Daud, A., Amjad, T., Hayat, M.K.: Group anomaly detection: past notions, present insights, and future prospects. SN Comput. Sci. **2**, 1–27 (2021)
30. Feuerriegel, S., Hartmann, J., Janiesch, C., Zschech, P.: Generative AI. Bus. Inf. Syst. Eng. **66**, 111–126 (2024)
31. Regulation (EU) 2016/679 of the European Parliament and of the council of 27 April 2016 on the protection of natural persons with regard to the processing of personal data and on the free movement of such data, and repealing directive 95/46/ec (general data protection regulation). Official Journal of the European Union (2018). https://eur-lex.europa.eu/eli/reg/2016/679/oj
32. Georgiadis, G., Poels, G.: Towards a privacy impact assessment methodology to support the requirements of the general data protection regulation in a big data analytics context: A systematic literature review. Comput. Law Secur. Rev. **44**, 105640 (2022)
33. Georgiou, D., Lambrinoudakis, C.: Data protection impact assessment (DPIA) for cloud-based health organizations. Future Internet **13**, 66 (2021)
34. Gharib, M., Giorgini, P., Mylopoulos, J.: Towards an ontology for privacy requirements via a systematic literature review. In: Mayr, H.C., Guizzardi, G., Ma, H., Pastor, O. (eds.) ER 2017. LNCS, vol. 10650, pp. 193–208. Springer, Cham (2017). https://doi.org/10.1007/978-3-319-69904-2_16
35. Gharib, M., Giorgini, P., Mylopoulos, J.: COPri vol 2 - a core ontology for privacy requirements. Data Knowl. Eng. **133**, 101888 (2021)
36. Gharib, M., Mylopoulos, J., Giorgini, P.: COPri - a core ontology for privacy requirements engineering. In: Dalpiaz, F., Zdravkovic, J., Loucopoulos, P. (eds.) RCIS 2020. LNBIP, vol. 385, pp. 472–489. Springer, Cham (2020). https://doi.org/10.1007/978-3-030-50316-1_28
37. Goldsteen, A., Ezov, G., Shmelkin, R., Moffie, M., Farkash, A.: Data minimization for GDPR compliance in machine learning models. AI Ethics **2**(3), 477–491 (2022)
38. Gong, W., Zhang, W., Bilal, M., Chen, Y., Xu, X., Wang, W.: Efficient web APIs recommendation with privacy-preservation for mobile app development in industry 4.0. IEEE Trans. Ind. Inf. **18**, 6379–6387 (2022)
39. Guizzardi, R., Amaral, G., Guizzardi, G., Mylopoulos, J.: An ontology-based approach to engineering ethicality requirements. Softw. Syst. Model. **22**, 1897–1923 (2023)

40. Guo, Y., et al.: A security protection technology based on multi-factor authentication. In: International Conference on Mobile Networks and Wireless Communications (ICMNWC), pp. 1–5 (2022)
41. Gutub, A.A.A., Khan, F.A.A.: Hybrid crypto hardware utilizing symmetric-key and public-key cryptosystems. In: International Conference on Advanced Computer Science Applications and Technologies (ACSAT), pp. 116–121 (2012)
42. Hartmann, S., Ma, H., Vechsamutvaree, P.: Providing ontology-based privacy-aware data access through web services and service composition. Transactions on Large-Scale Data-and Knowledge-Centered Systems, pp. 109–131 (2016)
43. Johnson, G., Runge, J., Seufert, E.: Privacy-centric digital advertising: implications for research. Cust. Needs Solut. **9**, 49–54 (2022)
44. Jordan, S.: Strengths and weaknesses of notice and consent requirements under the GDPR, the CCPA/CPRA, and the FCC broadband privacy order. Cardozo Arts Ent. LJ **40**, 113 (2022)
45. Khovratovich, D., Beltrán, M.M., Mennink, B.: Generic security of the SAFE API and its applications. In: Guo, J., Steinfeld, R. (eds.) Advances in Cryptology - ASIACRYPT 2023. ASIACRYPT 2023. LNCS, vol. 14445, pp. 301–327. Springer, Singapore (2023). https://doi.org/10.1007/978-981-99-8742-9_10
46. Kitchenham, B.: Procedures for performing systematic reviews. Keele, UK, Keele Univ. **33** (2004)
47. Koçi, R., Franch, X., Jovanovic, P., Abelló, A.: Web API evolution patterns: a usage-driven approach. J. Syst. Softw. **198**, 111609 (2023)
48. Konow, J.: Coercion and consent. J. Inst. Theor. Econ. JITE **170**, 49–74 (2014)
49. Kovic, Ž., et al.: Valid consent in the acute hospital setting: perspectives of patients and members of the public. Ir. J. Med. Sci. (1971-), 1–12 (2024)
50. Krasnashchok, K., Mustapha, M., Al Bassit, A., Skhiri, S.: Towards privacy policy conceptual modeling. In: Dobbie, G., Frank, U., Kappel, G., Liddle, S.W., Mayr, H.C. (eds.) ER 2020. LNCS, vol. 12400, pp. 429–438. Springer, Cham (2020). https://doi.org/10.1007/978-3-030-62522-1_32
51. Lala, S.K., Kumar, A., T., S.: Secure web development using OWASP guidelines. In: International Conference on Intelligent Computing and Control Systems (ICICCS), pp. 323–332 (2021)
52. Lamothe, M., Guéhéneuc, Y.G., Shang, W.: A systematic review of API evolution literature. ACM Comput. Surv. **54**, 1–36 (2021)
53. Li, C., Palanisamy, B.: Privacy in Internet of Things: from principles to technologies. IEEE Internet Things J. **6**, 488–505 (2018)
54. Liestyowati, D.: Public Key Cryptography. J. Phys: Conf. Ser. **1477**, 052062 (2020)
55. Majumdar, S., et al.: ProSAS: proactive security auditing system for clouds. IEEE Trans. Dependable Secure Comput. **19**, 2517–2534 (2021)
56. Manos, P., Konstantinos, F., George, S., Sotiris, I.: Defining IoT orchestrations with security and privacy by design: a gap analysis. IEEE Internet Things Mag. **4**, 80–87 (2021)
57. Mohamed, A.K.Y.S., Auer, D., Hofer, D., Küng, J.: A systematic literature review of authorization and access control requirements and current state of the art for different database models. Int. J. Web Inf. Syst. **20**, 1–23 (2024)
58. Nguyen, T.T., Backes, M., Stock, B.: Freely given consent? Studying consent notice of third-party tracking and its violations of GDPR in Android apps. In: ACM SIGSAC Conference on Computer and Communications Security (CCS), pp. 2369–2383 (2022)
59. Nyst, C., Falchetta, T.: The right to privacy in the digital age. J. Hum. Rights Pract. **9**, 104–118 (2017)

60. Oh, S.R., Kim, Y.G.: Interoperable OAuth 2.0 framework. In: International Conference on Platform Technology and Service (PlatCon), pp. 1–5 (2019)
61. Oliveira, Í., Sales, T.P., Baratella, R., Fumagalli, M., Guizzardi, G.: An ontology of security from a risk treatment perspective. In: Ralyté, J., Chakravarthy, S., Mohania, M., Jeusfeld, M.A., Karlapalem, K. (eds.) Conceptual Modeling. ER 2022. LNCS, vol. 13607, pp. 365–379. Springer, Cham (2022). https://doi.org/10.1007/978-3-031-17995-2_26
62. Oath, P.: The Hippocratic oath. Am. J. Med. Genet. **58**, 187–94 (1995)
63. Pallas, F., et al.: Towards application-layer purpose-based access control. In: Annual ACM Symposium on Applied Computing, pp. 1288–1296 (2020)
64. Pandita, R., Xiao, X., Zhong, H., Xie, T., Oney, S., Paradkar, A.: Inferring method specifications from natural language API descriptions. In: International Conference on Software Engineering (ICSE), pp. 815–825 (2012)
65. Papadogiannakis, E., Papadopoulos, P., Kourtellis, N., Markatos, E.P.: User tracking in the post-cookie era: how websites bypass GDPR consent to track users. In: Web Conference, pp. 2130–2141 (2021)
66. Phillips, M.: International data-sharing norms: from the OECD to the general data protection regulation (GDPR). Hum. Genet. **137**, 575–582 (2018)
67. Pozzobon, L., Ermis, B., Lewis, P., Hooker, S.: On the challenges of using black-box APIs for toxicity evaluation in research. arXiv preprint arXiv:2304.12397 (2023)
68. Rajmohan, T., Nguyen, P.H., Ferry, N.: A decade of research on patterns and architectures for IoT security. Cybersecurity **5**, 2 (2022)
69. Ramadan, Q., Strüber, D., Salnitri, M., Jürjens, J., Riediger, V., Staab, S.: A semi-automated BPMN-based framework for detecting conflicts between security, data-minimization, and fairness requirements. Softw. Syst. Model. **19**, 1191–1227 (2020)
70. Rao, P.M., Deebak, B.D.: Security and privacy issues in smart cities/industries: technologies, applications, and challenges. J. Ambient. Intell. Humaniz. Comput. **14**, 10517–10553 (2023)
71. Rivadeneira, J.E., Silva, J.S., Colomo-Palacios, R., Rodrigues, A., Boavida, F.: User-centric privacy preserving models for a new era of the internet of things. J. Netw. Comput. Appl. **217**, 103695 (2023)
72. Sadi, M.H., Yu, E.: RAPID: a knowledge-based assistant for designing web APIs. Requirements Eng. **26**, 185–236 (2021)
73. Sadi, M.H., Yu, E.: WEBAPIK: a body of structured knowledge on designing web APIs. Requirements Eng. **28**, 441–479 (2023)
74. Samariya, D., Thakkar, A.: A comprehensive survey of anomaly detection algorithms. Ann. Data Sci. **10**, 829–850 (2023)
75. Sánchez, D., Viejo, A., Batet, M.: Automatic assessment of privacy policies under the GDPR. Appl. Sci. **11**, 1762 (2021)
76. Saxena, U.R., Alam, T.: Provisioning trust-oriented role-based access control for maintaining data integrity in cloud. Int. J. Syst. Assur. Eng. Manag. **14**, 2559–2578 (2023)
77. Serbout, S., El Malki, A., Pautasso, C., Zdun, U.: API rate limit adoption - a pattern collection. In: European Conference on Pattern Languages of Programs, pp. 1–20 (2023)
78. Sinha, G.A.: A real-property model of privacy. DePaul L. Rev. **68**, 567 (2018)
79. Storey, V.C., Lukyanenko, R., Castellanos, A.: Conceptual modeling: topics, themes, and technology trends. ACM Comput. Surv. **55**, 1–38 (2023)

80. Sun, P., Shen, S., Wan, Y., Wu, Z., Fang, Z., Gao, X.z.: A survey of IoT privacy security: architecture, technology, challenges, and trends. IEEE Internet Things J. 1–1 (2024). https://doi.org/10.1109/JIOT.2024.3372518
81. Suphakul, T., Senivongse, T.: Development of privacy design patterns based on privacy principles and UML. In: IEEE/ACIS International Conference on Software Engineering, Artificial Intelligence, Networking and Parallel/Distributed Computing (SNPD), pp. 369–375. IEEE (2017)
82. Truong, N.B., Sun, K., Lee, G.M., Guo, Y.: GDPR-compliant personal data management: a blockchain-based solution. IEEE Trans. Inf. Forensics Secur. **15**, 1746–1761 (2019)
83. Unabhängiges Landeszentrum für Datenschutz: The standard data protection model - a method for data protection advising and controlling on the basis of uniform protection goals. Unabhängiges Landeszentrum für Datenschutz: Kiel, Germany (2019)
84. Voigt, P., von dem Bussche, A.: The EU General Data Protection Regulation (GDPR). Springer, Cham (2017). https://doi.org/10.1007/978-3-319-57959-7
85. Von Grafenstein, M., Jakobi, T., Stevens, G.: Effective data protection by design through interdisciplinary research methods: the example of effective purpose specification by applying user-centred UX-design methods. Comput. Law Secur. Rev. **46**, 105722 (2022)
86. Weiss, J.B.: Data processing agreements: coordination, drafting & negotiation. In: International Association of Privacy Professionals (IAPP) (2019)
87. Weng, J.H., Chi, P.W.: Multi-level privacy preserving k-anonymity. In: Asia Joint Conference on Information Security (AsiaJCIS), pp. 61–67 (2021)
88. Wolford, B.: What is GDPR, the EU's new data protection law? GDPR EU (2018). https://gdpr.eu/what-is-gdpr/
89. Wulf, A.J., Seizov, O.: Please understand we cannot provide further information: evaluating content and transparency of GDPR-mandated AI disclosures. AI Soc. **39**, 235–256 (2024)
90. Yasmin, J., Tian, Y., Yang, J.: A first look at the deprecation of RESTful APIs: an empirical study. In: IEEE International Conference on Software Maintenance and Evolution (ICSME), pp. 151–161. IEEE (2020)
91. Zeng, M.L., Qin, J.: Metadata. Facet Publishing (2020)
92. Zhang, Q.: An overview and analysis of hybrid encryption: the combination of symmetric encryption and asymmetric encryption. In: International Conference on Computing and Data Science (CDS), pp. 616–622. IEEE (2021)
93. Zhang, R., Liu, G., Kang, H., Wang, Q., Wan, B., Luo, N.: Anonymity in attribute-based access control: framework and metric. IEEE Trans. Dependable Secure Comput. **21**, 463–475 (2023)
94. Zhou, C., Barati, M., Shafiq, O.: A compliance-based architecture for supporting GDPR accountability in cloud computing. Futur. Gener. Comput. Syst. **145**, 104–120 (2023)

The Role-Artifact-Function Framework for Understanding Digital Identity Models

Frederico Schardong[1,2(✉)] and Ricardo Custódio[1]

[1] Universidade Federal de Santa Catarina, Florianópolis, Brazil
ricardo.custodio@ufsc.br
[2] Instituto Federal do Rio Grande do Sul, Rolante, Brazil
frederico.schardong@rolante.ifrs.edu.br

Abstract. Identity and Access Management (IAM) is a crucial aspect of online interactions, and researchers and practitioners have been exploring this area since the early days of the Internet. Over the years, many digital identity protocols and standards were created. While OAuth 2.0 and OpenID Connect (OIDC) are currently the most widely used and mature protocols, the emerging concept of Self-Sovereign Identity (SSI) and its underlying protocols promise greater user privacy and control. Although much emphasis has been placed on new protocols and implementations, the ontological and formal understanding of digital identity models still needs to be addressed. In this paper, we make three contributions: (i) introduce the Role-Artifact-Function (RAF) framework, which comprises a meta-metamodel and a metamodel; (ii) describe and compare digital identity models through the instantiation of the RAF metamodel; and (iii) present significant insights, including the conceptual equivalence between the established family of x509-based protocols and SSI, as well as the correlation between the chronological evolution of identity models and their increasing linguistic complexity.

Keywords: Identity and Access Management · Digital Identity · Self-Sovereign Identity · Metamodel

1 Introduction

During the early days of the Internet, Service Providers (SPs) established Identity Providers (IdPs) to authenticate users and offer customized services. This resulted in usability challenges, with users frequently resorting to weak password reuse across platforms, thus increasing vulnerabilities [27]. Third-party IdPs emerged, enabling users to register with a select few IdPs for access to various web services. This model concentrates valuable private information within a limited number of large repositories. In contrast, Self-Sovereign Identity (SSI) presents a digital identity paradigm centered on individual autonomy over their data. SSI empowers individuals as sovereign data guardians, granting them authority over its governance, storage, and sharing permissions [2].

W. Maass et al. (Eds.): ER 2024, LNCS 15238, pp. 377–395, 2025.
https://doi.org/10.1007/978-3-031-75872-0_20

Existing models lack formal descriptions on a shared ground, which will facilitate their comparison and evaluation. The increasing development of SSI has introduced new challenges and complexities to the field of IAM [2,18], making formal matters more urgent [29]. Formal studies can provide a common language and framework for evaluating digital identity models, allowing for more effective communication between researchers, practitioners, and policymakers. Additionally, such studies can help identify the strengths and weaknesses of different models, leading to the development of more robust and effective IAM solutions.

The IAM literature has often conceptualized digital identity models using a bottom-up approach, starting from real-world instances, such as the protocols and concrete implementations [29]. In contrast, this paper adopts a town-down approach, offering a structured methodology to describe and comprehend digital identity models. We introduce the Role-Artifact-Function (RAF) framework, which comprises a meta-metamodel and a metamodel. The latter is instantiated to formally describe three IAM models: (i) offline outsourced IdP; (ii) online outsourced IdP; and (iii) SSI. While this work does not cover the instantiation of these models to concrete identity systems or protocols, we offer high-level protocols that illustrate the foundational concepts of real-world protocols and applications implementing these models.

The remainder of this paper is organized as follows. In Sect. 2, we provide the required background on digital identity models. In Sect. 3, we introduce the RAF framework. In Sect. 4, we describe existing models using RAF, creating a shared ground to compare them in Sect. 5. We explore related work in Sect. 6 and conclude in Sect. 7.

2 IAM Preliminaries: Digital Identity Models

Different IAM models, also called identity models, can be categorized based on the responsibilities and interactions of the roles involved, namely user, IdP, and SP. Based on this classification approach, current identity systems and protocols can be generally categorized into three models, namely centralized (Fig. 1a), outsourced IdP (Fig. 1b), and SSI (Fig. 1c).

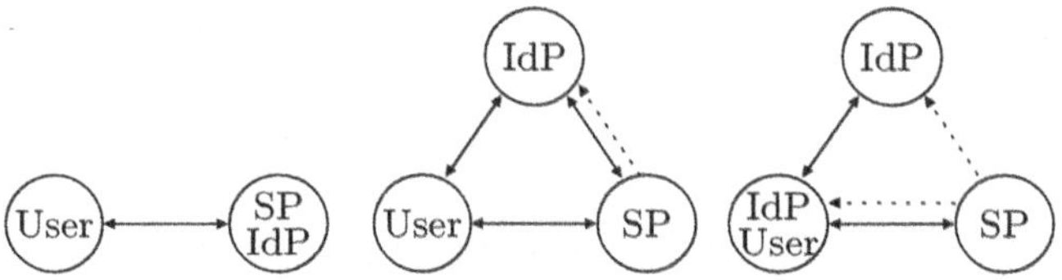

(a) Centralized. (b) Outsourced IdP. (c) SSI.

Fig. 1. Current digital identity models. Circles represent entities, labels represent roles, solid lines represent interactions, and dashed lines represent trust [29].

2.1 Centralized

In the early days of the Internet, SPs had no choice but to develop IdPs to authenticate consumers and offer customized products and services. Nevertheless, this resulted in the establishment of *centralized* authorities that served as both SPs and IdPs. Users frequently resorted to reusing weak passwords across multiple systems, resulting in many vulnerabilities and usability issues [27].

In considering adopting the centralized model, it is pertinent to acknowledge the establishment of the server-client architecture as standardized in 1996 through the Hypertext Transfer Protocol (HTTP) version 1.0. This initial version featured a rudimentary method for client identification and authentication, reliant on a straightforward comparison of usernames and passwords lacking cryptographic safeguards. Subsequently, in 1997, Digest Access Authentication was introduced to enhance security. This method introduced a nonce-based challenge, requiring the client to hash its response using MD5 before transmitting [11].

2.2 Outsourced IdP

The next logical evolution was to replace the centralized authorities with third-party IAM solutions, *i.e.*, IdPs. This paradigm shift allowed users to engage with a limited number of IdPs to access a diverse array of web-based services. While this approach streamlines the management of multiple identifiers and passwords for users, it also consolidates significant volumes of sensitive personal data within a few major silos. To standardize the interactions among IdPs, SPs, and end-users, token exchange protocols like SAML [14], OAuth 2.0 [13], and OpenID Connect [24] have been introduced. These protocols are used daily by billions of users through industry-leading IdPs like Google and Meta.

The OAuth 2.0 protocol introduced standardized procedures facilitating SPs to interact with IdPs[1] to obtain access to digital identity attributes or perform actions on behalf of users. However, its primary focus on authorization rather than authentication leads to the exclusion of crucial digital identity elements. OAuth 2.0 does not regulate how SPs should request fundamental digital identity attributes like name and email, leaving this determination to IdPs. Moreover, SPs cannot set a minimum Level of Assurance (LoA) acceptable for authenticating users. In response to these shortcomings, the OpenID Connect (OIDC) protocol was conceived as an extension of OAuth 2.0 [24].

2.3 Self-sovereign Identity

Self-Sovereign Identity (SSI) is a new approach to digital identity that emphasizes individual sovereignty over their data. Unlike previous identity models where individuals were viewed as mere users, SSI recognizes individuals as the sovereign owners of their data, granting complete control over it. They can manage and store their data and decide with whom to share it [29].

[1] OAuth 2.0 refers to SP as client and IdP as authorization and resource servers.

Christopher Allen [2] proposed ten principles an SSI system must fulfill. These principles, known as the ten principles of SSI, outline the characteristics of an SSI system and are as follows: (i) users must have an independent *existence*; (ii) users must *control* their identities; (iii) users must have *access* to their own data; (iv) systems and algorithms must be *transparent*; (v) identities must be *persisted*; (vi) information and services must be *portable*; (vii) identities should be *interoperable*; (viii) users must *consent* to identity use; (ix) disclosure of claims must be *minimized*; and (x) the rights of users must be *protected*.

Let us discuss the two most relevant principles for brevity: minimization and access. The *minimalization* principle enhances user privacy about attribute sharing. It allows users to share statements about their attributes, such as their age, rather than sharing their birthdate. This approach is advantageous because less information is shared and potentially retained by the SP. Zero-Knowledge Proof (ZKP) is a popular method employed to share predicates over one or more attributes of a credential without compromising authenticity or integrity [19,20, 28]. In brief, ZKP allows users to prove to SPs that some properties about attributes hold without revealing them [29]. The *access* principle means that users have complete control over their data without relying on IdPs to manage them. Users have autonomy over storing, managing, and sharing their data. ZKP also enables the implementation of the access principle by demonstrating the credential's validity without disclosing the credential to the SP [5]. Lastly, it is worth mentioning that trust is another critical aspect of SSI. Although individuals have the autonomy to issue their credentials, others are free to distrust them.

Let us move on from theoretical concepts to more practical topics. In the realm of SSI literature, Verifiable Credentials (VCs) [31] and Decentralized Identifiers (DIDs) [25] are crucial W3C standards [7,21,29]. The VC standard defines the terminology used in SSI, explaining that a *claim* is any statement made about a *subject*, and a *credential* is a collection of one or more assertions made about a subject. A VC is a credential that guarantees the credential's integrity, as well as the issuer's identification and non-repudiation. It contains a revocation list or another method of revocation. A *verifiable claim* or *Verifiable Presentation (VP)* is a tamper-resistant claim derived from a verifiable credential. Additionally, the DID specification outlines how SSI users can issue, update, and revoke identifiers independently without relying on other entities. These identifiers, digital wallets, and protocols, such as DIDComm [12] and DID Exchange [33] for exchanging personal information, are essential for SSI applications.

3 Role-Artifact-Function Framework

In this section's first part, the RAF meta-metamodel establishes a high-level abstract syntax, or a meta-language [17]. In the second part of this section, we introduce the RAF metamodel, an instance of the RAF meta-metamodel.

3.1 RAF Meta-Metamodel

The RAF meta-metamodel is grounded in set theory and is defined as follows.

Definition 1. *The RAF meta-metamodel is a triple* $(\mathbb{R}, \mathbb{A}, \mathbb{F})$*, where:*

- $\mathbb{R}$ is the set of *roles* played in the digital identity model.
- $\mathbb{A}$ is the set of *computational artifacts* employed by the roles.
- $\mathbb{F}$ is the set of *functions* in the metamodel with domain and co-domain in $\mathbb{R} \cup \mathbb{A}$. Subscript symbols represent the roles that can execute said function.

The *roles* are abstract entities with distinctive computational artifacts and functions that the real-world actors in an IAM system can play. For instance, in SSI, the end-user acts as an IdP and user. The *computational artifacts* represent algorithms, data structures, and other IAM-related artifacts. The *functions* are operations executed by roles. To instantiate this meta-metamodel into a metamodel, we need to provide instances for the sets $\mathbb{R}, \mathbb{A}, \mathbb{F}$ as described next.

3.2 RAF Metamodel

Definition 2. *The RAF metamodel is defined as an instance of the RAF meta-metamodel* $(\mathbb{R}, \mathbb{A}, \mathbb{F})$*, where:*

- $\mathbb{R}=\{s,\ i,\ v\}$ *represents the roles within the model.*
- $\mathbb{A}=\{\mathcal{C},\ \mathcal{R},\ \mathcal{M},\ \mathcal{P},\ \mathcal{L}\}$ *denotes the computational artifacts.*
- $\mathbb{F}=\{issue_i,\ revoke_i,\ status_{s,v},\ trust_v,\ authn_s,\ authz_s,\ request_v,\ present_s,\ verify_v\}$ *encompasses the set of functions.*

Next, we will describe each component in detail.
Roles ($\mathbb{R}$):

- s: subject, *i.e.*, the user, with a set of attributes $s_A \subset A$ (*e.g.*, age and name) where A is the set of all possible attributes[2].
- i: issuer, *i.e.*, the IdP.
- v: verifier, *i.e.*, the SP.

Computational Artifacts ($\mathbb{A}$):

- $\mathcal{C}$: set of credentials, and each credential $c \in \mathcal{C}$ asserts a set of attributes $c_A \subset s_A$ about subject s[3]. Each attribute $a \in c_A$ has an associated value, denoted by c_a.
- $\mathcal{R}$: set of revocation registries, where each registry $r_c \in \mathcal{R}$ associated with a credential c is associated with a boolean value indicating whether the credential c is valid.
- $\mathcal{M}$: general-purpose machine, *i.e.*, a Turing machine.
- $\mathcal{P}$: program for a general-purpose machine $\mathcal{M}$, *i.e.*, a tape with instructions for the Turing machine.
- $\mathcal{L}$: language for statements, *e.g.*, predicate or first-order logic, where $\mathcal{L}(c \cdot r_c)$ is a statement about a credential c and a revocation registry r_c in $\mathcal{L}$.

[2] We delegate the specifics, such as the value of attributes or how they change over time, to the instances of the metamodel.
[3] The expiration of credentials based on time is excluded for simplicity of abstraction.

Functions ($\mathbb{F}$):

- $issue_i : \{s\} \times \wp(s_A) \nrightarrow \mathcal{C} \times \mathcal{R}$—issuing a credential by issuer i takes the subject s, a subset of their attributes $s_{A'} \subset s_A$, and generates a credential $c \in \mathcal{C}$ with attributes $c_A = s_{A'}$ and a revocation record $r \in \mathcal{R}$.
- $revoke_i : \mathcal{C} \times \mathcal{R} \nrightarrow \mathcal{R}$—given a credential $c \in \mathcal{C}$ and its associated revocation record $r \in \mathcal{R}$, this function updates the record to indicate that c is revoked, producing a new revocation record $r' \in \mathcal{R}$.
- $status_{s,v} : \mathcal{R} \rightarrow \{\texttt{true}, \texttt{false}\}$—determines the revocation status of a credential c. If the revocation record r_c in the set $\mathcal{R}$ indicates that c is revoked, it returns `true`; otherwise, it returns `false`.
- $trust_v : \{i\} \rightarrow \{\texttt{true}, \texttt{false}\}$—the trust function of verifier v returns a boolean indicating whether it trusts issuer i.
- $request_v : \wp(\mathcal{L}(\mathcal{C} \cup \mathcal{R})) \nrightarrow \{s, i\}$—verifier v can inquire subject s or issuer i to provide a program $\mathcal{P}$ that meets the statements in the language $\mathcal{L}(\mathcal{C} \cup \mathcal{R})$.
- $present_{s,i} : \wp(\mathcal{C}) \times \wp(\mathcal{R}) \times \wp(\mathcal{L}(\mathcal{C} \cup \mathcal{R})) \nrightarrow \{\mathcal{P}\}$—presenting function takes sets of credentials, revocation registries, and statements as input and produces a program $\mathcal{P}$. The execution of $\mathcal{P}$ in $\mathcal{M}$ is designed to confirm the veracity of the provided statements without compromising the privacy of the associated credentials. Specifically, it ensures that no additional information about the credentials is disclosed.
- $authn_s : \{\mathcal{P}\} \rightarrow \{\texttt{true}, \texttt{false}\}$—the authentication function of the subject s takes a program $\mathcal{P}$ as input and returns a boolean value indicating whether the subject is the owner of the credentials expressed in $\mathcal{P}$.
- $authz_s : \{\mathcal{P}\} \times \{v\} \rightarrow \{\texttt{true}, \texttt{false}\}$—subject s authorization decision function receives a program $\mathcal{P}$ and a verifier v and returns `true` if program $\mathcal{P}$ can be shared with verifier v or `false` otherwise.
- $verify_v : \wp(\mathcal{L}(\mathcal{C} \cup \mathcal{R})) \times \{\mathcal{P}\} \rightarrow \{\texttt{true}, \texttt{false}\}$—verification function returns `true` if the execution of program $\mathcal{P}$ in $\mathcal{M}$ satisfies the set of statements in language $\mathcal{L}$ about credentials and revocation records and `false` otherwise.

As we conclude our exploration of the RAF metamodel, we focus on its practical applications in the next section. We apply the RAF metamodel to two pivotal identity models: outsourced IdP and SSI. This shift is a move from understanding the foundational elements of the RAF framework to seeing it in action, highlighting how it can be used to break down and analyze specific identity management approaches. By examining different digital identity models through the RAF lens, we aim to showcase the framework's utility in describing the nuances that transverse identity systems.

4 Digital Identity Models Through RAF

In this section, we instantiate the RAF metamodel into the outsourced IdP and SSI models. This process involves defining concrete instances of the abstract components of the RAF metamodel. For the sake of simplicity, we instantiate the most abstract and general elements of the metamodel, *i.e.*, we provide an instance of the language $\mathcal{L}$ and the function $present_s$ for each model. We demonstrate that these instances meet the functional requirements defined for each digital identity model. This study does not instantiate these models to actual digital identity protocols, but we provide high-level protocols that demonstrate the fundamental notions of real-world protocols implementing these models.

Firstly, we decompose the outsourced IdP model into two: offline and online. The former pertains to outsourced IdP interactions in which the IdP plays no active role in transmitting personal information when the end-user utilizes their credentials, which improves privacy. In contrast, the latter involves the IdP actively engaging in this process, reducing the end-user's privacy but easing the burden of storing and managing their credentials.

4.1 Offline Outsourced IdP Model

This section delineates the Offline Outsourced Identity Provider Model (OffOIdPM), a paradigm that allows the credential presentation to occur asynchronously. The model revolves around issuing a credential and a corresponding revocation record to the subject by the IdP, facilitating a verification process that does not necessitate continuous online access to the IdP. It has been a cornerstone of the Internet through the x509 digital certificate [15] and its family of protocols [1,3,4,16,22,26]. Definitions 3 and 4 lay the foundation for this model, which is further explored through Lemma 1 and Theorem 1.

Definition 3. *In the OffOIdPM, the issuer i issues a credential c and a revocation record r_c to the subject s through executing the $issue_i$ function.*

Definition 4. *In the OffOIdPM, subject s shares statements about themselves in language $\mathcal{L}(\mathcal{C} \cup \mathcal{R})$ with verifier v without the involvement of issuer i.*

Let us instantiate the RAF metamodel to describe the OffOIdPM.

Lemma 1 **($\mathcal{L}^\alpha$ as an instance of $\mathcal{L}$).** *In the OffOIdPM, the set of statements regarding credentials and their revocation status can be represented by the language $\mathcal{L}^\alpha$, which is an instance of the RAF metamodel's abstract language $\mathcal{L}$.*

Proof of Lemma 1. Proof by construction. The language $\mathcal{L}^\alpha$ is a regular language over the alphabet $\Sigma = \{c, r_c\}$, and can be defined by the regular expression $\mathcal{L}^\alpha = (cr_c)^*$. This formulation establishes $\mathcal{L}^\alpha$ as an instance of the abstract language $\mathcal{L}$, applicable to modeling offline credential verification processes. □

Corollary 1. *The regular language $\mathcal{L}^\alpha$ encompasses the empty string $\{\varepsilon\}$ and any sequence of credential c and its revocation record r_c. This regularity confirms that $\mathcal{L}^\alpha$ aligns with the formal requirements of $\mathcal{L}$, demonstrating its suitability for modeling credential and revocation record handling in the specified model.*

Lemma 2 **($present^\alpha_s$ as an instance of $present_s$).** *In the OffOIdPM, the function that produces programs $\mathcal{P}^\alpha$ to prove statements in $\mathcal{L}^\alpha$ is $present^\alpha_s$, which is a particular instantiation of RAF metamodel's abstract function $present_s$.*

Proof of Lemma 2. Proof by construction. The function $present_s^\alpha$ first ensures by a matching operation that the inputted credentials and revocation records are those referenced by the inputted statement in language $\mathcal{L}^\alpha$. Since the statements in language $\mathcal{L}^\alpha$ are plain sequences of credentials and revocation records, the program $\mathcal{P}^\alpha$ is a sequence of instructions to output the inputted statements. □

Theorem 1. *The instantiation of the RAF metamodel's* $issue_i$ *function following Definition 3 is trivial and is thus omitted. Language* $\mathcal{L}^\alpha$ *and function* $present_s^\alpha$ *are explicitly defined to align with the requirements specified in Definition 4. Together, these elements provide a complete description of the OffOIdPM.*

Proof. We prove Theorem 1 by construction using language $\mathcal{L}^\alpha$ and function $present_s^\alpha$. We present a high-level protocol that instantiates the OffOIdPM and describes the flow of information respecting Definitions 3 and 4. We refrain from instantiating other functions of the RAF metamodel as their implementation is straightforward. The protocol is depicted in Fig. 2 and proceeds as follows:

1. The issuer i generates a credential c and its revocation record r_c through the $issue_i$ function, dispatching both to the subject s.
2. The verifier v requests the credential c and its revocation record r_c from the subject s utilizing the $request_v$ function, specifying the desired language representation $\mathcal{L}^\alpha(c \cdot r_c)$.
3. Upon request, the subject s constructs program $\mathcal{P}^\alpha$ through the $present_s^\alpha$ function, embedding c and r_c within $\mathcal{L}^\alpha$ to fulfill the verifier's request, and transmits $\mathcal{P}^\alpha$ after evaluating $authz_s(P^\alpha, v)$ as `true`.
4. Authentication of ownership over program $\mathcal{P}^\alpha$ is achieved by s through the $authn_s$ function, establishing credibility in the presented credentials.

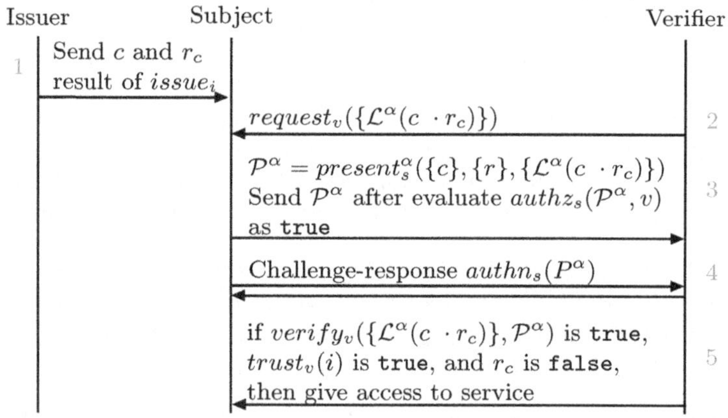

Fig. 2. The RAF-described OffOIdPM through a high-level protocol: the flow of information between issuer i, subject s, and verifier v. Numbers denote protocol steps, and arrows represent messages.

5. The verifier v grants access if it validates the received program $\mathcal{P}^{\alpha}$ against the requested information, the issuer's trustworthiness, and the credential's validity based on the revocation record, completing the verification process.

This high-level protocol exemplifies how the RAF metamodel's roles, computational artifacts, and functions can be instantiated to implement the OffOIdPM under Definitions 3 and 4. □

Our OffOIdPM model's description and the high-level protocol closely resemble the x509 certificate system and their related protocols [15]. For example, issuing x509 certificates, especially within national Public-Key Infrastructure (PKI) systems [1], involves rigorous verification steps to confirm the accuracy of subject attributes, akin to our $issue_i$ function. Similarly, the Automatic Certificate Management Environment (ACME) protocol allows internet servers to secure x509 certificates for domain names [3], another practical application of the $issue_i$ function. For revocation, the Certificate Revocation List (CRL) [4] serves as an example of revocation records R, with the Online Certificate Status Protocol (OCSP) [26] acting as an instance of the $status_v$ function. In our description, we emphasize offline verification, similar to how CRL might accompany a certificate without needing issuer contact due to both being digitally signed. Authentication is facilitated through the Certificate Management Protocol (CMP), a challenge-response system verifying private key ownership [16]. Finally, the Certificate Management over CMS protocol illustrates the $revoke_i$ function, showing how certificates are efficiently revoked [22].

The proposed high-level protocol and the digital certificate examples encounter two main problems: privacy and usability. Privacy is compromised because subjects cannot choose which credential attributes to share. Usability must improve since individuals must always have their credentials for verification. The privacy concern can be addressed with cryptographic schemes that enable selective attribute disclosure [23], which we present in Sect. 4.2. However, the usability issue is fundamental to the model and necessitates changing how information flows, which we explore in Sect. 4.3.

4.2 Self-sovereign Identity

The Self-Sovereign Identity (SSI) model is portrayed in the literature as a revolutionary identity model that gives individuals control over their credentials, including who can access them and how they are used [2,29,31]. However, it is simply a specialization of the OffOIdPM model, as seen below.

Definition 5. *In the SSI model, issuer i issues a credential c and a revocation record r_c to subject s by executing the $issue_i$ function.*

Definition 6. *In the SSI model, subject s shares statements about themselves in language $\mathcal{L}(\mathcal{C} \cup \mathcal{R})$ with verifier v without the involvement of issuer i.*

Definition 7. *In the SSI model, the language $\mathcal{L}(\mathcal{C} \cup \mathcal{R})$ must allow to: (i) express the disclosure of any subset of attributes of a credential c; and (ii) express properties and relations of any subset of attributes of a credential c.*

Note that Definitions 5 and 6 are copies of Definitions 3 and 4 from OffOIdPM framed for SSI. Thus, SSI is an extension of OffOIdPM that includes an extra bound. We formally describe SSI instantiating the RAF metamodel as follows.

Lemma 3 ($\mathcal{L}^\beta$ as an instance of $\mathcal{L}$). *In the SSI model, the set of statements regarding credentials and their revocation status can be represented by the language $\mathcal{L}^\beta$, which is an instance of the RAF metamodel's abstract language $\mathcal{L}$.*

Proof of Lemma 3. Proof by construction. The language $\mathcal{L}^\beta$ can be created using the First-Order Logic (FOL) constructs to encapsulate SSI's entities, relationships, and processes. The syntax and semantic integration of RAF with FOL forms language $\mathcal{L}^\beta$ as follows:

- Variables: Let RAF roles and computational artifacts denote the variables of $\mathcal{L}^\beta$.
- Predicates: Let RAF functions be incorporated as FOL predicates by aggregating the inputs and outputs of RAF functions as parameters of the FOL predicates. Non exhaustive list of examples:
  - $issue_i(s, s_A, c, r_c)$: reflects the RAF function $issue_i$, where issuer i issues credential c with attributes s_A and revocation record r_c to subject s. This predicate represents the action of credential issuance.
  - $trust_v(i, \texttt{true})$: reflects the RAF function $trust_v$ indicating that verifier v trusts issuer i.

  Moreover, auxiliary predicates to access and manipulate properties of RAF roles and computation artifacts are defined as follows:
  - $has(a, b)$: indicates if entity a posses, or contains entity b.
  - $comp(op, a, b)$: indicates if the boolean operator op (*e.g.*, $<$, $\geq$, $=$, $\not\to$, $\leftrightarrow$, etc.) between the operands a and b is $\texttt{true}$.
- Functions: No function is required besides standard FOL logical connectives and quantifiers. □

Corollary 2 (Direct mapping of $\mathcal{L}^\beta$ to RAF.). *By directly mapping RAF functions into FOL predicates, this construction ensures that the language $\mathcal{L}^\beta$ accurately reflects the operational semantics of the RAF framework. This direct mapping affirms the language's completeness in representing SSI dynamics.*

Language $\mathcal{L}^\beta$ enables the creation of comprehensive statements tailored for the SSI model, in alignment with Definition 7. To illustrate the capability of $\mathcal{L}^\beta$ in formulating such statements, we present two examples:

- A valid credential c which includes an *age* attribute and ensures that the value of this attribute exceeds 18.

$$\mathcal{L}^\beta(\exists c\, \exists r_c\, ((status_s(r_c) \Leftrightarrow \texttt{false}) \wedge has(c, age) \wedge comp(>, c_{age}, 18)) \tag{1}$$

– A valid credential c from issuer i (*e.g.*, a government body) with a *name* attribute whose value matches that of another credential c''s *name* attribute. Additionally, this second credential c' must be valid and possess a *category* attribute valued at *premium* and should be issued by issuer i' (*e.g.*, a ticket seller for a football game):

$$\begin{aligned}
&\mathcal{L}^{\beta}(\exists c\ \exists s_A\ \exists c'\ \exists s'_A\ (issue_i(s, c, s_A, r_c) \\
&\wedge issue_{i'}(s, c', s'_A, r_{c'}) \wedge (status_s(r_c) \Leftrightarrow status_s(r_{c'}) \Leftrightarrow \mathtt{false}) \\
&\wedge has(c, name) \wedge has(c', name) \wedge has(c', category) \\
&\wedge comp(\Leftrightarrow, c_{name}, c'_{name}) \\
&\wedge comp(\Leftrightarrow, c'_{category}, premium)))
\end{aligned} \tag{2}$$

Lemma 4 (*$present_s^{\beta}$* **as an instance of** *$present_s$*)**.** *In the SSI model, the function that produces programs $\mathcal{P}^{\beta}$ that proves statements in $\mathcal{L}^{\beta}$ without revealing additional information is $present_s^{\beta}$, which is a particular instantiation of the RAF metamodel's abstract function $present_s$.*

Proof of Lemma 4. Proof by construction. The construction of $present_s^{\beta}$ is demonstrated through the pseudo-algorithm presented in Algorithm 1. To fulfill Definition 7, we adopt ZKP and use a widely recognized notation [19,20,28], symbolized by $\Sigma = (Gen, Prove, Verify)$. Within this scheme, *Gen* generates common parameters, *Prove* for creating a cryptographic proof, and *Verify* for validating said proof.

Theorem 2. *The instantiation of the RAF metamodel's $issue_i$ function following Definition 5 is trivial and is thus omitted for brevity. However, language $\mathcal{L}^{\beta}$ and function $present_s^{\beta}$ are explicitly defined to align with the requirements specified in Definitions 6 and 7. Together, these elements provide a complete description of the SSI model.*

Proof. Proof by construction. Let $\mathcal{L}^{\beta}$, $present_s^{\beta}$ and $\mathcal{P}^{\beta}$ be employed in a protocol that describes the flow of information respecting Definitions 5, 6 and 7. We borrow the protocol from the Proof of Theorem 1, replacing $\mathcal{L}^{\alpha}$ by $\mathcal{L}^{\beta}$, function $present_s^{\alpha}$ for $present_s^{\beta}$, and program $\mathcal{P}^{\alpha}$ by $\mathcal{P}^{\beta}$. Moreover, the statement $\mathcal{L}^{\alpha}(c \cdot r_c)$ of steps two, three, and five are replaced by the FOL statement presented in Eq. 1. □

The SSI model preserves the user's privacy by allowing them to disclose only the necessary information. In this high-level protocol, the subject selects an attribute of one of their credentials to present to the verifier. The verifier does not receive the credentials or revocation registries directly. Instead, the subject constructs a program $\mathcal{P}^{\beta}$ using the selected credential and revocation registry and sends it to the verifier. The verifier trusts the program $\mathcal{P}^{\beta}$ because it is convinced of its truthfulness after executing it to verify the presented statements. The program $\mathcal{P}^{\beta}$ employs ZKP, a technique heavily used in the SSI literature [29].

The OffOIdPM requires users to disclose their credentials to the verifier, who may disseminate this information to other entities. On the other hand, the SSI

Algorithm 1: $present_s^\beta$

Input: Set of credentials $C \subset \mathcal{C}$, set of revocation records $R \subset \mathcal{R}$, query Q in language $\mathcal{L}^\beta$
Output: Program $\mathcal{P}^\beta$

```
Initialize P^β as an empty list.
Initialize CR'_s as an empty set.
Derive a set of conditions D from Q.
Create tuples linking each credential to its revocation record CR_s = {(c_1, r_c1),
  (c_2, r_c2), ..., (c_n, r_cn)} from C and R.
foreach d ∈ D related to attribute a, its value c_v or r_c do
    Add all tuples (c, r_c) to CR'_s in which any attribute a ∈ c_A
    its value c_v or revocation record r_c is relevant to d.
end
foreach (c', r_c') ∈ CR'_s do
    Establish common parameters p ← Gen().
    foreach d requiring verification of a, c'_v or r_c' do
        Extract witness w showing a, c'_v or r_c' satisfies d.
        Create ZKP: π ← Prove(p, {a, c'_v, r_c'}, w) without revealing w.
        Append Verify(p, π) to P^β.
    end
end
Combine all verification elements in P^β ensuring P^β ends with an evaluation that
  returns true if and only if all Verify operations are successful, otherwise false.
return P^β
```

model exhibits greater flexibility as it empowers users to generate statements regarding their credentials, enabling them to exert more precise control over disseminating their attributes on the Internet.

4.3 Online Outsourced IdP Model

Lastly, we diverge from the asynchronicity of OffOIdPM and SSI. This section delineates the Online Outsourced Identity Provider Model (OnOIdPM), which brings usability gains to the detriment of privacy towards the IdP. This model is today's *de facto* standard way of using digital identity on the web through the OAuth 2.0 and OIDC protocols. Let us formally define the OnOIdPM as follows:

Definition 8. *In the OnOIdPM, the issuer i issues a credential c and a revocation record r_c and either stores them or sends them to the verifier v.*

Definition 9. *In the OnOIdPM, the verifier v inquires the issuer i with statements about a credential c and its revocation record r_c.*

The Definitions 8 and 9 describe the OnOIdPM, which behaves very distinctively from OffOIdPM and SSI. From the beginning, it is evident that the user is not bothered by the need to store and manage credentials. Let us formally describe it, instantiating the RAF metamodel as follows.

Lemma 5 (**$\mathcal{L}^\gamma$ as an Instance of $\mathcal{L}$**). *In the OnOIdPM, the set of statements regarding credentials and their revocation status can be represented by the language $\mathcal{L}^\gamma$, which is a particular instantiation of the RAF metamodel's abstract language $\mathcal{L}$.*

Proof of Lemma 5. Proof by construction. The language $\mathcal{L}^\gamma$ can be created using a Context-Free Grammar (CFG), which allows for queries regarding attributes in a credential. Let us define the CFG as $\mathcal{L}^\gamma = (V, \Sigma, O, S)$, where V is a set of variables (non-terminal symbols), Σ is a set of terminal symbols, O is a set of production rules, S is the start symbol.

Variables (V):

- Q - A query.
- L - A list of attributes to return the value.
- B - An attribute.

Terminal Symbols (Σ):

- $age, name, ...$ - Attributes in A.
- s - The subject s.
- of - The subject from which to obtain the credential with the attributes.

Start Symbol:

- $S = Q$ - The start symbol is the query.

Production Rules (O):

1. $Q \rightarrow L\ of\ s$
2. $L \rightarrow B \mid B\ L$
3. $B \rightarrow age \mid name \mid ...$

Corollary 3. *The language $\mathcal{L}^\gamma$ facilitates querying one or more attributes from a credential. For example, the query "age name of s" is accepted by $\mathcal{L}^\gamma$, indicating it conforms to the grammar's rules for valid queries.*

Lemma 6 (**$present_i^\gamma$ as an instance of $present_i$**). *In the OnOIdPM, the function that produces programs $\mathcal{P}^\gamma$ to prove statements in $\mathcal{L}^\gamma$ without revealing additional information is $present_i^\gamma$, an instance of RAF metamodel's $present_i$.*

Proof of Lemma 6. The concrete function $present_i^\gamma$ has three steps. First, the query, *i.e.*, the statements in language $\mathcal{L}^\gamma$, are decomposed into a list of attributes and their credential using the CFG described in Proof 4.3. Second, for each existing attribute a in a queried credential c, an instruction is added to program $\mathcal{P}^\gamma$. This instruction outputs a and its value, namely c_a. Third, an instruction to output the revocation status of c, namely r_c, is added.

Theorem 3. *The instantiation of the RAF metamodel's $issue_i$ function following Definition 8 is trivial and thus omitted. Language $\mathcal{L}^\gamma$ and function $present_i^\gamma$ are explicitly defined to align with the requirements specified in Definition 9. Together, these elements provide a complete description of the OnOIdPM.*

Proof. We prove Theorem 3 by construction using language $\mathcal{L}^\gamma$ and function $present_i^\gamma$. We present a protocol that describes the flow of information respecting Definitions 8 and 9. The protocol is depicted in Fig. 3 and operates as follows:

1. Subject s requests a credential from issuer i, which creates a credential c with attributes *age* and *name* and the revocation record r_c, using function $issue_i$ and stores them.
2. Verifier v requests to issuer i for the attribute *name* of subject s using $request_v(\mathcal{L}^\gamma(\texttt{name of s}))$.
3. Issuer i uses $present_i^\gamma(\{c\}, \{r_c\}, \{\mathcal{L}^\gamma(\texttt{name of s})\})$ to obtain program $\mathcal{P}^\gamma$, then asks subject s to prove they are s referenced in $\mathcal{P}^\gamma$ through $authn_s(P^\gamma)$ followed by obtaining authorization to share program $\mathcal{P}^\gamma$ with v using the function $authz_s(P^\gamma, v)$.
4. Issuer i shares the program $\mathcal{P}^\gamma$ with verifier v, which grants access to subject s if $\mathcal{P}^\gamma$ satisfies the requested statements, and if they trust the issuer, and if the credential is not revoked.

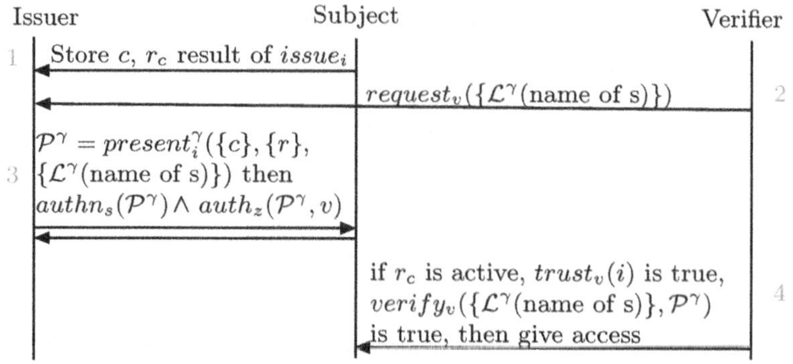

Fig. 3. Online outsourced IdP protocol: the flow of data between issuer i, subject s, and verifier v. Numbers denote protocol steps, and arrows represent messages.

The protocol describes a different information flow than the SSI model. The subject s does not have to store its credentials as the issuer i does that and shares programs with verifier v. This protocol is similar to OAuth 2.0 [13] in three ways. Firstly, the responsibility of implementing an authentication mechanism is delegated to the implementer. Secondly, it requires an expression of intention from the user for the issuer to share their data with the verifier, *i.e.*, the $authz_s$ function. Lastly, the program $\mathcal{P}^\gamma$ represents an `access token` containing the authorized user attributes intended for sharing with the verifier.

5 Discussion

The literature abstracts real-world applications that use identity in digital identity models. However, a thorough analysis demands more than abstracting roles and information flow. The RAF framework facilitates a deeper understanding, more effectively distinguishing between identity models. This section explores insights derived from the instantiation of models using the RAF metamodel.

The x509 Family and SSI have a Lot in Common. The literature points to SSI as a strong driver of innovation in the IAM field [21]. Indeed, significant innovation is happening in ZKP and privacy-preserving protocols [29]. Nevertheless, the Proof of Theorem 2 shows that SSI is, from a conceptual point of view, the result of the inclusion of privacy-preserving techniques to express statements about attributes, credentials, and revocation records to the OffOIdPM. This questions the need to abandon three decades of technological advances made in the x509 family of protocols and the myriad of applications that support them in favor of a new stack of technologies. Instead, integrating ZKP and similar modern technologies into existing x509 frameworks might offer users privacy benefits without discarding the existing infrastructure.

Chronological Development and Linguistic Complexity of e-ID Models. It is worth noting that the chronology of the creation and popularization of digital identity models aligns with Chomsky hierarchy [30], depicted in Fig. 4. Although we presented the models in the order of OffOIdPM, SSI, and OnOIdPM, their chronological development occurred as follows: first OffOIdPM, then OnOIdPM, and finally SSI. By analyzing the languages associated with these models in their chronological order and classifying them according to Chomsky hierarchy, we find that the languages $\mathcal{L}^\alpha$, $\mathcal{L}^\gamma$, $\mathcal{L}^\beta$ correspond to regular, context-free, and context-sensitive grammars, respectively. The adoption and widespread use of one model over another may be influenced by the increased expressiveness of the languages associated with each model, in addition to the improvements in privacy and usability.

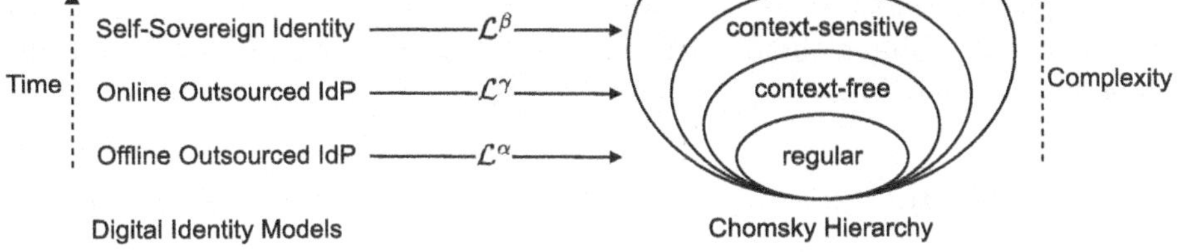

Fig. 4. Digital identity models and Chomsky hierarchy.

A Look Into the Future. The chronological development of digital identity models highlights the early establishment of OnOIdPM, which was distinguished by its usability improvement for the end-user. Despite SSI's later introduction, which conceptually echoed OffOIdPM's approach, there are research and market opportunities to leverage OnOIdPM's inherent usability advantages and tackle its privacy disadvantages. To this end, privacy-preserving techniques are being integrated into OnOIdPM's protocols, exemplified by OpenID for Verifiable Presentations, aiming to meld OAuth 2.0 and OIDC with ZKP to reconcile the privacy divide between SSI and OnOIdPM [32].

6 Related Work

There have been previous attempts to provide a meta-discussion on digital identity. The "The Laws of Identity" by Kim Cameron [6], for instance, attempts to develop an understanding of identity systems for the Internet. The author draws seven statements, named laws of identity, that they argue should guide the construction of digital identity systems. They range from user consent and minimal disclosure to the pluralism of technologies and consistent user experience. This work offers general guidelines instead of mathematically describing meta-identity with entities and their relationships as this paper does. This is also the case for the seminal work of SSI, *i.e.* the "The Path to Self-Sovereign Identity" by Christopher Allen [2]. Instead of detailing rules of a metamodel for identity or the SSI model itself, ten general directives for SSI are given. We have presented them in Sect. 2.

On the other hand, some related works formally describe identity models. In [9], an abstract identity model named the Digital Identity Model (DIM) is introduced. It defines domains of organizations, users, and their attributes, and a mapping between users, attributes, domains, and their values. In other words, users' attribute value depends on the domain. Other functions are also defined: *e.g.* $ident$, which returns the identifier for a given domain; $checkCredC$, which checks if an identifier and a credential with values match in a context. These are combined to describe existing identity models [8,9] and protocols [10]. In contrast to utilizing general functions as foundational elements that define identity models, *i.e.*, a bottom-up approach, our research presents a metamodel that is instantiated into a model, *i.e.*, a top-down approach. Through this process, entities, computation artifacts, and relationships are established, providing greater versatility and enabling the description of new models with novel relationships, a capability that DIM lacks.

7 Final Remarks

Engaging in meta-discussions about scientific subjects is an essential endeavor that facilitates a deeper understanding of the objectives and methods employed within a particular field of study. These attempts facilitate additional innovation by utilizing shared notation and establishing mutual knowledge about the various components and their interconnections.

This research paper introduced the RAF meta-metamodel and metamodel as a framework for examining identity and access management dynamics. It was used to formally describe three digital identity models, specifically the offline outsourced IdP, the online outsourced IdP, and SSI. The utilization of the RAF metamodel facilitated the comparison between the models, effectively highlighting their shared and distinctive characteristics. We hope future IAM-related works employ our suggested notation to articulate their novel contributions.

References

1. Adams, C., Lloyd, S.: Understanding public-key infrastructure: concepts, standards, and deployment considerations. Sams Publishing (1999)
2. Allen, C.: The path to self-sovereign identity. Available online: http://www.lifewithalacrity.com/2016/04/the-path-to-self-sovereign-identity.html (accessed on 04 June 2023) (2016)
3. Barnes, R., Hoffman-Andrews, J., McCarney, D., Kasten, J.: Automatic Certificate Management Environment (ACME). RFC 8555 (Mar 2019). https://doi.org/10.17487/RFC8555
4. Boeyen, S., Santesson, S., Polk, T., Housley, R., Farrell, S., Cooper, D.: Internet X.509 Public Key Infrastructure Certificate and Certificate Revocation List (CRL) Profile. RFC 5280 (May 2008). https://doi.org/10.17487/RFC5280
5. Camenisch, J., Lysyanskaya, A.: Dynamic accumulators and application to efficient revocation of anonymous credentials. In: Yung, M. (ed.) CRYPTO 2002. LNCS, vol. 2442, pp. 61–76. Springer, Heidelberg (2002). https://doi.org/10.1007/3-540-45708-9_5
6. Cameron, K.: The laws of identity. Available online: https://www.identityblog.com/stories/2005/05/13/TheLawsOfIdentity.pdf. Accessed 04 June 2023 (2005)
7. Čučko, Š., Bećirović, Š., Kamišalić, A., Mrdović, S., Turkanović, M.: Towards the classification of self-sovereign identity properties. IEEE Access **10**, 88306–88329 (2022). https://doi.org/10.1109/ACCESS.2022.3199414
8. Ferdous, M.S., Chowdhury, F., Alassafi, M.O.: In search of self-sovereign identity leveraging blockchain technology. IEEE Access **7**, 103059–103079 (2019). https://doi.org/10.1109/ACCESS.2019.2931173
9. Ferdous, M.S., Norman, G., Poet, R.: Mathematical modelling of identity, identity management and other related topics. In: Proceedings of the 7th International Conference on Security of Information and Networks, pp. 9–16. SIN '14, Association for Computing Machinery (2014). https://doi.org/10.1145/2659651.2659729
10. Ferdous, M.S., Poet, R.: Formalising identity management protocols. In: 2016 14th Annual Conference on Privacy, Security and Trust (PST), pp. 137–146. IEEE (2016). https://doi.org/10.1109/PST.2016.7906948
11. Hallam-Baker, P., et al.: An Extension to HTTP : Digest Access Authentication. RFC 2069 (Jan 1997). https://doi.org/10.17487/RFC2069
12. Hardman, D.: DIDComm Messaging. Available online: https://identity.foundation/didcomm-messaging/spec/. Accessed 04 June 2023 (2020)
13. Hardt, D.: The OAuth 2.0 Authorization Framework (Nov 2012). https://doi.org/10.17487/RFC6749

14. Hughes, J., Maler, E.: Security assertion markup language (saml) v2.0 technical overview. Available online: https://docs.oasis-open.org/security/saml/Post2.0/sstc-saml-tech-overview-2.0.html. Accessed 30 Aug 2024 (2005)
15. ITU-T: Recommendation x.509. Available online: https://www.itu.int/rec/T-REC-X.509-201910-I/en. Accessed 04 June 2023 (2000)
16. Kause, T., Peylo, M.: Internet X.509 Public Key Infrastructure – HTTP Transfer for the Certificate Management Protocol (CMP). RFC 6712 (Sep 2012). https://doi.org/10.17487/RFC6712
17. Kern, H.: Model interoperability between meta-modeling environments by using M3-level-based bridges. Ph.D. thesis, Universität Leipzig (2016)
18. Kuperberg, M.: Blockchain-based identity management: a survey from the enterprise and ecosystem perspective. IEEE Trans. Eng. Manage. **67**(4), 1–20 (2019). https://doi.org/10.1109/TEM.2019.2926471
19. Lee, J., Choi, J., Oh, H., Kim, J.: Privacy-preserving identity management system. Cryptology ePrint Archive 2021/1459 (2021)
20. Lee, J., Hwang, J., Choi, J., Oh, H., Kim, J.: SIMS: self-sovereign identity management system with preserving privacy in blockchain. IACR Cryptol. ePrint Archive **1**(2019/1241), 1–13 (2019)
21. Mühle, A., Grüner, A., Gayvoronskaya, T., Meinel, C.: A survey on essential components of a self-sovereign identity. Comput. Sci. Rev. **30**, 80–86 (11 2018). https://doi.org/10.1016/j.cosrev.2018.10.002
22. Myers, M., Schaad, J.: Certificate Management over CMS (CMC). RFC 5272 (Jun 2008). https://doi.org/10.17487/RFC5272
23. Polk, T., Lee, J., Park, S., Park, J., Lee, H., Lee, H.: Internet X.509 Public Key Infrastructure Subject Identification Method (SIM). RFC 4683 (Oct 2006). https://doi.org/10.17487/RFC4683
24. Recordon, D., Reed, D.: Openid 2.0: a platform for user-centric identity management. In: Proceedings of the Second ACM Workshop on Digital Identity Management., pp. 11–16. ACM, Alexandria, USA (2006). https://doi.org/10.1145/1179529.1179532
25. Reed, D., Sporny, M., Longley, D., Christopher, A., Grant, R., Sabadello, M.: Decentralized Identifiers (DIDs). Available online: https://www.w3.org/TR/did-core/. Accessed 04 June 2023 (2019)
26. Santesson, S., Myers, M., Ankney, R., Malpani, A., Galperin, S., Adams, D.C.: X.509 Internet Public Key Infrastructure Online Certificate Status Protocol - OCSP. RFC 6960 (Jun 2013). https://doi.org/10.17487/RFC6960
27. Scarfone, K., Souppaya, M.: Guide to enterprise password management. Available online: https://csrc.nist.gov/publications/detail/sp/800-118/archive/2009-04-21. Accessed on 04 June 2023 (2009)
28. Schanzenbach., M., Kilian., T., Schütte., J., Banse., C.: Zklaims: Privacy-preserving attribute-based credentials using non-interactive zero-knowledge techniques. In: Proceedings of the 16th International Joint Conference on e-Business and Telecommunications - SECRYPT,. pp. 325–332. INSTICC, SciTePress, Prague, Czech Republic (2019). https://doi.org/10.5220/0007772903250332
29. Schardong, F., Custódio, R.: Self-sovereign identity: a systematic review, mapping and taxonomy. Sensors **22**(15), 5641 (2022). https://doi.org/10.3390/s22155641
30. Sipser, M.: Introduction to the Theory of Computation. Cengage Learning (2013)
31. Sporny, M., Longley, D., Chadwick, D.: Verifiable Credentials Data Model 1.0. Available online: https://www.w3.org/TR/vc-data-model/. Accessed 04 June 2023 (2017)

32. Terbu, O., Lodderstedt, T., Yasuda, K., Looker, T.: Openid for verifiable presentations. Available online: https://openid.net/specs/openid-4-verifiable-presentations-1_0.html Accessed 30 August 2024 (2024)
33. West, R., Bluhm, D., Hailstone, M., Curran, S., Curren, S., Aristy, G.: Aries rfc 0023: Did exchange protocol 1.0. Available online: https://github.com/hyperledger/aries-rfcs/blob/master/features/0023-did-exchange. Accessed on 30 August 2024 (2019)

Ontological Foundations of Resilience

Pedro Paulo F. Barcelos[1,2,3(✉)], Rodrigo F. Calhau[3,4], Ítalo Oliveira[3], Tiago Prince Sales[3], Frederik Gailly[1,2], Geert Poels[1,2], and Giancarlo Guizzardi[3]

[1] Department of Business Information and Operations Management, Ghent University, Ghent, Belgium
[2] CVAMO Core Lab, Flanders Make @UGent, Ghent, Belgium
{pedro.favatobarcelos,frederik.gailly,geert.poels}@ugent.be
[3] Semantics, Cybersecurity and Services, University of Twente, Enschede, The Netherlands
{i.j.dasilvaoliveira,t.princesales,g.guizzardi}@utwente.nl
[4] LEDS, Federal Institute of Espírito Santo, Serra, Brazil
calhau@ifes.edu.br

Abstract. Amid rising global challenges, resilience is attracting increased interest across various disciplines. However, significant ambiguities, vagueness, and variations in its definitions present notable obstacles to interdisciplinary communication and practical application. These semantic issues negatively impact not only the applications that rely on these definitions but also undermine the integrity of the conceptual models built from them, rendering them unable to ensure interoperability and clarity for their intended users. Recognizing the need for a robust and clear definition of resilience, this work addresses the complexity inherent in the concept by performing an ontological analysis using the Unified Foundational Ontology (UFO) and creating a sound core ontology model with OntoUML, UFO's related conceptual modeling language. This research unfolds the conceptualization of resilience by investigating its fundamental categories and related concepts. We explore essential aspects of resilience, examining whether it preexists disturbances or is developed in response to them. We also identify its relational dependencies, establish how it is actualized, and determine the circumstances under which it becomes perceptible. Following our analysis of the ontological nature of resilience, the paper establishes an ontologically well-founded definition of this concept. To illustrate the practical application of our theoretical findings, we present a specific case in the field of production management.

Keywords: Resilience · Ontological Analysis · Unified Foundational Ontology · OntoUML · Ontology

W. Maass et al. (Eds.): ER 2024, LNCS 15238, pp. 396–416, 2025.
https://doi.org/10.1007/978-3-031-75872-0_21

1 Introduction

Resilience is an important concept across numerous disciplines, including strategic management, supply chain management, sustainability, disaster management, ecology, engineering, defense, political science, psychology, and sociology [11,45,70]. Both scientific and nonscientific literature reflect a rising use of this term, underscoring its broad importance and multidisciplinary roots [1,34,36,45,47,70,71,79]. However, definitions of resilience vary significantly across disciplines [34,57,68,78], leading to complexities, contradictions, and ambiguities that pose significant challenges in both theoretical and practical domains [38,57]. Furthermore, the polysemy of resilience leads to contradictory interpretations that undermine its utility in achieving a coherent discourse [57]. These issues hinder the development of operational definitions and generalizable metrics, complicating the application of resilience in normative settings [34,47].

Conceptual models aiming to represent resilience and their derived knowledge artifacts, such as schemas, data structures, inherit these definitional issues, impacting their clarity and interoperability. The literature presents examples of resilience models in UML and ER, created for diverse fields including small and medium-sized enterprises [72], industrial supply chains [2], maritime systems [41], extreme weather [80], and data ecosystems [26].

The literature underscores the necessity of a clear and general definition of resilience to facilitate interdisciplinary research and enhance empirical testability and operationalization [68,75,78]. Despite this recognized need, disambiguating resilience is challenging due to its complex nature and the nuanced interpretations across contexts [68]. Acknowledging that completely neutral perspectives are unachievable when defining resilience, it is evident that existing definitions rely on implicit ontological assumptions. To create a robust and reusable model, researchers must rigorously identify and declare their ontological commitments using a suitable well-founded ontology representation language [28,29].

This paper addresses the ambiguities surrounding resilience by performing an ontological analysis grounded in the Unified Foundational Ontology (UFO), which provides the necessary ontological foundations for clarifying the fundamental categories of resilience and their related concepts. We formalize this analysis in a sound ontology artifact using UFO's related conceptual modeling language, OntoUML [30] *(contribution I)*. We entitled the generated ontology 'Resilience Core Ontology', or simply **ResiliOnt**.

In our analysis, we explore fundamental aspects of resilience by questioning *(i)* whether resilience is an inherent quality of an object or an outcome observed only after an object has endured a disturbance, *(ii)* what are the necessary and *(iii)* the sufficient conditions for an object to possess resilience, and *(iv)* when resilience can be observed. Addressing these points helps to fill the gaps in the current understanding of resilience. Building upon the results of our analysis, we provide an ontologically well-founded definition of resilience *(contribution II)*.

The remainder of this paper is structured as follows. Section 2 presents the foundational ontological theory upon which we build our analysis. Then, Sect. 3 presents the contrasting views on resilience found in different paradigms. Our principal contribution is found in Sect. 4, where we analyze resilience to clarify its semantics. In Sect. 5, we present a case in production management to illustrate the application of the theoretical findings. The discussion in Sect. 6 contextualizes our findings within the existing literature, and Sect. 7 presents our conclusions by synthesizing our contributions, discussing implications, presenting limitations, and outlining future research directions.

2 Ontological Foundations

2.1 The Unified Foundational Ontology

UFO is a well-established foundational ontology that has been used successfully in numerous ontological analyzes in fields as complex as economics, software engineering, treatments, and decision-making processes [30,37,54,76].

Among all the applications of UFO, its role in the design of OntoUML is the most significant. OntoUML is a conceptual modeling language with explicitly defined formal and real-world semantics that reflects the ontological micro-theories of UFO. It serves as an engineering tool for enabling the use of formal ontological theories in the construction of conceptual models and domain ontologies [30,32]. OntoUML was also used to formalize both the Capabilities [18] and the Common Ontology of Value and Risk (COVER) [60] ontologies, which play a central role in establishing the groundwork for our research, making it the optimal choice for formalizing ResiliOnt.

UFO is organized into three main fragments: UFO-A (ontology of endurants), UFO-B (ontology of perdurants, partially represented in Fig. 1), and UFO-C (ontology of social and intentional entities). For our analysis, UFO-A and UFO-B are particularly significant. Extending UFO-A, UFO-B focuses on entities that occur over time, formalizing how Substantials, Situations, and Events relate to each other [10,31].

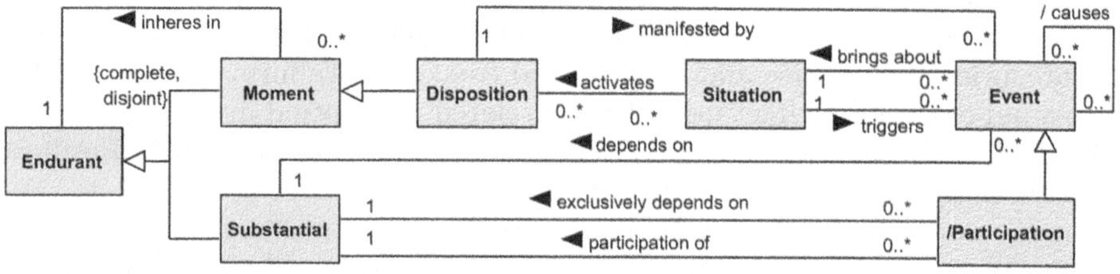

Fig. 1. Representation of UFO-B fragment as a class diagram illustrating the relationships among Substantials, Events, and Dispositions

Endurants are entities that persist through time while potentially undergoing changes in their properties. Independent Endurants are called Substantials, while those existentially dependent are named Moments. Disposition, a key concept in this work, belongs to the latter category.

Dispositions are properties that a Substantial ("object-like" Endurants) possess and have the potential to produce distinct effects within their context. They come into effect through Situations that provide the necessary conditions for latent qualities to manifest as Events. A classic example of Disposition is a magnet's ability (object) to attract (event) iron when they are close enough (situation).

Events are the realized outcomes of Dispositions. They represent changes or occurrences that may alter the state of affairs and are inherently linked to Substantials, arising from and acting upon these entities. Events and Situations relate in two distinct forms: an Event can bring about a Situation, making it a fact in the world, or Situations can trigger Events, causing them to occur because the Situations exist [31].

2.2 The Capability Ontology

In a series of recent studies, Calhau et al. [15–18] have expanded on Dispositions in UFO, exploring the relationships among them, with a particular emphasis on Capabilities. Defined as changeable [23] and composable [64] entities, Capabilities represent the ability to achieve specific effects or declared objectives [62]. This "beneficial" aspect is reflected in its definitions across different areas. For instance, it is defined as the "ability to do something useful" in enterprise architecture and systems engineering, and as the "ability to achieve a desired effect" in information systems [48,63]. In UFO, Dispositions can be characterized as 'Categories' (a rigid mixin, relationally independent type) due to their "neutral" nature regarding their impacts. Capabilities, in contrast, are understood as 'RoleMixins' (an anti-rigid, relationally dependent mixin type), reflecting their conditional and context-dependent nature.

There are numerous ways in which dispositions can be expressed [15], with Enabling and Disabling Dispositions being particularly important in this work. *Enabling Dispositions* lay the groundwork for the activation of other dispositions, such as the foundational IT infrastructure that enables cloud-based services. *Disabling Dispositions*, on the other hand, negate or suppress the function of other dispositions, such as in cybersecurity measures that disable unauthorized access. While Enabled Dispositions can manifest themselves in Events, Disabled Dispositions are unable to manifest.

2.3 COVER: the Common Ontology of Value and Risk

We now turn our attention to COVER, originally presented in [60] and later extended and reinterpreted in [51]. This ontology provides a well-founded conceptualization of value and risk, disentangling three perspectives: experiential, relational, and quantitative. These perspectives are crucial for understanding the nature of risk and its relationship with value. COVER introduces several key concepts that have implications for our analysis of resilience, such as the ones presented in Fig. 2.

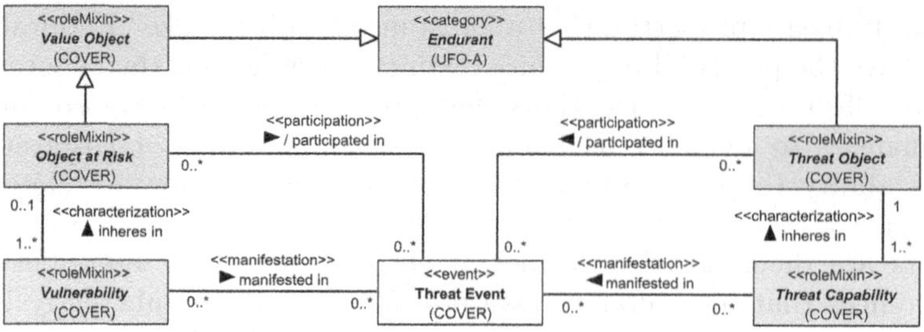

Fig. 2. OntoUML diagram adapted from COVER illustrating the relationships among Objects at Risk, their Vulnerabilities, and their potential participation in Threat Events

As seen in Fig. 2, the Object at Risk is central to the experience of risk. This specific type of Substantial is a Value Object, the bearer of value—and is consequently susceptible to losing it. In the context of this paper, value is considered binary, i.e., it is either fully preserved or completely lost. An instance of an Object at Risk is a worker in a factory setting, where the possibility of an accident could result in harm or injury. The occurrence of a threatening situation can activate the vulnerabilities of the Object at Risk, potentially leading to a Threat Event. This event has the potential to cause loss, whether intentional, such as a cyberattack, or accidental, like a spill that damages essential electronics. COVER introduced Threat Object as an important concept, embodying any entity or element that can cause a Threat Event. Examples of Threat Objects include environmental hazards (e.g., toxic chemicals, bacteria, or viruses), cyberattackers, or an aggressive agent (like a bullying peer or an abusive partner).

Objects at Risk are entities characterized by their inherent Vulnerabilities. These Vulnerabilities are Dispositions that predispose an object to potential detrimental events (i.e., they may participate in Threat Events). For example, the flammability of a structure renders a house vulnerable to fire, which, if realized, could result in substantial loss. COVER defines Vulnerabilities as 'RoleMixins', indicating their relation-dependent nature. Finally, in Fig. 2, note that the labels used by associations related to events are in the past tense. By incorporating events, the model's semantics transition to a historical perspective, affecting the events and their associated objects [4].

3 Resilience

Resilience, understood as a social construct, is shaped by the beliefs and worldviews of individuals or groups, leading to varied interpretations and applications in different fields [79]. Reghezza-Zitt et al. [57] provide a comprehensive overview of how resilience is defined across different disciplines. In material physics, resilience refers to the capacity of a material to absorb energy and resist breakage, emphasizing its ability to return to its original state after deformation. In psychology, resilience is understood as an individual's ability to adapt and recover from trauma, focusing on the processes and resources that enable overcoming stressors and maintaining well-being. It involves the ability to rebuild after traumatic experiences, leading to new development and strength. In ecology, resilience describes ecosystems' capacity to absorb disturbances and reorganize while maintaining critical functions, emphasizing persistence and adaptation over returning to a pre-disturbance state.

The authors also propose the classification of resilience into two major paradigms that offer distinct perspectives. These paradigms reflect broader differences in understanding resilience as either a static property or a dynamic process. The first is the *technocentric paradigm*, often referred to as *engineering resilience*. It aligns with the traditional view of stability and emphasizes the ability of systems to return to an equilibrium state after a disturbance. Engineering resilience tends to see resilience as a measurable state, often tied to technical and organizational capabilities to withstand and recover from disturbances. This paradigm focuses on resistance to shocks and the speed of recovery, suggesting that a resilient system is one that can bounce back to its pre-disturbance state. The second paradigm, known as *socio-ecological*, views resilience as the capacity of a system to persist through continuous change and adapt to new conditions, highlighting the importance of maintaining essential functions despite transformations. This approach considers resilience as an ongoing capacity to adapt and evolve in response to changing conditions, rather than simply returning to a previous state [57].

4 Ontological Analysis of Resilience

This section undertakes an ontological analysis to provide precise semantics to resilience. By addressing specific guiding questions, we incrementally refine our understanding of what resilience encompasses. Each step of the analysis is crafted to detail the mechanisms and intrinsic properties that define resilience.

Existing studies frequently concentrate on system-level resilience, whereas our approach additionally considers the resilience of individual components and elements not integrated into systems. In the context of this work, we use the term 'Object' to refer to COVER's 'Value Object' concept. Thus, for our purposes, 'Object' encompasses any entity to which resilience can be applied. This choice of terminology is grounded in the system ontology presented in [18] and aligns with the nomenclature used in the COVER ontology.

4.1 Resilience as a Risk-Dependent Capability

After analyzing fundamental characteristics of resilience by examining definitions from diverse disciplines, Daniel [21] argued that Resilience is a Disposition. Using the Basic Formal Ontology (BFO) [6], the study concluded that resilience, like other dispositions in BFO, inherently exists as a potentiality within a system.

Building on the premise that resilience enables an Object to preserve its value-defined in terms of an agent's goals-amidst disturbances, we further classify Resilience as a Capability, a specific type of Disposition. This classification is supported by extensive literature that conceptualizes resilience as a capability. Studies such as [12,20,22,24,52,59] corroborate this classification, though without explicit ontological commitment. Additionally, Kochan and Nowicki's supply chain literature review [39] identified resilience as an 'ability' and noted that the analyzed works used this term and 'capability' interchangeably.

Classifying Resilience as a Capability allows us to answer an important question in the resilience literature: "*Is Resilience an inherent quality of an Object, present before impact and revealed at the moment of impact, or is it an outcome observed only after an Object has endured a disturbance?*" Since Capabilities are intrinsic properties of Objects rather than contingent upon Events, we assert that the presence of Resilience in an Object is determined by a specific configuration of Dispositions, and therefore does not depend on experiencing a disturbance (an Event in UFO). Resilience, being a Capability, is a property only manifested in particular situations and that can also fail to be manifested. In other words, Resilience is only observable in certain scenarios and may not always be observable.

Acknowledging Resilience as an intrinsic quality that Objects may have leads us to the subsequent inquiry: *What are the necessary conditions for Objects to possess Resilience?* According to the COVER ontology, there is a clear dependency chain: no goal means no vulnerability, and no vulnerability means no risk. Extending this chain, we argue that there can be no resilience without risk. Since Resilience is proposed as an object's capability to avoid its loss of value in the face of an adversity, it logically follows that only Objects at Risk—those subjected to potential Threat Events or Loss Events—would be able to possess Resilience. COVER describes Risk as an assessment of potential negative outcomes, fundamentally associated with uncertain future events that could impact valued goals or assets. Objects at Risk have an ascribed value that is deemed worth preserving and that could be under threat from adverse events. Therefore, Resilience is primarily risk-dependent and, ultimately, goal-dependent. However, not all Objects at Risk possess Resilience; for instance, sugar is highly vulnerable to water and dissolves fast upon contact, with irreversible effects.

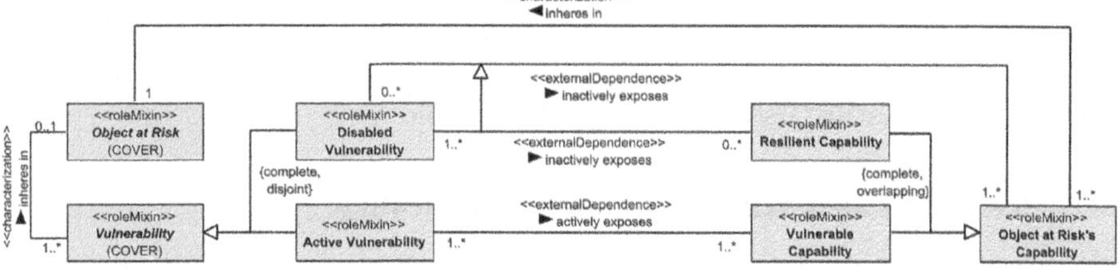

Fig. 3. OntoUML diagram representing the relations between Object at Risk's Vulnerabilities and Capabilities

The relationship between Object at Risk's Capabilities (capabilities that inheres in Object at Risks, such as a boxer's capability to fight) and Vulnerabilities, as depicted in Fig. 3, is characterized by the state of the latter. Active vulnerabilities expose their related capabilities, making them susceptible to threats. I.e., an active vulnerability is a point of weakness within the Object at Risk that could potentially be exploited. For example, using an outdated cryptographic algorithm (Active Vulnerability) may harm the system's confidentiality (Vulnerable Capability), making it susceptible to unauthorized access. Conversely, disabled vulnerabilities, as they are unable to manifest themselves, maintain a neutral stance, neither preserving nor exposing their related capabilities. Disabled vulnerabilities are inactive and cannot be exploited by Threat Capabilities, hence, they are not a source of risk. For instance, updating the cryptographic algorithm to a more secure version (Disabled Vulnerability) preserves the system's confidentiality. In summary, Object at Risk's capabilities can enable or disable related vulnerabilities, altering the Object at Risk's susceptibility to threats.

There is an important distinction between a disabled vulnerability and one that is absent. A disabled vulnerability refers to a condition where the vulnerability still exists, but its potential negative effects are neutralized through specific capabilities. For example, consider the human body's capability to regulate its appendix: a healthy appendix indicates the presence of a capability to counteract potential issues, effectively disabling the vulnerability to appendicitis. In this case, the vulnerability exists but cannot be manifested, and hence, does not lead to losses. The risk only manifests if this disabling capability ceases, potentially leading to appendicitis. Conversely, an 'absent' vulnerability refers to a context where the vulnerability does not exist or has been completely removed, such as in the case of an individual who has undergone an appendectomy and is no longer vulnerable to appendicitis. In this scenario, the vulnerability is not simply disabled but entirely eliminated. Thus, while a disabled vulnerability may become active again if the disabling mechanism ceases to function, a removed vulnerability permanently eliminates the risk.

4.2 Achieving Resilience

Having examined the ontological nature of resilience and its dependency on risk, we now address the question: "*What are the sufficient conditions for Objects to possess Resilience?*"

Considering the relationships between capabilities and vulnerabilities outlined previously, it becomes evident that Resilience does not exist in isolation; it is a capability that exists simultaneously with a given configuration of the capabilities and vulnerabilities of its bearer. Resilience represents the relational dynamics within the Object at Risk where one of its capabilities is affected by one of its vulnerabilities, and this vulnerability is disabled by another capability.

Figure 4 illustrates Resilience within an Object at Risk. It shows that a Disabling Capability becomes a Resilience-Producer Capability when it disables a Vulnerability. This prevents the Disabled Vulnerability from manifesting in a Threat Event, eliminating the opportunity for Threat Capabilities to exploit it, and establishing a Resilient Capability in the Object at Risk. In the OntoUML model shown in Fig. 4, three derived associations define the participation of Resilience in an Object at Risk. These associations' derivations can be obtained from a formula that asserts that if an Object at Risk o possesses both a capability c_2 and a vulnerability v, and another capability c_1 disables v that exposes c_2, then logically, Resilience r represents this configuration. This Resilience r inheres in o, is sustained by c_1, and specifically preserves c_2 despite v.

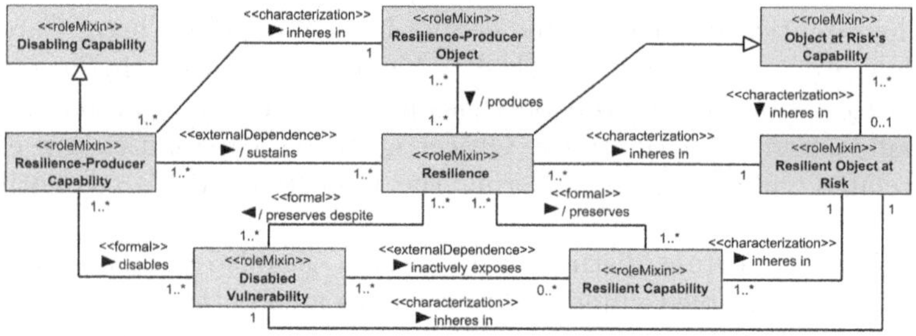

Fig. 4. OntoUML diagram depicting Resilience as the representation of a configuration within an Object at Risk

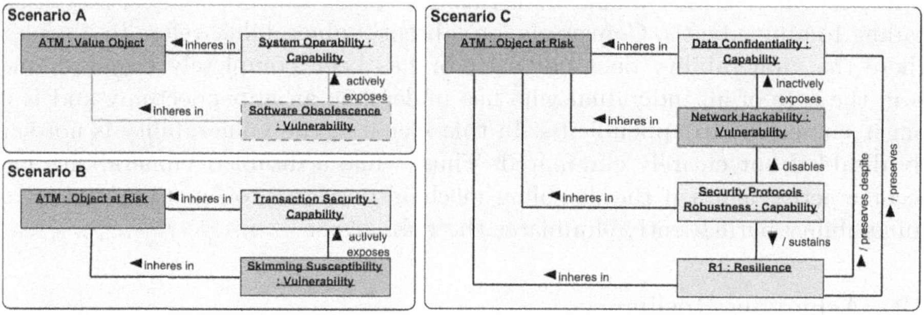

Fig. 5. Comparative analysis of ATM system resilience in three different scenarios: A) non-vulnerable case post-software update, B) vulnerable, non-resilient case subject to skimming, and C) non-vulnerable, resilient case with robust security protocols

To exemplify how Resilience can be achieved in a concrete context, Fig. 5 presents three simple practical scenarios within an Automated Teller Machine (ATM) system. We use UML Object Diagrams in all examples in this paper. Blue boxes represent Objects. Capabilities and Vulnerabilities are depicted as green and red rectangles, respectively, with black outlines indicating active dispositions and red outlines indicating inactive ones. Orange boxes denote Resilience instances. Dashed outlines in lighter classes and lighter associations represent past or future possibilities, to be defined in each example.

In Fig. 5, Scenario A represents a situation right after a software update nullifies the risk of Software Obsolescence (a change in the Object eliminated the vulnerability). Here, the non-resilient nature of the scenario is evident as the ATM's System Operability currently faces no vulnerabilities. Scenario B also depicts a non-resilient case, however, for a different reason. Here, the ATM's Transaction Security is susceptible to skimming, reflecting an active vulnerability that attackers can exploit, a direct threat to the system's integrity. In contrast, Scenario C exemplifies a resilient configuration; here, the ATM's Data Confidentiality is defended against Network Hackability, a vulnerability that is disabled by the Security Protocols Robustness, thereby achieving Resilience R1.

4.3 Perceiving Resilience

Previously, we described how resilience can be achieved within an Object at Risk. However, possessing resilience is not synonymous with manifesting it. As a capability, resilience only becomes apparent under specific, favorable circumstances during threat events. In this section, we ask "*When can resilience be observed?*" We examine its manifestation in scenarios where resilience prevails over threats and where vulnerabilities lead to loss. This involves a comparative analysis of Threat Events that occur with and without the presence of Resilience, demonstrating the conditions that allow Resilience to be effectively 'visible'.

In this paper, we expand the original idea of Threat Events from COVER to include both successful and unsuccessful outcomes. Understanding the manifestation of resilience begins with recognizing how a Successful Threat Event leads to a Loss Event, presenting the exploitation of an Object's Vulnerability by a Threat Object. Conversely, an Unsuccessful Threat Event occurs when the Object's vulnerabilities are not exploited, preventing the execution of the threat and demonstrating the Object's resilience. This comparative analysis clarifies the nuances of Resilience, emphasizing how it functions as a protective mechanism.

Loss Events represent the concrete realizations of adverse outcomes from risk experiences, such as the actual damages resulting from a cyberattack or an accident. A Loss Event typically occurs when an Object at Risk loses its value as defined by a specific goal of an agent. For instance, in a healthcare setting, a Loss Event might be the accidental exposure of sensitive patient records, where the value is the confidentiality that is critical to patient trust and regulatory compliance. Similarly, in manufacturing, a crucial machine's breakdown due to improper maintenance might constitute a Loss Event, significantly impacting production capacity and hence the company's ability to meet contractual obligations. These events underline the manifestation of loss as historically dependent on a preceding Threat Event. Together, these elements construct the pathway that captures the progression from an Object at Risk's inherent vulnerability through to the occurrence of a Loss Event. This clearly aligns the loss with the decline of valued capabilities or functions critical to the agent's objectives.

Figure 6 presents an OntoUML diagram depicting Successful Threat Events, where a Threat Object with a specific Active Threat Capability exploits an Active Vulnerability in an Object at Risk. This interaction, occurring within a favorable situation, leads to a Successful Threat Event and subsequently to a Loss Event, highlighting the sequence of risk realization that leads to the Object at Risk's loss of value.

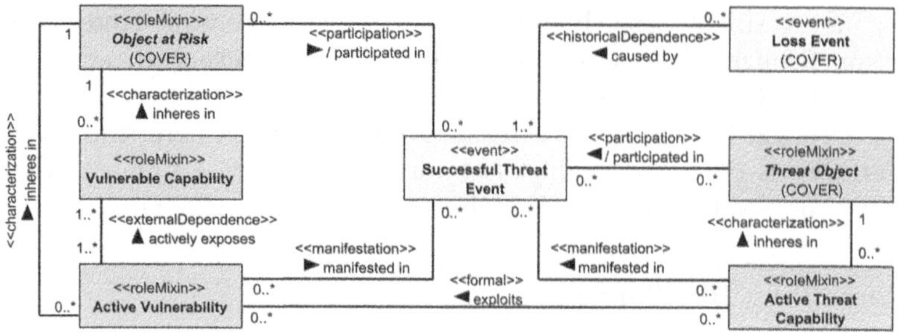

Fig. 6. OntoUML diagram representing a Successful Threat Event and the consequent loss of value of the Object at Risk

While an Object at Risk inherently faces potential threats due to its vulnerabilities, the impact of these Threat Events is primarily determined by the presence or absence of resilience preserving despite vulnerabilities. For instance, a building in a seismic zone, despite being exposed to earthquakes (Threat Events), will not experience structural failures (Loss Events) if it incorporates advanced engineering practices specifically designed for seismic resilience. This underscores that targeted resilience effectively protects against the adverse consequences of specific threats. Conversely, an Object at Risk with exposed vulnerabilities, such as a wooden house in a wildfire-prone area, is almost certain to be destroyed when exposed to fire. This exemplifies how Threat Events result in Loss Events when specific resilience measures are absent. Meanwhile, possessing resilience despite a vulnerability is crucial in preventing corresponding Loss Events. For example, vehicles equipped with advanced safety features, while susceptible to road accidents (Threat Events), can avoid severe damages or injuries (Loss Events) due to their built-in resilience specifically designed for road safety.

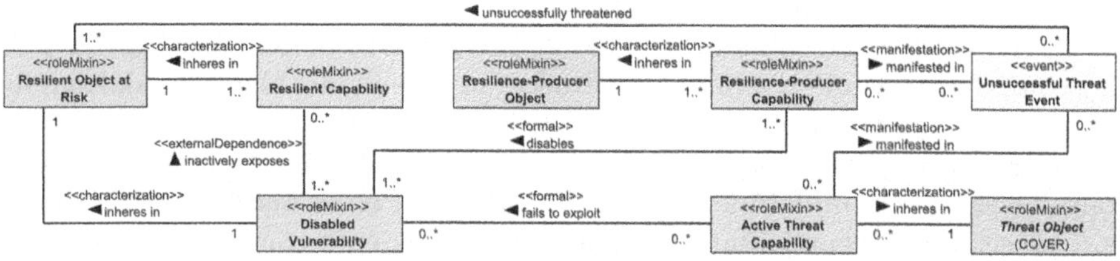

Fig. 7. OntoUML diagram representing the participation of Resilient Capabilities in an Unsuccessful Threat Event, without loss of value of the Object at Risk

Having discussed the dynamics of successful threat events, we now turn to Unsuccessful Threat Events. The OntoUML diagram depicted in Fig. 7 shows how a Resilience-Producer Capability plays a crucial role in preventing a Object at Risk from participating in Successful Threat Events. This capability ensures that even when a Threat Object manifests its Threat Capability, the outcome does not lead to a Loss Event. Specifically, the diagram highlights that Resilience-Producer Capabilities are directly related to Unsuccessful Threat Events, which are characterized by their inability to culminate in any Loss Event Types. By preventing the manifestation of vulnerabilities during Threat Events, Resilience-Producer Capabilities ensure that these events do not progress to cause actual losses, thus underscoring the essential function of resilience in safeguarding the Object at Risk against potential damages. Once outlined the dynamics of Threat Events, we next apply these concepts to the example depicted in Fig. 8, which examines a submarine's resilience to different pressure levels.

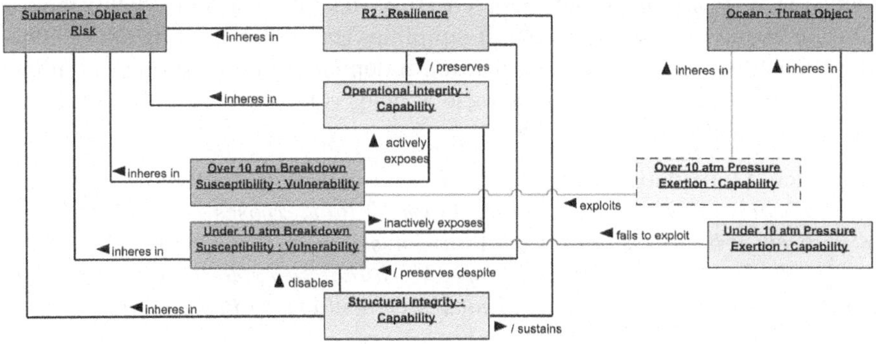

Fig. 8. UML Object Diagram depicting a submarine's pressure response: resilience under 10 atm and loss over 10 atm due to the exploitation of an active vulnerability

In the first possibility, which represents an Unsuccessful Threat Event, the submarine demonstrates its capability to withstand pressures under 10 atmospheres (atm). This resilience is evidenced by the submarine's inherent capabilities, specifically a disabling capability that neutralizes the "Under 10 atm Breakdown Susceptibility." As a result, Resilience R2 is achieved, maintaining the structural integrity of the submarine and preventing the vulnerability from being exploited. Consequently, the operational integrity of the submarine is preserved by the capability that prevents the vulnerability from manifesting.

In the second possibility, we outline a future Successful Threat Event where the submarine lacks resilience against pressures over 10 atm. Here, the "Over 10 atm Breakdown Susceptibility" vulnerability is exploited because of the absence of disabling capabilities, resulting in a failure to maintain structural integrity under high pressure. This results in the submarine's loss as the external ocean's pressure directly affected the operational integrity. The first scenario exemplifies how resilience, through specific protective capabilities, contributes to ensuring the submarine's continued functionality without loss by blocking the potential exploitation of vulnerabilities. In contrast, the second scenario depicts a case where the lack of resilience leads to the successful exploitation of a vulnerability, culminating in a negative outcome for the submarine.

Given the detailed examination of the role of resilience in threat events, we can now revisit this subsection's initial question and answer when resilience can be observed. While objects may inherently possess resilience, it becomes observable only during threat events through the specific capabilities that disable vulnerabilities. These capabilities act decisively to protect the object from loss of value, demonstrating the essential nature of resilience in preventing adverse outcomes under threatening circumstances.

4.4 Defining Resilience

Following our ontological analysis, we propose our own definition of resilience. Moving away from the practice of creating discipline-specific definitions, our definition is universally applicable. It simplifies the understanding of the concept and establishes a domain- and application-independent foundation that enhances its utility and applicability across various fields. Our ontologically well-founded definition of resilience is as follows.

Resilience Definition: *A resilience R is a capability that inheres in a value object O when O possesses a vulnerability V that exposes a capacity C_1 of O and is disabled by a capability C_2. As a consequence, R preserves C_1 despite V, prevents the loss of value of O because V cannot be exploited by capabilities of threat objects in threat events, and makes O resilient to these events.*

5 Resilience Modeling: A Production Management Illustration

In this section, we illustrate the application of ResiliOnt by presenting the example of ExCo, a fictitious electronics manufacturer. To manage the risks associated with supplier dependencies, this company has created a structured network consisting of two key suppliers. In a previous state, ExCo used dual suppliers, here named Supplier 1 and Supplier 2, to mitigate the risk associated with single supplier dependence, ensuring operational flexibility and continuous material supply. This section discusses the scenario represented in Fig. 9, where Supplier 1 experiences a disruption in its production capability. This scenario presents a complex interplay of capabilities and vulnerabilities, demonstrating that the ontology can be populated with meaningful data.

In the depicted scenario, the production capability of Supplier 1 was disrupted because its 'Political Instability Susceptibility' vulnerability was active, which exposed this capability. Without resilience, the exploitation of this vulnerability led to a loss of value for Supplier 1, resulting in its inoperability. In the original state, Supplier 1's 'Delivery Capability' played a central role in keeping ExCo's 'Single Supplier Dependence' and 'Input Material Shortage' vulnerabilities disabled—in Fig. 9, red lines represent the discontinued relations. However,

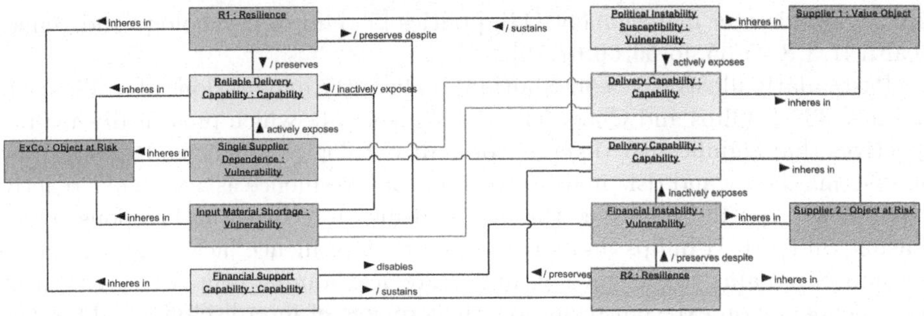

Fig. 9. UML Object Diagram illustrating resilience dynamics through the interplay of capabilities and vulnerabilities in a fictitious electronics manufacturer's supply chain

once Supplier 1 became non-operational, the absence of its capability affected these vulnerabilities in distinct ways.

The end of Supplier 1's 'Delivery Capability' does not enable ExCo's 'Input Material Shortage' vulnerability, as Supplier 2's 'Delivery Capability' still disables this vulnerability, keeping it inactive. This configuration results in ExCo's Resilience R1, which is supported by Supplier 2's 'Delivery Capability', preserving ExCo's 'Reliable Delivery Capability' despite 'Input Material Shortage'. Regarding ExCo's 'Single Supplier Dependence' vulnerability, the disruption of Supplier 1 means that only Supplier 2's contribution to disabling it is available (represented by the blue line in Fig. 9). Since this vulnerability requires contributions from at least two suppliers to be disabled, it becomes active when Supplier 1 is non-operational. An active vulnerability signifies that the 'Reliable Delivery Capability' is exposed and can be exploited. However, this does not mean that exploitation necessarily occurs, as seen in this scenario.

Finally, an operational Supplier 2 bears 'Financial Instability', a vulnerability that, if active, could expose and potentially disrupt its 'Delivery Capability'. Demonstrating proactive management, ExCo addresses this with its 'Financial Support' capability, effectively disabling the 'Financial Instability' vulnerability and ensuring the continuity of Supplier 2's delivery capabilities. This interplay results in Resilience R2 within ExCo's supply chain, preserving Supplier 2's 'Delivery Capability' despite 'Financial Instability'.

6 Related Works

After conducting an extensive, though not systematic, literature review, we observed that several academics have endeavored to explain the meaning of resilience with the aim of deepening the concept's understanding. However, these efforts employ methodologies that differ from ontological analysis. We can divide these efforts into two groups: *(i)* works that offer broad definitions applicable across multiple disciplines [11,19,33,36,38,45,55,58,70,74], and *(ii)* works that provide contributions to particular fields such as sustainability and ecology

[14,27,50], disaster management [44], politics [5], and to psychology and general health [1,3,8,25,35,46,56,66,67,79].

Particularly illustrative contributions include the explorations of resilience by Haimes [33], Phillips and Chao [55], and Walker [74], which present diverse perspectives that significantly diverge from our ontological analysis. Haimes draws on systems theory and risk analysis to emphasize resilience as a system's reactive capability to specific, identified threats, focusing on recovery and response mechanisms. Similarly, Phillips and Chao argue that resilience lacks inherent meaning and only gains significance within strategic planning contexts, highlighting its dependency on external scenarios; their review of interdisciplinary literature supports this viewpoint. In contrast, Walker critically examines existing definitions in ecological and social areas to propose that resilience is a dynamic capacity for systems to adapt and change in response to disturbances. His work emphasizes the importance of learning and transformation over mere resistance. Our presents resilience as a context-independent characteristic inherent to some Objects, independent of preceding or future disturbances. Unlike these perspectives, we assert that understanding a system's vulnerabilities is sufficient to conclude their potential resilience, thus extending the concept beyond reactive measures.

Regarding the use of foundational ontologies, we could identify two related works. In [53], Ortmann and Daniel propose an ontology design pattern for referential qualities anchored in the DOLCE foundational ontology [13]. Their study employs a generalized definition of resilience from the socio-ecological domain as a case study for the application of the proposed pattern. Although their discussion incorporates DOLCE's meta-properties for resilience, their primary goal was not to define resilience, but merely to model the adopted concept's definition. In a subsequent work, rooted in BFO but still using a resilience definition for the socio-ecological domain, Daniel [21] proposes resilience as a disposition that is realized through processes. We used the author's arguments as one justification for our work to classify resilience as a capability (a subtype of disposition in UFO). Although grounded in a foundational ontology, the analysis of the author takes as its premise the domain-specific definition of resilience and does not address other significant aspects of the concept, as noted by the author.

A major contribution of this paper is ResiliOnt, an OntoUML core ontology built following the ontological analysis presented herein. Ontology artifacts built with this language are ontologically well-founded, as they reflect the ontological principles of UFO. The use of an ontologically well-founded language contrasts with common practices in building resilience ontologies. Our literature review identified that lightweight languages such as OWL—chosen for their ease of implementation rather than their representational fidelity [28]—are typically used for the formalization of these artifacts. Using lightweight ontologies and their related construction methodologies, Van Wassenaer et al. [75] discuss the challenges of creating a resilience ontology due to the impossibility of achieving a unified resilience concept across disciplines, proposing a case-specific approach. Examples of ontologies found using these languages include resilience ontologies for the domains of cybersecurity [7, 9, 69], telecommunications networks [73], supply chains [40, 65], and urban systems [42, 43]. Lastly, Mock [49] used UML Class Diagrams to clarify resilience-related terminology within the engineering domain, rather than applying a foundational ontology. Although Mock's approach brings structured discussion within its scope, it does not create a conceptually sound resilience ontology that can be generalized across different disciplines.

7 Conclusion

In this paper, we addressed the key ambiguity problem associated with the concept of resilience by employing an ontological analysis using UFO and creating ResiliOnt, an OntoUML core ontology for the resilience domain *(contribution I)*. Considering the importance of adopting the FAIR principles (Findability, Accessibility, Interoperability, and Reuse) [77], we made ResiliOnt publicly available with a permissive license (Apache 2.0) in a git repository (https://w3id.org/resiliont/git), where the complete ontology can be accessed. Additionally, we added it to the FAIR OntoUML/UFO Catalog [61].

Through our analysis, we clarified that resilience is a capability inherent in objects at risk, defined by their vulnerabilities. Our findings demonstrate that resilience is achieved when an object possesses a vulnerability that is disabled, preventing the exposure of essential capabilities during threat events. We showed that resilience, while existing prior to threat events, can only be observed when such protective mechanisms actively prevent losses during these events. We concluded by developing a sound definition of resilience *(contribution II)*.

Our ontological analysis provides a robust foundation for addressing resilience, which is particularly relevant for managing risks and ensuring continuity in the face of increasing global uncertainties. The developed ResiliOnt ontology allows modelers to represent and analyze the interplay of capabilities and vulnerabilities across various domains, facilitating informed decision-making. Moreover, it extends the applicability of conceptual modeling to pervasive areas, such as resilience engineering, risk management, and system design. When used in the development of other models or systems, it allows for the creation of more precise and interoperable results, thereby enabling these artifacts to effectively incorporate resilience.

Our investigation clarified the conceptual core of resilience, yet it did not address its quantification or gradation, which is useful for many practical implementations. Resilience was viewed as being either present or not—a valid approach when analyzing systems at a granular level. Future studies will address the measurement of resilience, allowing for a spectrum of resilience levels. Once accepting gradation, ResiliOnt must be updated. Additionally, the study did not delve into the complexity of resilience's sub-capabilities, such as resistance and adaptability.

We also acknowledge that some authors argue that the vagueness of resilience may be beneficial, facilitating interdisciplinary connections and acting as a non-controversial 'boundary object' that promotes consensus and multidisciplinary collaboration without forcing a singular definition [47,68]. They claim that the flexibility of the resilience concept can be seen as advantageous, allowing it to adapt to various disciplinary contexts and expand research possibilities [14,57]. However, by establishing a clear, ontologically well-founded definition, our work aims to provide a framework that not only supports precise academic discourse, but also enhances the operationalization of resilience in diverse settings.

Finally, as highlighted by Thorén [71], resilience theorists face a central dilemma: to accept a 'thinner' version of resilience that may lack depth but is broadly applicable, or to embrace the substantial ontological implications inherent in more detailed conceptualizations. Our ontological analysis grounded in UFO contributes to the latter approach, providing strong ontological commitments that enhance the conceptual clarity and operational relevance of resilience.

References

1. Aburn, G., Gott, M., et al.: What is resilience? An integrative review of the empirical literature. J. Adv. Nurs. **72**(5), 980–1000 (2016). https://doi.org/10.1111/jan.12888
2. Ajalli, M.: Conceptual modeling of determining factors in the assessment of sustainability and resilience of the supply chain: a study of rubber industry suppliers in Iran. J. Rubber Res. (2024). https://doi.org/10.1007/s42464-024-00257-3
3. Allen, R.S., Dorman, H.R., Henkin, H., Carden, K.D., Potts, D.: Definition of resilience. In: Resnick, B., Gwyther, L.P., Roberto, K.A. (eds.) Resilience in Aging, pp. 1–15. Springer, Cham (2018). https://doi.org/10.1007/978-3-030-04555-5_1
4. Almeida, J.P.A., Falbo, R.A., Guizzardi, G.: Events as entities in ontology-driven conceptual modeling. In: Laender, A.H.F., Pernici, B., Lim, E.-P., de Oliveira, J.P.M. (eds.) ER 2019. LNCS, vol. 11788, pp. 469–483. Springer, Cham (2019). https://doi.org/10.1007/978-3-030-33223-5_39
5. Anderson, B.: What kind of thing is resilience? Politics **35**(1), 60–66 (2015). https://doi.org/10.1111/1467-9256.12079
6. Arp, R., Smith, B., et al.: Building Ontologies with Basic Formal Ontology. The MIT Press, Cambridge (2015)
7. Babiceanu, R.F., Seker, R.: Cyber resilience protection for industrial internet of things: a software-defined networking approach. Comput. Ind. **104**, 47–58 (2019). https://doi.org/10.1016/j.compind.2018.10.004
8. Barasa, E., Mbau, R., et al.: What is resilience and how can it be nurtured? A systematic review of empirical literature on organizational resilience. Int. J. Health Policy Manag. **7**(6), 491–503 (2018). https://doi.org/10.15171/ijhpm.2018.06
9. Bellini, E., Marrone, S.: Towards a novel conceptualization of cyber resilience. In: 2020 IEEE World Congress on Services (SERVICES), pp. 189–196 (2020). https://doi.org/10.1109/SERVICES48979.2020.00048
10. Benevides, A.B., Bourguet, J.R., et al.: Representing a reference foundational ontology of events in SROIQ. Appl. Ontol. **14**, 293–334 (2019). https://doi.org/10.3233/AO-190214
11. Bhamra, R., Dani, S., et al.: Resilience: the concept, a literature review and future directions. Int. J. Prod. Res. **49**(18), 5375–5393 (2011). https://doi.org/10.1080/00207543.2011.563826

12. Birkie, S.E.: Be lean to be resilient: setting capabilities for turbulent times. Ph.D. thesis, Politecnico di Milano, Milano (2015)
13. Borgo, S., Ferrario, R., et al.: DOLCE: a descriptive ontology for linguistic and cognitive engineering. Appl. Ontol. **17**, 45–69 (2022). https://doi.org/10.3233/AO-210259
14. Brand, F.S., Jax, K.: Focusing the meaning(s) of resilience: resilience as a descriptive concept and a boundary object. Ecol. Soc. **12**(1) (2007)
15. Calhau, R.F., Almeida, J.A.P.A., et al.: Modeling competences in enterprise architecture: from knowledge, skills, and attitudes to organizational capabilities. Softw. Syst. Model. (2024). https://doi.org/10.1007/s10270-024-01151-7
16. Calhau, R.F., Almeida, J.P.A.: Zooming in on competences in ontology-based enterprise architecture modeling. In: Sales, T.P., Proper, H.A., Guizzardi, G., Montali, M., Maggi, F.M., Fonseca, C.M. (eds.) EDOC 2022, pp. 198–213. Springer, Cham (2023). https://doi.org/10.1007/978-3-031-26886-1_12
17. Calhau, R.F., Kokkula, S., et al.: Modeling competence framework elements with an ontology-based approach. In: 2023 IEEE 25th Conference on Business Informatics (CBI), pp. 1–10 (2023). https://doi.org/10.1109/CBI58679.2023.10187498
18. Calhau, R.F., Sales, T.P., et al.: A system core ontology for capability emergence modeling. In: Proper, H.A., Pufahl, L., Karastoyanova, D., van Sinderen, M., Moreira, J. (eds.) EDOC 2023. LNCS, vol. 14367, pp. 3–20. Springer, Cham (2023). https://doi.org/10.1007/978-3-031-46587-1_1
19. Carlson, J.L., Haffenden, R.A., et al.: Resilience: theory and application. Technical report, Argonne National Lab., United States (2012). https://doi.org/10.2172/1044521
20. Chu, Y.H.: Resilience capabilities in the face of environmental turbulence: a case of Hong Kong small to medium enterprises. Ph.D. thesis, RMIT University (2015)
21. Daniel, D.: Resilience as a disposition. In: Formal Ontology in Information Systems - Proceedings of the Eighth International Conference, FOIS 2014, 22–25 September 2014, Rio de Janeiro, Brazil. Frontiers in Artificial Intelligence and Applications, vol. 267, pp. 171–182. IOS Press (2014). https://doi.org/10.3233/978-1-61499-438-1-171
22. Davey, J., Krisjanous, J., et al.: Editorial: service resilience in an increasingly ambiguous, dynamic and complex world - absorb, adapt and transform. J. Serv. Mark. **38**(4), 385–391 (2024). https://doi.org/10.1108/JSM-03-2024-0122
23. Dori, D., Sillitto, H.: What is a system? An ontological framework. Syst. Eng. **20**(3), 207–219 (2017). https://doi.org/10.1002/SYS.21383
24. Duchek, S.: Organizational resilience: a capability-based conceptualization. Bus. Res. **13**(1), 215–246 (2020). https://doi.org/10.1007/s40685-019-0085-7
25. Glantz, M.D., Sloboda, Z.: Analysis and reconceptualization of resilience. In: Glantz, M.D., Johnson, J.L. (eds.) Resilience and Development, pp. 109–126. Springer, Boston (2002). https://doi.org/10.1007/0-306-47167-1_6
26. Grabis, J., Deksne, L., et al.: A capability-based method for modeling resilient data ecosystems. In: Karagiannis, D., Lee, M., Hinkelmann, K., Utz, W. (eds.) Domain-Specific Conceptual Modeling, pp. 339–363. Springer, Cham (2022). https://doi.org/10.1007/978-3-030-93547-4_15
27. Gruemm, H.R.: Definitions of Resilience. IIASA Research Report RR-76-005, International Institute for Applied Systems Analysis (IIASA), Laxenburg, Austria (1976)

28. Guizzardi, G.: On ontology, ontologies, conceptualizations, modeling languages, and (meta)models. In: Proceedings of the 2007 Conference on Databases and Information Systems IV: Selected Papers from the Seventh International Baltic Conference DB&IS'2006, pp. 18–39. IOS Press, NLD (2007)
29. Guizzardi, G.: Ontology, ontologies and the "I" of FAIR. Data Intell. **2**(1-2), 181–191 (2020). https://doi.org/10.1162/dint_a_00040
30. Guizzardi, G., Botti Benevides, A., et al.: UFO: unified foundational ontology. Appl. Ontol. **17**, 167–210 (2022). https://doi.org/10.3233/AO-210256
31. Guizzardi, G., Wagner, G., de Almeida Falbo, R., Guizzardi, R.S.S., Almeida, J.P.A.: Towards ontological foundations for the conceptual modeling of events. In: Ng, W., Storey, V.C., Trujillo, J.C. (eds.) ER 2013. LNCS, vol. 8217, pp. 327–341. Springer, Heidelberg (2013). https://doi.org/10.1007/978-3-642-41924-9_27
32. Guizzardi, G., Wagner, G., et al.: Towards ontological foundations for conceptual modeling: the unified foundational ontology (UFO) story. Appl. Ontol. **10**(3–4), 259–271 (2015). https://doi.org/10.3233/AO-150157
33. Haimes, Y.Y.: On the definition of resilience in systems. Risk Anal. **29**(4), 498–501 (2009). https://doi.org/10.1111/j.1539-6924.2009.01216.x
34. Herrera, H.: Resilience for whom? The problem structuring process of the resilience analysis. Sustainability **9**(7) (2017). https://doi.org/10.3390/su9071196
35. Herrman, H., Stewart, D.E., et al.: What is resilience? Can. J. Psychiatry **56**(5), 258–265 (2011). https://doi.org/10.1177/070674371105600504
36. Hosseini, S., Barker, K., et al.: A review of definitions and measures of system resilience. Reliab. Eng. Syst. Saf. **145**, 47–61 (2016). https://doi.org/10.1016/j.ress.2015.08.006
37. Johannesson, P., Perjons, E.: An ontological analysis of the notion of treatment. In: Dobbie, G., Frank, U., Kappel, G., Liddle, S.W., Mayr, H.C. (eds.) ER 2020. LNCS, vol. 12400, pp. 303–314. Springer, Cham (2020). https://doi.org/10.1007/978-3-030-62522-1_22
38. Kaplan, H.B.: Understanding the concept of resilience. In: Goldstein, S., Brooks, R.B. (eds.) Handbook of Resilience in Children, pp. 39–47. Springer, Boston (2005). https://doi.org/10.1007/0-306-48572-9_3
39. Kochan, C.G., Nowicki, D.R.: Supply chain resilience: a systematic literature review and typological framework. Int. J. Phys. Distrib. Logist. Manag. **48**(8), 842–865 (2018). https://doi.org/10.1108/IJPDLM-02-2017-0099
40. Koot, M., Mes, M.R.K., et al.: Building an ontological bridge between supply chain resilience and IoT applications. In: Proper, H.A., Pufahl, L., Karastoyanova, D., van Sinderen, M., Moreira, J. (eds.) EDOC 2023. LNCS, vol. 14367, pp. 79–96. Springer, Cham (2024). https://doi.org/10.1007/978-3-031-46587-1_5
41. Laun, A., Mazzuchi, T.A., et al.: Conceptual data model for system resilience characterization. Syst. Eng. **25**(2), 115–132 (2022). https://doi.org/10.1002/sys.21605
42. Lestakova, M., Logan, K., et al.: Towards a common ontology for investigating resilience of interdependent urban systems. In: Proceedings of the Joint International Resilience Conference, JIRC 2020, 23 November 2020–27 November 2020, pp. 101–104. University of Twente, Twente (2020).https://doi.org/10.3990/1.9789036550956
43. Lombardini, G.: Dealing with resilience conceptualisation. formal ontologies as a tool for implementation of intelligent geographic information systems. TeMA J. Land Use Mobility Environ. (2014).https://doi.org/10.6092/1970-9870/2540
44. Manyena, S.B.: The concept of resilience revisited. Disasters **30**(4), 434–450 (2006). https://doi.org/10.1111/j.0361-3666.2006.00331.x

45. Martin-Breen, P., Anderies, J.M.: Resilience: A Literature Review (2011)
46. McCubbin, L.: Challenges to the Definition of Resilience. Information analyses; speeches/meeting papers, ERIC - Institute of Education Sciences (2001)
47. Meerow, S., Newell, J.P., et al.: Defining urban resilience: a review. Landsc. Urban Plan. **147**, 38–49 (2016). https://doi.org/10.1016/j.landurbplan.2015.11.011
48. Merrell, E., Limbaugh, D., et al.: Capabilities (2022). https://philpapers.org/rec/MERC-14
49. Mock, R.G., Leksin, A., et al.: An ontology of risk associated concepts in the context of resilience. In: Proceedings of the 29th European Safety and Reliability Conference, pp. 1320–1327. Research Publishing, Singapore (2019). https://doi.org/10.3850/978-981-11-2724-3_0246-cd
50. Myers-Smith, I., Trefry, S., et al.: Resilience: easy to use but hard to define. Ideas Ecol. Evol. **5**, 44–53 (2012). https://doi.org/10.4033/iee.2012.5.11.c
51. Oliveira, Í., Sales, T.P., et al.: An ontology of security from a risk treatment perspective. In: Ralyté, J., Chakravarthy, S., Mohania, M., Jeusfeld, M.A., Karlapalem, K. (eds.) ER 2022. LNCS, vol. 13607, pp. 365–379. Springer, Cham (2022). https://doi.org/10.1007/978-3-031-17995-2_26
52. Oppong Banahene, K., Anvuur, A., et al.: Conceptualising organisational resilience: an investigation into project organising. In: Proceedings of the 30th Annual ARCOM Conference, vol. 2, pp. 795–804. Association of Researchers in Construction Management, Portsmouth, UK (2014)
53. Ortmann, J., Daniel, D.: An ontology design pattern for referential qualities. In: Aroyo, L., et al. (eds.) ISWC 2011. LNCS, vol. 7031, pp. 537–552. Springer, Heidelberg (2011). https://doi.org/10.1007/978-3-642-25073-6_34
54. Almeida, J.P.A., Guizzardi, G.: An ontological analysis of the notion of community in the RM-ODP enterprise language. Comput. Standards Interfaces **35**(3), 257–268 (2013).https://doi.org/10.1016/j.csi.2012.01.007
55. Phillips, F.Y., Chao, A.: Rethinking resilience: definition, context, and measure. IEEE Trans. Eng. Manag. 1–8 (2022). https://doi.org/10.1109/TEM.2021.3139051
56. Pooley, J.A., Cohen, L.: Resilience: a definition in context. Aust. Commun. Psychol. **22**(1) (2010)
57. Reghezza-Zitt, M., Lhomme, S., et al.: Defining resilience: when the concept resists. In: Resilience Imperative, pp. 1–27. Elsevier (2015). https://doi.org/10.1016/B978-1-78548-051-5.50001-2
58. Reid, R., Botterill, L.C.: The multiple meanings of 'resilience': an overview of the literature. Aust. J. Public Adm. **72**(1), 31–40 (2013). https://doi.org/10.1111/1467-8500.12009
59. Reinmoeller, P., van Baardwijk, N.: The link between diversity and resilience: new research shows that the most resilient companies are those that continually orchestrate a dynamic balance of four innovation strategies. MIT Sloan Manag. Rev. **46**, 61+ (2005)
60. Sales, T.P., Baião, F., Guizzardi, G., Almeida, J.P.A., Guarino, N., Mylopoulos, J.: The common ontology of value and risk. In: Trujillo, J.C., et al. (eds.) ER 2018. LNCS, vol. 11157, pp. 121–135. Springer, Cham (2018). https://doi.org/10.1007/978-3-030-00847-5_11
61. Sales, T.P., Barcelos, P.P.F., et al.: A FAIR catalog of ontology-driven conceptual models. Data Knowl. Eng. **147**, 102210 (2023). https://doi.org/10.1016/j.datak.2023.102210
62. Saxena, M.: Capability Management: Monitoring and Improving Capabilities. Global India Publications, India (2009)

63. SEBoK Editorial Board: The Guide to the Systems Engineering Body of Knowledge (SEBoK), v. 2.9 (2023). www.sebokwiki.org
64. Sillitto, H.G.: 10.2. 1 "composable capability"–principles, strategies and methods for capability systems engineering. In: INCOSE International Symposium, vol. 23, no. 1, pp. 723–738 (2013). https://doi.org/10.1002/j.2334-5837.2013.tb03050.x
65. Singh, S., Ghosh, S., et al.: Enhancing supply chain resilience using ontology-based decision support system. Int. J. Comput. Integr. Manuf. **32**(7), 642–657 (2019). https://doi.org/10.1080/0951192X.2019.1599443
66. Southwick, S.M., Bonanno, G.A., et al.: Resilience definitions, theory, and challenges: interdisciplinary perspectives. Eur. J. Psychotraumatol. **5**(1), 25338 (2014). https://doi.org/10.3402/ejpt.v5.25338
67. Stainton, A., Chisholm, K., et al.: Resilience as a multimodal dynamic process. Early Interv. Psychiatry **13**(4), 725–732 (2019). https://doi.org/10.1111/eip.12726
68. Strunz, S.: Is conceptual vagueness an asset? Arguments from philosophy of science applied to the concept of resilience. Ecol. Econ. **76**, 112–118 (2012). https://doi.org/10.1016/j.ecolecon.2012.02.012
69. Thinyane, M., Christine, D.: SMART citizen cyber resilience (SC2R) ontology. In: 13th International Conference on Security of Information and Networks. SIN 2020. Association for Computing Machinery, New York (2021). https://doi.org/10.1145/3433174.3433617
70. Thorén, H.: Resilience as a unifying concept. Int. Stud. Philos. Sci. **28**(3), 303–324 (2014). https://doi.org/10.1080/02698595.2014.953343
71. Thorén, H., Olsson, L.: Is resilience a normative concept? Resilience **6**(2), 112–128 (2018). https://doi.org/10.1080/21693293.2017.1406842
72. Utami, I.D., Santosa, I., et al.: Conceptual modeling of resilience measurement during natural disasters for SMEs. IOP Conf. Ser. Mater. Sci. Eng. **1072**(1), 012050 (2021). https://doi.org/10.1088/1757-899X/1072/1/012050
73. Vlacheas, P., Stavroulaki, V., et al.: Towards end-to-end network resilience. Int. J. Crit. Infrastruct. Prot. **6**(3), 159–178 (2013). https://doi.org/10.1016/j.ijcip.2013.08.004
74. Walker, B.H.: Resilience: what it is and is not. Ecol. Soc. **25**(2) (2020). https://doi.org/10.5751/ES-11647-250211
75. van Wassenaer, L., Oosterkamp, E., et al.: Food system resilience: ontology development and impossible trinities. Agric. Food Secur. **10**(1), 38 (2021). https://doi.org/10.1186/s40066-021-00332-7
76. Weigand, H., Johannesson, P., et al.: Ontological analysis of policy-based decision making. In: Proceedings of the 17th International Workshop on Value Modeling and Business Ontologies. University of Twente (2024)
77. Wilkinson, M.D., Dumontier, M., et al.: The FAIR guiding principles for scientific data management and stewardship. Sci. Data **3**(1), 160018 (2016). https://doi.org/10.1038/sdata.2016.18
78. Wilt, B., Long, Suzanna, P., et al.: Defining resilience: a preliminary integrative literature review. In: Proceedings of the International Annual Conference of the American Society for Engineering Management, pp. 1–10. American Society for Engineering Management (ASEM), Huntsville, United States (2016)
79. Windle, G.: What is resilience? A review and concept analysis. Rev. Clin. Gerontol. **21**(2), 152–169 (2011). https://doi.org/10.1017/S0959259810000420
80. Zimmerman, R., Zhu, Q., et al.: Conceptual modeling framework to integrate resilient and interdependent infrastructure in extreme weather. J. Infrastruct. Syst. **23**(4), 04017034 (2017). https://doi.org/10.1061/(ASCE)IS.1943-555X.0000394

Conceptual Modelling Method for Digital Twins

Emilio Carrión[1,2(✉)], Óscar Pastor[2], and Pedro Valderas[2]

[1] Mercadona Tech, Valencia, Spain
emcarrio@mercadona.es

[2] PROS - VRAIN, Universitat Politècnica de València, Valencia, Spain

Abstract. Effective conceptual modelling is critical for accurately representing the physical world in digital twin implementations, yet existing methods often lack comprehensive guidance or overlook key aspects like communication modelling. This research proposes the Entity-Relationship Digital Twin (ERDT) modelling method tailored for industrial digital twins. Building on established Entity-Relationship (ER) models, ERDT extends them with constructs for handling historical data, and defining security interfaces and data flows between physical and virtual components. The method provides a systematic process covering digital twin objective setting, physical component selection, conceptual entity definition, interface specification, and communication modelling. It emphasizes principles like encapsulation and separation of concerns to enhance maintainability. Evaluated against ISO 25010 quality criteria, ERDT demonstrates strengths in functional appropriateness, usability, portability, and maintainability while identifying opportunities for further improvement. A logistics case study illustrates applying the method to a real-world industrial scenario. By bridging conceptual modelling with software engineering best practices, ERDT facilitates developing robust, maintainable digital twins.

Keywords: Digital Twins · Modelling method · Conceptual modelling

1 Introduction

This research is part of Mercadona Tech's efforts to develop and apply digital twins (DTs) technology in real industrial environments. DTs, which are real-time virtual representations of real-world systems and entities [30], have garnered significant interest due to their potential to optimize processes, improve efficiency, and enable predictive maintenance. Also, the use of conceptual models in DT development has been widely recommended [7,23]. And following the Model-Driven Architecture (MDA) philosophy, as with any software product, it is necessary to have production methods that allow us to specify and represent the Conceptual Schema of an Information System to then transition to the implementation phase [20].

P. Valderas—This author's work is part of the R&D&I project PID2023-146224OB-I00 funded by MCIN/AEI/10.13039/501100011033.

W. Maass et al. (Eds.): ER 2024, LNCS 15238, pp. 417–435, 2025.
https://doi.org/10.1007/978-3-031-75872-0_22

However, existing modelling methods often fall short in providing comprehensive guidance on conceptual modelling or fail to address the intricate details of representing a DT accurately. Furthermore, the modelling of communication channels and data flows between the real environment and the DT, as well as within the digital model itself, is frequently overlooked, leading to potential integration challenges [8].

This research aims to address these gaps by proposing the Entity-Relationship Digital Twin (ERDT) model, a conceptual modelling method specifically designed for modelling DTs and their data flows in industrial contexts. By drawing upon established software engineering practices and industry-recognized quality standards, such as ISO 25010 [1], our method seeks to enhance the applicability, maintainability, and functional suitability of DT implementations.

By grounding our work in real-world industrial requirements and leveraging Mercadona Tech's expertise in logistics and supply chain operations, this research attempts to contribute a pragmatic and effective method for DT development. The goal is to facilitate the adoption of DTs in industrial environments, enabling organizations to harness the potential of this technology for process optimization, quality control, and operational excellence.

This research is structured as follows: Sect. 2 contextualizes the definition of what a DT is and the main aspects we have focused on. Section 3 presents the background of this research. Section 4 presents the main contribution of this work. Section 5 showcases the proposed method with a real industrial scenario. Section 6 evaluates the proposed solution against evaluation criteria. Finally, Sect. 7 closes with the work's conclusions.

2 Digital Twin Contextualization

DTs are being used across various industries [30], including manufacturing, healthcare, urban planning, and infrastructure management. In manufacturing, DTs are used to simulate and optimize production processes. Healthcare utilizes DTs to create virtual models of patients, facilitating personalized treatment. Urban planners model cities and the construction industry relies on DTs to monitor and manage building projects.

Thus, the first step when defining a conceptual modelling method for a DT is to agree on one single definition of what a DT is, as it is being applied to many fields and there have been many conceptualizations [30].

2.1 DT Definition

Previous reviews on the state-of-the-art theory and practice of DTs [26] integrate the contributions of works about DT design and implementation to provide a holistic definition of DT. Based on their analysis, the different components of a DT are defined as follows:

The elementary components without which a DT cannot exist: Physical Asset, Digital Asset and Information flow between the physical and digital asset.

The imperative components that guarantee the uniqueness of DT: IoT devices (to collect sensors' information), Data (required to monitor the system), Machine learning (for predictions and feedback), Security of data and information flow among various components involved in the DT, and DT Performance evaluation.

And there are other properties inherent to any DT that are incorporated to a greater or lesser extent depending on the main application of the DT:

- Self-evolution: a DT can learn and adapt in real-time. The frequency of this synchronisation depends on the update scenarios, such as event-based, periodic intervals, and condition-based.
- Domain dependence: According to the domain, a DT may provide or prioritise services specific to the industry.
- Autonomy: A DT could either make changes to the physical asset itself, or a human in control could make changes to the DT.
- Synchronisation: Synchronisation of data could be either continuously or at certain time intervals.

2.2 Conceptual Modelling Requirements

Given this holistic definition provided by [26], we have selected key specific concepts of a DT which are essential for DTs definition and on which we have focused our efforts in our proposal:

- The *historical nature of data* required for machine learning and analysis applications. Often, DT functionality is oriented to behaviour analysis, predictions, and enhanced capabilities using automatic machine learning. These functionalities usually make use of historical data to extrapolate, learn, and make predictions based on real-time data. Thus, being able to model it is essential to defining DTs.
- The *security* of the data and the information flow management. Security is also a main concern when developing real-time digital replicas of physical entities, as in some cases it handles private information or data that can not be shared with unauthorized parties.
- The *data flow* between physical assets and digital environment. Their ability to synchronize and maintain an up-to-date virtual representation. This synchronization happens through a continuous exchange of data between the real and virtual components, either through periodic data exchange at set intervals or through event-driven updates triggered by changes in the physical system state. Effectively modelling these two-way synchronization mechanisms is crucial for realizing the real-time mirroring capability of DTs.

3 Research Problem

To identify the strengths and weaknesses of existing DT development methods, we conducted a systematic literature review [8] that revealed crucial aspects that show significant obstacles to the successful implementation of DT models.

One of the key limitations identified is the lack of detailed guidance on how to carry out the conceptual modelling of a DT [14,15,18,31,35].

Also, the reviewed methods frequently lack consideration for the specific context in which DTs operate. The unique characteristics of DTs, such as the historical nature of data or its security concerns are often overlooked, or insufficiently addressed [4,28,30,36].

Furthermore, our review identified a significant gap in the modelling of data flows between the real environment and the digital model, as well as between the different parts of the digital model itself [2,3,5,6,10–15,17–19,21,22,24,25,27–29,31–34,37,38]. The conceptual components underlying these data flows are rarely addressed in depth (apart of being mentioned), creating challenges for seamless integration and data exchange.

The justification for proposing a new method lies in the need to address these deficiencies as the lack of clarity in the conceptual modelling of a DT can result in inaccurate and ineffective models. Additionally, the separation between conceptual modelling and the development of the DT can lead to inconsistent implementations.

Although many of the works analysed in previous studies make use of hierarchical structures to model the nature represented by the DTs [2,4,16], our proposal choses a more direct modelling based on Entity-Relationship (ER) models [9].

The main contribution of this work is then a robust conceptual modelling approach, coupled with a structured framework for modelling historical data, security constraints and data flows between physical and digital environments, key aspects crucial for the accurate representation of physical systems and the effective integration of DTs in industrial environments.

4 Conceptual Modelling Proposal

To consider all the conceptual modelling requirements for a DT, our proposal extends ER models to clarify the nature of the data a DT handles, to consider its security requirements, and to include the modelling of its data flows.

ER models have several key advantages over other models such as ontologies and hierarchical models for DT modelling. Their simpler and more intuitive structure makes them easier to understand and apply, especially for more practical development teams. In addition, the data-centric approach of ER models aligns well with the typical requirements of DTs, which often involve managing and integrating substantial amounts of heterogeneous data received from a great variety of sensors.

While ontologies and hierarchical modelling methods offer more expressive power and semantic richness, the simplicity, data focus and ease of integration characteristics of ER models can be particularly beneficial in the initial stages of DT development or in cases where requirements are simpler and more data-centric.

The next subsection introduces the details of an Entity-Relationship Digital Twin (ERDT) model to describe the intrinsic characteristics of DTs. Subsection 4.2 proposes some practical guidelines for constructing this model.

4.1 Entity-Relationship Digital Twin Model

For ERDT models to more reliably represent a DT and its interactions between the real and virtual world, the following extensions of ER models are proposed:

Historical Nature of Data. According to [26], the DT data (gathered from different IoT components and software) is required to monitor the system, guarantee correct behaviour and provide input to the machine learning system. Thus, it requires big data analysis and storage tools to extract useful information from it.

Then, relevant aspects of this data are its heterogeneity and its historical nature.

The heterogeneity of data is already contemplated in the conceptual definition of value sets in ER models, so our proposal focuses on clarifying the need and representation of the historical nature usually present in DT-collected information. As DT functionality usually refers to the evolution of data on a given period, this nature should be included in the conceptual model representing the DT.

Our proposal extends the attributes definition of ER models to allow the representation of these historical values.

Let T be a value set, where its domain is a set of time values. A *historical attribute* is defined as a function (1) which maps from an entity set (E_i) or a relationship set (R_i) into an ordered set of pairs made of a non-empty subset (P) of value sets (V) and the value set T that indicates the occurring time of that data:

$$f : E_i or R_i \rightarrow P(P(V) \times T) \tag{1}$$

The proposed visual notation of historical attributes (as shown in Fig. 1) is a double circle representing that this type of attribute is not comprised of a value but a time-series of them.

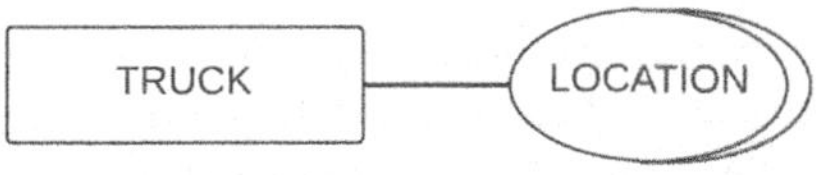

Fig. 1. Visual notation of historical attributes.

Besides, while sensor data and historical attribute tracking are core aspects of DTs, they often need to be combined with computational models and simulations to unlock capabilities like predictive maintenance, optimization, and what-if analysis [26]. The ERDT approach allows for such analytical models to be represented as derived attributes (already present in ER) calculated by applying physics equations, machine learning algorithms or other domain-specific simulations on the sensor data.

This allows the virtual components to not just mirror data, but also integrate sophisticated analysis and simulations tightly with the DT's representation of the physical system.

Security. Next, to consider the data security concerns on DT design and implementation, and to provide a base from which to build upon the DT data flow conceptualization, we propose the definition of interfaces for accessing to data and properties of the instantiated entities.

Through these interfaces, we allow various parts of the system to communicate and access information belonging to other entities. These interfaces also handle the conceptual security constraints guaranteeing that only allowed parties access the information or update the DT.

An *interface* is therefore formally defined as a function (2, 3) that takes the current attributes (F), an entity instance and a non-empty set of values which it assigns to that entity, returning the updated attributes:

$$I : F \times E_i \times P(V) \rightarrow F \tag{2}$$

$$I(f, e, v) = f' \text{ where } f'(x) = \begin{cases} v \text{ if } x = e \\ f(x) \text{ if } x \neq e \end{cases} \tag{3}$$

And its proposed visual notation is a capsule shape as shown in Fig. 2.

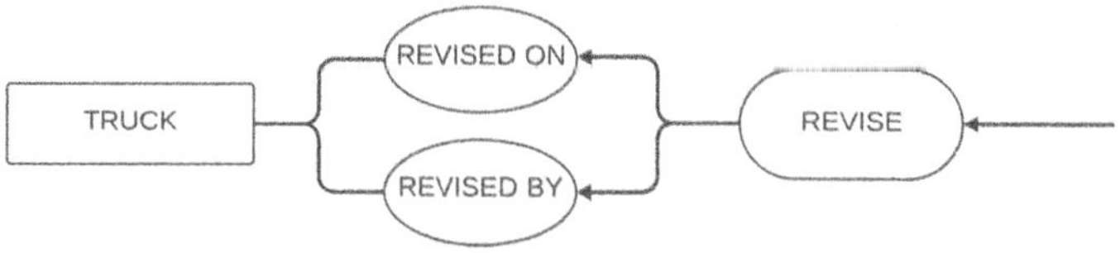

Fig. 2. Visual notation of interfaces.

Following data security requirements and to homogenise how data is updated in the DT, an interface must also be used to create the relationships between entities, as data coming from the physical world should always be communicated through interfaces, relationships are not an exception. Therefore, interfaces can also be formally defined as a function (4) that takes the current relationships, a non-empty set of entities and returns the updated set of relationships where new ones have been added and old ones (in case of unique constraints) have been removed:

$$I : R \times P(E_i) \rightarrow R \tag{4}$$

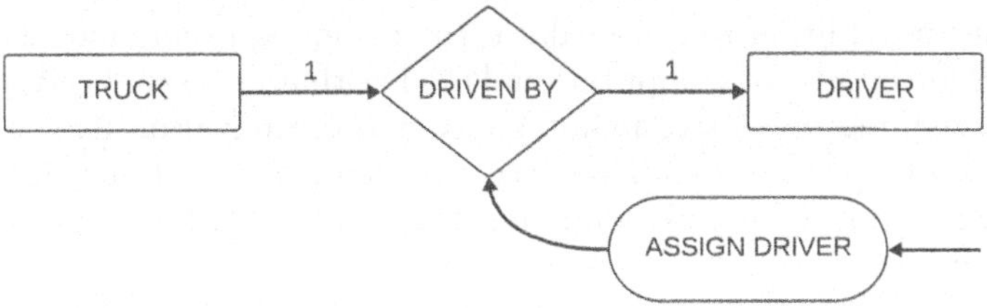

Fig. 3. Visual notation of interfaces assigning relationships.

A visual notation for this type of interface is shown in Fig. 3.

Finally, note that interfaces can also encapsulate more complex computational logic beyond just data access and updates. For example, an interface could apply a physics model to calculate derived analytical attributes like running an optimization routine to suggest ideal operational parameters. Just as derived attributes, such analytical interfaces unlock DTs' predictive capabilities.

Data Flows. An essential aspect of DT modelling is representing the communication and data flows that enable real-time synchronization between the physical entity and its virtual representation to ensure an up-to-date virtual model that accurately reflects the current physical system state.

To populate the DT with the necessary information we must obtain the information from somewhere. In real-time physical environments, this information is often distributed among the various parts of the physical system and can be obtained in many ways. As seen in Sect. 2.1, the most common are event-based (incoming information gathered from the physical entity), periodic intervals (asking a physical entity about its state), and condition-based.

The condition-based data will be modelled as derived attributes already present in ER models, that will be computed in real-time based on other entity attributes.

To model the other two data flow paradigms, we propose the following conceptual elements:

- Incoming event: emitted by the physical component, refers to a change in its state.
- Data request: when the DT system asks the physical entity about its current state to store it or compare it with the last version it had. It runs periodically or by demand.

Depending on the type of physical entity we are modelling, we can define one communication or another. There are many cases where physical entities are not able to emit events, and they only have an interface that can be accessed to get their status. In other cases, if the entity allows it, it is the entity that reports its status and changes using events or provided interfaces.

Note that in addition to sensor data, the incoming events and data requests can also include inputs for computational models that generate derived analytical attributes, enabling predictive maintenance and optimization use cases.

An *incoming event* IE can be formally defined as a function (5, 6) that receives some value (V) and populates the entity attributes or relationships using an interface I_i:

$$IE : F \times E_i \times V \rightarrow F \tag{5}$$

$$IE(f, e, v) = I_i(f, e, v) \tag{6}$$

A *data request* DR can be formally defined as a function (7, 8) that fetches a value from an external resource and then uses that information to populate the entity attributes or relationships using a given interface as the incoming events:

$$DR : F \times E_i \rightarrow F \tag{7}$$

$$DR(f, e) = I_i(f, e, v) \tag{8}$$

where v is the value fetched from the physical entity.

Both data requests and incoming events facilitate the real-time synchronization of the virtual model by updating it with the latest data from the physical counterpart. Also, both use defined interfaces to update the model, preserving the principle of least knowledge keeping the model low coupled and guaranteeing security constraints.

The proposed visual notations of incoming events and data requests (as shown in Fig. 4) are a signal-in arrow and a notched signal-in arrow respectively. Note that, as defined, data flows point to interfaces and not directly to attributes or relationships, as following encapsulation and the security requirements of DTs, mutating attributes should be only made through their defined entity interfaces.

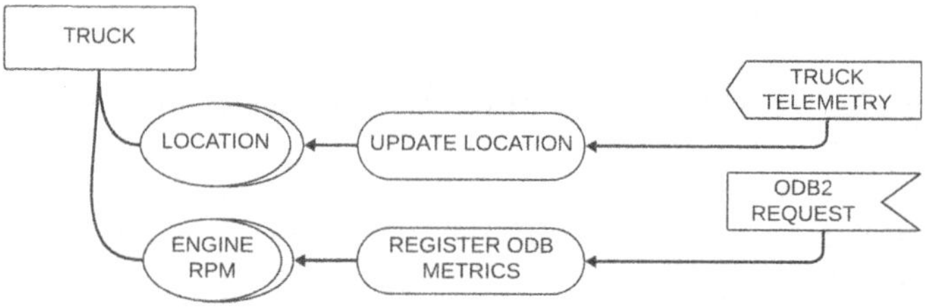

Fig. 4. ERDT diagram with communications.

While incoming events and data requests facilitate the flow of information from the physical entities into the DT, it is crucial to recognize that data exchange in DTs is inherently bidirectional. The digital model must not only ingest data from sensors but also be capable of issuing commands or triggers that can update or control the state of the represented physical components. To accommodate these closed-loop requirements central to many DT use cases, our ERDT models allow defining outgoing events or commands issued by the DT and received through actuator interfaces on the physical side. This outgoing interaction enables the virtual model to apply its analysis, predictions, or optimizations by actuating changes in the real environment through a conceptually modelled command flow.

- Outgoing Events: Issued by the DT, these represent instructions or actions that the DT wants to apply to the physical entity. These could be commands to actuators to change the state of the physical entity, trigger a process, or perform some operation.

As with incoming events and data requests, they are handled through interfaces. When an interface is invoked and the DT status has been modified, this change can trigger outgoing events that provide real-time feedback or execute automatic measures.

The proposed visual notations of outgoing events (as shown in Fig. 5) is a signal-out arrow. In the example, a "max rpm reached" event is issued when setting the ODB metrics. If the engine RPM surpasses a certain threshold, the DT issues an event to alert the driver and apply automatic safety measures.

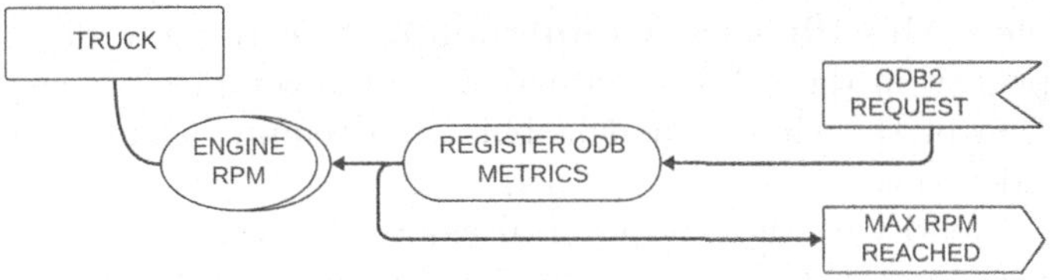

Fig. 5. Visual representation of outgoing events.

4.2 Modelling Step-by-Step Guide

Apart from the conceptual modelling method of the DT, we also propose a generalist step-by-step guide to be followed for the construction of this model. A weakness that we have observed in many of the methods analysed in our previous works (as seen in Sect. 3) is that many of them refer to or propose a conceptual modelling of the physical components but do not detail how to carry out this modelling. Our work tries to fill the gap by proposing a guided process with advice for the modelling and subsequent viable implementation of the DT.

Step 0: Select the Goal of the Digital Twin. The first step before defining a DT is to be clear about its objective or function. It is essential to be concise about whether a DT will solve the problem we are facing and narrow down its objective as much as possible to avoid unnecessary complexity as development costs can be severely affected by poor planning or by a definition of requirements that are too ambitious to solve our problem.

Also, defining the right objectives is especially important when developing DTs for non-manufacturing use cases like healthcare, urban systems, or autonomous vehicles, where the goals can be more complex and multi-faceted.

Step 1: Define a Common Vocabulary. When designing and building DTs, it is common to work with an interdisciplinary team. When working in a physical environment, software developers who build the systems typically work closely with other types of people such as operations staff, workers, and even staff from third party companies.

For this reason, we propose as an important first step to define a common vocabulary to avoid misunderstandings and redundant conversations.

This process should involve domain experts who have in-depth knowledge and experience in the specific field or industry where the DT will be applied. Collaborating with them is crucial to accurately capture the nuances, terminologies, and operational intricacies of the physical environment, ensuring that the DT accurately represents and simulates the real-world system.

Step 2: Select the Physical Components. Selecting the physical components to represent in the DT is a critical and often complex process that forms the foundation of the virtual model. This step requires significant effort and careful consideration.

Begin by identifying the key physical assets that are essential to achieving the DT's defined goals. This selection process should balance comprehensiveness with practicality, focusing on components that are most relevant to the DT's purpose rather than attempting to model the entire physical reality.

Once identified, conduct a thorough analysis of each component to determine the relevant attributes and relationships that need to be modeled. This phase often reveals challenges in attribute mapping and heterogeneous data integration, as physical assets may have diverse data formats, update frequencies, and levels of detail. Address these challenges by developing a robust data integration strategy that can handle various data sources and formats.

Throughout this process, involve domain experts to ensure accurate representation of the physical components and their interactions. Regularly reassess the selected components and their attributes as the DT project evolves, making adjustments as necessary to maintain alignment with the DT's objectives while managing complexity and resource constraints.

Step 3: Define the Entities. The next step is to establish the conceptual models that will define each entity. Several of the reviewed methods [15,34] suggest making use of a library or collection of components previously used in the DT or in other projects to avoid rework and take advantage of standardized models.

We propose the same conceptual structure in which we will record our models to use them again or extend them when we find similar entities. However, we suggest not making excessive use of standardization since it is often better to define a specific solution to the current problem before trying to adapt something already defined by force.

To define the ERDT model, we will define an Entity Set for each component selected in the second step.

Next, we will identify those that relate to other entities. We will establish a conceptual relationship between them to show a common link.

Finally, we will identify the set of attributes of each entity that are relevant to the goal of our DT. In this step, we can include attributes that we think may be useful, we recommend limiting this number as much as possible and focusing on those that intervene in the problem we want to solve. We will also identify those for which we need to know the historical values.

Step 4: Define the Interfaces of Each Entity. The next step is to define the interfaces that will allow the entities and system users to interact with each other, be modified, and communicate.

These data query and modification interfaces can be as simple or complex as needed. Query interfaces, for example, can make transformations on the data before it is returned, so interfaces can fulfil functions such as aggregating information, obtaining derived values, or making complex updates to the entity's attributes and relationships.

We will also define the security constraints each interface has and the permissions needed for accessing them.

Step 5: Define the Data Flows. The next step is to define the different data flows that our system has and that will allow our DT to be able to operate with updated information. Defining these data flows is key to enabling real-time synchronization.

We recommend, as well as selecting the entities and attributes to be represented by our DT, that we limit the number of communications and information flows and adapt them to the problem to be solved. The more communications we define, the greater the complexity and cost of implementation we will have.

We will define the list of incoming events, data requests and outgoing events that will be propagated to the physical entity to provide real-time feedback or execute automatic measures.

Once selected, we will relate them to the interfaces that will update our DT with the newly obtained information and trigger outgoing events.

Next Steps: Iterate. Software development is an iterative process, therefore the very development of the solution obtained after the application of this method can provide new information that can require the modelling to change, hence any of the steps can be reviewed later to modify and extend the model obtained to represent and adapt to the new information discovered.

5 Case Study

To showcase the modelling method and the proposed design method we propose a real case study existing in the Mercadona Tech logistics chain.

Our business is the delivery of online grocery orders. We sell, prepare, and deliver orders to homes, which involves a complex physical process that includes several entities that are related to each other.

We have a warehouse from which we prepare the orders, where we employ several workers and several last-mile trucks that deliver these orders and are driven by drivers.

For this case study, we want to define a DT that aims to locate all the workers in the geographical environment and within the warehouses to apply risk control measures in the working environment. One of the desired measures is to alert the operations team when a truck enters a certain geographical area, to prevent certain vehicles from accessing designated low-emission zones (LEZ). In addition, we want to analyse the route that drivers and workers have travelled during the day.

Step 0: Select the Goal of the Digital Twin. As mentioned above, the DT will aim to be able to locate each of the workers, both delivery and warehouse workers, alert the operations team when a truck has accessed a limited area, and to be able to consult their position at any time of the day.

Step 1: Define a Common Vocabulary. To speak the same language and ensure good communication between stakeholders, we have defined together with domain experts (mainly operations managers) the following ubiquitous language:

A *picker* (the name of the worker who prepares orders) works in a *hive* (the name we give to our warehouses) and always has an *indoor location.* A *driver* delivers orders using a *truck* that always has a *location* (its coordinates).

Step 2: Select the Physical Components. The physical components that will be represented in the DT will therefore be:

- Hive: the facility where we prepare orders.
- Picker: the person who prepares the orders.
- Truck: the vehicle that delivers the orders.
- Driver: the person who drives the truck and delivers the orders.

As we can see, physical elements like orders that do not serve to fulfil the DT goals are not included in the modelling, reducing the complexity needed for implementation.

Step 3: Define the Entities. From the selected physical components and the common language developed, we define the entities that we are going to represent in our DT (* historical attribute, ** derived attribute).

- Hive (Name, Blueprint).
- Picker (ID, Name, Indoor Location*).
- Truck (License Plate, Location*).
- Driver (Driver License, Name, Location**).

Note the location of the driver that is defined as a derived attribute. This is due to that information being related to the location of the truck the driver is driving and not an attribute of itself.

To relate the entities to each other, we are also going to define the following relationships:

- Works in: relates picker with hive.
- Delivers from: relates truck with hive.
- Driven by: relates driver with truck.

Step 4: Define the Interfaces of Each Entity. For the DT goals we have defined the following interfaces:

- Set location (picker): updates the indoor location of the picker.
- Get location (picker): returns the current indoor location of the picker. Can also be invoked using a specified datetime to retrieve the location at a given time.
- Set location (truck): updates the location of the truck.
- Assign driver (truck, driver): relates driver with truck.
- Get location (driver): returns the location of a truck driven by this driver, returns an empty value if it is not currently driving a truck. Can also be invoked using a specified datetime to retrieve the location at a given time.
- Get blueprints (hive): returns the visual representation of the hive's blueprints.

As we can see, the interface to get the location of a driver uses the information present in a related entity. This can be implemented in many ways, but the important part is that it respects encapsulation, as we do not speak to "strangers" to know the driver's location, keeping security constraints and ensuring better maintainability.

Step 5: Define the Data Flows. Finally, we define the communication flows that allow us to keep our DT updated with the actual status of the entities it represents:

- Picker telemetry (incoming event): updates the pickers indoor location using the set location interface.

- Truck GPS coordinates (data request): updates the truck's location using the set location interface.
- Driver assigned (incoming event): assigns a driver to a specific truck using the relationship interface.
- Truck entered LEZ (outgoing event): triggers an alert to the operations team to indicate that a truck has entered a restricted low-emissions zone.

Visual Representation. A visual representation of the defined DT model is shown in Fig. 6.

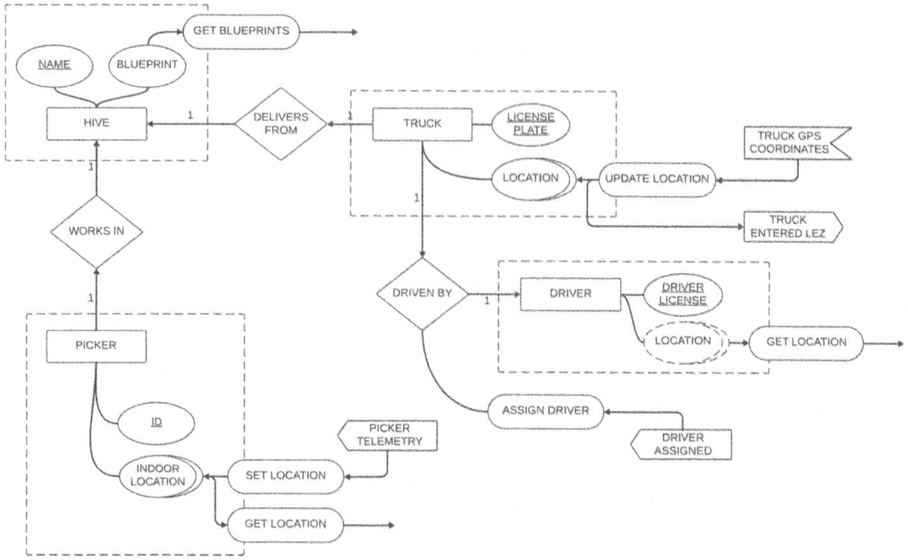

Fig. 6. ERDT diagram showing the modelling of the proposed DT.

6 Evaluation Against Quality Criteria

As this research focuses on the development of a modelling method with a primarily practical approach, we have based our proposals on software product quality criteria that are widely accepted in the industry. We have taken as a basis the quality criteria stipulated in the ISO 25010 (a standard that provides a comprehensive framework for evaluating the quality of software systems and products) to support the decisions taken in our proposed method.

This approach based on industry-recognised quality standards seeks to ensure the applicability and practical relevance of our modelling approach. By grounding ourselves in established quality guidelines, we aim to ensure that our proposals respond to the concrete needs and requirements of the software development environment.

And, while the case study shows the application of the ERDT modelling method to a real-world logistics scenario, further evaluating it against well-defined quality characteristics can provide additional validation and insights. Leveraging the quality models from ISO 25010, this section assesses the ERDT approach's strengths and potential limitations across key quality attributes.

Functional Suitability. A core driver of the ERDT method is improving the functional completeness and appropriateness of DT conceptual models. By extending ER models to explicitly represent historical data, interfaces and data flows, the ERDT models can more comprehensively capture DT requirements compared to simpler hierarchical approaches.

Compatibility. By building upon the well-established and widely adopted ER modelling approach, the ERDT models can co-exist with legacy data models and databases already using ER notations. This lowers adoption barriers for organizations with existing ER-based systems.

Also, the ERDT extensions like interfaces, historical attributes, and data flows are designed to be implementation-agnostic conceptual constructs. As such, the resulting models can potentially interface with diverse software components, facilitating interoperability between the physical and virtual components of the DT.

Usability. The visual notation, consistency with traditional data modelling approaches, and iterative nature of the method contribute to good usability for teams building DTs. Explicit consideration of ubiquitous languages and involving domain experts enhances understandability.

Maintainability. Applying principles like encapsulation, modularity, and separation of concerns is a key strength of the ERDT method. The emphasis on well-defined interfaces between components promotes loose coupling and better modifiability. The ability to evolve the models iteratively as new requirements emerge improves long-term maintenance.

Portability. By avoiding proprietary notations and grounding in well-established conceptual foundations like ER modelling, the resulting ERDT models exhibit a high degree of platform independence that aids portability. The models themselves are implementation-agnostic.

Potential Limitations. No evaluation is complete without considering potential limitations and areas for improvement. The ERDT method currently lacks quantitative evaluation criteria or benchmarks for assessing qualities like performance efficiency or reliability of the resulting DT implementations. Incorporating such analysis could be beneficial, particularly for resource-constrained or highly available DT deployments.

Additionally, the treatment of security aspects in the ERDT method is limited to defining access interfaces with constraints on which entities/users can interact with them. The explicit modelling of constructs for capturing systemic security policies could be addressed in future works.

7 Conclusion

The DT paradigm continues to gain traction across industries as a powerful approach for bridging the physical and virtual worlds. However, successfully realizing DTs depends on robust conceptual modelling methods that can accurately capture the complexities of real-world systems and environments.

This research has proposed the Entity-Relationship Digital Twin (ERDT) modelling method. It introduces key constructs for modelling historical data, security constraints, and data flows between physical and virtual components by extending the well-established Entity-Relationship model.

A core strength of the ERDT method is its ability to create conceptual models that are both comprehensive in scope yet grounded in proven software engineering principles like encapsulation and separation of concerns.

The logistics case study shows how the method can be applied to model a real-world industrial DT involving multiple entities such as warehouses, vehicles, and personnel. The resulting ERDT model captured important domain semantics, and relationships, and kept the virtual representation synchronized with the current physical state through well-defined data flows.

Evaluations against quality criteria based on the ISO 25010 standard provide evidence that the ERDT method promotes the development of DT systems exhibiting desirable characteristics like functional appropriateness, usability, portability, and strong maintainability.

As organizations across sectors increasingly seek to unlock the transformative potential of DTs, the ERDT conceptual modelling method represents a timely and pragmatic contribution. By bridging the gap between academic research and industrial practice, this work paves the way for more seamless and robust DT adoptions aligned with the realities of today's fast-paced software development environments.

Disclosure of Interests. The authors have no competing interests to declare that are relevant to the content of this article.

References

1. Iso/iec25010:2023 (2023), https://www.iso.org/standard/78176.html
2. Aivaliotis, P., Georgoulias, K., Arkouli, Z., Makris, S.: Methodology for enabling digital twin using advanced physics-based modelling in predictive maintenance. Procedia CIRP **81**, 417–422 (2019). https://doi.org/10.1016/j.procir.2019.03.072

3. Aivaliotis, P., Arkouli, Z., Georgoulias, K., Makris, S.: Methodology for enabling dynamic digital twins and virtual model evolution in industrial robotics - a predictive maintenance application. Int. J. Comput. Integr. Manuf. **36**(7), 947–965 (2023). https://doi.org/10.1080/0951192X.2022.2162591
4. Alam, K.M., El Saddik, A.: C2PS: a digital twin architecture reference model for the cloud-based cyber-physical systems. IEEE Access **5**, 2050–2062 (2017). https://doi.org/10.1109/ACCESS.2017.2657006
5. Andrade, M., Lepikson, H., Machado, C.: A new framework and methodology for digital twin development. In: 2021 14th IEEE International Conference on Industry Applications (INDUSCON), pp. 134–138 (Aug 2021).https://doi.org/10.1109/INDUSCON51756.2021.9529701
6. Benzon, H.H., Chen, X., Belcher, L., Castro, O., Branner, K., Smit, J.: An operational image-based digital twin for large-scale structures. Appl. Sci. **12**(77), 3216 (2022). https://doi.org/10.3390/app12073216
7. Bordeleau, F., Combemale, B., Eramo, R., van den Brand, M., Wimmer, M.: Towards model-driven digital twin engineering: 1st international conference on systems modelling and management, ICSMM 2020. In: Systems Modelling and Management - 1st International Conference, ICSMM 2020, Proceedings, pp. 43–54 (2020). https://doi.org/10.1007/978-3-030-58167-1_4
8. Carrión, E., Pastor, O.: A systematic review of methodologies for developing digital twins: insights and recommendations for effective implementation. CEUR Workshop Proc. (CEUR-WS.org) **3645** (2023)
9. Chen, P.P.S.: The entity-relationship model-toward a unified view of data. ACM Trans. Database Syst. **1**(1), 9–36 (1976). https://doi.org/10.1145/320434.320440
10. Constantinescu, C., Giosan, S., Matei, R., Wohlfeld, D.: A holistic methodology for development of real-time digital twins. Procedia CIRP **88**, 163–166 (2020). https://doi.org/10.1016/j.procir.2020.05.029
11. Dai, S., Zhao, G., Yu, Y., Zheng, P., Bao, Q., Wang, W.: Ontology-based information modeling method for digital twin creation of as-fabricated machining parts. Robot. Comput. Integr. Manuf. **72**, 102173 (2021). https://doi.org/10.1016/j.rcim.2021.102173
12. Ebrahimi, A.: Challenges of developing a digital twin model of renewable energy generators. In: 2019 IEEE 28th International Symposium on Industrial Electronics (ISIE), pp. 1059–1066 (Jun 2019).https://doi.org/10.1109/ISIE.2019.8781529, https://ieeexplore.ieee.org/document/8781529
13. Ensafi, M., et al.: A modeling methodology towards digital twin development in smart factories for the industry 4.0 human augmentation experiments (Oct 2021)
14. Gao, Y., Lv, H., Hou, Y., Liu, J., Xu, W.: Real-time modeling and simulation method of digital twin production line. In: 2019 IEEE 8th Joint International Information Technology and Artificial Intelligence Conference (ITAIC), pp. 1639–1642 (May 2019). https://doi.org/10.1109/ITAIC.2019.8785703, https://ieeexplore.ieee.org/document/8785703
15. Jia, W., Wang, W., Zhang, Z.: From simple digital twin to complex digital twin part i: a novel modeling method for multi-scale and multi-scenario digital twin. Adv. Eng. Inform. **53**, 101706 (2022). https://doi.org/10.1016/j.aei.2022.101706

16. Kirchhof, J.C., Michael, J., Rumpe, B., Varga, S., Wortmann, A.: Model-driven digital twin construction: synthesizing the integration of cyber-physical systems with their information systems. In: Proceedings of the 23rd ACM/IEEE International Conference on Model Driven Engineering Languages and Systems, pp. 90–101. MODELS '20, Association for Computing Machinery, New York, NY, USA (Oct 2020). https://doi.org/10.1145/3365438.3410941, https://dl.acm.org/doi/10.1145/3365438.3410941
17. Liu, S., Bao, J., Lu, Y., Li, J., Lu, S., Sun, X.: Digital twin modeling method based on biomimicry for machining aerospace components. J. Manuf. Syst. **58**, 180–195 (2021). https://doi.org/10.1016/j.jmsy.2020.04.014
18. Luo, W., Hu, T., Zhu, W., Tao, F.: Digital twin modeling method for CNC machine tool. In: 2018 IEEE 15th International Conference on Networking, Sensing and Control (ICNSC), pp. 1–4 (Mar 2018). https://doi.org/10.1109/ICNSC.2018.8361285, https://ieeexplore.ieee.org/document/8361285
19. Martínez, G.S., Sierla, S., Karhela, T., Vyatkin, V.: Automatic generation of a simulation-based digital twin of an industrial process plant. In: IECON 2018 - 44th Annual Conference of the IEEE Industrial Electronics Society, pp. 3084–3089 (Oct 2018). https://doi.org/10.1109/IECON.2018.8591464, https://ieeexplore.ieee.org/document/8591464/authors#authors
20. Pastor, O., Molina, J.C.: Model-Driven Architecture in Practice. Springer, Berlin, Heidelberg (2007). https://doi.org/10.1007/978-3-540-71868-0
21. Psarommatis, F.: A generic methodology and a digital twin for zero defect manufacturing (ZDM) performance mapping towards design for ZDM. J. Manuf. Syst. **59**, 507–521 (2021). https://doi.org/10.1016/j.jmsy.2021.03.021
22. Qamsane, Y., et al.: A methodology to develop and implement digital twin solutions for manufacturing systems. IEEE Access **9**, 44247–44265 (2021). https://doi.org/10.1109/ACCESS.2021.3065971
23. Rasheed, A., San, O., Kvamsdal, T.: Digital twin: values, challenges and enablers from a modeling perspective. IEEE Access **8**, 21980–22012 (2020). https://doi.org/10.1109/ACCESS.2020.2970143
24. Schroeder, G.N., Steinmetz, C., Pereira, C.E., Espindola, D.B.: Digital twin data modeling with automationml and a communication methodology for data exchange. IFAC-PapersOnLine **49**(30), 12–17 (2016). https://doi.org/10.1016/j.ifacol.2016.11.115
25. Schroeder, G.N., Steinmetz, C., Rodrigues, R.N., Henriques, R.V.B., Rettberg, A., Pereira, C.E.: A methodology for digital twin modeling and deployment for industry 4.0. Proc. IEEE **109**(4), 556–567 (2021). https://doi.org/10.1109/JPROC.2020.3032444
26. Sharma, A., Kosasih, E., Zhang, J., Brintrup, A., Calinescu, A.: Digital twins: state of the art theory and practice, challenges, and open research questions. J. Ind. Inf. Integr. **30**, 100383 (2022). https://doi.org/10.1016/j.jii.2022.100383
27. Sierla, S., et al.: Roadmap to semi-automatic generation of digital twins for brownfield process plants. J. Ind. Inf. Integr. **27**, 100282 (2022). https://doi.org/10.1016/j.jii.2021.100282
28. Singh, S., Weeber, M., Birke, K.P.: Advancing digital twin implementation: a toolbox for modelling and simulation. Procedia CIRP **99**, 567–572 (2021). https://doi.org/10.1016/j.procir.2021.03.078

29. Sleuters, J., Li, Y., Verriet, J., Velikova, M., Doornbos, R.: A digital twin method for automated behavior analysis of large-scale distributed IoT systems. In: 2019 14th Annual Conference System of Systems Engineering (SoSE), pp. 7–12 (May 2019). https://doi.org/10.1109/SYSOSE.2019.8753845, https://ieeexplore.ieee.org/document/8753845
30. Tao, F., Zhang, H., Liu, A., Nee, A.Y.C.: Digital twin in industry: state-of-the-art. IEEE Trans. Industr. Inf. **15**(4), 2405–2415 (2019). https://doi.org/10.1109/TII.2018.2873186
31. Tipary, B., Erdős, G.: Generic development methodology for flexible robotic pick-and-place workcells based on digital twin. Rob. Comput. Integr. Manuf. **71**, 102140 (2021). https://doi.org/10.1016/j.rcim.2021.102140
32. White, G., Zink, A., Codecá, L., Clarke, S.: A digital twin smart city for citizen feedback. Cities **110**, 103064 (2021).https://doi.org/10.1016/j.cities.2020.103064
33. Zhang, H., Qi, Q., Ji, W., Tao, F.: An update method for digital twin multi-dimension models. Rob. Comput. Integr. Manuf. **80**, 102481 (2023). https://doi.org/10.1016/j.rcim.2022.102481
34. Zhang, L., Zhou, L., Horn, B.K.P.: Building a right digital twin with model engineering. J. Manuf. Syst. **59**, 151–164 (2021). https://doi.org/10.1016/j.jmsy.2021.02.009
35. Zhao, P., et al.: The modelling and using strategy for the digital twin in process planning. IEEE Access **8**, 1-1 (2020). https://doi.org/10.1109/ACCESS.2020.2974241
36. Zheng, P., Sivabalan, A.S.: A generic tri-model-based approach for product-level digital twin development in a smart manufacturing environment. Rob. Comput. Integr. Manuf. **64**, 101958 (2020). https://doi.org/10.1016/j.rcim.2020.101958
37. Zheng, X., Psarommatis, F., Petrali, P., Turrin, C., Lu, J., Kiritsis, D.: A quality-oriented digital twin modelling method for manufacturing processes based on a multi-agent architecture. Procedia Manuf. **51**, 309–315 (2020). https://doi.org/10.1016/j.promfg.2020.10.044
38. Zhong, X., et al.: A multidisciplinary approach to the development of digital twin models of critical care delivery in intensive care units. Int. J. Prod. Res. **60**(13), 4197–4213 (2022). https://doi.org/10.1080/00207543.2021.2022235

26. Sleuters, J., Li, Y., Verriet, J., [illegible], M., Doornbos, R.: A digital twin method for automated behavior analysis of large-scale distributed [illegible] [illegible]

[illegible]

Author Index

A

Abbad-Andaloussi, Amine 18
Abel, Mara 152
Ackermann, Lars 38
Ahmad, Saad 337
Ali, Syed Juned 257, 295
Almeida, João Paulo A. 133
Arora, Udit 317
Attri, Sudhir 337
Avila, Caio Viktor S. 276

B

Bhatia, Sumit 317
Bonte, Pieter 317
Borgida, Alex 215
Bork, Dominik 257, 295
Burmester, Gerrit 355

C

Cabot, Jordi 94
Calhau, Rodrigo F. 396
Carrión, Emilio 417
Casanova, Marco A. 276
Chang, Jingfei 3
Cheng, Wen 3
Coelho, Gustavo 276
Custódio, Ricardo 377

D

Dwivedi, Ruchi 337

F

F. Barcelos, Pedro Paulo 396
Feijó, Lucas 276
Ferreira Pires, Luís 133
Fill, Hans-Georg 75

G

Gailly, Frederik 396
García, Grettel 276
Golipour, Reza 170
Guizzardi, Giancarlo 133, 396

H

Hartmann, Sven 355
Henrique Rodrigues, Fabricio 152

I

Izquierdo, Yenier 276

J

Jablonski, Stefan 38
Jaouhar, Ibrahim 195

K

Kampik, Timotheus 56
Kelsen, Pierre 94
Khan, Aasim 337
Khan, Shakil M. 170, 195, 215
Klímek, Jakub 235
Kumar, Shashikant 317

L

Leme, Luiz André P. Paes 276
Lemos, Melissa 276
Li, Yong 3
Liaskos, Sotirios 170, 195, 215
Lipovetzky, Nir 56
Liu, Yabin 112

M

Ma, Hui 355
Ma, Qin 94
Muff, Fabian 75
Muhammad Danish, Syed 195

W. Maass et al. (Eds.): ER 2024, LNCS 15238, pp. 437–438, 2025.
https://doi.org/10.1007/978-3-031-75872-0

Mutharaju, Raghava 317, 337
Mylopoulos, John 170, 215

N
Naganathan, Varun 295
Nascimento, Eduardo 276
Nečaský, Martin 235
Neuberger, Julian 38

O
Oliveira, Aiko 276
Oliveira, Ítalo 396

P
Pastor, Óscar 417
Pinheiro, João 276
Poels, Geert 396
Polyvyanyy, Artem 56
Prince Sales, Tiago 396
Priyadarshi, Praveen 337
Prokop, Dominik 235
Proper, Henderik A. 94

R
Reinhartz-Berger, Iris 257
Rezayat, Sarmad 355

S
Schardong, Frederico 377
Schreiber, Clemens 18
Shen, Qingtan 56
Shi, Gengyuan 112
Silva, Jonathan 94
Singh, Gunjan 317
Škoda, Petr 235
Stenchlák, Štěpán 235

T
Tommasini, Riccardo 317

V
Valadares Vieira, Lucas 152
Valderas, Pedro 417
van der Aa, Han 38

W
Wagner, Gerd 133
Wang, Chaokun 112
Weber, Barbara 18
Wu, Xunjin 3
Wu, Yunxiang 3

Y
Yaqoob, Muzamil 337

Z
Zeng, Lingfang 3

The manufacturer's authorised representative in the EU is Springer Nature Customer Service Centre GmbH, Europaplatz 3, 69115 Heidelberg, Germany. If you have any concerns regarding our products, please contact ProductSafety@springernature.com

Printed and bound by CPI Group (UK) Ltd, Croydon, CR0 4YY

30/09/2026

02225566-0017